TEACHING LABOURS OF SISYPHUS!

TEACHING LABOURS OF SISYPHUS! CLASS LACTURE SYNOPSES IN ENVIRONMENTAL SCIENCES

Volume - I

Basics and Resources

Prof. C.B.S.R. Sharma
Pondicherry University

KALPAZ

First Published, 2020

Published by

Kalpaz Publications
C-30, Satyawati Nagar,
Delhi – 110052
Ph.: 011-47034999, 9811692060
www.kalpazpublications.com
E-mail: kalpaz@hotmail.com

Printed at: G. Print Process, Delhi

Cataloging in Publication Data—DK
Courtesy: D.K. Agencies (P) Ltd. <docinfo@dkagencies.com>

Sharma, C. B. S. R., author.
Teaching Labours of Sisyphus! : Class Lecturer Synopses in Environmental Sciences / Prof. C.B.S.R. Sharma.
volumes cm
Contents: Volume I. Basics & Resources — Volume II. Impacts & Management.
ISBN 9789353242350 (set) (HB)
ISBN 9789353242367 (vol. I)

1. Ecology. 2. Environmental Sciences. 3. Biology. 4. Natural Resources. I. Title.

LCC QH541.S53 2020 | DDC 577 23

DEDICATION

TO

Innumerable teachers
who guided my Empathies
And influenced
My Conduct with Students
And Class Room Methods

Especially

SOUTHGATE [London, UK]
CROW [Wisconsin, USA]
GUNDURAO [BITS, Pilani]
SWAMINATHAN [IARI, New Delhi]
AVTAR KRISHNA KAUL [JAMMU & KASHMIR]

Contents

Foreword 9
Preface 11
Acknowledgments 15

VOLUME - I

BASICS AND RESOURCES

(*Series Page No. 1-426 See Below*)

1. Cytogenetics and Microbiology 17
2. Basic Ecology 75
3. Biodiversity & Germplasm Banking 141
4. Coasts and Wetlands 223
5. Bioenergy 277
6. Natural Resources 313

VOLUME - II

IMPACTS & MANAGEMENT

(*Series Page No. 427-807 See Below*)

7. Pollution and Toxicology 7
8. Environmental Mutagenesis 111
9. Environmental Philosophies, Politics and Activism 197
10. Applied Ecology 267

Appendices 313
Confessions 375

पांडिच्चेरी विश्वविद्यालय
PONDICHERRY UNIVERSITY
(केंद्रीय विश्वविद्यालय) (A Central University)

பேராசிரியர் குர்மீத் சிங்
துணைவேந்தர்
आचार्य गुरमीत सिंह
कुलपति
Prof. GURMEET SINGH
Vice-Chancellor

आर.वेंकटरामन नगर,
R. Venkataraman Nagar,
कालापेट / Kalapet,
पुदुच्चेरी -६०५ ०१४.
Puducherry - 605 014.
भारत. India.

Foreword

To write a foreword to the life's work of an Octogenarian Professor, "*Teaching Labors of Sisyphus*" is indeed a rare opportunity. Being ripe and mature was not his only privilege; he was considered the best teacher in his times. He was the pioneer in curriculum and Syllabus making for Ecology and Environmental Science as back as 1987. From Botany, through Ecology and Genetics, he graduated to the current field, Environmental Sciences which enabled him to teach about 10 subjects, a rare feat anywhere in the world.

There are some subjects not found Commonly in India, that he initiated such as Applied Ecology, Environmental Mutagenesis and Environmental Politics, the last still continues in the Department of International Studies. I was told that there is no other teacher in our University, to whose classes attend students from many departments, about 10 in all.

Participatory approach, value of questioning, practice of integrating information from diverse sources are some of the ingredients of his value system, not common in our present times. His present book is truly of student concerns and the labors, truly Sisyphean. Are these labors of painstaking teaching, heroic in effort or a punishment to those who cannot do anything else than teach?

This book is most useful to all students whether they are learning or teaching or competing. It is a stupendous effort of nearly encompassing 200 topics cutting across 10 subjects. In other words, one need not read 10 books. This one alone would suffice. A book that every University must possess and be emulated by every branch of Sciences and Humanities. Professor Sharma's Sustained efforts for 30 years to educate students are brought in this work. I am happy to have come across this rare Teacher.

He is also a student councilor who prescribed 20 characteristics on which teachers need to be evaluated. Bibliographies are rarely found now a days; consequently piracy of authorships increased! Hope and wish that this book should be widely distributed and revised in due course of time.

October 9, 2019

GURMEET SINGH
Vice-Chancellor

Preface

This is my Magnum Opus – my Life's work – Reading, Writing, Teaching, Syllabi, Curriculum, References, Bibliographies, and Evaluations of Courses, Students and Teachers. Class Lecture Synopses of the subjects I have taught, at the Universities of Berhampur, Madurai, Coimbatore and Pondicherry, truly form Sisyphus' labors, thankless in the current times! For this I had the Baptism at the Birla Institute of Technology and Science, Pilani and the Indian Institute of Science, Bangalore, where I was asked to teach to PG and Post-PG students. This compilation was preceded by a collection of articles in the Print Media [*SHARKS ON CAMPUS*], and a compendium of lectures on Environment in 35 Institutions in India [*ECOLOGY, ENVIRONMENT AND POLITICS*].

Dissatisfaction with the existing order is the mother of all new approaches This book is one such.

My first teachers were my mother and her brother. She has been a teacher to all who seek in scriptures and culture and my uncle, in literature and newspapers. Veerabhadram Mastar at Polavaram rescued me from vagabond urchins and admitted in the local middle school in the standard-6, lifting me from Second, and that too without the knowledge of my father.. Further inspiration came from Ayyagari Master, Parvatheesam Master and Ramayya Mastar from Manepalli and Rajole High Schools. A character was thus formed demanding more from teachers. At College I was utterly dissatisfied but for one good teacher in Botany, Gopala Rao and a fresh hand in Zoology, Ramakrishna.

At University level, my teachers at Pilani were excellent humans. But I am looking for more. satisfying experiences. The first I got was Dr. Gundu Rao of the Pharmacy Department - methodical, disciplined and pleasant - a versatile genius. I attended his classes in Chromatography and Microbiology.

The second was M. S. Swaminathan at the Indian Agricultural Research Institute, New Delhi, in Genetics, to whom I was sent by my Professor B.N. Muley sab. I soon became an Ekalavya. Talking with him for a few minutes is learning and impart to you readily for the asking. He has been maintaining a personal library even in those times. I had the privilege of his patronage during 3 summers of 1965 – 68.

The third one is Avatar Krishna Koul from the University at Srinagar. A chance meeting through Avtar Singh, my colleague kept me glued to him. I must have met him only a dozen times, from a few hours to few days each time, so far. He is a ready teacher. Even a mere conversation turns into a class - amusing and anecdotal, and make one long for more! When I became a teacher at Berhampur University, I tried to make a mix of these ideal teachers. Being different in my history, however I needed a new mechanism to practice and got it luckily.

It was from Prof. James Crow of Wisconsin. He came to I.A.R.I., New Delhi for a few weeks and I happened to meet him, by chance in Genetics Department. He presented me his Class Notes in Genetics which he was teaching in U.S.A. You can see this in many old Libraries. This notes is a Spiral Bound Volume printed only on one side with brief, but structured notes in sentences. The other side is for personal jottings. I gifted my copy to the Library of Pondicherry University along with 750 other books

This is my model. It needs conversion to Indian Scenario. Here comes my innovation. It involves an abridgment of Crow's model and a change in the usage of language. Sentences are replaced by keywords and key phrases. Each topic becomes half of the original in Crow's Notes.

I did this for Cytogenetics. The students liked it. I continued this practice ever since from 1975 with all the subjects taught by me until 2004. I called these 'Synopses'. These syllabus-based summaries have scope for expansion as well as abridging. Added are the relevant texts. Thus accumulated, is a huge bibliography. Mostly students took these as handouts; some gave feedback, helping me to improve. By the end of 2004, when I retired, there were 15 Booklets, one each for a subject, ranging from 25-80 pages!

A decade passed, I found that my hand-outs were used widely carefully camouflaging their origins. A whole paper, Environmental Politics, is run in the school of International Studies at Pondicherry University without acknowledging me. There must be a few more similar cases.

Most books are written in one of the Shakespearean ages - 4th or 5th or $6^{th.}$ But this book originates in all these, covers the 7th and an uncertain 8th age. A record of 5 ages took the draft. to me. It is my good fortune that I preserved my notes. Obviously this is not a 'FULL' book, but partly

'EXACT' and Fully a 'READY' book in a true Baconian sense. This is the first book of this kind. And It is my good luck that this innovation occurred.

It should be admitted that [1] Sequences of arrangements of topics are not perfect [2] Standards vary among the 194 topics [3] Repetitions occur, [4] There could be printer's devils and author's over-sights. These are the usual geriatric commissions.

During those bad years tormented by colleagues and authorities at Pondy, a solace was my association with Madras Institute of Development Studies in Madras. A glance of their library showed me many good books in social sciences. One such was the book by Prof. Southgate in economics. I found there a summary of the book in the form of synopses very similar to my present exercise. I was thrilled to realize that I am in the august company of a great teacher. Southgate developed this method in 1948 in Economics. A similar one has emerged from my system too in 1975 in Biology first and on Environment later.

History has many such instances. Mendel's work in 1866 was unknown until its rediscovery in 2001 laying the foundation of Genetics. Griffith's work in 1928 was not known until the work of Watson, Crick, Lederberg and Tatum, during 1950s when DNA was found to be the Genetic material. History is un-ignorable but too slow to discover truths. The story of this book is one such.

For convenience, the chapters are adjusted into Two Volumes. A unique feature is the involvement of students in evaluations, that I practiced and advocated. But no one heeded me. Thus the Courses we offer and the teaching we do are subjected to scrutiny by users. Many courses and most teachers were rejected by students. This is the reality which everyone hides, and everywhere.

This book is my story and exposes many evils in higher education, for a discerning reader. This is also an apology to the student world on behalf of the non-teaching cheaters in the all important field of Environment! Yet, students, competitors, and tutorial Institutions can use this effort. Most significant of all, anyone who wants to gain some knowledge of environment, can find a useful friend in my humble attempt.

Professor C.B.S.R. Sharma
e-mail: cbsrsharma42@gmail.com
Pondicherry University

Acknowledgments

Preparing for teaching to students continued through out my career, someties burning midnight oil! Doing a good job of this is not possible without the constant and continuous support and forbearance of my wife, **Ramadevi.** Only students who occasionally visit my house can tell about her virtues which buttressed my work.

Somewhere in 1990s, I wanted to discontinue this practice and work like my colleagues to distance their hostility from me. **Brother Kennedy,** a student of mine at Pondicherry, came to me alone and appealed to me to continue this effort.

After retirement, I stopped all works of past. But Last year, my **grand son, Aditya**, A lad of 3 years barges into my study at will and asks for a chosen book; reluctantly gets it from me; with trepidation. A child could tear it playfully! Lo! And behold! What I feared has not happened. Every day he came; selected a book and played with it and put it back. My spirits buoyed up that I took this old file and edited it into the present book of 800 pages in about 6 months.

The above one was computerized with equal spirit and efficiency by **V. Murugaiyan**, the Computer Specialist, daily visiting my house!

All the above are the superlative people that were brought by providence *to complete this work.*

1

Cytogenetics and Microbiology

1. ORGANISATIONAL COMPLEXITY OF LIFE
2. EVOLUTION
3. CYTOGENETICS & EVOLUTION –INTRODUCTORY
4. CELL BIOLOGY AND GENETICS -HISTORICAL
5. CELLS IN PLANTS, ANIMALS AND PROTISTS
6. PHYSICOCHEMICAL ORGANIZATION OF CELLS
7. CELL STRUCTURE AND FUNCTION
8. CELL DIVISIONS
9. CHARACTERISTICS OF MICROBES
10. MENDELIAN INHERITANCE
11. HYBRIDISATION, HYBRID VIGOUR
12. LINKAGE AND CROSSING OVER
13. MUTATIONS: CHROMOSOMAL AND GENIC
14. GENES AND ACTIONS
15. MAMMALIAN AND HUMAN CYTOGENETICS

SYLLABUS

MICROBIOLOGY

1. Introduction to Microbiology
2. Classification and General Characters of Microbes
3. Summary of Microbiology

CYTOGENETICS

1. Introduction to cytology, genetics and evolution
2. History of cytology, genetics and evolurion
3. Tools and techniques in cytology, genetics and evolution
4. Physico-chemical organisation of cells- colloidal properties of the protoplast
5. Physico-chemical organisation of cells - Biochemical properties of the cell
6. Cellular organisation in plants, animals and protists
7. Cell structure and function - general framework, boundary systems, cytoplasmic organelles, nuclear organelles.
8. Cell division - Mitosis, Amitosis and Endomitosis
9. Cell division - Meiosis
10. Mendelian inheritance
11. Modification of Mendelian inheritance by interaction of factors
12. Linkage, Crossing over and chromosome mapping
13. Gene-concept, nature, action, code
14. Mutation-Somatic, germinal - numerical, structural, genic
15. Cytoplasmic inheritance
16. Sex determination and sed inheritance
17. Hybridisation - Inbreeding, Outbreeding and hibrid vigour
18. History of evolutionary thought - Theories of evolution
19. Evidences for evolution
20. Spectrum of organisational complexity of organisms.
21. Patterns of evolution and Mechanism of evolutionary change

1. ORGANISATIONAL COMPLEXITY OF LIFE

I. INTRODUCTION

Life, evolution of characters; evolution of organisms, "Vertical" transmission. "Horizontal" development. Role of environmental factors and changeability of environment.

II. GEOLOGECAL TIME SCALE AND HISTORY OF LIFE

A. PRECAMBRIAN: archeozoic and proterozoic epochs; 10,000-3000 million years origin of earth and first life.

B. PALIOZOIC ERA: Cambrian, ordovonian, Silurian, Devonian, Carboniferous, permian epochs; 500-230 million year; all major invertibrate phyla, algae land plants, tree ferns gymnosperms, fishes amphibians and reptiles.

C. MESOZOIC: Triassic, Jurassic, Cretaceous epochs; 230-133 million years; flowering plants, Mammals.

D. CENOZOIC: Paleocene, Eocene, oligocene, Miocene, Pliocene, Pleistocene epochs. 135-1 million years; mammals insects, flowering plants; Cultural evolution of man.

III. SPECTRUM OF ORGANIZATIONAL COMPLEXITY OF LIFE

A. Non living systems increasing Living systems Complexity

B. Atom—molecule—cell—individual—population—species—community—Ecosystem.

IV. PRIMARY ACTION OF GENE AND FINAL EXPRESSION OF CHARACTERS

A. DNA—RNA—Protein Synthesis-Cell structure—Tissue Morphological— Elongation — Organ — character Differentiation Structure

B. Metabolic Processes intervening in the gene expression Synthesis of amino acids, bases, hormones, activity of respiratory enzymes, regulatory genes cell division and gene environment interactions.

V. MICROBES

1. Discovery: Hooke 1665, Leewenhock 1676.
2. "Spontaneous generation of life" Controversy and its importance in the acceleration of microbial studies

3. Germ theory of fermentation: Pasteur 1857.
4. Germ theory of disease
   (a) Fracartoro 1546 on the modes of transmissions of infections.
   (b) Robert Koch 1876, on Bacillus anthracis causing anthrax epidemic in sheep and cattle.
5. Technical advances
   (a) Schroeter, 1872, identification of colonial growth,
   (b) Hosse, 1883, introduction of agar
   (c) Petri, introduction of suitable glassware
   (d) Koch & others, selective enrichment of microbial cultures to isolate various bacteria,
   (e) Gram, 1884, 'gram' staining.
6. Discovery of viruses
   (a) Iwanowski, 1892: Tobacco Mosaic Virus
   (b) Loeffler & Frosch, 1898: Food mouth disease of cattle
   (c) Twort, 1915: bacterial virus
   (d) Stanley, 1935: crystallization of viruses
7. Immunity: Pasteur, 1881; Metchnikoff, 1884: Behring & Kilasato, 1890 and Wright and Douglas.
8. Chemotherapy: Ehrlich, 1900-10 wit arsephenamine (against Syphilis
9. Physiology & genetics: Beadle & tatum, 1940: gene-enzyme relations. Tatum & Lederberg, 1946: sexuality in bacteria.

VI. MICROSCOPES

Light, UV, Darkfield, Fluorescence, Phase contrast and Electron microscopes.

VII. DYES & STAINING

1. Chromophore or auxochrome dyes.
2. Simple or differential stains, gram stain.

VIII. CULTIVATION OF MICROBES

Recruitments: nutrients, energy source, pH, temp, etc.

Culture, pure culture, culture

2. EVOLUTION

I. EVOLUTIONARY THOUGHTS AND THEORIES

A. INTRODUCTION: of characters convergence and divergence. Evolution of organisms-speciation, progression and retrogression, Vertical and horizontal plane of evolution.

B. HISTORICAL ASPECTS:

1. Obscure period: Scripture—Bible, Vedas, Confusianism, Aristotle, Herodotus, Empedocles, Democritus Theophrastus.
2. Medieval period: Bacon(1561-1626) Leibritz(1649-1716)and Buffon(1707-88)
3. Formative period: Lamarck(1744-1829), Goethe(1748-1823) Cuvier(1769-1832) Prichard (1786-1848), Darwin (1809-1882)
4. Modern period: Wright,Fisher,Haldane, Mayr,Simpson, Dobzgansky, Stebbins Grant, Darlington, Varilov, Cronquist, Westergaard, Nomura, Huxley
5. Darwinism: Beagle, Origin of Species, Wallace, TH. Hyxley
6. Basic tenets: Overpopulation, struggle for existence variations and selection, survival of the fittest and adaptation, fittest variation carried over. Useful characters: for food, escape from enemies, resistance to climate, sex appeal, resistance to disease, fertility, individual plasticity.
7. Variations: Neutral, useful and harmful Natural selection operates on the existing variations at population level and at character level. Variation progressive as it brings new features, heredity conservative as it preserves variation.
8. Testing variations: Polymorphism: Ecotypes-genotypes.

C. OBJECTIONS

Theocracy's uneven and irrational fight-Fluctuating nature of variations.

Selection is random irrespective of the merit of variation—Adaptation not well explained. Fate of transitional forms during speciation.

D. NEODARWINISM

Mendelian, Meiotic and Mutational sources of variation—Natural selection as a filter-genetic polymorphism in transient populations

- adaptive value(s) of gene pools. — Impact of Malthus, Mendel, DeVries,—Modification by Haldane, Fisher, Wright, Huxley, Nomura etc.

E. LAMARCKISM

Basic lenets: increase of bulk of organism extending dimensions of parts, new organs out of necessity and conscious effort, degree of development depends upon employment, such acquired characters are inherited.

F. PROOFS

Crane, giraffe's long neck Vestigeal eyes of cave fishes, absence of digestive tract in tapeworm. Webbed feet and long legs of ducks with water-habit. Hormones and secondary sex characters.

G. EXPERIMENTS OF MCDOUGAL

With learning ability of fishes subjected to electricity, of Mammerer on the impact of climatic conditions on the laying ability of Salamander species

H. OBJECTIONS

Irreproducible experiments, Weismann's theory of soma and germline, Phillips and Castle's experiment on guinea pig ovary transplantation coupled by hybridization, lack of size increase in higher echelons of animal & plant kingdoms rejection of lamarckism

Neolamarckism: acceptance of a few tenets after modification

II. EVIDENCES FOR EVOLUTION

A. **UNITY IN DIVERSITY:** Sources and implications of evidences.

B. **CLASSIFICATION:** Likeness of organisms within taxon and between taxa.

C. **DOMESTICATION:** changes occurring in domestication indicate the same could happen in nature.

D. **COMPARATIVE ANOTOMY:** theory of convergence similarity of plant organs, homology among lizard foreleg, bat wing, horse foreleg, human arm insect mouth parts.

E. **EMBRYOLOGY:** Recapitulation theory, Atavism partial recapitulation of ancestry indicates relationships

F. **BLOOD TESTS:** Confirmatory, gives degree of kinship. (1) birds closely related to reptiles (2) Simidae (apes) closely resemble human blood followed by Thecidae (monkeys).

G. **PALEONTOLOGY:** geological time table, fossils; ascent of life

H. **GEOGRAPHIC DISTRIBUTION:** endemism at Galapogos islands - Tortoises (giant) different from mainland. Variation due to migration, isolation and variations. Marsupial distribution with great range of modifications due to geographical isolation of Australia with wide range of environment-tropical rain forest to desert.

I. **VESTIGAL ORGANS:** Once developed structures reduced to nonfunction during evolution: abortive stamens, rudimentary pistils, rudimintary tail and third eye lid in man.

J. **EXPERIMENTS:** genetic experiments, persentages (geneologies) of cultivated plants, Raphanobrassica,

K. **CONCLUSIONS:** Explorations, ecologic experiments on evolving species population genetics & polymorphism, genetic experiments for assessing kinships.

III. PATTERNS AND MECHANISMS OF EVOLUTIONARY CHANGES

A. BASIC PATTERNS OF EVOLUTION

1. Sequential evolution: modification of existing gene pools; never produces new populations from old; conservative nature of biological inheritance.
2. Divergent evolution: Origin of new populations from old; myriad modifications ensue.

B. **ELEMENTAL FORCES:** Factors that produce changes in the frequency of a pair of alleles from one generations to another.

C. LEVELS OF EVOLUTIONARY CHANGE

1. Sequential: Microevolution
2. Divergent: Speciation, macroevolution, megaevolution

D. **MICROEVOLUTION:** adaptive, neutral and non-adaptive changes in Gene combinations; evolution resulting from interaction between

(a) variation and mutation, (b) natural selection and (c) genetic drift to produce small population changes.

1. Variation and Mutation: Provides hereditary materials to be molded by natural selection and genetic drift Mendelian and meiotic variability.
2. Natural selection: Differential reproduction of certain alleles or gene combinations over others present in the

population, caused by the impact of the total environment; cannot produce new genes or combinations of genes only molds the existing genetic variation.

3. Genetic drift: Completely random fluctuations of alleles and gene combinations even under constant environment.

E. SPECIATION:

1. Species category: Evolutionary concept, tropological concept, nondimensional concept, multidimentional concept.
2. Types of speciation: Sympatric and allopatric
3. Intraspecific categories
4. Isolating mechanism
   (a) Spatial isolation:allopatric populations
   (b) Genetic isolation: allopatric& sympatric populations
      (i) Barriers between populations
         Ecologic: Prevention of mating
         Ethologic: Prevention of mating
         Morphologic: Prevention of mating
         Physiologic: Prevention of mating, fertilization or development
         Cytologic: Prevention of fertilization or development
      (ii) Barriers in hybrids between populations
         Hybrid non viability or weakness
         Hybrid failure to attain sexual maturity
         Hybrid sterility
         Hybrid non viability or sterility in later generations.

The mechanisms are prezygotic or postzygotic.

F. ADAPTATION:

1. Characteristic that is advantageous to a particular organism or population.
2. End product of evolutionary change is the establishment of orgnisms that function more efficiently, in a certain enviroment, than predecessors.
3. **The reality of adoption:** diversity of life & environments.
4. **Environmental factors:** Physical and Biotic.— extraspecific (community), interspecific (population) and internal (individual).

5. **Process of adaptation:** Original population -micro-evolutionary change by variation and selection—gene pool of more efficient interaction with environment - changes in variation- more favoured gene combinations by natural selection-adaptation.

G. MACROEVOLUTION:

1. Follows the acquisition of new general adaptation or
2. Entrance into a new adaptive zone.
   (a) A general adaptation and invasion of new adaptive zone through special adaptations in different divergent descendent lines—Adaptive radiation-sharing a common back ground of general adaptation.
   (b) Convergence in special adaptation with other distantly related groups differing in their general adaptation—reptiles and fishes.
   (c) Ultimate extinction—basic rule of macroevolution-due to rigid specialization to narrow adaptive sub-zones, their inability to move to new adaptive zones through newer modification—Fossil background.

H. MEGAEVOLUTION:

Rare Origin of new biological organisational plans; shares the features of micro and macroevolution

1. After evolutionary exploration and experimentation by divergent lines of the ancestral stocks (adaptive radiation) one of them crosses the ecological barrier into the new zone.
2. Break through and shift rapid, last it may fail
3. New zone devoid of competition and requires a new general adaptive type for its invasion.

I. COMMON FEATURES OF MACRO - AND MEGA-EVOLUTION: IRREVERSIBILITY.

3. CYTOGENETICS & EVOLUTION - HISTORICAL

I. INTRODUCTION

A. **Life:** Organisms and their characteristics; Plants, animals and protists.

B. **Major processes of life:** Development, Reproduction, Senescene and death.

C. **Development:** Cellular multiplication, growth, differentiation.

D. **Reproduction:** Fusion and fission; transfer or characters, inheritance, heredity, genetics.

E. **Senescence & death:** Work, wariness and collapse of the system.

F. Role of cells in development, reproduction and death and Cell as a unit of structure, function, perpetuation and decline

G. Basic architecture of cells.

H. Cellular uniformity in the living world, in

1. Organizational patterns: Structure & development
2. Working principles: Physiology during prime and ageing
3. Inheritance methods: Reproduction & heredity

I. General similiarity between plants, animals, and protists and within each of them:

Structure, multiplication, growth and differentiation of cells; energy conservations, waste disposal, senescence, sexuality & asexuality, fusion & fission of cells, recombination, variations and their transmission.

J. Division of labour among different organelles, role of membrane systems. Homology between organs and organelles.

K. Cellular descipline: In structure, development & reproduction; coordination of relay processes and their control; consequences of indescipline.

L. Levels of biological organisation and their pivotal role of cells. Historical role of cells:

Appearance, perpetuation & changeability.

Atoms — molecules — organelles — cells — tissues — organs — organism — population — species — community — Ecosystem.

M. Dividual & Individual organisms.

N. Life spans of organisms. Responses to environment. Variations in the gene pool during generations. Inheritance of variations & modification of organisms & their groups in time.

O. Vertical plane in evolution: Retrogression & progression in the ascent of life.

P. Horizontal plane in evolution: Divergence, Convergence & parallelism in individual traits or ascending species.

Q. Variety of and complexity in organisms.

R. Checks & balances in the web of life: Aesthetics of nature

II. HISTORICAL ASPECTS

A. MAJOR PERIODS OF PROGRESSION OF KNOWLEDGE:

1. 16th Century to 1900: Classical period
2. 1901 Century to 1921: Renaissance period
3. 1921 Century to 1953: Experimental period
4. 1953 Century to date: Modern period

B. MAJOR BREAK THROUGHS MADE AND PRINCIPLES EVOLVED DURING DIFFERENT PERIODS:

1. Classical period:
   (a) Compound lens system
   (b) Discovery of cells — Hooke, Leeuwenhoek
   (c) Concept of homology & epigenetic development of embryos.
   (d) Cell theroy — Schleiden and Schwann
   (e) Cell lineages, and germ layers
   (f) Mendelism, theory of origin of species: Darwin
   (g) Germplasm theory — Weismann
   (h) Discovery of nucleus, chromosomes, fertilization and cell division - Brown, Waldeyer, Strassbarger, Hofmeister.
   (i) Discovery of chemical fixation, microtome, staining.
   (j) Chromosome theory of inheritance; interrelationships between miotsis, meiosis, fertilization and
   inheritance: Origin of the hybrid science of Cytogenetics — Boveri, Sutton, Wilson.
   (k) Theories of protoplasmic structure:
   Granular / Fibrillar / Alveolar / Colloidal

2. Renaissance period:
   (a) Rediscovery of mendellism—Devries, Tshermak, Correns
   (b) Chromosome homology, linkage and crossing over.
   (c) Gene concept—Morgan, Muller, Sturtevant, Bridges, Emerson, Mc Clintock, Bateson.
3. Experimental period:
   (a) Development of phase contrast, electron, UV, & X-ray microscopy.
   (b) Feulgen-Rosenbeck nuclear reaction,micromanipulation, cytochemistry, centrifugation, biochemical techniques — autoradiography, tissue culture, photography.
   (c) Role of cytoplasmic organelles in protein synthesis - Brachet, Casperson.
   (d) Artificial induction of mutation — Muller
   (e) Nee Darwinism — Wright, Fisher, Haldane
   (f) Biochemistry of nuclear acids and cellular constancy of DNA —Chargaff, Davidson.
   (g) One gene-one enzyme hypothesis-Beadle, Tatum
   (h) Bacterial transformation—Avery et al
   (i) Transduction, lysogeny - Zinder, Lederberg, Wollman
   (j) Structural elucidation of proteins – Pauling
   (k) Double-Helix model of DNA - Watson, Crick, Wilkins, Franklin
4. Mixed period:
   (a) Biosynthesis of nucleic acids — Ochoa, Kornberg
   (b) Classification of genes - Benzer
   (c) Structural elucidation through electron microscopy — Palade, Porter.
   (d) Gene action and regulation, transcription, translation, replication, operon hypothesis, genetic code, codon dictionary, Central dogma—Crick, Jacob, Monod, Nirenberg, Holley, Khorana.
   (e) Semi conservative replication of chromosomes: Taylor.
   (f) Chromosome heterogeneity; Replication and banding patterns—Lima deFaria, Gesman, Casperson.
   (g) Euchromatin, heterochromatin, satellite and repetetive DNA.
   (h) chromosome inactivation - Lyon

(i) Organ, tissue and cell culture, totipotency of cells — Steward, Street, Nitsche.

(j) Haploid culture: Sunderland, Melchers

(k) Cell hybridization in plants and animals: Cocking, Carlson

(l) Development of monosomic lines—Sears, Riley

(m) Development of hybrid Maize — Shull

(n) Gene transfer: Nif gene fron Klebsiella to Lycopersicum through E.Coli — Dixon

(o) Cytoplasmic DNA—Ryan, Sager

(p) Chromatin Redundancy theory—Medvedev

(q) Cytophotometry and fluorescence microscopy

(r) Structural elucidation of proteins-Sanger

(s) Chromosome models—Taylor, Dupraw, Freeze, Whitehouse

C. CURRENT TRENDS:

Membrane permeability; cytoplasmic DNA; chromosome structure and function; Chromosome inactivation and heterogeneity; Cell cycles; in situ hybridization of DNA; Protoplast fusion, cell transformation, haploid culture; Mapping of genes in man through cell hybridization; Nucleic acid variation; Enzyme histochemistry & use of EM & autoradiography Nucleolar function.

D. MAJOR CELLULAR THEORIES AND THEIR SALIENT FEATURES:

Cell theory, Mendelism, Chromosome theory of inheritance, Gene concept, DNA as genetic material, Semi conservative replication of chromosomes, chromosome inactivation theory, Totipotency of cells, Operon hypothesis, Chromatin redundancy theory.

E. CONTRIBUTING FACTOS TO PROGRESS:

1. Spirit of enquiry sustained by constant increase in problems facing mankind
2. Progress in other desciplines of science and their corresponding application in cell biology
3. Refinement of old and development of new techniques.
4. Accidents
5. Necessity
6. Chronologically selected list of discoveries and break-throughs.

4. CELL BIOLOGY AND GENETICS-INTRODUCTION

I. INTRODUCTION

A. **BASIC ARCHITECTURE OF CELL:** Cell wall, ppm, cpm, nucleus, organelles and ground pm.

B. **PHYSIO CHEMICAL NATURE OF CELL**

1. Chemistry: Inorganic: water, anions and cations.
   Organic: Proteins, carbohydrates, lipids, nucleic acids etc.
   Physiological significance of the chemicals.
2. Forms of matter
   (a) Homogeneous
   (b) Heterogeneous
      1. Suspension
      2. Emulsion
      3. Colloids (sol, gel, coascervate, tactoid)
3. Cells as a polyphasic system warranted by their special features

C. **IMPORTANCE OF CELL**

1. Unit of structure, organization & physiology
2. Role in Reproduction (inheritance), Development (Growth and differentiation)

D. **DEVELOPMENT OF CELL BIOLOGY AND GENETICS**

1. Major break-throughs
   (a) Cell theory: Hooke, Brown, Schleiden, Schwann.
   (b) Mendelism: Mendel.
   (c) Chromosomes & Heredity: Waldeyer, Boveri, Wilson, Sutton.
   (d) Rediscovery of Mendelism: Correns, Tschermak, DeVries.
   (e) Gene concept: De Vries, Johannsen, Bridges, Morgan.
   (f) Mutations: Muller
   (g) DNA as genetic material: Griffith, Avery, McCleod and McCarty
   (h) DNA: Structure and genetic control: Beadle & Tatum, Brachet & Caspersson
   (i) Cell cylces, Sex determinations, Human & agricultural genetic, Chromosomal behviour and architecture.: Howard & Pele, Barr, Tjio & Levan, Ris, Kaufmann, Westerngard.

(l) Cell culture & Hybridization: White, Harris, Ephrussi, Ericksson.

E. TOOLS & TECHNIQUES:

1. Microscopes: Light, phase, and electron microscopes.
2. Stains: Feulgen reaction, Methylgreen - Pyronin.
3. Cytochemistry, microincineration, enzyme digestion.
4. Autoradiography.

II. CELL MORPHOLOGY

A. CELL STRUCTURE IN DIFFERENT ORGANISMS

1. Eukaryotic
   (a) Plant cell (b) Animal cell
   (c) Protozoan cell
2. rotokaryotic
   (a) Bacterial cell (b) Myxophycean cell
   (c) Yeast cell (d) Viral cell

B. SHAPE, SIZE AND NUMBER VARIATIONS AND THEIR SIGNIFICANCE

1. Shape
   (a) Factors controlling shape.
   (b) Different shapes & their significance.
   (eg) Nerve cell, Erythrocyte, Melanocyte.
2. Size
   (a) Variations in different organisms.
   (b) Factors governing the size
      1. Np Index, 2. A/V ratio, 3. Metabolic rate.
   (c) Cell size - a problem of structural engineering.
3. Number
   (a) Unicellular, Colonial, Rotifer type.
   (b) Multicellular - differentiated.
   (c) Differential cell division vis-a-vis time of occurrence and duration

C. DIFFERENT TYPES OF CELLS CONSTITUTING DIFFERENT TISSUES.

1. Animal cells
   (a) Epithelial (b) Blood (c) Nervous
   (d) Connective (e) Muscular

2. Plant cells
   (a) Epidermal (b) Undifferentiated
   (c) Vascular (d) Supporting (e) Supp. Fibrous

III. CELL STRUCTURE AND FUNCTION

A. MAIN DIFFERENCES BETWEEN PLANT CELLS ANIMAL CELLS AND UNICELLULAR ORGANISMS.

1. Cell wall, cetrosomes, pigments etc.,
2. Extra cellular architecture of unicellular organisms.

B. VARIOUS ORGANELLES OF A 'TYPICAL' CELL.

1. Boundaries: CEll wall and plasmalemma.
2. Cytoplasm: Ground plasm, Endoplasmic recticulum, Ribosomes, Golgi bodies, Lysosomes, Mitochondria, Plastids, Vacuoles, Centrosomes.
3. Nucleus: Nuclear membrane, Nucleolus and Chromosomes.

C. ORGANELLES - THEIR NATURE, STRUCTURE AND FUNCTION.

1. Cell wall
   (a) Hemicellulose, cellulose, pectin, lignin, suberin, chitin.
   (b) Lattice work of microfibrils of variable length.
   (c) Middle lamella and development of walls.
   (d) Nature of walls in different organisms.
   (e) Permeability to substances and importing mechanical strength.
2. Cell Membrane: Lipoproteinous (Robertson, 1958)
   (a) Arrangement of lipid and protein molecules.
   (b) Semipermeability to substances of different sizes.
   (c) Lability of membrane in forming invaginations and protrusions.
3. Ground substances
   (a) Subject to gelation and solation.
   (b) Theories explaining the nature of ground plasm
   (c) 1. Emulsion theory 2. Foam (alveolar) theory.
   3. Fibrillar theory. 4. Granular theory.
   (d) Cytonemata: Strugger, 1956-7.
   (e) Highly complex enviroment in which all others are maintained.
   (f) Enzymatic faculties working under gene control.

4. Endoplasmic reticulum"
   (a) Network of membrane bound cavities or canal system.
   (b) Tubules, vesicles, cisternal, enchylema.
   (c) Variations among bacteria, erythrocytes, spermatocytes, secretory tissues, etc.
   (d) Palade & Porter (1954): EM studies, lined by ribosomes.
   (e) Function: Intracellular transport, displacement of assimilates, protein, carbohydrate synthesis.
   (f) Effect of anaerobicsis and role in micronucler formation
   (g) Orign: de neve, from cytoplasmic or nuclear envelope

IV. CYTOPLASMIC ORGANELLES

A. RIBOSOMES (MICROSOMES)

1. Palade (1953): Free in the cytoplasm or attached to the endoplasmic recticulum.
2. Sizes and number - variable.
3. Ribonucleoprotein responsible for cytoplalsmic protein synthesis.

B. GOLGI COMPLEX:

1. Canalicular system associated with ER, with smooth surfaces, discovered by Golgi (1898)
2. Size and shape organization and density - Vary with different kinds of cells.
3. Possesses a unit membrane; localisation within the cell variable
4. Lipids, a few enzymes, like alkaline & acid phosphatases.
5. Occur mostly in animals less in plants, absent in fungi.
6. Dictyosomes - during cell division.
7. Origin: from nuclear envelope or endoplasmic recticulum.
8. Function: Synthesis of pancreatic secretions, mucilage, hemicellulose and cell wall matrix.

C. LYSOSOMES

1. Tail of a metamorphosing tadpole, absent in plants.
2. Unit membrane, enclosing hydrolytic enzymes.
3. Lysis - a defence mechanism.
4. Analogy with a phagosome.

D. VACUOLES

1. Plant vacuoles for osmotic regulation.
2. Animal vacuoles: Pinosomes, phagosomes and contractile vacuoles.

E. CENTROSOMES

1. Absent in plant cells.
2. Role in cell division, organization of spindle.
3. Centrioles and surrounding plaques - fibrillar proteins.

F. MITOCHONDRIA

1. Granular, rodlike, universally distributed among eukaryotes.
2. Characteristically aggregate in different types of of cells.
3. Proteins, lipids, -SH groups, trace of nucleic acids.
4. Matrix and cristae: Lamellar, tubular or zig zag.
5. Unit membrane and surfaces for enzymatic activity.
6. "Power houses of the cell": Oxidative metabolism.

G. PLASTIDS OF PIGMENTS

1. Lencoplasts, chromoplasts & chloroplasts.
2. Chloroplasts in plants, photosynthesis.
3. Variations in sizes, shapes, number per cell and distribution in different types of cells of plants.
4. Proteins, lipids, chlorophyll, carotenoids, xanthophyll, steroids and phosolipids, traces of DNA.
5. Unit membrane - Lamellar.
6. Grana - stroma - intergrana.
7. Size and number of grana - vary in different organisms and with light - darkness cycle.

V. NUCLEAR ORGANELLES

A. NUCLEUS (NUCLEAR MEMBRANE, NUCLEOLI & CHROMOSOMES)

1. Prochromosomal and metachromosomal.
2. Robert Brown (1865): "Fundamental unit of life"
3. Interkinetic, kinetic and differential nuclei.
4. Sizes, shapes, number per cell, position within cell vary with different organisms.
5. Extravagant shapes: Surfce/Volume, polyploids.
6. Hertwig's nucleocytoplasmic index.
7. Chromocenters, karyonema.

B. NUCLER MEMBRANE

1. Two layered unit membrane, outer sieve like and inner continuous thinner.
2. Continuous with endoplasmic recticulum.

C. NUCLEOLUS

1. No membrane, usually 1 or 2 per cell-connected with the ploidy level of the chromosomes.
2. Internuclear movements active or passive.
3. Nucleolonema and pass amospha.
4. Mitotic disappearance due to several reasons.
5. Origin: Prenucleolar bodies coalesced to form nucleoli.
6. A sort of reservoir for materials produced by chromosomes - indespensable for protein synthesis.
7. RNA, proteins, traces of DNA.
8. Nucleolus and spindle, Matrix.
9. Role may be auxillary - Ontomutations.

VI. CHROMOSOMES

A. INTRODUCTION

1. Structures connected with metabolism and heredity.
2. Number diploid and haploid is fixed for every species of plants and animals.
3. Shapes, morphology and behaviour constant.

B. MORPHOLOGY

1. Arms, primary construction, secondary construction, satellites and telomeres.
2. Homobrachial or heteroprachial - variations in the position of centromere and the nature of satellites.
3. Chromonemata coiled coil - major & minor coils - pellicke and matrix.
4. Aulocantha + 800 (n) Ophioglossum - 510(n) Ascaris = 1 (n) Haplopappus = 2 (n) number may be of taxonomic significance.
5. Size is no guide to the genetic content. minute in fungi and birds, largest in monocot plants, constant.
6. Secondary construction - nucleolar organizer.
7. Centromere: Micells, spherule and granule theories, role in chromosome movement.

C. EUCHROMATIN AND HETEROCHROMATIN

1. Differences between eu- & hetero chromatin.
2. Late replication, role in sex, staining.

D. ULTRASTRUCTURE

1. Fibrils & microfibrils, chelating substances.
2. Steffensen versus DNA structure and genetic function.

E. TYPES OF CHROMOSOMES

1. Autosomes.
2. Sex chromosomes - X and Y.
3. Supernumerary chromosomes - origin, role and fate.
4. Polycentric, dicentric and rign types: origin & fate.
5. Toccid type: Nature of centromeric material, mitotic behaviour.
6. Lamp brush chromosomes: Oocytes of amphibians, nature of chromonema, loops and their nature, crossing over between loops, loops and gene expression.
7. Polytene chromosomes: Salivary glands of dipherars, polyteny, bands, interbands, and bulges, Balbiani rings (or chromosome puffs) and gene expression, significance.

F. CHEMISTRY AND FUNCTION:

1. DNA, protein, RNA and phospholipids.
2. Constant per cell or any tissue of any organism
3. Arrangement of chemicals into the functional units.
4. Replication and transcription.

VII. APPLIED ASPECTS

A. IMPROVED VARIETIES OF FOOD PLANTS.

1. Hybrid vigour
2. Polyploidy
3. Mutation
4. Breeding and selection
5. Breeding for disease resistance.
6. Seedless fruits etc.
7. Cumulative effects of biocides.

B. HUMAN AFFAIRS

1. Medicine 2. Cancer
3. Environmental mutagenesis
4. Genetic counseling and eugenics
5. Inherited diseases, chromosomal and genic, mental retardation

5. CELLS IN PLANTS, ANIMALS AND PROTISTS

I. CELLS

A. INTRODUCTION

There are many more kinds of cells than there are organisms. Many organisms consists of more than a single cell type.

B. CELL SHAPE

1. Shape related to body plan and physiology of the organism
2. Unicellular organisms: Inherent effects
3. Multicellular organisms:Mechanical forces and cell function
4. Law of minimal spaces
5. Erythrocyte, melanocyte and neuron

C. CELL SIZE

1. Smallest and the largest and ratios between them.
2. Factors governing the size
   (a) Nucleocytoplasmic ratio b. Surface area to volume ratio
   (c) Metabolic rate.
3. A problem of structural engineering: A balance between small cells (for support) and large ones (for area/volume relationship).
4. Range of cell sizes.

D. CELL NUMBER

1. Definite numbers only in some organisms
2. Not all cells divide at the same time and for the same duration of time.

E. ANIMAL CELLS

1. Tissue: Mass of similar cells performing a common function usually forming a part of an organ.
2. Epithelial: Connective, muscular, nervous & blood tissues.
3. Epithelial tissue: Cell shapes, function & secretions
4. Connective tissue: Cartilage, tendon, bone, adipose & fatty tissues.
5. Muscular tissue: Smooth, Cardiac & skeletal
6. Nervous tissue: Neuron & its structure & function.
7. Blood: Leucocytes, lymphocytes & erythrocytes
8. Extracellular material in animal tissues

F. PLANT CELLS

1. Pigmented and vacuolated
2. Epidermal, vascular, supporting & undifferentiated
3. Epidermal tissue: lining of organs with pores & outgrowths
4. Vascular tissue: Phloem & xylem; their structure & function,
5. Supporting tissue: Collenchyma & fibres.
6. Undifferentiated tissue: Parenchyma, filling the space left out by other tissue. Chloroplasts too.

G. PLANT, ANIMAL & PROTIST CELLS: THEIR RELATIVE USES IN THE STUDY OF CELL BIOLOGY.

H. KARYOTIC ORGANIZATION OF CELLS

1. Eukaryotic cells: advanced, their characteristics & examples.
2. Protokaryotic cells: Primitive e.g. Actinomycetes, Spirochetes, bacteria, Mycoplasma, bluegreen algae-etc. Characteristics: absence of membrane systems, golgi complex, mitochondria, plastids, mitosis, nucleus, nucleolus, chromosomes, histones. Presence of one genonema with circular DNA. DNA fibrils soft and small; Replication and transcription simultaneous. Myxophyceae most complex.
3. Mesokaryotic cells: Intermediate. Dinophyceae. (pyrrophyta) Cell & nuclear envelope, chromosomes motochondria, plastids etc present. Histones absent, DNA fibrils small and soft, replication & transcription simultaneous.

6. PHYSICOCHEMICAL ORGANIZATION OF CELLS

I. INTRODUCTION

A. COLLOIDAL PROPERTIES

1. Systems of matter: homogeneous and heterogeneous
2. Types of heterogeneous systems:
   (a) Disperse phase & dispersion medium
   (b) Interfacial and surface tension.
3. Heterogeneous systems
   (a) Suspension
   (b) Emulsion
   (c) Colloid:
      1. Importance of surfaces
      2. Differences from crystalloids;
      3. Lyophilic & lyophobic colloids
4. Colloidal properties of proteins
   (a) Viscocity due to attraction between molecules & structural asymmetry,
   (b) Size ranges for different states of matter
   (c) Hydrophobic & hydrophilic radicals of proteins
   (d) Yield value, thixotropic flow & dilatancy
   (e) Hofmeister's series
   (f) Types of colloidal states
      1. Sol 2. Gel 3. Coaservate & 4. Tactoid.
5. Cells as a polyphasic colloidal system
   (a) Theories proposed for protoplasmic structure :
      1. Granular 2. fibrillar 3. alveolar & 4. Colloidal
   (b) Protoplasmic properties that should be explained by any theory
      1. Appearance of protoplast
      2. Rhythmic changes in appearance and function.
      3. Simultaneous occurrance of many chemical reactions without mutual interference
      4. In vitro requirements of higher temperature and/or, pressure to repeat cellular biochemical reactions.

(c) Some cellular facts

1. Centrifugation impact on

(a) organelles (b) endoplasmic reticulum &

(c) ground substance & their recovery from the disturbances.

2. Dynamic & flexible nature of ER and ground substances

(d) Cell is a complex multitude of chemicals dispersed in a chiefly aquatic medium constituting a polyphasic system.

(e) Development of membranous systems as a mechanical physiological barrier between different polyphasic system.

(f) Organelle as a polyphasic system by itself.

6. Interrelationships between

(a) simultaneous occurrance of a variety of reactions

(b) polyphasic nature of the physical system

(c) delimiting membranes

(d) division of labour among organelles.

7. Structure:

(a) Helical - helix (Pauling): Fibrous proteins

(b) Globular proteins have folded helices

(c) Bonds: Vanderwaal bond, hydrogen bond, ionic bond, covalent bond

8. Ionogenic groups

(a) Acidic groups: Negatively charged due to loss of protons

(b) Basic groups: Positively charged due to gain of protons.

9. Isoelectric point and electrophoresis

B. AMINO ACIDS

1. Carboxyl & amino groups
2. Peptide bond
3. Types of amono acids

C. CARBOHYDRATES

1. C, H. & O.
2. Energy sources for cells
3. Supporting elements for plant cells
4. Plant synthesise.
5. Monosaccharides, Disaccharides & Polysaccharides.
6. Monosaccharides: Cn (H2O)n: Number of C atoms vary.

(a) Trioses, pentoses, hexoses and heptoses.

(b) Pentoses parts of nucleic acids

(c) Hexoses (glucose) source of energy in the cell.

7. Disaccharides: C12 H22 O11 :

   (a) Condensation of two molecules of monosaccharides with the loss of a water molecule.

   (b) Sucrose, maltose: plants (c) Lactose: Animals

8. Polysaccharides: (C6 H10 O5)n :

   (a) Condensation of many molecules of monosaccharides with a corresponding loss of water molecules

   (b) Upon hydrolysis: yield simple sugars.

   (c) Starch: Mixture of two long polymers (amylose & amylopectin)

   (d) Glycogen:

      1. Starch of animal cells, composed of glucose;
      2. Energy reserve, mostly in liver & muscle
      3. Histochemical localisation through iodine reaction.

   (e) Cellulose: Units of cellobiose (C12 H22 O11), a disaccheride isomer of maltose.

   (f) Xylan: Xylose units.

9. Mucopolysaccharides: Ploymers of acetylated hexoseamine

   (a) Meutral mucoploysaccharides (chitin) composed of acetyl glucose amine or galactose or rhamnose.

   (b) Acid mucopolysaccharides: in addition to acetyl glucoseamine, glucoronic acid, sulfuric acid or phosphoric acid.

D. BIOCHEMICAL ORGANIZATION OF CELLS

1. Compounds found in cells of organisms
2. Relative number of molecules of various types in cellular materials.

   WATER:

   (a) Large quantities in more active cells

   (b) Free or bound (5%)

   (c) Medium of distribution, Osmotic regulation.

   SALTS:

   (a) Cations: (a) K (Cytoplasm) dominant, followed by Mg.Na (Nucleus) and Ca. (b) Combine with hormones, nucleotides & proteins e.g. homoglobin (Fe), Chlorophyll (Mg), Hemoeyanin (Cu) and Cytochromos (Fe).

(b) Anions: Phosphate dominant followed by bicarbonate and chloride.

(c) Some salts of cations, in minute quantities are necessary for the functioning of certain enzymes.

K = Cytoplasm; Na: nucleus

(d) Elements found in varius organisms.

(e) Importance of some ions:

CALCIUM: Blood circulation, bone & classified cartilage

POTASSIUM: High in the cytoplasm, especially of muscles & erythrocytes nerve conduction and muscle contraction.

SULPHUR: Essential component of many enzymes and coenzymes, sulfhydril linkages in proteins, protective capacity against ionising radiation.

E. PROTEINS

1. Salient features:
   (a) molecular weight
   (b) C.H, O, N, S. & P.
   (c) amino acids and their sequences.
2. Solubility: In water, alcohol, acidic and basic solutions, or insoluble
3. Zwitter ions: Positive as well as negative ions.
4. Denaturation:
   (a) causes changes in chemical, physical & biological properties.
   (b) Factors affecting denaturation
   (c) Irreversible d. Flocculation & coagulation
5. Globular & fibrous proteins: Corpuscullar & linear.
6. Classification:
   (a) Simple proteins: On hydrolysis yield amino acids e.g., albumins, globulins, protamines.
   (b) Conjugated proteins: On hydrolysis simple proteins & prosthetic groups.

e.g.		
Nucleoprotein	:	nucleic acid
Lipoprotein	:	fatty acids
Glycoproteins	:	Carbohydrate
Mucoproteins	:	

F. LIPIDS:

1. Food reserves
2. Parts of cell structure
3. Fats, waxes, phospholipids, carotenoids & sterols
4. Triglyceride ester of glycerol and three fatty acids, which may be of two or three kinds.
5. Phospholipids:
   (a) Zwitter ions
   (b) Hydrophilic and hydrophobic groups present
   (c) Important in cellular permeability
   (d) Some are characteristic of the species.
      1. Phosphatidyl - inositol: Plants
      2. Phospholipids with large number of unsaturated fatty acids: Animals.
6. Waxes:
   (a) Esters of higher aliphatic acids & long chain fatty acids.
   (b) Protective coatings c. Dipot lipids in seeds, sperms etc.
7. Sterols:
   (a) Aromatic alcohols with free-OH groups
   (b) Animals: Cholesterol
      Plants: Sitosterol
      Fungi: Ergasterol
   (c) Sex hormones, Vitamin D, Cell membrane.
8. Carotenoids:
   (a) Carotenes & Xanthophylls
   (b) Vitamin A, derived from carotene.

G. NUCLEIC ACIDS:

1. Deoxyribose Nucleic Acid: DNA
   (a) Nuclei, bacteriophages
   (b) Sugar, Phosphate, Purines (adenine & guanine) and pyrimidines (cytosine & thymine)
   (c) Nucleotides, Nucleosides, acid & alkaline hydrolysis
   (d) Constancy per cell & organism, A-T and G-C pairs.
   (e) Watson-Crick (1953) model, hydrogen bonding
   (f) Chain linking antiparallel
   (g) Complementarity of regions, hybridization, annealing process.

2. Ribose Nucleic acid: RNA
   (a) Cytoplasm, plant viruses
   (b) Sugar, Phosphate, purines (Adenine & Guanine), pyrimidines (Cytosine & Uracil)
   (c) Nucleolides, Nucleotides, acid and alkaline hydrolysis.
   (d) Ribosomal RNA (R-RNA): 70 - 80% smaller component with 16S and larger one with 23S.
   (e) Soluble / Transfer RNA (s-RNA or t-RNA): 10-15% Water soluble, 4S., aminoacid adaptor molecule.
   (f) Messenger RNA (m-RNA): 5-10%, unstable, single stranded transcription and translation.

H. VITAMINS & GROWTH REGULATORS:

1. Organic molecules of diverse chemistry
2. Act chiefly as parts of enzymes
3. Kinds of vitamins
4. Cytokinins, gibberellins and auxins

I. CYTOCHEMISTRY:

1. Localisation of chemicals in cells
2. Aims
   (a) Determine the localization
   (b) Quantity in each locus
   (c) Establish the function of the chemical

3. Freeze drying:
   (a) Frozen, minimising shrinkage embedded
   (b) Fixation: rendering proteins insoluble by chemicals

4. Colour reactions: Developing characterestic colour reactions employing specific chemical regents. e.g. Feulgen reagent.

5. Microincineration: Heating at high temperature electric furnace, leaving only ash.

6. Enzyme digestion: Removal of one cell constitutent making possible the identification of the other. e.g. Removal of protein by pepsin and trypsin and fix nucleic acid.

7. Cytophotometry: Quantitation of chemicals based on the light absorption by the dyes bound to them.

7. CELL STRUCTURE AND FUNCTION

I. GENERAL FRAME WORK:

A. CHIEF DIFFERENCES BETWEEN PLANT & ANIMAL CELLS & UNICELLULAR ORGANISMS

1. Cell wall, Centrosomes, pigments (b) Extra cellular architecture of unicellular organisms.

B. VARIOUS ORGANELLES OF A 'TYPICAL' CELL

1. Boundaries: Cell wall and plasmalemma
2. Cytoplasmic organelles & ground plasm: Ground plasm, Endoplasmic reticulum, ribosomes, dictyosomes, Lysosomes, mitochondria, plastids, vacuoles, Centrosomes.

II. BOUNDARY SYSTEMS

A. CELL WALL:

1. Chemical composition: Cellulose, Pectin, Lignin etc.
2. Fibrillar organization,
3. Middle lamella and development of walls.
4. Nature of walls in different organisms
5. Permeability & mechanical strength.

B. PLASMALEMMA:

1. Lipoproteinous,
2. Semipermeability
3. Membrane lability for protrusions & invaginations

III. CYTOPLASMIC STRUCTURES

A. GROUND PLASM:

1. Nature:homogeneous plasma;
2. Ectoplasm & endoplasm;
3. cytonemata;
4. Gelation & solution:
5. Theories of organization: Emulsion, Fibrillar, Granular & alveolar theories.
6. Function.

B. ENDOPLASMIC RETICULUM:

1. Discovery: Palade & Porter (1954)
2. Occurrence: In most cells except in prokaryotes
3. Nomenclature

4. Structure:
   (a) Tubular or Vesicular
   (b) Cisternae, Lumen, hyaloplasm;
   (c) Smooth or rough.
5. Ultrastructure:
   (a) Interlacing hollow system;
   (b) Number & location vary;
   (c) Lumen & enchylema;
   (d) Accessory nuclei.
6. Function:
   (a) Intracellular transport;
   (b) Protein & carbohydrate synthesis
   (c) Mitochondrial function during anaerobiosis
7. Origin:
   (a) de noveo:
   (b) Invagination of plasmalemma:
   (c) From nuclear envelope.

C. RIBOSOMES

1. Terminology: Microsomes, ribosomes, polysomes.
2. Ribosomes:
   (a) Discovery: Palade (1953)
   (b) Synonyms: Ergastoplasm, Nissl bodies (nerve cells)
   (c) Occurrence: Association with E.R., in all active cells.
   (d) Properties & function:Basophily,Ribonucleoprotein, protein synthesis.

D. LYSOSOMES:

1. Discovery: de Duve (1950-57)
2. Occurrence: Kidney and spleen
3. Structure: Membrane bound, granular
4. Function: Lysia of foreign bodies and lysis of decrepit cells of an organism (tail of tadpole).
5. Comparison with phagosome

E. GOLGI COMPLEX OR DICTYOSOMES:

1. Discovery: Golgi 1898; Lipochondria (Baker 1957), Dictyosomes (Heslop-Harrison 1965).
2. Structure:
   (a) Smooth canalicular ystems with double membrane,
   (b) Vesicles with inflated extensions.

3. Constitution:
   (a) Fluidy interior
   (b) Phospholipids & Phosphatases.
4. Occurrence:
   (a) Mostly in animals, less in plants
   (b) Polar, scattered, circumnuclear
   (c) Small, Large, reticulate
5. Origin:
   (a) From nuclear envelope
   (b) Special differentiation of ER.
6. Function:
   (a) Water balance, Secretary
   (b) Synthesis of mucilage, Hemicellulose
   (c) Cell wall matrix and phragmoplast (Heslop - Harrison 1965).

F. CENTROSOMES:

1. Occurrence: Animals, sperm cells of ferns & gymnosperms; in plants: Only as a diffuse polar body.
2. Structure: 2 Centrioles surrounded by 9 peripheral triplets.
3. Function: Spindle formation during cell division.

G. MICROTUBULES

1. Characteristics: Ectoplasmic, closer to centrioles or scattered microfilaments, (Bajer & Mole-Bajer 1967).
2. Function: Skeletal, Contractile, chromosomal movement in dividing cells.

H. Vacuoles

1. Plant cells have large central sap vacuoles
2. Animal cells, Pinosomes, phagosomes, contractile vacuoles.
3. Membrane bound.

I. MITOCHONDRIA

1. Occurrence:
   (a) Universal, granular or rod-shaped
   (b) Aggregations in characteristic manner in muscle, nerve and secretory cells.
   (c) More active in dividing cells.
   (d) Stained by Janus green B.

2. Chemistry: Protein (65-70%), Lipid (25-30%), DNA (0.5%) etc.
3. Structure:
   (a) Typical double membrance;
   (b) Tubular or cylindrical
   (c) Cristae
4. Function:
   (a) Power house of the cell (Siekevitz 1957)
   (b) Energy supply to the cites of synthesis.
5. Origin:
   (a) From microbodies:
   (b) From membrane system:
   (c) Transformation of symbiont into organelle.
6. General information:
   (a) Division during cell division
   (b) Traces of DNA of a primitive nature
   (c) Symbiotic theory.

J. PLASTIDS

1. Types: Leucoplasts, chloroplasts, Chromoplasts
2. Chloroplasts :
   (a) Shapes, number, size
   (b) Protein (56%) & Lipids (32%), chlorophyll (8%) & traces of DNA of a primitive type
   (c) Behaviour in hypotonic & hypertonic solutions
   (d) Disappearance in darkness
   (e) Structure: Lamellar, grana, stroma, quantasomes
   (f) Origin from amoeboid proplastids
   (g) Relationship with motochondria h. Transformation of a symbiont into organelle.

IV. NUCLEAR ORGANELLES

Nucleus: nucleolus, chromosomes and nuclear membrane.

A. NUCLEUS:

1. Introduction: Discovery (Brown), Fundamental unit of life, prochromosomal and metachromosomal systems, eukaryotic, protokaryotic & dinokaryotic organisation, classification.

2. Morphology: Nucleocytoplasmic ratios, number, position & size variations, tazonomic value, nuclear uniformity, chromocenters, karyomeres.
3. Structure: nuclear membrane, nucleolus, chromosomes.
   (a) Nuclear membrane: Elastic, 2-layered, lipoproteinous, continuous with E.R., significance.

B. NUCLEOLUS: BUSCH, SIRLIN

1. Introduction: discovery,nonmembranous, movements, variablity occurrence, nucleolonema & pars amorpha.
2. Chemistry: RNA, RN protein turnover, relationship with cytoplasmic RNA.
3. Function: role in spindle organization, protein synthesis, Matrix, nucleolonema & ontomutation
4. Formation: prenucleolar bodies & their assembly, Nucleolar organising chromosome.

C. CHROMOSOMES:

1. Introduction: discovery, definition, role.
2. Morpholoty: number, size variations, shapes & other characteristics, taxonomic importance of numbers, polidy levels & their significance.
3. Karyotype: Chromosome complements, symmetrical & asymmetrical karyotypes.
4. Structure: Brachea, Primary & secondary Construction
   (a) Primary construction: centromere, kinetochore, localised of diffused, or dicentric or polycentric, position characteristic, autonomous, structure: micell, spherule or granule theory, function: responsible for the diagnostic shapes of chromosomes & anaphase movements, chemistry.
   (b) Secondary construction: Olisthrzone, nucleolar or satellited, tertiary intercalary, heterochromatin, spiralisation.
   (c) Satellites: terminal or inter calary, micromacro and linear.
   (d) Telomeres: extremities of brachea, heterochromatic, affinity towards nuclear membrane.
   (e) Brachea: Matrix, chromation-eu-and heterochromatin. Chromonemata-major and minor coils, coiled coil hetero, homobrachial, heterochromatin & euchromatin

heterogeniety in banding and replication patpterns heteropyknosis, Nucleic acids & protein & their distribution, types of heterochromatin & their function, comings, Casperson, Limade-Faria, White.

(f) Strandedness of chromosomes: 2,4, strands, multistranded, steffensen's model. Fibrils and their sizes. Ris, Mazia, Kaufmann.

(g) Chromosome models: arrangement of chemicals in the chromosme (a) protein backbone hypothesis (b) Protein-bridge hypothesis (c) Super coil (d) rope (e) differential coiling hypothesis. Taylor, Steffensen, Dupraw.

(h) Gene structure and chemical nature of chromosomes: Gene-DNA, RNA, Nucleoprotein, chromomere, interchromomere.

5. Types of chromosomes: (a) autosomes (b) sex- chromosomes (c) B-chromosomes (d) polytene (e) Lampbrush (f) Coccid-type chromosomes.

(a) Autosomes: brachea, primary & secondary constructions, satellites, telomeres.

(b) Sex chrosomes: Sex / Chromatin, X,Y,Z, etc; Mittwoch.

(c) B-chromosomes: supernumarary or accessory, Maize Rye, Sorghum etc., acro-or metacentric; mitotically stable or unstable; origin; significance; Ostergren's parasitic theory' phenotypic effects: Muntzing, Ostergren, White.

(d) Polytene chromosomes: Discovery by Balbiani, occur in the salivary glands of Dipteran larvae; Drosophila: 6 strands of fused chromosomes; chromocenter; polyteny: painter, white & Gall; bands interbands, waists, doublets, capsules, puffs,- Beerman's work. Polytene chromosomes in plants.

(e) Lampbrush chromosomes: Diplotene chromosomes of oocytes in sharks, amphibians, reptiles and birds. Structure: Chromomeres, loops, their spinning out as functioning of the genes, dynamics of loop behaviour and heterozygosity, wooly nature, chemistry of the loop, chromomere and inter-chromomeric axis.

Analogy between lampbrush and polytene chromosomes and the role of polyteny and loops.

(f) Coccid-type: Luzula purpurea, Homoptera etc. Centromeric activity diffuse. Brown, Battaglia.

8. CELL DIVISION

I. MITOSIS

A. INTRODUCTION

1. Nuclear division with equitable chromosomal distribution.
2. Discovery: Flemming, Strassburger, Hertwig.
3. Mitotic rate, time and length of mitosis during which organisms grow depend upon adult size.
4. Mitotic components - chromatic and achromatic, mitotic stages.
5. Intranuclear mitosis in Barbulanympha, mitotic durations in different organisms.
   (a) Growth, regeneration and sexual reproduction
   (b) Dividing ability of tissues and mitotic duration variable.
   (c) Chromatic and achromatic apparatus.

B. BIOCHEMCIAL EVENTS

6. Cell division cycle: G1 S G2 M and C phase, and their relative durations in different systems - interphase - hydration—visibility and optical properties: Howard and Pelc, Taylor, Kimber.
7. Characteristics of G1, S, G2, M and C phases.
   (a) G1 (Gap 1 or Growth 1) phase.
   (b) S (Synthetic) phase.
   (c) G2 (Gap 2 or Growth 2) phase.
   (d) Synthesis of DNA, RNA and protein: Chromosome replication.
   (e) Late replication of some chromosome segments.
   (f) Variations in the durations of G1, S & G2 phases.

C. VISIBLE EVENTS: D OR M (DIVISION OR MITOTIC) PHASE

1. Prophase

(a) Changes in the surface tension, Viscosity
(b) Linear contractions of chromosomes by spiralisation.
(c) Nuclear membrane and nucleoli disappear.
(d) Homologous chromosomes, longitudinal duality, relic and relational coiling.

(e) Centrosome move 180 and organises spindle in animal cells. In plant cells spindle fibers ray out polar caps.

Spindle

1. Protein rich in -SH groups, traces of RNA.
2. Shape of spindle variable, spindle-isolaed.
3. Fibers: Continuous, chromosomal, interchromosomal
4. Microtubular organization of spindle.

2. Prometaphase and spindle organization

(a) Spindle organization from polar caps or centrosome.

(b) Types of spindle: pointed, truncated or flared out at the pole, unipolar multipolar, — continuous, chromosomal and interzonal fibres—Direct and indirect mitosis (Schrader 1953).

(c) Nature of spindle, isolation of spindle (Mazia & Das 1954).

(d) Microtubules - cytoplasmic, centromeric and chromosomal microtubules. (Bajer and Mole - Bajer 1969).

3. Metaphase

(a) Chromosome movements consist of Congression, Orientation and Distribution.

(b) Diplochromosomes - paranemic or plectonemic – centromere division.

(c) Chromosomal distribution - hollow spindle.

4. Anaphase

(a) Chromatid separation and their further movement towards poles - factors affecting movement - laggards and forwards - theories of chromosome movement.

(b) Movement of chromosomes synchronous

(c) Haplo chromosomes.

5. Telophase

(a) Chromosomes decondense, converge, relic coils

(b) Reverse of prophase, prenucleolar bodies, nucleolar organization.

(c) DNA content half of prophase nuclei

6. Cytokinesis

(a) No cytokinesis in coenocytic algae

(b) Can occur without karyokinesis - sea urchin

(c) Plants cell plate formation - dictyosomes – phragmoplast - future middle lamella.

(d) Animals: Furrowing by astral cleavage, or disjunctive.

7. **Cell cycle**
   (a) Reproduction of cells -generation time and factors involved.
   (b) DNA amounts versus cell cycle duration.
8. **Significance**
   (a) Constancy of species maintained, transmission of same genetic material.
   (b) Linear heredity established
   (c) Failure of cytokinesis, breakage, unequal segregation of daughter chromosomes, if perpetuated, lead to diversity within species.
9. **Deviations from normal behaviour**
   (a) Acceleration, depression, induction and inhibition of mitosis.
   (b) G1, S, G2 - initiated effects and their appearance in Mitosis = chromosomal and microtubular - spindle and cytokinesis.
   (c) Consequences of deviations.

Amitosis: Tapetal divisions

Endomitosis: Endoduplication, ploidy and DNA, endoprophase, and metaphase etc. differentialed tissues.

II. MEIOSIS

A. INTRODUCTION

1. Discovery by Hertwig, strassburger, Von Beneden, Weismann.
2. Meiosis is coexistant with functional bisexuality – an antithesis of fertilization.
3. Modification of two mitotic divisions where chromosomes divide only once.
4. Separation of homologous chromosomes of maternal and paternal origin.
5. Types: initial, intermediary or terminal

B. REPRODUCTION

1. Offsprings similar or identical with parents.
2. Monoparental and biparental.
3. Transfer of characters - inheritance.

C. LIFE CYCLE

1. Variable life cycle.
2. Genetic constancy of species maintained by meiosis.
3. Occurence: Sporic, gametic or zygotic.

D. SALIENT FEATURES OF MEIOSIS

1. Reduction of chromosome number by the separation of maternal and paternal chromosomes
2. Reshuffling of gene groups.

E. BIOCHEMICAL EVENTS

1. G1, S and G2
2. Variations in the duration of the above.
3. Late replication and synchrony in meiotic systems.

F. VISIBLE EVENTS

1. Prophase - I:

Chromosome replication. Riley, Bennett, Stern, Hotta.

Leptotene: Nuclei larger, DNA replication, beaded appearance, attraction between chromosome ends.

Zygotene: Mating thread stage, synapsis- proterminal, procentric, intermediate-between homologues.

Amphitene: Synezesis of synapsed chromosomes

Pachytene: long stage, nucleolus prominent, bivalents, 4-stranded chromosome contraction, crossing over of segments.

Diplotene: Wooly appearance, condensation, chiasmata—variability, beginning of terminalization, lampbrush chromosomes.

Dictyotene: Unusual, in mosses, sudden elongation (Dill)

Diakinesis: Maximum condensation and terminalization.

Nature of chiasmata: Crossing over, chiasmata, chiasmata frequency, terminalization quotient, breakage - union, precocity, synaptinemal complex, equational – reductional nature, 3-strand and 4 -strand doubles, chiasma interfearence; Moses, Moens, Darlington.

Prometaphase: dyad, bivalent, centromeres lying face to face, origin of spindle material, microtubules.

2. Metaphae - I:

(a) Bivalent arranged at the equatorial plate.

(b) Material & parental chromosomes separated from the bivalent by the action of spindle.

(c) Reduction versus equation.

3. **Anaphase - I:**
   (a) Paternal and maternal chromosomes segregated to the two poles.
   (b) The bipartite chromosome has recombined gene groups.
4. **Telophase - I:** relaxation of chromosome coiling, regrouping of chromosomes. No synthesis of nucleolus. May directly enter prohpase II.
5. **Metaphase II**
   (a) Origin of another spindle.
   (b) Orientation of chromatids at the new equatorial plate.
6. **Anaphase II**
   (a) Separation of chromatids into daughter chromosomes.
   (b) Poleward segregation of daughter chromosomes.
7. **Telophase II**
   Aggregation of chromosomes, decondensaton of chromosomes.
8. **Nature and Polarity of spindle.**
   Cytokinesis I: phragmoplast formation, furrowing etc. Successive type End products of meoisis: eggs, spores, sperms, haploid organisms.

G. **ANALOGY WITH MITOSIS.**

H. **CONSEQUENCES AND SIGNIFICANCE**

1. Results in the formation of spores or gametes.
2. Source of genetic variation through recombination.
3. Antithesis of syngamy.

Cell cycle: Several days in Barley, wheat, G1, S, G2 phase in one of the early prophases, synthesis at the time of crossing over, importance of bud size, meiotic stages and biochemical phase correlations.

Genetic significance

(a) Logical necessity as an opposite of fertilization, in transmission of parental charactors.
(b) Source of variability: segregational and recombinant.
(c) Crossing over percentages and linkage groups
(d) Study of homology between segments
(e) Differential distribution of genes in the 1st. and 2nd. divisions: Equational as well as reductional.

(f) Modification of 2 mitoses: (a) instead of 2 haplochromosomes of 2 homologues, diplochromosome of 1 only goes to pole (b) segments of these diplochromosomes partially changed and (c) contromere did not divide.

(g) A force in evolution — slow and gradual-conservative through variability.

Man with all his noble qualities,
with sympathy that feels for the most debased,
which extends not only to other men
but to the humblest living creature,
with his god-like intellect which has penetrated
into the movements and constitution of the solar system
-with all these exalted powers - still bears in his bodily frame
the indelible stamp of his lowly origin with benevolence

Darwin

9. CHARACTERISTICS OF MICROBES

I. SOME BASICS

A. SPECTRUM OF ORGANIZATIONAL COMPLEXITY OF THE LIVING WORLD CELINDIVIDUAL-POPULATION - COMMUNITY - ECOSYSTEM.

B. SPECTRUM OF LIVING FORMS - ORIGIN AND EVOLUTION

1. Plantae - Classification and characters.
2. Animalae - Classification and characters.
3. Protista - Classification.

C. PROTISTA AND THEIR GENERAL CHARACTERS

Unicellular, colonial, coenocytic and multicellular. Provide insights into the fundamental nature of life.

1. Viruses 2. Rickettsiales 3. Bacteria 4. Protozoa
5. Algae 6. Fungi 7. Yeast

D. ORIGIN OF MICROBIAL LIFE.

E. NATURE

1. Nutritional variations 2. Similarities to plants and animals 3. Prokaryotic and eukaryotic.

F. ECONOMIC IMPORTANCE.

1. Nitrogen fixing and agriculture 2. Plant pathogens 3. Animal and human pathogens 4. Sewage purification 5. Seaweeds, mushrooms and food 6. Industry: Fermentation, antibiotics, algin, agar, etc.

G. MICROBIAL DISTRIBUTION AND ECOLOGY

1. (a) Earth -Oceans between rocks - water on mountain depressions, atmosphere with H_2O vapour, CH4,NH4,H, NO, O or CO2
   (b) Organic compounds like sugars, glycerine, fatty acids, amino acids
   (c) Purines, pyrimidines, polysacharides and protiens
   (d) Nucleic acids, first self-replicating, 2 billion years passed
   (e) Primordial form a protovirus
   (f) Catalytic powers, O_2 using & CO_2 liberating
   (g) Pigmented ones & those that can use O_2 directly & utilise plant carbohydrates

(h) Oxygen Slowly accumulated above ocean surface, UV rays were prevented by it, Explosive multiplication and divergence of forms arose O_2 increased life passed on to land luxuriously - microbes too evolved with respect to multiplication, pigmentation, mobility, etc.

(i) Living world today is a spectrum of forms varying almost imperceptibly from one to the next, protists constituting a small part NA + P, Proto Bacteria-like Ancestral Virus organisms, flagellates, Green algae, Virus Bacteria, Higher animals, Fungi, Algae, Higher plants

H. DISCOVERY OF MICROBES AND ORIGIN

1. Hooke (1665) molds; Leeuwenhoeck (1676); Bacteria
2. Spontaneous origin: Needham (1748)
   from preexisting ones: Schrader & Dusch (1834)
   (cotton plugs and autoclave) & Pasteur
3. Importance: Scientific footing; stimulation of study; comparison of activities with other microbes;germ theories of fermentation, desease demonstrated.

I. GERM THEORY OF FERMENTATION AND DESEASE

1. Schwann & Kutzing (1831-38) founders (yeast): CO_2 evolution, Pasteur: lactic alcoholic acetic butyric fermentation confirmed.
2. Pasteur: anaerobic existence and growth of microbes
3. Microbes bringing specific substrate changes laid foundation to important industrial developments
4. Koch (1876):Bacterial induction of deseases demonstrated first Bacillus anthracis: anthrax epidemic of cattle
5. Koch's postulates
   (a) Fixing organism
   (b) Isolate pathogen and culture
   (c) Reproduce disease in healthy animals d. Reisolate

J. TECHNICAL ADVANCES

1. Schroeter 1872: formation of distinct colonies by different microbes Koch's Students
2. Brefeld: gelatin (sterile) plates
3. Hesse 1883): agar plates
4. Petri: 'Petri'dish of glass

5. Gram (1884): Gram staining
6. Selective enrichment to isolate various bacteria: Koch Beiferinck. Winogradsky

K. VIRUSES

1. Suspected: Pasteur
2. TMV: Ivanowski 1892
3. Animal virus: Loeffler & frosch 1898 (cattle)
4. Bacteriophage: Twort 1915, d'Herella (1917)
5. TMV crystallisation: Stanley (1935)

L. IMMUNITY

1. Once affected, becomes immune to it. Jenner, Pasteur 1881
2. (a) Cellular theory (phagocytosis): Metchnikoff 1884
   (b) Humoral theory (antibody Vs antigen) Behring, Kitasato 1890 (both valid)

M. CHEMOTHERAPY

1. Ehrlich (1900-10)No.606, Arsphenamine against Siphilis
2. Domagk (1935 around) sulfa drugs-Woods'1940 PAMBA explanation
3. Antibiotics: Flemming (1929) accidental finding of Penicillin 1943 Waksman: Streptomycion (Staphylococcus)

N. PHYSIOLOGY AND GENETICS

1. 1924 conference in Holland: Biochemical unity of plants, animals and microbes
2. Beadle and Tatum (1940): Enzymatic diferences vis-a-vis genetic ones: Gene - enzyme theory
3. Tatum & Laderberg (1946) Sexual conjugation and other methods of genetic changes involving DNA always.
4. Spread, recognisability render them admirable subjects of study,
   Aim: exact relationship between chemical structure and general constitution

O. TOOLS: Advances limited by the available equipment

1. Microscope (ordinary, Visible, light, compound) max.1000x, 1.2u R.P
2. UV microscope: 0.1u. UV invisible, short wave lengths, Quartz lenses dark field, good for photomicrography
3. Dark field microscopy: dark ground stop prevents light from entering objecitve except that replaced by objects which hence appear luminous

4. Flouroscence microscopy:
   Intense blue UV object with yellow body light filter auramine dye filter flourecent in E.P in dark field
5. Phase Contrast Microscopy: Slight differences in contrast intensified.

   Undefracted

   Condenser ring of Objective diaphragm light — Defracted

   Phase shifting element in the objective — Particles appear darker or lighter than surrounding medium, than before.
6. Electron Microscopy: Radiations shortest in vacuums Photographed
   (a) 3 Electromagnets (Condenser/Objective/E.P) — Image Observed on a flourescent screen
   (b) Quartz knives
   (c) 0.5 mu sections
   (d) Collodion/Cellophane
   (e) Shadowed by Au/Cr: 3 Dimensional
   (f) - General 10 - 50,000 times
       - 100,000 rare
       - 1,000,000 possible

P. STUDY OF BACTERIA

1. Wet mounting or hanging drop
2. Dyes chromophore (-NO2, N - NO): property of color to dye auxochrome (-OH NH2) Unite with object adsorption or chemical reaction.

   Simple: dye solution, differential = Primary stain - differentiate secondary stain or counter stain.
3. Gram stain, crystal violet, safranin, violet gram positive, red gram negative (95% alcohol differentiation)

Q. CULTIVATION: nutrients, energy source, pH, temp., etc

1. (a) Culture (b) pure culture
   (c) culture medium (d) infusion (tissue extracts)
2. Chemically defined/ synthetic first used by Pasteur
3. Sterilisation: steam at 120 degree C for 15 - 30 mts.
   15 lbs / Sq.inch for 15-30 M (Bunsen flame for mouths & tubes needles bottles etc.

10. MENDELIAN INHERITANCE

A. MENDEL'S EXPERIMENTS ON PEA AND THE CONCLUSIONS ARRIVED AT. The Characters are:

Plant hight	:	dwarf/tall
Flower position	:	axial/terminal
Fruit colour	:	green/yellow
Fruit texture	:	hard/soft
Seed colour	:	Colourded/white
Seed texture	:	smooth/wrinkled
Cotyledon	:	green/yellow

B. FIRST EXPERIMENT: SHORT VS TALL: 3:1 ratio

First law: Law of segregation Factors, dominance, recessiveness homozygosity, heterozygosity, pureline, reciprocal cross, felial generations, symbols, gamete, zygote, genotype, phenotype, back cross, test cross.

C. SECOND EXPERIMENT: Round and yellow seeded plants Vs green and wrinkled and yellow: round and green and wrinkled and green.

Second law: Law of independent assortment. Punnett's square. Factors for different characters segregate independently during reproduction.

D. PROBABILITY: Expected vs Actual, Data Processing,

E. MONOGENIC INHERITANCE, CHARACTERS ARE ON DIFFERENT CHROMOSOMES, APPROPRIATE EXPERIMENTATION AND MAINTENANCE, WIND BARRIERS, DATA COLLECTION, PLANT ASSEMBLY AND ACCURATE OBSERVATIONS, HYBRIDIZATION,

F. REDISCOVERY BY DE VRIES, CORRENS, TSCHERMAK.

G. TERMINOLOGY

1. Crossing & Selfing
2. Felial Generations.
3. Male and Female gametes
4. Phenotype & Genetype.
5. Homozygous & Heterozygrous
6. Dominant & Recessive.
7. Back cross/Test cross 8. Punnett square

H. SIGNIFICANCE

1. Relation to meiosis
2. Segregation as source of variation,

11. HYBRIDISATION, HYBRID VIGOUR

1. Hybridisation: Types, examples, historical aspects
2. Outbreeding and Inbreeding: Factors influencing: perennials and annuals.
3. Protection against self pollination: differential maturity, heteromorphy, separation of sexes, stigmatic protection, enclosure of sex organs.
4. Phenotypic effects - Vigour, metric & meristic characters
5. Quantitative variability -
6. Hybrid vigour - heterosis - Shull - Hybrid Maize.
7. Theories of heterosis
    (a) Physiologic stimulus theory
    (b) Greater initial output hypothesis
    (c) Dominant factor hypothesis
    (d) Linked favourable dominant genes hypothesis
    (e) Over-dominance theory
    (f) Cytoplasmic nuclear reaction
8. Inbreeding and the genotype: Intensity, loci involved, generations of inbreeding: S,F and M generations.
9. Coefficient of inbreeding
10. Inbreeding and selection
11. Inbreeding and qualitative characters - waxy gene of maize.
12. Causes of inbreeding consequences
13. Practical applications: Breeding system
    (a) Cross pollinated crops
    (b) Self pollinated crops
14. Large scale production of hybrid seeds
    (a) Self incompatibility
    (b) Male sterility

12. LINKAGE, CROSSING OVER

A. INTRODUCTION

Different pairs of genes are inherited independently of each other when genes are on different chromosomes. But when two genes are on the same chromosome they stay together in inherititance. This is called Linkage which can be broken only by crossingover in meiosis. (Recombination).

B. HISTORY OF DISCOVERY:

1. Crossing two varieties of sweet peas where parental combinations were in exaggerated proportions.
2. "Coupling and repulsion" theory.
3. Morgan's theory of linkage and crossingover.
4. First clear report of linkage in maize by Collins and Kempton in 1911 between waxy endosperm(wx) and aleurone color (C).

C. LINKAGE:

1. Example of chickens: with creeper, normal, rescomb and single comb genes
2. Diagram of crosses
3. Recombinant and non-recombinants, recombinants due to crossing over.
4. Percentage of crossing over is a direct function of gene distance on the linkage map.

D. CHROMOSOME MAPPING:

1. Extrapolation of linkage map to chromosome is chromosome map.
2. Drosophila, Maize etc.
3. Cross involving 3 pairs of factors necessary for checking the gene distances in the 2 pair crosses.
4. Positions of nearer genes determined by testing them with reference to the known one in 2 pair and 3 pair crosses.
5. Gene order, combining map segments, interference & coincidence.

E. TIME AND PLACE OF CROSSING OVER:

Meiosis, absence of C.O. in Drosophila male and female silk moth, significance of crossing over, factors affecting-crossing over frequencies, genetic and cytological crossing over, formation of chiasmata.

13. MUTATIONS: CHROMOSOMAL AND GENIC

I. GENERAL

A. INTRODUCTION

1. Source of variation in evolution
2. Source of useful characters for human use.
3. Discovered and named by Waagen (1869).

B. DEFINITION

Darwin-Continuous variation as in sports De-Vries and Korjinsky: Any sudden heretable change of not traceable to the genetic recombination & segregation. Mayr (1949): Discontinuous chromosomal change with a genetic effect.

C. CLASSIFICATION

Dobzhnansky 1953, Gaul 1964.

D. SOMATIC MUTATION: BLAKESLED

1. Genetic change in the axillary or terminal bud.
2. Cause-chromosomal or mutational, spontaneous or induced.
3. Mosaics in animals.
4. Classification. Sectorial/periclinal/mericlinal
5. Special chimaeras are important in horticulture/ Flower colour/ fruit colour in apple.
6. Examples - Datura, Solanum, Crepis.

E. GERMINAL MUTATIONS

II. DETAILS

A. NUMERICAL: Stebbins, Kihara, Eigsti, Dustin,

1. Introduction: Multiplication of whole set of linkage groups or addition/deletion of a few linkage groups.
2. Classification:
   - (a) Haploidy-only one set of linkage group
   - (b) Diploidy-Two sets of linkage group (Homologues/ Maternal/Paternal/Allelic)
   - (c) Euploidy- Multiplies of linkage groups

-	Triploidy	=	3	
-	Tetraploidy	=	4	Autotetraploidy
-	Pentaploidy	=	5	
-	Hexaploidy	=	6	Allotetraploidy

Aneuploidy - Addition or delation of same linkage group.

(a) Nullisomic - absence of two homologous linkage groupsresult in lethality.

(b) Monosomic - (2n-1) absence of one linkage group result in half of the spores without one linkage group. e.g. Triticum aestivum (2n=42)

Sears et al: Mono 1 to Mono 21 were evolved. The 21races each deficient in one linkage group show phenotypic deficiency corresponding to the missing linkage group.

(c) Trisomic - (2n+1) - Addition of one linkage group double trisomic (2n+1+1)

(d) Tetrasomic - (2n+2) addition of two linkage groups double tetrasomic (2n+2+2)

(e) Polysomic - (2n+n)

3. Causes: Restitution - Failure of spindle, Endoduplication of chromosomes Failure of cytokinesis.

4. Induction of polyploidy

   (a) Chemicals - especially colchicine-C. Mitosis—Acenaphthene, Griseofulvin, Vinblastine, Vincristine, Podophyllin.

   (b) Colchicine - alkaloid from Colchicine autuminale, inhibits spindle Has no effect on colchicum Blackslee (1937) Eigsti & Dustin (1945-1953).

   (c) Methods - seed treatment, Bud treatment

5. Changes due to polyploidy

   (a) Gigas character b. Increased growth rate

   (c) Increase in active principles of medicinal plants

   (d) Vitamins in fruits and vegetable increase.

6. Economic importance

   (a) Wheat, Sugarcane, Many horticultural plants are Polyploids

   (b) Seedless melon, grapes etc.

   (c) Gene mapping in complexes of Solanum, wheat (A B D) genome etc.

   (d) The evolution of monosomic lines in case of wheat was helped in mapping the economically important character and subsequently using them hybridization progress.

7. Evolutionary importance

   (a) No new species originate-only vigor and growth increase

(b) Associated with hybridization-eg-Solanum,Sisymbrium, Triticum complexes

(c) Not progressive but conservative as it involves only alternations in the existing linkage group.

(d) Variability may result in subspecies when vigorously acted upon by selection pressure.

B. STRUCTURAL

1. Breaks

(a) Chromosome break, Re-union may or may not take place

(b) Chromatid break

(c) Centromere break-mis division or isochromosome may result.

(d) Telomeric break-ring chromosome

(e) Spontaneous breaks-Rare

(f) Induced break-by many chemicals or irradiation.

2. Losses (Deletions)

(a) Portions of linkage group may break up & get lost.

(b) Meiotic consequence a heteromorphic pair with a deletion loop.

(c) If deletion includes important genes lethality or sterility of the gemetes will be caused.

(d) Rearrangements

(e) Causes and consequences

1. Occur after break and reunion

2. Reunion may be within the same chromosome or between homologous or between different homologues.

3. Reunion within the same chromosome in a reversed order of genes-Inversion.

4. Additions (Duplication) Dosage effect or suppressor effect

(a) Segments increase or added up

(b) Some genes hence will be represented more than once on each chromosomes.

(c) Results in increased phenotypic expression of the concerned genes.

5. Conclusion (a) Important in evolution of population, (b) Generally bivalent in population showing

polymorphism, (c) Besides usual effect, secondary position effects are also caused.

C. GENE OR POINT MUTATION

1. Occurrence

   (a) Gametogenesis (b) Sporogenesis (c) Zygotene

2. Types of phenotypic changes

   (a) Physiologic traits eg-nutritional requirement of adenine in Neurospora crassa.

   (b) Behavioural trait - eg- Reaction to light (Rats) and gravity (Rice).

   (c) Qualitative traits - eg- Quality of grain (lysine in wheat and maize) chlorophyll mutants.

   (d) Qualitative traits-eg

      1. Metric-Yield of a crop,
      2. Meristic - number of flowers & inflorescence

   (e) Homeostasis - eg –

      1. Petaloidy of cotton
      2. Antennae into legs in Drosophila

3. Randomness

   (a) Direction & types of mutation unpredictable,

   (b) Some genes may mutate any number of times while some never do.

4. Recessiveness

   (a) Mutant (mutated genes) is mostly recessive to the wild type. (nonmutated form)

   (b) Hence mutation appear late in the progeny.

5. Repeated occurrence

   (a) Gene changes are generally recurrent.

   (b) Frequency with which gene alters to another varies eg. Hemophilia once in 300.

6. Reversibility

   (a) Some examples are

      1. Forked mutant reversed to the wild type normal bristles.
      2. Paler mutant reverted to the wild type bright red eye.
      3. Streptomycin resistant—Streptomycin suceptible-Streptomycin dependent in E Coli.

   (b) Rates of forward mutations are always higher than the backward mutation.

7. Classification
   (a) Classification based on manner of occurrence:
      1. Spontaneous:
         (a) Reasons are metabolic
         (b) Hot spots in chromosomes more susceptible to spontaneous occurence than induction: Levine 1963.
         (c) Charactersitc of spontaneous and induced mutationos are different
      2. Induced:
         (a) Muller (1921) Drosophila, using x-rays (b) Target theory (c) Mutant / mutagenesis / mutagen (d) Mutagens
         1. Radiation- UV, X-ray - U-ray
         2. Chemicals - mustard gas/alkylatic agents
   (b) Classification based/on extent of mutation-
      1. Micromutation - Small
         (a) Manifest-expressed, (b) Cryptic - hidden,
         (c) Transpecific
      2. Macromuation – Large
         (a) Transpecific-Viable between different species also (b) Intraspecific - Viable only within the species.
         (c) Classification based on the mode of origin at the gene level
         1. Transition - Purine replaced by another purine / pyrimidine replaced by another pyrimidine eg- Bromouracil and 5-methyl cytosine.
         2. Transversion - Purine into pyrimidine & vice-versa.
         3. Substitution - atoms of purine and pyrimidine replaced by foreign radicals.
         4. Tautomerism and isomerism
8. Conclusion
   (a) Applied value and the quest for directed mutation: crop production and resistant to disease
   (b) A probable reason for malignant disease
   (c) Pollutants causing spontaneous variability (oten harmful) to human and other populations.

(d) Role in evolution of plants and animals by causing continuous variability. (Micromutation) as well as discontinuous (Macromutation) type.

III. ACTIONS OF CHEMICALS ON CELLS

A. DIFFERENCES BETWEEN PLANT AND ANIMAL CELLS.

B. RESPONSES OF DIVIDING CELLS TO CHEMICALS

1. Mitotic inhibition or retardation- G1, S and G2 phases.
2. Mitotic induction or acceleration - role of hormones, speeding up of cell cycle, differentiated cells.
3. Antispindle effects, C - mitosis
4. Antichromosomal effects
5. Inhibition of cytokinesis - bimitosis.

C. CONSEQUENCES OF ABERRANT CELL DIVISION.

D. SPECIFIC AND MULTIPLE EFFECTS, DELAYED AND NON-DELAYED EFFECTS

E. BIOCHEMISTRY OF THE ABERRANT MITOSIS

F. APPLIED ASPECTS OF ABERRANT CELL DIVISION - ENVIRONMENTAL MUTAGENESIS, AGRICULTURE, PHARMACOLOGY AND CANCER.

In every walk with nature one receives far more than he seeks.
When we try to pick out anything by itself, we find it hitched to everything else in the Universe.
The Sun shines not on us but in us. The Rivers flow not past, but through us.

John Muir

14. GENES AND ACTIONS

I. CLASSICAL CONCCEPTS

A. Rediscovery of Mendel's Work.

B. Presence and Absence Theory

C. Mosaic Theory

D. Gene Theory of Morgan and its Postulates.

E. Gene Complex Theory

F. Discovery Of Exceptions To Mendel's & Morgan's Postulates

1. Incomplete dominance 2. Pseduo = alleles & multiple alleles.
3. Pleotropism & polygeny 4. Position effect.

G. Mendel, Johannsen, Morgan, Goldshmidt

II. LINKAGE, CROSSING OVER AND GENETIC MAPS

A. LIMITATIONS OF MENDELIAN INHERITANCE.

B. RELEVANCE OF MEIOSIS TO MENDELISM.

C. LINKAGE OF GENES, their crossing over to the homologous & consequences.

D. EXPERIMENT 1:

Creeper and rose comb vs (chicken) normal and single comb.

Experiment 2:

Scute, echinus and crossvein-less vs wild type (Drosophila)

E. NON RECOMBINANTS AND RECOMBINANTS. Percentage recombination. Regions of crossing over. Single and double cross overs.

F. CROSS OVER PERCENTAGES as functions of gene distances - Construction of genetic map.

G. INTERFERENCE, COINCIDENCE.

III. GENE EXPRESSION AND INTERACTIONS

A. APPEARANCE OF CHARACTERS IN THE PHENOTYPE

1. Monogenic inheritance-Allelism, dominance, segregation, independent assortment (Mendal, Morgan)
2. Pseudoallele and multiple alleles (Green)
3. Digenic inheritance-gene interaction, supressers position effect. Emerson.
4. Polygenic inheritance.
5. Pleiotropism (Dobzhansky)

B. GENE EXPRESSION

1. Expressivity 2. Penetrance
3. Variations in different sexes 4. Control by environments

C. GENE INTERACTIONS

1. Epistasis 2. Modifiers 3. Suppressors

D. PSEUDALLELES: Tests of recombination and complimentarity

E. POSITION EFFECT (Cis - and trans- types)

IV. MODERN CONCEPTS

A. BASICS

1. Gene enzyme hypothesis 2. Gene polypeptide hypothesis
3. Terms - Cistron, Recon, Muton, Codon, Operon
4. Plasmagenes, Episomes.

   Operational unit of DNA controlling protein synthesis, recombination, Mutation.

B. CLASSIFICATION:

Recon = smallest element of the genetic map which is interchangeable but not divisible as shown by the test of (*) genetic map which when altered gives rise to mutant forms.

Cistron = A map segment corresponding to a function as shown by the test of complementarity (Benzer)

C. SIZE:

1. Position on the chromosome map
2. U.V. estimation by Muller and prokofyeva-1250 Ao
3. X-ray estimation based on target theory 40-90 Ao
4. Polypeptide theory — 35000 Ao

D. CHEMICAL NATURE:

1. Constancy of DNA from cell to cell.
2. Correlation of DNA with ploidy.
3. Transforming principle in Pnumococcus-DNA (Avery et al)
4. Radioactive P and not S was found infected by phages in Bacteria.

E. MODE OF GENE ACTION:

1. Gene-enzyme theory
   (a) Beadle and Tatum (1941) on Neurospora crassa*.
   (b) Use of mutation and differential nutrient culture and haploid ascospores.

(c) Tracing of characters ot Biochemical reactions and enzyme.

2. One gene one polypeptide theory
   (a) Yanofsky and Crawford (1959)
   (b) As a segment to the 3 di-mensional structure of proteins.
3. Operon Hypothesis-(Jacob and Monod 1961) Structural, operator, regulating genes, Respression, Induction initiator and terminator.

F. MECHANISM OF GENE ACTION:

1. Duplication, Replication
2. Transcription
   (a) RNA synthesis dependent on DNA
   (b) RNA polymerase, transcriptase.
   (c) Base composition complementary to that of DNA
   (d) Site for the protein synthesis.

   Gene (DNA) — Character (Phenotype)

   DNA-RNA-enzyme-Biochemical pathways-Character.
3. Translation
   (a) Site = Ribosomes
   (b) rRNA act as template for mRNA
   (c) tRNA hook aa and bring them to Ribosomes
   (d) tRNA = 1. small mol.wt.
   2. small No.of nucleotide
   3. short life span
   4. Specificity
   (e) Lineup of aa as peptide bond.
4. Reverse transcription: Temin, Baltimore

G. GENES OUTSIDE CHROMOSOMES: Plasmagenes, Sager, Ryan,

H. RECURRENT GENES: Zinder, Wollman, Jacob

1. Episomes eg (a) Prophage (b) Sex factors
2. Prophage
   (a) Phages of bacterial virus-free phage, vegetative phage and prophage.
   (b) Free-phage-non-living-cause lytic life cyclo prophage--causes lysogenic cycle

(c) Lysogeny—(1) Duplication (2) Recombination (3) Prophage has all attributes of a gene (4) Application: Nif gene transfer.

I. CODE FOR GENE ACTION:

1. Specificity of protein
2. Inter 1 relationships between DNA, RNA and Protein.
3. Complementarity between base sequences in DNA and a sequences to protein.
4. Nature of the code-coding hypothesis
5. Code composition—1,2 or 3 triplets
6. Reading of the code: (a) overlapping (b) Partially over lapping (c) Comma hypothesis (d) Non-overlapping.
7. Relation between the number of bases in the codon and the available amino acids.
8. Experiment to show the codon specificity to particular aa.
   (a) Poly U,-phenyl alanine.
   (b) Substitution of bases on DNA by mutation
9. Codon dictionary
   (a) Non-Sense code—Opal Ochre amber
   (b) Partial degenerancy
   (c) Sense code.

One cannot but wonder how an environment can make people despair and sit idle and then, by changing the conditions, one can transform the same people into matchless performers.

Muhammad Yunus

15. MAMMALIAN AND HUMAN CYTOGENETICS

A. MAMMALIAN SYSTEMS

1. Karyology
2. Polymorphism in populations
3. Sex chromosomes
4. Replication patterns of autosomes and sex chromosomes
5. Euchromatin, heterochromatin and late replication

B. HUMAN SYSTEMS

1. Karyology
2. Sex Chromosomes and abnormalities associated with them- Turner's syndrome, Kleinfelter's syndrome.
3. Chronology of chromosomal replication
4. Autosomal abnormalities - trisomics and deletions
5. Chromosomal aberrations and disease.
6. Induced chromosomal aberrations and their consequences - Psychedelics, contraceptives, food additives, drugs etc.

C. RELEVANCE OF MAMMALIAN CELL STUDIES TO HUMAN SYSTEMS

1. Heritable diseases
2. Birth defects
3. Cancers
4. Genetic Counseling
5. Organ transfer
6. Others

2

Basic Ecology

1. CONCEPTS AND HISTORY
2. ENVIRONMENTAL FACTORS
3. HABITAT CHARACTERISTICS
4. RESPONSES TO ENVIRONMENT
5. SUCCESSIONS IN HABITATS
6. CYCLES AND DISRUPTIONS
7. ACID RAIN
8. DISTURBED HABITATS
9. AUTECOLOGY AND GENECOLOGY
10. POPULATIONS
11. COMMUNITIES
12. ECOSYSTEMS
13. TERRESTRIAL ECOSYSTEMS
14. AQUATIC ECOSYSTEMS
15. BIOGEOGRAPHY
16. ZOOGEOGRAPHY
17. HUMAN ECOLOGY
18. ENVIRONMENTALISM

Syllabus

1. Environment, Ecology and Human Welfare: Threatened niches of man; Efforts to save the planet. History, Components, functions, current status and Scope, Ecology in India.
2. Environmental cycles, Biological Response, Biogoeochemical cycles Nutrient cycles and budgets,
3. Acid rain, Global Warming, Ozone depletion, Eutrophication, Desertification Chemicalisation and Irradiations, Soil Erosion: past, present and future
4. Variation and Adaptation, Natural Selection and Micro Evolution Population processes - structure, growth, dynamics, Regulation, Productivity, Food chains, webs and pyramids, Energy flow, Community Structure, Species diversity, Succession, Concepts and functions
5. Interrelationships - Predator - Prey & Host - Parasite, etc Competitions - inter & intra specific; Animal behaviour
6. Ecosystems of the world- Geology, geography, climate & biology, Evolution in time and space, Principles of Phytogeography and Zoogeography
7. Carrying capacity, Buffering ability and Diversity of the Biosphere. Germplasm depletions and conservation
8. Human population - Processes, Problems, Subsistence Systems – Agro - ecosystems, Urban ecosystems, Consumption, Environmental health.
9. Impact Assessments, Conservation & Restoration, Science & Technology Economics, Politics

References

1. Colinvaux, PA 1973. Introduction to Ecology. Wiley
2. Ehrlich, PR and Roughgarden J 1987. The science of Ecology. Macmillan
3. Krebs, CJ 1985. Ecology. Harper& Row
4. Lederer, RJ 1984. Ecology and Field Biology. Benjamin/Commings
6. Lloyd, JR 1980. Man and the Ecosystem. Macmillan
7. Luding, JA and Reynolds JR 1988. Statistical Ecology
8. Smith, RL 1986. Elements of Ecology. Harper & Row

1. CONCEPTS AND HISTORY

I. INTRODUCTION

1. The settled facts of ecological knowledge can be summarised in a conceptual form. Some of these assumed standard terminology. However all concepts cannot be embedded in terms. Nor are all terms embody concepts. Such conceptual terms are enumerated below to constitute a base line of ecological learning and awareness. These are expected to serve as scientific expressions of the "commandments" given earlier.
2. Species is a uniform interbreeding population spread over time and space.
3. Vegetation collective and continuous growth in space, which is described. Flora is the species content of a region irrespective of the number of each, which is listed. Population is a group of individuals of the same species in a given area.
4. Community is a group of populations of different in a given area.
5. Ecosystem is an system where communities interact with physical environment leading to clearly definable trophic structure and biotic diversity with flow of materials and energy.
6. Climax is a terminal community in equilibrium with the environment. There may be only one such community (monoclimax theory) or more (polyclimax theory).
7. Biome is a complex of several communities some in climax stage and others in different stages of sucession maintained under similar climatic conditions.
8. Succession is a natural process by which different groups or communities colonize the same area in a sequence over a period of time. If this starts on a substratum without life it is primary. If it starts on a biotically built substratum, it is secondary.
9. Standing quality is the amount of inorganic substances present in an ecosystem at any given time.
10. Standing Crop is the amount of living material present in an ecosystem/population/community which is expressed in numbers or weight per unit area.
11. Biomass is the standing crop expressed in weight.
12. Ecological Pyramids are the graphic representations of the structure and function at successive trophic levels of an ecosystem which may be shown in numbers, biomass or energy content.

12. Productivity is the amount of organic material accummulated in the living component per unit time. It is primary when the plants trap the radiant energy to produce organic substances. It is secondary when it is stored by the consumer. Total rate of photosynthesis is gross productivity. Deduction of material used up in respiration leaves out net productivity.
13. Food chain is the transfer of food energy from the plants through a linear series of organisms - primary & secondary consumers, etc.
14. Food web is the interlocking pattern of a number of food chains linked with each other at several points.
15. Adaptation is any feature of the organism that aids it to survive under the conditions of its habitat.
16. Ecad is a plant population that markedly differ from other populations of the species in vegetative features & these variations are temporary and reversible with the change in the habitat.
17. Ecotype is a plant populations that markedly differ from other populations of the species and these variations do not change with the habitat.
18. Ecotone is a zone of transition, presenting a situation of special ecological interest between two different types of communities.
19. Liform is the form of the plant with all its adaptations to climate.
20. Biological Specturm is the frequency of distribution of various life forms in the flora of a place.
21. Bioshpere is the part of the planet earth that supports life.
22. Biogeochemical cycles are the cyclic movements of chemical substances through soil, water, biota and atmosphere.

II. THE COMMANDMENTS

1. Plants and animals are products of evolution - genetics, selection and ecology. Therefore their distribution is limited by barriers.
2. Competitions exist among species for nutrients and space, food and eproduction. Therefore populations do not increase without limits.
3. All habitats are not equally good for any given species.
4. If exploitation of organisms is faster than renewability, extinction can ensure, preceded by depletion.
5. Balances among species can become strong in time which may be mutally beneficial. They may eventually become stable and permanent.

6. Plants and animals suffer from disturbances in the habitat but the former are more resilient to recover. Thereforeo communities can rebound from disasters.
7. The webs and chains for food etc throw up a dominant species. This keystone species may be ultimately very essential to a community.
8. Since the organisms have cycles of life span, habitats, the cycles of climatic conditions, elements too are re-cycled in all natural systems.
9. Climates may change globally due to a variety of reasons, affecting organisms over decades in many ways. Therefore communities too change.
10. Biological and environmental factors operate modifying the systems even drastically over centuries. Thus evolutionary changes in all the natural systems are a constant phenomenon.
11. Plant productivity, a resource to animal and humans is subject to the above conditions and is always greater in nature than in nurture, for, the former is balanced with minimum inputs.
12. Minor modifications/variations occur between plants and animals concerning the above due to their mobility, metabolism and nutrition.
13. The resourcefulness of organisms and others in the ecosystem led to domestication, agriculture, ownership commodification, consumerism and commerce, experience and experimentation, through (science and technology) Economics and Politics influence them first and finally determine them. Man therefore is a political animal. Inherting all the instincts and behaviour of the animal kingdom, useful to him, man dominated fellow men crisis depens.
14. Man, who is a basic igradient of the above ecological scheme, alienated himself and controlled the above scheme resulting in serious consequences. So, ecology became an important study and vital for human survival.
15. Thus ecology deals with all aspects of planetary life - not of sectors - Holistic. Therefore ecology is everyone's business - not of sections - Humanistic.

    Thus the roots of basic ecology of plants, animals, microbes in soil and water tend to be cut and curtailed by the most keystone species - Man. Thinking and concerned humans developed theories regarding the consequences and how to manage or live with them. More ponderously, can they be managed at all.

III. TAXONOMY, APPROACHES, RELATIONSHIPS

A. DEFINITIONS

1. Scientific Natural history (Elton 1927)
2. Study of structure and function of nature (Odum 1971)
3. All relations of all organisms to all environments (Taylor 1936)
4. Interactions determining distribution and abundance of organisms (Krebs 1987)
5. Study of Plants and animals in their relations to each other and to their environment (Kendrigh 1971)

B. OBJECTIVES

1. Geographic distribution and abundance
2. Temporal changes in occurrence, abundance and behaviour
3. Interrelationships with other organisms
4. Adaptations and adjustments
5. Behaviour
6. Evolutionary development of the above
7. Productivity
8. Modelling of Systems, processes and their progress
9. Disturbances and consequences
10. Management development for human welfare.

C. APPROACHES TO THE STUDY

1. Descriptive: Natural history (endless and aimless)
2. Functional: Relationships & Proximal causes (static)
3. Evolutionary: Ultimate causes (improbable theories)

D. METHODS OF STUDY

1. Mathematical 2. Laboratory 3. Field

E. SCHOOLS OF THOUGHT

1. Upsalla School
2. Zurich - Montpellier School (Braun-Blanquet)
3. Russian
4. British (Tansley)
5. American (Clements)

F. CLASSIFICATION

1. Utilitarian: Theoritical - Applied
2. Taxonomic: Plant-Animal-Insect-Avian-etc,
3. Geographical: Terrestrial - Aquatic - Marine - Estuarine
4. Conceptual: Individual, Population, Community, Ecosystem
5. Functional: Physiological, genetic, Evolutionary, behavioural, sociological
6. Sociological: Populations (Distribution: dispersal, light, moisture, temperature, water, soil, habitat, interelationships Abundance Growth, nutrition, competition) Community (Distribution, structure, changes, diversity, organisation, productivity,cycles)

G. CURRENT TRENDS

1. Systems of interacting species processing nutrients and energy - comparions on different continents
2. Evolution and Ecology: How natural selection moulded ecological patterns.

H. CONCLUSIONS

1. Ecology now is in a great growth phase - where Chemistry was in 18th century.
2. Ecology is for Environmental Studies, what physics is for engineering.

I. BRANCHES OF ECOLOGY

1. Ecology –Plants-Animals
2. Bio-/Zoo-/Phyto - geography
3. Population Ecology
4. Community Ecology
5. Ecosystems – general
6. Forests
7. Mangroves
8. Aquatic - lakes, rivers
9. Marine - Estuarine, coastal
10. Desert
11. Alpine
12. Grassland
13. Islands
14. Mountains
15. Vectors
16. Human Ecology
17. Pollution-Air, Water,
18. Toxicology
19. Urban Ecology
20. Systems Ecology/ Modeling
21. Wildlife Ecology
22. Natural Resources-Biotic & Nonbiotic
23. Management
24. Impact Assessments
25. Environmental Mutagenesis
26. Agro ecosystems
27. Eco development
28. Ecological Genetics/ Genecology
29. Evolutionary Ecology
30. Behavioural Ecology
31. Remote Sensing

IV. ORIGINS, GROWTH, CURRENT TRENDS

A. ROOTS

1. Religious scriptures recognised the value of ecology
2. Origins and development of agriculture demonstrated the ecological acumen of the then humans
3. Egyptians, Babylonians have experienced plagues of animals
4. High reproductive rate of Mice and locusts was noticed by Aristotle
5. Providential ecology (Herodotus & Plato). Nature is designed to benefit all organisms - Harmony being the ultimate goal. This is possible by operating balances in nature.

B. ORIGINS

1. Graunt (1662): Population of humans quantified in London. Doubling through reproduction expected in 65 years
2. Leewenhock (1687): Theoritical rate of increase in flies 1 pair, 3 months will give rise to 746, 496
3. In 1762, Mynah bird introduced to Mauritius from India to control locusts.
4. In 1775, Predatory ants from nearby mountains were brought to date palm orchards in Arabia.
5. Malthus (1798): Population increase geometrically (1-2-4-8-16) Resources increase arithmetically (1-2-3-4).
6. Mid 19th Century: Darwinian Natural history. Darwin, Thoreau, Wallace, Banks, Brown.
7. Natural Selection replaced Providential ecology i.e. harmony through balances (Malthus, Lyell, Sponcer, Darwin).
8. Foundations are thus laid by Natural history, Demography, Medicine and Agriculture.

C. GROWTH

1.	Buffon (1756)	Natural history - touched all modern ecological problems and concepts
2.	Forbes (E) (1844)	Marine animals, seasonality
3.	Haeckel (1869)	Total relations of animals to organic and inorganic environment
4.	Forbes (SA) 1887	Populations in lakes increase, checked in favour of a balance
5.	Warming (1895, 1909)	Communities, first course in Ecology
6.	Cowles (1899)	Plant succession on sand dunes

7.	Ross (1908-11)	Malaria - Mosquitoes - Infections - Human - ecological relationships at population level
8.	Zurich: Schroter Montpellier: Flahault	Phytosociology
9.	Clements (1916)	Succession of Vegetation
10.	Fisher (1939)	Quantification of Rare (1-2 nos) common (loose count) & abundant (bewildered)
11.	1935	Era of population and community ecology
12.	Tansley (1935)	Ecosystem approach - Energy flow Kendeigh - Odum, Whittaker, Pearsall etc
13.	Turesson: Ecotypes (1920s)	Genecology, Ecotypes and Ecological Genetics

D. CURRENT TRENDS

1. Until 1960s ecology was not considereid important. The awakening came due to destruction of nature by increasing populations and consumerism. (Therefore "ecology" is used for everything - not correct - This deals with organisms and environment only) These human environmental problems are the material broad of human concern and interest.
2. Applied ecology - Agriculture, Fisheries Wildlife managment, Conservation, restoration, Forestry, Silvicultures
3. Ecology applied to human affairs - Habitat disturbances and consequences
4. Ehrlich, Darling, Leopold, Hardin, Carson, Sax, Mellanby, Nicholson DuBois and many others have taken stands on social issues
5. Ecosystem approach, stress ecology, Modelling and predictious, conservation and restoration, Resources - Ecology- all habitats - deep sea to polar corners.

V. INDIAN SCENE

A. PHILOSOPHICAL ASPECTS

1. Ecological thoughts in Hindu way of life and scriptures. Panchabhootas, cycles of life, Dashavataras - evolution of life and doom.

2. Buddhism, Jainism and Hinduism: Concern for plants, animals and man as part of nature

B. BRITISH INDIA

1. Descriptive accounts of foresters
2. Floristic and faunistic surveys (Roseburgh et al)
3. Wildlife descriptions: Corbet et al)
4. Indeon (1921) Saxton (1922): Ecology of upper gangetic plains, Misra reviewed (1946-59)
5. Troup (1925): Forests, grasses
6. Bor (1947,48): Forests
7. Champion (1929, 35, 37): Forests
8. Agharkar (1924): Grasslands, Mangroves
9. Bharucha (1930,36): Grasslands

C. INDEPENDENT INDIA

1. Botanists
   - (a) Bharucha (Bombay): Grasslands, weeds
   - (b) Misra: Ecotypes, Autecology, ecophysiology, communities of a variety of habitats
     - (i) 1937-45: Banares (ii) 1946-55: Saugar
     - (iii) 1956-62: Banares (iv) 1963 - Others
   - (c) Pandeya (Rajkot): Productivity, Systems, Grasslands
   - (d) Ramakrishnan (Chandigarh-Shillong): Ecotypes, shifting cultivation
   - (e) Singh (JS) (Kumaon-Banares): Himalayan, Modelling
   - (f) Kaul (Srinagar): Lakes, eutrophication
   - (g) Varshney (Delhi): Pollutionv & Plants
   - (h) Gadgil (Bangalore): Theoritical aspects, Western ghats
   - (i) Joshi (Pilani): Desert
2. Zoologists
   - (j) Roonwal
   - (k) Ishwar prakash: Rajasthan vertebrates
   - (l) Mani: Insects - Himalayan - Biogeography Book
   - (m) Anantakrishnan: insects
   - (n) Panikkar: Oceanography
   - (o) Natarajan, Senapathi, Seshayya: Marine biology & Ecology

(p) Baker
(q) Salim Ali: Birds
(r) Datta Munshi: River ecology

D. INSTITUTIONAL WORKS
1. Botanical Survey of India
2. Zoological Survey of India
3. Anthropological Survey of India
4. Geological Survey of India
5. CAZRI, Jodhpur
6. NIO, Goa
7. F.R.I., Dehradun
8. W.I.I., Dehradun
9. Inst. Himalayan Ecology, Sikkim

E. PROGRAMMES
1. Biosphre Reserves
2. Western ghats, Himalayas, Easter ghats
3. Indian Ocean Expedition (Intern)
4. W.W.F.
5. B.N.H.S.
6. Tiger, Gir lion, Crocodile, Turtle

F. OTHERS
1. Ecology & Economics & Development
2. Ecology & Man - CSE
3. People: Chipko

2. ENVIRONMENTAL FACTORS

I. INTRODUCTION

A. HABITAT - where an organism lives

B. ENVIRONMENTAL CONDITIONS - the set - Environmental Complex

C. DIRECT FACTORS: L,T,H, nutrients, water
INDIRECT: Soil structure, organisms, wind, slope, Altitude

D. FACTORS

1. Climatic or Aerial
   (a) Light (b) Temperature (c) Rainfall (d) Humidity (e) Atmosphere gases & wind
2. Topographic or physiographic
   (a) Altitude (b) Direction of Valleys
   (c) Steepness & Exposure of Slopes
3. Edaphic: Soil
4. Biotic: Plants, animals, microbes

E. INTERACTION OF ECOLOGICAL FACTORS

F. ORGANISMS

G. ATMOSPHERE,

H. WATER, Habitat (S.A. rock)

II. CLIMATIC FACTORS

A. LIGHT - Wavelengths, penetration, canopies, water, energy

1. Chlorophyll formation, heating, stomata & transpiration, development photoperiodism (long & short day) Hello & Sciophytes
2. Animals - Metabolism, Reproduction, Development, eyes & vision, pigmentation, locomotion - Photoperiodism - rhythms

B. TEMPERATURE

1. Animals: metabolism, growth, reproduction, morphology, warm-blooded, cold blooded
2. Plants: Metabolism - Reproduction - Phenology - Zonation patterns with mean day temp - altitude & latitude

C. RAINFALL

1. Plants & Animals: hydrologic cycle - evapotranspiration & precipitation, water relations & habitats

D. AIR

1. Humidity - vapor - Relative humidity - wind, temp. Plant & animal processes
2. Gases = N = 78%, CO2 = 0.9%, others Bio-Tropo Sphere Strato————Meso————Iono

E. WIND

1. Lodging, uprooting, erosion, etc.

III. TOPOGRAPHY

A. ALTITUDES: temp, humidity, wind, radiation, etc.

B. VALLEYS: air circulation, winds, rain

C. SLOPES: water retention & vegetation, soil erosion

IV. EDAPHIC FACTORS

A. COMPOSITION

1. Mineral matter 2. Organic matter: humus
3. Water 4. Air spaces
5. Organisms

B. FORMATION

1. Weathering Physical Chemical Soil profile reveals
2. Parent material topography, time, rain, temp, evaporation, wind, phytosphere, zoosphere, microbes affecting factors, Water
3. Soil Profile

   O1 & O2 A1 A2 B C R

   Fresh decomposed Organic Mineral Clays, Minerals Bedrock, leaves, Minerals, Incompletely, Weathered, rocks

C. TYPES

1. Residual
2. Transported Colluvial (gravity), alluvial (water), glacial (snow), Eolian (wind)
3. Classification - USDA 10 types

D. PROPERTIES

1. Mineral matter: texture, porosity
2. Air - wet & dry conditions not available
3. Water physically dru/Physiologically dry Hygroscopic

   Capillary & gravitational - Field capacity

   Plants water table

E. SOIL SOLUTION - weak solution of salts - acidity - Soil types

F. HUMANS - litter - duff - humans

G. ORGANISMS - N. fixation, Root growth, antibiosis, soil formation

H. SOIL EROSION:

1. River sediments (ganges, kosi - top 8)
2. Top soil loss Maximum 4700 m tons
3. Water erosion (Sheets - hills - gully)
4. Wind erosion - Saltation - Suspention - Surface Creep
5. Landslides - Stream banks, deforestation - grazing
6. Conservation - Control/Stop the above by all means

> *Earthworms, though in appearance a small and despicable link in the chain of nature, yet, if lost, would make a lamentable chasm ... worms seem to be the great promoters of vegetation, which would proceed but lamely without them.*
>
> **Gilbert White**

3. HABITAT CHARACTERISTICS

I. CARRYING CAPACITY

A. Edwards & Fowle 1955. The Concept of Carrying Capacity

B. Standing crop: Individuals or biomass in a community

C. Productivity: Org. matter/unit or time/unit of area

Rate yearly (also months, weeks or daily)

- small crops may have high productivity
- large crops may have low

D. The largest standing crop which a habitat can support without deterioration or maximum number of animals that can survive the least favourable, yet tolerable environmental conditions during a stated period of time: Carrying Capacity

- amount of food - shelter - social tolerance etc

E. Malthus, Darwin - population size reduced

- stabilisation below the ultimate level
- density-independent or environmental factors set the ultimate limit or carrying capacity

F. Resource limits population (Malthus) Economics - limitation

- appropriation by a section (Marx) population, Resources & Environment (Darwin) Ecology

G. Populations growth Vs c.c. which is finite - 3 patterns

1. Stabilization at or below cc: Stabilization: Resource self-renewing, population checked by predation, parpasitism, limited reproduction such as territoriality
2. Oscillation around/below cc: Oscillations: Interdependent Population (Predator-Prey) dynamics out of phase with one another.
3. Overshooting the cc - extinction or incomplete recovery
    1. pests on managed ecosystems (insects in Agric)
    2. over exploit environment and starve-overshoot and collapse (grazing mammals, carnivores, are eliminated)
    3. Overshooting: population depends on a resource that cannot be replenished (bloom and bust of a test tube yeast culture)

H. Multiple Resource Constraints Vs. C.C.

1. Plants: light, water, nutrients - various in various habitats (water in desert)

2. If limiting resources is not available, it blooms until it
   (a) encounters another limiting factor
   (b) disrupt other populations that share the local environment e.g. Phosphorous in freshwater algae - algal bloom

II. STABILITY & DIVERSITY

A. No of species

B. Relative number of individuals in each

C. Genetic simplification - community less stable

1. Reduction of no. of species in a community
2. Genetic diversity of a population
3. Human lives can be taken by a virulent & drug resistant stain
4. Genetic simplification - Influences - How ?
5. Is it more characteristics? more interactions ? more combinations ? etc

III. ECOLOGICAL BUFFERING

More critical, Life supporting in tropics - decomposition more rapid

- Biosphere cushions the interface between air and geotopic surface
- Soil is held in place by plants, protected from falling rain
- Soil absorbs water, prevents runoff
- nutrients are bound and increase the carrying capacity Overgrazing, deforestation, overcultivation reduce this buffering
- i.e. life supporting
- Maintenance is straight, destruction also straight therefore consequences are clearest
- Site specific, climate & geography

4. RESPONSES TO ENVIRONMENT

I. PLANTS

A. INTRODUCTION

1. Humidity, fog, cloud, precipitation, soil moisture - SPAC
2. Land Plants: Water-balance - Warming (1909)

B. HYDROPHYTES

1. Free floating - Eichhornia, Pista
2. Rooted & floating - Nymphea, Mansilea
3. Submerged & floating - Ceratophyllum
4. Rooted submerged - Vallisneria, Hydrilla
5. Rooted emergent - adaptations: Roots, stems, leaves

C. MESOPHYTES

D. XEROPHYTES

1. Ephemeral annuals 2. Succulents 3. Nonsucculent adaptations

E. HALOPHYTES

- lithophytes (rock) - psammophytes (sand)
- pelophilous (mud) - helophilous (swamp) Mangroves

II. ANIMALS

A. HYDROCOLES: "Stream lined bodies", fine, muscles in bundles

B. AMPHIBIOUS: Body, neck immobile, bower light, nostrils & eyes shift

C. MESOCOLES: Water retention
- selective food habits sheathy structures,
- dry excretion, nocturnal habits, burrowing, coiling
- migration

Water conservation

1. Goats - food
2. C - blood
3. desert - metabolic
4. Imperious skin (mammals)
5. Chitinous skeleton (insects)

D. XEROCOLES: drought evaders , drought resistants

E. AERIAL: metabolism, muscles, wings for flight

A species is the result of the inter and intra relations of that. Some species with the biotic and abiotic factors around it.

III. ABIOTIC FACTORS:

A. WIND

1. Effects on transpiration,
2. Damage to the leaf surface,
3. Effects on photosynthesis,
4. Effect on the shaping of the tree,

B. LIGHT

1. Plant classification on the basis of response to light.
   (i) shade tolerant, (ii) shade intolerant.
2. Efficiency of light utilisation,
3. C_3 AND C_4 plants,

C. MOISTURE & WATER

1. Hydrological cycle.
2. Importance of water to plant body.
3. Division of the plants on the basis of availability of water.
   (a) Xerophytes. (b) Mesophytes.
   (c) Hydrophytes. (d) Psammophyetes.
   (e) Lithophytes. (f) Halophytes.
4. Leaf Structure, Road Structure and Stomatal physiology in relation to water availability.

D. TEMPERATURE

1. Role of temp. as on important ecological factor.
   (a) Diurnal Temp. Fluctuations.
   (b) Seasonal Temp. Fluctuations.
2. Temp. and Respiration.
3. Temp. and Transpiration.
4. Adaptation to temp
   (a) Heat stability. (b) Frost resistance. (c) Chilling resistance.
5. Independence of temp can be achieved in many Functions, but never in those of growth and development.

IV. BIOTIC FACTORS

A. COMPETITION

Distribution of vascular plants is largely the result of marked interspecific competition.

1. Intraspecific competition.
   (a) Nature. (b) Characteristics. (c) Effects - Self thinning in

plants. (d) Example of Lolium Perenne where Self-tuinning tanes place

2. Interspecific Competition.

   (a) Nature. (b) Ecological Niche (c) Examples.

   1. Additive Experiment (crop-weed Mixture). Effect of weed Avena fatua and A. indoviciana on the crop A. Sativa. The weeds succeed.
   2. Competition between Phalaris tuberosa and Lolium perenne. The later has reduced capacity to exploit its own nutrient supply in the presence of former, so the former one wins.

B. PREDATION

1. Patterns of Abundance
2. Convolution of prey and predator. Intensive plant eater tadpove is very long, as compared to adult cornivorous frog.
3. Specialisations among predators - Food preference (extreme slectivity) - Drosophila pacea is monophagous and is the only species capable of consuming the rotten tissues of cactus.
4. Effects of predators on plant fitness - plant pathogens reducing the photosynthetic area of an individual putting it in disadvantageous positionn than its competitors.
5. Mutual interference among predators.

C. ALLELOPATHY

1. Grevillea robusta, shows allelopathic function in producing some chemicals that kills its own saplings and helps to keep spacing between trees.
2. Toxicants, Repellants, Attractants etc. are allelopathc group of chemicals.

D. PARASITISM

1. The plants (or) animals which derive their food partially (or) entirely from other living organisms are termed parasites.
2. Examples: Orabanche, Rafflesia, Cusuta etc.

E. COMMENSALISM

1. Mutual Co-existence of two individuals, in which one individual derives benefit from the association while the other associate is neither harmed nor benefitted.
2. Examples - Epiphytes like orchids growing on branches of trees.

5. SUCCESSIONS IN HABITATS

I. INTRODUCTION

A. DEFINITION: Natural process by which the same locality becomes successively colonised by different groups of plant species.

B. HISTORY :

1. "Succession" was first used by Hult (1885) in Sweden authentic studies by Coroles & Clements
2. Also called as Ecosystem development (Odum 1971)
   - involves changes in species structure and community processes in time
   - modifies the physical environment
   - culminates in a stabilized ecosystem with maximum biomass and symbiotic function

II. CAUSES

A. INITIAL CAUSES

1. Produce bare areas or destroy existing populations
2. Erosion, deposits, wind, fire, etc. 3. Biotic effects

B. CONTINUING CAUSES

1. Edaphic features change
2. Migration, ecesis, aggregation, competition, reaction, etc.

C. STABILISHING CAUSES

1. Community stabilises 2. Climate is chief cause

III. SUCESSIONAL TRENDS

A. Change in the kinds of plants and animal forms

B. Increase in the species Diversity

C. Increase in the organic matter and biomass

D. Decrease in the net community production or annual yield

IV. TYPES OF SUCCESSION

SUBSTRATUM

A. PRIMARY :

1. Succession starts from the primitive substratum
2. No living matter previously
3. First organisms: Pioneers or Primary Colonizers

B. SECONDARY

1. Substrata built previously with some living matter
2. Some external force - biotic, climate, fire, etc. eliminates existing community, but substratum remains built up
3. Successions are rapid

INFLUENCING FORCES

C. AUTOGENIC

1. Community modifies its own environment

   Thus causing its own replacement by new communities

D. ALLOGENIC

1. Replacements caused by external conditions

E. AUTOTROPHIC

1. Continuous domination by green plants
2. Begins in a predominantly organic environment
3. Progressive decline in the energy content

V. MECHANISMS

A. NUDATION: Development of a bare area

1. Topographic: Soil erosion by gravity, water or wind landslide, volcanic activity
2. Climatic: Hails, frost, fire, drought
3. Biotic: Disease, epidemics, Man's denading activities

B. INVASION: Successful establishment of a species in a bare area

1. Migration : dispersal of seeds, spores & other propagules by air, water etc.
2. Ecesis : successful establishment by adjusting with the area's conditions. Only a few can do this
3. Aggregation: Many individuals of the established species are produced through reproduction & they tend to aggregate forming a colony

C. COMPETITION & COACTION: The large populations compete for space and nutrition. Individuals affect each other.

D. REACTION: Environment is modified by the living organisms-oil, water, light and temperature modify "inviting" better fitting organisms. Thus a series of communities sequentially replace each other with the changing environmental conditions: Sere Pioneers are small & need less nutrients.

E. STABILIZATION: The final unreplaced community is called climax community, the stage, climax and the process, stabilisation.

F. RETROGRESSIVE SUCCESSION: Due to destructive effects of organisms the usual development of community does not take place and reverses, (e.g. forest becoming shrubby or grassland).

G. DEFLECTED SUCCESSION: Instead of progressing towards the expected climax, the succession goes in a different direction yielding to different communities (e.g. Temporary ponds having different communities in each year).

VI. EXAMPLES

A. HYDROSERE OR HYDRARCH

1. Plants
   - (a) Phytoplankton stage: Bacteria, BG-algae, diatoms, algae, etc.
   - (b) Rooted submerged stage: Vallisneria, Hydrilla, etc.
   - (c) Rooted floating stage: Pistia, Lemna, Nymphea, Nelumbium, etc.
   - (d) Reed - Swamp stage: Scirpus, Typha, etc.
   - (e) Sedge-Meadow stage: Eleocharis, Cyperus, etc.
   - (f) Woodland stage: Populus, Salix, etc.
   - (g) Forest stage: Quercus, Acer, Ulmus (Temperate)
2. Animals: Nutritional basis
   - (a) Pioneers: protozoans, gill fish, sunfish, etc.
   - (b) Crustaceans - Daphnia, Cyclops, etc Insects: dragon flies, May flies, Submerged stage
   - (c) Coelenterates, snalis, frogs, water beetles floating stage
   - (d) Lung breathing animals, annelids, black birds, herons, sparrows, Reed-Swamp ducks, rats & Beavers
   - (e) Terrestrial forms
3. Functional Changes
   - (a) As structural changes take place (species composition and diversity) functional changes i.e. auto- & heterotrophs takes place.
   - (b) Living & dead organic matter increases progressively

B. LITHOSERE - A XEROSERE ON ROCK

PLANTS

1. Crustose lichen stage : poor moisture,high temperature, no organic matter

2. Foliose lichen stage : thallose, accummulate water & dust humus accumulation
3. Moss state : thin soil layer forms
4. Herbaceous stage : Minerals & humus change the habitat and allow eptemerals, animals, binneals and perennials gradually
5. Shrub stage : shrubs, perennials, long rooted and enrich soil Trees
6. Forest stage : Mixture of most of the above

   ANIMALS

   1. Ants, spiders: Pioneers
   2. Mites and other insects
   3. Invertebrates & Vertebrates; reptiles, rodents
   4. Complexity with plant complexity

VII. ECOSYSTEM DEVELOPMENT

1. Auto and heterotrophic successions result in increased species composition, diversity, coactions, and habitat enrichment.
2. Community energetics, structure, life histories, selection pressures and homeostasis stabilised as a climax.
3. Climax-Mono-& Polyclimax -Edaphic, Biotic,Topographic and fire climaxes
4. Biome
   (a) Biotic community of geographical dimension with a distinctive life form in the climax stage.
   (b) Bigger unit than a community embracing geographical regions - tundra, forest desert, etc.

6. CYCLES, DISRUPTIONS, CONSEQUENCES

I. BIOLOGICAL CYCLES

(a) Life history & life span
(b) Vegetations/Somatic growth
(c) Food and nutrition - feeding habits
(d) Space - niches, migration, territorialism
(e) Reproduction - Breeding seasons
(f) Defences - migrations, segregations

II. BEHAVIOUR CYCLES

(a) Solar (Diurnal)
(b) Lunar (tidal etc)
(c) Seasonal (temp, rainfall)
(d) Annual (basically seasonal)

III. ECOLOGICAL: SUCCESSIONS

IV. ENVIRONMENTAL CYCLES

(a) Geological: Phosphorous, Water
(b) Chemical: CO_2, N_2, O_2 Biogeochemical
   1. Gaseous   2. Nutrients: Nitrates, phosphates, etc

V. BUDGETS

(a) Minimum Requirements (b) Maximum tolerated level
   1. Food, space, reproduction
   2. Sunlight, water, nutrients - salts, nutrients - traces

VI. DISRUPTIONS:

(a) Additions and deletions (pollution of soil, water & air, loss of soil, germplasm, water)
(b) Biological cycles: Population growth, densities, behaviour cycles
(c) Ecological cycles: Interactions and balances
(d) Environmental cycles: Regional changes & global changes
   1. CO_2 increase: Greenhouse effect, warming, sealevel raises (global).
   2. Sx, Nx increase: acid rain (regional)
   3. Nutrient raise: eutrophication (regional/local)
   4. Water loss/absence: desertification (regional)

VII. CONCLUSIONS

(a) DIRECT AND INDIRECT EFFECTS - Acid rain, Plants, Water, Soil, Animals

(b) INTERACTIONS AMONG CYCLES - long & short term consequences

(c) HABITAT DISRUPTION: Carrying capacity, Buffering ability & stability through diversity

(d) Restorative Practices

1. Pollution of soil, air, water abatement
2. Reduce consumption
3. Soil binding through vegetation
4. Water management
5. Conservation

> *"An attitude to life which seeks fulfillment in the single-minded pursuit of wealth - in short, materialism - does not fit into this world, because it contains within itself no limiting principle, while the environment in which it is placed is strictly limited."*
>
> **Ernst F. Schumacher**

7. ACID RAIN

I. INTRODUCTION

In 1872, a British chemist discovered a link between acid in rain falling near Manchester and the SO_2 given off when coal was burned. 70 years later research in Europe confirmed his discovery.

II. ACID POLLUTION

(a) SO_2, NO_2 produced when fossil fuels get burnt covert in the atmosphere as sulphates and nitrates and then into acids.

(b) These return to earth in rain, snow, hail, fog or mist.

III. ACID POLLUTION CHAIN

(a) EMISSION

(b) TRANSPORT

(c) POLLUTION

IV. ACID POLLUTION RECEPTORS

(a) PRIMARY RECEPTORS

(b) SECONDARY RECEPTORS

(c) TERTIARY RECEPTORS

> *We do not inherit the earth from our ancestors; we borrow it from our children*
>
> **Chief Seattle**

8. DISTURBED HABITATS

I. Patch Dynamics

A. REASONS / IMPLICATIONS

1. (a) "Patch" implies a relatively discrete spatial pattern but does not establish any constraint on size, internal homogenity or discreteness

   (b) "Patch implies a relationship of one patch to the surrounding unaffected or least affected matter.

   (c) "Patch Dynamics" implies patch change.
2. Perturbation
3. Disturbance
4. Endogenous and Exogenous causes of disturbance.

B. DISTURBANCE REGIMES IN TEMPERATE FORESTS

1. Components
   (a) Average disturbance Rates.
   (b) Distribution of Disturbance in space.
   (c) Disturbance distribution in time.
   (d) Severity of Disturbance.
   (e) Rates of Recovery.

C. TROPICAL FOREST COMMUNITY

1. Tree Fall Regimes.
   (a) Gap Creation.
   (b) Gap Environment.
2. Regeneration Behaviour.
   (a) Primary Tree species.
   (b) Pioneer Tree species.
3. Regrowth.

D. SAND PRAIRIES

1. Perspective on Grassland disturbances.
2. Biological setting.

   (a) Persistents. (b) Ephemerals. (c) Peripherals.

II. DISTURBANCE AND PATCH DYNAMICS

A. ON ROCKY INTERTIDAL SHORES

1. Kinds of Open space produced by disturbance

2. Characteristics.

   (a) Areal Extent. (b) Intensity. (c) Frequency and (d) seasonality.

3. Modes of Patch colonization.

   (a) Patch Type. (b) Patch location. (c) Patch surface characteristics. (d) Patch size and shape.

B. VERTEBRATES

1. Vertebrate Adaptations.

   (a) Type of Disturbance.

   (b) Regime of Disturbance.

   (c) Type of Biological system.

   (d) Regional context.

   (e) Type of Response.

III. ADAPTATIONS OF PLANTS AND ANIMALS IN A PATCH DYAMIC SETTING

A. RESPONSE OF WOODY PLANTS

1. Seed Production and Dispersal.
2. Seed Storage and germination.
3. Seedling Establishment.

B. FOREST HERBS VS CANOPY GAPS

1. Gap Environmental.

   (a) Size, Shape, & Despatch. (b) Modification of Gap characteristics. (c) Light. (d) Temperature. (e) Soil Moisture. (f) Nutrients. (g) Animals - Nutrients resources.

2. Responses

   (a) Temperature. (b) Light. (c) Water (d) Nutrients.

3. Herb Responses.

   (a) Sun Herbs. (b) Light flexible Herbs. (c) Shade Herbs.

C. INSECT ADAPTATIONS

1. Factors affecting response.

   (a) Dispersal (b) Host Selection.

   (c) Resource Quality and Quantity.

2. Insect Propagation of Disturbance Effects.

   (a) Increased plant mortality. (b) Patch predisposition.

3. Insects as Regulators.

   (a) Community Organisations. (b) Disturbance Reliability.

D. NATURAL DISTURBANCE AND ECOSYSTEM ENERGETICS

1. Ecosystem changes during stand development.
   (a) General Development Patterns.
   (b) Biomass Accumulation.
   (c) Net Primary Productivity.
   (d) Autotrophic Respiration and Gross Primary Productivity.
   (e) Heterotrophic Respiration and Net Ecosystem Productivity.

IV. ECOLOGICAL ADAPTATIONS TO NATURAL DISTURBANCES

A. PLANTS

1. Aquatic Plants - Hydrophtes
2. Terrestrial Plants
   (a) Mesophytes (b) Xerophytes
3. Marshy plants - Melophytes.
   (a) Lithophilous (b) Psammophilous
   (c) Pelophilous (d) Helophilous

B. ANIMALS

1. Hydrocoles. 2. Amphibious animals
3. Mesocoles 4. Xerocoles
5. Adaptations

V. FIRE FACTOR

A. EFFECTS

1. Injuiry.
2. Death.
3. Alteration in Physical and Chemical Factors.
4. Removal of Competition.
5. Stimulation of growth and mutation.

B. ADAPTATIONS

1. Hard seed-coats.
2. Short Life cycles.
3. Development of fire-resistance [Oils, resins].
4. Lignotubers.
5. Serotinous Cones.

9. AUTECOLOGY AND GENECOLOGY

I. POPULATION LEVEL

A. INTRODUCTION: In any given community species of plants and animals appear and disappear periodically. At any given time, similarly they are in different stages of life. Thus a spectrum of life and its activities can be seen at any given time. This is because of three reasons.

1. Diversity of species
2. Diversity of life histories of species
3. Diversity in the interactions of the stages of life histories with environmental factors climatic, edaphic & biotic

B. ANTECOLOGY

Life histories of plant species including the environmental interactions - Ecological life histories/biological flora/antecology Ecological clocks

C. PHENOLOGY

1. Seed output
2. Seed dispersal Animals, wind, water etc
3. Seed viability
4. Seed dormancy Mocrobes, chemicals etc of soil
5. Seed germination water temp, light (W.T.L)
6. Seedling growth drought, wind, T.L.W.
7. Vegetative growth TLW Energy
8. Reproductive growth TLW Energy
9. Pollination Animals, wind, etc
10. Inflorescence, seeding,
11. Death and decay & biomass - Microbes – soil
12. Vegetative propagation - influences

D. ECOLOGICAL AMPLITUDE & ENVIRONMENTAL REQUIREMENTS: RANGE conditions a species can tolerate and grow. Best performance obtained when environmental requirements are fulfilled.

E. LAW OF THE MINIMUM: Minimum amounts/quanitites of nutrients etc needed for growth and reproduction

F. LAW OF TOLERANCE: Limiting effect of maximum narrow spectrum of tolerances with Temperature, Water, Broad salinity

II. COMMUNITY LEVEL

A. FACTOR COMPENSATION: Species may adopt to reduce limiting effects ecotypes: Species with wide range of distribution always duely populations adapted to local conditions

B. MORPHOLOGY, TAXONOMY, GEOGRAPHY, NATURAL DISTRIBUTION - abundance, density, etc.

C. INDICATOR SPECIES - Narrow ranges & spectra

D. VARIATIONS AND ADAPTATIONS

1. Ecads - ecophenes, habitat, induced environmentally
2. Ecotypes - genotypical response to environment, inter fertile
3. Ecospecies - 1 or more types of ecotypes

III. ECOSYSTEMS LEVEL

A. ECOLOGICAL NICHE

Ecads, ecotypes and ecospecies are distinct populations of the same species. Such distinctions help in widening the range of distribution. When these ranges of occurrence & growth differ widely they are said to have developed their own "niches" - significant segregation.

1. Spatially (habitat niche): (different location Millepedes of forest floor
2. Functionally (trophic niche): Darwins' herbivores, insectivores (variations)

B. ECOLOGICAL EQUIVALENTS

1. Organisms occupying same/similar niches in different geographical regions.
2. Taxonomically different, usually.
3. Grasses (producers) & grazers (herbivores) different in grasslands of different continents e.g. Kangaroos of Australia, bison & Antelopes of N. America

C. GENECOLOGY

1. Turesson 1922, ecotypes, origin or variations, development of species, niches, widening distribution ecology of genes - origin and spread
2. India: Ramakrishnan (Euphorbia hirta)

IV. ANIMALS

A. DEFENCE AGAINST PREDATION (reduced mortality)

1. Chemical (toxins, frogs, molluscs)

2. Anatomical (stinging cells) speed increasing devices
3. Morphological (colorations, no-shadows-flattening)
4. Behavioural (similar to mimicrops, the morphological + escape + tough abitats)
5. Codistribution (mutualism)

B. REPRODUCTIVE ECOLOGY

1. Site
2. Timing togetherness, parental support
3. The young - energy, predation
4. Age
5. Mating systems
6. Sex ratios - parthenogenesis & Vegetative propagation: exception
7. Brood parasitism - others nests

C. FEEDING ECOLOGY

1. Quantity
2. Food preferences
3. General & Special
4. Foraging - food gathering

D. SPACING SYSTEMS

1. Proximity advantages & disadvantages
2. Habitat preferences: dominance, gradients, territoriality for defense, food, reproduction
3. Groups – Home ranges overlap when individuals move in flocks

10. POPULATIONS

AUTECOLOGY, GENECOLOGY, POPULATION DYNAMICS

I. INTRODUCTION

A. Plants and animals

B. Genetic statuses in time and space

C. Plants and productivity management

D. Animals and human management

II. INDIVIDUALS: Ecological life

A. PLANTS

1. Phenology
2. Ecological Amplitude
3. Variations & adaptations
4. Niches
5. Ecological equivalents

B. ANIMALS

1. Spacing: proximity & distance
2. Feeding: preferences, quantity, foraging habit
3. Reproduction: Site, age, time, sex ratios, Broods, Mating
4. Defence: Morphological, anatomical, behavioural, chemical and codistribution

III. POPULATIONS: CHARACTERISTICS

A. PLANTS

1. Genetic structure
2. Frequency, abundance, density
3. Reproductive capacity
4. Habit
5. Inter relationships with other plants, animals and environment

B. ANIMALS

1. Genetic structure
2. Size, density & dispersion
3. Ages, natality, mortality & life tables
4. Interrelationships with other animal & plants and environment

IV. DYNAMICS OF GROWTH

A. PLANTS

1. Reproductive capacity
2. Pollination and seed dispersal
3. Dormancy, viability, perennation, reproduction
4. Herbivory

B. ANIMALS

1. Geometrical vs Arithmetic increase
2. Intrinsic rate (i.r) or natural increase: No environ. resistance
   (Mortality-natality or Nat-Mort.)
   (no emigration, immigration etc.)
3. Carrying capacity limits this exponential growth, logistics of resources makes the natural increase (i.r) progressively reduce, as the population increases towards the carrying capacity.
4. Logistic theory
   (a) Envt. constant that C.C. and natural increase do not change
   (b) No time lags in response of the population to change in its density
   (c) Individuals have identical characteristics in their responses to density, irrespective of age or sex
   (d) Growth is continuous
   (e) Age structure does not change in successive generation
   (f) Modifications
      1. Time lag exists
      2. Fluctuations in cc
      3. Chance events for survival/death
      4. Discontinuous growth of some populations

C. HOW PLANTS DIFFER FROM ANIMALS

1. Plants are modular - develop from a single zygote but produce repetetive structures vegetatively - modules. Thus there are two structures
   (a) genet: from one zygote one plant
   (b) ramet (tiller): off shoots
2. No movement - water, wind, animals, gravity, used
3. Growth is density related
   - density increases - dry weight or individuals decrease
   thinning law: inverse proportion

V. REGULATIONS OF POPULATIONS

A. PLANTS INCOMPLETE REPRODUCTION

1. Viability, dormancy,
2. Herbivory - nutritional ethology
3. Biotic interferences
4. Climatic changes

B. ANIMALS

1. Regulation around/below carrying capacity
2. Factors influencing population density increase natality, immigration, decrease mortality, emigration density dependent or independent
   (a) Density Dependent factors - predation & competition increase - Population increase
   (b) Density Independent factors - foci, flood, etc.
3. Keyfactor analysis
   Among mortality factors, one or two may be the most important. This is called Key-Factor.
4. Self regulation: Death and mating-failure accumulation of wastes social bahaviour - food and breeding
5. Immigration and emigration.

VI. EVOLUTION

A. PLANTS : Variations, Selection
adapatation, niches, varieties, species loss
interfertility

B. ANIMALS: Variations, Selection, Competition, predation, mutualism/adapatations commensalism

VII. HUMAN RELEVANCE

A. ECOLOGY: natality, mortality, population, regulation, resources, immigration, emigration, niche segregations, Race formation, population, diversity within races & between

B. SOCIAL & ECONOMIC ISSUES: Resoruces, Science & Technology, artificial niches (made by man)
Consequences - Marxism, Hardinism, Gaia, Spaceship - Ecocentrie - vs Anthropocentrism

VIII. CONCLUSIONS: Population trends : Life Boat ethics ?

A. CO EVOLUTION

B. SOCIOECONOMIC CHANGES VS ECOLOGICAL PRINCIPLES

C. POLICY INPUTS FOR SCIENCE & TECHNOLOGY

11. COMMUNITIES

I. DEFINITION & HISTORY

1. A group of several species of plants and/or animals living together and interacting in a habitat
2. Theophrastus (370-250 BC) existence of plant communities in different environmental areas recognized
3. Grisebach (1838): Plant formation as an important unit of vegetation, recognized
4. Forbes (1844): different types of assemblages of animals at different depths in the Aegean sea, (while studying molluscs) found.
5. Mobius (1880): Biocoenosis was coined to describe an association of organisms in an oyster bed community
6. Schroter & Kirchner (1902): The term synecology was introduced for the study of the plant community in the ocean bed
7. Five lines of traditional thought
   (a) USA: Cowles (1899), Clements (1905): Succession
   (b) UK: Tansley (1904), sucession, ecotypes, evolution
   (c) Sweden: Hult (1881), Du Rietz (1930), Phytosociology, Dominance, (Uppsala) Indicators,
   (d) France (Zurich - Montpellier): Braun-Blanquet, Phytosociology, phytogeography Raun Kier (1934): Physiognomy of the plants
   (e) USSR: accent on physiology and environment

II. CHARACTERISTICS

A. SPECIES DIVERSITY :

1. Plant, animal, microbial species and their characteristic populations differ from habitat to habitat. This diversity may be studied locally (small regions) or regionally (major geographical zones)

B. DOMINANCE

1. Some species exert a major influence in a community

C. GROWTH FORMS

1. Trees, shrubs, herbs, lianas, Creepers, broad-leaved, narrow-leaved.
2. Horizontal/Vertical stratification - gives a characteristic appearance

3. Horizontal: Vegetational types based on altitudes (non common)
4. Vertical: most common, storyed vegetation - subterranean, floor, herbs, shrubs and trees

D. SUCCESSION
1. Development in a direction - different in various habitats.
2. Migration, seedling establishment (ecesis), colonization - animals, - This complex either replaced or become complex

E. TROPHIC STRUCTURE
1. Nutritional behaviour of plants and animals with degrees of auto - & heterotrophy

III. INTERRELATIONSHIPS

A. Stratification: The plants of one layer modify the environment for the another - microenvironment. the strata may also be interdependent.

B. Cohabitation: Togetherness for nutrition, spatial, reproductive and other needs, allelopathy and allelogeny.

C. Competition: Space, nutrition, etc. Replacements happen by better ones - succession - stoppage when stability is reached through balances of interelationships - climax.

IV. CLASSIFICATION OF COMMUNITIES

A. CONCEPTS
1. Principle of species individuality:
   (a) Each species has its own individuality - genetic adaptibility, physiology, population dynamics - within its total range of tolerance to environmental factors (ecological compltitude).
   (b) They are distributed independent of others where it can disperse and survive.
   (c) Organisms of a habitat are simply an assembly of species finding the habitat within their tolerances.
   (d) Objections: Coactions, Coevolutions ignored.
2. The theory of Community Unit or Association Unit
   (a) Communities are organised basic units
   (b) They are equivalent to a species of an organism
   (c) A particular species exists constantly in a particular community - dominantly.

(d) The community is named after the dominant species.

(e) Five classifications exist all differing only in terminology and sub classifications (French, Swedish, British, Russian, American Schools)

3. The Concept of Vegetational Continuum

(a) Communities are supposed to vary continuously in space. No distinct communities with boundaries but a gradual change in space and composition forming gradients.

(b) Environmental gradient and Vegetational gradient occur (mountains changing altitudes & vegetation)

(c) No clearcut separation of vegetation and environmental conditions in nature.

(d) Communities give the landscape a characteristic pattern

(e) Environmental gradient parallels with vegetation gradient - Ecocline

(f) 5 major ecoclines in different geographic area

(g) 20 biomes cover all communities

(h) Where one community and another starts: No point or line - but a transition zone with elements from both communities - Ecotone.

(i) Principle of edges: greater number of species, densities of many are higher in the ecotones.

B. CLASSIFICATIONS

1. Physiognomic: habitat & growth form

(a) Humboldt (1808): 19 groups

(b) Griesbach (1875): 7 main and 60 subsidiary

(c) Warming (1909-23): 2-Auto-and Heterotrophs

Autotrophs: Many classes of Hydro & terrestrial plants

(d) Raunkier (1934): Lifeforms - 5 major classes based on perennating bud & protection under adverse climate

(e) Braun-Blanquet (1932): modifications over Raunkeer

(f) Schimper (1898, 1903): 15 formation types - forest, scrub, grassland, savannah, meadow, steppe, etc.

2. Phytosociological: species dominance, successions, trends in vegetation stability, community boundaries - variations minor.
   (a) Zurich-Montpellier School: (Flahault & Schroeter 1910): fundamental unit floristic composition definite physiognomy uniform habitat conditions uniform has a characteristics species (Braun-Blanquet): fidelity Association - Alliance - Order – Class.
   (b) Uppsala School: Fries (1913) Dr Reitz (1918-21) constancy of a species present in 90% stands Quantification initiated.
   (c) Russian School: Sukachev (1929) formation, association, etc.
   (d) American School: Cowles (1899, 1901) Clements (1916) Community dynamics & succession Cause - Effect philosophy begins Climax community - Formation - the major unit Association Consociations Societies locations (local variants).
   (e) British School: Tansley (1904) American & European thoughts Physiognomy of Warming, Succession of Clements.

V. PARAMETERS OF STUDY

A. QUANTITATIVE CHARACTERS

1. Frequency : (a) % of occurrence in the sampling units
   (b) Frequency classes 0.20, 21-40, 41-60, 61-80, 81-100 (ABCDE)
2. Density : (a) Numerical strength of a species in a community
   (b) Degree of competition indicated
   (c) Total no. of individuals in all sampling units divided by total no. sampling units
3. Abundance : (a) No. of individuals of any species/sampling unit
   (b) as (c) above & total no. of sampling units of species occurrence.
4. Cover : herbage cover occupying the ground area by the above ground parts (Chart Quadrat % Cover =Groups 1-6. Braun – Blanquet.

5. Basal area : ground actually penetrated by the stem (by Callipers).
6. Dominance : (a) area occupied or biomass
   (b) Importance Value Index (IVI)

$$\text{Relative Density} = \frac{\text{Density of the Species}}{\text{Total density of all species}} \times 100$$

$$\text{Relative Frequency} = \frac{\text{Frequency of the Species}}{\text{Total Frequency of all Species}} \times 100$$

$$\text{Relative Dominance} = \frac{\text{Dominance of the Species}}{\text{Total dominanace (cover) of all}} \times 100$$

B. QUALITATIVE CHARACTERS

1. Physiognamy: growth form of dominant species
2. Phenology: periodicity of growth changes in seasons - phenograms
3. Stratification: Vertical layers of plant species (Bisect method)
4. Sociability: The degree of association between species - 5 groups (Braun-Blanquet 1932).S1 = Singly, S2 = 4-6 plants, S3 = Scattered groups (many), S4 = Bigger groups (many), S5 = a large group over a large area
5. Vitality: Capacity for normal growth and reproduction Daubenmire (1968): V1 = Seedlings die, V2 = unable to reproduce, V3 = Vegetative Reproduction, V4 = Uncommon Reproduction Sexual, V5 = Reproduction sexual, common & grow regularly
6. Life-forms: 5 major types - bud position

VI. METHODS OF STUDY

A. FLORISTIC

B. PHYSIOGNOMIC

C. SOCIOLOGICAL

1. Qualitative
2. Quantitative
   (a) Quadrat (b) Bisect
   (c) Transect - line, belt (d) Others

12. ECOSYSTEMS

I. INTRODUCTION

A. Tansley (1935): System resulting from the integration of all the living and non-living factors of the environment.

B. Parallel terms: Biocoenosis (Mobins 1877), Microcosm (Forbes 1887), Geobiocoenosis (Dokuchev in Sukachev 1944) Holocoen (Frederichs 1930), Biosystem (Thienemann 1959).

C. Area, Organisms, Communities, Coactions, interactions, material cycles, energy flow, trophic structures (food chains & webs.)

D. Gaian ecosystem = Biosphere, Smaller ones = forest, desert, grassland, marine, fresh water, cropland, Very small one = pond.

E. Bio energetic approach is the ecosystem approach.

II. KINDS

A. NATURAL

1. Terrestrial: Forest, grassland, desert
2. Aquatic :
   (a) Marine: deepsea, surface, shallow, estuarine
   (b) Freshwater
      1. Lotic: Stream 2. Lentic: lake, pond,, pool, ditch, swamp

B. ARTIFICIAL

1. Croplands   2. Urban systems

III. STRUCTURE

A. Ranges & gradients of climate: light, temperature

B. Species, Numbers, biomass, distribution, life histories : living materials

C. Quantity and distribution of non-living materials

A. CLIMATIC RANGES

1. Light: diurnal, seasonal   2. Temperature: diurnal, seasonal
3. Rainfall: seasonal, annual

B. ABIOTIC COMPONENT

1. Amounts of distribution of inorganic substance : P, S, C, N, H: Standing Quality
2. Amounts & Distribution of organics
3. Climate of the region

C. Biotic Component: trophic structure

1. Autotrophic Component: Producers-Photosynthecising organisms
2. Heterotrophic Component: Consumers - Utilisation, rearrangement and decomposition.
   (a) Macro-concumers: herbivores, carnivores & Omnivores - primary, secondary and tertiary consumers
   (b) Micro consumers: docomposers, saprotrophs - release inorganic nutrients into environment making them available again to autotrophs.
3. Trophic level: food level of organisms
4. Standing Crop: Amount of Living material in trophic levels
   (a) number of organisms per unit area
   (b) organism mass in unit area

   -living weight, dry weight, carbon weight, calories, etc.

D. ECOLOGICAL PYRAMIDS

1. Trophic structure is characteristic of each ecosystem.
2. This structure and interrelationships can be shown graphically, producer forming the base and the tertiary consumer the apex.
3. Pyramid of Numbers (at each trophic level): Standing titration

   = grassland and pond (base very large)

   = forest parasitic food chain

   do not give a true picture of food chain
4. Pyramid of Biomass (at each trophic level): Standing titration Quantitative relationships: grasslands forest pond
5. Pyramid of Energy (at each trophic level): rates of passage of food all ecosystems

IV. FUNCTIONS

A. PATHWAYS: Energy and nutrients

Biological pathway: Radiant energy converted into chemical

energy by plants - This energy flows unidirectionally

through herbivores, carnivores and decomposers.

Biogeochemical Pathway: Mineral flow in a cyclical manner.

B. PRODUCTIVITY: Organic matter accummulated in a unit time

1. Primary: Plants-Photosynthetic
   (a) Grosss: depends on chlorophyll content - amount of CO_2 fixed/gm chlorophyll/hour.
   (b) Net: Gross photosynthesis minus respiration - storage of organic matter (increase in biomass)
2. Secondary: Consumers - heterotrophs
   (a) Utilise food in their respiration and distribute energy to different tissues - assimilation
   (b) Secondary productivity mobile and does not remain in situ like primary productivity
3. Net Productivity: net primary production minus composition by the heterotrophs

C. FOOD CHAINS

1. Transfer of food energy from the produces through a series of organisms-herbivores, carnivores & omnivores.
2. Taxnomically very different but occupy same trophic level.
3. Grazing food chain: greenplant and upwards
   a. grass - rabbit – fox b. Plankton - small fish - big fish - birds
4. Detritus food chain: dead organic matter to microbes. Mangroves leave detritus of plant leaves - destritivores (small no. of species in large numbers) small carnivores, fish game fish Birds

D. FOOD WEBS

1. Food chains are not isolated unidirectional sequences
2. Several chains interlinked constitutes web

grass	hopper	hawk	lizard
grass	rabbit	mouse	snake

3. macrophytes small fish game fish

macrophytes	small fish	game fish
	larvae of insects,	
	molluses, etc.	
phytoplankton	zooplankton	

4. Each species is kept under a natural check
5. Complexity depends upon the length of food chain and food habit diversity
6. Alternatives at different points of consumers in the chain determine the interlocking pattern.

V. ECOLOGICAL ENERGETICS

A. 1/50 millionth of solar radiation reaches earth's atmosphere.

B. 300 mu-10 u and above 1 cm enter earth's outer atmosphere. (28 km).

C. 390-760 mu (Visible light) reaches earth's surface.

D. 34% sunlight reaching earth's atmosphere is reflected back into its atmosphere - 10% is held by ozone layer, water vapour - 56% reaches earth's surface.

E. Radiant energy reaching earth surface: 10% Uv - 45% Visible and 45% infrared.

F. Plants absorb blue and red light.

G. Ecological Energetics

1. Quantity of solar energy reaching the ecosystem
2. Quantity of energy used by green plants for photosynthesis
3. Quantity of energy flow from producers to consumers
4. Path of energy flow from producers to consumers

H. 1-5% of energy is used by green plants for photosynthesis, and the rest absorbed as heat by water, vegetation & ground.

I. 0.02% of the sunlight reaching the atmosphere is used in photosynthesis. It is on this all organisms of an ecosystem depend.

VI. ENERGY FLOW IN ECOSYSTEM

A. IMPORTANT FACTORS

1. Efficiency of producers in absorbing and converting solar energy.
2. Use of this converted chemical form of energy by consumers.
3. Total input of energy in the food and its efficiency of assimilation
4. Loss of energy through respiration, heat, excretion, etc.
5. The net production.

B. SINGLE CHANNEL ENERGY FLOW (e.g. Fresh water ecosystem)

1. Single radiation gross productivity autotrophs herbivore consumptioncarnivore consumption decomposition unutilised and Respiration
2. More energy available for herbivory than is consumed (111)
3. More energy available for carnivory that is consumed (15)

4. More is last through respiration by herbivores (4-5/15) & carnivores (1.8/3) than by producers (23/111).
5. Utilisation more efficient as the chain proposes (15 mt of 111 - 3 out of 15).

C. DOUBLE CHANNEL ENERGY FLOW (e.g. grazing & detritus)

1. Grazing and detritus food chains combined - realistic and practical.
2. Conforms to the basic stratfied structure of ecosystems
3. Separates grazing (consumption of living matter) from detritus (utilisation of dead matter) in time and space.
4. That micro- & micro consumers differ greatly in size - metabolism relations, is recognised.

   herbivores predators producers Grazing food chain detritus food chain

D. UNIVERSAL MODEL :

1. Most applicable to all ecosystems and all levels

I	=	Irigested Energy	P = Production
NU	=	Not used	B = Biomass
A	=	Assimilated	S = Stored
R	=	Respiration	E = Excreted

2. Food webs very complex, multichannel flows occur in nature
3. Measurements in field conditions difficult

VII. NUTRIENT CYCLES

A. MACRONUTRIENTS N-C-H-O-P-K- (atmosphere & soil) Micronutrients - Cu, Fe, Co (soil - very conservative and finite in nature - atmospheric, edaphic, biological and chemical.

B. ATMOSPHERIC CYCLES

1. Hydrological 2. Carbon

C. EDAPHIC CYCLES

1. Nitrogen 2. Minerals: N, P, K, Ca, Mg & S
3. Micronutrients - trace elements - (Fe, Zn, Mn, Fe, Bo, Mo, Co, etc.).

D. UPTAKE AND ACCUMMULATION

E. DECOMPOSITION

F. RATE OF CYCLING

VIII. ECOSYSTEMS

A. PONDS: Standing state, macrophytes, phytoplankton, Benthos, Zoolplankton, Primary and secondary and tertiary consumers, decomposers

B. MARINE (70% of earth's surface) Plankton, macrophytes, primary, secondary and tertiary consumers and decomposers

C. GRASSLANDS: Producers, primary and secondary consumers and decomposers

D. FORESTS:Producers, primary, secondary and tertiary consumers & decomposers

E. DESERT (17% of the land mass) Producers, consumers and decomposers

F. CROPLANDS

IX. PRODUCTIVITY

1. Maximum productivity - net plant production 1 year - Tropical forests
2. Total % primary production of the planet, tropical forests (17.3) and wooded savanrahs (19.2). These too have very poor conversion rate of 0.001%. Reasons are
   (a) Energy losses between the outer atmosphere and canopy.
   - 15% and 8% of the solar radiation reaching the earth come to tropical and temperate zones.
   (b) Interception of light by plants.
   - interruption efficiency dependence on leap area index
   (c) Plant biochemistry: C_4 plants, lower respiration good.
   (d) Below-ground production
   Temperature plants (25%) translocate greater amount to root systems than do tropical plants (10%)
3. Secondary Production
   (a) Assimilation efficiency: ingested energy left after waste disposal
   (b) Production efficiency: assimilalted energy used to increase the energy content of the population

	(C)	(A)		
Poeciloerus Pictus	67	25	10	(P)
		42	15	(R)

C = Consumption, A = Assimilation , (FU)
FU = Feces + Urine, P = Production,
R = Respiration

13. TERRESTRIAL ECOSYSTEMS

I. ECOSYSTEM

Interaction between the organism and the non living environment, each influencing the properties of the other and necessary for the maintenance of life on earth.

1. Basic kinds of ecosystem :Four major types of aquatic habitats - Freshwater, Marine, Estuarine, Terrestrial
2. Terrestrial ecology is concerned with the study of organisms growing on land that is much variable in terms of both, time and geography.
   (a) BIOMES: Easily recognised terrestrial community unit. In a given biome the life form of the climax regetation is uniform and is the key to reognition. [ODUM],

A. DESERTS

1. Less than 10 of annual rainfall on that regions where there is more rainfall but unevenly distributed in the annual cycle.
2. Two types of North America desert - cold desert, Washington and the hot desert, Arizona.
3. Four distictive life forms - annuals, desert shurbs, succulents and microflara.
4. Animals - reptiles, insects, nocturnal rodents, birds and camels
5. Decomposers - very few, poor vegetation, thermophiles,

B. GRASSLANDS

1. In regions of a rain betweem 10 -30 inches - depeneding on temperature, seasonal distribution of rainfall, water - holding capacity of soil.
2. Present in North America, Eurasian contients, southern South America, central and south Africa and Australia.
3. Dominant plant life - grasses 5-8 ft, forks and woody plants may be present.
4. Large herbivores, large mammals, large grazing birds.
5. Grasslands soil - best suited for corn and wheat.

C. FORESTS

1. Occupy 40% of land,
2. Depicts a picture of ecological succession - non forest variety and forest variant.

3. Trees, shrubs and a variety of ground vegetation, depends on the geographical position of forest.
4. Temperature decidous forest - Quercus, Acer, Betula, Picea etc.
5. Temperate coniferrous forest - Abies, Picea, Pinus, Cedrus, Juniperus etc.
6. Ants, flies, beetles, elephants, deer, males, squired, shrews, snakes, birds, lizards.
7. Wide variety of micro organisms - fungi, bacteria, actinomycetes

D. TUNDRAS

1. Wet arctic grasslands, cold marsh, frozen for a partion of the year.
2. This vegetation made - lichens, grasses and sedges.
3. Breeding migratory birds, emerging insects during summer, permanent resident mammals - ox, caribou, reinder, polar bears, wolves and bennings.

The ecological crisis is doing what no other crisis in history has ever done - challenging us to a realization of a new humanity.

Jean Houston

14. AQUATIC ECOSYSTEM - FRESH WATER AND MARINE

I. INTRODUCTION

A. ECOSYSTEM:- Interaction between the biotic and abiotic components of the environment amongst themselves and with environment.

B. TYPES OF ECOSYSTEM:- (a) Aquatic ecosystem, (b) terrestrial ecosystem.

C. AQUATIC ECOSYSTEMS: are divided into a. fresh water ecosystem eg. Ponds, lakes, streams. b. Marine ecosystems eg. seas and oceans.

D. DIFFERENCE BETWEEN FRESH AND MARINE ECOSYSTEM:- Fresh water;- (a) fresh water, dry up during the dry periods. Marine ecosystem;- (a) saline water bodies, (b) they never dry up.

E. TEMPORARY WATER BODIES :- I. Fresh water bodies; (a) natural bodies of water, (b) experience recurrent dry phases of varrying duration.

F. FACTORS GOVERNING THEIR FORMATION :- (a) preciptation, percolation capacity [low] (b) clay soils, such slicons formed are called ephemeral streams . (c) run off from surface, (d) topographic features, (e) overland flow, (f) ground water flow.

G. ABIOTIC FACTORS ;- (a) Temperature :- (i) varies not only on seasonal but even daily or even hourly basis, (ii) variation due to turbidity, shallow waters, (iii) temperature variation effects fauna-leading to thermal death of insects. (b) Turbidity;- 1. may be due to clay particles, 2. microrganisisms-prevants penetration of light. (c) dissolved CO_2 and O_2; do fluctuate diurnally due to photosysnthesis and respiration. few mortalities in fish were reported. d. Other chemical parameters;- dissolved substances, conductivity of waters, cone of chemicals.

H. BIOTIC FACTORS OF TEMPORARY WATERS:- considered similarities in fauna between two or more locations seen eg. 1. snails-physa fonticola. 2. copepods-eucyclops serratulus; acanthocyclps vernaties. 3. beetles-rhanthus pul resources, 4.leeches-melobdella stagnails. 5. microsustaceans-canthocamptus staphylinroides, cupricerces ovum. Aquatic invertebrates; 1. sponges, 2.alderflies, 3. caddisfies. Other inhabitants include;

1. Bacteria, 2.fungi, 3. macrophytes, 4. protozoans, 5.fishes, 6. amphibious, 7.greyteals and pink necked duck.

I. RIVER AS AN ECOSYSTEM:- river - a tree like arrangement of small channels joining to form progresively large channels.

   1. Sources of water in rivers; 1. preciptation, 2. surface drainge, 3. melting of snow ice, 4. ground water
   2. Phyico - chemical characters; 1. currentrnajor controlling limiting factors, 2. land water interchange. 3. oxygen tension - variation in oxygen level, 4. temperature, 5. turbulence - irregularity in the movement of water molecules.

J. ESTUARINE ECOSYSTEM: Estuary - place where river meets the sea, intertidal zone between fresh water habitat and marine habitat

   1. Variations in the estuary - water level, salinity, temperature.
   2. Classification of estuaries based on geo - morphology, a Fjord type estuaries eg. Norweguan Fjord, b tectonic estuaries eg. Sanfrancisco Bay, c. river delta estuaries eg. Nile river delta, based on salinity variations in the estuary a. highly stratified eg. Mouth of Mississippi river, b. Moderatly stratified eg. chesapeake bay, c. vertically homogenous estuary,
   3. Components of an estuary :
      (a) Abiotic components;
         1. Salinity -during high and low tides, it varies.
         2. Turbulance - caused due to mixing up of fresh and sea water,
         3. Siltation - reduces illumination thus effecting growth of plants.

      (b) Biotic components :
         1. Permananent fauna: all spend complete life in the estuary eg. polycheats likes Neries, Arenicola, amphitrilt and crustaceans like balances, palaemon.
         2. Temporary fauna; spend part of their life in the estuary or pass through them on their way from the river to oceans and vice versa.
         3. Characteristics of estuary: (a) vertical zonation, (b) mineral cycle, (c) energy flow.
         4. Estuarine adaptations: (a) live in burrows - not effected by changes in salinity, (b) live in shells - saved from death. (c) euryhaline and eurythernal.

(d) eyes - covered by conjunctival sacs - danger of drying up.

K. MARINE WATER ECOSYSTEM; They include the saline water bodies eg. seas and oceans;

1. Physical and chemical parameters:-

   (a) tides, (b) waves, (c) currents, (d) temperature - thermocime. (e) density, (f) light.

2. The ocean floor; 1. ocean depth - slightly over 3,798 meters. 2. continental shelf - shelf of land gently sloping from the surfline to a depth of 135 to 180 metres off most of the continents of the world. 3. shelf formed - combination of wave action during glacial periods, when the oceans level was lower. 4. Animal life planktonic population, 5. shelf area is called - neritic zone.

3. Influence on man; (a) recreation - beaches, scuba diving, swimming, (b) a place to dump. (c) transportation, (d) commercial fishing, (e) mining the sea (f) source of fresh water, (g) electricity generation - tides, currents.

4. Features of the marine environment

   (a) The coastal environment,

   (b) Estuaries and marshes,

   (c) Zonation of the sea

   (d) Two main life forms seen - corals [Coelenterata], Mangroves [plant sps]

L. Animals of the marine environments

1. protozoa;

   (a) Class ciliata eg. Paramecium,

   (b) Class rhizopoda eg. toranuifera, radiolaria,

   (c) Class flagelata eg.euglena.

2. porifera - bearers eg.sponges.

3. coelenterata 3 classes ;

   (a) Hydrozoa eg.obelia, hydr (a)

   (b) Anthozoa eg.sea anemones.

   (c) Scyphozoa eg. jelly fishes.

4. Mollusca;

   (a) Polyplacophora eg. chitons,

   (b) Gastropodea eg. pila globosa,

   (c) Bivalvia eg. freshwater russel
   (d) Cephalapoda eg. octopus.

5. Arthropoda; classes;
   (a) Crustacea eg. crabs,
   (b) Archnida eg. spiders and scorpions,
   (c) Myriapoda eg. milipedes,
   (d) Insecta eg. all insects.
6. Fchinodermata classes;
   (a) Asthenoidea; eg. star fishes
   (b) Crinoidea eg.sea lilies,
   (c) Echinoidea eg. sea urchins, and dollars,
   (d) Molothuroidea eg.sea cucumbers.
   (e) Ophiuroidea eg.britle stars.

M. EFFECTS OF LIGHT ON THE MARINE ANIMALS: [JOHN RESECK pg 182] ;-

1. Effect on growth and development, 2. Effect on pigmentation and colour
3. Effect on eyes,
4. Effect on locomotion-
   (a) phototaxis, (b) photokinesis, (c) phototrophism
5. Lunar periodicity,
6. Bioluminiscence,
7. Photoperiodism.

N. EFFECTS OF TEMPERATURE ON MARINE ORGANISMS

1. Range of temperature tolerance,
2. Effect on growth and development,
3. Effect on animal distribution,
4. Effect or reproductive behaviour.

O. ADAPTATIONS OF ANIMALS IN BENTHIC REGIONS:

1. Lung fish; bladder gets compressed when fish moves down expands when it moves up.
2. Whales; withstand great pressures by allowing their lungs to be completely flattenend.
3. Seals; can store increased amount of O_2 reserves for the brain, heart and vital organs by cutting off their circulation to other parts of the body.

15. BIOGEOGRAPHY

I. INTRODUCTION

A. Solar system, earth, rotation & climate

B. Evolution of life, continental drift & biota

C. Flora and Fauna

D. Community, Ecosystem & Biome

II. PHYTOGEOGRAPHY

A. BASIC PRINCIPLES

1. Climatic zones
2. Homoclimes
3. Distribution and barriers
4. Age and area
5. Endemism - Land, water, islands
6. Latitude and Altitude

B. FLORISTIC REALMS OF THE WORLD

1. Holarctic: Eurasia, N. America, Greenland small differences
2. Paleotropic: Old world, large differences
3. Neotropic: New world, large differences
4. Australian: Australia, extreme isolation
5. Capensis: S.W. tips of Africa
6. Antarctic: South American tips, sub antarctic islands

C. VEGETATION TYPES OF THE WORLD

1. Tropical evergreen forests: low altitude zones near the equator with heavy rain all through year excepting for a few dry spells.
   (a) Amazon basin and Central American isthmus
   (b) Cango, Niger & Zambesi basins & Madagascar
   (c) Highly stratified
2. Tropical scrub & deciduous forests: Rain less than the tropical evergreen forests and unevenly distributed. Deciduous due to dry spells Africa, Australia & Brazil.
3. Tropical Savannahs: Grasslands with scattered trees. Lesser rainfall than deciduous forests. Dry season prolonged, Africa, lesser extent in S.America & Australia. Grasses tall. Trees, palms and Euphorbias.
4. Subtropical evergreen forests: Warm-temperate climate of Japan and South Atlantic. High moisture and less seasonal variations in temperature.

5. Temperate deciduous forests: Seasonal variations in temperatures. Moisture abundant dry spells. Europe, NE America, Australia, tip of South America.
6. Temperature moist coniferous Forests: Temperate rain forests, low temperature, high moisture, conifers. California to Alaska.
7. Temperate Grasslands: Rainfall very low (10-30") but higher than the deserts. Tall grasses. North America. Forested areas with degraded soil also support grassland.
8. Subtemperate coniferous forest:Evergreen conifers. North America, Eurasia.
9. Desert: Less rain fall (10"). Ephemerals, succulents, thorny shrubs. N. Africa, Australia, Tibet, S. America.
10. Tundra;Arctic.Dwarf treeless community. Grasses, sedges, etc. dwarf shrubs.

III. PHYTOGEOGRAPHY OF INDIA

A. FLORISTIC REGIONS

1. Western Himalayas
2. Eastern Himalayas
3. Upper gangetic plain
4. Lower gangetic plain
5. Indus Plain
6. Deccan - Peninsular
7. Western Peninsular
8. Andamans

B. VEGETATIONAL TYPES

1. Tropical Rain Forests - Evergreen: West Coast, Assam, Andaman.
2. Tropical dry Deciduous forests: Bihar, Orissa
3. Sub tropical forests: Hill stations
4. Temperpate forests: Nilgiris, Himalayan regions
5. Deserts: Rajasthan 6. Mangroves: Bengal, Andamans, Deltas
7. Sandy sea shore: East Coast
8. Savannahs: Haryana, Punjab, A.P., Mysore, Maharashtra, etc.
9. Alpine forests: Sikkim, Kashmir

IV. ZOOGEOGRAPHY

Distribution

Living: Horizontal areas Altitudinal/Vertical distribution

Extinct geological

A. HORIZONTAL

1. Palaearctic: largest, Europe, Russia, N. China Subdivided into European, Medeterranian, Siberian, Manchurian (B5 families of terrestrial Vertebrates)
2. Eturopean: Arabia, Africa (161 families - 30 endemic)
3. Oriental: India, Lanka, S. China, Malaysia, Indonesia, Phillippines [153 families).

   Sub Region: Indian, Ceylonese, Inco-Chinese, Indo-Malayan
4. Australian: Australia & New Zealand (134 families)
5. Neotropical: Mexico, C. & S. America, West Indies (155 families).
6. Neoarctic: N. America & Greenland (120 families)

B. VERTICAL: Coastal, intertidal, surface, middle and deep, Coral reefs

Dispersal

1. Wind and gales:
   (a) aerial nektons like insects, birds, bats, etc.
   (b) Seeds, pollen of plants
2. Migration
   (a) Seasonal - temporary - animals
   (b) Permanent - racial groupings – animals
3. Land bridges: extinct – extanct
   (a) Panama, Suez, Bering, Gibraltar, Ceylon, Indonesian islands, etc.
4. Water as a Vehicle
   (a) Plant seeds, whole plants, vegetative propagules
   (b) Animals on the rafts and drift wood or Vessels
5. Animals: for plants & plant parts

Barriers

1. Topographic : Mountain Ranges, High seas, Andes, Rockeys, Himalayas, Cancacus
2. Climatic : Extremes of temperature & moisture
3. Vegetational : Food & shelter for animals confining the animals

16. ZOOGEOGRAPHY

I. ZOOGEOGRAPHY

A. DEFINITION

Zoogeography is the study of the distributin of animal life on the earth and the factors controlling it.

B. HISTORY

1. Buffon (1707 - 1788) held formal ideas about animal distribution.
2. Earnest Haeckel made a zoogeographical approach in dealing with ecological phemomenon.
3. In 1857, Dr. Sclater devided the world into six regions, based on the distribution of birds.
4. Russel Wallace is called the "Father of Zoogeography". His book 'The Geographical Distribution of Animals.' (1876).

C. FACTORS CONTROLLING ANIMAL DISTRIBUTION

1. Prodigality of production
2. Barriers: The different kinds of barriers are
   (a) Topographic - water currents, depth, salinity, impurity, land masses, large water holder, mountain ranges. eg. Himalayas.
   (b) Climatic - temperature, light, humudity.
   eg. extremes of temperature and moisture are important, thus amphiluans and reptiles are more common in tropical than temperate arear, decreasing considerably towards the poles
   (c) Vegetation - depending upon the selective food habits of organisms
3. Dispersal:
   (a) Migration - the permanent and temporary movements of organisms from one region to another.
   (b) Land Bridges - eg. Suez, Panama Isthamus
   (c) Natural rafts and driftwoods - drifting materials like ice, timber scene as means for transporting organism from place to place.
   (d) Wind, storms - organisms are easily carried long distances.
   (e) Flying animals - eg. birds that are flown off-course.

(f) Human agency - Travelling human population have introduced 'alien' organisms into habitats. Eg. rabbits were introduced by man into Australia.

4. Enviromental conditions and geologic changes:

1. Adaptation 2. Population density.
3. Predation. 4. Competition.
5. Diseases 6. Extinction.
7. Influence of man.

D. PLANES OF ANIMAL DISTRIBUTION

1. Distribution in Space.

- Geographic distribution i.e. Horizontal or superficial
- Psychozoic era: age of man

E. KINDS OF ANIMAL DISTRIBUTION

It is the method of spreading and reaching an area not premously inhabited bythe specus or groups. There are four kinds of pattern of distribution.

1. Cosmopolitan: (or Universal or Continuous) distribution eg. rats, bats, man, mytilus, Artemia, ralima.
2. Discontinous (or Disjunctive): distribution eg. camel, peripatus, notodulur, belosloma.
3. Isolated distribution:

   Eg. Tantara lizard in New Zealand; Ornithornynchur (duck carried platypus) in Australia & Tasmania; Enhnida spiry anteater in Australia & Tasmania & New Guinea.

4. Bipolar distribution:

   Animals are found to inhabit only the North Pole (Arctic) and South Pole (Antartic) region with no representatives in the intermediate ocean.

   Eg. Lampsa, Mysiothela (coelenterata), Chione (molluse), Oncorhynchur (Salmon).

F. ZOOGEOGRAPHIC REALMS

1. Realm Megogaea or Arctogaca 2. Realm Notogaea

   (a) Ethiopian Region (b) Oriental Region
   (c) Palaertic Region (d) Nearctic Region
   (e) Australian Region.

3. Realm Neogae

   (a) Neotropical Region

(b) Bathy metric distribution i.e. nuetral or altituclinal

- Malolinotic realm	pelagic, benthic
- Lumnobiotic realm	lotic, benthic
- Geoluotic realm	(Terrestiral)

G. INSULAR FAUNA

The term 'Insnular fauna' is used to describe the fauna of islands. A.R. Wallace has classified islands as:-

1. Continental Island(s) 2. Oceanic Islands.

H. EXAMPLE OF SPECIES ISOLATION

Australian isolation started about 90 million years ago, it separated from Antartica, before the continent has been reached by placental mammals. Therefore, the marsupials had no competition from placentals and colonised all the different ecological niches available.

Terminologies

1. Geographical range
2. Ecological range
3. Geological range
4. Barrier
5. Metamorphic migration
6. Ecesis
7. Endemic
8. Prodigality
9. Dispersal
10. Adaptation
11. Density
12. Competition
13. Extinction
14. Cosmopolitan
15. Discontinuous

I. ZOOGEOGRAPHICAL REALMS, DIVISIONS, TYPICAL FAUNA

REGION	SUB - REGION	FAUNA
ETHIOPIAN	1. East African	Catfish, Clawed toad,
	2. West African	gecko, ostriches,
	3. South African	Giraffe,
	4. Malagasy	
ORIENTAL	5. Indian	Carp, Myla, Draco,
	6. Ceylonese	Pheasants, flying
	7. Indo-China	Lemur, lour.
	8. Indo - Malayan	
PALAEARCTIC	1. Europian	Cyprimaler, salamander,
	2. Mediterranean	Alligator, Warbler,
	3. Siberian	Hedgeogar
	4. Manchurian	
NEARCTIC	1. Californian	
	2. Rock Mountain	Garpicke, howfin,
	3. Allegophany	Amblystoma, Bufo,

	4. Canadian	Gilo monster, wild turkeys pocket gophens.
NEOTROPICAL	1. Brazilian 2. Mexican 3. Chilean	Electric cells, pipid fugs, turites, Rhea, sloths, Lama.
AUSTRALIAN	1. Austro - Malayan 2. Australian 3. Polynesion 4. New Zealand	Osteoglossid, lung fish, frogs, spencolon, Crocodiles, Cassouranier, Lemur, echidna, duck lulled platypur.

> *Nature shrinks as capital grows. The growth of the market cannot solve the very crisis it creates*
>
> **Vandana Shiva**

17. HUMAN ECOLOGY

I. OBJECTIVE

1. To assess and delve deep into the relationship of Man with the biosphere in terms of obtaining food, clothing and shelter.
2. To review the development and impact of modern human life styles upon the ecosystem of the earth in comparison to ethnoecology and a more traditional natural community.
3. To discuss the principal ecological effects and climatic implications of air, water, soil pollution, together with means whereby these effects can be controlled. To elate humans to specific problems like energy option over population, extinction of species, depletion of natural resources etc.,

   A. ORIGIN AND EVOLUTION OF MAN
      1. Races of Mankind - Major, minor & mixes
      2. Pangea and gondwana land
      3. Mono centrism and Polycentrism
      4. Ancestors of modern man: Paleontology (S & E. Africa)

   B. ANCIENT CIVILISATIONS
      1. Nubia & Egypt 2. Palestine 3. South America
      4. Indian 5. Chinese

   C. PROGRESS OF HUMAN SOCIETIES
      1. Ancient (until the arrival of Islam): Greek, Roman, Chinese, Indian, Central Asian & Religions
      2. Medieval (until Industrial revolution and colonialism): Colonisation, Plundering others resources
      3. Modern - Early (until 1 world war)
         Recent (1914 to 1970 - I & II & III W.Ws)
         Current (Environmental Consciousness)
         Future (Ecocentrism or Anthropocentrism)

D. ECOLOGICAL PRINCIPLES OF POPULATIONS
   1. Habitat and Niche
   2. Genetics and Variations
   3. Growth of populations and their regulation
   4. Geographical distribution, races, migrations
   5. Interactions with plants, animals and themselves

E. SOCIOLOGICAL PRINCIPLES OF POPULATIONS
   1. Interaction with nature's resources: Economics activity
   2. Economic Interactions among individuals: Sociology of Settlements
   3. Management Mechanisms of economic and social activities: Political Processes
   4. Marxian outlook of Socioeconomic Primacy (Malthus, Darwin
   5. Free-enterprise outlook (Smith & Mills)
   6. Keynesian outlook of Social Control
   7. Abnormal outlooks - Racial, Military, Dictatorships

F. BASIC REALITIES OF CURRENT HUMAN SOCIETIES
   1. Rich Nations and Rich People
   2. Poor Nations and poor people
   3. Urban Systems-their basic parasitism
   4. Rural Systems -their productivity
   5. Industry as a bridge between Urban & Rural Economics
   6. Settlements & Cities, Resources & Commodities, barter and Market depend on Science, Technology, Mechanisms of economic change, political processes and political systems.
   7. Indian Situation and similar or worse scenarios

G. ECOLOGY OF HUMAN NEEDS
   1. Food - Global reality of Producers - have not Nations
      Production - Consumerism - have nots
   2. Water - Indian Scene: Mismanagement vs Self sufficiency
      - Excess resources, cases, Indian Scene
   3. Shelter- Settlements Philosophies- Vertical vs Horizontal growth – Shelterless -Urban vs Rural Settlements. Indian Scene
   4. Clothing - Have nots - Psyche of charity vs Psyche of dependence

5. Health - Biological and chemical sources of illhealth. Epidemics, genetic diseases, tutored microbes and accidental monstrocities

H. EDUCATION, SCIENCE, TECHNOLOGY

1. Human Resources as an agent of change for better
2. Global realities
3. Indian Scene
4. The last hope or the lost hope

I. CONSEQUENCES

1. Global - Regional – Local
2. PP & RN and RP & PN Violence at the tunnel mouth
3. Ecocentrism and Limits to growth vs the Onslought of Consumerism

J. CURRENT ISSUES

1. Divisions & Migrations programmed shuttling
2. Refugees - Economic, Ecological, religious, political
3. Marginalisation and violence d. Sucking effects
4. Noah's ark can hold only some

II. AGRICULTURE, FOREST AND NATURAL RESOURCES

(1) Agriculture can be viewed as simplified, artificial means of obtaining food which ultimately accumulates into the human biomass. Product of population boom.

(2) Agricultural communities are unstable, dependant on human intervention for its basic needs.

(3) Natural community more stable, genetically diverse and self sustainable.

(4) Agricultural community is simpler than natural community i.e. monoculture and therefore only desirable for humans which make it unstable and dependant an artificial means (methods to procure water, nutrients i.e. fertilizers, pesticides). The whole system is synthetic.

(5) All this leads to imbalances in the natural functioning of ecosystem and increases pollution in the long run.

(6) This mostly affects the developing countries and the poor.

(7) The gene pool of cultivated organisms is a subset of the gene pool of wild ancestors and relatives. The Consistents removal of undesirable characters (for human but may be desirable for wild

life) has in the process, left us with accountable genes. The genetic loss is most felt in the developed countries and the under developed are relatively safe.

(8) Forests were considered the source of livelihood in terms of its scientific and aesthetic value. History proves that trees were loved by one and all (e.g. Bishnois movement).

(9) Alarming felling of trees during and after Industrial Revolution.

(10) More prevalent in countries, scarce of fossil fuel.

(11) Timber and paper industry major consumption

(12) Felling of trees came changes in the global hydrological cycle, erosion, loss of diversity and therefore extinction of species.

(13) Natural resources apart from the one mentioned above include (unused land of the world, landscapes, recreation and tourism, water, minerals, conventional energy, wastes and pollution) have been under high pressures and have reached a threshold limit in its carrying capacity.

(14) St Francis of Assissi asserted that although man might be at the apex of creation, this did not mean that all life was for him and at his disposal.

(15) Short sighted gains, induced man to exploit nature to the most, without returning its due and therefore the immediate need for sustainable development.

III. ENERGY OPTIONS, OVERPOPULATION AND POLLUTION

1. Rapidly advancing depletion of oil, natural gas, coal reserve and forest because that too many people consume too many goods that require energy input for use or for manufacture.
2. Therefore the necessity to implore conventional energy sources (wind, sun and water) and a now & more modern one; nuclear energy (but its safety itself is questionable), tide, geothermal & Oceans are being considered.
3. Energy consumption by 20% of the global population living in North is much more (80%) than consumed by the remaining 80% (20%).
4. Therefore North recommended to mend its ways.
5. Underdeveloped countries should adopt sustainable and efficient methods for resource utilization.

6. Optimium population is one that can be sustained in stable balance with the resources.
7. Fossil fuel used gives rise to extensive pollution.
8. Two very important energy options being discussed are unclear power and solar power.
9. Questions about environmental impact, availability of uranium ore and safety have seriously threatened the nuclear power industry.
10. Solar power is a safe & viable alternative as it has few environmental hazards.
11. But in the near future, it is not likely that man is going to turn (decrease) away from fossil fuel use, unless we avoid waste, reduce the growth of energy demand.
12. Human population should not be left at the hands of nature (i.e. limiting factors cause a drop or eliminate populations) as there would be widespread misery, starvation and warfare.
13. Humane methods of limiting it are desirable.
14. More people means more food, clothing, homes, schools roads, automobiles, television sets, energy and the material goods our society holds so dear.
15. Therefore increased pressure on environment.
16. 1/3 of world's population in developed countries consume 85% of earth's resources.
17. World population estimated to be 8 billion by 2100: - poverty.
18. Threat to national security?
19. Increased population leads to increased pollution.
20. Pollution is reduction in the quality of water, air, land standards.
21. Caused by wastes disposed by traffic, industries, domestic consumption.
22. Pollution has damaging effect on public health, property, Ecosystem or aesthetic values.
23. Pollution abatement costs us a great deal.
24. Polluters compel society to bear the costs of pollution.
25. Wasteful consumption increases pollution.
26. Pollution makes the earth unsustainable.
27. Life of ecosystems of the world questioned?

IV. FUTURE

(1) Most problems linked with illiteracy, overpopulation in the south and increased affluence and consumerism in the North.

(2) Ecologically harmful and irrational practices to be altered or eliminated.

(3) Humans share the common fate of other living organisms.

(4) Humans should reflect on meaning of life and make this world a better place to stay on for generations.

(5) Simplistic and holistic attitude recommended.

(6) Alternative solution for population control, pesticide usage etc to be sought.

(7) Redefinition of urban settlements (proper management).

(8) Efficient land and energy resource use.

> *What is in the pencil is greater than what is around it. The talents in you are greater than the environment surrounding you. Your potentials will change your environment.*
>
> **Israelmore Ayivor**

18. ENVIRONMENTALISM

I. INTRODUCTION

II. PHILOSOPHIES

A. RESOURCES - PAST, PRESENT & FUTURE
- DOOM OR BOOM ?

B. INDUCTIVE AND DEDUCTIVE METHODS

C. ACCENTS :

1. Ecocentrism
2. Anthropocentrism
3. Existentialism

III. Historical

A. ANCIENT : Live with and share

B. MEDIEVAL : Exchange or own

C. MODERN : Exchange, appropriate or exclude

1. War 1 2. War 2 3. War 3 4. War 4

IV. Environmental Consciousness

Resource crunch, Survival & human rights

V. STATE OF THE WORLD

VI. PERSPECTIVES

A. 3rd world B. 2nd world C. 1st world

VII. ACTIONS

A. Global - Regional - Local

B. United Nations - Governments - Societies - Individuals

VIII. CONCLUSIONS

A. Philosophies revisited B. Consequences to face

C. Psychology of man D. Plain truth and the hope

3

Biodiversity & Germplasm Banking

1. BIODIVERSITY
2. BIOSPHERE RESERVES
3. ECOSYSTEMS
4. BIOGEOGRAPHY
5. ANIMAL RESOURCES AND GERMPLASM BANKING
6. WILD LIFE TRADE
7. DEFORESTATION PROBLEMS
8. ECOLOGICAL VALUES OF PLANTS
9. GRASSES
10. FOOD & CEREALS
11. PULSES, OILS & SPICES
12. FIBRES AND TIMBER
13. GUMS, RESINS & RUBBER
14. GENERAL FEATURES OF SOME PLANT MEDICINAL PLANTS
15. HISTORY AND EHNOBOTANY OF DRUGS
16. MARINE PLANTS

Syllabus

1. NATURAL ENDOWMENT: Biodiversity a result of evolution: Genetic, ecological and taxonomic. Phytogeography and Zoogeography. Principles of plant and animal distribution, Continental drift. Vegetational types and Floristic realms of the world.

   Evolutionary convergence and divergence, Age and area concept, Endemism, Continuous and discontinuous distribution. rainfall types, seasons, temperature, dry period, secondary factors. Macro, Meso, Micro-climates. monsoon mechanisms, vagaries of weather, El Nino, concept of probable climate

   Origin and diversification of cultivated plants
2. GERMPLASM BANKING: Economic Values, Domestication, Agriculture. Ethnobiology. Gathering all of one utility at one place- Concepts of Banking and Germplasm. Colonial Countries-UK, Holland.
3. CONSEQUENCES: Exploitation of global resources - Migrations – Inequalities; Encroachments - reduces the habitat Endangerment, Extinction, Monopoly: Loss of genes, ownership and trading in genes Globalisation of resources and privatisation of expertise.
4. PERSPECTIVES: Conservation, Restoration, Exploitation: Ex-situ, In-situ, Gardens, zoos, Parks, Sanctuaries, Biosphere Reserves. Barriers of time and space: Micropropagation, Cryopreservation, Engineering, Geographical Limits, NBPGR, NBAGR, NBMGR, ICAR etc, International: WTO, Intellectual Property, Rights.

References

1. Good, R. 1970. Phytogeography. McGraw-Hill, New York
2. Mani, M. S. 1978. Biogeography of India. Dr Junk Publishers, Amsterdam.
3. Kendeigh, S.C. 1974. Ecology. Prentice-Hall,
4. Grainage, M. and Ahmed S. 1988. Handbook of plants with pest control properties, John Wiley.
5. Andrewartha, H.G. And L.C. Birch,1954. The distribution and Abundance of Animals.
6. Brown, J.H. and A.C. Gibson, 1983 Biogeography.

1. BIODIVERSITY

I. PERCEPTIONS AND PROACTIONS

A. BASIC PERCEPTIONS

1. Introduction
2. Spectrum of information
3. Two functions of biota
4. BENEFITS FROM DIVERSITY
   (a) Stability of the system (b) Buffering Ability
   (c) Carrying Capacity
5. CONSEQUENCES OF EXTINCTION
   (a) Loss of a gene pool (b) Loss of an ecological Links
6. AGRICULTURAL PERSPECTIVES

B. CONCERTED PROACTIONS

1. TARGET SYSTEMS
2. AGENDA FOR ACTION
   (a) Inventories of plants and animals
   (b) Repositories of plants
3. MECHANICS OF ACTION
   (a) Organisation (b) Associates
   (c) Activitics at ground level
4. LEGAL ASPECTS
5. UNIFIED COACTIONS
   (a) Role models (b) Natural and Idealistic leadership

II. CONSERVATION OF BIODIVERSITY

A. DIVERSITY OF LIFE

1. Genetic diversity 2. Species diversity
3. Ecosystem diversity 4. Cultural diversity

B. VALUE OF DIVERSITY

C. LOSSES OF DIVERSITY- CAUSES

1. Plant diversity 2. Animal diversity
3. Habitat diversity 4. Genetic diversity
5. Cultural diversity

D. MECHANISMS OF LOSS

E. STRATEGIES TO CONSERVE BIODIVERSITY

III. BIODIVERSITY: VARIETY AND MEASUREMENT

A. DIFFERENT LEVELS OF BIODIVERSITY

1. Genetic diversity 2. habitat diversity 3. Cultural diversity

B. MEASUREMENT OF BIODIVERSITY

1. Species richness measure
2. Limitations
3. Proportional abundance indices

C. SAMPLING DIVERSITY

1. Choosing the right measure for diversity

D. APPLICATION OF SPECIES DIVERSITY MEASURE

1. Concept of species richness
2. Measurements
   (a) Rare faction Method - Procedures, assumptions, limitations, suitability
   (b) Jackknife Method - description, limitations suitability
   (c) Bootstrap Procedure - procedure, difference from Jackknife method, limitations, suitability.

E. HETEROGENEITY

1. Concept of Heterogeneity
2. Measures of Heterogeneity
   (a) Logarithmic Series (b) Log normal Distribution
   (c) Simpson's Index (d) Shannon-Wiener Index
   (e) Brillorim Index

F. EVENNESS MEASURES

1. Estimation 2. Drawbacks

G. BACKGROUND PROBLEMS

1. Practical difficulties 2. Assumptions 3. Limitations

IV. FACTORS CAUSING BIODIVERISTY

INTRODUCTION

Biodiversity is commonly used to describe the number variety and variability of living organisms. The factors that cause or force biodiversity in a region can also be called as barriers which prevents animals to disperse.

A. Natural Factors

Environmental conditions are determining or limiting factors of distributions. These factors like

1. Temperature: This affects species even a range from low temperature at are exteare to high temperatures at other and these constitute temperature gradient.
2. Light: Light is fundamental importance because it privides energy that green plants fix into carbohydrates during photosynthesis.
3. Salinity: In water salinity affects organisms in their distribution.
4. Interactions factor: Population of the species can live in those areas where there are favourable environmental gradients.
5. Climatic patterns: Many of the most important physical factors of the land environment have very distinet patterns of variations in different parts of the world which are called as climatic patterns.
6. Soil: Soil influences the development and distribution of certain plant species.
7. Ecological succession: The communities in an ecosystem under go developmental procers called succession.

B. Biological factors:

The biological factors causing biodiversity are as follows.

1. Food and Feeding: The availability of food material determines the species of that area.
2. Competitions: The competition for basic needs among animals determines the species number in that areas.
3. Predators and Prey: The simplest influence that predators hight hare to eliminate species by eating them or alternatively to prevent the entire of new ones into a habitat.
4. Niche: In a ecosystem there are different niches and each niche supports only some groups of organisms to survive.
5. Natural selection: The nature itself supports only a group of organisms with particular adaptation.
6. Isolating forces within the organisms: Genetic system leads to diversity in two ways. One is cumlation and the other is isolation.
7. External isolating forces: No two patches of wood lands, no two patches of fresh water bodies will be obsolutely save. The difference in these acts as external isolating forces.
8. Age and Area: There is a direct relation ship between age of a group or species and the even it spreads.

9. Adaptation for survival: Adaptation for survival results in the formation of new species.

2. ARTIFICIAL FACTORS

   (a) Industrialisation (b) Urbanisation (c) Intensive Agriculture

3. DISJUNCTIONS

   (a) Geomorphological disjunctions: Geomorphological disjunctions are caused due to the sudden fragmentations of the continents dritting away from each other, mountains etc.

   (b) Climatic disjunctions: The subranges privide different niches to different organisms and cause biodiversity increase in that range.

   (c) Evolutionary disjunction and Migrations: Migrations of species increases the biodiversity.

4. EVOLUTIONARY FACTORS

   Evolution results in increase of genetic biodiversity

   (a) Segregations: This results in the development of new species in the sense of new genes.

   (b) Recombinations: Recombinations is the source of variations.

   (c) Mutation: Mutations causes variation which are the basis for species diversity.

C. CENTERS OF ORIGIN

All groups tend to speciate most actively in a limited area that constitute a center of origin. When these ancestral species splits to yield daughter species. one is advanced than the other.

e.g. The origin and development of maize and wheat.

D. SPREAD OF DIVERSITY

Spread of diversity is the disposal of the organism. In plants it is by seed dispersal and in animals there are 3 main types.

1. Jump dispersal: Jump dispersal is the movement of organisms across great distances, followed by the successful establishment of a population of original disperse dereudants at the dextinations.

2. Diffusions: Diffusion is the gradual movement of populations across hospitable terrain for a period of many generations.

3. Secular migration: This is a kind of diffusion taking place so slowly that the diffusing species undergoes appreciable changes in the process.

E. WHY ARE THERE MORE SPECIES IN SOME PLACES THAN OTHERS

The results of evolution up to now is a world supporting a rich variety of species, with more in some places than others.

F. LIMITS TO THE NUMBER OF SPECIES

Diversity varies from place to place because the stability of the environment varies from place to place. The mechanism that links low diversity to low stability is the greater rate of extinction.

G. IS DIVERSITY REGULATED

The diversity of a population regulates randomly or is regulated around an equilibrium by density dependence factors.

V. BIODIVERSITY IN ARTIFICIAL ECOSYSTEMS

A. INTRODUCTION

Diversity is a concept which refers to the range of variations or differences among some set of entities. Thus Biological Diversity refers to variety within the living world. The word BIODIVERSITY is commonly used to describe the number, variety and variability of living organisms. The ecosystem in itself holds a very important bearing on global biodiversity.

B. BIODIVERSITY AT ECOSYSTEM LEVEL

The concept of biodiversity is most commonly defined in terms of genes, species and ecosystems. While its possible to define in principle what is meant by genetic and species diversity, there is no unique definition and classification of ecosystem at global level. Ecosystems explicitly include abiotic factors.

C. CLASSIFICATION OF ECOSYSTEMS

1. Natural Ecosystems: A natural ecosystem is a set of organisms occuring together, plus their interonediete environment, which interact with one another over a period and thus constitute a system. They depend largely on internal processes and often show a degree of isolation.
2. Artificial or manmade Ecosystems: Artificial ecosystems lie in between natural and fabricated systems. Artificial ecosystems are solar powered as in natural but differ in that:
   (a) ancillary energy sources are processed fuels rather than natural
   (b) diversity is greatly reduced.
   (c) dominant plants and animals are under artificial selection

(d) control is external. Classified into -

1. Agroecosystems 2. Aquaculture
3. Silviculture

D. AGROECOSYSTEMS

Agroecosystems are created in the physical sense by human interventian and they are essentially economic in nature. Agroecosystem is classified or includes :

1. Agriculture: Agriculture or cultivation of soils meant culturing a certain size of average for production of food and fibers for man's oven demand.

   (a) Diversity in agroecosystems: Man's interference effects the normal species interaction quite adversely.

   (b) Unifying concept for an Ecological Agroculture:

   Development of suitable strategies where agriculture is based on the principles of nature's ecosystems.

2. Animal Husbandary: Animal Husbandry or bioindustry refers to mans use of animals for his own needs. It also involves animal breed stock conservation.

E. AQUACULTURE

Aquaculture is the traditional extensive management in large bodies of freshwater such as lakes and reservoirs, to semi intensive and intensive culture in small freshwater tanks and ponds and brackish water areas.

1. Classification of Aquaculture

   (a) Freshwater Aquaculture: includes pond fish culture comprising Mono sex culture, composite fish culture, predator-prey culture etc.

   (b) Mariculture: involves exploitation of marine animals for food.

   (c) Brackish water aquaculture: Traditional brackish water farming is a dual system with alternate crops of fish and paddy. Salinity upto 20-30 ppt is ideal. Salt resistant variety of paddy is grown.

   (d) Metahaline culture: These are restricted to super saline salt pan areas where the salinity exceeds 200%. Brine Shrimp (Asternia salina) is extensively cultured.

2. Environmental aspects of Aquaculture

   (a) Extensive system: have no feed or fertilizer inputs.

(b) Semi-intensive system: some feed and/or fertilizer inputs are received. Man plays a governing role.

(c) Intensive system: mainly receives an external feed inputs.

F. SILVICULTURE

Silviculture is dying as a process by which the crops constituting a forest are tended, removed and replaced by new crops, resulting in the production of woods of distinctive form. Its an artificially raised forest crop.

1. Classification

   (a) Monoculture (b) Forest plantation

   Also classified based on method of felling :

   (a) High forest system (b) Coppice system

2. Displacement of older Ecosystems

   Conversion of one ecosystem into another due to establishment of plantation has various effects. Ecological and direct effect cause of felling, logging burning etc.

3. Susceptibility to diseases and Pests :

   This is a serious danger for plantations. Thus stability of a system does depend on diversity.

4. Risks associated with plantation Ecosystem :

   There are many but few are listed.

   (a) Single species crops provide an ideal habitat for pests.

   (b) Rapid colonization of injection

   (c) Disease build up over a period of time.

G. BIODIVERSITY AND ECONOMICS

The application of economics to naturel will lead to substantial losses of biological diversity. Manmade ecosystems in its present form of functioning and maintenance as such does not contribute to global biodiversity and is rather unstable.

2. BIOSPHERE RESERVES, SANCTUARIES & PARKS

A. DEFINITION OF BIOSPHERE

(a) Composition & Components (b) Habitats & Diversity

(c) Survival Strategy & Conservation

B. BIOSPHERE MODELS: ECOSYSTEM APPROACH

(a) Ecosystem Control Mechanism (b) Constancy in Ecosystems

(c) Feedback Mechanisms

C. MAN AND THE BIOSPHERE

(a) Evolution and impacts of man

(b) First Attempts at Biosphere Management

(c) Agriculture as an ecosystem management technique.

(d) Technology and Ecosystem changes

(e) Improvements to the Biosphere.

D. SANCTUARIES AND NATIONAL PARKS

(a) Definitions, Boundaries, limits

(b) Controlling / Governing Authorities

(c) Legislation, rules, regulations

(d) Global & National Conceptual Frameworks

(e) Role of the Forest Department

(f) Case Studies - National & International

E. CONSERVATIONS

(a) Role of Reserves, Sanctuaries & National Parks

1. Inherent limitations & advantages
2. Scope in environment management programs

(b) Conservation Ethic

1. World Conservation Strategy 2. Eco-development

(c) Conservation Law: (Case studies)

1. Organisation of the system 2. Acts & Legislation
3. Schedules & Sanctions

3. ECOSYSTEMS OF THE WORLD

I. ECOSYSTEMS

A. Biospheres
B. Geographic Realms
C. Climatic zones
D. Vegetation zones
E. Definition
F. Classification

Manmade / Managed Ecosystems

Natural Ecosystems

II. AQUATIC ECOSYSTEMS

Primary producers Consumers The decomposers

A. FRESH WATER

Stream, Rivers, Lakes and Ponds - Lentic and Lotic

Flora * Fauna * Adaptations * Variations Dynamics.

B. SHORELINE / Transition SYSTEMS

Marshes, Mangroves

Characteristics, FLORA, FAUNA, variations, adaptations, Dynamics, Importance

C. ESTUARINE AND COASTAL ECOSYSTEM

Rocky shore, sound beach, inter-tidal mudflat, tidal estuary

Characteristics, FLORA, FAUNA, variations, adaptations, Dynamics, Importance

D. CORAL REEFS

Distribution, Composition, Formation, Fauna, Flora, Types of Reefs, Values of Coral Reefs, Threats to Coral Communities

III. TERRESTRIAL ECOSYSTEMS

A. FORESTS

Primary Producers Consumers Decomposers

1. Cool temperate forests
2. Warm temperate forests
3. Oceanic Temperate Forests
   - (a) Characteristics
   - (b) Climatic conditions
   - (c) Distributions
   - (d) Flora & fauna
   - (e) Dynamics
   - (f) Nutrient cycling
4. Tropical Rain Forests
   - (a) Definition
   - (b) Distribution
   - (c) Salient Features
   - (d) Threats to Tropical Forests

(e) Estimation of Forest area in historical time

(f) Management Aspect

B. GRASSLANDS

1. Polar Grasslands
   (a) Tundra (b) Taiga
   1. Characteristics - Abiotic Components, Climatic conditions
   2. Distributioniv. Flora, Fauna, Ecosystem Dynamics
   3. Nutrients, Importance of Polar grasslands
2. Temperate Grasslands
   (a) Steppe (b) Prairie (c) Pampas
   1. Characteristics - Abiotic Components
   2. Climatic conditions 3. Distribution
   4. Flora, Fauna 5. Ecosystem Dynamics
   6. Nutrient Cycling
3. High Altitude grasslands
   (a) Characteristics (b) distribution
   (c) Flora & Fauna

C. SAVANNAS

1. Characteristics 2. Climatic conditions
3. Distribution 4. Flora & Fauna
5. Dynamics 6. Nutrient Cycling

D. SCRUBLANDS

1. Medeterranean Vegetation 2. California Chapparals
3. Cape Flora 4. Australian Scrubland
5. Chilean Scrubland
   (a) Characteristics (b) Climatic conditions
   (c) Distributions (d) Flora
   (e) Fauna (f) Dynamics

E. DESERTS

1. Distribution 2. Flora 3. Fauna 4. Adaptation
   (a) Subtropical hot Deserts
   (b) Subtropical coastal Deserts
   (c) Warm Temperate and cool temperate deserts
   (d) Temperate deserts
      1. Characteristics 2. Climatic conditions
      3. Distributions 4. Flora
      5. Fauna 6. Dynamics

F. HIGH ALTITUDES

1. Flora
2. Fauna
3. Distribution
4. Structure
5. Stratification
6. Climatic conditions
7. Dynamics
8. Importance

IV. AQUA-TERRESTRIAL ECOSYSTEMS

A. WETLAND ECOSYSTEMS

1. Definition
2. Geographical distribution
3. Values of Wetlands
4. Threats to wetlands
5. Conservation of wetlands

B. Salt Marshes / Mud Flats

1. Definition
2. Geographical Distribution
3. Flora of Salt Marshes
4. Fauna of Salt Marshes
5. Values of Salt Marshes
6. Human Impacts

C. Mangrove Ecosystem

1. Definition
2. Geographical Distribution
3. Community of Mangroves
4. Faunal Community of Mangroves
5. Values of Mangroves
6. Threats to Mangroves Communities

V. MAN-MADE ECOSYSTEMS

A. CROPLANDS

1. The primary Producers
2. Consumers
3. Decomposers
4. Transformers

B. PONDS

1. Abiotic Substances
2. The Primary Producers
3. The Consumers
4. The Decomposers and Transformers

4. BIOGEOGRAPHY

I. INTRODUCTION

A. Solar system, earth, rotation & climate

B. Evolution of life, continental drift & biota

C. Flora and Fauna D. Community, Ecosystem & Biome

II. BIOGEOGRAPHY

A. Introduction to biogeography

The study of patterns of distribution of organisms in space and time is called biogeography. It is broadly classified into 2 categories

1. Phytogeography: Study of plant distribution
2. Zoogeography: Study of animal distribution

B. Classification

1. Terrestrial Biosphere
2. Marine Biosphere
   - (a) Continental Shelf } Study of fauna
   - (b) Deep Ocean } in these Regions
3. Ecological Classification of Earth
   - (a) Terrestrial biomes (b) Marine Biomes
   - (c) Littoral Biomes
4. Each region with its endemic fauna
5. Zoogeographic Realms
   - (a) Realm megogaea (b) Realm notogaea
   - (c) Realm neogaea

C. Continental Drift: Effect on

1. Vertebrate distribution Sphenodon (Marsupial, Reptiles, Lystrosaurus)
2. Invertebrate distribution

D. Quartenary ice age: Effects of

1. Changing sea levels
2. Nunataks, Reliefs & Refugia
3. Glaciation in regions for ice

E. Marine Biosphere

1. Classification Pelagic and Benthic fauna
2. Latitude zonation present and past
3. Vertical dispersal in sea

F. Island Zoogeography - insular fauna
   1. Continental Islands   2. Oceanic Islands and Endemism
   3. Jaseon cycle.

G. Geographical Ecology: Geographical distribution of different types of communities and geographic variation in the ecological processes within communities case study: Sea Bird community.
   1. Kinds of Animal Distribution
      (a) Cosmopolitan   (b) Discontinous
      (c) Isolated distribution   (d) Bipolar distribution
   2. Factors Controlling Animal Distribution
      (a) Prodigality of production
      (d) Environmental condition and geologic changes
      (c) Planes of animal distribution   (d) Barriers
      (e) Dispersal   (f) Adaptation
      (g) Population   (h) Predation
      (i) Competition   (j) Diseases
      (k) Extinction   (l) Influence of man

H. Spread of a species
   1. Dispersal   2. Diffusion
   3. Secular migration   4. Effects of continental drift on this spread.

I. SPECIES ISOLATION - Disjunction: Causes
   1. Geomorphological   2. Climatic   3. Evolutionary
   4. Natural   5. Man Made

III. PHYTOGEOGRAPHY

A. Basic Principles

1. Climatic zones   2. Homoclimes
3. Distribution and barriers   4. Age and area
5. Endemism - Land, water, islands
6. Latitude and Altitude

B. Floristic realms of the world

1. Holarctic : Eurasia, N. America, Greenland small differences
2. Paleotropic : Old world, large differences
3. Neotropic : New world, large differences
4. Australian : Australia, extreme isolation
5. Capensis : S.W. tips of Africa
6. Antarctic : South American tips, sub antarctic islands

C. Vegetation types of the world

1. **Tropical evergreen forests:** low altitude zones near the equator with heavy rain all through year excepting for a few dry spells.
   (a) Amazon basin and Central American isthmus
   (b) Congo, Niger & Zambesi basins & Madagascar
   (c) Highly stratified
2. **Tropical scrub & deciduous forests:** Rain less than the tropical evergreen forests and unevenly distributed. Deciduous due to dry spells Africa, Australia & Brazil.
3. **Tropical Savannahs:** Grasslands with scattered trees. Lesser rainfall than deciduous forests. Dry season prolonged, Africa, lesser extent in S.America & Australia. Grasses tall. Trees, palms and Euphorbias.
4. **Subtropical evergreen forests:** Warm-temperate climate of Japan and South Atlantic. High moisture and less seasonal variations in temperature.
5. **Temperate deciduous forests:** Seasonal variations in temperatures. Moisture abundant dry spells. Europe, NE America, Australia, tip of South America.
6. **Temperate moist coniferous Forests:** Temperate rain forests, low temperature, high moisture, conifers. California to Alaska.
7. **Temperate Grasslands:** Rainfall very low (10-30") but higher than the deserts. Tall grasses. North America. Forested areas with degraded soil also support grassland.
8. **Subtemperate coniferous forest:** Evergreen conifers. North America & Eurasia.
9. **Desert:** Less rain fall (10"). Ephemerals, succulents, thorny shrubs. N. Africa, Australia, Tibet, S. America.
10. **Tundra:** Arctic. Dwarf treeless community. Grasses, sedges, etc. dwarf shrubs.

D. Floristic Regions of India

1. Western Himalayas
2. Eastern Himalayas
3. Upper gangetic plain
4. Lower gangetic plain
5. Indus Plain
6. Deccan - Peninsular
7. Western Peninsular
8. Andamans

E. Vegetational Types of India

1. Tropical Rain Forests - Evergreen: West Coast, Assam, Andaman

2. Tropical dry Deciduous forests: Bihar, Orissa
3. Sub tropical forests: Hill stations
4. Temperpate forests: Nilgiris, Himalayan regions
5. Deserts: Rajasthan
6. Mangroves: Bengal, Andamans, Deltas
7. Sandy sea shore: East Coast
8. Savannahs: Haryana, Punjab, A.P., Mysore, Maharashtra, etc.
9. Alpine forests: Sikkim, Kashmir

IV. ZOOGEOGRAPHY

A. DEFINITION

Zoogeography is the study of the distribution of animals on earth and the factors controlling it.

B. HISTORY

1. Buffon (1707 - 1788) held formal ideas about animal distribution.
2. Earnest Haeckal made a zoogeographical approach in dealing with ecological phenomenon.
3. In 1857, Dr. Sclater divided the world into six regions, based on the distribution of birds.
4. Russel Wallace is called the "Father of Zoogeography". His book 'The Geographical Distribution of Animals.' (1876).

C. PLANES OF ANIMAL DISTRIBUTION

1. Distribution in Space
   (a) Geographic distribution i.e. Horizontal or superficial
   (b) Psychozoic era: age of man

D. KINDS OF ANIMAL DISTRIBUTION

It is the method of spreading and reaching an area not previously inhabited by the species or groups. There are four kinds of pattern of distribution.

1. Cosmopolitan

   (or Universal or Continuous) distribution eg. rats, bats, man, mytilus, Antemia, ralima.
2. Discontinous

   Distribution eg. camel, peripatus, notodulur, belosloma.
3. Isolated distribution

   Eg. Tantara lizard in New Zealand; Ornithornynchur (duck carried platypus) in Australia & Tasmania; Enhnida spiry anteater in Australia & Tasmania & New Guinea.

4. Bipolar distribution

   Animals are found to inhabit only the North Pole (Arctic) and South Pole Antartic) region with no representatives in the intermediate ocean. Eg. Lampsa, Mysiothela (coelenterata), Chione (mollusc), Oncorhynchur (Salmon).

E. FACTORS CONTROLLING ANIMAL DISTRIBUTION

1. Prodigality of production
2. Barriers: The different kinds of barriers are
   (a) Topographic - water currents, depth, salinity, impurity, land masses, large water bodies, mountains. eg. Himalayas.
   (b) Climatic - temperature, light, humidity. eg. extremes of temperature and moisture are important, thus amphibians and reptiles are more common in tropical than temperate areas, decreasing considerably towards the poles
   (c) Vegetation - depending upon the selective food habits of organisms

F. DISTRIBUTION

1. Horizontal
   (a) Palaearctic: largest, Europe, Russia, N. China Subdivided into European, Mediterranean, Siberian,
   Manchurian (B5 families of terrestrial Vertebrates)
   (b) Ethiopian: Arabia, Africa (161 families - 30 endemic)
   (c) Oriental: India, Lanka, S. China, Malaysia, Indonesia, Philippines (153 families)
   Sub Region: Indian, Ceylonese, Inco-Chinese, Indo-Malayan
   (d) Australian: Australia & New Zealand (134 families)
   (e) Neotropical: Mexico, C. & S. America, West Indies (155 families).
   (f) Neoarctic: N. America & Greenland (120 families)
2. Vertical

   Coastal, inter tidal, surface, middle and deep, Coral reefs

G. DISPERSAL

1. Environmental conditions and geologic changes:
2. Adaptation
3. Population density
4. Predation.
5. Competition
6. Diseases
7. Extinction.
8. Influence of man.

1. Wind and gales:
   - (a) aerial nektons like insects, birds, bats, etc.
   - (b) Seeds, pollen of plants
2. Migration
   - (a) Seasonal - temporary - animals
   - (b) Permanent - racial groupings – animals
3. Land bridges: extinct - extanct
   - (a) Panama, Suez, Bering, Gibralter, Ceylon, Indonesian islands, etc.
4. Water as a Vehicle
   - (a) Plant seeds, whole plants, vegetative propagules
   - (b) Animals on the rafts and drift wood or Vessels
5. Animals: for plants & plant parts
6. Flying animals - eg. Birds that are flown off-course
7. Human agency - Travelling human population have introduced 'alien' organisms into habitats. Eg. rabhits were introduced by man into Australia.

H. BARRIERS

1. Topographic: Mountain Ranges, High seas, Andes, Rockeys, Himalayas, Caucasus
2. Climatic: Extremes of temperature & moisture
3. Vegetation: Food & shelter for animals confining the animals

I. INSULAR FAUNA

The term 'Insular fauna' is used to describe the fauna of islands. A.R. Wallace has classified islands as:-

1. Continental Island(s) 2. Oceanic Islands.

J. EXAMPLE OF SPECIES ISOLATION

Australian isolation started about 90 million years ago, it separated from Antartica, before the continent has been reached by placental mammals.

Therefore, the marsupials had no competition from placentals and colonised all the different ecological riches available.

K. TERMINOLOGIES

1. Geographical range	2. Ecological range
3. Geological range	4. Barrier
5. Metamorphic migration	6. Ecesis
7. Endemic	8. Prodigality
9. Dispersal	10. Adaptation

11. Density
12. Competition
13. Extinction
14. Cosmopolitan
15. Discontinuous

L. ZOOGEOGRAPHIC REALMS

1. Realm Megogea or Arctogea
   (a) Ethiopian Region
   (b) Oriental Region
   (c) Palaertic Region
   (d) Nearctic Region
2. Realm Noto gea
   (a) Australian Region.
3. Realm Neogea
   (a) Neotropical Region
   (b) Bathy metric distribution i.e. nuetral or altituclinal
      - Malolinotic realm pelagic, benthic
      - Lumnobiotic realm lotic, benthic
      - Geoluotic realm (Terrestiral)

M. DISTRIBUTION IN TIME: GEOLOGIC OR DURATIONAL DISTRIBUTION.

Paleozoic era, Meszoic era and Cenozoic era

N. ZOOGEOGRAPHICAL REALMS, DIVISIONS, TYPICAL FAUNA

REGION		SUB - REGION	FAUNA
ETHIOPIAN	(i)	East African	Catfish, Claued toad,
	(ii)	West African	geckor, ostriches,
	(iii)	South African	Giraffe,
	(iv)	Malagasy	
ORIENTAL	(i)	Indian	Carp, Myla, Draco,
	(ii)	Ceylonese	pheasants, flying
	(iii)	Indo-China	Hemur, lour.
	(iv)	Indo - Malayan	
PALAEARCTIC	(i)	Europian	Cyprimaler, salamanden,
	(ii)	Mediterranean	alligator, warbleir,
	(iii)	Siberian	Hedgeogar
	(iv)	Manchurian	
NEARCTIC	(i)	Californian	
	(ii)	Rock Mountain	Garpicke, howfin,
	(iii)	Allegphany	Amblystoma, Bufo,
	(iv)	Canadian	Gilo monster, wild turkeys pocket gophens.
NEOTROPICAL	(i)	Brazilian	Electric cells, pipid fugs,
	(ii)	Mexican	turites, Rhea, sloths,
	(iii)	Chilean	Lama.
AUSTRALIAN	(i)	Austro - Malayan	Osteoglossid, lung fish,
	(ii)	Australian	flogs, spencolon,
	(iii)	Polynesion	Crocodiles, Cassouranier,
	(iv)	New Zealand	emur, echidna, duck lulled platypur.

5. ANIMAL RESOURCES AND GERMPLASM BANKING

1. ECONOMICS

A. TYPES OF BENIFIT

1. Food
   - (a) Terrestrial animals
   - (b) Aquatic animals
   - (c) Bait
   - (d) Invertebrates & vertebrates
2. Non-Food
   - (a) Fibre
   - (b) Load Bearing etc
   - (c) Medicine
   - (d) Miscellaneous
     1. Commercial
     2. Ornamental/Decorative
     3. Money & Barter
     4. Medical
     5. Biomedical & Research
     6. Work assistants
     7. Pollinators
     8. Game/sport Hunting
     9. Recreation & Education
     10. Tourism
     11. Pets/Comparison
     12. Biological Control
     13. Domestic
3. HARMFUL
   - (a) Predators
   - (b) Harm by contact
   - (c) Posionous/Stingers
   - (d) Pests
   - (e) Parasites
   - (f) Vectors
   - (g) Intermediate Hosts

B. MAN & WILD ANIMAL

1. Exploitation of wild species
   - (a) Food
   - (b) Fibre, Hides etc
   - (c) Medicines
   - (d) Miscellaneous
2. Genes from wild Species for modifying domesticated stocks
3. Potential for further Domestication
   - (a) in recent times
   - (b) Some potentially interesting species.

C. EXPORTATION OF ANIMALS

1. Economic Significance of Domestic Stock
   - (a) Developing Countries
   - (b) Developed Countries
2. Wild Exploitation
   - (a) Developing countries
   - (b) Developed countries
3. Animal Resources & Bio Economics

II. DOMESTICATIONS

A. MAN & ANIMALS: EVOLUTIONARY HISTORY

B. DOMESTICATION OF ANIMALS BY MAN

1. History
2. Extent of Domestication
3. Resourcefulness of animals
   (a) Food : Invertebrates & vertebrates
   (b) Fibre
   (c) Load Bearing etc
   (d) Medicine
   (e) Miscellaneous

C. RESOURCES

(a) Cattle and Buffaloes
(b) Sheep
(c) Goats
(d) Pigs
(e) Horses
(f) Donkeys and Mules
(g) Camels
(h) Yaks
(i) Poultry

D. OTHER RESOURCES FROM DOMESTIC ANIMALS

(a) Aquaculture
(b) Food from organic wastes
(c) Animal manures
(d) Fuel from wastes

III. MANAGEMENT PRINCIPLES & MANAGEMENT

A. CONSERVATION OF DIVERISTY

B. WILDLIFE IN TROUBLE

C. WILDLIFE IN TRANSIT - A CRUEL TRADE

1. Livestock
2. Insect resources
3. Ocean resources
4. Living resources
5. Cephalopods
6. The peruvian anchoveta
7. Coral resources
8. Marine mammals
   (a) Classification
   (b) Habit and Habitat
   (c) Exploitation in Global water
      (i) Causes
      (ii) Extinction of species
   (d) Exploitation in Indian ocean
   (e) Exploitation in Bering sea
9. Marine and freshwater resources
10. Problem of over exploitation
11. International marine mammal project: tuna-dolphin pact
12. Sea turtles conservation
13. The great whales: international whaling industry

D. FRESHWATER FISHES

E. STRATEGIES FOR CONSERVATION

F. EPISODES

1. Direct Extermination
   - (a) Meat and Eggs
     1. American bison (the kansas tragedy)
     2. Doclo (raphurs circullatus)
     3. Passenger pigeon (ectopistes migratorius)
     4. Steller's sea cow
     5. Great auk
     6. Whaling
   - (b) Purposes of hunting
     1. Hides Furs And Feathers
     2. Souvenirs
     3. Superstitious beliefs
     4. Trophy hunting and pleasure
     5. Animals as competitors
2. Indirect Extermination
   - (a) Ravaged Waters (b) Domestic animal Diseases

G. LEOPOLD'S SEQUENCES & HICKEY'S PHASES

1. Action Phase 2. Awareness Phase
3. Generalising in Wildlife Management

H. LAWS AND TREATIES IN WILDLIFE MANAGEMENT

1. Project Tiger 2. Gir Lion Santuary Project
3. Project hangul 4. Himalayan Musk Deer Project
5. The Indian Elephant

I. CAN ANIMAL EXTINCTIONS BE PREVENTED?

J. CONTROLLING ANIMAL POPULATIONS

K. INTERNATIONAL COMMERCE

L. ECOLOGICAL EVALUATION OF SPECIES

IV. CONSERVATION AS MANAGEMENT

A. INTRODUCTION

1. Why Conserve ? 2. Definition of Wild Life
3. World Conservation Strategy

B. HABITAT

1. Tundra 2. Steppes
3. Tropical Rain Forest 4. Decidous Forest
5. Deserts

C. DISRUPTION OF THE HABITAT
   1. Primary Disruption   2. Secondary Disruption
D. HUNTING FOR FOOD   E. HUNTING FOR SPORT
F. PREDATOR LOSS   G. EXTINCTION HISTORY
H. ENDANGERED SPECIES   J. WILD LIFE ANAGEMENT
K. PARK AND RESERVES   L. SANCTUARIES
M. PROJECT TIGER   N. CROCODILE FARMING
O. LEGISLATION

V. GERMPLASM BANKING

1. Definitions   2. History   3. Techniques
   A. SCOPE
      1. Improvement of Domestic Stock
      2. Conserving native varieties of Domestic Stock
      3. *IN SITU* Conserving Wild species, Zoos & germplasm Banking
   B. ORGANIZATIONS INVOLVED
   C. INDIAN SCENARIO
      1. Livestock Germplasm   2. Wild Species Germplasm
   D. FUTURE OF GERMPLASM BANKING: PROSPECTS/ POTENTIAL
   E. NEED FOR RESEARCH: REQUIRED DEVELOPMENTS
   F. DIRECTION OF GROWTH

6. TRADE IN WILD LIFE

A. INDIAN WILDLIFE

B. HIMALAYAN RANGE

C. GANGETIC PLAINS

D. DECCAN PLATEAU

1. Primates 2. Pholidota 3. Carnivora
4. Perissodactyla 5. Artiodactyla 6. Rodentia
7. Cetecea 8. Sirenia 9. Proboscidea

E. WILDLIFE TRADE

1. Introduction 2. Coffee trade in brazil
3. Jasmin trade 4. Killing for fashions
5. Whaling industry 6. Pet trade

F. WILDLIFE PRODUCTS

1. Ivory 2. Musk 3. Medicinal value
4. Bear bile 5. Peacock oil 6. Tiger fat
7. Uromastic oil 8. Great indian bustard
9. Tanned and untanned skins
10. Fur skins 11. Bird feathers 12. Stag horns
13. Live animals 14. Meat

G. NEEDS OF CONSERVATION

H. ROLE OF INTERNATIONAL AND REGIONAL ORGANISATION

I. NATIONAL PARKS

J. WILDLIFE SANCTUARY

K. THE PROJECTS ARE

1. Gir lion sanctuary project
2. Himalayan musk deer project
3. Project tiger

L. CAUSES FOR THE TRADE

1. Commercial 2. Social

M. CLASSIFICATION OF TRADES

1. Live individuals
   (a) Pet trade
      1. Birds 2. Tortoises 3. Reptiles
   (b) Zootrade
   (c) For collectors (d) Falcorny

(e) Cactus (f) Orchid

(g) Butterfly collection (h) Biomedical research

2. Dead individuals

(a) Meat

1. Aquatic
2. Terrestrial

(b) Skin and fur (c) Cora (d) Oil

(e) Ivory (f) Horns/antlers (g) Shells

N. REGULATING THE TRADE

1. Global scenario
2. Indian

(a) The wild life protection act

(b) The wild life protection amendment act,1971

(c) Special projects

1. Project tiger
2. Gir-lion sanctuary project
3. Himalayan musk deer project
4. Manipur brow antlered
5. Project hangul
6. Project elephant
7. Crocodile project

> *"We are being made aware that the organization of society on the principle of private profit, as well as public destruction, is leading both to the deformation of humanity by unregulated industrialism, and to the exhaustion of natural resources, and that a good deal of our material progress is a progress for which succeeding generations may have to pay dearly."*
>
> **T.S. Eliot**

7. DEFORESTATION PROBLEMS IN INDIA

I. INTRODUCTION: Disappearance of this precious resource

(1) Cultivation
(2) Wood as a fuel
(3) Overgrazing by cattle
(4) Submergence due to Hydroelectric projects
(5) Construction of road ways and communications
(6) Replacement of forest by plantation

II. HISTORY OF EXPLOITATION: State scenario

(1) Problems in Himalayas
(2) Jammu and Kashmir
(3) Himachal Pradesh
(4) Uttar pradesh
(5) Problems in North East India
(6) Problems in Western Ghats
(7) Central India

III. CONSEQUENCES

1. Soil erosion
2. Floods
3. Climate
4. Genetic resources
5. Wild life
6. Carbon dioxide

IV. EPISODES of DESTRUCTION

1. The 'Exxon Valdez' Accident (Alaska)
2. Destruction of the Brazilian Rainforest

V. Conservation

A. BIOSPHERE - SOME BASIC DEFINITIONS
B. HUMAN ENVIRONMENT
C. THREE FUNDAMENTAL FACTORS
   1. Conservation of the Soil
      (a) Management
      (b) Engineering methods
      (c) Biological methods
      (d) General management
   2. Use of Chemicals
   3. Conservation of Water
      (a) Water distribution in the biosphere
      (b) Expected global demands
      (c) Water pollution
   4. Conservation of the Wild-Life - RESTORATION
   5. Conservation of the Forest – Management, Prectices
   6. Conservation of the Urban Systems - Management

7. Impact of Population on Conservation - Control Measures
8. Conservation of Energy - Action for Conservation
9. Conservation of the Vanishing Heritage
10. Aesthetic and Ethical Values

D. LAND CLASSIFICATION

VI. Tissue Culture For Conservation

A. INTRODUCTION

B. TECHNIQUES

1. Micro propagation
2. Clonal propagation

C. APPLICATIONS

1. Plant pathology
2. Production of genetically variable plants
3. Viral eradication
4. Plant breeding, and plant tissue culture

VII. Policy For Forests and People

1. Perceptions of forest crisis and resource scarcity lead to normative government statements of policy and the imposition of cumulative layers of formal control.
2. Policy mechanisms are too complex and incoherent to function well.
3. Sectorialism and Polarisation of views increase with The uncertainty and complexity of forest issues.
4. Pro-timber emphasis.
5. Communications and perceptions of local foresters and national policy makers.
6. Informal policy.
7. Policies from outside the forest sector have more influence than forest sector policy.

8. ECOLOGICAL VALUES OF PLANTS

A. INTRODUCTION

B. PLANT RESOURCES

1. Tropical Forests: Past and Present
2. Forest Resources
   (a) Global (b) National
3. Causes for Species Extinction
4. Germplasm Resources
   (a) Medicinal (b) Agricultural c. Others
5. Conservation Strategies

C. CLIMATE - VEGETATION RELATIONSHIP

D. ENVIRONMENTAL ROLES OF PLANTS

1. Controlling Wind Erosion
2. Adding O2 to the Air
3. Removing CO2 from the Air
4. Filtering dust from the Air
5. Maintaining Vegetative Cover
6. Organic mulches
7. Wind breaks
8. Watershed
9. Wildlife
10. Cooling the Air
11. Mangroves
12. Food chain
13. Nitrogen fixation
14. Nutrient cycling
15. Forest trees
16. Pollution control
17. Air Pollution
18. Reducing noise
19. Pollination

E. VALUES OF NON FLOWERING PLANTS

1. Indicators of air Pollution
2. Indicators of water Pollution
3. Ecological uses of Bryophytes
4. Sponges for Acid rain
5. Ecological Condition
6. Erosion prevention
7. Seed banks
8. Nitrogen Fixing

F. TREATMENT & WASTE WATER

G. SEAGRASSES

1. Characteristics & Habitat
2. Resource potential
3. Productivity
4. Man-induced Depletion
5. Natural Depletion
6. Management
7. Restoration

H. GERMPLASM CENTRES – GROUNDNUT

I. OTHERS

1. Pollen Transport
2. Seed dispersal
3. Nector of the plant
4. Apiculture
5. Biopesticides of mosquito
6. Dragon fly nymphs
7. Pest eating pests
8. Predator - prey reationship
9. Fishes-gambusia, minnows eat mosquito larvae

> *Do not go where the path may lead; go instead where there is no path and leave a trail*
>
> ***Emerson***

9. GRASSES

I. FOOD

Rice	:	Oryza sativa
Wheat	:	Triticum aestivum
Pearl millet	:	Peninsetum typhoides
Millet	:	Setaria italria
Giant millet	:	Sorghum.
Maize	:	Zea mays
Common millet	:	Panicum miliaceum

II. HIGHER ATTITUDES

Coix lacryma	:	brew beer from grains, eat them as porridge
Secale cereale	:	Rye
Hordeum vulgare	:	Barley
Avena sativa	:	Oats
Eleusine corocona	:	Ragi (finger millet): agricultural classes of India.
Saccharum officinarum	:	Sugarcane.

III. OTHER GRAINS USED

Digitaria cruciata	:	Khasi hills (for fooder also)
Paspalum scrobiculatum	:	South India
Echinochloa frumentosa	:	tribes of N.E. India

There are non - recognised cereals eaten by poorer people at times of want. They include various species of Brachiaria, Cenchrus, Dactyloctenium, Echinochloa etc.

IV. GRASSLAND AND GRAZING

No grassland in India is a climax type. True grassland is developed in a climate characterised by

1. Frequent precipitation of rain adequate to keep the upper layer of soil moist during the veg, period.
2. Sufficient warmth during the growing season. So Indian grasslands are seral although the above climate is present.
3. Species colonising them are those with high seed productivity.
4. Imperata cylindrica perennial with above features, and with a firm rhizome.

5. Saccharum spontaneum Erianthus & Phragmitis: enormous root system & lightest seeds.

Several grasslands are mainly due to grazing and fire. Fire maintains grasslands of tall grasses in the early stages and if grazing is added the tall grassland will be replaced by grassland of depauperate species. Thus Saccharum, Erianthus etc. could be replaced by Imperata and this inturn is replaced by Eupatorium odoratum in (a forest climate) S.america. Showing grassland instability.

Grasses develop fibrous nature, have a well developed rhizome or root system & produce seeds adopted to transport by air or animals to survive fire & browsing. Cattle do not like mature grasses. The herdsmen hence rearch the jungle for telinder shoots. Tall grassland therefore is usually the result of fire plus the ordinary grazing. The short & turf grassland is brought about by burning plus high incidence of grazing.

All grazing animals - sheep, goats, cattle, camels eliminate the more palatable and nutritions forms of fodder from the grassland. Overgrazing can reduce a tall grassland to a depauperate turf of Chrybopogon aciculatus and Imperata cylindrica in Assam.

In drier parts the disappearance due to grazing is even more rapid. Their places are taken by Xanthium strumarium or Euphorbia sp.

Thus grazing troubles in India are caused by

1. Too many cattle for the available grass.
2. Grassland in India is unstable.

V. FODDER GRASSES

(1) Plains : Andropogon (3 sp) Chrysopogon (4) Cynodon (2) Bothriochloa (2) Echinochloa (2) Dactyloctemium Brachiaria (4) Eragrostis (2) Dichanthium (2) Cenchrus (3) Panicum (2) Digitaria

(2) Deserts & sea coasts : Cenchrus priuri, Tragus biflous Dactyloctenium sindicum, Aristida (3) Desmostrachya bipinnata

Hills, humid: Agrostis (4) Lolium (2) Phalaris (2) Poa (4)

Hills, arid: Bromus (5) Bothriochloa (2)

(3) Gross output : Botriochloa ischaemum: 8-17 tons/acre
Cenchrus ciliaris: 4 1/2 -20 tons/acre
Apluda mutica: 10-26 tons
Pennesetum purpureum: 19-70 tons

VI. OILS

Cymbopogon, Vetiveria, Bothriochloa etc. from leaves & sheaths, roots, glumes & spikelets, also

1. C. nardus & C. winterianus: citronella oil, Quality of oil from the latter is higher.
   (a) Scenting of soaps, disinfectants, polishes etc.
   (b) The oil is used for the synthesis of many complicated organic compounds like synthetic menthol.
2. C. schoeranthus: Oil has phollandirene used as a diuretic.
3. C. caesius: oil has dipentene, limonene, geramiol & perillic alcohol
4. C. martimin : Plamarosa oil, exported from India as teraniol (80-90%) 90 tons/year. Gives a lasting odour of roses, flavour tabacco, manufacture of soap, perfume.
5. C. flexuobus: oil of lemon grass. composed of Citral perfumery, cosmetics, soaps, 750 tons/yr exported.
6. Vetiveria: roots. Women into baskets, curtains or tatties and when moistured cool and secent the air.

VII. PAPER MAKING

1. Saccharum spontaneum
2. S.bengalense — spp. of Bothriochloa
3. Arundo donax — Cymbopogon
4. Desmostachya lipinnata — Erianthus etc.

Straw board : Vetiveria zizanioides

Packing paper : Themeda arundinacea

Unfortunality the fibre length of all these grasses is short and hence can be employed in the manufacture of a first-class writting paper only after mixing with Bamboo.

VIII. ORNAMENTAL GRASSES

1. Bamboo
2. Rhynchelytum repens: pink feathery panicles
3. Lagurus ovatus: dense woody panicles
4. Lamarckia aurea: golden spikelets.
5. Arundo donax, Phalaris aurndinacea, Holcus mollis : variegated leaves.
6. Lawn grasses

Natural lawn	: Imperata cylindrica & Chrysopogon aciculatus
Higher attitudes	: Pennisetum clandestinum
Dry areas	: Dichanthium annulatum, Bothniochloa pulisa
Cynodon dactylon	: best
Europe	: Agrostis tenuius

7. Soil binders and moisture conservers
   (a) Sand dunes in area of low rainfall (40 cm per annum): panicum antidotale, P. lingidum, hasiurus hirserlis, s. munja, cenchrus sp.
   (b) Seashore: Spinifex littoreus, Paspalum vaginatum, Irchaemum muticum, Paspalum vaginatum.
   (c) Soil binders of plains: Brachiaria spp (3) a few spp. of Dactyloctenium & Eragrostis also.
   (d) Hills, humid: Pennesetum clandestinum
   Hills with low rain fall: Dichanthium annulatum
   (e) Heavy rainfall (Assam): Imperata cylindrica rhizomes combat erosion

IX. MEDICINAL IMPORTANCE

1. Agropyron repens: treatment of diseases of the genito-urinary tract. Rhizome used. Constituents.: triticin, dextrose, mannitol, inosited etc.
2. Cymbopogon schoenanthus: Rheumatism. Promote dissolution of stones in the bladder. Oil used: gout., fever, cholera, indigestion etc, are used. C. iwarancusa: stimulant also used in gout and rheumatism. C. citratus: laxative.
3. Vetiveria zizanoides: snake & scorpion bite. roots used paste used to treat bruises, swellings and burnings.
4. Demostachya bipinnata: dysentery menorrhagia
5. Triticum aestivum: laxative, an aphrodisiac.
6. Setaria italica: (grains) diuretic & astringent.
7. Saccharum officinarum: ayurvedic prescriptions as diuretic, cooling and aphrodiseac.
8. Panicum artidotale: smoke used as disinfectant in small pox.

X. MISCELLANEOUS USES

Thatching grass	: Imperata cylindrica, Saccharum spontaneum Desmestaehya bipinnata

Wattle walls	:	Arundo donax, Themedia arundinacea, Phragmites karka etc
Matting	:	Phragmites, Arundo, Vetiveria zizaniodes
Ropes	:	Eulaliopsis binata & Desmostachya bipinnata
Ornament	:	Cymbopogon spp leaves twisted into rings & bangles for their pleasant odor. The roots of vetiveria also are made into rings and necklaces buy tribals
Stuffing pillows	:	Imperata cylindrica: fruits with silky callus Brooms: Aristida setacea, A. hystix, A. adscensionis etc. Cigarette & cheroot wrappers: sheaths of infls. of zea mays are used for wrapping Bidis & cheroots.
Rodent repellents	:	Baskets with fruiting heads of Setaria verticillata are used to store grain. Their scabridities act against mice & rats.

Rosaries, beads, beadwork: fruit cases of Chionachne koenigii & those of Coix gigantea are used.

Musical instrument	:	hollow stem of Arundo donax & Phragmites karka

> *It is horrifying that we have to fight our own government to save the environment.*
>
> **Ansel Adams**

10. FOOD CROPS

I. GENERAL

A. THE HISTORY OF FOOD PLANTS

B. ORIGIN AND DISTRIBUTION OF FOOD PLANTS

C. THE NATURE OF FOOD PLANTS

D. THE LOWER PLANTS AS SOURCES OF FOOD

(a) Fungi:

1. Mushrooms 2. Truffles
3. Other Fungi

(b) Algae

1. Chondorus crispus 2. Rhodymenia palmate
3. Agar

E. THE MAJOR CEREALS

F. THE NATURE OF CEREALS

(a) Wheat

1. Characteristics 2. Kinds of wheat
3. Wheat Products

(b) Maize

1. Characteristics 2. Kinds of Maize
3. Products of Maize

(c) Rice

1. Characteristics 2. Use of Rice

G. MINOR AND SMALL GRAINS

(a) Barley (b) Rye (c) Oats
(d) Sorghum (e) Broom corn (f) Sweet Sorghum
(g) Grain Sorghum

H. MILLETS

(a) Setaria italica (b) Echinochloa frumentacea
(c) Panicum miliaceum (d) E. Crusgalli
(e) Eleusine coracana (f) Pennisetum glancum

I. OTHER GRAINS

(a) Wild Rice (b) Jolis teans

J. PSEDUO CEREALS

(a) Bud Wheat (b) Quinoa

K. NUTRITIVE VALUE OF FOOD

(a) Food for health and growth (b) Protein food

(c) Why protein is necessary (d) Carbohydrate

(e) Value of minerals (f) vitamin

L. FOOD SCARCITY IN DEVELOPING COUNTRIES

M. EXPORTS AND IMPORTS OF FOOD

N. PLANT BREEDING FOR HIGH YIELD

O. AGRICULTURE AND ENVIRONMENT

P. INTERNATIONAL AGRICULTURE INSTITUTES

Q. INDIAN AGRICULTURAL RESEARCH INSTITUTE

II. CEREALS

A. INTRODUCTION

1. Most important group of food plants - Gramineae
2. Caryopsis -wall of the seed fuses with the ovary wall -grain fruit
3. True cereals - Rice, Wheat, Maize, Barley, Oats and Rye.
4. Rice, Wheat, Maize - important part in the growth of civilisations
5. High in carbohydrate, proteins and fats considerable.
6. Millets and Soghums are not cereals.

B. RICE: Oryza sativa Linn.

1. PRINCIPAL FOOD CROP OF TROPICS

   (a) S.E. Asia: 85% world area, 50%- India & China, 25% - Japan, Thai, Burma, Indoneshia.

   (b) Largest area: India 79 million acres. 28 million tons/year.

   (c) Centres of origin: India and Indochina: Cultivation in India 3000 BC.

   (d) Antiquity and place in the life of the people: Connection with Hindus - birth, marriage, death, one of the oldest economic plants. From delta to 3-5,000 ft above sea level., self pollinated.

   (e) O. sativa, O. glaberrima (West Africa): Origin from O. perennes complex wild sp = 23-28. 2n

   (f) India - Egypt, Europe, Australia, Africa, America China - Japan & Korea

2. CULTIVATION

   (a) Damp soils - (a) Shallow water (1.2 m waters) (b) deep water/floating (3.5 m) (c) Upland (d) High attitude vars (short duration, low temp).

(b) Japan: Cultural practice + manuring + Protection measures high yeilding.

(c) Iaponica: (high yeilding) X indica (tillering better, resistance to disease and adverse climate).

(d) Fields ploughed - Seedbed - transplantation of seedlings 9-10". - Water circulation until ripering - dried out - harvested - stacks are stacked upto drying.

3. MANURING

(a) Role of 6-5' algae; green manure, - Sesbanea aculeata, Lens esculentus, Crotalaria juncea

4. PROCESSING

(a) Threshing: Grains removed - winnowed - caryopses without grain goes & grains remain Paddy/Rough rice.

(b) Husking: Husk removed by pounding in wooden "Mortar & Pistil" Brown Rice or

(c) Milling: grain moved between millstones.

(d) Chaff removed by blowers - Chaff

(e) Grain pounded in huge mortons - bran layer

(f) White rice is polished by friction - the outer, more nutritive parts one removed due. Milled Rice White

5. USES

(a) More people use this as food than any other cereal

(b) Rice and pulses, especially soya beans

(c) Quality Head Rice = Whole grain / 3/4th.

Total Rice = Total. Parboiled: Soaked, boiled, dried. Milling easy Vitamins & other nutrients retained. Less breakage: more head rice.

(d) Rice bran oil: Soaps and cosmetics

(e) Straw: Straw boards, Paper Mats.

(f) Intoxicating beverages in Indochina, A.P. and Orissa in India.

(g) Indica: India, Ceylon Taiwan, S.China
Japonica: Japan, Korea N.China
Javanica: Indonesia (partly)

h. Taichung, I.R.,

C. WHEAT

1. TRITICUM AESTIVUM

Leading gain crop of temp. climates. cultivated in a wide range of climates cool winters & Hot summers = Extensive cultivation.

(a) 3.5% of Global wheat production, 2nd in importance in India, 29 millions of acres. 3rd in acreage.

(b) 10% of the total area under foodgrains, 14% (under cereals' acreage).

(c) North & central regions of India, 5th acreage, 7th in production (World).

(d) Indus Valley civilisation: Mohenjo-Daro excavations Probably T. sphaerococcum endemic to India - Indian ancestry. 5000 yrs. BC.

(e) Relatively short cycle in India 4-6 months, upto 9 months in the west. (Hilly regions in India) self pollinating.

(f) 18 recognised species: 5 cultivated in India

1. T. aestivum: bread wheat - largest area (North)
2. T. durum: macaroni wheat (Central & West)
3. T. dococcum: emmer wheat Origin = S.W. Asia
4. T. turgidum: the rivat wheat 2n = 14,28,42
5. T. sphaerococcum: Dwarf Wheat.

(g) First crop to be attended by plant breeders.

(h) New series of improved wheats - adaptability to regions yield, grain quality resistance.

2. CULTIVATION

(a) October - November - March - April

(b) Sour, manured, irrigated, cut, dried, threshed, winnowed - mechanical or traditional.

3. USES

(a) Wheat flakes, flour - Suji, Ata, Maida - bread, chapatis, puries, biscuits, cakes, pastry.

(b) Beer and other alcoholic beverages

(c) Straw: seating chaing, stuffing mattresses. (12a) Red & white Kernel & Hand texture = high

(d) fodder: in Protein and gluden (bloats bread for bigger leaf) Soft textured ones = low in protein and bread making qualities.

(e) A = T.bicocicum, T.monococcum D = T.aestivum
B = Aegelops speltoides
Triticale: Riley (Australia), Sonora (Mexico) varieties
Mutation breeding in India, germplasm collections

(f) Nomenclaurne = (Poosa, New Poosa), Man Place Station No. Descriptor short concise words.

D. MAIZE: Zea mays: Corn, Indian corn

1. Important in U.S.A.: 57% of the maize of the world.
2. 1.4% of the world in India, 4.4% (China) 3.3% (USSR) 2.3% (Mexico) 2.9% (Mandura) 2.4% (Yugoslavia)
3. Introduced in India in 16-17th century from Tropical America. Staple food in (portaguese) tribal areas, hilly & uplandish regions.
4. 9.6 million areas, 3 million tons/year. Khanif crop, N.E. hilly parts. June-July - September-October.

   5th place in acreage & 4th place in yield in the world.
5. Well irrigated, heavy loamy &/or coaise grand soil of hilly tracts.
6. Food for man and livestock, cattla, poultry innature ones eated after roasting, corn flakes.
7. Corn starch, Industrial alcohol, glucose
8. Corn oil: Soap, lubrication, Salad oil
9. Stalk fibre = Paper and yarn
10. Zein, the protein of the grain: artificial fibres with teisle strength and wool-like qualities.
11. Artiquity 3-5,000 yrs: central America, red Indian used.
12. Hybird Maize: Shull 1909, East 1909. inbread sterile X inbred fertile hybrid regiour.

E. BARLEY: Hordeum vulgare

1. Great antiquity. Used before wheat. Oldest of all cultivated plants.
2. Known to all ancient civilisations
3. 8.4 million acres, 2.7 million tons/year.
4. Cultivation, harvesting etc are similar to wheat
5. Rabi crop: October - December - February-April.
6. Solo or mixed with legumes peas, lentils, mustard, linseed.
7. Flour used
8. Children's food - 6 rowed varieties have higher protein content, breakfast food.
9. Alcoholic beverages (especially from 2 rowed varieties)

F. OATS: Avena sativa

1. Temperature climate of N.Europe
2. One-sided spreading panicle, plant 2.5'.
3. Limited in India - N.W. Himalayas: A. Sterilis var culla

4. Human food and fodder for cattle: high fat, protein & minerals.
5. Cakes, biscuits, breakfast food.
6. Oatmeal

G. RYE: Secale cereale Linn.

1. More recent than other cereals.
2. Native: Central Asia - Black sea & Caspian sea
3. Habit: resembles wheat and Barley. Grains are like wheat.
4. Leaves bluish.
5. Bread in Europe, black bread because of the dark colour (Gluten).

> *People would rather believe than know.*
>
> **Edward O. Wilson**

11. PULSES, OILS AND SPICES

I. PULSES

A. INTRODUCTION

1. Leguminosae
2. next in importance to cereals, as human ford
3. More protein than any other vegetable
4. as aleuron grains in the cells along with Starch grains
5. Animal nutrition
6. Companion cropping and crop rotation
7. 1/7 of cultivated area in India, 25 million hectares, 10-12m metric tons.
8. 37% chick pea gram, 13% pigeon pea, black gram, green gram, lentil, pea, ground nut, soya bean.
9. Make soil fertile.

B. GRAM: CICER ARIETINUM

1. Native of S.Europe grown in U.P, M.P, Punjab, Bihar, Maharashtra 84 types
2. Brown: desi
3. White: kabuli
4. Rabi crop at the end of rainy season: Sept-Nov —> Feb-April
5. Dal - split seed, & husk removal.
   self pollination: 48 hours. flowering
6. Flour is 'Baisan' - sweets, bread
7. Raw grain - roasted, soaked, boiled
8. Cattle & horse

C. PIGEON PEA: CAJANUS CAJAN

1. Asia and/or Africa. tropics and subtropics East Indies, West Indies, India.
2. MP, A.P., U.P., Maharashtra, Mysore selfing = 36-48 hrs
3. 2nd in importance in India. flowering.
4. 'Kharif' crop May-July —> (6-8 months) Dec-March.
5. 6 million acres. 2m tons/year
6. Dry crop mixed with millets
7. protein source: immature and ripe seeds
8. leaves & twigs: fodder
9. husk = cattle feed

10. Popular in S.India
11. Livestock poultry feeds
12. Urease extracted on large scale:estimation of urea in blood & Urine

D. SOYABEAN: GLYCINE MAX

1. Nature of SE Asia. Crop area in India is small, developing crop.
2. Drier areas upto 6000 above sealevel. Assam, Orissa, W Bengal, U.P.hills.
3. Varieties: Palmetto, Monetto, Clemson, Creole, Charlee,
4. high protein and oil
5. more minerals, Ca, P than any ceral, peas and beans.
6. Fe, K, Mg & Vitamins.
7. Soyabean oil: cooking, oilcake = cattle feed
8. Fdour & cooked bean for diabetics
9. Biscuits and Chapatis by mixing with wheat flour
10. Vegetable milk and curd, even ghee
11. Industry: Soaps, food products, paints, varnishes, plastics, poultry food.

E. GARDEN PEA: PISUM SATIYUM

1. Native of S Europe - chiefly UP, HP, Punjab
2. Annual, trailing herb with white/coloured flowers
3. Raw seeds or canning, peameal, split meal
4. Forage and green manuring

F. BLACK GRAM: PHASEOLUS MUNGO

1. U.P., M.P., Punjab and Bengal - origin S & SE asia.
2. Small, oval black seeds.
3. South Indian Menu of a great variety
4. Fodder for cattle

G. GREEN GRAM: PHASEOLUS AUREUS

40 varieties - macrosperma (large), microsperma (small seeds)

1. M.P. U.P. Rajasthan, Bihar, Bengal - origin S & SE Asia
2. One, the ancient pulses of India
3. Pods green, seeds oval small and green
4. split-seeds or full seeds
5. selfing: < 12 hrs

H. LENTIL: LENS CULINARIS

1. Nature of SW Asia, Cultivated AP, MP, UP, Maharashtra, Rajasthan, Bengal.
2. One of the most ancient food plants mentioned even in Bible
3. Black-clayey soils, lens-shaped seeds. Buch branched annual.
4. Selfing

I. KIDNEY BEAN: PHASEOLUS VULGARIS

1. Native of America: throughout India
2. Soil rich in lime necessary
3. Twining annuals with slender pods
4. Young pods, unripe seeds, dried seeds: human consumption
5. Plants: fodder

J. COWPEA: VIGNA SINENSIS

1. Bushy trailing annual. Through out India
2. Nature of Central Africa 3. cattle and poultry

K. BROAD BEAN: VICIA FABA

1. SW Asia. NW India now. prehistoric cultivation known.
2. Erert annual with large seeds
3. Youngpods, seeds
4. The only legume in Europe before the time of Columbus
5. Fodder

L. LABLAB: DOLICHAS LABLAB

1. twining herb cultivated through out India
2. Pods, unripe seeds: vegetable
3. fodder for horses, cattle.

M. PEANUT: ARACHIS HYPOGEA

1. Native of Brazil S.India, Maharashtra, U.P., N.Gujarat most famous.
2. fruit ripens under soil - sandy oil
3. roasting or salting
4. Peanut butter
5. oil: cooking, highest calories 1lb=2700 cals nuts
6. oil cake = fodder
7. Vegetable ghee after hydrogenation

II. OILS

A. SOME INDIAN OIL-YIELDING PLANTS

1. Arachis (Groundnut)
2. Brassica (Rape, mustard)
3. Carthamus (safflower)
4. Cocos (coconut)
5. Croton (Oleum crotonis)
6. Cucumis (Wild musk melon)
7. Cucurbita (Pimpkin)
8. Elaeis (African oil palm)
9. Eruca (Taramira)
10. Glycine (Soyabean)
11. Gossypium (Cottonseed)
12. Helianthus (Sunflower)
13. Juglans (Walnut)
14. Linum (Linseed)
15. Madhuca (Mahua)
16. Olea (Olive)
17. Pongamia (Pongam oil)
18. Prunus (Alamon oil)
19. Ricinus (Castor)
20. Salvadora
21. Sapindus (Soapnut)
22. Sesamum (Sesame)
23. Shorea (Salbutter)
24. Telfaria (Gyster nut)
25. Theobroma (Cocoa)
26. Xanthium
27. Ximenia

B. FATTY OILS

liquids at ordinary temperatures. Usually contain Oleic acid. Stored usually in seeds. do not evaporate. Usually edible as cooking media containing solid & liquid fats.

C. FATS

Fats are solid at ordinary temperatures contain stearic and palmitic acid decomposed by alkalis & react to form soap.

D. CLASSIFICATION

1. Drying and Semi-drying Oils
   (a) Edible: refined/unrefind
   Hemp oil Sunflower foil Linseed oil
   Soybean oil Walnut oil Niger-seed oil
   (b) Soaps,varnishes paints, candles
   Sufflower oil Cotton Sarson oil Indian Rape oil
   Pappy oil Corn oil Sesame oil Margosa oil
2. Non drying: Castor, Groundnut, Olive
   (a) Edible (b) Soap, lubricants
3. Vegetable fats: Coconut, Mahua, Pongamia
   (a) Edible (b) Soap & Candle

1. Drying and Semidrying oils

(a) Linseed oil: Linum usitatissimum, Linaceae

1. Seed is crushed into meal, heated after moistening oil is expelled by using rotary mills, hydraulic presses or expellers.
2. Possess sweet taste with pleasant falvour. Yellowish brown to pale yellow. Stored in non metallic containers unexposed to air and light.
3. Most important drying oil.
   (a) Paints, varnishes
   (b) Linoleum, oil cloth, printing & lithographic oils
   (c) Adulterant for mustard, groundnut & coconut oils
   (d) Pharamacopoea: external application
   (e) Veterinary: lalxative
4. MP, UP, J&K, Punjab, Partly Orissa

(b) Niger - seed oil: Geizotica abyssinica, compositae

1. Herb, native of tropical Africa, Seeds important.
2. Edible, cooking, oil cake as fodder
3. Illuminant, in paint
4. Soap & varnish industries
5. MP, AP, & Orissa

(c) Hemp Oil: Cannabis sativa, Cannabinaceae

1. Under shrub, native of Asia, seeds.
2. Illuminant, paint, soap & varnish
3. UP, MP, Bengal, Maharashtra, Orissa

(d) Soybean oil: Glycine max Papilionaceae

1. Herb, South East Asia, seeds
2. Cooking, cake as fodder
3. Candles, varnishes, soap, paints, greases, linoleum, rubber substitutes, insecticides disinfectants.
4. Plastics, adhesives, foanuing solutions
5. HP, Assam, Bihar, Bengal, Punjab.

(e) Sunflower oil: Helianthus annus,

1. Very important oil seed crop. 40-50% oil, high yields
2. Cooking oil, nutritimally high quality with proteins & vitamins A,D & E.
3. Paint, varnish & soap
4. Vanaspati ghee

(f) Walnut oil: Juglans regia,

1. Tree, native of Iran, mature & old Kernds
2. Fresh & cold pressed oil edible, pleasant smell & flavor
3. Hot pressed oil: White paint, oil paints of artists, printing ink & soap
4. Kashmir, HP & hills of Punjab & Assam.

(g) Safflower oil: Carthamus trictorius

1. Shrub, native of India, seeds
2. Edible & similar to ground nut oil
3. Illuminant, soap, varnish & paint
4. MP, UP & AP, Mysore, Maharashtra.

(h) Pappy oil: Papaver somniferum,

1. Herb, native of West Asia, seeds.
2. First cold pressing yields a white edible oil. 2nd hot pressing - reddish oil - used for burning soap and oil paints (after bleaching).

(i) Cotton seed oil: Gossypium sp.

1. Kernels crushed, heated, hydrantically pressed. Oil pumped into tanks. Impurities settle as sediment.
2. Vanaspati ghee, cake as fodder
3. Impure residue: soap, washing powders, artificial leather, roofing tar

(j) Corn oil: Zea mays

1. Embryo with about 50% semi drying oil
2. Crude oil for rubber substitutes, cheap paints cake is cattle feed.
3. UP, Punjab, J & K.

(k) Sarson oil: Brassica compestris, Cruciferae.

1. Herb, seed with 30-45% oil, extracted by solvents or expression
2. Cooking and burning

(l) Indian Rape oil: Brassica compestris, Cruciferae

1. Herb, seed, extracted by solvents and expression
2. Edible, cattle feed and manure
3. UP, West Bengal, Punjab.

(m) Sesame oil: Sesamum indicum,

1. Herb, seed with 50% oil, extracted by cold pressure

2. Cooking, soap, cosmetics, hair oils, fodder (cake) sweatmeats, illumination, anrinting body.
3. UP, MP, AP, TN, Maharashtra.

(n) Margosa oil: Azadirachta indica,
1. Tree, native of Burma, seeds
2. Antiseptic, burning, cake as fertilizer & manure

III. SPICES

A. INTRODUCTION

1. Prominent part in the civilisations of antiquity - India, China
2. Spices orginated in Asiatic tropics
3. First objects of Commerce between East and West and played an important role in history, Columbus, Magellan
4. No nutriture value, but render eating a pleasure; aromatic oils
5. Spice: all aromatic vegetable products used for flavouring foods, sometimes restricted to hardened plant parts, used after pulverisaton.
6. Condiment: possess sharp taste, usually added to food after cooking

B. ROOTS AND UNDERGROUND STEMS

1. ASAFOETIDA: FERULAASAFOETIDA, UMBELLIFERAE
   (a) Perennial herb, Punjab, Kashmir.
   (b) gum-resin exuded from the roots
   (c) flavouring
   (d) Medicinal: asthma, cough and indigestion
2. GINGER: ZINGIBER OFFICINAIS,
   (a) Erect perennial herb. Rhizomes branch digitately "hands"
   (b) Nature of SE Asia. Early users: India & China. Cultivated in KERALA, & WEST COAST, U.P., W.B, Maharashtra.
   (c) Tropical climate, rich moist soil with partial shade.
   (d) Rhizomes: Yellow outside, greenish-yellow inside. Starch, gums, deo-resin, essential oil dug out after aerial parts wither.
   (e) 48,000 acres under this crop, 24,000 tons crude ginger (mostly West Coast) dried ginger (Sonthi) exported to West & Arabian countries.
   (f) aroma: essential oil, pungency: gingerin (oleoresin) CONDIMENT

(g) medicines; carminative and digestive stimulant

(h) flavouring beverages: ginger beer.

3. TURMERIC: CURCUMA DOMESTICA ZINGIBERACEAL

4. CURCUMA AMADA, MANGOGINGER

(a) Perennial, tubers cleared, washed and dried in sun. Yellow colour, pungent bitter taste.

(b) Native of Cochin, china, East Indies. Tropical.

(c) 60-100,000 acres. Maharashtra, Orrisa, Bengal, A.P., T.N.

(d) Exports - West, Ceylon & Pakistan

(e) condiment - flavour & colour - pickles & curries

C. BARKS

1. Cinnamon: CINNAMOMUM ZEYLANICUM DALCHINI

(a) One of the oldest. Native of Ceylon. Evergreen tree.

(b) Nilgiris, Assam, South Canara, Malabar, Kumaon

(c) Sheltered situations upto 1000 mtrs attitude receiving 200-250 cm. rainfall

(d) Seed propagation

(e) 2-cutting seasons - determined by sap passage into the corky layer-indicated by the ready separation from a test cut.

D. FLOWER BUDS AND FLOWERS

1. SYZYGIUM AROMATICUM Clove

(a) One of the most ancient and has a unique position in the International spice trade.

(b) Native to Moluccas - spice islands - East Indian Archepelugo.

(c) Introduced in India around 1800 A.D by the East India Company.

(d) Western Ghats, Nilgiris, Kerala - Zanzibar 90% of world production.

(e) Clove: dried, unopened flower bud of evergreen tree of about 10-12 meters.

(f) Seed propagation

(g) Aromatic, warming, flavouring of pickles, curries etc, clove oil medicinal.

2. CAPPARIS SPINOSA - CAPER BUSH

(a) Nature of Medeterranean - Punjab, Gujarat, Western Ghats

(b) Unopened flowers - Capers

(c) Condiment - meat, sauces and pickles.

E. FRUITS

1. Red pepper - chillies - CAPSICUM FRUTESCENS SOLANAEEAE

   (a) native of West Indies - cultivated through out India.

   (b) fresh, ripe, dry, or powdered - flesh, seed and rind has pungent principles.

2. BLACK PEPPER - PIPER NIGRUM, PIPERACCAE

   (a) One of the most ancient Crops of India - probably originated in the hills of S.W India - Kerala.

   (b) Moist parts of India, Ceylon & other tropics: branching, climbing perennial

   (c) Mixed crop in homesteads - productive for 100 yrs.

   (d) Vegetative or seed propagation. Humus-rich soil.

   (e) Pepper: BLACK = dried fully developed unripe fruits, wrinkled pericap WHITE = dried ripe fruits, no pericap

   (f) Spice or condiment, oleoresin pungent> stimulates salivation & gastric juices.

3. Coriander, Coriandrum Sativum

   (a) Aromatic herb. In ancient Sanskrit, Egyptian and Roman literature mentioned.

   (b) Nature of Mediterranean - India: MP, Mysore, Bihar etc.

   (c) Fruit = 2 one-seeded carpels/meri carps with numerous oil ducts.

   (d) Oil is medicinal - flavours beverages, (giss, whisky etc).

4. Cuminum, Cyminum, Zira, Umbelliferae

   (a) Nature of Mediterranean; Punjab, U.P., annual herb. Exported.

   (b) elongated oval fruits aromatic.

   (c) Spice and condiments.

   (d) Soup, curries, pickles, bread, cheese etc.

5. Anise, Pimpenella Anisum Linn, Saonf, Umbelliferae

   (a) Native of Mediterranean - U.P., Punjab, Assam, Orrisa

   (b) Condiment. Carminature, prevnent Fatulence. oil in medicines and beverages.

F. SEEDS

1. Cardamom, Eletaria cardomomum Zinzeberaceae
   (a) native of India - Kerala, Mysore, T.N., Assam, Sikkim.
   (b) 'MAJOR' = larger fruits but short panicle 'MINISCULA' = Smaller fruits but long panicle.
   (c) Perennial herb, 6-12' height, Triangular fruits borne through out the gear.
   (e) USE: Masticatory flavouring all dishes & bevereges.
2. Fenugreek, Trigonella foenum - Graecum, (Methi) Papilionaccae
   (a) Native of S.Europe & Asia - North India - annual legume
   (b) Spice and condiment seeds Leaves aromatic: vegetable & fodder
   (c) medicinal - carminative
3. Indian Mustard, Brassica Juncea Cruciferae
   (a) Punjab, W.B, U.P.
   (b) Seeds: Condiment in pickles. Oil: cooking purposes.

G. LEAVES

1. Basil, Ocimum basilicum, Labiateae
   (a) native Africa, India. Small shrub cultivated through out India.
   (b) Condiment, golden yellow oil used in perfumery and beverages.
   (c) Seed = dysentery and chronic diarrhoea.
2. Mint, Mentha longifolia Pudina Labiateae,
   (a) Aromatic herb. Native of Europe & Asia - Kashmir, U.P., Punjab
   (b) flavouring agent
   (c) dry leaves carminative and stimulant
3. Peppermint, Mentha piperata, Labiateac
   (a) Aromatic herb. Nature of Europe - Maharashtra, Punjab & Kashmir.
   (b) flavouring food stuff - persistent cooking taste.
   (c) oil - carminature, stimulant, allays nausea & vomiting
   (d) oil - perfume, soap industry
4. Tarragon, Artemisia dracunculus
   (a) Native of W.Asia - Western Himalayas
   (b) Aromatic leaves - condiment. seasoning soups and salads
   (c) essential oil: perfumery

IV. Germplasm Resources

(a) genetic conservation
(b) need for germplasm conservation
(c) genetic erosion
(d) pattern of genetic conservation
(e) storage
(f) information system
(g) pattern of genetic conservation
(h) germplasm maintenance
(i) acquisition and exchange problem
(j) biotechnology and gene banks
(k) political scenario of gene banks
(l) organisations involved in germplasm conservation

> *"I am glad I will not be young in a future without wilderness."*
>
> **Aldo Leopold**

12. FIBRES AND TIMBERS

I. FIBRES

A. INTRODUCTION

(a) bow strings
(b) nets for food catching
(c) clothing
(d) nearly 2,500 species
(e) long thick walled tapering sclerenchyma
(f) lignin & cellulose

1. Natural fibre: Rough substitute to cloth. bast separated from tree trunks
   (a) Broussonetia papyrifera: Tapa cloth, clothing of natives in polynesia until 1920 s.
   (b) Ficus nekbunda (Moraceae)
   (c) Hibicus elatus some minor purposes.
2. Brush & broom: Tough & stiff fibred turgs whose ends make a brush Strong, stiff, elastic & flexible. Leaf stalks, twigs & even roots

   Palmae
   (a) Caryota urens: Sub Himalayan. Leaf sheaths, soft and fine, fibrous cords, fishing nets, brooms ropes
   (b) Borassus flabellifer: Stem, leaf, stalks, midribs,
   (c) Cocos nucifera: loose fibre, carpets, brooms, ropes
   (d) Raphia vinifera: West african coast, long brushes.
   (e) Attalia furnifera: brown fibre, street brushes

Gramuneae

   (a) Sorghum zulgare: Inflorescence, Carpet brush.
3. Rough weaving fibre: Interlacing for hats, baskets, chains Used after splitting roots, stems,etc. hats, mats, baskets etc.
   (a) Pandanus tectorius: thatching roofs, hats
   (b) Erianthus munja: stem, fibre, ropes
   (c) Calamus ratoon: Chair making
4. Filling fibre: Filling cushions, pillows, packing material Stuffing pillows, protection of valuables.
   (a) Calotropis procera Calotropis gigantia Seed sourse (Asclepiadeceae
   (b) Ceiba pentandra Bombacaceae Pods
   (c) Solanalia malabarica, Bombacaceae

5. Textile fibre: Fibres twisted into threads & threads woven into cloth
   (a) surface fibres
   (b) soft
   (c) hard fibres. Long, fine, uniform, Cohesive, strong
   (a) Surface fibres: Cotton (Gossypium) 70%
   (b) Soft fibres: Bast fibres from secondary phloem and pericycle.
      1. Linum utitatissimum (Linsed/flax): Linaceae, length, fineness, durability (stem)
      2. Cannabis sativa (Hemp): Stem of male plants - pericycle ropes, twine, carpets, nets (hill tribes)
      3. Corchorus (Jute): Secondary phloem different types of cloth, paper, fine yarn curtains, sacs etc.
      4. Crotalaria (Sun Hemp): Coarse fibre, gunny cloth, sacs.
      5. Hibiscus Cannabinus: Coarsa canvas, fishing nets
   (c) Hard fibres
      1. Musa (Manila hemp): Phillippines, light, elastic, strong & resistant to water.
      2. Agave americana (Agave): Twine, rope, sacs.
      3. Cocos nucifera: Fruit mesocarp several purposes.
6. Paper fibre: Wood fibres of bamboo, sugarcane or even textile fibers. Cellulose important.

   Cellulose of fibres used in paper industry. Chinese used first Bamboo, sugarcane, Imperata etc.

   (a) Manufacture of wood pulp
   - Mechanical process: Removal of fibres from wood, removal of impurities from fibres, removal of water, sheet making.

     Yellow: 1. resins, lignin and suberin not removed

     2. News print, wrapping paper.
   - Chemical process: Fibres with pure cellulose only extracted.

   (b) Manufacture of paper from pulp
      1. Bleaching and washing
      2. Dye-addition if colour is required

3. Passage through machinery of rollers for
   (a) Squeezing of water, and
   (b) Sheeting of interlacing fibres.

B. Important Fibre Plants of India

1. Agave (Sisal)
2. Aloe
3. Boehmeria
4. Borassus (Palmyra)
5. Calotropis
6. Cannabis (Tree hamp)
7. Caryota (Kittul)
8. Ceiba (White silk cotton)
9. Cocos (Coir)
10. Corchorus (Jute)
11. Coryota (Fan palm)
12. Crotalaria (Sun hemp)
13. Erythrina (Indian Coral tree)
14. Furcrnea (Mauritius hemp)
15. Gossypium (Cotton)
16. Hibiscus (Kenaf)
17. Linum (Flax)
18. Luffa (ridged gourd)
19. Musa (Banana)
20. Pandanus
21. Pengularia
22. Phoenix (Date-palm)
23. Phormium (New Zealand flax)
24. Sabal (Cabbage palm)
25. Salmalia (Silk Cotton tree)
26. Sansveria
27. Tillandsia
28. Triumfetta
29. Typha
30. Urena
31. Urtica
32. Yucca

II. TIMBER

A. INTRODUCTION

1. Third necessity of mankind: shelter
2. Strength, hardness, stiffness: density, moisture wood preservation-insects, fungi
3. Boats, utensils, furniture, fuel, construction, package, petroleum, coal, cards, plywoods, shipping
4. Secondary xylem
   TRACHEA porous: non ring type, ring type
   TRACHEIDS nonporous, Vessels, Fibres, Wood pasenchyma
5. Properties: STRENGTH: No breakdown
   HARDINESS: no yielding to cutting
   STIFFNESS: no change of shape
   TOUGHNESS: bear shocks
   CLEARABILITY: no splitting
6. Fuel wood: heat and power - directly or indirectly
   Timber wood: Construction, MP/Assam 75% species, 20% forest trees

B. ORISSA

1. Terminalia 2. Ficus 3. Cedrula
4. Acacia 5. Artocarpus

C. EXAMPLES

1. Teak	:	TECTONA GRANDIS, Verbenaceae, TN, Kerala, Maharashtra B&O moderately heavy, immune to pathogens.
2. Shorea	:	SHOREA ROBUSTA, Depterocarpaceae: Assam, MP, B&O Heavy
3. Deodar	:	CEDQUS DEODARA, Conifera, light, moderately hard, durable
4. Dalbergia	:	DALBERGIA SISSOO, leguminosae,: Assam, Punjab, U.P. harder than Teak, durable (Redwood)
5. Pine	:	PINUS LONGIFOLIA, Western Himalayas
6. Jarul	:	LAGERSTRONIA FLOSREGINA, Assam, West Coast
7. Mahogany	:	SWIETENIA MAHAGONI, all over India
8. Siris	:	ALBIZZIA spp., Leguminosae, all over India.
9. Mango	:	MANGIFERA INDICA, Anacardiaceae all over India
10. Iron	:	XYLIA XYLOCARPA, AP, MP, very hard

D. THREE VALUABLE TIMBERS: SAL: SHOREA ROBUSTA

E. WORLD PRODUCTION AND TRADE IN TIMBER

13. GUMS, RESINS AND RUBBERS

A. GUMS: Decomposed product of cellulose of inner tissues. Gummosis

Allied to pectines & contain sugar

Swell in water and then soluble: Colloidal

Exudation through injury from bark, wood & cambium

June-July / September, October

Seal over plant wounds, adhesives

Printing and Finishing textiles.

Sizing for paper.

1. ACACIA GUM (Acacia arabica): bark, viscosity, high textile printing, polish-making, confectionaries, paints, inks pottery. Emulbifying agent in medicines, Food = delivery after cooking with sugar.
2. GUM ARABIC (Acacia senegal): Arabian countries, Sinegal river, and adhesive for textile printing.
3. BABOOL GUM (Acacia scopioides)
4. GUM TRAGACANTH: Astraglus gummifer, Bark (Papilanacue) integration of pith and medullary rays. Turkey, Iran, adhesive, medicine, printing.
5. KARAYA GUM (Sterculia urens): white, bark
6. INDIA GUM: MP, creams, glycernic, soaps, sugars, pastes, cosmetics, icecreams.
7. KINO GUM (Pterocarpus marsupium): bark (Leguminosoe) South & central India. Medicines Bengal kine gum: Butea frondona: Inferior to above (papilionaceae)
8. GHATHO GUM (Anogeissus latyelia): India, Ceylon, adhesion
9. LOBAT BEAM GUM (Ceratonia siliqua): Caesalpiniaceae enderperm of the seed. Burma gum, Java gum, Cherry gum (prunus) U.S.A.
10. GOWER GUM (Cyamopsis tetragonoloba): Tapinonaceae Seed. food, paper & textile industries.
11. AGAR AGAR LIKE GUM: Gracilaria.

II. TYPES OF NATURAL RUBBERS & THEIR SOURCES

	TYPE- SOURCE	EXTRACTION METHOD	TYPE OF PRODUCT
1.	Rubber Tree (Hevea Brasilienusis) family Euphosbiaceae. South America, cultivated in Srilanka and Malay archipelago.	Incersion tapping of latex.	Rubber, high purity
2.	Rubber plant (Ficus elastica) South East Asia	Shredding of leaves and shoot	Rubber High purity
3.	Panama rubber tree (Castilla elastica) and other species of of castilla. Moraceae Tropical America.	Incrsion tapping of latex	Rubber high purity
4.	Guayule shrub (Parthemium argentatum) composita(e) Mexico and Texas.	3-5 yr old shrub shredded, leached	Rubber, plus 13-18% resin.
5.	Russian Dandelion (Taraxacum, compositae Turkestan	Shredded, leached with hot water.	Rubber high purity
6.	Rubber nice (Cryptostegia grandifloria) Asclepidiaceae. Africa Gutter Percha	Latex from stems	Hard Plastic softens to rubber with heat
7.	Trees of Genera Pelagium,Payena Sapotaceae, Malaya	Leaves or branches shredded and leached with hot water	Hard Plastic and softens to rubber with heat.
8.	Chicle- Sapodilla tree (Manilkaea zapota) sapotaceae, Mexico and central America, cultivated in tropics	Latex tapping	soft rubber.
9.	Balata -Balata Tree (Manilkeae bidentata) Sapotaceae, Tropical america	Latex tapping	tough hard rubber, softens with heat.

14. ETHNOBOTANY GENERAL FEATURES OF MEDICINAL PLANTS

I. INTRODUCTION

1. Some Important plant derived medicines: Colchicine, Papaverine Quinine, Morphine, Cocaine, Digitonin, Reserpine, Ephedrine, Vinblastine.
3. Countries : India, Mexico, Poland, New Guinia, China, Lebanon, NZ Phillipines, Nigeria, Burma, Malaya, Greece, USSR, Argentina
4. Nevada : Train, S. America: Schultes [Amazon], Russia, Peter the Great. Breynius, 1716

II. SOME HISTORICAL ASPECTS

1. Snake root against insanity: Reserpine Hindu belief on Rauwolfia serpentina high blood pressure
2. Radiation burns: Aloe vera: Cleopatra used
3. Cabbage eaten before alcohol consumption - soup / eaten before banquets. amino acids
4. Curare: Chondodendron tomentosum
5. European Belladona: Australia's Dubosia
6. Explorers: Goodspeed, Shultes, Klug, Brecher, Farnsworth [Pharmacognacist]
7. First Bot. drug search: 3500 yrs ago / Queen Hatshepsut [Egypt]

III. ETHNOBOTANY

1. Fundamental Principles
2. Ancient civilization
3. Tribal of India
4. Cultivated Plants orgains
5. Ethnobotanical history drugs
6. History of ethnobotany
7. Drugs in different plant parts
8. Active Principles

According to Schultes (1962) Ethnobotany is the study of the relationship which exists between people of primitive societics and their plant environment"

India is very rich in ethnobotanical information About 80% of India's population lives in villages, and a considerable proportion comprises tribals living in remote forest areas.

Phytogeographically India is divisible into some regions

(a) Himalayas and far eastern states

(b) Central and eastern India

(c) Western India

(d) Southern India

(e) Andaman & Nicobar Islanda

IV. SACRED GROVE

purest of vegetation ranging in extent from a few trees to forty hectares or more which is left undisturbed because of its assocation with some deity. In its original form, this protection forbade any interference with the grove

V. CLASSIFICATION OF MEDICINAL PLANTS

Changes / variations in groups / families / genera / species

1. Taxonomic: Algue, Fungi, Pteridos, Gymnos, Dicot, Monocot
2. Organ-wise: Stem, root, leaf, seed, flower
3. Active principles: 1. Alkaloids, 2. Glycocides, 3. Saponins, 4. Flavonoids, 5. Tannins, 10. Resins, 6. Coumarins, 7. Anthroquinones, 12. Phenols, 8. acids, alcohols, esters, 9. Volatile oils, 11. Carbohydrates, 13. Vitamins & harmones, 14. Toxins. Some can be identified in anatomical sectors.
4. Pharmacological Activity: 1. Antineoplastic, 2. Antimicrobial 3. Antiviral, 4. Antimalarial 5. Insecticidal, 6. Hypoglysemic, 7. Cardiotonic, 8. Andro & estrogenic

Vinca rosea: all varieties do not have activity only some from West Indies and Madagascar.

Cinchona: All species may have activity but variable

Strophanthus: All species may not have activity

Solanaceae / Apolyanaceae: many genera may have activity

VI. PLANT ORGANS USEFUL

1. **Underground Parts:** Podophyllum, Aconitum, Colchicum, Curcuma, Zinger, Glorioa, Urginea, Allium, Rauwolfia, Ferula
2. **Barks:** Cinchona: Quinine, Alastonia scholaris: Chromic dysentry Bauhinea variegata: Syphilis, leprosy, Cinnamomum zeylanicum: aromatic
3. **Stems:** Ephedra , Calotopis: leprosy, rheumatism, Santalum: Skin diseases.
4. **Roots**
   (a) Atropa belladonna (Solanaceae): European, stimulant antispasmodic, external pain reliever.
   (b) Atropa acuminata (Solanaceae): Indian (Kashmir) tinctures, Plasters
   (c) Hemidesmus indicus (Asclepiadaceae): Indian sarsaparilla (S. India), blood purifier, siphilis, urino-genital diseases

(d) Plumbago rosea (Plumbaginaceae): throught India, stimulant, Abortifecient, stomach Dyspepsia, higher doses - narcotic

(e) Plumbago zeylanica (Plumbaginaceae): Bengal, S.India, Plumbagin - poison – Abortions

(f) Rauwolfia serpentina (Apocyanaceae): Himalayan Foot hills, Sikkim, Western Ghats largest sp, Africa & S. Africa. ajmaline, reserpine, yohimbibe ajmalinine, ajmalicine, serpintine, serpentinine,

1. Charaka samhita 1000 BC as Sarpagandha against snake bite, Madness
2. Mongoose eating prior to fighting with cobra.
3. French Bot. Plumiers (17th centry) in honour of 16th century German physician - Botanist - Traveller - author - Rauwolf.
4. Rumphius - Radix mustletoe - India, Java against all poisons
5. Roxburgh - Andhra physicians using against poisons & promote delivery in tedious cases.
6. Oleoresins - hypnotic & sedative action
7. Lowering B.P., sedation, hypertension, neuropsychologic & gynaecological, menstrual and menopausal problems. Insomnia.

(g) Withania Somnifera (Solanaceae): Semi arid regions of India. Aphrodisiac, rejuvinator, nervous disorders Rhenmatic pains inflammation of joints.

Leaves: Ulcers, boils, swellings, skin-diseases.

(h) Ferula asafoetida (Umbelliferae): Punjab, Kashmir. Oleo-resin gum exudes from rootstock, carminative, anti-spasmodic, diuretic, anthelminthic

5. Underground Stems

(a) Curcuma longa (Zinzeberaceae): Turmeric. Maharashtra, Bengal, Madras, AP, Orissa, stomachic, stimulant, carminative (opp) flatulence) fresh juice anthelminthic, cleans foul ulcers. decoction - eye wash, dressing for spains, wounds.

(b) Curcuma amada (Zinzeberaceae): Mango ginger, Bengal, AP, TN, wild in Konkan stokachic, cooling, carminative

(c) Allium cepa (Liliaceae): Onion, Throughtout India, perennial raw: diurctic, juice: Piles, decoction = cough with vineger - Jaundice

(d) Allium sativum (Liliaceae): Garlic, Throughtout India - Perennial bulbils or cloues. Great value, fevers, coughs, flatulence, nervous disorders, bonehitis, asthma, Disinfectant, earache, insecticidal

(e) Zingiber officinale (Zinzeberaceae): Ginger, Perennial herb. Native of S.E. Asia, Kerala, UP, HP, AP, Bengal, Maharashtra stimulant, carminative, dyspepsia, dropsy Paste - headache and tooth ache.

6. Barks

(a) Cinnamon zeylanicum [Lauraceae]: native of ceylon- Nilgiris, Dalchini, S. Kanara, Malabar, Assam, Kumaon, Cinnamon, tooth ache,

1. aromatic, carminative: Powder, decoction
2. neuralgic pains, headache: Paste
3. astningent, antiseptic, carminative: oil

(b) Cinchona officinalis & other species (Rubiceae)

1. Native of Andes in South America
2. Khasia hills, Nilgiris, Sikkim, MP.
3. 29 alkaloids e.g.s. cinchonine, Quinidrice, Quinine
4. Life saving drug against Malaria

(c) Saraca indica (Caesalpiniaceae): Asoka

1. Native of India, western peninsula, C & E. Himalayas Bengal
2. Astringent, uterine disorders, piles
3. Diabetes - dried flowers

(d) Bauhimia variegata (Caesalpiniaceae): Mountain Ebony

1. Through out India
2. anthelminthic, liver complaints
3. Skin diseases like leprosy.

7. Stems And Woods

(a) Ephedra gerardiana (gymnosperm): Most speices in South America small shrub of Himalayas, 7-16000'. Kashmir to Sikkim. Ephedrine against asthma. Plant tincture: cardiac stimulant. Stem decoction - rheumatism (USSR).

(b) Santalum album (Santalaceae): Chandan. White Sandal Wood. Tree found in Western Peninsula, Mysore and forests of TN. and Kerala. Wood: Cooling, cardiotonic and diretic paste cools inflammatry skin diseases, headache essential oil -

stimulant, antiseptic, demulcent (soothing effect on skin & membrances).

(c) Pinus roxburghii (gymnospem): Pine Tree of Western & Eastern Himalayas olco-resin, stomachic and stimulant (ingredient of medicinal plasters & ointments, disorders of urinos-genital disorders.

(d) Acacia catechu (Mimosaceae): Catechu, Famous astringent - bleeding piles, chromic dysentery, bleeding gums, hypertrophy of the tonsils. Tincture: painful mammaries.

8. Leaves

(a) Adhatoda vasica (Acanthaceae): Perennial shrub: throughout India upto 4000' sub Himalayan tract. Twigs, fls. collected before summer and dried and sold in medicinal markets. Alkaloid vascine. chest diseases. powerful expectorant. Asthma-dried leaves are smoked decoction / powder.

(b) Aloe barbadensis (Liliaceae): Fleshy, tapering to a bluntness. thorny prickles on the margin - through out country after skin removal, the flesh is given for the enlargement of liver, spleen etc. Juice: menstrual suppression, jaundice, rheumatism, intestinal worms in children.

(c) Crinum asiaticum (Amaryllidaceae): Purgativs & tonic. Warm Juice useful in ear and skin diseases.

(d) Bryophyllum pinnatum (Crassulaceae): Throughout India, diarrhoea, cholera, astringent and antiseptic, toasted leaf (slight) presents swelling, irritation stopped, heals rapidly: wounds, boils, cuts, bites of venomous insects etc.

(e) Calotropis procera (Aesclepiadaceae): Most places of India. Dropsy, enlargement of Viscera. Dry leaves smoked for relief from Asthma, Leaf juice: skin diseases. Latex: leprosy, dropsy, abortifacient taken internally or applied at the mouth of Uterus.

(f) Centella asiatica (Umbelliferae): Throughout India. Alterative, toxic. children - early stages of dysentery. Powder (leaf) with milk - mental weakness, memory, improves blood & nervous system among children. Leaf juice & lanoline great value in elephantiasis.

(g) Jatropha curcas (Euphorbiaceae): Native of tropical America. Cultivated along the coromandel coast and Trarencose. Latex: styptic - applied to bleeding wounds, piles, eczema, ringworm. Decoction: galactagague - applied to breaste of nursing mothers

(h) Ocimum Sanctum (Labiateae): Aromatic herb. Through out India. Stomachic. Anthelminthic, Gartic and liver diseases of children dyspepsia.

(i) Piper betle (Piperaceae): Climbing shrub. Cultivated Antiseptic, sialogogne, aphrodisiac, carnivative juice with honey to children - indigistion, diarrhoea - eye diseases. Oil-coated leaves - dressing on ulcers & blistered surfaces.

(j) Tylophora asthmatica (T. indica): Trailing creeper, N.India, B&O Bengal, Assam. Leaves thick, deep green Chewing and swalling leaves, reliever Asthma.

9. Seeds

(a) Daucus carota (Umbelliferae): Carrot - Gajar. Annual herb. UP, MP, Punjab aphrodisease, neroine toxic, dropsy, utermine pain & diseases of kidney.

(b) Elettaria cardamonum (Zinzeberaceae): Herb. native of India. Cultivated in Kerala, Mysore, Assam, Madras etc. aromatic stimulant, abortifacient, emmenagogue diseases of kidney, liver, rectum, throat & aches of ear, head & teech.

(c) Pongamia pinnala (Papilionaceae): Common tree on both peninsular. Skin diseases, rheumatism - seed paste & oil bark, roots, leaves are also useful.

(d) Ricimus communis Euphorbiaceae): Small tree cultivated in AP, Maharashtra,Mysore, Orissa. Ricinine alkaloid, effective purgative, congectivitis leaf = headache & as poultice for boils.

(e) Strychnos nux-vomica (Loganiaceae): Tree found in Orissa, Bihar, AP, TN, dried ripe seeds - toxic stimulant, treatment of epilepsy, paralysis, nervous disorders, impotence, hydrophobia, intermillent fevers.

(f) Trigonella foenum-graecum (Papilionaceae): Methi Fenugreek. Native of S.Europe, Trigonelline aromatic, nutritive, lactagogue, aphrodisias dropsy, sheumatism. Seed paste - roasted or boiled + leaves in Ayurvedic.

10. Fruits

(a) Aegle marmelos (Rutaceae): Tree. Ripe fruit aromatic, laxative & cooling. Unripe or Half ripe one. Cotringent, digestive alternative constipation and diarrhoea.

(b) Cassia festula (Caesalpixiaceae): Ornamental tree with yellow flowers. Throughout India pulp from the pods: pleasant & suild purgative even to children & expectant mothers. Confection = diabetes. Leaves & root also useful.

(c) Coriandrum sativum (Umbelliferae): Aromatic herb, native of medeterranean. Cultivated in MP, Mysore, Bihar, especially. Stimulant, aphordisease, refrigerant, flatulence, neuralgia. Waterpaste - garglings - mouth and throat ulcers.

(d) Cuminum cyminum (Umbelliferae): Native of Mediterranean. Cultivated N.Gujarat, Punjab, UP. Source of thymol. Emmenegoque (promosing menotruatioon & regularising it). dippepsia, checks nausea.

(e) Emblica officinalis (Euphorbiaceae): Tree found throughout India. Richest source of Vitamin C. fresh fruit: refrigerent, divertic, against habitual constipation & other digestive trouble, dried fruit: stomachia, astringent, blood pionfier, seed infusion: opthalmic diseases.

(f) Foeniculum vulgare (Umbelliferae): Medeterranean herb. Cultivated in Gujarat, Punjab, Maharashtra & Assam. fruit: Appetizer, lexative, aphrodisease, carminative diseases of eye, spleen, kidney. Also Emmenagogne. Leaves & seed also valuable.

(g) Papaver somniferum (Papaveraceae): Native of W.Asia. Cultivated in UP, Punjab, J & K. Unripe capsules - scratch - milky sap exudation - dried spoxtaneously. Medicinal opium comes from ASIA

Minor (W.Asia, N.East) from 2000 yrs. India: Banores, Putna, Malvia famous. Indian opium = commercially important: smoken, drunk, eaten in Asia, especially China.

Primary: stimulant, cerebrospinal system - effects every organ of the body.

Secondary: narcotic, anodyne, antispasmodie, poison if overdosed.

(h) Piper nigrum (Piperaceae): Creeping undershrub, native of India, Malaya cultivated in Western Ghats unripe dried berries = black pepper alkaloid piperine ripe, cover removed berries = white pepper, infusion or powder. nerve toxic, emmenagogne, disorders of the urinary system.

(i) Solanum khasianum (Solanaceae): 1. Wild perennial herb of hill tracts, especially Khasi, Jayantia hills, plant hirsute, prickly, deeply lobed leaves, berry about 1" dmt. with 3-400 seeds. 2.

Solasodine - a base for many drugs, analogue of diosgenin and good source of Sapogenin sapogenin a base for cortisone and allied steroid products. 3. Cortisone - arthritis refer strophanthus Dioscorea 4. Other steroids - Discorea - Trigonella Sex hormone balance though oral contraception.

11. All Parts Of Plants

(a) Andrographis paniculata (Acanthaceae): Throughout India, herb. decoction of plant. Powder of seeds. bronchits, dysentery, dyspepsia.

(b) Azadirachta indica (Meliaceae): Native of Burma, grown all over India. Leaves: Carninative, diurctcic, insecticidal, anthelminthic, Jaundice, skin diseases wounds, swellings, Barks: as leaves Seed: laxative gum:demulcent seedoil = leprosy, fruit: urinary diseases, intestinal worms.

(c) Datura metel (Solanaceae): Throughout India. All parts = intoxicant, narcotic, aphrodisiac, toxic, anodyne (pain reliever) fruit juice = dandruff & hair loss seed paste = decaying teeth, piles. alkaloid rich.

(d) Achyranthes aspera (Amaranthaceae): Through out India, piles, boils, purgative, diuretic, astingent.

(e) Solanum nigrum (Solanaceae): Throughout India, cardiotonic, diuretic, anodyne, diaphoretic Dropsy (excessive water in tissues) berries toxic, Hot leaves against sweller & painful testides. alkalids.

(f) Solanum xanthocarpum (Solanaceae): Through out India. Astringent, divertic, anthehunthic. Against flabulence, dropsy, asthma, heart diseases alkaloid.

(g) Tenospora cordifolia (Menispermaceae): Tropical India, Andamans, aliane, hepatic, stimulant, diuretic, Against fever, rheumatism, siphilis, dyspepsia impotence, gonorrhoea, Jaundice.

(h) Vinca rosea (Apocyanaceae): Native of Madagarcar, White or pink flowers, allower India. Always flowers. Antineoplatic Alkalids: Vinblastine, Vincristine, Lochnerinine, Vindoline. Anti diabetic (India, SriLanka, S.Africa).

Improvement: TISSUE CULTURE, BREEDING, Floristics & Vegetation studies 1. Hydrid seed function, 2. Nursery Technology

Datura innodia X Atropa belladonna

Lycopersicum esculentum X Solanum tuberosum

Arabidopsis thaliana X Brassica compestris

F. CONSERVATION

1. Presence of alkaloids and other useful active principle is often not confined to one or a few species of the genus.
2. Related species of medicinal plants need to be studied in detail.
3. The botanical, pharmacognostic, phytochemical and other aspects of most of the Indian species remain to be studied.

G. CITES - CNVENTION ON THE NTERNATIONAL TRADE IN ENDANGERED SPECIES

1. 1989 - Elephants added to CITES list - Meeting in the Geneva
2. Ivory exports and imports banned

> *"A nation that destroys its soils destroys itself. Forests are the lungs of our land, purifying the air and giving fresh strength to our people."*
>
> **Franklin D. Roosevelt**

15. HISTORY AND ETHNOBOTANY OF SOME PLANT DRUGS

I. Some Important Plant Drugs

300 million drugs. 47% are of natural origin: Plants provide blue prints for thousands of synthetics. Came from only 4% of the plants analysed.

- Total plants 3,50,000
- Flowering plants 1,75,000
- Newer findings/year 2,000

A. CINCHONA

1. C. ledgeriana C.officinalis C.pubescens C.succisubra - 70 species, alkaloid, native of S.America. into Europe 1640s. Landenbergia malacophylla, Remiijia pedunculata: alternatives
2. (a) Quinine, Cinchonine, Totaquine and 30 others
   (b) Syntheties: Chloroquine, primaquine etc, Atebrine
   (c) Resistance developed, but not to Quinine.
   (d) Doering & Woodward (1944) Quinine synthesized.
   (e) Chloroquine: Germans in War II.
3. Isolation: Pelletier & Caventou (Fr) did not patent
4. Discovery: Father Calamcha 1633
   (a) Storm - trees fell into pools - water bitter - stranger passing by with fever & thrist forced to drink- CURED. Cinchona bark in water is bitter.
   (b) Jesuits chewing barks to identify trees & differentiate - on experimentation found.
   (c) Surgeon on a stranded Pirate ship found lions seeking this tree & eating the bark.
   (d) Countess Cinchon, beautiful wife of Vicery of Peru - fever -governer of Loja - Quina Quina (bark of barks) - Relieved - went to Spain - popularised. 1638.
5. Cinchona Linnaeus, Quinine (Quina Quina)
   (a) 1. Cardinal de lugo cured Louis XIV. Jesuit Priest 1633-1658)
   2. Archduke of Austria too cured - relapsed - died as the medicine was not given 2nd time.
   3. the drug was condemned.
   4. "Jesuits want to exterminate the protestants"
   5. Oliver Cromwell - died rather than accepting it !

(b) Talbor - a Quack. Condemned. used a concoction containing the same "Jesuit powder". - rose leaves + lemon juice + Vine(s) cured Louis IV again. Died at 39. Sold secnet to Louis IV who published after Talbor's death. Astonishment to people.

(c) de Jussieu & La Condamine: Several sps, cultivation practice - the most beautiful tree - 1735 - 1761 - collection - Treasure- Sailing Buenos Aires - the night before, the Indian watchman left into the jungle with the treasues ! Tragedy left him broke. 1771 returned to Paris - died tragically in the Asylum.

(d) Haasskar (Dutch) in disguise - to Jawa - seeds & seedlings - Honoured - but as tourist in S.A. (1852) found to be cheated by Indians - seeds etc failed - Removed from job.

(e) Ledger: 18 yrs of faithfulness & friendship with his (1843-65) helper -asked for the best -refused & left - 4 yrs. returned with seeds hidden in hair - tortured to death by Indians - seeds sent to UK ignored sold on streets by Dutch - Java - Best investment in History - controlled world's Quinine - 9/10 ths of supply.

(f) Fischer 1927 - Smuggled from Java to Phillippines. 1942: Amsterdam by Germans, Java by Japanese, Phil. factory by Japanese Americans strads & paralysed.

Fischer though sick - harvested secretly in phillipines & emplaned the cargo - the plane shot down. Special plane - C. ledgeniara seeds - U.S.A. (via Australia)

MALARIA: Ronald Ross: fever important because it offsets 1/3 rd population the misery it inflicts and serious opposition to the March of civilisation

1897 proved that mosquitoes carry the disease. no deserts, no savage races, no geographic difficults have proved as inimical as this one.

B. RAUWOLFIA: Apocyanaceae, 175 species

1. 30 centuries in India folk remedy. Sarpagandha - antidote to snake bite. Pagal - ke - dawa - insanity herb.
2. MK Gandhi drank tea from this.
3. Meditating holymen chew it regularly, 1000 BC charaka Samhita, Europe 1563 AD - Garcia de Orta - Book on Hindu medicine. Mangoose fortifies itself before attacking a snake. If bitten, seeks out this herb, eats leaves.

4. Plumer named it in 1703 in honour of a 16th century physician - explorer Leonhard Rauwolf.
5. Large doses - paralysis & death
6. Discovery
   (a) 1920's Indian researches on indigenous bot. drugs, Rig-veda = 4,500 - 1600 BC, oldest repository of human knowledge. plants as medicine . Ayurveda - drugs listing, Susruta sanhita = not later than 1000 BC therapy Charaka Samhita = 2,000 remedies given - toxicology etc. Buddhist period = med. pl. cultivated. Contacts with Greece, Rome, Arabia, Pesia, enriched Materia medica, Hindu, Ayurveda = 1/8th of world's population other system = Unani (Moslems) Tibbi.
   (b) 1931, Siddique & Hussin, Rauwolfia 1. Ajmaline & 2. Serpentine types Ajmaline, ajmalinine, ajmalicine in honour of Hakim Azmal Khan - founder of Ayurvedic / Unani / Tibbi college.
   (c) 1930's Sen & Bose - sedation, drop in BP insomnia reduction. Urged the medical men of the world to try it.
   (d) 1949 Vakil confired the imporotance
   (e) 1953 Raudixin (Squibb's), 44% deaths in US – Cardiovascular climinated, Reduced electric shocks & brain surgery,
   (f) Snake roots of US are not Rauwolfia but, Polygala senega, Eryngium aquaticum
   (g) Bengal collection - "Elephant killed 17 collectors. others donot go to forest. delivery delayed"
   (h) R. vomitoria africa best source of reserpine, 2-3 leaves swallowing produces vomiting. central Africa from Senegal - Lake Victoria in East Africa. Congo is the best.
   (i) R. canercens - native of caribbean introduced to India [R. tetraphylla] accidentally seeds in the ballast of ships.
   (j) R. serpentina, R. vomitoria, R. canescens 6th among all prescription for natural products. Brainites ? like colites, diabetes, hepatitis hypertension - most species of Rauwolfia still await screening.

C. YAMS: Dioscoria 600 sp. [Dioscorides: Greek physician], from 1705

1. Arthritis, steroids
2. Sex hormons, cortical hormones

3. Diosgenin, 70-75% of steroid harmons from Yams.
5. Steriod: Sterols, cortical hormones, sex hormones, bile acids
6. Cortical hormones: arsthritis, rheumatism, eye & skin infections, male hormonoes build bodies wasted by illness - harmones ease menopausal symptoms, overcome disabling conditions.
7. Marker: father of steriod hormones. 147 papers 1935-43, 75 patents (Parke Davis & Co.). Recognised the value of Liliales: Yucca, Agave, Dioscorea, etc. Saponin altered to harmones - isolated sapogenins - Smilax -(sarsaparilla) root - sarsapogenin.
8. Diosgenin -5 steps - Progestesone - pregnancy hormone -8 steps - testosterone - male hormone
9. Strophanthus Expedition of Up John & Penick: brought soil. It contained bacteria "fermenting" progesterone etc - cortisone & 11-02 - hormones.

   66 Lbs of dryroot -> 11b of diosgenin & 2 oz of cortisone.

D. PERIWINKLES: newly-formed = cancer, neoplastic

1. Historical folk remedies - clues for modern research
   (a) Jivaro head hunters of Eucador - "tsantsa" potion of about 30 plants for shrinkling heads - same action on tumours.
   (b) Penobscot Indian remedy for cancer. Podophyllum peltatum (American mandrake May apple) - Sandoz Ltd - anticancer drug. Ancient mandrake - Mandragora – Sedative.
   (c) Graeco - Roman times - Aristolochia- Aristolochic acid.

   Plants have more chemicals than chemists can ever synthesize - Natural less likely to be poisonous than synthetics, as they are developed in association with life.
   (d) Hodzkins disease = cancer of lymph glands, spleen, liver. 1958 - VLB - isolated by Beer, Noble, [Canada]. Svoboda - 23 new alkaloids - Vincristine. 6 weeks supply - i.e. 1 gm - 2 tons of crushed leaves - several thousand dollars.
   (e) Folklore - Phillipines, India, Africa, Jamaica = Diabetes. No where as a cancer cure. Noble from his brother in Jamaica - lead (1944) Beer (1954) Calts (1956) - discovery work. Oral feeding = no reduction but many animals died -no bacteria - WBC are reduced. Protection /resistance

has fallen. This selective action on leukoblasts - rended it a candidate anticancer drug. - Vinca - leuko - blastine/ VLB - roots, stems, leaves. (Vinblastine, velban).

E. STROPHANTHUS, APOCYANACEAE

12 times all the bulls of USA needed to cure american patients alone. Ouabin - like ergotamine & LSD in some respects.

1. African Arrow Poison (David Livingstone)
2. Arthritis -S. sarmentosus, Cortisone - Sarmentogenin
3. Strophanthin, strophanthidin - Glycoside bitter taste, first to be extracted.
4. 1 ton of seed = 12,500 tons of beef animals
5. Laurence = President Truman, USDA expedition for sarmenloius
6. Expeditions by several drug comparies.
7. Nobel prizes for three [Reichstein, Kendall, Hench]
8. Pulitzer & Lasker Award - One Journalist (2nd time) William Laurence
9. Banned in colonies as witch doctors used then to despatch troublesome persons = a little in the finger nails.

F. CHONDODENDRON TOMENTOSUM, MENISPERMACEAE

1. Curare: S.American Arrow poison, Tubocurarine, King 1935.
2. Paralysis, multiple sclerosis, Parkinson's disease,
3. Climbing liana (Ruiz & Pavon 1798), Grapelike clusters & purple fruits
4. Shock therapy: against breakage of spine, armbones
5. Surgery: muscle relaxation
6. Last stages of rabies to ease
7. Tetanus - trauma - painful muscular contraction - cured [or C. toxicoferum]
8. Curare: upto 30 ingredients ! differ from region & tribe.
   One - tree curare , two - tree curare: Monkey behaviour
   Head drop test of rabbit
8. Curare filled bullets: Eisenhower mooted
9. Meat of animals killed by hunting (fear) tasteless - poison used Therefore
   (a) Bamboo can - tubocurare
   (b) Calabash can - emptied gourds - most potent
   (c) Pot can - clay vessels

10. Effective for 30 yrs. Antidote is Calabar bean - another poison - Physostigma venerosum - physostigmine.
11. Blood stream - not oral feeding - paralysis - skeleton muscles - nerves - chest - breathing - death with knowledge.

G. DIGITALIS

1. Number one drug for the heart - stimulates the vagus center, the 10th cranial nerve - the most important one.
2. Patients drew his attention (Dr. Withering) to a family recipe (dropsy) kept as a secret by an old woman from whom he obtained - Digitalis.
3. On Erasmus Darwin's request through, saved a patient friend of him.
   - Lunar society - James Watt, Benjamin Franklin, Joseph Priestley.
   - Withering's contribution - Witherite mineral, Witheringia genus
4. Other plant of similar use: Urginea maritima; Depression of over active hearts = Aconitum napellus aconite, buttercup family "Queen mother of poisons"; Digitoxin - glycoside, cardiotoxic - kidney - Dropsy cured.

H. MUSHROOMS

Betle Quid	- India	Brain washing -	Hyocyamine
Doubosia Quid	- Australia		Scopalamine
Coca Quid	- S. America		Morphine
		Even L.S.D.	

I. FUNGI

Antibiotics

J. HALLUCINOGENS

1. Peyote cactus: Mescalin
2. Ergot (Claviceps): L.S.D.
3. Cannabis: Marijuana, only female plants
4. Papaver: opium - Morphine - Heroin (Pain killer)
   Ololinqu - Rivea corymbosi / Mexico
5. Spain, N. France incident - Bread and Aspergillus
6. Datura: Hyocyanine, Scopolamine: Atropa - Atropa X Datura ?

16. MARINE PLANTS

A. INTRODUCTION

1. Algae occupy thrice, the volume occupied by bacteria
2. Highly vital Nostoe muscorum & Nodularia harneyana: 70 years.
3. P.K.De (1939): It was felt that bacteir growing int he sheaths of blue green algae that fix nitrogen. But it was shown they have little value. Bacterial free cultures of Anabaena gelalinosa & Aulowia fertilissima, have effeciently fixed Nitrogen.
4. Application of blue green algae to rice fields

   Watanabe 1951 & 2196, 1759 lb/acre/year: Tolypothrix

   increase in leaf length = 17%: tenuis

   increase n ear no. = 30%

   Allen (1955) 2900 lb/acre/year: Anabaena cylindrica
5. Venkataraman & Dutta (1958): Many myxoplyceae capable of N2 fixation.
6. R.N.Singh(1950) Kaul(Lucknow) Reclamation of alkaline usar soils, Nostic, scytonema and Arabaena; after 1 year of reclamation 1576 - 2000 lb. of rice (transplanted), pH 9.7 - 7.6; Exchangeable 20% - 33%, Water holding capacity increased by 40%
7. G.E. Fogg (1861): N2 fixaction as well as photosynthesis by the same organism (generally not so), Anabaena cylindrica N2 + 3 H2O - 2NH2 + 1 1/2 O2, like the photolysis of water.
8. Food for the land

   (a) Ulva, Enteromorpha intestinalis, Soleria chordalis etc Ireland: West and South west coasts.

   Fucus vesiculosus generally

   Scotland: 1915: 25,000 tons were used. (potash)

   England: Scilly & channel Isles: seaweed, an integral part of their agriculture.

   Fucus scoratus - fresh for root crops, - ash for wheat

   (b) Seaweed manure dug into the soil to a foot below the surface increases the fruiting period & also renders them free from blight (in Tomatoes)

   America: Alaska: Alaria fistulosa employed for potatoes

   New England coast: Kelp day as a holiday when people went to beach to collect the weeds.

New Zealand: Macro cystin pyrifera, Lessoina variegata & Ecklonia radiata (bottom weeds) Carpophyllum, Blossevillea & Sargassam (rock weeds).

Seaweed manure excellent for it contains no weeds or fungal pests

9. Greater variety in the process of development
10. Indian work.

B. ECONOMIC IMPORTANCE

1. China & Japan: industrial utilisation suire many centuries
2. Rhodymania & Phyllophora (Rhodo): Iodine
3. Gelidium, Gracillaria & Gigarhina: agar agar, Japan
4. Porphyra & gelidium: China & Japan food.

C. FODDER

1. Norway, Scotland, France, USA & N.Z. 2. Prohemiacers
3. Cattle factories for this purpose in USA, Danmark & Norway.
4. Milk yielding & egg laying capacity of cattle & poultry increased
5. Water =10%, Protein =7%, Fat =4%, Ash =15%, Fibre =3%, Carbo =61%
6. Water blooms - cattle
4. 20% of the total ration of cattle in USA.
5. Dried sea weeds increased milk-yielding & egg-laying capacity.
7. In one of the Orkney (Scot land) Islands, a race of sheep exclusively feed on seaweeds.
8. Fucus, Ascophyllum, Laminaria: Common stock feed.
9. Iceland: horses prefer Laminaria sacetarina (sugar) Cattle: Rhodymenia palmata, Finland: Laminaria & Alaria for cattle.
10. Laninarin: a polypaceharide, easily digestible.
11. Mannitol in small quantities is converted to glycogen
12. Netherlands: Utrecht Veterinary University: increase in blood haemoglobin: 10-20% , increase in milk & convert Vitamin A.
13. Norway: no riboflamin deficiency increase in iodine content of eggs - poultry.
14. U.K.: no Tb, Foot & mouth disease, coutagious abortion: due to sea weed.
15. Canada: Turkey breedess association of British Columbia: annual mortality checked

16. India: temperate waters: more brown algae
    : tropical waters: brown, red & green equal.
17. U.S.A.: factory at Los Angles, for cattle, poultry & pig feed.: Other factories in Denmark, Norway, Orkneys

D. FISH FOOD

1. Plankton & attached forms in sea as well as fresh water.
2. Near the drainage mouth - forms grow - seashore (max growth).
4. Red alga, bron alga & blue - green alga.
5. Philippines fish - Alga 1 Alga 2 Alga 3
   (blue green) cladophra or Entero-chactomorpha morpha
6. Mirgation of sardius consulated to diatous flora. (Malabar coast)
7. Physiological activity of algae influence water medium
   a. Remove CO_2. b. Water purification
8. Filamentous algae - directlu as fish food.
9. The seashore constitutes the richest food producing region in the entire sea. Owing to the richness brought by the drainage from the land.
10. The great fishing grounds are found where algae grow abundantly (attached or plankton).
11. Zebrasoma (Surgeon fish): on red alga
    Amausia: Ectocarpus
    Forcipiger (of Hawaii): Hydrocoleum (blue green)
12. Oedugorium, spirogyra, Mirospora, Ulothris, cladophora & Pithophora - fish food.
13. Malabar coast: Sardines & diotoms (Fragillaria oceanica) close correlation established.
14. Philippines: Milkfish
    Fry Lyngbya 3 Months Cladophora & Enteromorpha
    aestuani later Chactomorpha a few months
15. Physciological role of algae: by influencing the water medium. O_2 release & CO_2 removal.
16. Extra cellular products form a major source of food.
    - glycollic acid, oxalic acid, galoctose, arabinose
    - also fucose, shammose, uronic acid Chalmydomona
    - antibiotic (a fatty acid from chloella).

- Monodus subterraneus: Glutaminase
- Ectocarpus: carotenoids, polypeptides, volatile substances etc

E. SOIL RECLAMATION

Extracellular products Antitioties etc.

Dixare producing Harmful.

1. high in N_2 & Potash but low in P.
   (a) N_2 not reality available takes time
   (b) Potash & organic matter quickly used up.
   Red sea weeds produce lime (Calcium carbonate)
   Lithothamnion: (submerged) France & connemara (Ireland)
   every 2nd or 3rd year: lucerne fields
   3rd or 4th year: pasture meadows.

F. HUMAN FOOD

G. INDIA

1. Thivy (1961)
   (a) Minerals & micronutrients unrepresented in chemical fertilizers. (I & P).
   (b) Brinjal, Tapioca, Cyamopsis, Doliehos, Guards, Amaranthus, Papaya: Good results at CMFRS Mandapam.
      1. Vitamin A,B,C & E.
      2. Nitzschia (diaton): Vit A.— source in liver oil of many fishes
      3. Vit B: Ulva & Posphyra
      4. Vit C: Alaria valida, Ducoids & Porphyra
      5. Josephine tilden: “Extra ordinary physical capacity & endurance”, “high intelligence, unusual artistic, literary & scientific achievements of this race”.

      6.7. Kinds of weeds.

H. OTHER COUNTRIES

Europe & America

Chlorophyceae: Ulva lactuea, Enteromospha, Monostroma

Phacophyceae: Laminaria seacharina

Rhodophyceae: Rhodymenica palmata, Porphyra (South wales)

Laurencia, pinnatifida, Iridaca edulis (Scotland.

Mn.Griffiths: Pickles of Gracilaria compressa

Dictyopheris polypodiodes

Carragheen (Iriph moss); Chondrus crispus: imp.

South Africa

soak in water, simer in mulk Ecklonia maxima

South East Asia

Hawaii	:	no feast complete without limu
Black limu	:	Enteromospha flexuosa or E.intestinalis
Plousefoot limu	:	Codium muelleri
Long limu	:	Gelidium sp
Dry lium	:	Gymmogongrus vermicularis
Hidden limu	:	Hypnea nidifica
Red limu	:	Asparagopeis sanfordiana
Mananea limu	:	Gracilaria coronopifolia
Lipoa limu	:	Haliseris platiogramma

Hulu hulu waena limu: Gratelonpia filicina

Limu: 5000 lbs annually at Honolulu

South America

1.	Chile	:	Durvillea antarctica
	Cachiyugo	:	algae dried & satled in santrago.
	Phyllogigas	:	stems chewed.
	Yuyucho	:	eaten by Indians. Prepared from Nostive

commune

Australia

aborigines	:	Sarcophycus potatorum & Durvellia antarchica

New Zealand

porphyra, Gigartima & Gracilaria

China

throughtout the coastlands. interrior: terrestrial Nostoe, commune

Japan

principal uses of algae. Some old stamps should intrepied young girls scarcting in the sea for sea weeds.

Tokyo bay

inversion of twigs 5-10 fathons.

twig plantation: September, harvest: Jaunary - March.

"Reed burning" cultivation dependent on direction of fresh water currents, salinity temp etc. if not favourable 1,200 mile is loss.

1913 : & 8,00,000 value of algae food industry "Laver industry"

1927: 34 kilometer: 23,827

1936: 50 kilometer: 31,540

Cutting near the base of the blade better because, a new blade grows more rapidly than a new plant.

Laminaria diabolica : more deliearier prepared.

Undaria pinnatifida

Arthothamnum bifidus

Mesoglvia crassa

Japanese statistics laminaria

Principal components : carbohydrats (Sugars & vegetable gum)

: small quantities of protein and fat

: ash (salts of Na & K), 80 -90% water.

I. COMPOSITION

1. Proteins

Protein as well as fat contents vary within the same species.

Some are soluble, others not.

The price of the alga propotioral to its proteins content.

2. Carbohydrates

(a) Some digestible & others not.

(b) Pentasaus easily digestable, 4-11% of the total carbohydrates galaotaus also are used.

(c) 25% - 70% of the total carbohydrate is generally digcotic.

(d) Carbohydrates are not generally well attacked by digestive juices.

(e) Sea weed food is more valuable to sick aniamsl & persons than those in normal health.

(f) Sea weeds are employed usually in countries where the standard of living is too low.

3. Iodine & Goitre

(a) Use of algae and algal products is the principal reasons for the lack of goitre in the orient. (probably due to I2).

(b) Iodine content ppm

ulva lactina 31

Gelidium amancii 1600

Laminaria religiosa	240 - 11,580
Porphyra tevera	18

4. Vitamins

a : Ulva lectuca, Daminaria digitala, codium tomentosum Nitschia

b : Alaria ralida, Porphyra nereocystis, Rhodymerina pertusa

c : Prophyra raiadum, Gigarhina, papillata. algae has hald or even more of the irtative as an orange has. (especially pophyra) The Eskimo of Greenland obtains 50% of his vitamin C from algal foods.

Rats growth faulting when fed on pure synthetic diet which disappeared when 5% again was added. Even breeding was induced. Iscorbic and content

Laminaria digitata	Himanthalia sp.
Arcophyllum nodosum	Incus resiculsus
Porphyra umbilicalis	

5. ASH

Kelp: burnt ash of sea weeds. For Soda and Iodine, Potash. As iodine sources are otherwise meagre, one has to remost to sea weeds, in duecourse.

(a) Laminaria
(b) Ascophyllous
(c) Saccosliza bulbosa
(d) Himanthalis lorea
(e) Fucus vericulosus
(f) Chorda filum
(g) F.Serratus
(h) Alaria esculenta

J. AGAR - AGAR

1. Name is of malayan origin refering to the red sea weeds of the genus Encheuma
2. Sources: Gelidium (USA), Gigartima (UK) Plerocladia (New Zealand), Suhria (South Africa), Ahnfeldtia (Russia), Gracilaria (Australia)
3. Japan is the principal producer as well as user
4. Uses
   (a) Microbiological cultures (resists liquefication of bacteria)
   (b) Sizing of fabries silks etc.
   (c) Lubricant
   (d) Photography - in making plates & films
   (e) Food - China & Indochina

(f) Brewing of beer, manufacture of wines & coffee

(g) Laxalimes

(h) Cosmetics

(i) Bakery & confectionary industries

K. ALGIN

1. Stanford in 1883.
2. Soluble sodium salt of alginic acid (in cell walls)
3. Laminaria digitata Laminaria Baccharima

   Alaria esculenta Ascophyllum

   Fucus serratus Fucus vesiculosus
4. Seasonal fluctuations in its contents
5. Can absorb 200-300 times its wt. of water.
6. Textile industry: dressing & polishing material
7. Waterproof clothes - tents, wagon covers etc.
8. Stabilizer to give smooth body & texture to ice-cream.
9. Artificial fibre production - silk - for wears ! like glass dresses sea weed dresses - water proof & fire proof may come in vogue. As some fibres are coloured, no need of dying.

L. MEDICINE

1. Carraghun, agar-agar, laminaria & Fucus in (Germen list of medicines)
2. Chondrus crispius: diurshoea, dysentery, irritations of alimentarty canal.
3. Agar-agar: lutricant in cases of contropation prepn. of pills, supportories & plashers in the emulsification of ointments.
4. Fucus: in goitre
5. Digena simplex: treatment of worms Chondria, Rhodymenia

   Laminaria bracteata: Menstural troubles

   Laminaria saccharima: goitre & siphilis

   Carraglieen: anticoagulent substance for blood.

   Durvillea: antidote to scabies.

   Fuscus: for reddering faces in some parts of Russia

   Chondrus: paints, creams etc. Promoting curly hair

M. OTHER USES

Adhesive: Chondrus, Gigartive & Grateloupia

String:	Chorda (French coast)
String:	Nereocystics (fishing lives)
Ceramics & Pottery:	grazing (Soda)
Leather smoothing:	Chondrus
Strengthening paper:	agar & lacquer (China)
Insulating material:	alginic acid
Like gum arabic:	Fucoidin (ca. salt of a carbohydrate etherical sulphate) Knife handles: stipes of lessonia (as thick as man's thighs)

Keeping the cooling towers alga-free

1. Chlorella pyremidosa, phormidium inundatum & P.retzil.
2. K2 MnO4, CuSo4 & Algimgim MT4. (most powerful) (Wiscousin).

Wealth from sea

1. Mineral wealth
2. 40,000 million tons/yr by river, winds & materials
3. P, Mn, Fe, Cu, & Co.
4. Calcareous materials of 15 million tons/yr: from the plakton remains

Algal tannins can prevent fouling

1. Sargassum natans & S.fluitants (branch tips) antimicrobial
2. Can prevent fouling due to algae & barnacles in temperate as well as tropical conditions.

Algae produce Ca Co3 :

1. "Kerogen' of ancient rocks which is responsible for producing crude oil.

Algae can increase the yield:

1. Presoaking for 24 hours in algae extract of Phormidium foveloarum.

4

Coasts and Wetlands

1. ECOSYSTEMS OF THE WORLD
2. FUNCTIONAL ASPECTS
3. MARINE SYSTEMS
4. MARINE PLANTS
5. MOLLUSCS AND TURTLES
6. CORALS
7. SEA BEDS
8. RIVERS
9. LAKES
10. ISLANDS
11. AVIAN TOXICOLOGY
12. MANGROVES
13. WET COASTAL ECOSYSTEMS
14. TANKS
15. WETLANDS
16. COAST LINES
17. EAST COAST OF TAMILNADU

Syllabus

1. Introduction to Ecosystems and Climate, Hydrologic cycle, Water resources of the world, Rainfall, runoff, infiltration, evaporation.

   Physical and chemical properties of water, Aquatic systems -Marine and fresh water.
2. Wetland types, distribution, characteristics, structure and function
3. Rivers; reservoirs - small and big - natural and man made; Islands
4. Coastline of India - East Coast and West Coast, Coasts of Tamil Nadu Orissa, Andhra Pradesh and Bengal, Sundarbans, Kutch, Andamans Wet and dry coastal systems.

   Back waters, Estuaries, Deltas, Mangroves, Corals, Sea Beds, Flora and Fauna
5. Ecological and Economic values
6. Developmental aspects - Land over wetness, Agricultural wetlands
7. Sociology, Economics and Politics: Wetlands and Coastlines
8. GNRL - Global, National, Regional and Local aspects
9. Conservation and Restoration

References

1. Alan. H. Brush & Clark, G.A. 1983. Perspectives in Ornithology. Cambridge University Press.
2. Nybakken, J.W. 1988. Marine Biology: An ecological approach. Harper & Row, New York.
3. Shaeffer, C.T. 1987. Marine Ecology; J. Hopkins University Press, Baltimore.
4. Long, S.P & Mason, C.F. 1983. Salt marsh Ecology. Blackie and Son Ltd.
5. Jeffries, M.& Mills,D. 1990. Freshwater Ecology: Principles and Applications. CBS Pub.
6. Tomlinson, P.B. 1986. The Botany of Mangroves. Cambridge U. press.
7. Cherley, R(ed) 1969. Water, Earth and Man. London. Methuem & co.

1. ECOSYSTEMS OF THE WORLD

I. ECOSYSTEMS

A. DEFINITION: "Webster". "Assemblage of objects joined in a regular interaction and inter dependence".

B. CLASSIFICATION: Ecosystems are classified on the basis of their origin (or) existence and further on the basis of Biological aspects.

1. Biospheres
2. Geographic Realms
3. Climatic zones
4. Vegetation zones
5. Definition
6. Classification

Manmade / Managed Ecosystems   Natural Ecosystems

II. TERRESTRIAL ECOSYSTEMS

A. FORESTS

1. Cool temperate forests
2. Warm temperate forests
3. Oceanic temperate forests
4. Tropical rain forests

B. GRASSLANDS

1. Polar Grasslands
   (a) Tundra
   (b) Taiga
2. Temperate Grasslands
3. High Altitude grasslands

C. SAVANNAS

D. SCRUBLANDS

E. DESERTS

F. HIGH ALTITUDES

III. AQUATIC ECOSYSTEMS

A. FRESH WATER

Stream, Rivers, Lakes and Ponds - Lentic

Flora, Fauna, Adaptations, Variations and Dynamics.

B. INLAND WATERS

1. Potable water
2. Irrigation
3. Fisheries
4. Transport

C. MARINE SYSTEMS (ISLAND ESTUARIES)

1. Fisheries
2. Transport
3. Minerals

IV. AQUA-TERRESTRIAL ECOSYSTEMS

Transition communities

They form, transition ecosystems in between terrestrial and aquatic ecosystems.

A. **SALT MARSHES/MUD FLATS:** They are areas of alluvial deposition with low shrubby, Terrestrial vascular plants.

B. **ESTUARINE AND COASTAL ECOSYSTEM**

1. Rocky shore, sound beach, inter-tidal mudflat, tidal estuary
2. Characteristics, FLORA, FAUNA, variations, adaptations, Dynamics, Importance
3. Geographical distribution: Global in distribution restricted to

   28 N & 25 S in Neotropics.

   28 N & 38 S in Palaeotropics.
4. Values of salt marshes: Optimal places to carryout Ecological studies, highly productive ecosystems, serve as feeding ground for many birds, fishes, etc.
   (a) Definition
   (b) Geographical Distribution
   (c) Flora of Salt Marshes
   (d) Fauna of Salt Marshes
   (e) Values of Salt Marshes
   (f) Human Impacts

C. **MANGROVE ECOSYSTEMS:** They are littoral communities formed at sheltered low lying tropical & sub tropical coasts

1. Distribution: Restricted to tropical and subtropical areas.
2. Flora and Fauna: Major floral communities are likes Acetabularia, Caulerpa, Dictyosphaeris, mosses, marine algae fauna has Mudskipper (Characteristic of mangroves) Nematodes, Copepods, Amphipoda, Mollusca, etc.
3. Values of mangroves: Timber yield, pulp, particle board, commercial fishing, Aquaculture purposes (shrimps and prawns).
4. Threats to mangroves: Commercial clearance, Aquaculture, alternation of freshwater flow in to them. Traditionally considered as waste land, hence conversion occurs.
5. Management: Management aspects requires wide range of ecological considerations, conservation & public education & legal activities.

(a) Definition

(b) Geographical Distribution

(c) Community of Mangroves

(d) Faunal Community of Mangroves

(e) Values of Mangroves

(f) Threats to Mangrove Communities

D. CORAL REEFS: They are shallow aquatic ecosystems restricted to tropical seas, formed by CaCO3 deposits of polyps.

1. Distribution: Restricted to seas lying in between 30 N & 30 S latitudes.
2. Values: They have high degree of ecological utility in sustained development. Maintain proper shoreline, provides nutrients for many fishes and shelter to molluscs, crustaceans, etc
3. Threats: Natural - storms, climatic change, predation
   Artificial - oil slicks, siltation, pollution

Distribution, Composition, Formation,
Fauna, Flora, Types of Reefs, Values of Coral Reefs,
Threats to Coral Communities

V. MAN-MADE ECOSYSTEMS

A. CROPLANDS: They are nothing but Agricultural fields (paddy etc) Plantations, Afforestations etc.

B. POND ECOSYSTEMS: They are freshwater ecosystems (not always) managed by man. (ed) Aquaculture Fisheries etc.

C. WETLANDS: They are mostly semi-natural and managed eg. paddy field, peat mining.

They are areas with water logged condition comprise fresh brackish lotic or lentic ecosystems

D. BOGS: Peat producing, present in moist climate.

E. FENS: prolific peat producing wetlands

F. SWAMPS: with little (or) no peat accumulation with water logged stage.

G. **FLOOD PLAINS:** periodically flooded areas with considerable variations in vegetations.

- Distribution: It is global, but the datas are not sufficient., (Compiled by UNESCO, Navigation charts etc)
- Values of wetlands: Generation of fisheries & wild life, recharging inland water supply, recreational values.
- Conservation: Designation, promote conservation motto in sensitive parts, establishment of natural reserves, training personnel for conservation efforts.

1. Definition
2. Geographical distribution
3. Values of Wetlands
4. Threats to wetlands
5. Conservation of wetlands

Animals kill other animals for food.
They also kill them for protection.
Man also kills animals.
But wilder is that man
Who kills the spirit of man in others?
Nehru

2. FUNCTIONAL ASPECTS

I. COMPOSITION OF WETLANDS

A. WATER

The properties of wetland determine considerbaly, its functioning. Dissolved solids, Dissolved gases and organic status.

1. Dissolved solids - compounds of Nitrogen, Posphorus, Iron, Manganese.
2. Dissolved gases - 02, $C0_2$, Methane, H2S and Nitrogen
3. Organic solutes

B. FLORA AND FAUNA

They are the second major composition of wetlands which are typical of each wetland and play a major role in its functioning.

Listing a few important species of plants and animals, including micro-organisms.

C. SEDIMENT

The foundation of the wetlands & its composition.

II. WETLAND DYNAMICS

A. PRIMARY PRODUCTION

Products of wetlands and factors responsible for the rate of productions.

1. Plant Productivity
   (a) Primary productivity - its dependence on external factors
2. Distribution of producers

B. SECONDARY PRODUCTION

Materials and energy budget of consumers

C. PRIMARY CONSUMPTIONS

D. SECONDARY CONSUMPTIONS

E. TYPES OF NUTRIENTS CYCLED AND FACTORS INFLUENCING CYCLING

F. TRANSPORT OF MATERIALS AND ENERGY FLOW

G. DECOMPOSITION

1. By Microorganisms
2. Other species

H. NITROGEN RETENTION IN WETLANDS

1. Sedimentation
2. Uptake by vegetation

3. Distribution
4. Uptake by macrophytes and micro organisms.

I. GAS PRODUCTION IN WETLANDS

Because of decomposition, different organic gases are shunted into atmosphere, unequally. Total annual methane emission estimated to be 0.54 gt of which 0.09 GT - 0.07 GT from natural wetlands and tropical wetlands emit 0.04 Gt.

III. FUNCTIONING OF SALT MARSHES

Focus on variations / deviations.

IV. FUNCTIONING OF ESTUARIES

Focus on natural disturbances.

IV. FUNCTIONING OF TIDAL SALT MARSHES

Important functional aspects of tidal falt marshes.

V. FUNCTIONING OF MANGROVES

VI. FRESH WATER MARSHES

In science it often happens that scientists say, 'You know that's a really good argument; my position is mistaken,' and then they would actually change their minds and you never hear that old view from them again. They really do it. It doesn't happen as often as it should, because scientists are human and change is sometimes painful. But it happens every day. I cannot recall the last time something like that happened in politics or religion.

Ralph Waldo Emerson. *He who knows the most, he who knows what sweets and virtues are in the ground, the waters, the plants, the heavens, and how to come at these enchantments, is the rich and royal man.*

Carl Sagan

3. MARINE SYSTEMS

I. INTRODUCTION

A. COASTLINES AND ESTUARIES

B. SEABED

C. ISLANDS, REEFS AND BARS

D. GEOGRAPHICAL DISTRIBUTION

II. TAXONOMY

A. OCEANS

B. COASTLINES

C. ISLANDS

D. REEFS

E. ESTUARIES

F. MARSHY LAND

G. ROCKY SHORES

H. SEABED

I. BRACKISH WATER

J. TIDAL WAVES

III. OCEANS

A. MAJOR OCEANS AND SEAS

B. OVERVIEW OF THE WORLD'S FERTILE ZONES

IV. ECONOMICS

A. FISHERIES AND ALGAE

Fisheries as a factor in strategic policies and action

World Catch and Consumption

Legal regimes in oceanic fisheries

Territorial Seas

Fishery disputes-focus on Indian ocean

B. MINING FOR FOSSIL FUELS, OTHER MINERALS

C. BIOSPHERE RESERVES NECESSARY

D. HARDLY ANY INDIGENOUS RESEARCH WORK

E. ANTARCTICA RESOURCES AND EXPEDITIOUS

F. 20 OR 200 MILES TERRITORIAL WATERS

G. MILITARY ACTIVITIES: REGIONAL AND GLOBAL POWERS

H. DUMPING OF WASTES BY FOREIGN COMPANIES

I. COASTLINES PRESERVATION AND UTILISATION BY LOCAL PEOPLE

J. OCEAN AS AN ENERGY RESERVE

V. COASTLINES

A. Mangroves

1. Distribution: Global & regional
2. Flora
3. Fauna
4. Resourcefulness
   (a) Ornamental (b) Wood and timber
   (c) Medicines (d) Thatching
   (e) Consumption for intoxication

B. Other Biotic Systems

Distribution, composition, exploitation and consequences

1. Algae: classes, families, genera many
   (a) Food (b) Medicine
   (c) Chemicals (d) Others
2. Angiosperms
   (a) Sea grasses -13 Gen.& 50 Spp[global] 13 species [India]
   (b) Food and shelter for fauna
   (c) Packaging, compost, paper
   (d) Prevention of erosion
3. Vertebrates
   (a) Food (b) Medicinal (c) Others
4. Invertebrates
   (a) Food (b) Medicinal (c) Others

C. Salt Marshes

(1) Distribution (2) Composition
(3) Economic importance (4) Exploitation

VI. ISLANDS, REEFS ETC

A. GEOGRAPHY AND DISTRIBUTION
B. FLORISTIC VARIATIONS
C. FAUNISTIC VARIATIONS
D. HUMAN POPULATION DIVERSITY

VII. SEABED

A. FLORISTIC COMPOSITION

B. FAUNISTIC COMPOSITION

C. MINING ACTIVITIES

1. Minerals 2. Oil 3. Natural gas

VIII. TIDAL WAVES: TYPES AND EFFECTS

Effects: Biological, Chemical & Geological

Adaptations: Resistance

IX. RESOURCES

A. FISHERIES

B. OTHER VERTEBRATES

C. MOLLUSCANS & CRUSTACEANS

D. OTHER INVERTEBRATES E. PLANTS F. MINERALS

X. RESOURCEFULNESS

A. FOOD B. MEDICINES

C. ENERGY D. OTHERS

XI. PROBLEMS

A. BOUNDARIES AND CONFLICTS

B. COASTAL POLLUTIONS

C. DEPLETIONS

D. WASTE DUMPING

E. CONSERVATION ISSUES

F. INEQUALITIES IN SCI. & TECHNOL

A. DEPLETIONS BREED DEPLETIONS

B. CONSERVATION

C. LAWS, NORMS & PRACTICES

E. LOCAL PEOPLE VS HIGH TECHNOLOGY

4. MARINE PLANTS

I. INTRODUCTION

A. **ALGAE OCCUPY THRICE, THE VOLUME OCCUPIED BY BACTERIA**

B. **HIGHLY VITAL NOSTOC MUSCORUM & NODULARIA HARNEYANA:** 70 years.

C. **P.K.DE (1939):** It was felt that bacteria growing in the sheaths of blue green algae that fix nitrogen. But it was shown they have little value. Bacterial free cultures of Anabaena gelatinosa & Aulowia fertilissima, have effeciently fixed Nitrogen.

D. **APPLICATION OF BLUE GREEN ALGAE TO RICE FIELDS**

Watanabe 1951 & 2196, 1759 lb/acre/year: Tolypothrix

increase in leaf length = 17%: tenuis, increase in ear no. = 30%

Allen (1955) 2900 lb/acre/year: Anabaena cylindrica

E. **VENKATARAMAN & DUTTA (1958):** Many myxoplyceae capable of N2 fixation.

F. R.N. Singh (1950) Kaul (Lucknow) Reclamation of alkaline usar soils, Nostic, Scytonema and Anabena; after 1 year of reclamation 1576 - 2000 lb. of rice (transplanted), pH 9.7 - 7.6; Exchangeable 20% - 33%, Water holding capacity increased by 40%

G. **G.E. FOGG (1861):** N2 fixaction as well as photosynthesis by the same organism (generally not so), Anabaena cylindrica

N2 + 3 H2O - 2NH2 + 1 1/2 O2, like the photolysis of water.

H. **FOOD FOR THE LAND**

1. Ulva, Enteromorpha intestinalis, Soleria chordalis etc

   Ireland: West and South west coasts.

   Fucus vesiculosus generally

   Scotland: 1915: 25,000 tons were used. (potash)

   England: Sicily & channel Isles: seaweed, an integral part of their agriculture.

   Fucus scoratus - fresh for root crops, - ash for wheat

2. Seaweed manure dug into the soil to a foot below the surface increases the fruiting period & also renders them free from blight (in Tomatoes).

   America: Alaska: Alaria fistulosa employed for potatoes

   New England coast: Kelp day as a holiday when people went to beach to collect the weeds.

New Zealand: Macrocystis pyrifera, Lessoina variegata & Ecklonia radiata (bottom weeds) Carpophyllum, Blossevillea & Sargassum (rock weeds).

Seaweed manure excellent for it contains no weeds or fungal pests

I. GREATER VARIETY IN THE PROCESS OF DEVELOPMENT

J. INDIAN WORK.

II. ECONOMIC IMPORTANCE

A. CHINA & JAPAN: Industrial utilisation suire many centuries

B. RHODYMANIA & PHYLLOPHORA (RHODO): Iodine

C. GELIDIUM, GRACILLARIA & GIGARHINA: Agar agar, Japan

D. PORPHYRA & GELIDIUM: China & Japan food.

III. FODDER

A. NORWAY, SCOTLAND, FRANCE, USA & N.Z.

B. PROHEMIACERS

C. CATTLE FACTORIES FOR THIS PURPOSE IN USA, DANMARK & NORWAY.

D. MILK YIELDING & EGG LAYING CAPACITY OF CATTLE & POULTRY INCREASED

E. WATER =10%, PROTEIN =7%, FAT =4%, ASH =15%, FIBRE =3%, CARBO =61%

F. WATER BLOOMS - CATTLE

G. 20% OF THE TOTAL RATION OF CATTLE IN USA.

H. DRIED SEA WEEDS INCREASED MILK-YIELDING & EGG-LAYING CAPACITY.

I. IN ONE OF THE ORKNEY (SCOT LAND) ISLANDS, A RACE OF SHEEP EXCLUSIVELY FEED ON SEAWEEDS.

J. FUCUS, ASCOPHYLLUM, LAMINARIA: COMMON STOCK FEED.

K. ICELAND: HORSES PREFER LAMINARIA SACETARINA (SUGAR) CATTLE: RHODYMENIA PALMATA, FINLAND: LAMINARIA & ALARIA FOR CATTLE.

L. LANINARIN: a polypaceharide, easily digestible.

M. MANNITOL IN SMALL QUANTITIES IS CONVERTED TO GLYCOGEN

N. NETHERLANDS: Utrecht Veterinary University: increase in blood haemoglobin: 10-20% , increase in milk & convert Vitamin A

O. NORWAY: no riboflamin deficiency increase in iodine content of eggs - poultry.

P. U.K.: no Tb, Foot & mouth disease, coutagious abortion: due to sea weed.

Q. CANADA: Turkey breedess association of British Columbia: annual mortality checked.

R. INDIA: temperate waters: more brown algae
: tropical waters: brown, red & green equal.

S. U.S.A.: factory at Los Angles, for cattle, poultry & pig feed.
: Other factories in Denmark, Norway, Orkneys

IV. FISH FOOD

A. PLANKTON & ATTACHED FORMS IN SEA AS WELL AS FRESH WATER.

B. NEAR THE DRAINAGE MOUTH - FORMS GROW - SEASHORE (MAX GROWTH).

C. RED ALGA, BRON ALGA & BLUE - GREEN ALGA.

D. PHILIPPINES FISH - ALGA 1 Alga 2 Alga 3
(blue green) Cladophra or Entero-Chactomorpha morpha

E. MIRGATION OF SARDIUS CONSULATED TO DIATOUS FLORA. (Malabar coast)

F. PHYSIOLOGICAL ACTIVITY OF ALGAE INFLUENCE WATER MEDIUM

1. Remove CO_2. 2. Water purification

G. FILAMENTOUS ALGAE - DIRECTLY AS FISH FOOD.

H. THE SEASHORE CONSTITUTES THE RICHEST FOOD PRODUCING REGION IN THE ENTIRE SEA. OWING TO THE RICHNESS BROUGHT BY THE DRAINAGE FROM THE LAND.

I. THE GREAT FISHING GROUNDS ARE FOUND WHERE ALGAE GROW ABUNDANTLY
(attached or plankton).

J. ZEBRASOMA (SURGEON FISH): on red alga
Amausia: Ectocarpus
Forcipiger (of Hawaii): Hydrocoleum (blue green)

K. **OEDOGONIUM, SPIROGYRA, MIROSPORA, ULOTHRIX, CLADOPHORA & PITHOPHORA - FISH FOOD.**

L. **MALABAR COAST:** Sardines & diatoms (Fragillaria oceanica) close correlation established.

M. **PHILIPPINES: MILKFISH**

Fry Lyngbya 3 Months Cladophora & Enteromorpha

aestuani later Chactomorpha a few months

N. **PHYSIOLOGICAL ROLE OF ALGAE:** by influencing the water medium. O_2 release & CO_2 removal.

O. **EXTRA CELLULAR PRODUCTS FORM A MAJOR SOURCE OF FOOD.**

- glycollic acid, oxalic acid, galoctose, arabinose
- also fucose, shammose, uronic acid Chalmydomonas
- antibiotic (a fatty acid from chlorella).
- Monodus subterraneus: Glutaminase
- Ectocarpus: carotenoids, polypeptides, volatile substances etc

V. SOIL RECLAMATION

Extracellular products	Antibiotics etc.
Dixane producing	Harmful.

A. **HIGH IN N_2 & POTASH BUT LOW IN P.**

1. N_2 not reality available takes time
2. Potash & organic matter quickly used up.
   Red sea weeds produce lime (Calcium carbonate)
   Lithothamnion: (submerged) France & connemara (Ireland)
   every 2nd or 3rd year: lucerne fields
   3rd or 4th year: pasture meadows.

VI. HUMAN FOOD

VII. INDIA

1. Thivy (1961)
   (a) Minerals & micronutrients unrepresented in chemical fertilizers. (I & P)
   (b) Brinjal, Tapioca, Cyamopsis, Dolichos, Gourds, Amaranthus, Papaya: Good results at CMFRS Mandapam.
      1. Vitamin A,B,C & E.
      2. Nitzschia (diatom): Vit A.— source in liver oil of many fishes

3. Vit B: Ulva & Posphyra
4. Vit C: Alaria valida, Ducoids & Porphyra
5. Josephine Tilden: "Extra ordinary physical capacity & endurance", "high intelligence, unusual artistic, literary & scientific achievements of this race".

6.7. kinds of weeds.

VIII. OTHER COUNTRIES

Europe & America

Chlorophyceae: Ulva lactuea, Enteromorpha, Monostroma

Phacophyceae: Laminaria sacharina

Rhodophyceae: Rhodymenica palmata, Porphyra (South wales)

Laurencia, pinnatifida, Iridaca edulis (Scotland.

Mn.Griffiths: Pickles of Gracilaria compressa

Dictyopheris polypodiodes

Carragheen (Iriph moss); Chondrus crispus: imp.

South Africa

Soak in water, simer in mulk Ecklonia maxima

South East Asia

Hawaii : no feast complete without limu

black limu : Enteromorpha flexuosa or E.intestinalis

plousefoot limu : Codium muelleri

long limu : Gelidium sp

dry limu : Gymmogongrus vermicularis

hidden limu : Hypnea nidifica

red limu : Asparagopeis sanfordiana

mananea limu : Gracilaria coronopifolia

lipoa limu : Haliseris platiogramma

hulu hulu waena limu: Gratelonpia filicina

limu : 5000 lbs annually at Honolulu

South America

1. Chile : Durvillea antarctica

Cachiyugo : algae dried & satled in santrago.

Phyllogigas : stems chewed.

Yuyucho : eaten by Indians. Prepared from Nostive commune

Australia

Aborigines: Sarcophycus potatorum & Durvellia antarctica

New Zealand

Porphyra, Gigartima & Gracilaria

China

throughtout the coastlands. interrior: terrestrial Nostoc commune

Japan

Principal uses of algae. Some old stamps: young girls searching in the sea for sea weeds.

Tokyo bay

Inversion of twigs 5-10 fathoms.

Twig plantation: September, harvest: January - March.

"Reed burning" cultivation dependent on direction of fresh water currents, salinity temp etc. if not favourable 1,200 mile is loss.

1913: & 8,00,000 value of algae food industry "Laver industry"

1927: 34 kilometer: 23,827

1936: 50 kilometer: 31,540

Cutting near the base of the blade better because, a new blade grows more rapidly than a new plant.

Laminaria diabolica: more deliearier prepared.

Undaria pinnatifida

Arthothamnum bifidus

Mesoglavia crassa

Japanese statistics : on Laminaria

Principal components: carbohydrates (Sugars & vegetable gum)
: small quantities of protein and fat
: ash (salts of Na & K), 80 -90% water.

IX. COMPOSITION

A. PROTEINS

Protein as well as fat contents vary within the same species.

Some are soluble, others not.

The price of the alga proportional to its protein content.

B. CARBOHYDRATES

1. Some digestible & others not.
2. Pentoses easily digestable, 4-11% of the total carbohydrates galactoses also are used.
3. 25% - 70% of the total carbohydrate is generally digested.
4. Carbohydrates are not generally well attacked by digestive juices.

5. Sea weed food is more valuable to sick animals & persons than those in normal health.
6. Sea weeds are employed usually in countries where the standard of living is too low.

C. IODINE & GOITRE

1. Use of algae and algal products is the principal reasons for the lack of goitre in the orient. (probably due to I2).
2. Iodine content

Iodine content	ppm		
Ulva lactina	31		
Gelidium amancii	1600		
Laminaria religiosa	240	-	11,580
Porphyra tevera	18		

D. VITAMINS

1. Ulva lectuca, Laminaria digitala, Codium tomentosum, Nitschia
2. Alaria ralida, Porphyra nereocystis, Rhodymerina pertusa
3. Prophyra riadum, Gigarhina papillata. algae has half or even more of the c-vitamin as an orange has. (especially pophyra) The Eskimo of Greenland obtains 50% of his vitamin C from algal foods.

   Rat growth failed when fed on pure synthetic diet which disappeared when 5% algin was added. Even breeding was induced.

   Ascorbic acid content

   Laminaria digitata, Himanthalia sp. Arcophyllum nodosum Incus resiculus, Porphyra umbilicalis

E. ASH

Kelp: burnt ash of sea weeds. For Soda and Iodine, Potash. As iodine sources are otherwise meagre, one has to remost to sea weeds, in duecourse.

1. Laminaria
2. Saccosliza bulbosa
3. Fucus vericulosus
4. F.serratus
5. Ascophyllum
6. Himanthalis lorea
7. Chorda filum
8. Alaria esculenta

X. AGAR - AGAR

A. NAME IS OF MALAYAN ORIGIN REFERING TO THE RED SEA WEEDS OF THE GENUS ENCHEUMA

B. **SOURCES: GELIDIUM (USA), GIGARTIMA(UK) PLEROCLADIA (NEWZEALAND) SUHRIA (SOUTH AFRICA), AHNFELDTIA (RUSSIA), GRACILARIA (AUSTRALIA)**

C. **JAPAN IS THE PRINCIPAL PRODUCER AS WELL AS USER**

D. **USES**

1. Microbiological cultures (resists liquefication of bacteria)
2. Sizing of fabries silks etc.
3. Lubricant
4. Photography - in making plates & films
5. Food - China & Indochina
6. Brewing of beer, manufacture of wines & coffee
7. Laxatives
8. Cosmetics
9. Bakery & confectionary industries

XI. ALGIN

A. **STANFORD IN 1883.**

B. **SOLUBLE SODIUM SALT OF ALGINIC ACID (IN CELL WALLS)**

C. **LAMINARIA DIGITATA**

Laminaria baccharima — Alaria esculenta

Ascophyllum — Fucus serratus

Fucus vesiculosus

D. **SEASONAL FLUCTUATIONS IN CONTENTS**

E. **CAN ABSORB 200-300 TIMES ITS WT. OF WATER.**

F. **TEXTILE INDUSTRY: DRESSING & POLISHING MATERIAL**

G. **WATER PROOF CLOTHES - TENTS, WAGON COVERS ETC.**

H. **STABILIZER TO GIVE SMOOTH BODY & TEXTURE TO ICE-CREAM.**

I. **ARTIFICIAL FIBRE PRODUCTION** - silk - for wears like glass dresses, sea weed dresses - water proof & fire proof may come in vogue. As some fibres are coloured, no need of dying.

XII. MEDICINE

A. **CARRAGHUN, AGAR-AGAR,LAMINARIA & FUCUS IN**[German list of medicines)

B. **CHONDRUS CRISIPUS:** diarrhea, dysentery, irritations of alimentarty canal

C. **AGAR-AGAR:** lubricant in cases of contraception pills, supportories & plashers in the emulsification of ointments.

D. **FUCUS:** in goitre

E. **DIGENA SIMPLEX:** treatment of worms Chondria, Rhodymenia

Laminaria bracteata: Menstural troubles

Laminaria saccharima: goitre & siphilis

Carraglieen: anticoagulent substance for blood.

Durvillea: antidote to scabies.

Fucus: for reddering faces in some parts of Russia

Chondrus: paints, creams etc. Promoting curly hair

XIII. OTHER USES

Adhesive	: Chondrus, Gigartive & Grateloupia
String	: Chorda (French coast)
String	: Nereocystics (fishing lives)
Ceramics & Pottery	: grazing (Soda)
Leather smoothing	: Chondrus
Strengthening paper	: agar & lacquer (China)
Insulating material	: alginic acid
Like gum Arabic	: Fucoidin (Ca. salt of a carbohydrate, etherical sulphate)
Knife handles	: stipes of lessonia (as thick as man's thighs)

A. KEEPING THE COOLING TOWERS ALGA-FREE

1. In industrial towns: measure of high turning standard
2. Chlorella pyremidosa, phormidium inundatum & P.retzil
3. K2 MnO4, CuSo4 & Algimgim MT4. (most powerful) (Wisconsin)

B. WEALTH FROM SEA

1. Vishnu produced all kinds of wealth by churning the ocean.
2. Mineral wealth
3. 40,000 million tons/yr by river, winds & materials

4. P, Mn, Fe, Cu, & Co.
5. Calcareous materials.

   15 million tons/yr: from the plakton remains after death.

C. ALGAL TANNINS CAN PREVENT FOULING

1. Sargassum natans & S.fluitants (branch tips)
2. antimicrobial
3. Can prevent fouling due to algae & barnacles in temperate as well as tropical conditions.

D. ALGAE PRODUCE CA CO3

1. by algae
2. "Kerogen' of ancient rocks which is responsible for producing crude oil

E. ALGAE CAN INCREASE YIELD

1. Presoaking for 24 hours in algae extract.
2. Phormidium foveloarum

> *"Earth provides enough to satisfy every man's needs, but not every man's greed."*
> **Mahatma Gandhi**

5. MOLLUSCA AND TURTLES

I. MOLLUSCA

A. INTRODUCTION
B. MALACOLOGY AND CONCHOLOGY
C. HISTORICAL
D. HABIT AND HABITATS
E. SIZE AND FORM
F. NUMERIFIC STRENGTH
G. ECONOMIC IMPORTANCE

II. TURTLES ON THE EAST COAST OF INDIA

A. LEGAL STATUS
B. DISTRIBUTION

1. TAMIL NADU
2. ANDHRA PRADHESH
3. ORISSA
4. WEST BENGAL

C. TRADE

1. TAMIL NADU
2. ANDHRA PRADESH
3. ORISSA
4. WEST BENGAL

D. MEASURES FOR CONSERVATION

6. CORALS

I. INTRODUCTION

A. Classification

PHYLUM - Coelenterata

CLASS - Anthozoa

ORDER - Stolonifera Eg. Tubipora

ORDER - Telestacea , Eg. Telesto

ORDER - Alcyonacea, Eg. Alsyonium

ORDER - Coenothecalia

ORDER - Gorgonaceae

ORDER - Pennatulacea

Sub Class Hexacorallia

ORDER - Madreporia

II. FORMATION OF REEF TYPES

A. Fringing Reefs - Along coastline

B. Barrier Reefs - Separated from land by lagoon.

C. Aiocles - Ring shaped reefs around central lagoon.

D. Patch Reefs - Circular irregular reefs from lagoon floor.

E. Fossil Reefs

III. GEOMORPHOLOGY OF REEFS

A. Reef accummulation

1. Light - clear water. Growth & to light intensity.
2. Turbidity - High turbidity low growth.
3. O2 - High
4. PO4 - From the bacterial decomposition.

B. Geochemistry

Mg, Sr, Ba, Mn trace quantities.

IV. FORMATION / REEF BUILDING

A. Sexual reproduction

B. Sperms & ova released.

C. Planula larva

D. Polyp forms.

E. Adult asexual.

F. Budding into daughter polyps.

V. NUTRITION, CACIFICATION AND GROWTH

1. Feed on zooplankton.
2. Photosynthates produced by zooxanthellae are used by the corals.
3. Formation of caco3 by zooxanthellae in gastrodermics-theroy not accepted.

VI. REEF FORMATION - DISTRIBUTION &LIMITING FACTORS

1. Temperature - 23-25 c - greatest growths.
2. Light - essential for zooxanthellae - 20-30 m.
3. Salinity-low salinity, sedimentation. Freshwater-reduction of corals
4. Wave - strong wave action - thrive

VII. ZONATION

Atoll - lagoon - windward Reef - Vigorous coral growth - seaward Reef - Reefflat - lagoon, leeward Reef - narrow

VIII. DARWIN'S SUBSIDENCE THEORY

A. Atoll Takes Shape Former Land.
B. Coral Reefs in Areas of Sinking of Land
C. Darwin (1831)

IX. NUTRITION

A. Zooxanthellae - Hermatypia Corals.
B. Zooplankton - Also Source of Nourishment.

X. PRODUCTIVITY

A. Primary Producers of Reef
   1. Zooxanthellae 0.9 - 2.48 X 10 6 Cals/cm2 Total - 0.9 gcm-2 d-1.
B. Net Productivity
   1. Indian Reefs: 2.4 - 9.1 g cm-2 d-1

XI. INDIAN CORAL REEFS

A. Lakshadweep, Andaman archipelago, Tuticorin, Mandapam.
B. Productivity - 2.4 - 9.1 gcm-2 d-1
   Mannar - 7.3 gcm-2 d-1.
   Lakshadweep - 9.1 gcm-2 d-1.
C. Resources: foodfishes, demeseral, molluscan reserves.

D. Constraints on sustainability

   1. Oil Pollution 2. Mining 3. Building 4. Dredging

E. Management

   1. Declaring areas as Marine Sanctuary - Gulf of Kutch
   2. National Park - Gulf of Mannar.

XII. FUTURE

A. Tourism - Corals Shouldn't be Touched or Picked.

B. Exploitation of Coral Reserves to End.

XIII. World Distribution of Corals and Current Status

A. Refer Global Biodiversity Pp. 304-321.

"What we are doing to the forests of the world is but a mirror reflection of what we are doing to ourselves and to one another."

Chris Maser

7. SEABEDS

I. INTRODUCTION

The mysteries of the deep sea floor were opened to man by an invention brought into use around world war I. The greatest part the sea floor is below the euphotic zone where the light intensity is too attenuated to support photosynthesis. The organisms that live there are therefore forced to rely on a supply of food from above sinking through the water column and settling on the interface between water and sediments.

II. HISTORICAL FEATURES

The systematic exploration of the deep sea began with the voyage of the HMS challenger 1872-1876. In 1948 the Swedish deep sea Expedition in the Atlantic developed new techniques for trawling and the winch used by later expeditions.

III. PHYSIOLOGICAL FEATURES

Sea has an average depth of about 4000 m and provide living apace for communities of animals and plants. Sea is classified vertically. Up to 100 meter – Photozone; 0 to 200 - epipelagic zone; 200 to 4000 bathypelagic zone in this 200 to 100 meropelagic zone below 4000 m to 6000 is a byssopelagic zone

A. Type of Benthic Plants and Animals

There are various kinds of plants attached to the sea bed

1. Laminarids
2. Rock weeds Fucales
3. Sea Grasses
4. Marsh Grasses

B. Animals

1. Organisms that live within the bottom deposits eg.
   Polychaete worms, Burrowing crustacean clams.
2. Epifauna, those that live on or above the sea floor eg. Scallops, starfish, sea urchins, and mussels.
   (a) Sea fan [umbellula]
   (b) Sea cucumber [elpidis glacialis]
   (c) Head, fore part and the trunk of Pogonophoran Birsteinia witjasi
   (d) Isopod crustacean (macrostylus hadalis)
   (e) Bathypteriod fish (bemthosaurus)

C. Attached

Porifera, coelenterate, certin hydroids, sea fans, black corals, sea anemones, madrepone corals, crastacea, Echinodermata, Notochordata.

1. **Benthic crawlers and swimmers:** This group comprises the freely moving animals, Annelida, Gephyrea, Crustacea, Pychnogonida, Mollusea, one group of cartilaginous fishes Holocephali 8600 to 10,000 m the mainly anemones, echiuriod and polychaete worms, bivalves, isopod and amphipod crustaceans, sea cucumbers and Pogonophora.
2. **Micro organisms:** Bacteria and possibly diatoms live on the sea floor with the hydrostatic pressures up to 1000 atm.

IV. THE DEEP SEA ECOSYSTEM

The main regions of deep sea ecosystem lie under the warm ocean. They may be divided by depth into mesopelagic (200 to 1000m) bathypelagic (>1000m) benthopelagic near the deep sea floor.

A. Coral Reef Ecosystem

Coral reef grow best where the mean annual water temperature is between 23°c to 25°c

B. Coastal Upwelling Ecosystem

Up-wellings are most active. There is a great blooming of the phytoplankton and fishes

Shelf - Sea ecosystem: Apart from coral reef and coastal upwelling the most productive marine ecosystems are in sea over the continental shelves of temperate region.

V. RESOURCES FROM THE DEEP SEA & SEA BEDS

A. **Marine Mining:** The process of recovering minerals from sea water and from seabed and under sea floor. e.g. red clay, calcareous ooze, siliceous ooze, metaliferous ooze.

B. **Food:** World fisheries expanded steadily from 1945 to 1970.

C. **Energy:** The potential for energy from the sea's motion and processes.

D. **Marine sediments:** The accumulation of minerals and organic remains on the sea floor.

E. **Sediments of Continental Margins:** These include the deposits of the sediments of the continental shelf.

F. Deep Sea Sediments: Sediments covering the floor of the deep sea were first systematically described and classified during the late 19th century by Murray and Renard 1884-1891.

1. Benthic Sediments: Biogenic sediments formed from the skeletal remains of marine organisms.
2. Non biogenic sediments: They are silicate materials.
3. Studies of deep sea sediments are a relatively recent phenomenon

G. Deep Sea Current: These currents are sluggish with average speeds only (about 100 ft/hr) and generates clouds of very fine sediment.

VI. POLLUTION

Ocean floor dumping: Since the dumping of munitions and poisonous gases around world war II, disposal of toxic and radioactive wastes on the ocean floor increased.

VII. MARINE LAW

There is probably no topic that is more complex than international marine law prior to 1958.

> *"Oh Beautiful for smoggy skies, insecticided grain,*
> *For strip-mined mountain's majesty above the asphalt plain.*
> *America, America, man sheds his waste on thee,*
> *And hides the pines with billboard signs, from sea to oily sea."*
>
> **George Carlin**

8. RIVERS

I. INTRODUCTION

A. CRADLES OF CIVILIZATION

B. DEFINED AS A FLOWING WATER BODY IN A CHANNEL WITH DEFINED BANKS

II. HISTORY

Development of civilizations resulted in development of irrigation systems, agricultural systems, trade and commerce.

1. Memphis & Thebes on Nile
2. Babylon on Euphrates & Tigris
3. Mohenjo-Daro & Harappa on Indus

III. GEOLOGY & CLASIFICATION

1. One of the earliest geomorphological phenomenon
2. Water in Liquid state produced during transition from Archeozoic to proterozoic era
3. Genesis of a river involve both tectonic processes (endogenous) and climatic processes (exogenous).

A. Direction of Flow (Slope)

1. Atlantic Ocean
2. Pacific Ocean
3. Indian Ocean
4. Arctic Ocean

   This comprises the peripheral or centrifugal drainage system.
5. Interior barriers - Centipetal flow.

B. Periodicity

1. Perennial or permanent rivers Humid climate regions.

   Most rivers are of this category
2. Periodic Rivers

   Arid climates where evaporation exceeds precipitation
3. Episodic Rivers

   Irregular stream flow - run off channels of arid regions

C. Course

1. Autochtonous (indigenous or native)

   Entire course runs through regions of relatively uniform climatic conditions.

2. Allochtonous (non-indigenous or exotic origin). Origin in humid or polar regions flow into dry area.

D. Length of Channel & Drainage Area

		Length	*Drainage Area*
1.	Minor river (small)	100-200km	1000-10,000
2.	Minor river (large)	200-500km	10,000-100,000
3.	Major river (small)	500-2,500km	100,000-1 million
4.	Major river (large)	>2,500km	>1 million km

IV. ECOLOGY

1. Origin from springs, glacier lakes.
2. Highest point in course is the origin
3. Importance of the water cycle.
4. Catchment area region from where water of the river is obtained
5. Watershed area demarcation area between catchment and drainage area
6. Greater the discharge greater the amount of suspended material
7. Effect of temperature on salinity and solubility of nutrients
8. Seasonal and daily variations in discharge effect biological and physical aspects.

V. RESOURCEFULNESS

A. Fishing
B. Hydro-electric power
C. Irrigation
D. Urban activities
E. Industrial activities
F. Recreation

The socio-economic development is closely related to the ability to manage water resources so as to sufficiently and sustainably provide for the above.

VI. ECONOMICS AND POLITICS

1. Boundaries of nations
2. Activities of commerce and trade
3. Governmental control over allocation of water rights
4. Ground water usage
5. Industrialisation and water consumption
6. Oldest existing written laws to distinguish between public and private rivers is the systematic compilation ordered by emperor Justinian (528) - *corpus juris civilis*

VII. SCIENCE & TECHNOLOGY

1. Hydro-electric power-dams, reservoirs, turbines etc, power industry development.
2. Navigation and shipping industries.
3. Fisheries and aquaculture.
4. Tourism and sports

> *"To waste, to destroy our natural resources, to skin and exhaust the land instead of using it so as to increase its usefulness, will result in undermining in the days of our children the very prosperity which we ought by right to hand down to them amplified and developed."*
>
> **Theodore Roosevelt**

9. LAKES

I. INTRODUCTION

Any relatively large body of slow moving or standing water that occupies an inland basin. Lakes occur throughout the world but are more abundant in high latitudes and mountain regions, particularly those that have been recently glaciated. Many lakes are also found in lowlands near the sea.

II. ORIGIN OF LAKES

1. Geological changes
2. Geographical changes
3. Volcanic activity
4. Submergence of geological history of a region
5. Natural presence of lakes depending upon the water tables, rainfall and mineral resources of the place.
6. Type of glaciers present.

III. GEOGRAPHICAL DISTRIBUTION

Common in places subjected to geographical changes recently

A. Lakes Around Glaciated Regions of N. Europe, Canada, Northern United States.

B. Recent Upliftment From The Sea - Florida.

C. Recent Volcanic Activity - Western Canada

IV. WORLD'S LARGEST LAKES

A. Caspian Sea (USSR / Iran) - Brackish Water

B. Lake Superior(USA / Canada)

C. Lake Victoria (E. Africa)

D. Aral Sea (USSR) – Brackish

E. Lake Huron (USA / Canada)

F. Lake Michigan (USA)

G. Lake Tanganyika (E. Africa)

H. Lake Baikal (USSR)

I. Great Bearl (Canada)

J. Lake Malawi (East Africa).

K. Great Slave (Canada)

L. Lake Erie (USA / Canada)

M. Lake Winnipeg (Canada)

N. Lake Ontario (USA/ Canada)

O. Lake Ladoga (USSR)

P. Lake Balshas (USSR)

Q. Lake Chad (Central Africa)

R. Lake Tilicaca (South America)

S. Lake Yre (Australia)

V. CLASSIFICATION

A. OLIGOTROPHIC- EUTROPHIC SERIES

1. Depends upon nutrient richness. typical oligotrophic lakes are deep, have low primary productivity.
2. Eutrophic lakes - rich nutrient content, low dissolved oxygen, shallow, great productivity eg lake Mendota and Linsehy Pond.

B. SPECIAL LAKES

1. Dystrophic lakes - brown water, humic and bog lakes - high concentration of humic acid, bog lakes have peat filled margins.
2. Deep, ancient lakes with endemic fauna - deepest lake in the world formed by tectonic movements - Lake Baikal in Russia includes 98% of 36 species of food are endemic.
3. Desert-salt lakes - In arid climates where evaporation exceeds precipitation. eg, great salt lake, Utah.
4. Desert alkali lake: Occurs in igneous drainages in arid climates with high pH and concentration of carbonates. eg. pyramid lake of Nevada.
5. Volcanic lakes: Acid or alkaline lakes associated with active volcanic region. Extreme chemical condition restrict biota eg. some Japanese & Philippine lakes
6. Chemically stratified, neromictic - permanently stratified by the intrusion of saline water creating a permanent density difference between surface and deeper water. Free oxygen and aerobic organisms are absent in bottom waters eg. Soda lake in Nevada.
7. Polar Lakes: Surface temperature remains below 4c or rise above it for only a brief period during summer. Plankton population grow very rapidly during summer.

C. IMPOUNDMENTS

Artificial lakes are characterised by fluctuating water levels and high production of benthos.

VI. ZONATION

Depending on structure of the lake basin (i) Littoral zone - extends from shore to a depth where the light is barely sufficient for rooted plants to grow. (ii) Photic zone - extends from the lake surface down to when light is about 1% of that at surface.

VII. TERMINOLOGY- PHYSICAL STRUCTURES

A. **Pelagic zone** - The area beyond the influences of this shore or bottom. Fauna adapts for swimming, smpemion & floatation. Water has a characteristic vertical thermal statification - 3 zones

1. Epilimnion 2. Thermocline 3. hypolimnion.

VIII. TERMINOLOGY - CHEMICAL STRUCTURE

Distribution of chemicals through lake water provide major element of lake structure (a) chemocline - depth at which rapid changes in a substratum occurs.

Characteristic Features: The littoral zone of the body of a shallow lake provide a good habitat for bottom dwelling animals whose foraging, burrowing and excretion help in recycling nutrients from the bottom.

IX. TERMINOLOGY - BIOLOGICAL STRUCTURE

A. **PLANKTONS:-** floating or swimming organisms. Two types a) zoo Plankton and phytoplankton. zooplankton include flagellates, ciliates, rotifers, crustacea, arthropods, worms, mollusca, annelids, nematodes, excreta of amphibians, reptiles, birds and mammals. Phytoplankton include algae, diatoms, dinoflagellates, euglenoids and fungi.

B. **NELETON** - Organisms inhabiting pelagic zone

C. **NEETONS** - inhabit surface of water.

D. **BEATHOR** - Organisms present at the bottom of the lake.

X. HUMAN IMPACTS

1. Eutrophication
2. Increase in number of bacteria in a river
3. Over exploitation of zooplankton.
4. Thermal pollution
5. Increase in the microbial content through industry
6. Growth of weeds
7. Commercialization of lakes led is the disturbance of lake ecosystem.

XI. RESOURCEFULNESS

A. Fishery

B. Hydro electric projects

C. Aesthetic appeal – tourism

D. Aqua culture

XI. Policies

Government trying to curb water pollution by controlling the amount of toxic effluents flowing into lakes and iritiate conservation programmes.

10. ISLANDS

I. INTRODUCTION

Islands smaller than a continent or an ocean, a visibly discrete object that can be labeled with a name and its resident populations. In the science of bio-geography, the island is the first unit that the mind can pick out and begin to comprehend. It has complexity of continents and oceans. Islands offer an additional advantage in being more numerous than continents. And variation is shape, size, degree of isolation and ecology. Islands provide the necessary replications in natural experiments. E.g., Galapagos islands.

II. HISTORY

The orderly relation between island area and species diversity has lead to measure the contributing factors. e.g., Carribean islands. And some islands show the effect of the increase in the open water season and the importance of wave action.

III. TAXONOMY

Many types of islands exist in the world. Some important ones:

Melanesia	Florida
Fiji	Mallaccas
Oceania	New caledonia
New Guinea	Soloman islands

Ice effected coastal islands

1. North west-Queen elizabeth islands
2. Eastern malville islands
3. East central arctic islands
4. South-east beffin islands
5. Northern canada etc.

IV. CHARACTERISTICS

1. Numerous river deltas of all sizes protrude offshore.
2. It has lateral channel deflections.
3. Absence of well developed wave-built of erosional features along shore, eg. Sand bars.
4. Terrestrial built features persist across modern beach slope. eg, sand drifts & earth flow levels
5. Vegetation extends to high tide line.

6. Large mounds of sediments offshore and concentric gravel berms built around small inter Channel Islands by sea ice.

V. BIOSPHERE

Islands have many types of flora and fauna similar to the nearby terrestrial country. e.g., Andaman & Nicobar Islands

1. Giant ever green forests.
2. Andaman tropical evergreen forests.
3. Southern hill top tropical forests.
4. Andaman semi - evergreen forests.
5. Andaman moist deciduous forests.
6. Littoral forests.
7. Mangrove forests etc.

VI. FLORA

In addition to endemic flora, other, trees, shrubs, and herbs also are found in some places of islands.

VII. FAUNA

In addition to endemic fauna, other land animals are also found in some places of islands.

VIII. DATA

1. Ice-dominated islands
2. Wave environment islands
3. Reduction and fragmentation of island
4. Equilibrium model of biota of a single island
5. Breeding birds of islands

11. AVIAN TOXICOLOGY

I. INTRODUCTION

A. Avian toxicology is the study of the toxicity of chemicals and other anthropogenic materials on bird fauna.

B. Toxic substances may be present in wetlands in small doses, may not be directly toxic and becomes toxic to birds by processes of bioconcentration, bio-accumulation & biomagnification etc.

Many wetland birds like heron, oyster, catches, sand pipes, and ducks are easily affected.

II. CLASSIFICATION OF TOXINS & SOURCES OF TOXINS

A. PLASTICS

2 types (1) user-plastics - fragments of plastic cups, toys, tornpieces of synthethic netting, etc (2) Plastic pellets - raw materials from which user-plastics are moulded.

B. OILS

2 types (1) Crude oil - released ethrough accidental oil tanker Wrecks, oil-well blowouts or small spillages. (2) Waste oil - realeased through washing & flushing of oil-tankers with sea-water on deposition of drilling mud.

C. PESTICIDES

Application on vegetation and land washed off with rain to enter wetlands. Also factory efftuents.

1. Insecticides eg, organochloines, organo-phosphate, etc.
2. Fungicides: carbamates, hitrogen compounds, hexachlor-benzenes, etc.
3. Herbicides eg phenolic acids, etc.
4. Fumigants eg methyl bromide etc.

D. HEAVY METALS

Mostly essential trace minerals but toxic when conentrations increase. Main toxic heavy metals are:

1. Mercury- effluents from electrolysis, electrical appratuses control instruments, amalgamations, pharmaceuticals, paper & pulp and other processes.
2. Lead- sources like mining & milling, refinary processes industries, exhaust of internal conbustion engines.
3. Cadmium - from industries producing fungicides, nuclear reactors, florescent lamps, photo & lithrography. nicklex cadmium batteries etc.

4. Arsenic- from insecticides, fungicides, herbicides, detergents
5. Copper- from mining chemical wastes, antifouling paints etc.
6. Other heavy metals- Zinc, Strontium, Aluminium, Titanium, Selenium, Chromium etc.

E. RADIOACTIVE SUBSTANCES

Levels greatly increased in the seas, released initially through pulses from nuclear explosion fall outs, now mainly by Reactor wastes, Radio-isotopes, and other nuclear - propelled uses.

III. ROUTES OF EXPOSURE & EFFECTS

Each pollutant has its own route of exposure & specific effect Bio concentration, biomagnification also take place.

A. PLASTICS

Birds could mistake floating plastic particles for zooplantion or fish eggs etc and consume them. The prey animals of birds could also have eaten them.

Plastic reduces the functional volume of the birds gizzard & leads to reduction in digestive capabilites.

B. OILS

Oils mat plumage of birds, make their flight impossible & lead to loss of bouyancy. Heat insulation ingestion causes gastro- intestinal problems, damage to liver & kidney besides general shock. Oil in the eyes cause irritation. In some cases blindness, amd affect embryos.

C. PESTICIDES

Essentially run off from fields & factories, reaches upto the food chain up to birds. Many of these accumulate in fatty tissues.

Pesticides mainly damage resources of birds.

Other effects: (1) Hormonal interactions mimicking hormones (2) Egg shell thinning (3) Reduced breeding success.

D. HEAVY METALS

Mostly cummulative cellular poisons, with a strong tendency to be deposited in bones. Mercury, lead, cadmium & arsenic are the most dangerous of the heavy metals.

All these severely affect various vital systems, wherever they are present. They also biomagnify.

E. RADIOACTIVITY

Damage to reproductive & somatic cells leading to chromosomal aberration etc.

IV. CONSEQUENCES: ECOLOGICAL & ECONOMICAL

Danger is greater in land locked wetlands

1. Plastics - harmful to a variety of animals like commercial fishes. Bird mortality leads predation in this food chain.
2. Oils - danger is greatest for breeding population Torrey Canyon disaster(1967) shattered the breeding of auks; guano produce affected greatly;
3. Pesticides - egg shell thinning causes decline in population.
4. Heavy metals - migratory bird could carry there toxic metals to other breeding or nesting sites in wetlands.
5. Radioactivity - decreases the nesting of birds.

> *"Let every individual and institution now think and act as a responsible trustee of Earth, seeking choices in ecology, economics and ethics that will provide a sustainable future, eliminate pollution, poverty and violence, awaken the wonder of life and foster peaceful progress in the human adventure."*
>
> **John McConnell**

12. MANGROVE ECOTOXICOLOGY

I. INTRODUCTION

1. Mangroves are basically tropical and are resplacements to salt marshes which are temperate.
2. Zonation of mangals

   (a) Proximal zone (b) Middle zone

   (c) Distal zone (d) Cihoral zone.
3. Primary productivity: Mangroves are highly productive.
4. Flora and fauna of mangroves; Nutrient uptake by plants: Uptake of Mg, fe and Mn, salt tolerance.

II. MINERALS AND METALS IN MANGROVES

Inputs and outputs: Main inputs are through the river and tidal action. Inputs: Nutrients and polluants. Pollutants mainly by river. Industrial effflents, domestic wastes and agricultural run off are the important inputs.

III. ECOTOXICOLOGY

Factors influencing toxicity: Exposure, organism and chemicals. Concentration response relationships, LD 50, Theshold units.

IV. TOXICITIES OF VARIOUS METALS AND COMPOUNDS

Trace metals toxicities of Mn, Fe, Zn, Mg, Pb, Cu, Cd, etc; General effects of specific metals: Zinc, Copper, Lead, Mercry, Ammonia, Nitrite, Nitrate.

V. PESTICIDE TOXICITY

Inputs and effects (Acute and chronic), Physical and chemical characteristics of pesticidies; stability and persistence; Transport and fate of pesticides in aquatic environments; Absorption; metabolism and elimination of pesticides in fish.

VI. OIL POLLUTION: Effects of PAH

VII. ECOPHYSIOLOGICAL STUDIES ON COASTAL ECOSYSTEMS

13. WET COASTAL ECOSYSTEMS

I. INTRODUCTION

Coastlines of the World over 44,00,00 kms in length represent one of the most dynamic of natural environs and one of the most important contexts in which human activity and geomorphological processes interact. All coastal zones contain at least 2 obvious habitats.

A. **MARITIME ZONE-** Home for many terrestrial animals and pets

B. **SEA-**as another habitat.

C. **INTERTIDAL ZONE**

1. **Classification of Coasts**

   (a) Primary coasts.

   - land erosion coasts
   - Land deposition coasts
   - Coasts shaped by volcanic activity

   (b) Secondary Coasts

   - Barrier coasts
   - Mud flats
   - Coral Reef coasts
   - Mangrove coasts.

2. **Principal Features of Coasts**

   Coastal environs are affected by five main types of sea-water movement namely waves, tides, currents and aerial transport of spray. An outline of the coast is primarily determined by its geological composition and structure and by inshore topography.

3. **Basic Types of Coasts Formed**

   (a) Embayed (b) Plain coasts (c) New coasts

4. **Essential Features**

   (a) Protected coastlines (b) Shallow shores

   (c) Currents (d) Tidal Range & salt water

   (e) Substrate formation

D. **GEOGRAPHICAL DISTRIBUTION**

Stable sand areas are colonised by mangroves and salt marshes are common in areas where sand is admixed with salt.

II. DIFFERENT TYPES OF COASTS

A. BRACKISH WATER ENVIRONS

Estuaries/brackish waters is defined as semi-enclosed coastal waters which retain a connection with the open sea.

There is a mixture of sea and fresh waters of terrestrial oxygen

1. **Classification**
   (a) Coastal plain estuaries
   (b) Semi enclosed Bays
   (c) Tectonic estuaries.
2. **Biota of Estuaries**

   Relatively few species have evolved the necessary adaptation required. Tolerating excess salinity is another factor. Three faunal groups recognised - Marine, freshwater and brackish. Freshwater sp. tolerate salinities more than 5%, and occur at the head of the estuary.
3. **Adaptations of Estuarine organisms**
4. **Productivity and food webs** - can be exceedingly productive comparable to TRF's. contribution by phytoplanktons (for nutrients), benthic algae & rooted plants in primary production is large.
5. **Hypersaline environment**
   (a) Lagoons (b) Tide pools

B. CORAL REEFS

60% occur in the Indian Ocean, 14% in the Caribbean, 13% in the South Pacific and 12% in the N. Pacific. 'Reefs' refers to population of strong corals which continues growth on products of its own making.

1. Classification
   (a) Fringing Reefs (b) Barrier Reefs (c) Atolls
   (d) Patin Reefs (e) Bank Reefs
2. Physical disturbances
   (a) Destruction from tropical storms
   (b) Anthropogenic disturbances such as overharvest & mining.

C. SALT MARSHES

Salt marshes are semi natural halophytic grasslands on the alluvial sediments.

1. **Most prominent flora**
   (a) Salicornia Spp. (b) Spartina Spp.
2. **Most prominent Fauna**
   (a) Fiddler crabs (b) Mud skippers

(c) Geese & duck sp. rats, moles which have a controlling effect on vegetation.

(d) Uca sp. excavate as much as 20% of the bank contributing to soil erosion.

3. Management of salt marshes

Land cultivation and mining activities have big effects on water and silt inflow into estuarine basins and hence on the life cycle of salt marshes.

4. Reclamation of salt marshes

(a) Reclaim the pollution affected areas.

(b) Restricting coastal sediments.

(c) Improved sedimentation process.

D. MANGROVES

Characteristic littoral plant communities of shelters, low lying tropical and sub-tropical coasts.

1. Adaptations

(a) Mangroves have laterally spreading cable roots.

PNEUMATOPHORES - are above ground roots and facilitate development on anoxic sediments.

(b) Viviparous in nature Eg. Brugiera etc.

2. Fauna

(a) Prawns (b) Fiddler crabs

(c) Ghost crabs (Dotella) (d) Mudskippers

(e) Molluscs / Echinoderms

III. IN-SHORE HARVEST AND EXPLOITATION

A. Coral Reef B. Crustacea C. Molluscs.

D. Commercial Fish, E. Seaweed etc. F. Plankton

IV. COASTAL MANAGEMENT

The potential resource use in the coastal areas is

A. PHYSICAL RESOURCES

1. Space
2. Power Generation

B. MINERAL RESOURCES

1. Lime-rich deposits
2. Gravel

C. EFFECTS OF POLLUTION

1. Pollutants can increase the natural biological intake leading to toxic levels.
2. Pesticide impact is magnified when received from fresh-water zones. Often 5-10 times greater concentration in estuaries than off shores.

D. NATURE RESERVES

1. Establishment of coastal Nature Reserves.
2. Necessary to determine composition and control mechanisms before establishing a nature reserve.
3. Criterion for establishing a marine/coastal reserve is the extent available
4. Ecology of Rocky Coasts
5. Ecology of Coastal Vegetation

> *"We find ourselves ethically destitute just when, for the first time, we are faced with ultimacy, the irreversible closing down of the earth's functioning in its major life systems. Our ethical traditions know how to deal with suicide, homicide and even genocide, but these traditions collapse entirely when confronted with biocide, the killing of the life systems of the earth, and geocide, the devastation of the earth itself."*
>
> **Father Thomas Berry**

14. IRRIGATION TANKS IN SEMI ARID REGIONS

1. **Introduction**
2. **Waterbodies of India**
3. **Perinnial concerns**
4. **State of the knowledge**
5. **Tamilnadu Scenario / Other States**
   (a) Background (b) Irrigation
   (c) Tanks (d) Perspectives
7. **Characterstics of Tanks -A Model**
   (a) Soil (b) Water
   (c) Flora (d) Fauna
   (e) Agriculture (f) Aquaculture
   (g) Villages (h) Peoples perceptions
8. Habitats
9. Biodiversity
10. Resourcefulness
11. Human Ecology
12. Conservation
13. Development
    (a) agriculture (b) aquaculture
    (c) sericulture (d) apiculture
    (e) social forestry
14. Imperatives
    (a) Government (b) NGOs
    (c) People (d) Acadamics
15. Perspectives
    (a) Socio ecology (b) Accounting and valuing
    (c) Diagnosis - Expert systems (d) Rapid Evaluation
    (e) Conservation & Development (f) National Tank Authority
    (g) Diagnosis - Taxonomy
16. Managerial Inputs

15. WETLANDS

I. INTRODUCTION

A. DEFINITIONS

1. Ramsar convention Definition: Areas of Marsh, Fen, peat land or water where natural or artificial, permanent or temporary with water that is static or flowing, fresh, brackish or salt, including areas of marine water the depth of which at low tide does not exceed six meter".
2. Macmillan Dictionary: "An area covered permanently, occasionally or periodically by fresh or salt water up to the depth of six meters".
3. Coward (1979): "Wetlands are transitional between terrestrial and aquatic systems were the water table is usually at or near the surface of on the land is covered by shallow water.

B. CONDITIONS FOR RECOGNISING A WATER BODY AS WETLAND

1. At least periodically the land supports hydrophytes
2. Substrate is predominantly un-drained soil.
3. Substrate is non-soil and saturated with water or covered by shallow water some time during growing season of each year

II. GLOBAL DISTRIBUTION OF WETLANDS

Different Data bases used for compiling and estimating.

A. REGIONAL EXTENT AND DISTRIBUTION

1. Europe and Mediterranean basin
2. North America
3. Latin America and Caribbean
4. African wetlands
5. Asia and middle east
6. Australia and oceania.

B. ASIAN WETLAND TYPES

22 types of wetlands recognised according to Directory of Asian wetlands Published by UNEP.

III. WETLAND HABITATS OF INDIA

A. MARSHES
B. CORAL REEFS
C. WETLAND SITES
D. RAMSAR SITES

IV. WETLAND LOSS: GROWING CONCERN

A. DATA: U.S.-54% of original wetland lost, (1,85,000 hectares) 87% of the wetland losses in U.S. Urban development claim 8% and other development 5%

B. INDIA: Main reasons /threats. Draining, waste dumps pollution

V. WETLAND TYPES

A. MARSHES

1. Main tidal marshes , Distribution, habitat peculiarity
2. Tidal fresh water marshes - main land Marshes in U.S eastern coasts
3. Fresh water marshes - Those dominated by grasses and sedges but are very different in origin and appearance. About 90% of wetlands U.S. are freshwater marshes.

   Cat tails (Typha), Reeds (Phragmites), Sedges (Carex) eg. Florida Everglades, 10,000 km2

B. SWAMPS

1. Still water area, margins and part of flood plains such as sloughs and Oxbows types - Herbaceous swamps & Mangrove swamps
2. Man made Wetlands :Importance

C. MIRES (PEAT LANDS)

1. Bogs: characteristics. 2. Fens :

D. FLOOD PLAINS: Definition and importance

1. Inland deltas 2. Coastal delta flood plain 3. Wetland forests

VI. VALUE OF WETLANDS

A. VALUE :

Economic	
Direct values	Indirect values
Other values	Recreational values

B. RECREATION VALUES AN EXAMPLE FROM U.S.

Travel cost approach and contingent valuation methods.

C. ECOLOGICAL VALUES OF WETLANDS

1. Improvement of water quality
2. Controlling of flow of nutrients
3. Wastewater treatments
4. Flood control: by reducing flood peaks
5. Storm protection and shoreline stablisation

6. Wetland biodiversity
7. Wetland species as bio indicators

VII. THREATS TO WETLANDS

A. ANTHROPOGENIC THREATS

1. Drainage for agriculture
2. Dredging and stream channelisation
3. Filling for degraded spoil
4. Construction of dykes, dams etc,
5. Discharge of Materials (Pollutants)
6. Mining of wetland soils for peat, coal, sand, gravel etc.

B. INDIRECT THREATS

1. Sediment diversion by dams deep channels
2. Hydrological alteration by canals spoil banks, roads and other structures
3. Subsidence due to extraction of ground water, oil, gas sulfur and other minerals

C. NATURAL THREATS

Subsidence, Drought, Hurricane, Storms, erosion, biotic factors

VIII. Conservation of Wetlands

(a) Conservation by declaring as protected areas

(b) Ramsar convention and conservation, aims, achievements

(c) Management of wetlands

16. COAST LINES

I. INTRODUCTION

1. Coastal Geomorphology
2. Ecology of Rocky Coasts
3. Inter tidal fauna and flora
4. Ecology of Coastal Vegetation
5. Mangroves and Estuaries
6. Seaweeds
7. Fisheries
8. Plankton Resources
9. Wet Coastal Ecosystems

A. COASTLINES

1. Mangroves
   - (a) Distribution: Global & regional
   - (b) Flora and Fauna
   - (c) Resourcefulness: Ornamental Wood and timber Medicines Thatching Consumption for intoxication
2. Other biota: Distribution, composition, exploitation & consequences
   1. Algae: classes, families, genera many
      - (a) Food (b) Medicine
      - (c) Chemicals (d) Others
   2. Angiosperms
      - (a) Seag rasses: 13 genera & 50 species global; 13 sp in India
      - (b) Food and shelter for fauna
      - (c) Packaging, compost, paper
      - (d) Prevention of erosion
   3. Vertebrates
      - (a) Food (b) Medicinal (c) Others
   4. Invertebrates
      - (a) Food (b) Medicinal (c) Others

B. SALT MARSHES

1. Distribution
2. Composition
3. Economic importance
4. Exploitation

II. WET COASTAL ECOSYSTEMS

A. INTRODUCTION

Coastlines of the World over 44,00,00 kms in length represent one of the most dynamic of natural environs and one of the most important contexts in which human activity and geomorphological processes interact. All coastal zones contain at least 2 obvious habitats.

- MARITIME ZONE - Home for many terrestrial animals and pets.
- SEA-as another habitat.
- INTERTIDAL ZONE

1. **Classification of coasts**

   (a) Primary Coasts:
   - land erosion coasts
   - Land deposition coasts
   - Coasts shaped by volcanic activity

   (b) Secondary Coasts:
   - Barrier coasts
   - Mud flats
   - Coral Reef coasts
   - Mangrove coasts

2. **Principal features of coasts**

   Coastal environs are affected by five main types of sea - water movement namely waves, tides, currents and aerial transport of spray. An outline of the coast is primarily determined by its geological composition and structure and by inshore topography.

3. **Basic types of Coasts formed**

   (a) Embayed (b) Plain coasts (c) New coasts

4. **Essential features**

   (a) Protected coastlines
   (b) Shallow shores
   (c) Currents
   (d) Tidal Range & salt water
   (e) Substrate formation

5. **Geographical distribution**

   Stable sand areas are colonised by mangroves and salt marshes are common in areas where sand is admixed with salt.

B. DIFFERENT TYPES OF COASTS

1. **Brackish water environs:** Estuaries / brackish waters is defined as semi-enclosed of coastal waters which retain a connection with the open sea. There is a mixture of sea and fresh waters of terrestrial oxygen.

(a) Classification: Coastal plain estuaries; Semi enclosed Bays; Tectonic estuaries

(b) Biota of Estuaries: Stressful environments and is perhaps not surprising that relatively few species have evolved the necessary adaptation required. Tolerating excess salinity is another factor. Three faunal groups recognised - Marine, freshwater and brackish water sp. Freshwater sp. tolerate salinities more than 5%, and occur at the head of the estuary.

(c) Adaptations of Estuarine organisms.

(d) Productivity & food webs: Can be exceedingly productive comparable to TRF's. Contribution by phytoplanktons (for nutrients), benthic algae & rooted plants in primary production is large.

(e) Hypersaline environment: a. Lagoons b. Tide pools

2. Coral reefs

60% occur in the Indian Ocean, 14% in the caribbean, 13% in the South Pacific and 12% in the N. Pacific. 'Reefs' refers to population of strong corals which coatenues growth on products of its own making

(a) Classification: (a) Fringing Reefs (b) Barrier Reefs (c) Atolls (d) Patin Reefs (e) Bank Reefs

(b) Physical Disturbances:

1. Destruction from tropical storms
2. Anthropogenic disturbances such as overharvest & mining.
3. Salt marshes: Salt marshes are semi natural halophytic grasslands on the alluvial sediments breeding saline water bodies

   (a) Most prominent flora: (a) Salicornia Spp. (b) Spartina Spp.

   (b) Most prominent Fauna :

   1. Fiddler crabs (b) Mud skippers
   2. Geese & duck sp. rats, moles which have a controlling effect on vegetation.
   3. Uca sp. excavate as much as 20% of the bank contributing to soil erosion.

(c) **Management :** Land cultivation and mining activities have big effects on water and silt inflow into estuarine basins and hence on the life cycle of salt marshes

(d) **Reclamation :** Reclaim the pollution affected areas; Restricting coastal sediments; Improved sedimentation process

4. **Mangroves:** Characteristic littoral plant communities of shelters, low lying tropical and sub-tropical coasts.

   (a) **Adaptations:** laterally spreading cable roots; PNEUMATOPHORES - are above ground roots and facilitate development on anoxic sediments; Viviparous in nature Eg. Brugiera etc.

   (b) **Fauna:** (a) Prawns (b) Fidder crabs (c) Mudshippers. (d) Ghost crabs (Dotella) (e) Molluscs / Echinoderms

C. INSHORE HARVEST AND EXPLOITATION

1. Coral Reef 2. Crustacea 3. Molluscs
4. Commercial Fish, Seaweed

D. COASTAL MANAGEMENT: The potential resources in the coastal areas

1. Physical resources: (a) Space b. Power Generation
2. Mineral resources: (a) Lime-rich deposits. b. Gravel.
3. Effects of pollution
   (a) Pollutants can increase the natural biological intake leading to toxic levels.
   (b) Pesticides impact is magnified when received from fresh water zones. Often 5-10 times greater concentration in estuaries than offshores.

E. EFFECTS OF POLLUTION

1. Establishment of coastal Nature Reserves.
2. Necessary to determine composition and control machanisms before establishng a nature reserve.
3. Criterron for establishing a marine/coastal reserve is the extent available

17. EAST COAST OF TAMILNADU

A. PLACES OF INTEREST

1. Markanam
2. Cuddalore
3. Tirumalaivasal
4. Poompuhar
5. Tanquebar
6. Karaikal
7. Velankanni
8. Kodikkarai
9. Vedaranyam
10. Muthupet
11. Manora
12. Tondi
13. Kilakkarai
14. Narippayur
15. Tuticorin
16. Tiruchendur
17. Manappadu
18. Ovari
19. Koodangulam
20. Kanyakumari

B. ECOSYSTEMS

1. Yedayanthittu
2. Chunnambar
3. Pichavaram Mangroves
4. Muthupet Mangroves
5. Athirampattinam - Ramnad
6. Tuticorin Mangroves
7. Tamraparni
8. Koodangulam
9. Sand dunes

C. FEATURES

1. Water bodies - Flowing
2. Water bodies - Nonflowing
3. Aquaculture
4. Salt pans
5. Mangroves
6. Harbours
7. Agriculture
8. Fisheries
9. Potable water
10. Industries
11. Coastal check posts
12. Wetlands
13. Land Marks
14. Wastelands
15. Sand dunes
16. Beaches
17. Beach sands
18. Social forestry
19. Boat Making / Repairs
20. Brick works

D. ASPECTS OF STUDY

1. Religious
2. Historical
3. Ecological
4. Resources
5. Livelihoods
6. Geography
7. Tourisism
8. Archeological

9. Fisheries
10. Agriculture
11. Aquaculture
12. Social Forestry
13. Climate

E. AREAS FOR

1. Research
2. Conservation
3. Development

> *"Considering the whole span of earthly time... Only within the moment of time represented by the present century has one species – man – acquired significant power to alter the nature of his world."*
>
> **Rachel Carson**

5

Bioenergy

1. BIOENERGY - I NTRODUCTION
2. BIOENERGETICS
3. DIRECT COMBUSTION
4. THERMAL CONVERSION
5. CHEMICAL EXTRACTION
6. ANAEROBIC DIGESTION
7. FORESTS OF INDIA
8. BIOTECHNOLOGY and BIOMASS
9. ENERGY FROM ANIMALS AND HUMANS
10. BIOENERGY - FUTUROLOGY
11. ENERGY - FUTUROLOGY

Syllabus

1. Introduction to energy and biological resources
   Principles of energy from plants, animals and others
   Bioenergetics
   Photosynthesis and secondary plant products
2. Plants as resources for energy.
   Direct combustion: carbohydrates
   Chemical extraction: secondary plant products
   Alcohol production: carbohydrates
   Thermal conversion: chemical technology
   Anaerobic digestion: converting into microbial physiology
3. Animals as resources for energy
   Human as Source of Energy
4. Social forestry, wastelands, Forests, Energy Plantations, Fuel wood
5. Biotechnology in breeding of biomass
6. Sustainable Management of Bioenergy

References

1. Calvin, M,1980. Renewable Energy Resources. Petroleum plantations and synthetic chloroplasts in) Renewable Energy prospects (Eds: Bach W, Manshared W, Mathews WH, Brown H) Pergamon
2. Hall DO, 1982. Solar energy through Biology - Fuels from Biomass, Experientia 38, 3-10.
3. Kishimoto, S, 1982. Wood fuels in Japan(in) Energy from Forest biomass(Ed: Smith (WR) Academic Press.
4. Palz, W, Chartier P (Eds) 1980. Energy from biogass in Europe. Applied science publishers., London.
5. Slesser, M, Lewis C, 1979. Biological Energy Resources, John Wiley
6. Sporn.1977. Energy in an age of limited availability. Pergamon press, Toole, J.O. 1977. Energy and social change. The M.I.T press.

1. ENERGY RESOURCES

I. INTRODUCTION

A. **Taxonomy:** Renewable & Non-renewable Direct & Indirect, etc.

B. **Anthropology:** Muscle and wood, Wind and wave, Sun and fire

C. **Nature:** Kinetic & potential, Production, Conversion, transport & use

II. TAXONOMY

A.	Solar	: Inexhaustible, source of all resources
B.	Phytomass	: Product of solar energy conversion
C.	Muscular	: Human and animal. Product of secondary/ tertiary consuming solar energy
D.	Biogas	: Combustion of animal excrement
E.	Wind	: Transport of particles and even human loads
F.	Tidal	: Transport of particles through force of movement
G.	Geothermal	: Site specificity
H.	Coal	: Direct combustion and conversion- Industrial revolution & Steam engine Fossil source
I.	Fossil oils	: A very major hydrocarbon energy source. Different grades useful for different purposes - Fossil source
J.	Natural gas	: Fossil source related to fossil oils
K.	Hydroelectric	: Generated from the force of falling waters. Transportation Technology.
L.	Nuclear	: Most recent. Power of the atom the ultimate part of matter fission and fusion

III. ANTHROPOLOGY

A. Usage of Muscle power
B. Discovery of fire
C. Use of Phytomass
D. Knowledge of wind and wave
E. Usage of wind and wave

IV. RESOURCEFULNESS

A. Solar

1. Cooking, heating
2. Solar ponds
3. Photovoltaics

B. Phytomass

1. Solar energy conversion into chemical form by plants
2. Primary producers on which all else depends

3. Efficiencies of energy conversion different
4. Direct combustion
5. Conversions to alcohol, hydrocarbons
6. Conversions to gasification
7. Energy contents are variable in various plants and parts

C. Biogas (Gobar gas)

1. Methane generation from animal dung
2. Cattle dung slung as a fertilizer
3. Part of animal husbandry and large agricultural holdings
4. Methane enhancement by plant adjuncts

D. Muscular

(a) Human muscular energy as a work force earning wages - Head loaders, Cart pullers, Vehicle pedlars

(b) Animal energy for cart pulling, water pulling, load carriers - Donkey, Camel, Cattle, Horse, Mule, etc.

E. Wind

1. Site specific - "Wind mills", "Water pullies"
2. Seasonal - "trade winds"
3. Converted to do mechanical work or electricity
4. Canada, U.S.A., India (Gujarat, TN)
5. Limited local needs

F. Tidal

1. Site specific
2. Converted to mechanical work or electricity
3. Coastal European countries
4. Limited local needs.

G. Geothermal

1. Only some places in the world
2. Heat of the interior earth converted to electricity

H. Coal

1. Fossilised and carbonised plant material
2. Coal mines in many places of the world
3. Associated with steam engines & industrial revolution
4. Thermal Power and electricity
5. Conversions to liquid and gaseous fuels
6. Non renewable and exhaustible

7. Pollutants many of which carcinogens
8. Exhausting - stocks last a century more

I. Fossil Oil

1. Most efficient of all - Hydrocarbons
2. Refinement yields different grades including gas-for different purposes
3. Mining is done on land, shorelines, offshore, seabed
4. Fast exhausting, another 200 years only
5. 2/3 resources in Middle East and North Africa
6. Highly versatile energy source

J. Natural Gas

1. Bye-product of fossil oil
2. Some grounds have only gas
3. Limited in use due to its physical state
4. Offshore & seabed
5. Siberian & Alaskan pipelines
6. HBJ pipeline in India
7. May lost for 60 years.

K. Hydroelectric

1. Falling waters used to generate electricity
2. Land gradient and rivers
3. All over the world where rivers flow
4. Rainfall and glacier based
5. One of the best-Nature-Science-Technology & Uses Never ending as long as climate & ecosystems are healthy

L. Nuclear

1. Nuclear energy discovered over 50 years ago
2. One of the most peaceful uses of energy
3. Never ending source
4. High technology 5. Fusion energy yet to be accomplished

V. EMPIRICAL KNOWLEDGE

Plant products, animal use, direct combustion, usage of wind and wave, sun and fire were all intuitive developments prior to industrial revolution

VI. SCIENCE & TECHNOLOGY

1. Mostly in Conversions and Usages

2. Phytomass plants, fast growing, high calorific values, conversion technology conversion
3. Biogas methanogenic systems,
4. Solar energy conversions and usage = 20 years
5. Wind, wave, geothermal - conversion systems = 20 years
6. Fossil energy sources - Conversion, transport, usage, conservation, efficiencies, and exploration - 50 years.
7. Hydroelectric: Most stabilized even several decades ago !
8. Nuclear - enormous science & technology inputs prior to production, high predictability and controls

VII. ECONOMICS

1. Inputs vs outputs
2. Necessity for development of other sources
3. Phytomass vs poverty
4. Zero costing to commodification and pricing
5. Absence of sources to resource generation
6. Productivity of a polity depends upon energy availability

VIII. POLITICS

1. People vs ruling systems vs ruling classes
2. Source to Resource: Have-nots' generation, Inequalities
3. Politics of the grids connected to industrialisation, employment, migrations
4. Science & Technology vs National Politics
5. International haves of Energy vs Have-nots
6. Energy Rich vs Development rich countries
7. Exploration, Conversion, transport, Usage politics
8. Oil shocks I (73-74), II (79-80), III (90-91)

IX. CONSEQUENCES

X. MANAGEMENT

1. Alternatives
2. Reduced consumption
3. Efficiency
4. Improved chulahs, Kerosene lamps, Stoves,
5. Solar heaters, cooking, ponds, pumps & Photovoltaics
6. Sewage/Garbage based systems.

2. BIOENERGETICS

I. INTRODUCTION

A. First Law of thermodynamics

$E = Q + W$ E = Total Internal Energy

Q = Heat given out by a system W = Work done by the system.

B. Second Law of thermodynamics

- Energy always transforms from nonrandom form to random forms
- Potential energy by bomb calorimeter.

C. Energy transformation

- Solar Energy Assimilation = Chemical energy of growth + Heat energy of respiration.
- Energy assimilation in carnivorous more than that in herbivores

D. Animal energetics

- At 3 levels

1. Organism level 2. Cellular level 3. Molecular level

- Animal energetics at organism level

$C = P + R + F + U$ $R = C - (P + F + U)$

C = Food consumed P = Productivity or growth

F = Faeces U = Urinary products

II. PHOTOSYNTHESIS

A. Definition

Photosynthesis is the process by which living organisms convert light energy into chemical energy of organic resources.

- Finally due to photo 4 recp. Light energy — heat energy

B. Light

Photosynthetically active radiation is 400 - 680 n.m.

- Light energy usually measured as mol. quantum

C. Global Photosynthesis

Co2 turnover = 3*10 power 12 tons/yr by prs.

PS. produces 5*10 power 11 tons organic matter/yr,

D. Light Absorption & Photosynthesis

10 mol. released per 8-1 photons absorbed

2400 cul. mol. are excited to produce 10 base 2 mol.

To reduce 1 Co2 we need 460 KJ Mol power -1 of quantum energy

E. Electron transport

Due to cyclic or non-cyclic light energy trapped into ATP, NADPH

F. Chemistry of photosynthesis: Co2 assimilated by using ATP & NADPH base 2 either through

1. C base 3 or Calvin cycle
2. C base 4 Hatch & Slack pathway.
3. CAM pathway.

- (RUBIS) = $\frac{Vc}{Vo}$ Vc = Velocity for Co2, Vo = Velocity for O2

- If more than 1 it is beneficial

G. Global photosynthetic productivity

III. THE VARIOUS PATHWAYS

1. C3 cycle (Rice) Mesophyll cell
2. C4 cycle (Maize) Mesophyll, Bundle sheath
3. Calvin or C3 or Reductive Pentose (P) Pathway (P) —> Phosphate
4. Hatch & Slack or C4 pathway
5. CAM —> Crassulacean acid metabolism pathway (semi succulent plants) Opuntia, Bryophyllum

Transfer of a gene from C4 to C3 increased the efficiency

C3 crops = 12gm-2 ground day -1 (2.5 tons/hect)

C4 = 22gm-2 ground day (5.7 tons/hectare)

IV. REASON FOR LOW FOOD PRODUCTION

1. Nutrient stress - reduced by using nitrogen
2. Pathogens —> introduction of Oxygenases (Insect resistance genes)
3. Temperature —> Drought stress (Heat shock proteins)

3. DIRECT COMBUSTION

I. DIFINITION

Burning of plant materials in the presence of Oxygen

II. SOURCES OF PHYTOMASS

A. Vegetation on non-farm lands

Forests, marginal lands

B. Vegetation on farm lands

1. Crops cultivated for energy usage
2. Crop remains from agricultural practices

C. Wastes and by products

Several plant based industries(Lumbering, Carpentry, Saw mills)

D. Miscellaneous

Dry fallen wood, trimmings from felled trees, residues from Saw mill, wood processing, etc.

III. CHARACTERISTICS

A. Calorific Value

1. 1 gm of O2 content of phytomass liberates 3349 cals of heat
2. Varies within the same plant at different times

B. Moisture content

1. 3.5-4.5 mj of heat energy is required to reduce 1 Kg of water
2. Increase in moisture content lowers heating values.
3. Feed stock must have 15% Moisture content

C. Ash content

1. Depends on the mineral content which varies with the plant and soil types;
2. Ideal firewood must have 2% ash content

D. Organic content

1. Forms - Cellulose, hemicellulose, lipid, hydrocarbon, phenolic compounds, Carbohydrate, proteins.
2. Compactness of wood material abundance and of hemicellulose

E. Others

1. Fast growing
2. Wide range of environment
3. Unpalatable to grazers
4. Erect without much branches
5. High density planting (energy farming)

IV. Uses

A. Domestic: Cooking, warming of the house

B. Industrial: Boilers, other usage

C. Electricity generation: Hawai-50% from phytomass, Tamilnadu

D. Automobile Fuel: World War II- USA, Trains, tractors, cars, river boats

> *"The fundamental principles of ecology govern our lives wherever we live, and ... we must wake up to this fact or be lost."*
>
> **Karin Sheldon**

4. THERMAL CONVERSION

I. DEFINITION

Decomposition of substrates in the presence of heat thermally converted

Dry phytomass --------------------------------Energy rich fuels

1. Absence of O2
2. Presence of limited amount of O2
3. Presence of hydrogen

II. SOURCES (any dry phytomass)

A. Wood sources

an ideal source

B. Herbaceous crops

Weedy terrestrial plants, (herbs & shrubs)

C. Agricultural wastes

Crop remains

D. Agro-industrial wastes

Plant raw materials based industries

E. Municipal solid wastes

Papers, clothes, etc., of phytomass origins, Human waste

Organic waste

III. PROCESS

A. Pyrolysis/ Direct combustion

1. Definition

Decomposition of polymeric organic materials into simple form by heating in the absence of air

2. Products

(a) Charcoal (19 KJ/Kg) (b) Liquid (25 Mj per Kg)

(c) Gas (15 MJ per M3)

3. Yield efficiency

20-40% charcoal, 20% pyrolytic oil, 20% gaseous products. Yield and heat content of the products varies with source

4. Use

(a) Charcoal: Home cooking, blacksmiths

(b) Oil: diesel substitute

(c) Gas: electricity generation, synthesis of methanol, petroleum substitute

B. Gasification

1. Definition

Conversion of solid or/liquid to gas in the presence of limited air.

2. Products

(a) Producer gas: Co+ N2+H2=CH4 small proportion
Calorific value: 1200 K.cal/NM(Low energy gas)

(b) Synthesis gas or
syngas: CO & H2
Hydrocarbons
Calorific Value

(c) Substitute: calorfic value: 38 MJ/m3
Natural gas Methane has high pr. & low temp.

(d) Methanol: syn gas --------------------methanol
upgraded

(e) Ammonia: syn. gas------------------ Ammonia

(f) Electricity

3. Uses

(a) Producer gas generators or gasifiers
Tractors, auto-mobiles, buses in Europe (World War

(b) Present
Producer gas engines are manufactured.

(c) Syn gas
As pipeline gas, fuel for boiler, internal combustion engines, substitute for natural gas

(d) Methanol
To power phosphoric acid cell used in vehicles, with ethanol & substitute used as petroleum substitute

(e) Gases
Electricity generation, to power engines

C. Hydrogasification

1. Definition

Phytomass is gasified in the presence of hydrogen to produce high energy gas (Methane & Ethane with or without a catalysis.

2. Products

High energy gas rich in methane & ethane & hydrocarbons

3. Uses

Substitute to natural gas liquid field gas used as a diesel substitute.

5. CHEMICAL EXTRACTION

I. DEFINITION

Extraction and upgrading of the vegetable products to high grade transportation fuels by catalytic cracking.

II. SOURCES

A. Isoprenes

1. History
   (a) Origin-Italian
   (b) 1938-in Ethiopia
   (c) Veg. gasoline-Euphorbia sps.
2. Pioneer: Calvin - Father of this field
3. Chemistry
   (a) Structure
      1. Long chain hydrocarbons
   (b) Occurence
      1. As natural terpenoids
   (c) Mol.formula: C5-H8)n
      1. Mono and sesquiterpenoid: essential oils
      2. Di- and triterpenoid: latex
      3. Poly terpenoid: rubber
4. Plant Examples
   (a) Rubber plants: Heavea brasiliensis, Parthenium argentatum
   (b) Petro plants: Capifera multijuga, Pinus, Euphorbia

B. Terpenoids

1. **Chemistry**
   (a) single repeting units, (polymers) isoprenoid
   (b) long chain or cyclic corbohydrates
2. Classification
   (a) Low Terpenes
      1. $C_{10}H_{16}$ – Monoterpenes
      2. $C_{15}H_{24}$ – Sesquterpenes
      3. $C_{20}H_{32}$ - Di terpenes
   (b) Carotenoids
      $C_{40}H_{56}$ - Tetra, sesquiterpenes
   (c) Rubber and Guttapercha $(C_5H_8)_n$ - Poly sesquiterpenes

3. Plant Examples
   (a) Monoterpene - Ocimum basilicum (myrene) (Ocimene)
   (b) Di terpene - Mayflower and lime flower (farnesol)
   (c) Sesqui terpene - Bergamat oil and some essential oils (Bisabtalene C15 H24)
   (d) Tri terpene - less occuring in plants, as terpene alchohols, or acids of aliphatic in three barks,

   balsams and resins or milky saps, with sugars, Eg. Antirrhinum majus
4. Biogenesis
   (a) Monoterpenes - derived from acyclic precursor geraniol orlinalo
   (b) Di terpene - geranyl geranid
   (c) Plant sterols & tri terpnes - derived from squalene
   (d) Sesqui terpne - derived from farnesol

C. Glycerides

1. History
   (a) Ancient – lighting (b) Recent - diesel substitute
2. Chemistry

   Identical with fats, composed of glycerdes of fatty acids, depending on No. of acid groups

   - monoglycerides
   - diglycerides
   - triglycerides
3. Classification
   (a) Use: (i) edible oil (ii) nonedible oil
   (b) Type: (i) drying (ii) semidrying (iii) non-drying
4. Plant Examples
   (a) G.max - 130,000 but/gal energy
   (b) Cocos nucifera, Zea mays, H.tuberosum – diesel substitute

D. Waxes - Lubrication of engines

1. Chemistry

   Simple liquids - one molecule of fatty acid & one high mol.wt.alcohol.
2. Properties

   Insoluble in H20 resistant to oxidation at high mp.

3. Types & Examples
   (a) Carnauba Wax
       Vegetable wax from leaves of wax palm (Copernica carifera)
   (b) Myrtle wax
       Berries of Myrica sps.
   (c) Candellib wax
       Stem of E. antisyphilitica
   (d) Jojoba wax
       Seeds of Simmondsia chinensis

> *Everyone who considers themselves a realist will be forced to justify their behavior in light of their contribution toward the preservation of the environment.*
>
> **Ernst von Weizacker**

6. ANAEROBIC DIGESTION - BIO-GAS

I. INTRODUCTION

A. Energy

B. Bio-energy

C. Bio sources

1. Organic residues
   (a) Animal wastes
   (b) Forest wastes
   (c) Crop residues and byproducts
   (d) Firewood trees and shrubs
2. Aquatic biomass

D. Technologies to convert biomass into energy

1. Biological   2. Thermo-chemical

II. DEFINITION

Biologically mediated transformation of organic material to a combustible gas-biogas (in absence of oxygen)

III. SOURCES

1. Aquatic plants, submerged & floating - weedy
2. Terrestrial plants, Marginal lands - weeds
3. Wastes: Agricultural, Agro-industrial, Homestead, Municipal
4. Forest sources: Rich in organic material like Forest litter, green plant matter-felled wood.

IV. HISTORICAL BACKGROUND IN INDIA

A. Traditional dung cake and gobar gas

Scale of operations

Alternate designs and operations

Operation and maintenance

B. Night soil   **C. Other wastes**

D. Gas   **E. Slurry**

F. Integrated systems   **G. Community plants**

Background in other countries

1. Korea   2. Japan   3. Nepal   4. Taiwan

V. ENERGY CONVERSION PROCESS

A. Organic matter-------------------- methane

+ bacteria   + CO_2 + H_2O

+ Water   + Stabilized effluent

B. Biochemistry & microbiology of methanogenesis

Polymeric substances (Phytomass)

(a) mono-or dimers (glucose, Xylose, maltose, amino acids & fatty acids)

(b) Degraded

(c) Acetic acid, propionic acid, Hydrogen & CO_2

(d) Converted

(e) Methane & CO_2 (Biogas)

C. Methanogenic Organisms

1. Examples: Clostridium, Escherichia, Methano bacterium M. brevibacter, M. bacillus
2. Properties
   (a) Sensitive to pH (6.6-7.6 pH optimum)
   (b) Temperature (35oc-54oc optimum)
   (c) Carbon: Nitrogen (30:1 optimum)
   (d) Solid content (7-9% by wt.)

IV. CHARACTERISTICS OF BIOGAS

1. 60-70% methane, 30-40% Co2, traces of hydrogen, nitrogen Water vapour & H2S.
2. 68% Methane, 31% Co2 & 1% Nitrogen gives 5871 K cal. m3 (calorific value).

V. USES

A. Rural families, Automobile fuel, electricity generation cooling, lighting, heating, engine fueling.

B. Sludge used as on organic manure in agriculture, improves Environmental health in rural areas, and reduces drudgery of women

VI. Limitations & Improvement

1. Rectification of techniques & process involved - biogas technology
2. Production to be increased - N2 Fixing plants – and by
   (a) Increasing phytomass production
   (b) Plant breeding
   (c) Plant growth regulators
3. Constraints on biogas production and use
4. Fermentation installation
5. Storing and using biogas

6. Storing and using effluent
7. Present economic viability
8. Interests of international agencies
9. Technological aspects of regional operations
10. Biochemical and other operational aspects
    (a) Poor digestibility of the dung
    (b) Use of other inputs
    (c) Frequency of feeding
    (d) C/N ratio
    (e) Removal of toxic materials
    (f) Fertilizer value of slurry and it's loss in drying
11. Design aspects: Gas holder
12. Problems of evaluation
13. Alternation and choices
    (a) Pyrolysis
    (b) Ethyl alcohol

> *The ecological crisis is doing what no other crisis in history has ever done — challenging us to a realization of a new humanity.*
>
> **Jean Houston**

7. FORESTS AND SOCIAL FORESTRY IN INDIA

I. SOURCES OF ENERGY

A. Renewable and non-renewable energy

B. Conventional and non conventional energy

II. BIOENERGY

A. Introduction to bioenergy

B. Average energy yield

III. FORESTRY

A. Introduction

B. Role of forestry

C. Classification of forests

1. Natural forests
2. Man-made forests

D. Benefits of trees and forests

1. Direct benefits
   - (a) Fuel wood
   - (b) Charcoal
   - (c) Round wood products
   - (d) Saw timbers
   - (e) Pulp wood
   - (f) Fodder
   - (g) Secondary metabolites
2. Indirect benefits

E. Protective role of forests

F. Amenity benefits

IV. FORESTS

A. Early scenes

B. Awakenings

C. War and after independence

D. Extension of agriculture

E. Forest area

F. Comparisons

G. Industrial wood

H. Cottage industries and subsidiary occupations

I. Animal rearing

J. Environment

V. SOCIAL FORESTRY

A. Main objectives of social forestry

B. Social forestry plantation

1. Strip plantation
2. Canal side plantation
3. Plantation along road side and railway lines

C. Silviculture systems

1. Definition
2. Essence

3. Classification
   (a) Short rotation forestry
       Selection of species
       Study of culture techniques
       Advantages
       Disadvantages
   (b) Coppice
4. Improvement of forest biomass

VI. CHOICE OF SPECIES AND PLANNING

A. Climatic regions
   1. Temperate regions
   2. Subtropical regions
   3. Tropical regions
B. Difficult and special sites
   1. Coastal areas
   2. Island areas
   3. Wetlands
   4. Parks and gardens
   5. Saline and alkaline areas
   6. Fruit growing areas in hills
   7. Planting for non-wood products and for cottage industries
      (a) Fibres and grasses
      (b) Essential oils
      (c) Oil seeds
      (d) Tans and dyes
      (e) Gums and resins
      (f) Lac
      (g) Bidi leaves
      (h) Honey

VII. EXOTICS IN SOCIAL FORESTRY

A. Eucalyptus,
B. Leucena leucocephala[subabul],
C. Acacia auriculiformis[akshmuui],
D. Populus spp[poplars]
E. Casuarina equisetifolia[suru],
F. Prosopis juliflora[vilayati babul]
G. Acacia torilis[israeli babul]

VIII. NURSERIES: GROWING AND SUPPLYING OF SEEDLINGS

A. Nurseries Growing and Supply of Seedlings
   1. Size of Nursery
   2. School Nurseries
   3. Kisan Nurseries
   4. Eco-Development task forces
   5. NGOs
   6. Supply of seedlings
B. Mass involvement and extension
   1. Target group
   2. Van mahotsav
   3. Incentives for tree planting
   4. Sharing of benefits

IX. Fuelwood

A. Fuel Wood Requirement In India
B. Amount used as fuel wood
C. Centers of consumption
D. Production
E. Fuel values
F. Factors determining Fuel values
G. Preference Of Wood For Fuel Farms
H. Comparison Of Wood Fuel With Other Energy Source
I. Defects in wood
J. Good Fuel woods, Bad wood fuels
K. Porous Fuel wood
L. Fuel wood charcoal
M. Fuel from woods & saw mill wastes
   1. Production
   2. Woods used & yields
   3. Process of manufacturing
   4. Utilization of charcoal)
O. Fuel wood trends

X. Plantations

A. Energy plantations
B. Characteristic of energy plantation
C. Selection Criteria Of Species
D. Water Hyacinth As Energy Source
E. Advantages of Energy plantation
F. Constraints In Energy Plantation
G. Yield In Energy Plantation

A. Energy plantation forestry

1. Sub-divisions of energy plantation
   (a) Silviculture energy farming
   (b) Agroforestry
   (c) Social forestry
   (d) Block plantation
   (e) Strip plantation
   (f) Monoculture plantation
2. Scientific tools employed in energy plantation
   (a) Methods
   (b) Spacing
   (c) Manure, fertilizer
   (d) Transplanting
   (e) Protection of plantation
   (f) Irrigation
   (g) Inter culture and soil working

3. Basic requirements of energy plantation
   (a) Rural firewood (b) Farm forestry

B. Land use systems involving trees

1. Natural vegetation management
2. Agroforestry
   (a) Rural development forestry (b) Alley farming
   (c) Silvipastoral system
3. Industrial plantation forestry

C. Constraints and opportunities of land use systems

> *It is time for us now as a nation to exercise the same reasonable foresight in dealing with our great natural resources that would be shown by any prudent man in conserving and widely using the property which contains the assurance of well-being for himself and his children.*
>
> **Theodore Roosevelt**

8. BIOTECHNOLOGY IN BREEDING FOR BIOMASS

I. INTRODUCTION

II. LONG RANGE APPLICATIONS

III. TRANSFORMATION TECHNOLOGY

A. Technique

B. Uses

1. Plant biotechnology
   genetic improvement in Brassica
   -oil yielding plants
2. Somaclonal variations
3. Exploitation of wild germplasm in Brassica

IV. TISSUE CULTURE

V. GENETIC MANIPULATIONS

VI. DNA TECHNOLOGY

VII. *in vitro* POLLINATION AND FERTILIZATION

VIII. *in vitro* OVULE EMBRYO CULUTRE

IX. EMBRYO RESCUE

X. PROTOPLAST ISOLATION AND PURIFICATION IN FOREST TREES(CONIFERS)

A. Cell wall degradation in plants

B. Plasmolisation of mixtures

C. Isolation time

D. Purification of protoplast fraction

E. Determination of protoplast viability

XI. PROTOPLAST CULTURE OF FOREST TREES

XII. REGENERATION OF PLANTS - FROM PROTOPLAST OF LINUM

A. Protoplast isolation

B. Protoplast culture

C. Plant regeneration from protoplast

XIII. SOMATIC HYBRIDS

XIV. AGROBACTERIUM TUMIFACIENS MEDIATED GENETIC TRANSFORMATIONS

9. ENERGY FROM ANIMALS AND HUMANS

I. ENERGY: USE AND DEMAND

Energy is the capacity of doing work. It may exist in potential, kinetic, thermal, chemical, Nuclear or other forms.

A. Importance of energy

B. Energy shortage

C. Worldwide consumption of energy

D. Patterns in developed and developing countries

In ancient days man is used as source of energy but latter it changed to slavery and this state prevails till now. And now-a-days modern slavery also exists even after ban on slavery by united nations.

II. ENERGY SUPPLY

A. Coal

B. Oil and Natural Gas

C. Nuclear Power

D. Hydro Power

E. Geothermal

F. Wind Power

G. Tidal Power

H. Wave Power

I. Biomass

J. Solar energy

1. Current usage and Potential in future and
2. Limited supply of all the above and need for alternatives

III. HUMAN ACTS AS SOURCE OF ENERGY

A. By providing physical labour

B. By his mental ability

C. By providing food

D. Excreta

E. Waste & Sewage

F. Fossil fuels

G. Land fillings

H. Labour

IV. HARNESSIBLE ENERGY FROM ANIMALS AND HUMANS

A. MUSCLE ENERGY: Muscular energy of human used for physical labour

1. AGRICULTURE: ploughs lands, raises crops and provides food
2. INDUSTRIES: His muscular power is used in building up machines which produce the items used in our daily life.

3. CONSTRUCTIONS: His muscular power is used in constructing industries & houses
   - (a) Numbers, varieties (b) Distribution
   - (c) Productivity (d) Urban Scenario
   - (e) Head Loaders - Construction workers, Agriculture, Transport
4. MIGRATIONS: people migrate from one place to another for work
5. BONDED LABOUR: If father takes money and dies in debt his son has to work until the debt is cleared.
6. CHEAP LABOUR: Labour get less wages for more work.
7. COSTLY LABOUR: Labour get high wages for less work.
   - (a) Working population in India
   - (b) Sectors of employment, in transport (rickshaw & hand-cart pullers, porters etc.) agriculture, construction, energy per individual

From Animals

Members, distribution, utility of cattle, donkeys, mules, horses camels, elephants, zebra Breeds and Germplasms - World and India.

B. BIOFUELS: Animal Excreta and human Excreta

1. Livestock and manure generation

- (a) Manure content - residues of feed origin, undigested, indigestible products of metabolism.
- (b) Process of methane/biogas generation - Bacteriological, anaerobic digestion
  - The Process, Excess thermal energy usage
  - Potential uses of the Biogas and the effluent
  - Biogas- an alternative energy source in India
- (c) Potential of Biogas and effluent
  - Limitation of storage due to gaseous form, difficulty in liquefaction, corrosiveness,
  - Uses in small units for heating, fuel to generate electricity, not large scale.
  - Effluent use as fertilizer excess heat recycled.
- (d) Biogas as an Alternative Energy source
  - in agricultural, developing countries
  - efficiency to be greater
- (e) Biogas in India

- National programme on Biogas Development ’82
- 14.02 lakh family units, 700 community units installed

2. Direct burning of dung

- less efficient recovery of energy
- creates (indoor) pollution

C. FOOD ENERGY: Energy contribution

1. Agriculture: staple food such as rice, jowar, bajra, pulses like red gram, bengal gram, fruits and vegetables
2. Dairy: cows, buffaloes, goats, camels, donkeys etc for milk
   (a) Nutrient content important to health
   (i) carbohydrates (ii) proteins (iii) Fats (iv) vitamins
3. Meat: Meat is obtained from many sources and are reared.
   (a) Birds: Hens, cocks, pegions, ducks, geese, turkey, Emu, Ostrich
   (b) HERDS: Sheep, goats & pigs
   (c) CATTLE: Cows, Buffaloes, camels & donkeys etc
   (d) WILD ANIMALS: Deers, Antelopes, rabbits etc
   (e) FISH: fresh water fish, salt fish, shell fishes
4. Eggs:- Eggs are obtained from birds like hens, pigeons, gulls, lapwings pheasants, ducks, turkeys & Ostriches etc. Eggs contains proteins in addition with vitamins.

D. WASTE & SEWAGE: Waste & sewage created by man is used as source of energy in the following ways.

1. BIOGAS: Production of biogas.
2. MANURE: This waste which is slightly separated and decomposed is used as manure
3. COMPOSTING: Composting is done from this waste& sewage. This is added to soil to increase fertility
4. LANDFILLINGS: for treatment of solid wastes
   (a) Biodegradation of polymers - proteins carbohydrates, fats etc.
   (b) Methanogenesis: Production of biogas.
5. FOSSIL FEULS

   Fossil fuels are formed by decomposition remains of human, animals & plants. Petroleum products are obtained in the form of crude oil & natural gas.

E. OTHERS: Human is an intelligent animal. This trait lead to the discovery & invention of many, starting with wheel

1. ELECTRICITY: electric energy is the form of energy required in daily life and is generated from following sources.

   Water - Hydroelectric power

   Coal - Thermoelectric power

   Nuclear - Nuclear electric power

   Wind - Wind electric power

2. TECHNOLOGY: Many new techniques are developed by developing new machines which makes work fast and saves both energy and time.

3. PETROLEUM PRODUCTS: Petroleum products like crude oil & gas are obtained from fossil fuels, a great source of energy.

4. COMPUTERISATIONS: A machine which process data very fast & accurately according to the instructions this made work automatic with less energy and time.

5. GENETIC ENGINEERING: By this advanced technique living thing with desired traits are developed and unwanted genes are removed. Thus the energy is saved and crop is obtained with greater yield.

F. CONCLUSION

* Importance of energy from animal and humans
* Limited supply
* Need for alternative

10. FUTUROLOGY - PHYTOMASS

I. QUANTUM OF PHYTORESOURCES

A. More than 500 species hold promise

B. Through Ethno-botanical enquiries: many plants are awaited

C. Plants suitable to different ecosystems: to be

D. Distribution of Forest land of India

1. 52.2% as Reserved area
2. 31% as Protected area
3. 16.8% as Unclassified area

E. Contribution of Forest Revenues to different states (1980-81)

1. Total revenues from all sources - Rs.1,450.518
2. Total percentage contribution of Forests 3.19

II. HISTORICISM IN PLANT SELECTION

A. Introduction and improvement

1. Priority to the local species

B. Archaeological screening

1. Abandoned human settlements, ancient monuments

C. Identifiable and plants and their relatives are re introduced

D. Re generation of ecosystem

III. ADVANTAGES

1. Plants are good stores, versatile in products convertibility and energy contents.
2. To utilise their regeneration and inexhaustible resource, implementation of phytomass scheme is essential.

IV. DISADVANTAGES

1. Acquiring new land areas and land use
2. Change in existing pattern of agriculture
3. Manpower diversion, uncertainty of costs and initial supply

V. LAND USE PATTERNS

1. Grow as many varieties of plants, in as many places, and as soon as possible.
2. According to 6th five - year plan (1980-85)
   (a) 29% of land area Reserved forests
   (b) 71% of land area Social forestry
   (c) Determines the extent of phytomass exploitation

VI. SOCIAL FORESTRY

1. Every strip of available land - vegetated by useful plants
2. International organizations - SIDA, World Bank, USAID, NSFP

11. ENERGY RESOURCEFULNESS

I. INTRODUCTION

The kind of stuff fundamentally make up the universe are matter and energy. Energy is tantamount to power, the key to the social and economic development of a technologically sophisticated society.

Derived from the Gk: energea: en-in, ergon-work.

Conversion of energy: a low holding good for all natural phenomenon.

1. Urban fuel wood comes from deforestation.
2. Self sufficiency unlikely in spite of Hydroelectric, fossil fuel and nuclear programmes. Wastage is one major scourge.
3. There may be enough food, but not energy to cook it.
4. Coal is preferred.
5. Oil: more explorations and gas.
6. Nuclear: Eleven new reactors.
7. Solar energy inputs
8. With the rate, purpose and efficiency of use.
   (a) Preservation (b) Restoration
   (c) Benefication (d) Maximization
   (e) Re-utilization (f) Substitution.
   (g) Allocation (strategy of use)
   (h) Integration of resource management.

I. Firewood as fuel

The present estimate of consumption of wood as fuel in India is more than 130 milion tons. A long term programme has to be devised

1. To estimate the damage done by felling
2. To restrict the extent of felling.
3. To establish new forest plantations for fire wood consumption.
4. To increase the supply of substitute fuel for fire wood.

II. HISTORY

A. Discovery of fire

The use of fire and domestication of animals are considered to be the historical sources of energy. It can be raid that the evolution of man largely depended on the sources of energy which appropriate technology has enabled him to master.

B. Early sources are the following.

1. Asphalt: used in Middle East in 600 BC. Technology advances of Babylonian empire Mesopotamia in 2500 BC-538 BC; diminished after 538BC.
2. Natural Gas: Used in China before 1000 BC transported through bamboo pipe lives.
3. Coal: Initiated by china, used in Roman times, Because an article of commerce in the 13th century. Discovery of use of who, for reduction of acres, in 1709.
4. Petroloum: Known to Babylonians though not used extensively.

   Promminace in 17th century 1640, Medena, Datty oil well drilled for duel for lighting street lamps.

   Romania - wamer - gas oil wells in 1650. Oil discovered in U.S. Early oil well drilled in 1859 in western Pennyslvamia.
5. Wind: Ship properlsion since early times; windmills in China spread the middle east and Europe.
6. Water: Babylomain irrigation 3000 yers ago using watersheds - Romans used them for flourmills and raw units.
7. Stream: Power used in 18th century

   19th century: revolution in use and exploitation of energy sources

III. CONCEPTS

1. Galileo, 17th century, idea of energy related to the pulley system.
2. Vis viva (living force) & mv concept developed in 17th century.
3. 19th century term energy applied to vis viva.
4. 19th century concept of conversion of energy.

IV. TYPES OF ENERGY

1. Gravitational	2. Kinetic	3. Heat
4. Electrical	5. Chemical	6. Radiant
7. Nuclear	8. Solar	9. Wind
10. Ocean	11. Tidal	12. Biomass
13. Geothermal	14. Natural gas	15. Hydro
16. Fossil fuels.		

V. RESOURCEFULNESS

Applications of the different types of energy in various fields.

1. Agriculture 2. Transport 3. Communication 4. Industry - petroleum, steel, metal, etc.

VI. ECONOMICS & POLICIES

1. Allocation, prices, taxation, trade - energy as a commodity.
2. Correlation between GNP and energy inputs.
3. Markets governed by public policy or private monopoly, eg OPEC
4. Impact of energy and economics is felt in unemployment, GNP, inflation and trade.
5. Changer in energy market place results in redistribution of economic wealth.
6. Policies in order to balance supply and energy consisted with economic, social and environmental goals.

VII. ENVIRONMENTAL IMPACTS

1. Air pollution 2. Water Pollution 3. Thermal heat waste 4. Climatic changes
5. Problem created at each stage
   - Production, upgrading, transport, utilization

VIII. ENERGY IN NATURE

Man lives in an ocean of energy. The falling water of rivers could yield enough hydro electric power to meet 80% of man's total energy consumption, though he uses 1 or 2%.

If the winds are tethered, they could turnout twice as much electricity as water power now does.

The most colossal dynamo of all is Sun. As the world's non - renewable energy supplies dwindle, the virtually unlimited and inexhaustible supplies that abound in nature must be ingeniously adopted to provide man's future power needs.

A. Sun

The sun is an atomic furnace that turns mass into energy. Every second it converts 657 million tons of Hydrogen into 653 million tons of Helium. The missing 4 million tons are discharged into space as energy. The earth is receiving only one two- billionths of this.

B. Wind

The sun's rays, stronger near the equator than in the Polar Regions, cause tropical air to warm and rise while cooler polar air moves into replace it. The result is wind.

C. Water

About a third of Sun's energy reaching the earth involves in evaporation. Every year it evaporates and lifts 417,000 km3 of the moisture a third hits the land as rain, snow etc,. This helps form the rivers, streams, glaciers that have reshaped the earth and provided man with a valuable source of power.

IX. ENERGY IN INDIA

Energy is an essential input for economic development and for improving the quality of life. per capita consumption of commercial energy is only one - eighth of the world average.

A. Energy requirements for India

About 1/4 th public sector investment allocation goes to energy sector. Energy demand in the following four sectors are considered - Industries, Transport, Agriculture, Household and commercial.

B. Regional distribution of energy demand

Issues relating to the distribution of energy in India. Trends of regional shares.

-The mix of energy -The efficiency of use -The agriculture needs

In the present state of scientific and technical knowledge it is convenient to list the main energy resources of India under five headings. Four of these fall under commercial energy.

C. Coal

1. Total resources - 81 billion tons.
2. Out of 21 billion tons - 58% non-coaking coal
3. Lignite - 2 billion tons which will least for 300 years found in Neyveli.
4. Problem is working and marketing:
5. The seams of coal tend to be very thick,
6. High ash content of coals.
7. Production and transport.

Distribution in India: No coal fields in north west regions.

Fields - Singareni, Neyveli, Renigani in WB, Jharia in Bihar

D. Oil and Natural gas

Total sedimentary area of India, on shore and off-shore comprises 27 basins. Cambay basin, North-East including Assam, Bombay high, Godavari, Kaveri river deltas. Natural gas is found both alone and with crude oil.

E. Hydro electric power

1. East flowing and west flowing rivers.
2. Some major projects bakra-Nangal, Hirakud, Mettur, Nagarjima-sagar, Kundah, Narmada, Tehri.

3. Contreoueeial as forests are eubmearged, decreasing life time due to liltation, Mega projects
4. Small dams are suggested.

F. Nuclear power

1. Nuclear fission releaser large amount of energy.
2. Fuels are ussanim 235, U236, Thorium.
3. Stations: Trombay, Kalpakkam, Kaiga, Tarapur, Koodenkulam.
4. Cotastrophic if there is an accident (Esplosion)
5. Ratio-active radiation leaks which causes ualions ailments such as cancer and even death.
6. Fusion power as future resource.

G. Thermal power stations

1. Using coal, lignite-burnt and water evaporated producing steam- turbine power.
2. Air pollution - Green house gases.
3. Water pollution - hot water bltout into marine environment causing severe damage to biota.
4. South and west are remote form coal fields - Transportation.

H. Environmental impacts

1. Transportation, processing, tranmission of power to different regions, water dieprosal activities all associated with environmental effects.
2. Uncontrolled production.
3. Unnecessary use of power - wastage.

X. UNTAPPED SOURCES OF RENEWABLE ENERGY

Solar energy, geothermal energy, tidal power and wind power

A. Solar energy

This seems to have the greatest potential for India in the long run, because of the large amount of solar energy which it receives. It means exploiting solar energy, either directly or after conversion into electricity. Conversion of solar energy into electricity can be achieved with present techniques only at very high cost. further research needed. A simple and common mode in solar energy utilisation is solar thermal conversion. Some of the commercial ways are cooking, water heating, desalination space heating, crop drying etc.

B. Geothermal energy

If might well be a more immediately useable source, and an

exploratory work is going on. The total potential, appears to be very limited.

-Himachal pradesh region is a potential area.

C. Tidal power

The no of possible sites have been identified however in this are the potential appears small. While in the present rate of technical knowledge, electric power could not be generated from tides at costs which would compare with other means of generation.

D. Wind power

The use of wind power for electricity generation is a costly method. If can be exploited in windy areas which are remote from other resource of power. If can be used for water pumping also. Wind farms area installed in coastal areas of Gujarat, TamilNadu, Maharashtra and orissa.

XI. NON-CONVENTIONAL ENERGY SOURCES

A. Biogas

If is the most important component of renewable energy supplies. As a byproduct, it gives enriched fertilizer also. It can be used for cooking, lighting and power generation.

B. Energy from urban waste

A pilot plant to utilise solid municipal waste for conversion into energy in the form of electricity is developed in Delhi.

C. Energy plantation

Woody biomass Waste and denuded lands are used for raising plantation of fast growing and high calorific value trees and shrub species. The out put provides fuel wood, fodder, power and substantial employment.

Power through gasification or incineration.

XII. COOKING ENERGY

The greatest share of energy consumed in our villages is used by kitchens.

1. National improved chulha programme.
2. Health hazards for women.
3. Conserving fuel wood.
4. Improving environmental conditions.

XIII. INDIA'S ENERGY POLICY

1. Accelerated exploitation of domestic conventional energy resources - Oil, coal, hydro and nuclear power.

2. Increase in indigenous production of oil and gas.
3. Management of demand for oil.
4. Energy conservation and management.
5. Development and exploitation of renewable sources of energy.
6. Austerity measures.

The present estimate of consumption of wood as fuel in India is more than 130 million tons. A long term programme has to be devised in relation to the use of wood as fuel.

(a) To estimate the damage done by felling
(b) To restrict the extent of felling.
(c) To establish new forest plantations for fire wood consumption.
(d) To increase the supply of substitute fuel for fire wood.
    1. Shortage of electric powers,
    2. National grid, state electricity boards,
    3. Rural electrification,
    4. Failure of monsoon rains
    5. Delays in civil works,
    6. Delivery of equipments
    7. Inadequacy of transmission and distribution facilities

XIV. CONCLUSION

Every individual should follow some ethics in living; Should realise that energy is for essential needs and nor for luxury. Conserving energy and understanding the problem can only help save the country from the energy crisis.

6

Natural Resources

1. RESOURCE EXPLOITATION
2. HUMAN DESTINIES IN NATURE
3. BASIC PRINCIPLES
4. BIOSPHERE RESERVES
5. SYSTEMS & RESOURCES
6. ATMOSPHERE AND ABOVE
7. MARINE SYSTEMS
8. FOREST SYSTEMS
9. COAST LINES
10. WASTELANDS
11. HUMAN ECOLOGY AND RESOURCES
12. RESOURCEFULNESS OF ANIMALS
13. TRADE IN WILDLIFE
14. PLANT RESOURCES
15. FOOD SOURCES
16. GERMPLASMS
17. LAND AND SOIL
18. MINERALS
19. WATER
20. ENERGY
21. CULTURED SYSTEMS
22. AGROECOSYSTEMS
23. ECOLOGICAL AGRICULTURE
24. REMOTE SENSING OF RESOURCES
25. MANAGEMENT OF RESOURCES
26. LIMITS TO ECONOMIC GROWTH
27. RESOURCE DEPLETION
28. INTERNATIONAL RELATIONS
29. INDIAN CONCERNS

Syllabus

1. Paradigm shift from Economics to Ecology after Club of Rome; Resources: Food, Shelter, Clothing, Education, Health, Security Depletion, Renewability and Non-renewability; Basic Needs, Consumption, Limits to growth and Sustainability; Basic Needs versus Consumption, Quality of Life,

   Harmony- Security- Resource illiteracy- Global 2000 projections The concept of Primary, Secondary and Tertiary Resources
2. Exploration and Exploitation of Natural Resources - Historical Perspectives and Philosophical perceptions.
3. Conceptual frame work for the study of Natural Resources - Ecology, Society and Politics
4. A Survey of Resources - Sectorial Considerations - Soil, Water, Animals, Minerals, Plants, Energy and Air. Characteristics, Exploitation and Consequences. primary and secondary.
5. A Survey of Resources - Holistic Approach - Conceptual Framework - Terrestrial and Aquatic Ecosystems - Geological and Atmospheric Components
6. Resource Amplification: Monocultures - Conceptual Framework, Agriculture, Aquaculture, Other Cultures and Germplasm Resources.
7. Human Resource Development - Concept and Contents
8. Politics of Natural Resources - Local, Regional and Global
9. Monitoring and Management: Secondary resourcefulness, Biosphere reserves and other conservation strategies, Modelling, GIS, EIA, Remote Sensing.

References

1. Barney, GO 1980. Global 2000 Report, Penguin
2. CSIR. 1970s Wealth of India, CSIR, New Delhi
3. India: Botanical, Zoological, Anthropological, Geological & other Surveys
4. Meadows, DH et al 1972. The Limits to Growth. Universe, New York
5. Owen, OS 1987. Natural Resource Conservation- An Ecological Approach, Macmillan, New York
6. Ramade, F. Natural Resources
7. Rao, KL 1979. India's Water wealth, Orient Longman
8. Simmons, IG 1981. Ecology of Natural Resources. John Wiley, New York
9. Westing, AH. 1986. Global Resources & International Conflict, O.U.P

1. HISTORY OF NATURAL RESOURCE EXPLOITATION

History of mankind is but a story of mutual exploitation - from river banks to maritime routes of trade to science and technology co-operation, for the empire building of the Ps.—pleasure, profit, power and popularity War is a constant phenomenon- Grief a fixed star. Peace is an occasional visitor - Joy, a vane that veers

I. HISTORY OF NATURAL RESOURCES

A. PREHISTORIC TIMES

1. Human settlements started and flourished wherever natural resources are bountiful especially water and soil. They grew in area and population size depending upon the resources and environment.
2. Trading started among these settlements for exchange of resources. Trade routes became the channels of information about the relative wealths of human settlements due to their natural resources.
3. Attempts to annex the neighbouring settlements along with their resources and further such advances have been a legion until the middle of 15th century. Enslavement of human resources have been very common during these times.

B. PRE INDUSTRIAL REVOLUTION / MEDIEVAL TIMES

4. Maritime advancements and the advent of industrial revolution bestowed tremendous advantages on the human resources in Europe. These advantages were used to colonise Africa, Asia and the Americas. Not only the lands were taken over, native human populations were exterminated (North America, South America, Africa) or enslaved (Africa). In Asia neither could be attempted due to population size and cultural status. Thus the resources of three continents have been appropriated by the European Nations, leading to conflicts among these countries in sharing the spoils. Consequently Europe determined the destinies of the most of the World's nations.

C. AFTER INDUSTRIAL REVOLUTION / MODERN TIMES

5. First World War

   Constitutes the First major conflict involving a land-locked Germany longing for colonies and their wealth. The designs were foiled. As a concession the Arctic was internationalised.

6. Second World War

   A frustrated Germany ganged up with two other nations similarly longing for the wealth of other nations devoid of industrial revolution. Once again, the desire to share the spoils of the colonial appropriation having failed, Antarctica, high seas, sea beds and outer space were internationalised as a probable compensation for the likely loss of colonies.

7. First and Second World wars were thus waged between two groups of developed countries for hegemony over world's resources i.e. between colony holder and non holders.

8. Third World War (1950s - 1970s)

   The third world war was unleashed by the entire developed world on the nondeveloped countries for resource draining through political domination i.e. Neocolonialism and Neoimperialism. This happened for three reasons.

   (a) Marshall plan for Europe was initiated with US and through which enormous development took place by the military - industrial complexes both for war purposes and rapid consumerism. This has raised standards and costs of life of people together with the national wealth in all the war-torn developed countries. All this could happen chiefly from the resource appropriation from the third world carried out for three centuries - which functioned like a fixed deposit - capital from the rest of the world.

   (b) Most of the decolonised countries unfortunately opted for the kind of development their colonial masters had in their own countries little realising that they had neither the "colonial capital" nor the scientific and technological bases (except China, Cuba perhaps). They had to therefore depend upon their former colonial rulers of Europe & their allies - USA, Canada and Australia for almost everything.

   (c) The developed countries began to assist the countries which have chosen their developments models with capital and manpower - Science, Technology, Aid for specific projects, loans and concessions. Wherever the above could not happen to their satisfaction (or not in their own interests) regional wars have been engineered. These embers are still burning or smouldering around a few dozen places.

(a) As a consequence of the above, enormous pollution of the entire globe was unleashed by he fierce development of the European nations - a king of war on the environment.

(b) The Natural Resources of the developing countries systematically depleted at a rate fastest in the history.

(c) The development has not been satisfactory due to outmoded technology, lack of scientific manpower, pressures of fiscal deficits and finally the development model (disregarding land/man ratio) unsuitable to the local peoples.

(d) Balance of Trade, Aid with strings, balance of payments of loans, migrations/sucking of trained manpower resulted in the further impoverishment of these nations despite the apparent facade of growth. Many countries reel under debt burdens. While other have an ever increasing population below poverty line. Divisions and conflicts; Hatred and Violence is the order of the day everywhere. The entire world got entangled in the strangle hold of their former colonial powers.

(e) Poor people, poor nations, pollution, depletion of resources, debt burdens, starvation, insanitation, energy crises, appropriation of others' wealths, overpopulation resulted in conflicts and violence all over the world. f. Environment on the inexorable march of degradation threatens the global future.

(f) Some of the above have been done in an indirect way through global organisations.

9. Fourth World War (1970s onwards)

The activities during the post war period have been affecting the entire globe, though some people more preferentially, very adversely threatening the entire future. This could however be delayed, even averted only by cooperative efforts by all nations thinking globally, and acting locally. The 4th WW therefore essentially constitutes follow-up actions against boomerangs from the 3rd WW

10. Inferences

(a) Exploiters also cannot escape environmental back lashes

(b) Developmental models should depend on the history, demography, resources and productivity of nations and cannot be borrowed.

(c) There cannot be open-ended growth as envisaged by both capitalism & communism; Policies cannot be right or left but front, conscious of writings on the wall in the front.

(d) Values cannot be neutral but socialistic and righteous. Means are as important as the ends. Agroecosystems are far more determinative of future of mankind than the urban systems. The only realistic solutions appear to be the idealistic ones.

11. Fifth World War [1990 Onwards]

With the breakdown of the Soviet System the most major check and balancing force of colonial exploitation ceased to exist. Consequently the 2nd world's disappearance resulted in the change of gears within all the other worlds. A kind of triage principle is being implemented in the name of globalisation. The paradigm of Think globally and Act locally "stands mutated to" Think locally and Act locally". Marginalisation of classes within the countries and between has begun.

12. Perspectives

The fourth world war is basically a war between the present & future generations while the fifth one is a scramble for owning private resources as far and as much as possible. Only some of the present generation bother to support the interests of the future people. If these forces win, there is hope for the globe. If the dark forces of the past triumph, ignoring future generations, doom is inevitable.

13. Intellectual activities

(a) 1938 W G Moore - Geography of Capitalism, WORLD FOOD BOARD. Post 2nd World War Phenomenon - World Resource Board - Hope for Future

(b) 1940. 8th American Science Congress made 5 Observations and 2 Recommendations.

(c) Club of Rome - Limits to growth - Overpopulation; depletion of resources; hygiene and sanitation, energy crises and pollution.

(d) World Models (1-5) by Pestel, Messarovic, Leontief, ...

U.N.World Model & Government Model (Carter-USA): Scenario exercises.

(e) The green philosophers.

(f) International activities: UNCHE (1972-Stockholm), UNEP, IMF, WB, ILO-UNEP-WHO-FAO, IUCN-FAO.

(g) Governmental and Intergovernmental activities.

North-South Dialogues, South-South Cooperations, Technology Transfers, Trade Practices, Debt burdens and Reliefs, Scientific collaborations, Aid Strings, Cancun - Williamsburg - Paris. Roles of Brandt, Carter, Indira Gandhi, Palme etc. USA, Canada, UK, Australia, China, Scandinavia, Japan's Questionable role.

(h) Peoples / Greens' Movements

Green Peace, Friends of the Earth, Local Movements in India, USA, Europe, Malaysia, South America, Scandinavia

D. MECHANISMS OF COLONIALISM

Continent	*Then Status*	*Actions*
1. North America	Civilised partly, developing thick population Strong	Kill
2. South America	Uncivilised not dense embedded in nature	Avoid
3. Australia	Uncivilised not dense	Avoid
4. Africa	Uncivilised dense in Pockets embedded in nature Strong	Enslave
5. Asia	Civilised thick populations Organised	Trade Divide & Rule

E. GLOBAL WARS IN SUMMARY

War & Duration	*Adversaries*	*Victims*	*Purpose*
Perennial wars			
1. 1914-18	Colonialists-1 vs Colonialists-2	Colonies	Sharing of Others' Resources
2. 1939-45	Colonialists-1 vs Colonialists-2	Colonies	Sharing of Others' Resources
3. 1950-70	Colonialists-1 & 2	Ex-Colonies	Indirect Exploitation of Former Colonies & similar Nations
4. 1972-90	All vs All Within & Between	Poor Countries Poor People	Averting Backlashes, Boomerangs For all
5. 1990 -	All vs All Within & Between	Poor Countries Poor People	Division of Countries into 8 Classes [Super triage] & each country into 3 classes [triage]

2. HUMAN DESTINIES IN AN INFINITE NATURE

I. CURRENT SCENARIOS

A. DEPLETION OF NATURAL RESOURCES

1. Overpopulations
2. Increased demand
3. Over exploitation
4. Habitat destruction
5. Excessive consumerism
6. Hedonism
7. Technological Advancements
8. Improper monitoring
9. Improper management

B. PREDICTABLE FACTORS

1. Long-term
2. Short-term
3. Mid-term

C. UNPREDICTABLE FACTORS

1. Natural disasters
2. Civil disturbances

D. GENERAL CONSEQUENCES

1. Deforestation - soil loss - floods - cycle
2. Air pollution and acid rain
3. Human settlement congestion - social & political crises
4. Prey-Predator relationships among humans
5. Water pollution and health
6. Chemicals in consumption: Irreversible health damage

E. SPECIFIC EPISODES

National

1. Underground water depletion
2. Salinity in the coastal fresh waters
3. Silent valley
4. Kashmir lakes
5. Interstate disputes
6. Chamouli & Chipko
7. Western Ghats
8. Indian Dams
9. Thana creek
10. Minerals & Tribals of Chota Nagpur

International

1. International disputes
2. Brazilian Rain forest
3. Sarawak & Indonesian timber
4. Antarctica exploitation
5. Defoliants and Pesticides
6. Alaskan Pipeline
7. Trans Siberian Pipe line
8. Trans Amazonian Highway
9. Karakoram Highway
10. Mombasa - Kampala Railline
11. Rhine - Maine – Danube
12. Nepal-India-Bangladesh Rivers
13. Aswan Dam
14. Sahel Region
15. Oil spills - Gulf war
16. Minamata Bay
17. Ethiopia - Somalia tangles
18. European lakes
19. North American Lakes
20. Lake Beikal

F. ULTIMATE DENOMINATORS

1. Cost-Benefit ratios
2. Population - Resources ratios
3. Populations & Productive lands
4. Per capita productive land

II. HINDSIGHT WISDOMS

A. INTRODUCTION

1. Holism and Humanism
2. Warning Signals & Sounds inaudible and deafening

B. PHILOSOPHICAL ROOTS: Baseline thoughts of Mankind

1. Religions: Nature supreme. No religion anticipated supremacy of man and matter over spirit and nature except Hinduism which has predicted ultimate doom due to man's dominion over matter.

   Evolution of Religions in different Regions of the World: Paganism to Vedic Dharma, Hinduism, Jainism, Budhism, Christianity, Islam, Taosism, Bahai, Bishnoi, Amish, Bioethics, Ecodestruction, Spiritualism vs Materialism, Religion and Future.
2. Philosophers: Theoreau, Emerson, Tolstoy, Gandhi. Essence of all religions is that man is a part of nature and has to live accordingly.
3. Marxism: Nature is a resource

C. LITERARY ROOTS: Predictions and prophesies

1. Verne, Wells, Orwell, Huxley
2. Snow, Clarke, Toffler, Flechtheim, Marxists

D. HISTORICAL ROOTS: The tangible facts

Ancient times

1. Nomads - Herds - Civilisations
2. Communes - Resource Consciousness - Balances
3. Societies - Territories - Religions - Trades - Conquests
4. Empirical Science and Technology

Medieval times

1. Trade Routes + Barters - Conquest
2. Industrial revolution - Origin of the first world
   Maritime conquests - Colonialism - Competition
   Enslavement - Murder - Slow acquisition techniques,
   Market - Military - Missionary axis, social Darwinism

Modern times

1. **World war I:** Colonialists Vs Colonialists

   Dragging colonies along, reparations as well as sharing spoils; Feudalism vs Capitalism - Origin of the 2nd world, matter over natural quests for ownership of own resources in colonised nations.

2. **World War II:** Colonialists Vs Colonialists

   Theaters of war in the colonies' Reparations, - Victor and Vanquished suffer equally - international treaties - loss of colonies and their resources - Marshall Plan and consumerism - Emergence of 2nd World as an alternative.

3. **World War III:** Former Colonialists Vs former Colonies

   Extensive development - conversion of raw materials into commodities for consumption and commerce - Militarism and industry - Neocolonialism through Science, Technology and trade - Aid, loans, balances of trade, interest and loan repayments - Regional wars - Second world vs Neocolonialism in the 3rd world.

III. ENVIRONMENTAL CONSCIOUSNESS WORLD WAR IV

A. THE WARNINGS

1. Club of Rome predictions
2. The data from Global 2,000 Report
3. The realities from state of the world reports
4. The philosophies: Leopold, Mumford, Darling, Boulding, Carson, Ehrlich, Commoner, Mead etc.
5. Philosophers - Doomists Vs Boomists

B. THE DILEMMAS OF NATIONS

1. Third World: Depleted resources, over population, Poor Science and Technology. Balance of payments, Debt burdens, unpatriotic exploitation of all sorts, Militarism and human rights, violations of today or Environment for tomorrow?
2. Second World: S&T, R&D geared for basic needs, Militarism and aid to the third world - Raising aspirations of peoples within & their sacrifices - Abdications, collapses and revolts against the political economics - change of values and abandonment of the third world - colonial resources and the communication systems of the first world and the utter irresponsibility and dishonesty of the 3rd world pulled down the second world - A tragedy of human destiny.

3. First World: Triumph of market economy - Scaling down of Militarism - Consumerism, pollution, S&T, R&D, Trade and Aid - Guardians of the planet - PPPN & RNRP a settled fact? Environmental imperialism or trusteeship can effluence be scaled down for basic needs.

IV. RECENT DEVELOPMENTS

A. UNITED NATIONS: UNEP, IUCN, UNCHE, ICFR, ICPEMC
First, Second & Third Worlds: North and South

B. NON-GOVERNMENTAL AGENCIES: FOE, WWI, Greenpeace etc

Efforts of COR, UNEP, WCS, Movements

C. COUNTRIES: Green Political Parties, Governmental Actions

V. CONCLUSIONS: ENVIRONMENTALISM

A. PSYCHES: appropriation, dispossession, alienation, preservation

B. CONSEQUENCES Divisions - Conflicts - hatreds and violence

C. PRECEPTS

1. Each organism takes what it needs and gives what it can. Consequently productivity of the whole is greater than the sum totals of the constituents. This leads of Harmony.
2. Therefore whatever is ethically wrong cannot be ecologically right.
3. Ecology: The new god that never fails and replaces all others, A way of life, ethos and ethics

D. PRACTICES: Autarkism + Humanism + Asceticism + communism

VI. HIGH IDEALISM IS THE REALISTIC METHOD

A. BOOM: Simon, Kahn Growth

B. DOOM: Violent Economics Paddock, Hardin, Myers
Triage, Life Boat, Noah's Ark

C. EQUILIBRIUM

Marx: Socialism, Gandhi: Non-violent Economics

Schumacher: Balanced Reductionism

Boulding, Mead, Ward, Stevenson: Spaceship Earth

Brown: Anticonsumerism, Steady-state Existentialism

D. BOOM FOR EQUILIBRIUM OR A CERTAIN DOOM: A Synthesis

Marx Boulding: Green Philosophy

Mead: Radical Humanism Gandhi

Schumacher: New Religion

E. PROVIDENTIAL ECOLOGY: Ethics, Old Values
Conservatism without being Conservative
Radical/ Revolutionary Conservatism

F. TYPES OF BOATS
Full: No space - Enough
Empty: Space - Surplus
Over-crowded: Sinks - Leave them

G. TYPES OF COUNTRIES
1. Recover without Medicines
2. Recover with Medicines
3. No Recovery despite Medicine

VIII. SELECTED BIBLIOGRAPHY

1. Barney 1982 : Global 2000 report
2. Huxley 1963 : Politics of Ecology
3. Hardin 1959 : Nature and lifeboat theory
4. Farvar & Milton 1972 : Careless Technology
5. Idris 1988 : Has humankind a Future ?
6. Kahn 1983 : Resourceful Earth
7. Meadows et al 1972 : Limits to growth
8. Myers 1980 : Pre-sinking ark
9. Nash 1977 : Progress as if survival Mattered
10. Osborne 1953 : Limits of the Earth
11. Simon 1984 : Ultimate resource
12. Spretnak & Capra 1985 : Green politics
13. Toffler 1970 : Future shock
14. Tolba 1983 : Earth Matters
15. Ward and Dubois 1972 : Only one Earth
World Food Board 1938
World Resource Board 1940
World in 1984

Geddes:
Radhakamal Mukherjee:
Pathak: Religion and Economy of the Himalayas

3. BASIC PRINCIPLES

ORIGINS OF THE ETHOS

(a) 1940 8th Amer. Sci. Congr. Clauses

(b) 1947 Moore - Worlds Wealth, World Resource Board

(c) Some significant contributors/contributions

  (a) Burnham: [1973] Blue Print for survival (Brit. Assoc. Adv. Sci)

  (b) Mumford: Built Environments

  (c) Darling: Reith lectures, Children & Plenty

  (f) Ehrlich: Population

  (g) Dubois: Cycling and diagnosis

  (h) Hardin: Sinking Ship

  (i) Others: Leopolds, Keunen, Dorst, Gates, Haldac, Mellanby, Wilson

1. Ecology Vs Economy Vs Society in time and space

2. Orient / Occident, Old / New World First, Second & Third Worlds

   Countries : G-7, G-15, G-18, G-77

   Wars : GW-1 GW-2 GW-3 GW-4 GW-5 RW-continuous

3. Prehistoric, Ancient, Medieval, Premodern, Modern, Post Modern

4. Resources: Primary/Secondary/Tertiary, Renewable/non-Renewable, Shared / Unshared, Basic Needs / Consumerism

5. Human Resources: Evolutionary, Industrial Revolution, Education, Science, Technology

6. Products: Ecological & Economic —> Agricultural & Industrial balanced by Detriments, Backlashes and Feed Backs

7. Ecological Surplus = EP > AP+IP =Buffering Endowment = Nationhood

8. BUYERS AND SELLERS ONLY

   Exclusion — Socially — Marginalisation — 70: 30

   Exclusion — Ecologically — 30: 70

9. Management

   (a) Local Vs Regional Vs Global outlooks

   (b) Exploration, alternatives, Conservation, Frugality & Altruism, Technological Efficiency, Renewability

10. Policies of the Governments on Science, Technology, Industry, Basic Needs, Consumerism, Social Distribution, Trade and

Finances are the keys.

Ideals: Scientific cooperations Technology transfers Industrial collaborations, Balance of trade (GATT) Balanced Payments.

11. Importance of Trade
    (a) Exports and Imports depend upon wealth, productivity and markets
    (b) Production by Binational and Multinational or National Enterprises

1. Bi-Multinationals	:	Technology & Markets available Profits and Capital fly Loss of Resources Consumerism
2. National	:	Local Technology, Local industry, Local Markets, Local Science, No flight of capital, No loss of resources Local needs - Basic needs Enormous Research (Science) & Development (Technology)

12. Role of Militarism: Diversion of Resources for Non-Developmental destructive purposes

    Role of Detente: Availability of Resources for peoples needs
13. Role of Political Systems and Changes

(a)	Basic Need		
	Centralised Economies	:	Essential Goods 'Technology, & productivity & distribution limited inputs Science, Technology directional
(b)	Market Economics	:	Excessive Consumerism
	Capitalistic Economics	:	Dominates basic needs Abundant inputs Science, Technology diverse
(c)	Mixed Economies	:	Essential commodities &distribution is the prime justice Capital intensive, therefore market oriented External Aid, Science, Technology, Markets etc essential

Changes in the economics alter national perspectives and international activities, commitments e.g. Eastern Europe.

14. Role of Internal Policies
    (a) Regional imbalances, Social strife and violence
    (b) Solution: Appropriate distribution through decentralisation and development based on ecological sustainability
15. Role of External Policies
    (a) Excessive dependence on the leader of technology, industry and capital
    (b) Solution: Development of indigenous expertise for satisfying national needs and not market economy
16. Imperatives: Plan Documents
    (a) Surveys of resources - Quality, quantity
    (b) Scientific knowledge availability
    (c) Technological amenability for exploitation
    (d) Ecological balances,
    (e) Targets of receipt
    (f) Ecologically viable political Units
        - Agroecosystems - Small towns - Small states
17. Cultural Economics of Ecological Resources
    (a) The Geography, Sciences, Technology, Development, Culture, Politics (Systems, Policies, Humans)
        Economics (Trade, Industry & Human resources) and Ecology of Natural Resources (Depletion & degradation in one N.R.)

People	Economics	Forest	Politics
Soil	Culture	River	Dam

        No enumeration of details of any single resource Not a resource based instruction, but a need based interaction More of concepts, trends & prospects and Alternative perspectives rather than listing of details of items
    (b) Thesis, Antithesis and Synthesis
        A. Taxonomy
        B. Exploitation / Development
        C. Motives / Objectives Targets
        D. Consequences E. Management F. Others
           - Carrying capacity, Biodiversity, Buffering - WCS
           - The six friends WWWWWH For whom and by whom

1. Formations: Geological, Biological, Both, Planetary
2. Longevity: Finite / Infinite, Large in Quantity or Renewable

3. Associations: Physical and Biological, Interactions, Chain Reactions - Everything is connected to everything
4. Usage: Reversible/Irreversible = Renewable / Exhaustible, Renewability Rates, Principle of Optimal Usage and Optimal depletion: Ecology of Resources
5. Secondary & Tertiary Resources: Science of Resources
6. Tradition / Heritage / Empiricism vs Intellectual Property Rights
7. Triage: Survivabiity of the Recipient / Victim 1918, 1970s
   Survivability of the Donor / Oppressor 1992 —>
8. Greed for Resources and Products :
9. Duties vs Rights of Leaderships and Followers

SWADESHI VS VIDESHI

1. NORTH will not take Goods from SOUTH due to Poor Quality: Improve Quality by buying their TECHNOLOGY through their CURRENCY
2. SELL NRs for Exchangeable Currency because of No Goods, because of No Good Technology, because of No Good Science, because of WHOM ?
3. Selling NRs leads to DEPLETIONS and they to Poverty of Resources
4. Science dominated by Higher Castes and now Higher Classes [or New Entries into them]. They build Personal empires in India or migrate to NORTH
5. Vicious Circle of Trade and Technology - Technology Transfers — Appropriate Technology - Latest Scientific improvements
   Old Products —> New Resources Wastes —> New Resources
6. Competition Impossible; Consumerism Indefensible.
   Therefore Production for local People is a Priority = SWADESHI

Example in India on Oil Seeds: The Cooking Medium

Resource	Science		Trade
Land Resource —>	Agriculture —> Oil Seeds —>		Imports —> Prices
Governance			
	Consumerism		Social Justice
Prices	Demands vs Needs		Population
	Consumers		Poverty line
Decrease <—	Resources	Limited <—	Augmentation by S,T,T
Increase <—	Demand, Consumer Population, Poverty		

Central Dogma: Conceptual Frame Work of Studying Nature's Resources

Resources	*Exploitation*	*Usage (Targets)*	*Consequences Ecol/Econ/Social*
(a) Types (SwampeaH)	(a) Science (R)	(a) Essential Basic Needs	(a) Depletion
(b) Geography			
(b) Distribution	(b) Technology(D)	(b) Nonessential consumerism Sustainable Vs Unsustai-nable	(b) Degradation
(c) Quality	(c) Trade Exports Imports		(c) Dependence (S&T; R&D)
(d) Quantity			(d) Trade Deficits
(e) Ecology Other Resources	(d) Industries Development		(e) National Income insufficient
			(f) Debt Burdens
			(g) Inequalities
			(h) Poverty
			(i) Division & Conflict

CONSTRAINTS & HOPES:

1. INFORMATION —> KNOWLEDGE —> WISDOM
2. NIMbyism, NODMYtism, NIMYltism, Nerlicofism

> *All nature wears one universal grin.*
>
> **Henry Fielding**

4. BIOSPHERE RESERVES

A. INTRODUCTION

The biosphere reserve concept; the need for biosphere reserves; the main criteria for establishing biosphere reserves; the conservation and legal status of these reserves and their advantages over other established modes of conservation.

Development	: Resources & Economics
Human society	: Anthropology & Sociology
Evolution	: Biology & Ecology

1. Nature: diversity of climate, substrata habitat life forms,
2. Ecosystems: Defined similarity of climate, habitat, life forms, cycles, foodchains and webs
   (a) Nonbiological Components: Air, water, climate, substratum (High longevity & longer history)
   (b) Biological Components: Consequences more severe (Lower longevity & long history)
3. Biospheres : Biological components of one ecosystem or a few continuing ecosystems, Andes (Peru) Himalayas (India)

   1. Preservation   2. Regeneration

   (a) Diversity: Plants, Animals, microbes

- Frequency	- Survival	- Density
- Stability	- Genetics	- genepool
- heritage		

   Ecological - Stability through Webs Chains [ideal]
   Economic Use [Real]

   - How many in a system   - Microhabitats
   - Each in how many systems

   (b) Germplasm Resources - extinction - Genetic Death
   Biological Resources - depletion - Physical Death

   (c) Productivity - Economic utility, Ecological balance

		Stages
Total productivity	Sum of totals of Surplus Constituents	4
Exploitation Equilibrium Conservation		3
Degradation of system Endangered Protected		4
Depletion of resource Extinction		5

(d) Buffering ability - climatic factors prevented from affecting substratum
   1. Physical - Middle layers between Core & Periphery
   2. Evolutionary

(e) Carrying capacity (Managing Sustainability
   1. Deserts = nil 2. Forests = Full
   3. Others = Intermediary
   Mountains, Islands, Grass lands, Waters

(f) Balances - 1. Territorial symbiosis
   2. Nutritional symbiosis
   3. Reproductive interdependences
   4. Checks & Balances - Predator-Prey, Chains, Webs, links

4. Biosphere Reserves
   (a) Economic utility & human habitations endanger ecological balances, endanger and deplete resourcefulness, eliminate buffering ability
   (b) The above threaten human survival
   (c) Imperative: Protect & regenerate the remaining ecosystems by reserving them for conservation
5. Ecological Development (based on ecological resourcefulness i.e. infrastructure)
   (a) Man Nature
   Ecosystems Man Man Man
   Biosphere Living conditions
   (b) Communism means ecological principles in a community
6. Ecological Regeneration
   Habitat - Buffering agents - frequency - diversity, productions, balances, webs, etc not mere populating by useful plant (i.e. Social Forestry).
7. Habitat cannot be viewed merely as a Life Supporting System.
   It has to be an ecological regenerating system
8. Biogenesis Vs Noogenesis
   Man is like any other animal depending on plants, animals & non living world and not a slave of Science & Technology
9. Space Ship Earth / Sinking Ship / Noah's Ark :
   Commonsense Vs Temptation

B. HISTORY

1. International Biological Programme [IBP] Man & Biosphere Programme [1974]. Idea initiated by UNESCO during 1973-74 under the Man and Biosphere programme.

   IUCN-UNEP-WWF (1980) set priority requirements. International Union for conservation of Nature, United Nations Environment Programme & World Wildlife Fund

2. Concept of Reserving Biological heritage, lest their spaceship Earth will loose its self sustainability and breaks off to disintegrate irrevocably.

3. Multidimensional Approach lead to the Biosphere Reserve concept

   (a) Resources : The ultimate resource base (Club of Rome, OR)

   (b) Economy : "Goods" Vs "bads", costing of "bads" impossible therefore keep the balance in favour of goods (Boulding) Greenhouse & Ozone (Caron)

   (c) Ecology : Everything being related to everything else, disturbance of any single component, may alter many others, consequences of which may be immeasurable. (Replacement of Oaks by Pines in the Himalayas; Amazon basin clearance for ranching, roadways, etc.) Leopold: forestry & Wildlife

   (d) Biology : Source of Germplasm Resources of Plants & animals, Ethnobotany, Wild relatives of cultivated plants - Rice, wheat, maize, sunflower, etc. Centres of origin & diversity of cultivated plants. (Darling (FAO, IUCN, IBPGR)

   (e) Anthropology: Native people - Forest Culture (Aranya; Mead)

   (f) Sociology : Population Explosion bound to pressurise the biosphere and under it fragile and disintegrate Protection & Education (COR, Ward)

   g. Fragility : The concept of Fragility: Irreversible breakdown of exploitation exceeds the limits of bearability

4. Characteristics of a Biosphere: Primarily biological, others secondarily

   (a) Diversity of organisms

(b) Buffering between litho - atmosphere

(c) Carrying capacity

5. Sustainable Development : Exploitation possible within the limits of bearability, i.e. without rendering the ecosystems fragile

6. Interventions :

(a) Policy : national, international appropriate or harmful

(b) Technology : national, international appropriate or harmful

(c) Anarchy

7. Dangers to the Biosphere

(a) Greenhouse effect: Destruction of terrestrial biosphere

(b) Ozone layer depletion: Melting pot Diversity due to uv rays

(c) Consumer ethos: Accelerates greenhouse effect
Destroy and develop, sell & buy
i.e. No cycling approach

(d) Poverty and its social pressures

(e) International Relations - Trade/Tourism/Aid and Debt/Wars

8. If the "bads" / "letoffs" / "imbalances" can be cycled development possible: Ecodevelopment; if not possible: Conservation

9. 70 countries, 270 resources, transboundary (details elsewhere)

10. Modalities and mechanisms of operating biosphere resources (details elsewhere)

C. CONSTRAINTS & PROBLEMS PERCEIVED BY TWO TYPES OF CASES

1. Time Variation: 7

(a) Hunter-gatherer : 1 day

(b) Traditional peasant farmer : 1 year

(c) Politician : Next Election

(d) Plant breeder : 10 years

(e) Forester : 30-50 years

(f) Crop Evolutionist : 100 years

(g) Genetical Conservationist : 10,000 years

2. Perception Variation: 4

(a) Individuals

(b) Social groups

(c) Historical cultural context

(d) Geographical regions

D. INTERNATIONAL SCENE

1. Priority requirements
   (a) Reservation of prime quality crop land for crops
   (b) Management for productivity in crop, grazing lands and forests
   (c) Prevention of soil degradation or restoration of degraded soil
   (d) Protection of catchment areas
   (e) Maintenance of support systems for fisheries
   (f) Control of pollution
   (g) Prevention of species extinction
   (h) Preservation of germ plasm
   (i) Establishment of a network of protected areas
   (j) Regulation of living resource utilization
   (k) Reduction of incidental cake (fisheries, forestry, etc)
2. Priority National Actions
   (a) Preparation of conservation strategies
   (b) Adoption of anticipatory environmental policies
   (c) Preparation of ecosystem evaluations
   (d) Advance assessment of environmental effects of all actions
   (e) Land and water use allocation based on assessments
   (f) Legislation concerning living resources and enforcement
   (g) Establishment of soil and water conservation body
   (h) Management of Marine living resources
   (i) Training facilities at professional, technician and used levels
   (j) Improvement of living resources management
   (k) Greater public participation
   (l) Education campaigns for users of sources, legislators, decision makers, and students.
   (m) Rural development with short and long term measures

E. FACETS OF STUDY

1. Long - term

   Meteorology, Hydrometry, Geology, Vegetation, Fauna, Soil Anthropology, Economic plants, Plants from Medicinal families, In situ germplasm

   Developmental activities: agriculture, industry, trade, tourism Impacts from development: Economic, Social, Biological

2. Short - term

   Afforestation, Weeds, Biological Pest Control, Tribal Medicine, Fuel Values of Pioneer Species, MFP [NTFP]

F. INDIAN SCENE

The implementation of the Biosphere Reserve Concept in India - requirements, advantages, disadvantages, range etc.

1. Man and Biosphere programme committee constituted in 1979
2. India: The Background

Location	: 8-38 N 60-98 E	Origins of Economic
Area	: 330 million hectares	plants: 150
Populations	: 800 million	Centres or origin: 1
Animals	: 65,000	Phytogeographic
Plants	: 45,000 species	realms: 2
		Regions: 12

3. Conservation efforts: 10 outmoded legislations
4. Indian Wild Life Act of 1972: Species and habitats
   (a) National Parks: 44
   (b) Sanctuaries: 207
   (c) Area: 88,000 Sq.Km. 3% of total and 12% of forested area
5. Biosphere Reserves: Biotic community as a whole

(a) Nilgiri (TN, Karnataka, Kerala)	(g) Kaziranga (Assam)
(b) Namdapha (Arunachal)	(h) Sunderban (Bengal)
(c) Nandadevi (U.P.)	(i) Thar desert (Rajasthan)
(d) Uttarakhand (U.P.)	(j) Manas (Assam)
(e) North Andamans	(k) Kanha (M.P.)
(f) Gulf of Mannar (TN)	(l) Nohrek (Meghalaya)

6. Action Plan

(a) Central Cell	(b) Concept development
(c) Declaration of select areas	(d) Legal protection
(e) Local participation :	
(f) Research and Monitoring:	Baseline data, Monitoring, Manipulation, Restoration

   (g) Education and training h. International Co-operation

G. AN EXAMPLE: NILGIRIS BIOSPHERE RESERVE

1. Location	: 76-74 45' E and 11 15' to 12 15 N		
2. Altitude	: 300 - 2700 m		
3. Area	: 5700 Sq. Km.		
	Core zone	: 2000 S(q) Km.	

		Forestry	: 2300 S(q) Km.
		Agriculture	: 1300 S(q) Km.
		Degraded	: 50 S(q) Km.
4. Fauna	:	Reptiles	: 80(endangered)
		Mammals	: 100 (5)
		Birds	: 550 (1)

5. Flora: 3500 (13,000 in India), 1500: Endemic
6. Tribals: About 20
7. Sub-Regions: About 15
   (a) Coorg Wynad
   (b) Kerala Wynad
   (c) Nilgiri Wynad
   (d) Nilambur
   (e) Amarambalam
   (f) Silent valley
   (g) Upper Nilgiri Plateau
   (h) Attapadi valley
   (i) Attapadi plateau
   (j) Siruvani Hills
   (k) Nilgiri S.E. slopes
   (l) Nilgiri E. Slopes
   (m) Sigur Plateau
   (n) Mysore Plateau S
   (o) Mysore Plateau N
8. Research Concepts:
   (a) Baseline data
   (b) Monitoring
   (c) Manipulation
   (d) Restoration

H. TYPES OF PROJECTS FOR NILGIRI BIOSPHERE RESERVE

1. Environmental history from the early records: Degradation in time.
2. Baseline data: flora, fauna, inventory of useful plants economically and ecologically and their characterisation.
3. Baseline data :climate, geography, geology, water, people
4. Impact Monitoring of agriculture, industries, forestry, tourism, trade and people
5. Ecological regeneration: Reclamation of degraded ecosystems
6. Ecorehabilitation: Integrated Rural Development, Past, Present and Future. Resources of Tribals, Resurrection of time-honoured practices

I. ANOTHER CASE STUDY: NANDADEVI BIOSPHERE RESERVE:

The historical events which lead to the degradation of the area which is presently under the protective status of a biosphere reserve area.

Landmark events in conservation action; present status and future of the reserve - how much of a difference has it made ?

J. SANCTUARIES, PARKS ETC.

The fundamental differences between sanctuaries, National parks and Reserves and the rules that govern them. Can we afford sanctuaries and National Parks ?

1. Indian scenario

Percentage of forested area order the legal protection of sanctuaries and National parks-the legal differences, areas/regions covered by them. number of sanctuaries and National Parks in each of the Indian states.

1. National Parks	:	75 —> 148
2. Sanctuaries	:	421 —> 503
3. Area	:	4.2% —> 4.6 %
4. Animals	:	81 000 [6.4% of the World] 62 % Endemic Endangered: 81 Mammals 47 Birds 15 Reptiles 3 Amphibians
5. Plants	:	45 000 [7% of the World] Flowering: 15000 Endangered: 15000 Endemic: 4900, Himalayan [2500] Peninsular [1800]

2. International scenario

USA

The National Conservation strategy of the United States of America and how it has lead to the formation of the worlds first National Park. The country's role in providing a major stimulus for "Conservation-through legal power" and establishing a nation-wide conservation ethic. The National Park Service (NPS) and the Outdoor Recreation Resources Review Commission (ORRRC), the wildlife and conservation related Acts and the reasons for the longterm success of the American National Park system.

USSR AND EASTERN EUROPE

The Soviet bloc although presently obsolete had a vastly different conservation strategy-the pros and cons of this method of protection and its longterm success or sustainability are discussed, as well as the global reaction to this approach.

SUMMARY

The protection of wilderness lands such as sanctuaries, parks and reserves is an affordable luxury or a global imperative - a purely personal opinion.

3. Biosphere Reserves of the World

Country	*Total area of reserves (ha)*	*Country*	*Total area of reserves (ha)*
Argentina (4)	2,005,180	Italy (3)	33,738
Australia (12)	4,742,673	Ivory Coast (2)	1,480,000
Austria (4)	27,600	Japan (4)	116,000
Benin (1)	380,000	Kenya (4)	851,359
Bolivia (2)	300,000	Korea, Republic (1)	37,430
Bulgaria (17)	27,602	Mali (1)	771,000
Byelorussian SSR	76,201	Mauritius (1)	3,594
Cameroon (3)	850,000	Mexico (3)	473,200
Canada (4)	375,147	Nigeria (1)	460
Central African	1,640,200	Norway (1)	1,555,000
Republic (2)		Pakistan (1)	31,355
Chile (7)	2,589,375	Panama (1)	575,000
China (3)	425,645	Peru (3)	2,506,739
Colombia (3)	2,514,375	Philippines (1)	23,525
Congo (1)	110,000	Poland (4)	25,576
Costa Rica (1)	500,000	Portugal (1)	395
Cuba (1)	10,000	Romania (3)	41,213
Czechoslovakia (4)	176,909	Rwanda (1)	15,065
Denmark (1)	70,000,000	Senegal (3)	1,093,756
Ecuador (1)	766,514	Spain (10)	614,977
Egypt (1)	1,000	Srilanka (2)	9,412
France (4)	344,527	Sudan (2)	1,900,970
Gabon (1)	15,000	Switzerland (1)	16,870
German Democratic	3,497	Tanzania, United	2,337,900
Republic (2) Republic (2)			
German, Federal	13,100	Thailand (3)	26,100
Republic (1)		Tunisia (4)	32,425
Ghana (1)	7,770	Ukraine (2)	120,655
Greece (2)	8,840	USSR (15)	4,134,541
Guinea (2)	133,300	UK (13)	44,308
Honduras (1)	500,000	USA (43)	14,158,855
Hungary (5)	128,883	Uruguay (1)	200,000
Indonesia (6)	1,319,440	Yugoslavia (2)	350,000
Iran (9)	2,609,701	Zaire (3)	297,700
Ireland (2)	8,808		
( ) number of reserves		66 (252)	1,56,870,317

5. SYSTEMS & RESOURCES

All resources of man are distributed in the various ecosystems. When one is exploited preferentially/exclusively, others get disturbed as they are linked together - leading to ultimate loss of balances. Taking care of these unexpected effects is necessary. Therefore exploitation of a resource should be on an ecosystem basis - i.e. covering all its resources holistically and not a few sectorally.

When copper is extracted in a tropical rainforest of Brazil, the soil, plant & animal life are destroyed simultaneously/concurrently. This is true with most mining operations - mineral, timber etc. in all the pristine ecosystems. So Management practices based on systems approach has to begin with the very beginning - to obtain maximum utility, avoid wastage of associated sources and manage the degradation of the ecosystem.

A. TROPICAL FORESTS

1. Plants - Timber & others
2. Fertile humus soil
3. Animals
4. Minerals - May be
5. Plant & animal physiology & behaviour

B. DESERTS

1. Minerals
2. Plant & animal physiology & behaviour

C. GRASSLAND & SAVANAHS

1. Water
2. Minerals
3. Plants
4. Animals - game animals, etc.
5. Plant and animal physiology & behaviour

D. TEMPERATE FORESTS

1. Plants - Timber & others
2. Fertile humus soil
3. Animals
4. Minerals
5. Plant & animal physiology & bebahaviour
6. Less extent except minerals

E. INLAND WATERS

1. Potable water
2. Irrigation
3. Fisheries
4. Transport

F. MARINE SYSTEMS (islands, estuaries)

1. Fisheries
2. Transport
3. Minerals

II. ECOSYSTEMS

A. ECOSYSTEM

1. Definition: "Webster". "Assemblage of objects joined in a regular interaction and inter dependence".
2. Classification: Ecosystems are classified on the basis of it origin (or) existence (ie) Manmade/managed and Natural and further on the basis of Biological aspects.

B. MANMADE/MANAGED ECOSYSTEMS: Artificial and Semi-natural

1. Croplands: They are nothing but Agricultural fields (paddy etc) Plantations, Afforestations etc. Social Forestry
2. Aquatic Ecosystems
   (a) Pond Ecosystems: They are freshwater ecosystems (not always) managed by man. (ed) Aquaculture, Fisheries etc.
   (b) Wetlands: They are mostly semi-natural and managed. eg. Paddy field, peat mining

C. NATURAL ECOSYSTEMS: Climate, Substratum, Habitat, Cycles, Others

A. TERRESTRIAL ECOSYSTEMS

1. Tropical Moist Forests:
   (a) Definition: Evergreen, hygrophilous With woody lianas, herbs and massive trees forming distinct canopies
   (b) Distribution: Global and in Tropical areas.
   (c) Salient features: Shelter for many endangered species, food, fuel, medicine, Timber, NTP, etc.
   (d) Management: IUCN Publication (Poora & Sayer 1991) Gives six key principles of management.
2. Transition communities
   (a) They form, as the mediator,transition ecosystems in between terrestrial and aquatic ecosystems.
   (b) Salt marshes / mud flats: They are areas of alluvial deposition with herbivorous, low shrubby. Terrestrial vascular plants.
      - Geographical distribution: Global, restricted to 28 N & 25 S in Neotropics. & 28 N & 38 S in Palaeotropics.

- Values of saltmarshes: Optimal places to carryout Ecological studies, highly productive ecosystems, serve as feeding ground for many birds, fishes,etc.

(c) Mangrove Ecosystems: They are littoral communities formed at sheltered lowlying tropical & sub tropical coasts

- Distribution: It is Global & restricted to tropical and subtropical areas.
- Flora & Fauna: Major floral communities are likes Acetabularia, Caulerpa, Dictyosphaeris, Mosses, marine algae fauna has Mudskipper (Characteristic of mangroves), Nematodes Copepods, Amphipoda, Mollusca etc.
- Values of mangroves: Timber yield, pulp, particle board, commercial, fisting, Aquaculture purpose (shrimps and prawns)
- Threats to mangroves: Commercial clearance, Aquaculture, alternation of freshwater flow in to them. Traditionally considered as waste land, hence conversion occurs.
- Management: Management aspects requires wide range of ecological consideration, conservation & public education & legal activities.

3. Aquatic ecosystems: It includes all freshwater & Saline water ecosystems of the worlds (Bays, seas, oceans).

(a) Wetland ecosystem: They are areas with water logged condition comprise fresh brackish lotic (or) lentic ecosystems

- Types of wetlands - Bogs: Peat producing, present in moist climate. Fens: prolific peat producing wetlands, swamps with little (or) no peat accumulation with water logged stage. Flood plains periodically flooded areas with considerable variations in vegetations.
- Distribution: It is global, but the datas are not sufficient., (Compiled by UNESCO, Navigation charts etc)
- Values of wetlands: Generation of fisheries & wild life, recharging inland water supply, recreational values.
- Conservation: Designation, promote conservation motto in sensitive parts, establishment of natural reserves, training personnel for conservation efforts.

(b) Coral reefs : They are shallow aquatic ecosystems restricted to tropical seas, formed by CaCO3 deposits of polyps

- Distribution: Restricted to seas lying in between 30 N & 30 S latitudes.
- Values coral reefs: They have high degree of ecological consideration in sustained development. Maintain proper shore line, provides nutrients for many fishes & shelter to molluscs, crustaceans.
- Threats: Natural - storms, climatic change, predation
  Artificial - oil slicks, siltation, pollution.

A true teacher makes oneself Progressively unnecessary to his students

6. ATMOSPHERE ABOVE

A. GASEOUS COMPOSITION

1. **Nitrogen:** Growth. Amino acids, Proteins, Enzymes, Bases, Nucleic Acids, Regulations
2. **Oxygen:** Primary Metabolism, Respiration
3. **Carbon Dioxide:** Primary production, Photosynthesis
4. **Ozone:** O -Liberation, Prevention of UV rays passage to Earth
5. **Others :**

B. BIOLOGICAL COMPOSITION

1. Viruses
2. Bacteria
3. Fungal Spores
4. Plant Pollen
5. Dust Particles
6. Insects
7. Birds

C. PHYSICAL FEATURES

1. Temperature: Altitude, Latitude and Longitude Variations
2. Light Fall :
3. Rain Fall
4. Wind Movement & Cloud Travel: Direction and Velocity, Trade Winds Rainfall Variations, seeding of Clouds, Stealing Rains

D. DYNAMIC QUALITIES

1. Water Cycle
2. Diurnal Cycles
3. Seasonal Cycles
4. O, C, N Cycles

E. MAJOR PROBLEMS

1. Warming Gases
2. Ozone Depletion

F. COMPLEXITIES: INTERACTIONS

1. Acid Rain
2. Floods
3. Rising Water levels in Seas
4. Glaciers
5. Icebergs

G. OTHERS

1. Solar Energy
2. Green House Gases
3. Ozone Depleting Chemicals
4. Trade and Consumption
5. Science and Technology
6. Economics
7. Politics

7. MARINE SYSTEMS

A. INTRODUCTION

1. Major oceans and seas
2. Coastlines and Estuaries
3. Seabed
4. Islands, Reefs and bars
5. Geographical distribution

B. RESOURCEFULNESS

1. Food: Biotic resources: Fishes and Algae
2. Medicines 3. Energy: Tidal and Thermal 4. Others

C. RESOURCES

1. World's fertile zones
2. Fisheries
3. Other vertebrates
4. Molluscans & Crustaceans
5. Other invertebrates
6. Plants
7. Minerals

D. COASTLINES

1. Coastal Geomorphology
2. Ecology of Rocky Coasts
3. Intertidal fauna and flora
4. Ecology of Coastal Vegetation
5. Mangroves and Estuaries
6. Seaweeds
7. Fisheries
8. Plankton Resources
9. Wet Coastal Ecosystems

E. SALT MARSHES

1. Distribution
2. Composition
3. Economic importance
4. Exploitation

F. ISLANDS, REEFS ETC

1. Geography and distribution
2. Floristic variations
3. Faunistic variations
4. Human population diversity

G. SEABED

1. Floristic composition
2. Faunistic composition
3. Mining activities
   (a) Minerals (b) Oil (c) Natural gas

H. PROBLEMS / ISSUES

1. World catch and Consumption: Depletions breed depletions
2. Local people vs High technology:Inequalities in Science & Technology

3. Laws, Norms & Practices: Boundaries and Conflicts Legal regimes in oceanic fisheries; Territorial seas
4. Fishery Disputes - focus on Indian Ocean
5. Coastal pollutions
6. Waste Dumping
7. Strategic policies and action
8. Military activities
9. Conservation issues
10. Antarctica

I. INDIAN SCENARIO

1. Coastlines preservation and utilisation by local people
2. Mining for fossil fuels in Krishna-Godavari basin
3. Biosphere reserves necessary
4. Hardly any indigenous research work
5. Antarctica Expeditious 6. 20 or 200 miles territorial waters
7. Military activities: regional and global powers
8. Dumping of wastes by foreign companies
9. Desalination as an imperative

> *Politics is about the improvement of peoples' lives*

8. FOREST SYSTEMS

I. INTRODUCTION

A. Forests - a major natural resource

B. Ecological importance of forests

C. Characteristic featuresd. Geographical distribution

E. Animal life
F. Plant life

G. Watersheds
H. Timber

1. Forest as resources, distribution, composition.
2. Trees-uses-timber.
3. Timber-uses, types, products and its uses.

II. CHARACTERISTIC FEATURES

A. Storeyed vegetation

B. Balances and climax community

C. Diversity, long standing nature and resourcefulness

III. GEOGRAPHICAL DISTRIBUTION

A. Equatorial and tropical
B. Subtropical and tropical

C. Temperate zones
D. Wet and dry

E. Islands and mainlands

IV. ANIMAL LIFE: GEOGRAPHICAL / ECOSYSTEM VARIATIONS

A. Food

B. Skin and other organs: ivory, birds, rhesus monkey,

C. Hedonistic pursuits

D. Invertebrates

E. Vertebrates including birds

V. PLANT LIFE: GEOGRAPHICAL / ECOSYSTEM VARIATIONS

A. Life cycles,
B. Seed banks,

C. Sprouting nature,
D. Dispersal,

E. Dormancy, viability,
F. Rooting nature

G. Canopies and stories

VI. SOURCES

A. Roots
B. Stems

C. Leaves
D. Fruits E. Seeds

VII. USES

A. Foods
B. Medicines
C. Chemicals
E. Housing: timber
F. Clothing: fibre
G. Ornamentals:
H. Timber
D. Industrial purpose: plant products

VIII. TIMBER

A. Ancient woodland and traditional management
B. Ecological characteristics of ancient woods
C. Recent secondary woodlands
D. Silviculture
E. Timber needs - state/country/international
F. Trade-within the country/outside
G. Impacts (international impacts)
   1. Ecological
   2. Economical
   3. Social
H. Futurology
I. Management of woodlands (international trade also included)

IX. WATERSHEDS

A. Rainfall
B. Streams, waterfalls & gradients
C. Rivers and reservoirs
D. Soil carriage

X. PERSPECTIVES

A. DEPLETIONS BREED DEPLETIONS
   1. Demand for forest products
   2. Demand for land
   4. Depletion of forest resources & its impacts (Immediate & far reaching)
   3. Damning of rivers
   5. Forest Management & its problems
B. LOCAL PEOPLE
C. ECOLOGICAL CONSEQUENCES
   1. Balances & population sizes
   2. Watersheds
   3. Soil erosion
D. CONSERVATION
   1. CITES, IUCN, MAB, WWF, IBPGR, IBAGR, SCOPE
   2. Biosphere Reserves, Sanctuaries, Zoos, Parks,

E. ECONOMICS AND POLITICS

1. Forests economics & Economic assessment of forests.
2. Forests & economic development.
3. Forest based industries
4. Forests - Solution to the energy crisrs.
5. Contributions of forests to national development.

XI. FORESTS IN INDIA

1. Annual loss 1.3 million/hectare. 8 times more than put up by forest departments.
2. Wood shortage and therefore prices are so high that boat, cart and even toy making is affected.
3. Bastar: Indravati dams, & Mining will render the people refuges. Narmada sagar/Tehri-Gharwal
4. Social forestry: trees for commercial value. Not for basic needs or ecology.
5. Eucalyptus: 1/2 million hectares, water and nutrient depletion.
6. Landless involved in afforestation: can be the biggest input towards national progress by land giving.
7. Westoby 1960s Social forestry
8. 1928 village based Forestry Royal Commission

9. COAST LINES

A. **INTRODUCTION**

1. Coastal Geomorphology
2. Ecology of Rocky Coasts
3. Inter tidal fauna and flora
4. Ecology of Coastal Vegetation
5. Mangroves and Estuaries
6. Seaweeds
7. Fisheries
8. Plankton Resources
9. Wet Coastal Ecosystems

B. **COASTLINES**

1. Mangroves
   (a) Distribution: Global & regional
   (b) Flora and Fauna
   (c) Resourcefulness: Ornamental Wood and timber Medicines Thatching Consumption for intoxication
2. Other biota: Distribution, composition, exploitation & consequences
   1. Algae: classes, families, genera many
      (a) Food (b) Medicine (c) Chemicals
      (d) Others
   2. Angiosperms
      (a) Seag rasses: 13 genera & 50 species global; 13 sp in India
      (b) Food and shelter for fauna
      (c) Packaging, compost, paper
      (d) Prevention of erosion
   3. Vertebrates
      (a) Food (b) Medicinal (c) Others
   4. Invertebrates
      (a) Food (b) Medicinal (c) Others

C. **SALT MARSHES**

1. Distribution
2. Composition
3. Economic importance
4. Exploitation

II. WET COASTAL ECOSYSTEMS

A. INTRODUCTION

Coastlines of the World over 44,00,00 kms in length represent one of the most dynamic of natural environs and one of the most important contexts in which human activity and geomorphological processes interact. All coastal zones contain at least 2 obvious habitats.

- MARITIME ZONE - Home for many terrestrial animals and pets.
- SEA-as another habitat. Third obvious habitat in some is
- INTERTIDAL ZONE

1. Classification of coasts

   (a) Primary coasts: - land erosion coasts

   - Land deposition coasts

   - Coasts shaped by volcanic activity

   (b) Secondary Coasts: - Barrier coasts

   - Mud flats

   - Coral Reef coasts

   - Mangrove coasts

2. Principal features of coasts

   Coastal environs are affected by five main types of sea - water movement namely waves, tides, currents and aerial transport of spray. An outline of the coast is primarily determined by its geological composition and structure and by inshore topography.

3. Basic types of coasts formed

   (a) Embayed (b) Plain coasts (c) New coasts

4. Essential features

   (a) Protected coastlines (b) Shallow shores

   (c) Currents (d) Tidal Range & salt water

   (e) Substrate formation

5. Geographical distribution

   Stable sand areas are colonised by mangroves and salt marshes are common in areas where sand is admixed with salt.

B. DIFFERENT TYPES OF COASTS

1. Brackish water environs: Estuaries / brackish waters is defined as semi-enclosed of coastal waters which retain a connection with the open sea. There is a mixture of sea and fresh waters of terrestrial oxygen (pritchard 1967)

   (a) Classification: Coastal plain estuaries; Semi enclosed Bays (bar built estuary); Tectonic estuaries

(b) Biota of Estuaries: Stressful environments and is perhaps not surprising that relatively few species have evolved the necessary adaptation required. Tolerating excess salinity is another factor. Three faunal groups recognised - Marine, freshwater and brackish water sp. Freshwater sp. tolerate salinities more than 5%, and occur at the head of the estuary.

(c) Adaptations of Estuarine organisms.

(d) Productivity & food webs: Can be exceedingly productive comparable to TRF's. Contribution by phytoplanktons (for nutrients), benthic algae & rooted plants in primary production is large.

(e) Hypersaline environment: a. Lagoons b. Tide pools

2. Coral reefs

60% occur in the Indian Ocean, 14% in the caribbean, 13% in the South Pacific and 12% in the N. Pacific. 'Reefs' refers to population of strong corals which coatenues growth on products of its own making (Stoddart 1969).

(a) Classification: (a) Fringing Reefs (b) Barrier Reefs (c) Atolls (d) Patin Reefs (e) Bank Reefs

(b) Physical Disturbances :
   (a) Destruction from tropical storms
   (b) Anthropogenic disturbances such as overharvest & mining.

3. Salt marshes: Salt marshes are semi natural halophytic grasslands on the alluvial sediments breeding saline water bodies

(a) Most prominent flora:
   (a) Salicornia Spp. (b) Spartina Spp.

(b) Most prominent Fauna:
   1. Fiddler crabs b. Mud skippers
   2. Geese & duck sp. rats, moles which have a controlling effect on vegetation.
   3. Uca sp. excavates as much as 20% of the bank contributing to soil erosion.

(c) Management: Land cultivation and mining activities have big effects on water and silt inflow into estuarine basins and hence on the life cycle of salt marshes

(d) Reclamation: Reclaim the pollution affected areas; Restricting coastal sediments; Improved sedimentation process

4. Mangroves: Characteristic littoral plant communities of shelters, low lying tropical and sub-tropical coasts.

(a) ADAPTATIONS: laterally spreading cable roots; Pneumatophores - are above ground roots and facilitate development on anoxic sediments; Viviparous in nature Eg. Brugiera etc.

(b) FAUNA: (a) Prawns (b) Fidler crabs
(c) Mudshippers. (d) Ghost crabs (Dotella)
(e) Molluscs / Echinoderms

C. INSHORE HARVEST AND EXPLOITATION

1. Coral Reef
2. Crustacea
3. Molluscs
4. Commercial Fish, Seaweed

D. COASTAL MANAGEMENT: The potential resources in the coastal areas

1. Physical resources: a. Space b. Power Generation
2. Mineral resources: a. Lime-rich deposits. b. Gravel.
3. Effects of pollution

(a) Pollutants can increase the natural biological intake leading to toxic levels.

(b) Pesticides impact is magnified when received from fresh water zones. Often 5-10 times greater concentration in estuaries than offshores.

E. Effects of Pollution

1. Establishment of coastal Nature Reserves.
2. Necessary to determine composition and control machanisms before establishng a nature reserve.
3. Criterron for establishing a marine/coastal reserve is the extent available

10. WASTELANDS

A. Wastelands and Restoration

Connotation of the word 'wasteland'

Extent of Wastelands in India

Kinds of Wastelands -

- Cultivated land affected by soil erosion
- Waterlogged land (Wetlands excluded)
- Saline and Alkaline lands
- Degraded forests
- Sedimented land
- Shifting cultivation 'Slash and Burn'

Consequences of depletion: Ecological and Socioeconomic

Reclamation potential: Ecorestoration

Suitable trees

Costs of Wasteland development

Governmental Policies: N.W.D.B.

Priorities for future action

B. INTRODUCTION

1. Why Restoration ? 2. History of land use.

C. DEFINITION AND CLASSIFICATION

1. Wastelands are " lands so damaged by industrial/ other developments that it is incapable of beneficial use without treatment.
   (a) Derelict land: land abandoned or relinquished by the owner
   (b) Disturbed land: Unporductive but not abandoned land.

D. CONTRIBUTING FACTORS

1. Deep mines
2. Strip mines or Open cast mines.
3. Quarries
4. Industrial & domestic wastes.
5. Naturally occurring wastelands.

E. RESTORATION

1. Planning and Management.
2. End uses of Restored land.
3. Nature conservation.

F. SOLUTIONS

1. Top soil conservation
2. Top soil application
3. Other materials
   (a) Sewage sludge
   (b) Domestic refuse
   (c) Pulverised fuel ash
   (d) Chemical wastes.
4. Hydraulic seeding
5. Direct improvement
6. Grasses & legumes
7. Trees & shrubs
8. Costs vs Benefits
   (a) Cost of land restoration.
   (b) Benefits of land restoration

> *Facts are stubborn things*
> *And whatever may be our wishes, Our inclinations,*
> *Or the dictates of our passion,*
> *They cannot alter the state of facts and evidence.*

11. HUMAN ECOLOGY AND RESOURCES

A. INTRODUCTION

1. For Millennia and Centuries in different parts of the world
   (a) human resources dominated over the other resources
   (b) competitively over fellow societies
   (c) by improving themselves in strength, competence and efficiency
2. Then Why this accent Now on HRD, prefaced by education in Environment
   a. NOW = 1970s in the North b. NOW = 1990s [?] in the South
3. Because acceleration of Human Resource Development urgently warranted due to the 5 dangers [LG] faced by Humanity, although to different extents in time and space.
4. Env. Edu. Initiated in late 1990s, legalised by Supreme Court intervention, in 2003
5. All round Development in quantity as well as quality in all areas of Human Endeavour, which may have direct or indirect bearing on a successful response to the challenges posed by the Limits to Growth and other Scenarios is the HRD
6. Development vs Detriment Backlashes and Feed backs
7. Human efforts to upgrade and improve themselves to meet challenges.

B. HISTORI CAL ASPECTS

1. Arab-Israeli war —> COR —> LG other Models on Future —> Several Worlds on the Planet —> several Worlds in each Polity —> Efforts Needed —> How, When By Whom —> Global 2000 — What Next ?
2. UNCHE —> UNCED-1 —> UNCED-2 —> UNCED-3 —> UNCED-4 1972 1982 1992 2002 2012
3. Suspicion / Allegation at UNO: Conspiracy of the Capitalism to block the progress of Developing Countries.
4. Marcuse, Mead, Ward, Stevenson, Leontief, etc: Marxism revised, 7% Tribals, Women & Asia, Peace Core to save Space ship Earth.

C. ANTHROPOLOGY

1. Africa —> Homo sapiens —> Races —> Negroid, Caucasoid, Mongoloid, Australoid
2. Nordic / slav / saxon / aryan / ural / siberian / arab

3. West, east, Central, bush, pigmy, sudan,
4. Chinese, mongols, polynesian, red indian
5. Tasmanian, andaman, dravidian, petagonian, eskimo,
6. Migrations and Mixtures
7. Others - Tribes, Ecotonal Populations, Special Habitats
8. Hair, Head, leg, Muscle, Joints, Brain etc

D. GENETICS

1. Galston to McKusick: Eugenics
2. Good, Bad, Homozygous, Heterozygous
3. Gene flows
4. Special characeristics of Raaces
5. Detrimental Characteristics

E. CIVILISATIONS: WILL AND ETHEL DURANT

1. Mesapotomia
2. Indus Valley
3. Egyptian
4. Incas
5. Aztecs
6. Others

F. CULTURES

1. Languages and Communications, Literatures, Music, Arts, Commodities and their Modifications, Travels
2. Life Styles: Habitat, Food, Reproduction
3. 30000 - 100000 years: Hunter —> Gatherer —> Settler —> Population —> Communities —> Society —> Rural —> Urban —>
4. Education: 10 Centuries / 40 centuries

G. MIGRATIONS & GENE FLOWS

1. Historical
   pre-industrial ireland and england
2. Causes and characteristics
   Religions Opportunity Disasters
3. Rural -Urban
4. Natural Inquisitiveness / curiosity of the Yonder
5. The Frontier Spirit: Ready to Move for Good with hope
6. Consequences and solutions

H. CURRENT SOCIETIES

1. Accelerated Education: Focused / Selective
2. Materialism, Discoveries & Inventions, Tools Technology, Fall of Values: Sell or Buy or Die

3. Churning [Manthan]
4. Information — Knowledge — Wisdom
5. Skills and Tools
6. Learning: See, Observe, Listen, Read, Ask
7. Self Crimes: Suicides, Addictions, Depressions, Abnormal psyches
8. Crimes on Others: Murders, Cheating, Outraging, Thieving, Lying
9. Ill-Health and Incapacity

I. PERSPECTIVES

1. 8:2 & 2:8 Syndrome — 5:5 Ideal
2. Critical Time in Human Life 20 -30;
3. 950 % Effort —> Global / Local Actions —> 10 Point Club —> 4 point actions.
4. Ecological Thinking that all are connected to each other
5. Value education to distinguish right from wrong and infuse morality and empathy for social justice
6. Improve positives for human welfare and decrease negatives

J. EXAMPLES: AT LEAST 50

1. Energy Productivity Revolutionised
   (a) Passivhaus of Darmstadt
   (b) Super Windows and Large Offices
   (c) School of Engineering & manufacture, De Montfort University, Leicestor, U.K.,
   (d) Renovating Masonry Houses
   (e) Cutting Danish Appliances Energy Use by 74 %
   (f) Lighting, Office Equipment,
   (g) Photovoltaics - 48 % Volts direct Current
   (h) Low Energy Beef
   (i) Breeding the Red Ones
   (j) Fans, Pumps and Motor Systems 11. Air Conditioning
   (k) Energy and Waste Savings
   (l) Super Refrigerators
2. Material Productivity
   (a) Water Efficiency in Manufacturing
   (b) Electronic Books and Catalogues
   (c) Steel vs Concrete
   (d) Subsurface Drip irrigation

(e) Residential Water Efficiency
(f) Perennial Poly culture
(g) Biointensive Minifarming
(h) Wood in Home Building
(i) Recycling wrapping plastic
(j) Rehabilitating vs Demolishing Buildings
(k) Reusing Bottles, Cans, large Containers

3. Transport Productivity - Revolutionised
   (a) Videoconferences
   (b) Electronic Mail
   (c) Capacity of the Existing Railways
   (d) Car-sharing
   (e) Car-free Mobility
4. Others
   (a) Electronic vs paper messages
   (b) Using solar energy
   (c) Afforestation
   (d) Reusing Materials
   (e) Recycling Products
   (f) Fullest use - One side Paper use
   (g) New Materials
   (h) Biotechnological Advances

Anti-Examples

1. Campus Plantations where none required
2. Water engineered into the sea
3. Excessive Computers but No Gadgets for lab studies, Field Studies, Academic Studies etc
4. Time and Life Managements
5. Perceptions and talent discovery and grooming

12. RESOURCEFULNESS OF ANIMALS

I. INTRODUCTION

A. A brief Evolutionary History: Man & animals co-existed for several thousands of years prior to domestication.

B. Man has been a major selective force in the life of fauna

C. Taxonomy: Vertebrates and invertebrates

D. Distribution: geographical, ecological

E. Anthropology: Domestication, food wildlife

II. USES OF ANIMALS & THEIR PRODUCTS

A. FOR FOOD: As meat, milk, eggs, blood etc. Important animals from the food present of view are

1. Cattle 2. Sheep 3. Pigs 4. Goats
5. Poultry 6. Fish 7. Shrimps & Prawns
8. Molluscs 9. Honey bees

B. FOR FIBRE, FUR, WOOL etc.: Animals explored for this are :

1. Sheep 2. Camel 3. Alpaca 4. Yak
5. Lynx

C. LOAD BEARING & DRAFT ANIMALS: Animals used for various purposes

1. bearing load - donkeys, elephants, horses, mules
2. Riding - horses, donkeys
3. Pulling carts - bullocks, horses etc.
4. ploughing & other agricultural works - Oxen, horses etc.
5. Sport - horse racing, bulls
6. Army - Cavalry

D. IN MEDICINE

1. Animals are useful in medicine in the following ways :
   (a) Alkaloids extracted from Insects, muskdeer etc.
   (b) Cancer Research - bison, molluscs
   (c) Animals products eg.
   Alantsin - European Blesten beetle, for urinogenital disorders
   Hundin - leeches, as anti coagulant.
   (d) As 'models' in research. eg. Manatees - Haemophilia
   Mangabey - Leprosy

E. MISCELLANEOUS

1. Pets
2. Animal products like hooves, leather, horn
   - (a) Fertilizer: excrement
   - (b) Transport: energy
   - (c) Household Companionship: dog, cat, etc.
   - (d) Skin, Teeth, feathers
   - (e) Ornamental purposes

III. EMPIRICAL KNOWLEDGE

Food, Energy, leather, musk, etc.

IV. DOMESTICATION

A. Domestication means 'human control' or breeding in captivity!

B. Dogs & wild pigs were first animals to be domesticated (about 12,000 years ago) as they were attracted to human camps and are hence said to be 'SELFDOMESTICATED'.

C. Domestication happened as animals could provide products like blood, meat, milk, skin. And can be good pets, hunters & used in sports.

D. The progress of domestication was as follows

1. The 'self-domesticated' species of dogs
2. The ruminants, cameloids, equines etc.
3. Animals adapted to inhospitable environment eg. camels in deserts, yaks in high attitudes.

E. The animals domesticated were - Dogs, Sheep & Goats, Cattle, Donkeys & Horses, Poultry, Camels, Reindeer, Cat etc.

F. Animals influenced man most significantly. Domestication & 'civilization' went hand in hand.

V. EXTENT OF DOMESTICATION IN VARIOUS PHYLA

A. Though there are millions of faunal species very few are domesticated/used

B. Mostly mammals are domesticated.

C. Very few invertebrates are used.

VI. WILD ANIMAL SPECIES

A. WILDLIFE - A short definition - Wildlife as a natural Resources Depletion - Causes and concern

B. TRADE IN WILDLIFE - Wildlife products: Live animals, products etc. Regulation of trade in Wildlife and conservation - CITES, Indian Wildlife Protection Act, 1972 etc.

C. COMMERCIAL FARMING OF WILDLIFE. Alternatives to Wildlife products

D. EXPLOITATION OF SOME WILD ANIMAL SPECIES

1. For food
   - (a) Marine animals - whales, fish etc.
   - (b) Mammals (terrestrial) - deer (various species)
     Reptiles (terrestrial) - iguanas, monitors etc.
     Birds - pheasants, pigeons, curlews etc.
   - (c) Has caused many an animal to be 'endangered'.
2. For Fibre, Hides, Fur etc.
   - (a) Animals used for their pelt, skin etc are chinchillas, leopards, vicuanas, others, Tiger, Kaola etc.
   - (b) Animals are hunted for this inspite of legislation prohibiting this (CITES etc).
3. Miscellaneous products
   - (a) Some examples are
     Tusks - elephants, walrus
     Bones - various animal (eg. tiger)
     Feathers - horn, shell, casque etc.
   - (b) Hunting - as a sport 'TROPHY HUNTING' eg. big cats like tiger, cheetah etc.
     - PREDATOR HUNTING by farmers etc to protect livestock eg. foxes, wolves, Black Bear etc.

VII. GENES FROM WILD ANIMALS AS A SOURCE FOR MODIFYING DOMESTIC STOCK

A. Improve hardness or yield from domestic stock of bovines etc. by using genes from wild species another eg. Jungle fowl & poultry.

B. Successful for fish eg. Carp.

VIII. POTENTIAL FOR FURTHER DOMESTICATION

A. Animals resembling already existing species are more likely to be domesticated in the future as a MARKET-NICHE for their product already exists.

B. Some eg are Capybara, Walrus and Red Deer etc.

C. There is a need to rear animals species who are endangered in the wild due to hunting for their products eg. Chinchillas, Iguanas etc.

IX. EXPLOITATION OF ANIMALS

A. ECONOMIC SIGNIFICANCE OF DOMESTIC STOCK

1. The 3rd world has most of the livestock but its less productive than livestock in 1st world.
2. Developing countries depend on livestock in many ways - the animals are said to have MULTIPLE - USES.
3. The productivity of livestock can be described by the following relationship.
   (a) Feed Efficiency = Outputs / Inputs
   Outputs / IM + IR.
   (b) IM = Feed resources required for maintenance
   (c) IR = Remainder of Feed resources-which is available formilk, drought power etc.
   (d) IR is lesser in livestock of developing countries.

B. WILD SPECIES EXPLOITATION - ECONOMIC SIGNIFICANCE

1. As in 'Sanctuaries, national parks' which attract tourists
2. Source of all the animal products mentioned earlier. The richer developed nations have a market for animal products from developing countries.
3. Exploitation of marine species is of great commercial value to countries like Norway, Japan etc.

C. ANIMAL RESOURCES & BIOECONOMICS

1. BIOECONOMICS means Biological Resource Economics
2. Competitive exploitation of the annual resource is cauvery depletion of the same eg. fish stock (anchovy in Peru)
3. Biological Resources have to be 'MANAGED' or 'REGULATED'.

   This can be managed by the following :

   (a) Charging a fee for the utility

   (b) Rationing eg. on whaling, hunting.

X. GERMPLASM BANKING

A. DEFINITIONS

1. Germplasm: The special type of protoplasm present in the reproductive cells or gametes of the plant & animal which Weismann suggested passed on unchanged from generation to generation.

2. Germplasm banks: Depositories where germplasm of animals is stored in the form of frozen semen, oocytes etc.
3. Types of animal germplasm banks

IN - VIVO (Live animals)		IN - VITRO (animal germplasm separated from animal)
IN - SITU	EX - SITU	
animals in their natural habitats eg. national parks, sanctuaries et(c)	animals out side their natural habitats e(g) Zoos et(c)	Semen Through banks. Cryopreseg. ervation etc.

B. HISTORY

1. Establishment of just national park in U.S.A. - Yellow stone
2. 1960s Germplasm banks started with a view to preserving commercially important genes.
3. Semen preservation techniques started for bulls, rooster etc.

C. TECHNIQUES

1. Mostly three freezing - CRYOPRESERVATION: That why they 're called FROZEN ZOOS'.
2. sperm, non-fertilized egg cells, embryo etc. stored in different ways. For eg. non fertilized egg cells are sensitive to freezing temperature while embryos can be frozen & stored.
3. Further research & perfection of techniques is necessary.

D. GERMPLASM BANKING - SCOPE

1. IMPROVEMENT OF DOMESTIC STOCK
   (a) sperm of hardy males used to improve some 'quality' of progeny.
   (b) Used on bovine species, roosters & fish.
2. CONSERVING NATURAL VARIETIES OF DOMESTIC STOCK
   (a) Hybrids' have replaced natural varieties of livestock in commercial breeding enterprises therefore there is a need to preserve the genes from the natural varieties.
   (b) This is done in germplasm banks.
3. IN CONSERVATION OF WILD SPECIES
   (a) Preserving genes of animals as safety deposits.

(b) Use of GERMPLASM is ASSISTED REPRODUCTION to produce live young

(c) Ways of ARTIFICIAL BREEDING are

- Artificial insemination (a.i)
- in vitro fertilization (i.v.f.)
- embryo transfer. (e.t.)

4. ZOOS & GERMPLASM BANKING (G.B)

    1. Actually investigating possibilities of Germplasm Banking for conservation of species through capture breeding.
    2. A.I practised on European & Siberian Ferret

       I.V.E. tries on Siberian Tiger, Indian Desert cat.
    3. Eg. Cincinnati zoo (U.S.A.), Coimbatore Zoo (India)

E. ORGANIZATIONS INVOLVED IN G.B.

1. No systematic collection of animal germplasm has been tried
2. International organizations affiliated to U.N. eg. Bureau of Protection of Genetic Resources (FAO)
3. Livestock germplasm banks in all nations
4. Zoos.

F. INDIAN SCENARIO (Prof. N.S. Ramaswamy, chairman, A.W.B. of India)

1. 400 million livestock: 200 million poultry, dogs, cats etc
2. Wealth Rs. 45,000 crores: equal to food grains (Products: 23M; Work & Fertilizer: 16 & Others: 6).
3. Farmers: 300 million
4. Slaughter houses: 3000: legal: 30,000: illegal Modernisation: 3000 crores (1/5 of the food grain sector) Annual earnings: Rs.3000 crores to farmers and owners of animals
5. Milk by 1995 440 lakh tons ——610

   Cooperatives: 270 districts

   158 gms —— 186 gms/day
6. LIVESTOCK GERMPLASM

    (a) Special Livestock Breeding Programme (SLBP) involves G.B.

    (b) National Dairy Research Institute (N.D.R.I.)

    (c) VIIth 5 year plan lead to establishment of 2237 A.I centres & 17 Frozen semen Banks In 1990-91, there were 825 semen Banks.

(d) Kerala, Andhra Pradesh etc. have important research institutes involved in G.B. techniques

7. WILDLIFE GERMPLASM

(a) In - situ ones are the best.

(b) Zoos involved in G.B. for capture Breeding Programme (eg. of Indian Desert cat etc.) Eg. Coimbatore Zoo.

G. FUTURE OF G.B.

1. Some of the uses of G.B. are

(a) Economic benefits from this are great as it is a great tool to manipulate livestock quality.

(b) In overcoming reproductive infertility among wild species by Assisted Breeding

(c) To enhance 'Reproductive Efficiency' of animals.

2. The advantages of G.B. are follows

(a) Can be used to interact with live germplasm from another generation.

(b) Risk in transporting wild animals is reduced.

(c) Risk of elimination to small populations due to catastrophe may be less alarming if the germplasm is safe.

H. NEED FOR RESEARCH

1. The reasons for research in cryopreservation are:

(a) Understanding the efficiency of frozen sperm from one species to another.

(b) Finding out the 'optimal' cryoprotectant.

(c) Knowing the viability of sperm/embryo.

(d) Finding techniques to make possible the production of live young.

(e) Finding out how to protect germplasm from diseases.

2. In future the preservation of wild Taxa will get more attention

XI. SCIENCE & TECHNOLOGY

A. New food animals - fattening - hormonic, non-hormonic

B. Improvement of animals for food - diet, hormones, genetics

C. Food processing as an industry

D. Stocking food for later use

E. Acceleration of milk production

F. Milk processing for various products

G. Acceleration of egg production

H. Food additives as an industry

I. Separation of fertilizer and energy in the excrements

J. Leather & skin tanning processes and commodities

K. Ivory, musk, silk, etc - technology

L. Taxidermy

M. Animal behaviour in human welfare, psychology, warfare

N. Breeding dogs, horses and others

O. Animals for the advancement of science monkeys,pigs,rabbits,rats

XII. ECONOMICS

A. Animal husbandry: operation flood

B. Milk & dairy products industry

C. Eggs & poultry - small scale industry

D. Leather industry

E. Miniscale activities with other animals

F. Exports, incentives, turnovers: economic processes

G. Bovine economics

XIII. POLITICS

A. Dogs and crime detection

B. Regional development through small scale industry

C. Industrial locations, licensing

D. Prawn, fisheries appropriation from historical ownership

E. Employment potentials vs actuals, regional disparities

F. Decision making - implementation - political mechanisms - lobbies - vote banks - election - power - agents of change

G. More national than international politics excepting in transfer of technology and science - intellectual property rights (1). Appropriate technology transfer with riders.

XIV. CONSEQUENCES

A. Depletion of resources:fisheries,game animals, birds, prawns, frogs

B. Pollution killing animals. Amazon river - small fish loss lead to the loss of big fish

C. Biomagnification of pollutants reaching man

D. Endangerment and extinction

E. Overgrazing, loss of plants and soil erosion

F. Excessive animals & loss of food rats taking 10-25% of human cereals

G. Deforestation, hunting, poaching, dams, agriculture & human settlements depleted animal populations

H. Consumerism on the increase.

I. Captive breeding

XV. MANAGEMENT

A. Conservation - biosphere reserves - sanctuaries, parks

B. Specific animal conservation projects - tiger, crocodile

C. Breeding in captivity

D. Animal energy to full harness

E. Accelerating food habits towards aquatic & terrestrial animal consumption as an incentive to mass scale & economic production of animal foods

F. Vector biology

XVI. CONCLUSIONS

A. Global data on various aspects mentioned above

B. Episodes/examples pertaining to the above

13. TRADE IN WILDLIFE

A. INTRODUCTION

1. The biodiversity is acknowledged to be a condition for the longterm sustainability of the environment, & the maintenance of its integrity. No species can exists alone, least of all man for he has exploited about 7,000 species for food alone.
2. Trade in wildlife - both animals & their products is the second most important cause pushing them towards extinction.

B. CAUSE FOR THE TRADE

1. Commercial

A rhino's horn has a market value of Rs. 9 lakh for 1/2 a kilo. Such phenomenal sums of money that is in wildlife trade makes it worth-while despite the ethical & legal implications. The trade in wild birds is estimated to be at least 7 1/2 million annually.

2. Social

Demand for rhino horn, tiger bone, bear bite ... widely used in oriental medicine & cuisine

C. CLASSIFICATION OF TRADE

1. Live individuals

(a) Pet trade

(b) Bio medical / Research trade

(c) Zoo Trade

(d) For collectors:

- (a) Falconry
- (b) Butterfly collections
- (c) Cactus collections
- (d) Orchid collections

2. Dead individuals

(a) Heat

1. Aquatic: marine, Fresh-water
2. Terrestrial

(b) Skin/Fur

(c) Corals

(d) Oil

(e) Ivory

(f) Horns/Antlers

(g) Shells

D. REGULATING THE TRADE

1. International scene

(a) 1900 - Lacey Act

(b) 1911 - PRIBIL of fur sea convention.

(c) 1916 - Convention on Migratory birds I

1936 - Convention on Migratory birds II

1972 - Convention on Migratory birds III
1976 - Convention on Migratory birds IV

(d) 1931 - Whaling convention.
(e) 1940 - Convention on nature protection & wildlife.
(f) 1958 - Convention on the high seas
(g) 1959 - Antarctic treaty.
(h) 1963 - Convention for N.W. Atlantic fisheries
(i) 1968 – International convention for the conservation
(j) 1973 - CITES
(k) 1976 - Convention on the conservation of Polar Bears.

2. Indian scenario

(a) 1873,1879 Madras Elephant Preservation Acts
(b) 1879 Nilgiri game & fish preservation Act.
(c) 1878 Indian Forests Act.
(d) 1887 Wild birds & game protection Act.
(e) 1912 Wild birds & animal protection Act.
1932 Bengal rhinoceros preservation Act
1933 Punjab wild birds & Wild Animals Act.
1951. Bombay Wild animals & Wild Birds Act.

E. WILDLIFE (PROTECTION) ACT - 1972.

F. WILDLIFE (PROTECTION) AMENDMENT ACT - 1991.

G. SPECIAL PROJECTS

1. Project Tiger
2. Gir lion Sanctuary Project
3. Himalayan musk deer Project
4. Manipur - brow-anteleved deer
5. Project Hangul
6. Project Elephant
7. Crocodile breeding project

H. CONCLUSIONS

1. International trade is a well-coordinated & managed threat to conservation. It is important to remember that because controls exist, monitoring is possible & a perpetual challenge for the policy makers & law enforcers.
2. There exists DATA & STATISTICS but what's known is far less than what isn't & the restrictions against Trade in Wildlife is.

14. PLANT RESOURCES

I. BASICS

A. INTRODUCTION

1. Universally present
2. Being primary producers they are the sources of sustenance to animals, microbes and man
3. The five Fs - Food, Fuel, Fodder, Fertilizer & Fibre
4. All round target of scientific and technological exploitation - Economic Botany to Biotechnology
5. Tropical world affected by colonising countries and natives' attraction to their food habits

B. TAXONOMY

1. Habitats: Aquatic - Terrestrial
2. Evolutionary level: Flowering - Nonflowering
3. Utilization: Cultivated - Wild
4. Actual Economic Use
   (a) Foods: Primary - Secondary - Tertiary
   (b) Fodder and Fertilizer
   (c) Fuels
   (d) Fibres and words
   (e) Phytochemicals
      1. Pesticides
      2. Perfumes & oil
      3. Fumigants & Mastications
      4. Narcotics
      5. Rubber
      6. Gums, resins, tannins & dyes
      7. Medicines

C. ANTHROPOLOGY

1. Dependence for food, shelter and clothing
2. Animals depend on plants 3. Domestication and Agriculture

II. RESOURCEFULNESS

Plants - Allelopathy - Seed Banks - Animals - Habitat - Food

3000 plants used by man for various purposes

A. FOODS

1. 150 cultivated for food; 20 are currently in use
2. Rice, Wheat, Maize, Barley, Potato, Sugarcane, Cocoanut, Banana
3. Primary foods: Cereals
4. Secondary foods: Legumes, Tubers, Oilseeds, Vegetables, Cane
5. Tertiary foods: Fruits & nuts, Beverages, Spices & Condiments
6. Algal macrophytes & mushrooms

B. FODDER AND FERTILIZERS (Indirect foods)

1. Fodder for Cattle: Legumes, Grasses, Others
2. Fertilizer to the soils
   - (a) Legume nodules
   - (b) Leaves of many plants as mulches
   - (c) Blue green algae

C. FUELS

1. Direct combustion; Selection criteria all plants
2. Petro plants: Cacti; Euphorbias, Brosium galactodandron
3. Alcohol yieldlers: tuber crops and sugarcane

D. FIBRES AND WOODS

1. Fibres
   - (a) Textiles: Cotton
   - (b) Paper: Bambusa, Dendrocalamus, Kenaf, Flax
   - (c) Weaving: Jute, Agave, Banana
   - (d) Plaiting: Cononut, Jute, Banana
   - (e) Mats, Stuffing
2. Woods / Timber

   Timber-uses, types, products and its uses.
   - (a) Temperate: Cedar, Fir, Hemlock, Larch, Pine, Sequoia, Birch
   - (b) Tropical: Teak, Deodhar, Shorea, Dalbergia
     1. Ancient woodland and traditional management.
     2. Ecological characteristics of ancient woods.
     3. Recent secondary woodlands.
     4. Silviculture.
     5. Trade-within the country/outside

6. Impacts (International impacts)
   (a) Ecological, (b) Economical, (c) Social.

3. Futurology.
4. Management of woodlands (International trade also included)

E. PHYTOCHEMICALS

1. Pesticides: Rotenoids, Pyrethrum, Neam
2. Perfumes & oils: Rose, geranium, citronella, lemongrass, Vetivera, Lavender, Eucalyptus, Sandal, Cedar
3. Fumigants and Masticatories: Tobacco, Betel, Sapoteceae latex, Colenut, Areca nut
4. Narcotics: Opium, Coccaine, Cannabis, Mushrooms
5. Rubber 99% world rubber trade - S.E. Asia
   75% crude rubber - tyre industry
   (a) Hevea braziliensis (95-98%)
   (b) Panama Rubber (c) Manicoba
   (d) Indian Rubber (e) Guyayule
   (f) Others

6. Gums, Resins, tannins & Dyes
   (a) Gums: Arabic, Tragacanth
   (b) Resins: Gum, Oleoresin, Hard resins, Anacardiaceae, Guttiferae, Conifers, Dipterocarpaceae
   (c) Tannins: Barks, roots, fruits, leaves & woods
   (d) Dyes and inks: Woods, roots, tubers, seeds, lichens
7. Medicines
   (a) Alkaloids, glycosides, flavanoids, oils, etc. from all organs from most plants
   (b) Name, part used disease curing, major producers, nativity
   (c) China, India, Native people developed these resources
   (d) Roots: Aconite, Colchicum, Ginseng, Gloriosa, Rauwolfia
   (e) Barks: Quinine, Curare
   (f) Stems: Ephedrine, Squills
   (g) Leaves: Aloe, Belladona, Digitalis, Ocimum, Solanum, Henna
   (h) Fruits and Seeds: Nuxvomica, Croton, Datura
   (i) Lower plants: Penicillin & other antibiotics, Ergot alkaloids

III. EMPIRICAL KNOWLEDGE

A. Medicinal plants
B. Food, Fodder, fertilizer, fuel and fibres

C. Exploration, domestication, cultivation and usage pattens

D. Scriptural, Traditional, Cultural

IV. SCIENCE & TECHNOLOGY: 5 FS & PHYTOCHEMICALS

A. FOOD PLANTS: Agricultural practices, Introductions, habitat selections, genetic improvement, Biotechnology, yield protection in field and Store house,food technologies

B. FUEL PLANTS: Photosynthetic efficiency, Calorific values, conversions, petroplant, agronomy, extraction and conversions, alcohol from canes and tubers, automobiles.

C. FIBRE PLANTS: Agronomy and genetics, fibre and fabric, new uses, refinements

D. FERTILISER AND FODDER: Genetics and Agronomy, new sources, new feeds, biofertilizers

E. PHYTOCHEMICALS

1. Insecticidal plant exploration, testing and usage techniques
2. Medicinal chemical principles, - Survey, pharmacognacy, Synthesis and testing, Biotechnology (Tissue culture)
3. Others -New sources, survey, Introduction, increasing yields through genetics and agronomy refinement, mass production, Tissue culture technology, leads for synthesis, commodification

V. SOCIOLOGY

A. Aesthetics, Economic Value, Ecological Value, Social Relevance

B. Individual shares and stakes C. Community shares and stakes

D. Regional shares and stakes [intercommunity]

E. Trans boundary concerns

VI. ECONOMICS AND POLITICS

The priceless products of nature from times immemorial had to be subsidised by political powers (through political mechanisms) for their continuity and improvement

A. FOODS, FODDERS, FERTILIZERS

Cost of productivity, Procurement & selling prices, land holdings, economics of green revolution, Food aids, Food subsidies, Public Distribution systems -Oil seed issues - Conflicts between staple foods - secondary foods and tertiary ones - The Politics and economics of food industry and Biotechnology

B. FUEL

Economics of fuel wood, Social forestry - economic wealth and political Leverage -Eucalyptization and monetary returns without reforestation or revegetation or meeting the fuel needs of the poor, targets vs potentials vs realities

C. FIBRES

Natural fibres vs synthetic fibres. Competitive pricing vis-a-vis other crops - Exports vs Imports - Resource vs Technology - Cotton & jute

D. PHYTOCHEMICALS

1. Rubber: Natural vs synthetic, Pricing and imports
2. Tobacco and the hard habits - economy & power
3. Narcotics trade, smuggling and political power, addictions and Society
4. Medicinal plants - Economics of cultivation, economic returns

VII. INTERNATIONAL RELATIONS

1. Hybrid maize 1944, 1956
2. Rubber / Cinchona
3. Plant Introduction
4. Germplasm Banks
5. Energy Plants
6. Tropical Forest Produce - Bases for Research
7. Biodiversity vs Biotechnology & Genetic Engineering, GM Plants

VIII. CONCLUSIONS

1. Germplasm depletions of all plant resources in favour of monocultures of a few selected/favoured plants
2. Agriculture, housing, industries, fuel wood result in deforestation and loss of yet unknown resources -the finite ones
3. Loss of infinite resources - ecobalances
4. Renewability far slower than consumption
5. Zero cost resources are commodified and priced depriving the common resource in favour of selected few - Biotechnology
6. Management issues - Agriculture, Agroforestry, social forestry, Cash crops, pastures & animal husbandry, Endangered species and Biosphere reserves
7. Presence of alkaloids and other useful active principle is often not confined to one or a few species of the genus.
8. Related species of medicinal plants genera need to be studied in detail.
9. The botanical, pharmacognostic, phytochemical and other aspects of most of the Indian species of the remaining genera remain to be studied.

SOME IMPORTANT MEDICINAL PLANTS

1. Aconftium 2. Adathoda 3. Alphinia 4. Artemisia
5. Atropa 6. Berberis 7. Cassia 8. Curcuma
9. Datura 10.Mentha 11.Piper 13.Solan

Success is the ability to go from one failure to another with no loss of enthusiasm
Success is the sum of small efforts repeated day in and day out
The secret of success is to know something nobody else knows
Along with success comes a reputation for wisdom

15. FOOD SOURCES

A. INTRODUCTION

1. What is food? (Renewable but destructible)
2. Importance of food and its dietary significance.

B. EXISTING FOOD RESOURCES

1. Plant - Terrestrial, Aquatic
2. Animal - Terrestrial, Aquatic

C. REASONS FOR DEPLETION OF FOOD RESOURCES.

1. Increased consumption with population explosion
2. Increasing areas of agricultural land brought under wastelands
3. Calamities - Natural and Man-made.
4. Wastage
5. Unequal distribution of global food resources
6. Economic development. Frog's legs and its effects
7. Land-use policies
8. Government policies - Internal, Export

D. ALTERNATIVE FOOD RESOURCES

1. Plant resources: bio-technology in improving food resources e.g. some sea weeds, algae, mushrooms.
2. Germplasm resources, Changing food patterns, New food resources
3. Animal resources, Rodent meat Sea food - oysters

E. PROBLEMS OF IMPLEMENTATION OF ALTERNATIVE FOOD RESOURCES

1. Attachment to conventional food practices
2. Religious dogma
3. Inadequate research
4. Lack of education on alternate food resources

16. GERMPLASMS

A. INTRODUCTION

1. Genetic resources - their care and preservation.
2. Strategic importance of genetic resources - the "New Imperialism" by advanced countries over developing countries
3. Threat to genetic diversity due to an exploding population
4. Importance of genetic diversity and its preservation
5. Reasons for the loss of genetic diversity

B. VALUABLE INDIAN GENES

1. Insect germplasm
2. Medicinal herbs
3. Crop genetic resources: Varieties of rice
   Vulnerable plant species
4. Animal genetic resources:
   a. Cattle and buffaloes
   b. Breeding sheep
   c. Goats
   d. Pigs
   e. Camel husbandry
   f. Horses, ponies, donkeys
   g. Poultry development
5. Fish genetic resources: Inbreeding of fish
6. Tree genetic resources: Depleting species

C. PLANTS

1. Importance of germplasms (gene pool): IBPGR
2. Loss of sources before exploitation is attempted
3. Reasons for Loss of Germplasm: Along with the loss of plants from the ecosystems other cohabitations are also lost which may have traits useful to man.
4. Examples
   (a) Sugarcane
   (b) Rice - gene for resistance to leaf rust from Silent Valley
   (c) Wheat - brown rust resistance gene form Mexico

D. CONSERVATION MEASURES

1. Stocks for plant improvement and new plant sources necessary
2. Botanical gardens, field stations, habitat reserves of natural vegetation types

3. Scientific Collaboration: International Network of Genetic Resource Stations
4. Catalogues of available resources

E. IUCN AND NATIONAL BODIES

1. Red books of endangered plants and animals
2. Breeding in captivity

F. INDIAN SCENARIO

1. Natural diversity in India: one of the richest in the world.
2. 50,000 varieties of rice known in India.
3. A sample of Rice from Eastern UP gave Asian farmers a gene against Grassy Stunt virus.
4. Silent valley revealed 9 new species and Andamans one
5. Buffaloes yield much less than a few decades ago
6. 9000 tons of frogs exported in 1981 earning Rs. 12 crores
7. People are turning against conservationists as 25% of forested lands including their wildlife are reserved.
8. Medicinal plants depleting, Ayurvedic medicine affected
9. Hardly any evaluation on animal especially marine systems
10. Wild life conservation synonymous with germplasm preservation.
11. Biosphere reserves necessary. Andaman & Nicobar, Nilgiris and 11 others
12. WWF, IBPGR active

G. FUTURES

1. Gene banks - World hunger.
2. Control of Third World Genetic resources and World food by multinational corporations.
3. Genetic engineering - Recombinant DNA technology
   Biotechnology, tissue culture and plant breeding
4. 1 out of 10 sp. in the danger of extinction / extinct already
5. 20,000 species are in need of protection

17. LAND AND SOIL

I. INTRODUCTION

1. Top soil is the root of productivity and therefore civilisations
2. Soil - water - plant - air continuum
3. Modified by climatic and biotic factors
4. Site variations

II. TAXONOMY

A. BASED ON PHYSICAL PROPERTIES

1. Sandy 2. Clayey 3. Loamy

B. BASED ON CHEMICAL NATURE

1. Acidic 2. Basic

C. BASED ON WATER

1. Waterlogged (wetlands, Marshes)
2. Physically dry - Sandy
3. Physilogically dry – Salty
4. Physical & Physiological dryness- Ice

D. BASED ON USAGE

1. Agricultural 2. Silvicultural
3. Permacultural 4. Forest
5. Grasslands 6. Wastelands

E. PROPERTIES

1. Particle Size and weight 2. Porosity
3. Temperature 4. Chemical nature
5. Water holding capacity 6. Acidity/alkalinity
7. Biotic life 8. Water table

III. ANTHROPOLOGY

A. Fertile lands determined settlements of humans

B. Fertile lands attracted forced seizures and ownerships

C. Origin and spread of human societies, and domestication of plants and animals followed fertile lands

IV. RESOURCEFULNESS

A. LIFE SUPPORT SYSTEMS

1. Root of all the biosphere 2. Agricultural productivity
3. Permacultural resource 4. Source of fertility
5. Water source 6. Biomass source
7. Primary producer 8. Seat of biogeochemical cycles

B. HUMAN SETTLEMENTS

1. Open air - tree shade - hutment to permanent dwellings of varying sizes

C. CULTURAL ACTIVITIES

1. Transportation
2. Artificial irrigation
3. Industrial & developmental agencies

D. SINKS AND MODIFIERS

1. Landfills
2. Receivers of wastes, dead biota and converters

E. AESTHETIC VALUE

V. EMPIRICAL SCIENCE

1. Relative Fertility
2. Soil nature and Crop productivity
3. Soil nature and quality of plant products
4. Water holding capacity

VI. SCIENCE & TECHNOLOGY

1. Water table exploitation
2. Chemical nature of nutrients and minerals
3. Physical nature of soil particles & interactions
4. Microbial activity augmentation
5. Soil classification based on their suitability for different uses
6. Usage of soil for commodities, housing
7. Increasing the utility of soils by additives/amendments
8. Microbial resourcefulness

VII. ECONOMICS & POLITICS

1. Base of all economic activity and conflicts
2. Land to the tiller, land reforms, land hunger, land ownership, land Vs people ratio etc for agriculture and homing have played major roles although history continue to do so
3. Urbanisation, land squeeze, landless men and the resulting social unrest are current phenomenon in thickly populated societies
4. Housing policy with minimal land spaces Vs ethics of previleged classes

A. LAND AND SOIL IN INDIA

1. 1/40 of the world land supports 1/2 of the world's buffaloes. Goats and cattle are additional; grazing land turning into agricultural lands, what is the future? Encroachment on forest land? Violent clashes in future? Social forestry programmes mainly plant non-brow species.
2. Wastelands of India: 100 million hectares, 40 million are still in some use. Affected by Salinity, alkalinity and erosion by wind and water.

   Ravines swallowed 4 million hectares. 10% of villages in chambal valley depopulated. Then same happened in a few other states.
3. Per capita land availability decreasing constantly. 0.2ha/by 2000 AD
4. Soil from forests silting the dams.
5. Agricultural land constantly turned into housing and industrial habitats (urbanisation) - 1.5 million hectares.
6. Land reclamation efforts hardly under operation.
7. Himalayas highly vulnerable on watersheds. Pine Vs Oak Meera Behn 1950.
8. Desertification in U.P., Haryana, Gujarat.

VIII. CONCLUSIONS

1. Loss of topsoil, by deforestation, drought and flood cycles
2. Desertification by overgrazing
3. Loss of fertility, fertilizers and dust bowls
4. Shrinking land to Man ratios
5. Urbanisation and loss of Agricultural and forest lands as a sequel
6. Interrelationships with other resources - Plant, animal, water
7. Improper land use - Settlements
8. Science & Technology to preserve natural systems
9. Global nutrient levels - Macro - & Micro

18. MINERAL RESOURCES

I. INTRODUCTION

1. Clay, sand & rock to Gold & Diamond
2. Directly connected to industrial revolution
3. No technology, no consumer product no daily life is possible without several minerals.
4. Part of earth, none in pure from except natural gas

II. TAXONOMY

A. BASED ON FORM
   1. Gaseous minerals, natural gas
   2. Liquid minerals, petroleum
   3. Solid minerals, most other

B. BASED ON AVAILABILITY
   1. Surface of earth
   2. Depths of earth
   3. Sea bed surface
   4. Depths of seabed

C. BASED ON ORIGIN
   1. Biotic-Coat, Petroleum, gas - extinct biomass
   2. Non biotic - all others

D. GENERAL USAGE
   1. Ferrous - Iron, etc.
   2. Nonferrous
      (a) Heavy: Zn, Cd, Cu, Hg, etc.
      (b) Precious: Ag, Au, Pl, etc.
      (c) Rare Earths :
   3. Radioactive - Uranium, Monazite, etc.
   4. Energy related Biotics: Coal, Petroleum, etc.

III. ANTHROPOLOGY

1. Extinct biomass for energy
2. Stone age to iron age to bronze age

IV. RESOURCEFULNESS

1. Antimony
   (a) Ores: Stibiute (b) Uses: (c) Global occurrence :
2. Arsenic
   (a) Ores: Orpiment, Realgar, Arseno - pigrute
   (b) Global occurrence (c) Major producers (d) Uses

3. Barium — a. Ores: Barite (BaSO4)
4. Bismuth — a. Bismuthinite
5. Cadmium — a. Greenockite
6. Cobalt — a. Ores: Cobalisite
7. Copper Chelopyrite, — a. Ores: Cuprite, Malachite, Covalute, Tetrahedrite, Chalecite, Boinite
8. Gold — a. Tellurides, Kalgoolite, Silverite, Calverite
9. Iron — a. Ores: Magnesite, Hematite, Pyrite, Ileminite, Limonite, Sidenite
10. Lead
11. Manganese
12. Magnesium — a. Ores: Dolomite
13. Mercury — a. Fulminate
14. Molybdenum — a. Molybdenite (MoS2), Wulfenite (Pb Mo O4)
15. Nickel — a. Niccolite, Millerite
16. Potassium — a. Sylvite
17. Silver — a. Argentile
18. Sodium — a. Halite
19. Tin — a. Stamite
20. Uranium — a. Uranite
21. Zinc
    - (a) Ores: Sphaberite, Wurtzite
    - (b) Global occurrence :
    - (c) Major Producers: d. Major uses :
22. Mica (Complex alumino selicate)
    - (a) Ores: Muscovite, Phlogopite, Lepidolite, Biotite, Zinnocoaldite
    - (b) Global occurrence: India
    - (c) Major Producers: India
23. Coal a. Ores: Peat, Lignite, antracite
24. Diamond
25. Graphite
26. Quartz
27. Asbestos
28. Building stones
    - (a) Granite (b) Marbles (c) Sandstone
    - (d) Limestone (e) Shale

V. EMPIRICAL KNOWLEDGE

1. Stones
2. Iron and bronze
3. Gold & silver
4. Silversmith, goldsmith, blacksmith & foundries before Industrial Revolution.

VI. SCIENCE & TECHNOLOGY

1. Detection and exploration methodology
2. Extraction of ore from habitat
3. Isolation/concentration
4. Commodification
5. Efficiency of material production at all stages
6. Industrial revolution - coal & iron to antarctic and seabed minerals
7. Alloy making
8. Conversions from one to another forms
9. Old uses, new uses
10. Science & technology of all the above directly connected to development of industries national wealth & international domination. Therefore these are kept 'secrets'.

VII. ECONOMICS & POLITICS

1. Science & technology gives strength to industry, builds National wealth & international domination.
2. Costs of life & standards of life better in some countries
3. Foreign markets, foreign wealth
4. Seeking others resources by science & technology Domination through trade practices
5. Political processes, mechanisms within one's and foreign Countries may be influenced through control of economics (energy minerals, heavy industry, machine tools)

VIII. MINERALS IN INDIA

1. Mineral production increased 50 fold in the last 3 decades.
2. A few million hectares of crop and forest land destroyed.
3. Hundreds of villages depopulated.
4. 50% of mining output comes from 40 contiguous districts of eastern and central india. Other important area is rajasthan.
5. Tribals are worst affected.
6. Mining pits, mining disasters, quarrying, collieries.

7. Health hazards to workers and people around.
8. Trading with foreign countries disadvantageous to india.
9. Industries, end products, social sectors receiving.

IX. CONCLUSIONS

1. Developing countries without adequate science & technology of mineral resources. Various degrees exist.
2. Developing countries without efficient/updated technologies leading to loss of natural resources through trading practices.
3. Developing countries' inability to produce commodities at competitive prices in a market economy !
4. Mining of common resources/others' resources - antarctica, seabed
5. Impacts on ecosystems & balances
6. Human ecological problems - migrations/displacements, consumerism and poverty
7. Stockpiling strategic minerals (20) by some countries + general poverty + independence
8. Inefficient technology + high costs of products efficiency, low costs + dependence + affluence for some
9. Depletion of mineral resources and alternatives

19. WATER

I. INTRODUCTION

1. Biosphere depends on water
2. No human civilisation without water
3. Mother of other resources and many inventions

II. TAXONOMY

A. SOLID: Ice, Icecaps, - polar, tropical, temperate

B. GASEOUS: Water vapour

C. LIQUID:

1. Rainfall - variations on earth - Humid tropics
2. Inland
   (a) Running/Flowing
      1. Perennial Rivers-Amazon, Missisipi, Missouri, Nile, Ganges
      2. Seasonal Rivers, streams
      3. Manmade channels - canals

   (b) Stationary
      1. Overground
         (a) Natural Lakes: N. American, Scandinavian, African, Russian, Indian
         (b) Man-made Resources allover the world's rivers
      2. Underground
3. Marine
   (a) Estuaries & lagoons
   (b) River months
   (c) Seas, gulfs, Bays, Straits Persian gulf, Red sea, Baltic, Adriatic
   (d) Oceans - Pacific, Atlantic, Indian

III. ANTHROPOLOGY

1. Most civilisations started and flourished around water sources Nile, Mesapatomian, Indus
2. Most of the world was colonised by maritime powers and the latter still continue as major world powers-Portugal, Spain, France, Holland, Britain

IV. RESOURCEFULNESS

A. SNOW

1. Source of potable water - Arctic & Antarctic
2. Origin of rivers – Himalayas

B. RAINFALL

1. Source for rivers, lakes, groundwater
2. Reduces temperature
3. Lifeline for all Biospheric components
4. Basis for agriculture

C. MARINE SYSTEMS

1. Transport and navigation
2. Biota and food sources
3. Salt
4. Tides as sources of energy
5. Industrial usage

D. INLAND WATERS

1. Transport and navigation
2. Drinking purposes
3. Agriculture
4. Aquaculture
5. Industrial uses
6. Uses in Science and technology
7. Energy production and Conversion (Electricity)
8. Source for all biota
9. Storage medium for rainfall

V. EMPIRICAL KNOWLEDGE

1. Cycle of water, vapour, life and death
2. Source of all other sources
3. Transport and navigation
4. Underground water (wells), Reservoirs (tanks)

VI. SCIENCE AND TECHNOLOGY

1. Water and climate relationships
2. Towing icebergs for potable water
3. Impounding waters for irrigation
4. Electricity generation
5. Steam and locomotion

6. Waters for cooling
7. De-salination of saline waters
8. Prospecting underground water
9. Water transport mechanisms
10. Water purification
11. Salt making technologies
12. Aquacultural technologies
13. Transport systems on and under waters

VII. ECONOMICS AND POLITICS

1. Irrigation schemes and riparian issues
2. Deforestation - Catchment & Command area conflicts
3. Hydroelelctric energy and distribution
4. Trans-boundary issues between political units
5. Overexploitation of groundwater - politics of wealth Appropriation of common property
6. Pollution of common waters by economic activity
7. Problem of national boundaries of seas Maternal & paternal seas
8. Dam - displaced peoples - Economy & politics

VIII. CONCLUSIONS

1. Drinking water shortage in the most world
2. Only a few countries have excess of potable water
3. Damming of rivers and the consequences
4. Water pollution and human health
5. Desalination of marine waters
6. Water Conservation of rainfall to reclaim wasted lands
7. Protection of catchment areas
8. Recharging of water tables - percolation systems
9. Sedimentation of reservoirs, floods, droughts & soil loss
10. Migrations of people for want of water
11. Waste disposal - Eutrophication - depletion and pollution of human food
12. Radioactive waste dumped into others' waters
13. Oil slicks and other major episodes
14. Acid rain
15. Global warming, Polar cap melting & sea level raise
16. Connecting rivers - Rhine - Maine - Danube etc.

17. Management of floods
18. Cropping patterns and water needs
19. Potable water loss into seas - conservation

IX. WATER AND ITS RESOURCES

1. Total precipitation 400 million hectare meters

   Soil: 215 Surface: 115 Evaporation :70

2. % used = 25 i.e. 20% = Surface = 13 i.e. 60%

   (a) India use 1/10 of the rainfall storage, necessary

   (b) Ground water resources substantial but are gradually depleting

   (c) Tanks, ponds neglected and even filled up.

   (d) Most high altitude lakes are dying excepting a few

   (e) Ecological value of wetlands not realised fully

   (f) Increasing pollution affect fisheries, fisher folk

   (g) Dam water covering 1% of land area. Produce little fish

   (h) Important cities facing water crisis

   (i) Poor of the country hardly having access to clean drinking water

   (j) 175 major & 450 minor dams drown 1/2 million hectares of forest

   (k) Canal irrigation benefited 5 million hectares of land

20. ENERGY

I. INTRODUCTION

The kind of stuff fundamentally make up the universe are matter and energy. Energy is tantamount to power, the key to the social and economic development of a technologically sophisticated society.

History:-Discovery of fire led to the first use of energy from a source external to the body. The use of fire and domestication of animals ar considered to be the historical sources of energy. It can be raid that the evolution of man largely depended on the sources of energy whch appropriate technology has enabled him to master.

Concepts: - Galileo, 17th century, idea of energy related to the pulley system

- living force concept developed in 17th century.
- 19th century term energy applied
- 19th century concept of conversation of energy.

Types of Energy:- (1) Gravitational (2) Kinetic
(3) Heat (4) Nuclear
(5) Electrical (6) Chemical
(7) Radiant

Conversion of energy: a fundamental law holding good for all natural phenomenon.

Taxonomy: Renewable & Non-renewable Direct & Indirect, etc.

Anthropology: Muscle and wood, Wind and wave, Sun and fire

Nature: Kinetic & potential,

Production, Conversion, transportation & use

Importance of energy and Energy shortage

Worldwide consumption of energy

Patterns in developed and developing countries.

EARLY SOURCES

1. **Asphalt:** used in middle east in 6000 BC technology advances of babylonian empire Mesopotamia in 2500 BC - 538 BC recovered the diminished after 538 BC.
2. **Natural Gas:** Used in China before 1000 BC transported through bamboo pipe lives .
3. **Coal:** invented by china, used in Roman times, Became an article of commerce in the 13th century. Discovery of use of who, for reduction of ares, in 1709.

4. **Petroloum:** Known to Babylonians though not used extensively. Prominence in 17th century 1640, Medena, Datty oil well drilled for duel for lighting street lamps . Romania - wamer - gas oil wells in 1650. Oil discovered in U.S. early oil well drilled in 1859 in western Pensylvania.
5. **Wind:** For ship propulsion since early times windmills invented in China spread the middle east and Europe.
6. **Water:** Babylonian irrigation 3000 years ago using watersheds - Romans used their for flour mills and saw units.
7. **Steam:** Power used in 18th century; 19th century began the revolution in use and exploitation of energy sources.

II. TAXONOMY

1. Current usage
2. Potential in future and
3. Limited supply of all the above and need for alternatives

   Application of different types / sources of energy in various fields:

   (a) Agriculture

   (b) Industry - petroluem, steel, metal etc

   (c) Transport

   (d) Communication.

A. **Solar:** inexhaustible, source of all resources

B. **Phytomass:** Product of solar energy conversion

C. **Muscular:** Human and animal. Product of secondary/tertiary consuming solar energy

D. **Biogas:** Combustion of animal excrement

E. **Wind:** Transport of particles and even human loads

F. **Tidal:** Transport of particles through force of movement

G. **Geothermal:** Site spepcificity

H. **Coal:** Direct combustion and conversion- Industrial revolution & Steam engine Fossil source

I. **Fossil oils:** A very major hydrocarbon energy source. Different grades useful for different purposes -Fossil source

J. **Natural gas:** Fossil source related to fossil oils

K. **Hydroelectric:** Generated from the force of falling waters. Transportation Technology.

L. **Nuclear:** Most recent. Power of the atom the ultimate part of matter fission and fusion

III. ANTHROPOLOGY

A. Usage of Muscle power B. Discovery of fire
C. Use of Phytomass D. Knowledge of wind and wave
E. Usage of wind and wave

IV. RESOURCEFULNESS

Man lives in an ocean of energy. As the world's non - renewable energy supplies dwindle, the virtually unlimited and inexhaustible supplies that abound in nature must be ingeniously adpoted to provide man's future power needs.

A. SOLAR

The most colossal dynamo of all is Sun.

The sun is an atomic furnace that turns mass into energy. Every second it converts 657 million tons of Hydrogen into 653 million tons of Helium. The missing 4 million tons are discharged into space as energy. The earth is receiving only one two- billionths of this.

1. Cooking, heating 2. Solar ponds
3. Photovoltaics

B. PHYTOMASS

1. Solar energy conversion into chemical form by plants
2. Primary producers on which all else depends
3. Efficiencies of energy conversion different
4. Direct combustion
5. Conversions to alcohol, hydrocarbons
6. Conversions to gasification
7. Energy contents are variable in various plants & plant parts

C. ANIMALS

Biogas (gobar gas)- Using Animal and Human Excreta & Wastes

1. Methane generation from animal dung
2. Cattle dung slung as a fertilizer
3. Part of animal husbandry and large agricultural holdings
4. Methane enhancement by plant adjuncts
   (a) Member of livestock and manure generation
   (b) Manure content - residues of feed origin, undigested, indigestible products of digestion and metabolism.
   (c) Process of methane/biogas generation - Bacteriological, aerobic digestion

(d) Potential of Biogas and effluent

- Limitation of storage due to gaseous form, difficulty in liquefaction, corrosiveness,
- Uses in small units for heating, fuel to generate electricity, not large scale as concentrated supply of manure needed.
- effluent use as fertilizer excess heat recycled.

(e) Biogas as an Alternative Energy source

- in agricultural, developing countries
- efficiency to be greater

(f) Biogas in India

- National programmeon Biogas Development '82
- 14.02 lakh family units, 700 community units installed

(g) Direct burning of dung

- less efficient recovery of energy
- creates (indoor) pollution

1. Similar process as for animal manure
2. Not widespread practice

D. MUSCLE ENERGY (LIVESTOCK AND HUMAN LABOUR)

1. Human muscular energy as a work force earning wages - Head loaders, Cart pullers, Vehicle pedlars
2. Animal energy for cart pulling, water pulling, load carriers - Donkey, Camel, Cattle, Horse, Mule, etc.

(a) Members, distribution, utility of: (world & India)

1. cattle
2. donkeys, mules
3. camels
4. elamas
5. elephants

(b) Breeds and Germplasms - World and India.

Humans :

(a) Working population in India

(b) Sectors of employment, in

1. Transport (rickshaw-pullers, hand-cart pullers, porters etc.)
2. agriculture
3. construction.

Food Energy (meat, milk, honey etc.) Honey from bees Insects as food

A. MEAT: 1. From wildlife 2. From fisheries
3. From livestock

B. MILK: 1. nutrient content of milk and importance to health
2. demand & production

CONCLUSION

1. energy demands are not being met
2. energy from animals and humans as a contribution to above
3. Used for greater exploitation of resources.

E. WIND

The sun's rays, stronger near the equator than in the polar regions, cause tropical air to warm and rise while cooler polar air moves into replace it. The result is wind.

If the winds are tethered, they could turnout twice as much electricity as water power now does.

1. Site specific - "Wind mills", "Water pullies"
2. Seasonal - "trade winds"
3. Converted to do mechanical work or electricity
4. Canada, U.S.A., India (Gujarat, TN)
5. Limited local needs

F. TIDAL

1. Site specific
2. Converted to mechanical work or electricity
3. Coastal European countries
4. Limited local needs.

G. GEOTHERMAL

1. Only some places in the world
2. Heat of the interior earth converted to electricity

H. COAL

1. Fossilised and carbonised plant material
2. Coal mines in many places of the world
3. Associated with steam engines & industrial revolution
4. Thermal Power and electricity
5. Conversions to liquid and gaseous fuels
6. Non renewable and exahustible
7. Pollutants many of which carcinogens
8. Exhausing - stocks last a century more

I. FOSSIL OIL

1. Most efficient of all - Hydrocarbons
2. Refinement yields different grades including gas-for different purposes
3. Mining is done on land, shorelines, offshore, seabed
4. Fast exhausting, another 200 years only
5. 2/3 resources in middle east and North Africa
6. Highly versatile energy source

J. NATURAL GAS

1. Byeproduct of fossil oil
2. Some grounds have only gas
3. Offshore & seabed
4. Siberian & Alaskan pipelines
5. HBJ pipeline in India
6. May lost for 60 years.
7. Limited in use due to its physical state

K. HYDROELECTRIC

About a third of Sun's energy reachng the earth involves in evaporation. Every year it evaporates and lifts 417,000 km3 of the moisture a third hits the land as rain, snow etc,. This helps form the rivers, streams, glaciers that have reshaped the earth and provided man with a valuable source of power.

The falling water of rivers could yield enough hydro electric power to meet 80% of man‘s total energy needs, though only 1 - 2% is used

1. Falling waters used to generate electricity
2. Land gradient and rivers
3. All over the world where rivers flow
4. One of the best-Nature-Science-Technology & Uses Never ending as long as climate & ecosystems are healthy
5. Rainfall and glacier based

L. NUCLEAR

1. Nuclear energy discovered over 50 years ago
2. One of the most peaceful uses of energy
3. Never ending source
4. High technology
5. Fusion energy yet to be accomplished

V. EMPIRICAL KNOWLEDGE

1. Plant products, animal use, direct combustion, usage of wind and wave, sun and fire were all intuitive developments prior to industrial revolution

VI. SCIENCE & TECHNOLOGY

1. Mostly in Conversions and Usages
2. Direct Creation: nuclear
3. Phytomass plants, fast growing, high calorific values, conversion technology conversion
4. Biogas methanogenic systems,
5. Solar energy conversions and usage = 20 years
6. Wind, wave, geothermal - conversion systems = 20 years
7. Fossil energy sources - Conversion, transport, usage, conservation, efficiencies, exploration - 50 years.
8. Hydroelectric: Most stabilized even several decades ago !
9. Nuclear - enormous science & technology inputs prior to production, high predictability and controls

VII. ECONOMICS

1. Inputs vs outputs
2. Necessity for development of other sources
3. Phytomass vs poverty
4. Zero costing to commodification and pricing
5. Absence of sources to resource generation
6. Productivity of a polity depends upon energy availability

VIII. POLITICS

1. Allocation , prices, taxation, trade grotas ie energy as a commodity.
2. Corelation between GNP and energy imputs.
3. Market machincs influenced by public policy or private monopoly eg OPEC
4. Impact of energy and economics is felt in unemployment, GNP, inflation and trade.
5. Changes in energy market results in redistribution of economic wealth.
6. Policies in order to balance supply and energy consisted with accuphatle economic, social and environmental goals.

Year	*Population (Billions)*	*Gross world product (trillion 1980 dollars)*	*Fossil fuel consumption (billion tons of coal equivalent)*
1900	1.6	0.6	1
1950	2.5	2.9	3
1986	5.0	13.1	12

World population economic output & fossil fuel consumption - state of the world 1987.

1. People vs ruling systems vs ruling classes
2. Source to Resource: Have-nots generation, Inequalities
3. Politics of the grids connected to industrialisation, employment, migrations
4. Science & Technology vs National Politics
5. International haves of Energy vs Have-nots
6. Energy Rich vs Development rich countries
7. Exploration, Conversion, transport, Usage politics
8. Oil shocks I (73-74), II (79-80), III (90-91)

IX. ENVIRONMENTAC IMPACTS

1. Air pollution
2. Water Pollution
3. Thermal heat waste
4. Climatic changes
5. Problem created at each stage - Production, upgrading, transport, utilization.

X. MANAGEMENT

Concerned with the rate, purpose and efficiency of use.

1. Preservation 2. Restoration 3. Benefication
4. Maximization 5. Reutilization 6. Substitution.
7. Allocation (strategy of use)
8. Alternatives
9. Integration of resource management.
10. Reduced consumption
11. Efficiency
12. Improved choolhas, Kerosene lamps, Stoves,
13. Solar heaters, cooking, ponds, pumps & Photovoltaics
14. Sewage/Garbage based systems.

XI. INDIAN SCENARIO: GENERAL

1. Yearly consumption of firewood: 14-20 million tons (Rs.500 crores). This is more than what is spent on afforestation during the last 3 decades. 8 Solar energy inputs.
2. Urban fuelwood comes deforestation.
3. Self sufficiency unlikely inspite of Hydroelectric, fossil fuel and nuclear programmes. Wastage is one major scourge.
4. There may be enough food, but not energy to cook it.
5. Coal is preferred.
6. Oil: more explorations and gas.
7. Nuclear: Eleven new reactors.

   Energy is an essential input for economic development and for improving the quality of life.

   India's per capita consumption of commercial energy is only one - eighth of the world average.

   (a) Energy requirements for India

   About 1/4 th public sector investment allocation goes to energy sector. Energy demand in the following four sectors are considered - Industries, Transport, Agriculture, Household and commercial.

   (b) Regional distribution of energy demand:-

   Issues relating to the distribution of energy in a neat country as India.

   - Trends of regional shares. - The mix of energy.

   - The efficiency of energy use. - The agriculture needs.

   (c) Energy resources of India

   In the present state of scientific and technical knowledge it is convenient to list the main energy resources of India under five headings. Four of there under 1 commercial energy.

   Coal, oil and natural gases, hydro electric power, and nuclear fuels, both actual and potential.

21. CULTURED SYSTEMS

I. MONOCULTURE

A. DEFINITION

1. Large population of only one species

B. EXAMPLES

1. Agriculture - Silviculture - Pomoculture etc
2. Agriculture: Wheat, Rice, Maize, Barley & Rye (Major 5)
3. Forestry: Pine, Casuarina, Eucalyptus, Prosopis & Bamboo (Major 5)

C. REASONS FOR ADOPTING MONOCULTURE

1. 2-3 times more yield due to industrialization of agriculture. But reached stability within 10 years.
2. Package: Pesticides - Fertilizers - Genetics - Irrigation Mechanisation

D. INDIA

1. Population doubled in 25 years (1985) and treble in 35 yrs (2000). While food production remains constant until 2 decades ago.
2. Per capital food reduced in man, from what it was a decade ago

E. DISADVANTAGES

1. Pest losses can lead to epidemic proportions leading to famines
2. Sapping nutrients of one kind only
3. Pollution due to intensive agriculture - pesticides & fertilizers
4. Trade Blackmail
   (a) Ghana - Tapioca
   (b) Cuba - Sugarcane (1960s)
   (c) Malaya - Rubber (2nd World War)
5. Disasters: Some Examples
6. Bengal famine
   (b) Irish famine (c) Meat 'Famine' in Europe
7. Punjab Problem (e) Russo-American 'SALT'

F. MEASURES: VARIABILITY DESIRABLE

1. Companion Cropping 2. Rotation Cropping
3. Fallowing 4. Food habit change
5. New crops

II. AGRICULTURE

A. INTRODUCTION

1. Agriculture - The need it serves.
2. Proto - agriculture - Features.
3. Survey - explore - domesticate - select - improve 10,000 years
4. 3,000- 200- 20- 5 major crop plants
5. Primary food - Secondary food - Tertiary foods and 5 Fs
6. Primary, secondary and tertiary resourcefulness
7. Population - 1B to 6 Billions

B. AGRICULTURE TILL NOW

1. Selection
2. Hybridisation (inter and intra - specific)
3. Gene manupulation, somatoplasm fusion.
4. Modern agriculture (with machinery)
5. Trends in research - To produce better yielding resistant varieties and to create diversity.
6. Productivity Package
   (a) Varieties - new varieties - water - Fertilizer - Pest control
   (b) Pestilence, Population, Political unit, Economics

C. EVIL EFFECTS

1. chemicals in water, food, soil
2. loss of fertility of soil
3. losses due to new pests

D. LACUNAE IN AGRICULTURE

1. Lack of fertilisers, pesticides etc.
2. Depletion and destruction of soil.
3. Defects of monoculture.

E. SOLUTIONS

1. Dry-land farming - water use
2. Wasteland productivity
3. Reclamation of nitrogen-deficient soils - soil.
4. Salinity resistant agriculture - soils.
5. Mountains - terrain.

F. AGRICULTURE AS AN ECOSYSTEM

1. Replace Fs, Replace Ps,
2. Multiple, alternate, inter, companion cropping patterns

G. ECOAGRICULTURE - UTOPIAN AMONG UTOPIAS

1. No inputs of F & P 2. No weeds 3. More varieties

H. WATER, GEOGRAPHY, NEEDS, BIOTECHNOLOGY, GERMPLASM RESOURCES

III. AQUACULTURE

A. WATERBODIES – OCEANIC

1. oceans 2. lagoons 3. estuaries 4. coastlines 5. islands

B. WATERBODIES - TERRESTRIAL

1. Rivers 2. Lakes 3. Reservoirs 4. Canals

5. Channels 6. Paddies 7. Tanks 8. Ponds

Boundaries, Temporary / Permanent, Flora & Fauna

C. UTILITY

1. Food 2. Nonfood purposes

D. BIOLOGICAL SYSTEMS

1. Plants 2. Fishes 3. Amphibians
4. Other vertebrates 5. Echinoderms 6. Molluscs
7. Annelids 8. Crustaceans 9. Coelenterates
10. Other invertebrates

E. TRADITIONAL CAPTURES AND CULTURES VS SCIENTIFIC MONOCULTURE

F. ISSUES AND PROBELMS

1. Historical property rights
2. Native people - native techniques
3. Technology as an overriding factor
4. Depletions without biological knowledge
5. Hinduism - Temples - Tanks - Cultures of Plants & Animals - Native - Hygiene
6. Transboundary issues
7. Exploitation for augmentation of food need and modernising the native crafts or commercialisation and profit making ?

22. MANAGEMENT OF AGROECOSYSTEMS

A. INTRODUCTION

1. History of management of agrosystem

(a) Traditional knowledge: Symbolic and ritual system that served to regulate land use practice.

(b) Traditional knowledge: Generational and lateral transfer of knowledge that incorporated subtle changes in the agroecosystem

2. Destruction of traditional knowledge bases due to colonialism

(a) Branding rural ceremonies as witchcraft

(b) Slaving of native populations

(c) Dying out of nature populations due to disease

(d) Restructuring the agricultural base of communities for colonial and market processes eg. plantations of tea and coffee

3. Impacts

(a) The transfer of agronomic knowledge -generational and lateral hindered or stopped.

(b) Destruction of hard technologies, eg. irrigation,

(c) Destruction of soft technologies eg. cultivar types, cropping mixes and techniques of biological control.

4. Resurgence of agroecological thought

(a) Upto 1970s stress was on Historical, Technological & Socio - economic factors as determinants of crops to be raised in a region

(b) Important scientists:

(i) Klages [1928], (ii) Papadalis [1938],

(iii) Tischlis [1965], (iv) Azzi [1956],

(c) Modern agroecological viewpoint upto 1980s: Stress on the social component in agricultural literatures and Traditional agricultural practices recognised for their ecological soundness.

B. CHARACTERISTICS OF AGROECOSYSTEMS

1. General characteristics

(a) As semidomesticated Ecosystem

(b) Impact of humans varying from low to very high

(c) As the solar powered ecosystem with energy subsidies in the form of

(i) Labour,

(ii) Fossil fuels + Labour,

(iii) Nutrients - manure fertilizers.

(iv) pesticides - organic or biological, chemical.

2. **Modern agroecosystem [western model] characteristics**
   (a) Auxiliary sources of energy, Heavily mechanised with large input of fossil fuels
   (b) Diversity can be greatly reduced, monocultures over vast areas
   (c) The dominant animals are under artificial rather than natural selection. eg. Use of pesticides and weedicides
   (d) The controls of the system are largely external rather than by subsystem feedback i.e.constant weeding, irrigation, application of fertilizers.

3. **Traditional tropical agroecosystem characterists**
   (a) The inputs are basically removable,
      (i) Labour and not machines are used,
      (ii) fossil fuels may not be used at any stage.
   (b) Diversity may be quite high -upto 600 species in some systems
   (c) Interactions between the biological components and environment are intensive.
      (i) Pest and predator populations balance each other.
   (d) The controls may reflect the level of intensity and usually taper off.
      (i) Fallow periods in agriculture.

C. BASIC MANAGEMENT APPROACHES IN AGRICULTURE

1. **Aim:** Using of ecological processes and relations to manipulate agroecosystems for producing better with fewer negative
   (a) environmental (b) Social impacts, (c) more sustainbility. (d) fewer external inputs.

2. **Agricultural technology approaches**
   (a) Enhancement of photosynthetic activity
   1. Important of plant architecture for better light interuption
   2. Genetic selection of varities with grater efficiency.
   3. Reduction of photorespiration and night respiration
   4. Use of varities of prolonged growth period
   5. Artificial enrichment with CO2.
   6. Hormonal stimulation of net photosysnthesis

7. Hormonal stimulation of crop senescence
8. Genetic incorporation of Cu or CAM mechanism into C3 crops
9. Efficient planting patterns
10. Use of plastic mulches that reflect light back to the undersides of leaves.

(b) Environmental Modification

1. Wind modification with windbreaks and shelter breaks
2. Frost control with wind breaks, heating fans and irrigation
3. Control of soil temperatures through mulching or application of Black charcoal and asphalt

(c) Soil management

1. Genetic selection of crops tolerant to nutritional deficiencies or toxicities.
2. Application of fertilizers at lower rates and increasing the efficiencies of applied fertilizers.
3. Minimum or reduced tillage.
4. Use of manure, compost, covers crops and green manure.
5. Enhancement of biological N2 fixation and selection of bacteria able to fix N2 in the rhizosphere of non-legume plants.
6. Use of Azolla in rice production.
7. Utilization of micorhizal association.
8. Direct use of primary fertilizer sources [i.e phosphoric rock]

(d) Water management

1. Drip irrigation,
2. Mulching, reduced tillage,
3. Control of stoma aperture with chemicals [u.PMA],
4. Cover management for shade control,
5. Wind breaks,

(e) Insect pest management

1. Preventive actions
   (a) Resistant varieties,
   (b) Manipulation of crop planning data,
   (c) Tillage and now spacing,
   (d) Crop rotation,
   (e) Improve field hygiene,
   (f) Use of attractants,
   (g) Pheromone traps,
   (h) Crop diversification.

2. Suppressive actions
   (a) sterile male technique,
   (b) sex attractant phenomena,
   (c) Introduction, augmentation and conservation of parasites and predators,
   (d) microbial and botanical insecticides,
   (e) use of mechanical or fire removal,
   (f) induction of behavioral changes.
   (g) pesticidal control when economic threshold is reached.

(f) Disease management

1. Resistant varieties,
2. Crop rotation, uses of sub-optimal fungicide doses,
3. Multilines or variety mixtures, biological control with antagonists
4. Multiple cropping, e. reduced tillage.

(g) Weed management

1. Design of competitive crop mixtures,
2. Rapid transplant of vigorous crop seedlings to weed free bed,
3. Use of cover crops, d. Narrow row spacing,
4. crop rotation.
5. Keeping crop weed free during critical competition period,
6. Mulching, h. cultivation regimes and allelopathy.

(h) Agrononmic system

1. Multiple Cropping system
   (a) inter cropping, b. strip cropping, c. ratoon cropping,
   (d) relay cropping, e. mixed cropping.
2. use of cover crops in orchards and vineyards
3. sod strip inter cropping and vegetable living-mulch system
4. agroforestry system
5. cropping system analogous to the natural succession of the area

D. MANAGEMENT OF AGROECOSYSTEMS IN THE INDIAN CONTEXT

1. Main types of agricultural systems in India

(a) shifting cultivation system, eg. north east India,

(b) semi permanent rainfed cultivation system. eg. most unirrigated arable areas excepting some in Kerala and West Bengal,

(c) permanent rainfed cultivation system-parts of Kerala & West Bengal.

(d) Arable irrigation system,

1. The gangetic belt-Punjab, Haryana, Western U.P.,
2. Canal irrigated areas of Tamil Nadu, Karnataka, Kerala etc.
3. Areas when the water table is sufficiently high for installation of pump sets.

(e) Perennial crop system.

2. Current managing approaches in Indian Agriculture: Green Revolution

(a) high levels of inputs to maximise output,

(b) management intensity is very high,

(c) highly centralised control over inputs.

(d) infrastructural dependence is very high.

(e) Ecological ramifications - inherent danger of pest epidemics associated with monoculture, the genetic base is narrowed down to an extent where there is increased dependence on the agriplat, soil erosion, salinity, pesticide pollution, fertilizer pollution, soil depletion of nutrients, excessive use of Natural resources. vital inputs are imported, unsustainable, traditional methods of farming are destroyed,

(f) Social problems: traditional agricultural practices are thrown out of gear, eg. elimination of the family farm, connections of land, resources and production Forms of access to land and resources changed. eg. share cropping, labour tenancies, access to water supplies and grazing lands,

(g) Economic and Political shortcomings: only resource rich farmers benefit increasing rural inequality, based on artificial subsidies, vital decisions about the farmers are out of their hands.

3. Towards Holistic Agriculture

(a) Tapping traditional knowledge,

(b) Decentralized approach,

(c) Taking ecological facts and principles to their logical application

(d) Making location specific decisions regarding the level of technology and external inputs.

(e) Incorporating the socio-economic-political equity in the package,
(f) Use of environmentally sound technologies,
(g) Sustainability and increased productivity of are the keywords

> *If COURAGE wasn't a standard result of a gain, it meant that the young could somehow acquire it as well*

23. ECOLOGICAL AGRICULTURE

A. INTRODUCTION

1. Ecological agriculture is the right combination of sustainable farming systems.
2. Can be practiced at various levels-small farms to large - scale agriculture.
3. Maximal use of land resources, available labour and capital.
4. Disadvantages of intensive chemical farming - soil erosion, deterioration of human content, adaptation of pests to pesticides, spiralling capital inputs.
5. Informational and technological input for advanced ecological farming is needed.
6. Optimal utilization of agro-waste products.

B. SOIL

Retention of mechanical structure by correct farming methods - minimum tractor usage, maintenance and enhancement of humus content.

1. Mineral Fraction: bedrock, nutrient status, crop suitability
2. Organic Matter: Cation Exchange Capacity, degrees of humification
3. Soil Organisms: Convert living matter to colloidal state - conditions must be maintained for their optimal performance.
   (a) vertebrates: burrowing rats and moles, predating snakes.
   (b) invertebrates: earthworms - churners and aerators.
   (c) microorganisms: protozoa, yeasts, algae, BG-algae, mycorrhizae fungi and bacteria
   (d) - ectotrophic - endotrophic - soil bacteria
4. nitrogen - fixing symbiosis: legumes, nodules and bacteria
5. bioconversion of organic nitrogen to nitrate: complex to simpler n-compounds, ammonia and its salts, nitrification
6. the ethylene cycle: depletion of o, anaerobes & ethylene, o-accummulation & aerobes, depletion—cyclic ethylene-nutrients into soluble form, turnover of organic matter.
7. soil reconditioning: aeration & its many good effects
8. plantation of tree-belts around fields: wind-breaking, pest control, rebuilding lost habitats

C. PLANT NUTRIENTS

1. MACRO-NUTRIENTS

A. Nitrogen (in nitrate form):for proteins, susceptibility to pests

(b) Phosphorus: healthy root system

(c) Potassium: carbohydrate metabolism, leaf efficiency, resistance

(d) Calcium: neutralise acidity, good for earthworms & other soil fauna

(e) Magnesium:

2. MICRO-NUTRIENTS: essential in small quantities,

D. BIOFERTILIZERS: FARM-PRODUCTED

1. Farmyard manure: composting hostile to pathogens and weeds. Builds organic content acting with insoluble nitrogen
2. Urine: N and K fertilizer.
3. Slurry: mixture of urine and faeces
4. Compost: all organic farm wastes, safe and best

E. GREEN MANURING AND GREEN LEAF MANURING: NON-FARM PRODUCED

Greens of legumes, soil structure, microbes, crop nutrition improves

1. Blood meal: protein source
2. Bone meal: slow acting Phosphorus fertiliser
3. Hoof and horn: slow acting Nitrogen and Phosphorus fertiliser

F. BIOPESTICIDES

1. Use of micro organisms
   (a) Insect pests: chemical pesticides harmful, microbes pathogenic to pests are used
   (b) Herbicides: biological control through pathogens
2. Natural pesticides

   Pyrethrum, Nicotiana, Derris, Neem and a few dozens

G. BIOCONVERSION OF AGRICULTURAL WASTES

Mushrooms

H. CONCLUSION

Ecofarming sustainable, low yielding, holistic but research inputs needed

24. REMOTE SENSING OF RESOURCES

A. INTRODUCTION

Major geographic problems and issues. Remotely sensed data as a tool for comprehensive understanding and identifying natural resource exploitation and the problems thereof.

B. PROBLEMS

1. **Water:** Scarcity, floods, irrigation problems. Remote sensing and its broad applications to these problems.
2. **Food:** Problems faced due to food scarcity as a direct result of pest problems; soil fertility loss due to slash and burn cropping and water scarcity.
3. **Natural disasters:** Intrinsic physical effects on human beings, vegetation and natural resources. Remote sensing as a forewarning tool.
4. **Physical communications:** Remote sensing and its inputs to plan new communication.
5. **Physical resources:** Remote sensing and its use in mineral & oil exploration, understanding future exploitation of other deposits with efficiency exploitation.
6. **Natural environments:** Threats to nature from various industrial and allied activities, Remote sensing as a tool to conserve and restore natural vegetation.

C. GETTING THE INFORMATION

1. **Electromechanical methods:** Use of 'snap shots' (visible and very near infrared Range VNIR), line scanners and linear arranges in imaging the earths surface.
2. **Passive microwave imaging:** Usage of sophisticated state detectors / fixed antennae to build up profiles of limited microwave energy- basis of passive microwave imaging.
3. **Active microwave or rader imaging:** Use of high speed radar for microwave imaging of the Earth's surface.
4. **Source of remotely sensed data:** Visible Infra-red Spim-Scan Radiometers (VISSR), VISSR Atmospheric or VAS, Geo-stationary satellites.

D. RADIATION CHARACTERISTICS OF NATURAL PHENOMENA

1. The atmospheric absorption spectrum: Atmospheric radiation spectrum of various gases, absorption 'atmospheric windows'.

2. Recording reflected and/or emitted radiation: Broad wave band sensing, narrow wave band sensing, Bispectral sensing, multispectral sensing.
3. Spectral signatures of the earth's surface: Characteristic emission pattern of various topographical features.

E. SENSORS FOR ENVIRONMENTAL MONITORING

1. Sensors in the visible wavelengths: Photographic and video cameras.
2. Sensors ontside the visible wavelengths: Infra red sensors, microwave radiometers, microwave radar, LIDAR (Laser Radar), Absorption spectrometers.

F. COLLECTING IN-SITU DATA FOR REMOTE SENSING INTERPRETATION

1. The need for in-situ data: Need to check remotely sensed with that of ground truth observations.
2. Selection of ground truth sites: Criteria for selection, time constraints affecting the collection of data, study objectives, statistical considerations.
3. Ground truth for crop stuides: Site morphology, crop/vegetation cover characteristics, cultivation /husbandry futures, soil surface conditions.
4. Sea truth observations: Sea-born platforms for collecting information.

G. MANUAL DATA ANALYSIS AND INTERPRETATION

1. The role of manual data analysis and interpretation
2. The methods of photo-interpretation: Basic tasks of photo interpretation.

H. WEATHER ANALYSIS AND FORECASTING

1. Advantage of remote sensing for weather studies
2. Weather and climate: Remotely sensed data for understanding weather phenomena, methods to identify and interpret raw data for later use.
3. The sea: Use of solar, Laser and infra-red imageries to study sea-bed morphology, plankton, movement of sea currents etc.

I. THE LAND

Remote sensing data for studying topographical features.

J. NATURAL VEGETATION

1. Spectrual reflectance of the vegetated surface:Understanding vegetation heterogeneity by differences in spectral reflectance pattern.
2. Wild life studies: Animal population studies and management programmes.

K. CROPS AND LAND USE

1. Aerial photographic surveys: Crop production, pest control and management strategies.
2. Thermal infra-red sensing in crop studies: Environmental determinants of crop studies - temperature and moisture.

L. ROCKS AND MINERAL RESOURCES

THE USE OF AIR PHOTO INTERPRETATION IN GEOLOGY: To study folding, faulting, joints, dig, bedding, foliation and structure and lithology of rocks.

M. PROBLEMS ENCOUNTERED

1. Security Restrictions
2. Handling Large Quantities Of Data
3. Interface between Technologists and Users

25. MANAGEMENT OF RESOURCES

I. ECOLOGICAL PARADIGM / PERCEPTIONS

1. Everything has a history
2. Everything is connected with everything else
3. Everything must go somewhere
4. Everything grows at somethings' expense (no free lunch)

II. ANTHROPOLOGICAL PARADIGM / PERCEPTIONS

1. Populations grow - biological & economic dimension
2. Consumption more for some - cultural & economic dimension
3. Poverty increases for many - economic & political dimension

III. MANAGERIAL PARADIGM / PERCEPTIONS

A. Conserve resources

B. Substitute resources

C. Educate people

D. Communicate with everyone

E. Generate income / resourcefulness: mcnamara

F. Coordinate all activities

G. Cooperate regarding science & technology

IV. I.U.C.N.'S PERCEPTIONS

A. WORLD CONSERVATION STRATEGY

1. Conservation to support long-time sustainable level of development
2. Maintenance of essential ecological processes & life support systems
3. Preservation of Genetic Diversity
4. Minimal interference with environmentally sensitive areas/ fragile ecosystems

B. PLANNING AND MANAGEMENT CONCEPTS

1. Development of National & Regional conservation strategies
2. Development of policy-making and management institutions
3. Rational resource allocation, environmental planning institutions and associated legislative and administration arrangement
4. Improvement of research, management and training processes to facilitate sustainable development
5. Education and participation of public in conservation

C. PROTECTED AREA CATEGORIES

1. Scientific and strict nature reserves
2. National and provincial parks
3. Natural monuments and landmarks
4. Managed nature reserves and wildlife sanctuaries
5. Protected land and sea-scapes
6. Resource reserves
7. Anthropological reserves
8. Multiple use Management reserves
9. Biosphere reserves
10. World heritage sites

V. ENVIRONMENTAL ETHICS

A. MORAL VALUES

1. Consciousness of human rights
2. Paramountcy of truth and natural justice
3. Intelligence and might are used for hedonism and exploitation of others
4. Righteousness in thought and action can set right the wrongs
5. European environmental movements - ethics based

B. LEVELS OF ETHICAL CONCERNS

1. Personal: Truthfulness & social consciousness, conservation, less consumption, avoiding wastage
2. Local: Sanitation, transport, occupational health,Education
3. Regional: Rivers, habitats, developing projects
4. Global: Vietnam war, Colonization of resources, acid rains, transboundary issues, Politics in Trade, Science & Technology

C. EDUCATION AS AN ETHICAL DUTY

1. Environment is everyone's business
2. Absence of Sectarian considerations
3. Awareness of Experimenting & Experiencing
4. Schools & Colleges
5. Sections of employees and employers
6. Nongovernmental organisations/clubs
7. Movements of Public conscience
   (a) Nader (b) Chipko & Appiko
   (c) Greens (d) Narmada - Patkar

(e) Ehrlich & Commoner (f) Antinuclear movements

(g) Australian Example -Stolen Futures

8. Institutional Learning - all sectors to be taught ecology and environment

VI. CONCLUSION

1. Potential Vs actual resourcefulness/resources
2. Reality Vs Ideal situations
3. Tragedy of Commons and the life boat ethic (Triage)
4. Marketing Conservation Strategy

Associate yourself with men OF GOOD QUALITY if you esteem your own reputation for it is better to be alone than in bad company.

26. LIMITS TO ECONOMIC GROWTH

Bases for International Cooperation

A. PRINCIPLES IN EXPLOITING THE BIOSPHERE FOR DEVELOPMENT

1. Carrying capacity: Since resources are limited population cannot grow beyond the size established by the resource limit. Malthusian logic
2. Stability & Diversity: More genetic diversity, more ecological stability. Agriculture: Reduction of crop losses due to modernisation may never materialise.

   "Ecological Nightmare".
3. Ecological Buffering: Biological matter buffers air and the geologic surface. If this matter is not in sufficient quantity, carrying capacity will be reduced - Warmer climates

   All the above may be site specific

B. CLUB OF ROME (CR)

June 1970, VolksWagen Foundation, Peccei, Kind, Pestel

C. MODELS PREDICTING CONSEQUENCES & ADVOCATING RAPATTERING OF GROWTH

1. **World I Model: (worldwide)**
   - (a) Forrester: Population, Capital, Resources, Pollution, Food
   - (b) Forrester, Pestel: World Dynamics 1971
2. **World II Model: (worldwide)**
   - (a) Meadows & Meadows (MIT): Limits to Growth (1972)
   - (b) Meadows & Meadows (MIT): Dynamics of Growth in a Finite World 1974.
3. **World Integrated Model (WIM)**
   - (a) Mesarovic (Hanover), Pestel (Cleveland) (1974) : Mankind at the Turning Point
   - (b) Interactions among Many aspects
   - (c) Global Cooperation to avoid Catastrophes, Division & Conflict, hatred & violence.
4. Model of Integrated Relations in Agriculture (MOIRA)
   - (a) Bruckmann (ed): "MOIRA: Food and Agriculture Model" (1975).
   - (b) Linnemann, (Amsterdam): Model of Integrated Relations in Agriculture

5. Latin American World Model
   (a) Herrera et al (Rio de Janeiro) 1976
   (b) Catastrophe or New society
   (c) Socio-political power
   Exploitation & Destructive Values in Society
   (d) Poor Peoples & Poor Nations (PPPN) vs Rich Peoples & Rich Nation (RPRN)
6. UN World Model
   (a) W, W2, W3, & WIM are frightening and unpalatable to the poor nations.
   (b) Strategies to improve PPPN through economy
   (c) Leontief (Brandeis U. & Harvard U.) 1973
   Future of the World Economy
   (d) Carter, Petri, Stern
   Physical limitations to Economic growth.
7. Governments Global Model (1982): Resource depletion & Effects

D. IMPROVEMENT OF WORLD ECONOMY

1. Growth rates of Agriculture in High Income regions: 200%
2. Growth rates required in the Low Income regions: 500%
   - LA & Asia, Africa & China: 4-5000
3. 9 critical geologic sources
   Cu Coal
   Fe Petroleum
   Ni Natural gas
   Mn
   Pb Critical by 2000 AD
   Zn
   70% remain in 2000 AD. Most critical by 2020 AD.

27. RESOURCE DEPLETION

I. PREDICTIONS BY GLOBAL 2000 REPORT

1. **Population:** 6.5 billion by 2000, more effects on L.D.C.s
   10 billion (2030)
2. **Arable land:** Increase by 4%
3. **Food:** Increased yields, only source
4. **Higher yields:** Fertilizer, pesticides, power for irrigation, fuel for machinery: Energy ?
5. **Energy from wood:** 25% increase only possible, bleak prospects, needs 25% more than supplies
6. **Fossil energy:** Coal, gas, oil, oil shale, tar sands,Uranium
   - finite
   - economic disparities among countries
   - environmental impacts everywhere
7. **Non-fossil Minerals:** The DC [25%] absorbs 75% of the total resources of the world
8. **Water:** - more severe, in many regions
   - 50% the world already need 100% increase
   - deforestation is the major culprit
9. **Forests:-** timber sources decline by 50%
   - 20 million hectares/year - disappear annually
   - most losses: Africa, Asia, South America 40% will totally go
10. **Agricultural Soils:-** deterioration serious
    - erosion, organic matter, salinisation, water logging, alkalization desert-like conditions
11. **Air:-**
    - CO_2 increased
    - Ozone depletion
    - Acid rain
12. **9 critical geologic sources -** Cu, Pb, Fe, Ni, Mn, Coal, Petroleum, Natural gas may be used up by 2000 AD
    - Zn 70% only remain in 2000 A.D.
    Most critical by 2020 A.D.
13. **Wastes:-** radioactive, - non-radioactive

14. **Extinction of germplasm:** 20% of the existing tropical forests irretrievably lost
15. **Future of the World Economy**
    1. Growth rate of agriculture now less than 200% in the High Income countries
    2. Requirements in the low Income Regions
        (a) 500% - Latin America;
        (b) 4-500% - Africa, China, Asia
        (c) 950% - Middle East

> *Our lives improve only when we take chances- and the first and most difficult risk we can take is to be HONEST WITH OURSELVES*

28. INTERNATIONAL RELATIONS

A. TRADE

Burma Europe

1. **Timber:** India Japan

Malaysia Indonesia

2. **Fossil fuel**

USA

OPEC Non-Islamic
Islamic India nations
nations (Islamic minority)

3. **Minerals**

CCE (Centrally Controlled Economics)

LDC Japan & EEC

No Technology others

4. **Trading Groups:** ECM, ASEAN, CIS, NAFTA, G-7, G-15, G-77, G-17 Intellectual Property rights - Heritage & Empirical Knowledge

B. AGRICULTURE

- Monocultural Practices of land use, pesticides, fertilisers
- Consumptive culture in human systems
- Oil seeds crunch
- Cash crops

C. WASTES DUMPING IN FOREIGN SEAS

D. TRADE IN WASTES: importing wastes and using them as secondary resources

E. NEOCOLONIALISM

Technology, Trade, Science, Treaties, Political actions within a country - between neighbours - between distant countries

(a) Africa Loss of local technologies

(b) Asia Loss of Traditional Technologies

(c) S. America Forest products / Minerals

Centrally controlled Economics

nonessential

CCE LDCs --------------------

technology

(Consumerism) Japan, EEC others

Social problems

F. POLITICS OF AID & DEBT CLEARANCE

To encourage a kind of development that will deplete resources, encourage consumption; discourage self reliance Debt - Aid - and Aid to clear debt - A Never ending cycle

G. STRATEGIC IMPORTANCE OF FOSSIL FUEL

1. Resource, Natural Resource, and what kind of natural resource is fossil fuel (ie non renewable, energy etC.)?
2. Why fossil fuel is a Mother of resources ?
3. Main fossil fuels (ie coal & petroleum).

H. GLOBAL DISTRIBUTION OF FOSSIL FUELS (coal & petroleum).

1. World's largest producers (coal/petroleum).
2. What portion comes to the world market ?
3. Who are the principal buyers and sellers ?

I. WHY THERE HAS TO BE A STRATEGY (ie its role) ?

1. What is the prevalent strategy of the buying and selling nation?
2. How these fossil fuels affects world economy?

J. SPECIAL REFERENCE TO INDIA IN ALL THE ABOVE POINTS.

India's internal and external strategies or situation.

K. OTHERS

1. Fossil Oil: West Asia Policy based on this
2. Minerals: Extraction vs Technology
3. Wastes: Radioactive / non - Radioactive / dumping / Reprocess
4. Rivers: Internal Regions / Countries
5. Sea: Coast lines / Islands
6. Trans Amazonian Highway: Amazonian Fires
   Land = No people
   People = Inadequate land
7. Evolutionary endowment never to be privatised

FOREST TIMBER

Scandinavia

Malaya —> Sarawak —> Restoration
Tribals / Bans

Japan —> Europe

Indonesia —> Kalimantan —> Migration
1970s ——> 1997: Burning, Haze

29. INDIAN CONCERNS

A. LAND AND SOIL

1. 1/40 of the world land supports 1/2 of the world's buffaloes. Goats and cattle are additional; grazing land turning into agricultural lands, what is the future? Encroachment on forest land? Violent clashes in future? Social forestry programmes mainly plant non-fuel species.
2. Wastelands of India: 100 million hectares, 40 million are still in some use. Affected by Salinity, alkalinity and erosion by wind and water. Ravines swallowed 4 million hectares. 10% of villages in chambal valley depopulated. Then same happened in a few other states.
3. Per capita land availability decreasing constantly. 0.2ha/by 2000 AD
4. Soil from forests silting the dams.
5. Agricultural land constantly turned into housing and industrial habitats (urbanisation) - 1.5 million hectares.
6. Land reclamation efforts hardly under operation.
7. Himalayas highly vulnerable on watersheds. Pine Vs Oak Meera Behn 1950.
8. Desertification in U.P., Haryana, Gujarat.

B. MINERALS IN INDIA

1. Mineral production increased 50 fold in the lalst 3 decades.
2. A few million hectares of crop and forest land destroyed.
3. Hundreds of villages depopulated.
4. 50% of mining output comes from 40 contiguous districts of Eastern and Central India. Other important area is Rajasthan.
5. Tribals are worst affected.
6. Mining pits, Mining disasters, Quarrying, collieries.
7. Health hazards to workers and people around.
8. Trading with foreign countries disadvantageous to India.
9. Industries, end produces, social sectors receiving.

C. WATER AND ITS RESOURCES

1. Total precipitation 400 million hectare meters

   Soil: 215 Surface: 115 Evaporation :70

2. % used = 25 i.e. 20% = Surface = 13 i.e. 60%
   (a) India use 1/10 of the rainfall storage, non-pollution necessary
   (b) Ground water resources substantial but are gradually depleting
   (c) Tanks, ponds neglected and even filled up.
   (d) Most high altitude lakes are dying excepting a few
   (e) Ecological value of wetlands not realised fully
   (f) Increasing pollution affect fisheries, fisher folk
   (g) Dam water covering 1% of land area. Produce little fish
   (h) Important cities facing water crisis
   (i) Poor of the country hardly having access to clean drinking water
   (j) 175 major & 450 minor dams drown 1/2 million hectares of forest
   (k) Canal irrigation benefited 5 million hectares of land

D. OCEANS

1. Coastlines preservation and utilisation by local people
2. Mining for fossil fuels in Krishna-Godavari basin
3. Biosphere reserves necessary
4. Hardly any indegenous research work
5. Antarctica Expeditious
6. 20 or 200 miles territorial waters
7. Military activities: regional and global powers
8. Dumping of wastes by foreign companies
9. Desalination as an imperative

E. ANIMALS (PROF. N.S. RAMASWAMY, CHAIRMAN, A.W.B. OF INDIA)

1. 400 million livestock; 200 million poultry, dogs, cats etc
2. Wealth Rs. 45,000 crores: equal to food grains (Products: 23M; Work & Fertilizer: 16 & Others: 6).
3. Farmers: 300 million
4. Slaughter houses: 3000: legal: 30,000: illegal Modernisation: 3000 crores (1/5 of the food grain sector) Annual earnings: Rs.3000 crores to farmers and owners of animals
5. Milk by 1995 — 440 lakh tons ——610
   Cooperatives: 270 districts
   158 gms —— 186 gms/day

F. FORESTS IN INDIA

1. Annual loss 1.3 million/hectare. 8 times more than put up by forest departments.
2. Wood shortage and therefore prices are so high that boat, cart and even toy making is affected.
3. Bastar: Indravati dams, & Mining will render the people refuges. Narmada sagar/Tehri-Gharwal
4. Social forestry: trees for commercial value. Not for basic needs or ecology.
5. Eucalyptus: 1/2 million hectares, water and nutrient depletion.
6. Landless involved in afforestation: can be the biggest input towards national progress by land giving.
7. Westoby 1960s Social forestry
8. 1928 village based Forestry Royal Commission

G. GERMPLAM

1. Natural diversity in India: one of the richest in the world.
2. 50,000 varieties of rice known in India.
3. A sample of Rice from Eastern UP gave Asian farmers a gene against Grassy Stunt virus.
4. Silent valley revealed 9 new species and Andamans one
5. Buffaloes yield much less than a few decades ago
6. 9000 tons of frogs exported in 1981 earning Rs. 12 crores
7. People are turning against conservationists as 25% of forested lands including their wildlife are reserved.
8. Medicinal plants depleting, Ayurvedic medicine affected
9. Hardly any evaluation on animal especially marine systems
10. Wild life conservation synonymous with germplasm preservation.
11. Biosphere reserves necessary. Andaman & Nicobar, Nilgiris and 11 others
12. WWF, IBPGR active

H. ENERGY

1. Yearly consumption of firewood: 14-20 million tons (Rs.500 crores). This is more than what is spent on afforestation during the last 3 decades. 8 Solar energy inputs.
2. Urban fuel wood comes deforestation.
3. Self sufficiency unlikely in spite of Hydroelectric, fossil fuel and nuclear programmes. Wastage is one major scourge.

4. There may be enough food, but not energy to cook it.
5. Coal is preferred.
6. Oil: more explorations and gas.
7. Nuclear: Eleven new reactors.

   Energy is an essential input for economic development and for improving the quality of life.

   India's per capita consumption of commercial energy is only one - eighth of the world average.

All human beings are born with unique gifts. The healthy functioning of our community depends on its capacity to DEVELOP EACH GIFT

TEACHING LABOURS OF SISYPHUS!

TEACHING LABOURS OF SISYPHUS!
CLASS LACTURE SYNOPSES IN ENVIRONMENTAL SCIENCES

VOLUME - II
IMPACTS & MANAGEMENT

Prof. C.B.S.R. Sharma
Pondicherry University

First Published, 2020

Published by

Kalpaz Publications
C-30, Satyawati Nagar,
Delhi – 110052
Ph.: 011-47034999, 9811692060
www.kalpazpublications.com
E-mail: kalpaz@hotmail.com

Printed at: G. Print Process, Delhi

Cataloging in Publication Data—DK

Courtesy: D.K. Agencies (P) Ltd. <docinfo@dkagencies.com>

Sharma, C. B. S. R., author.

Teaching Labours of Sisyphus! : Class Lecturer Synopses in Environmental Sciences / Prof. C.B.S.R. Sharma.

volumes cm

Contents: Volume I. Basics & Resources — Volume II. Impacts & Management.

ISBN 9789353242350 (set) (HB)
ISBN 9789353242374 (vol. II)

1. Ecology. 2. Environmental Sciences. 3. Biology. 4. Natural Resources. I. Title.

LCC QH541.S53 2020 | DDC 577 23

Contents

Foreword 9
Preface 11
Acknowledgments 15

Volume - I

Basics and Resources

(*Series Page No. 1-426 See Below*)

1. Cytogenetics and Microbiology 17
2. Basic Ecology 75
3. Biodiversity & Germplasm Banking 141
4. Coasts and Wetlands 223
5. Bioenergy 277
6. Natural Resources 313

Volume - II

Impacts & Management

(*Series Page No. 427-807 See Below*)

7. Pollution and Toxicology 7
8. Environmental Mutagenesis 111
9. Environmental Philosophies, Politics and Activism 197
10. Applied Ecology 267

Appendices 313
Confessions 375

7

Pollution and Toxicology

1. AIR POLLUTION
2. MARINE POLLUTION
3. FRESH WATER POLLUTION
4. GROUND WATER POLLUTION
5. INDOOR POLLUTION
6. NOISE POLLUTION
7. SOLID WASTES
8. SEWAGE POLLUTION
9. PESTICIDES POLLUTION
10. THERMAL POLLUTION
11. RADIATION POLLUTION
12. INTRODUCTION TO TOXICOLOGY
13. GENERAL, GENO & ECO-TOXICOLOGY
14. TOXICITY TO LIVER, KIDNEY AND SKIN
15. NEUROTOXICITY
16. RESPIRATORY TOXICITY
17. REPRODUCTIVE & DEVELOPMENTAL TOXICITY
18. ECOTOXICOLOGY - TERRESTRIAL SYSTEMS
19. ECOTOXICOLOGY: AQUATIC SYSTEMS
20. OCCUPATIONAL HEALTH
21. COMMUNITY HEALTH
22. MANAGEMENT STRATEGIES
23. BIOMONITORING OF POLLUTIONS
24. LAWS FOR POLLUTION CONTROL
25. MONITORING BY INSTRUMENTATION
26. REMOTE SENSING

Syllabus

1. POLLUTION and POLLUTION LAWS

   Surface water, Ground water, Marine, Soil, Air, Noise, Radiations Thermal, Pesticides , Solid/liquid wastes,
2. TOXICOLOGY: Basic Tenets, Taxonomy
3. TOXICITY TO THE ORGANS: Liver, Kidney, Skin
4. TOXICITY TO THE SYSTEMS: Respiratory, Nervous, Reproductory, etc.
5. GENETIC TOXICOLOGY: Origins, Basic Principles, Mechanisms, Consequences, Perspectives,
6. ECOTOXICOLOGY: Terrestrial Systems, Aquatic Systems
7. OCCUPATIONAL HEALTH
9. MANAGEMENT STRATEGIES
8. MONITORING SYSTEMS: Laboratory and Field
10. BIOMONITORING AND POLLUTION
12. INSTRUMENTATION TECHNIQUES
11. INDIAN SCENARIO

References

1. American Public Health Association APHA) Standard Methods for the Examination of Water and Wastewater. APHA, Washington
2. Albert. A. 1987 Xenobiosis, Chapman & Hall, London
3. Brown. AW 1978, Ecology of Pesticides, John Wiley, New York
4. Butler GC 1978. Principles of Ecotoxicology. Wiley, New York
5. Dixon HM 1981. Environmental Pollution, Wiley, New York
6. Eisenbud M, 1963. Environmental Radioactivity, McGraw-Hill
7. Hollaender and de Serres, 1971-1990. Chemical Mutagens. Vol. 1-12, Plenum
8. Nurenberg, HW [ed]1985. Pollutants and their Ecotoxicological significance
9. Rand. G.M. and Petrocelli, S.R. 1985. Fundamentals of Aquatic Toxicology - methods and application. Hemisphere Publ. Washington
10. Stern A.C. 1979. Air pollution Vols. 1-3.,Academic Press
11. Treshow.M.1970.Environment and Plant Response, McGraw Hill

1. AIR POLLUTION

I. INTRODUCTION

A. DEFINITION: Air pollution is the presence in the ambient atmosphere of substances in sufficient concentration, present for a sufficient time and under circumstances which interfere significantly with the comfort, health or welfare of persons or with full use or enjoyment of property.

B. CLASSIFICATION OF AIR POLLUTANTS

1. ORIGIN: PRIMARY - Directly emitted from a source, eg. SO2

   SECONDARY Pollutants - forms due to interaction of two or more primary pollutants eg. PAH
2. CHEMICAL COMPOSITION - ORGANIC or INORGANIC
3. STATE OF MATTER - PARTICULATES, GASEOUS ORGANIC and GASEOUS INORGANIC
4. SOURCES:
   - (a) Point source: large stationary source eg. Industrial processing
   - (b) Area sources: small stationary sources and mobile sources with indefinite routes. eg. Residential heating, Railyard locomotive
   - (c) Line sources: Mobile sources with definite routes. eg. High way vehicles

II. METEEROLOGICAL ASPECTS

A. FACTORS RESPONSIBLE FOR DISPERSION OF AIR POLLUTANTS.

1. Wind
2. Lapse Rate / The rate of change of temperature
3. Atmospheric stability
4. Inversion
   - Radiation
   - Subsidence

B. LAPSE RATE AND PLUME BEHAVIOR

1. Looping 2. Lofting 3. Looning
4. Fanning 5. Fumigation 6. Trapping

C. MIXING DEPTH

D. WIND ROSE

III. INDOOR AIR POLLUTION

1. Indoor /outdoor relationship
2. Personal Air pollution aspects
3. Sick Building syndrome
4. Sources of Indoor toxic contaminants.
5. Abatement Measures
6. Indoor Air quality standards
7. Regulatory Limitations.

IV. EFFECTS OF AIR POLLUTION

A. ATMOSPHERIC ASPECTS

1. Visibility
2. Turbidity
3. Thermal air pollution
4. Precipitation
5. Acidic Deposition
6. Ozone layer
7. Climate

B. HUMAN HEALTH

1. Suspended particulate matter
2. Sulfur Dioxide
3. Oxides of Nitrogen
4. Carbon Monoxide
5. Hydrocarbons
6. Ozone
7. Lead
8. Hazardous Air Pollutants

C. VEGETATION

1. Leaf tissue collapse with necrotic pattern
2. Chlorosis or other colour changes
3. Growth alterations.
4. Common Pollutants considered for the study: Sulfur dioxide, Oxidant smog gases, Ozone, Nitrogen Oxides, Fluorides, Peroxyacetyl Nitrate, Mercury, Chlorine, Hydrogen chloride Ammonia, Hydrogen sulfide and Hydrogen cyanide

D. ANIMALS

1. Arsenic
2. Lead
3. Fluorides

E. MATERIALS

1. Dyes
2. Textiles
3. Paper
4. Leather
5. Paints
6. Building materials
7. Rubber
8. Metals

V. REGULATORY ASPECTS

1. Legal Remedies - Common Law
2. Air quality management strategies
3. Emission standard
4. Air quality standard

5. Emission taxes
6. Cost Benefit Analysis
7. Legislative history
    (a) 1955 Clean air act (b) 1963 clean air act
    (c) 1967 Air quality act (d) 1970 clean air act
    (e) 1977 clean air amendments
8. State & local Air pollution control Measures & their effectiveness.

VI. CONTROL STRATEGIES

A. COLLECTION EQUIPMENT: Controls at the sources

1. Settling chamber 2. Cyclones
3. Scrubbers & wet collectors !
    (a) Spray towers (b) Ventus scrubbers
    (c) Cyclone scrubbers (d) Packed scrubber
4. Filters
    (a) Fabric or cloth filters (b) Fibrous or Deep bed Filters
5. Electrostatic Precipitator

B. CONTROL OF SPECIFIC GASEOUS POLLUTANTS

1. Combustion - incineration systems used are
    (a) Direct flame incineration (b) Thermal incinerators
    (c) Catalytic incineration
2. Absorption
    (a) Bubbler (b) Continuous
3. Adsorption
    (a) charcoal silica gel (b) Static sampler
    (c) Free freeze out.
4. Mechanical Retention
    (a) Evacuated Bottle (b) Continuous

SUMMARY

1. Nitrogen more abundant (78%) than oxygen (20.9%) in the atmosphere.
2. Carbon dioxide plays important role in photosynthesis and in maintaining global heat balance.
3. The nature of pollutants vary according to its source like gases, metallic pollutants, particulates, Hydrocarbons.
4. Sources of primary pollutants may be mobile or stationary, combustion or non-combustion, area or point source, direct or indirect.

5. Dispersion is influenced by micro, meso and macro scale motion.
6. By impacts or experiments the pollution is measure.
7. Green house effect, ozone layer depletion and acid rain are manifestations of air pollution on the ecosystem.
8. Bio-indicators used as an indicator for a particular pollutant.
9. Management strategies play important role in controlling the air pollution or to counteract the impact.

The Real Education Consists of DRAWING THE GOODNESS AND THE BEST Out Of our students. Which books can be better than the book of HUMANITY?

2. MARINE POLLUTION

I. INTRODUCTION

A. **MARINE RESOURCES:** A brief overview of the resourcefulness of the sea and its complexity and diversity of life forms.

B. **FOCUSSING PERSPECTIVES:** Focussing the varied perspectives of naturalists, environmentalists, conservationists and economists and the potential of the marine environment as they perceive it.

C. **EXPLOITATION OF MARINE RESOURCES:** A review of major landmarks in marine use and exploitation in recent historical times.

II. ORIGIN OF WASTE WATER

The pathways that lead to marine pollution - rivers and coastal outflows; atmospheric transports; direct and indirect inputs from ships, oil rigs and off-shore structures. Their relative contributions to local and diffused pollution.

III. TYPES OF POLLUTANTS

A systematic discussion of the various categories of pollutants, their sources, impact on biota and local habitats and the stages and processes involved.

A. **OXYGEN DEMANDING WASTES:** Sewage, food processing plants, pulp and paper mills, tanning operations and other organic waste producing activities.

B. **SYNTHETIC ORGANIC COMPOUNDS:** Pesticides, synthetic organic chemicals, detergents and the non-biodegradable effluents of major industries.

C. **PLANT NUTRIENTS:** Nitrogen and Phosphorus compounds entering water in large quantities because of large scale fertilizer use, by products of sewage treatment and processing of biological materials like textiles and food.

D. **INORGANIC CHEMICALS AND MINERALS:** Includes inorganic salts, mineral acids, finely divided metals and metal compounds.

E. **SEDIMENTS:** Soil, sand and mineral particles washed into the aquatic environment by storms & floods. This category also includes particulate matter carried in by rain.

F. **RADIOACTIVE SUBSTANCES:** Disposal of radioactive wastes, bioaccumulation and related concepts.

G. **THERMAL DISCHARGES:** Effects of heat on local biota around sources of water used as coolants in power plants.

H. **OIL:** Industrial effluents, oil refineries, spills and wastes.

IV. EFFECTS ON BIOTA

Effects of the above mentioned pollutants on specific taxa.

A. **AUTOTROPHIC ORGANISMS:**

1. Phytoplankton
2. Marine micro-algae
3. Higher Plants

B. **HETEROTROPHIC ORGANISMS:**

1. Zooplankton
2. Bivalves
3. Crustaceans
4. Fish

The importance of the above mentioned taxa as indicators of pollution and their role in bio-accumulation is significant

V. WATER POLLUTION LAWS AND STANDARDS

Acts, laws and legislative organisations equipped with handling, curbing, controlling, preventing or managing marine pollution. Policies and decisions regarding pollution at National and Global levels.

VI. TREATMENT OF WASTE WATERS

A. **BASIC PROCESSES OF WATER TREATMENT:** Physical, chemical and biological processes; Primary, secondary tertiary and advanced water treatment methods.

B. **DISPOSAL VERSUS REUSE:** Effectiveness of recycling waste material to combat disposal problems.

C. **USING ALTERNATIVE MATERIALS:** The success of substituting toxic compounds used in manufacture of essentials and its drawbacks.

D. **OCEAN DISPOSAL VERSUS LAND DISPOSAL:** Comparative study of ocean and land dumping of wastes.

VII. RESEARCH NEEDS

Sampling and analysis of marine pollution methods and technologies available.

VIII. CASE STUDIES

A. **MINAMATA:** Industrial metal contamination in coastal waters (Japan) - a very brief report of impacts.

B. **SAN FRANCISCO BAY (USA):** Effects of coastal outflow on local marine environment.

C. **RICHARDS BAY (SOUTH AFRICA):** Possible impacts of a proposed industrial unit along the coast.

IX. LASTWORD

Future of the ocean is at stake due to the wastes that the world generates.

Education means inspiring some one's mind, not just filling their head

3. FRESH WATER POLLUTION

I. INTRODUCTION

Of the entire Earth's water resources 'HYDROSPHERE' consists of less than 1% fresh waters; some 2% of fresh water ice and the remaining 97% is of sea water. Some 1500 substances are listed as pollutants in fresh water ecosystems.

II. NATURE AND COMPOSITION OF FRESH WATERS

1. Surface water: Rivers, Streams & Lakes
2. Ground waters.

III. SOURCES OF POLLUTION

A. POINT SOURCE: Discharges of waste waters from sewage works, factories & farms.

B. NONPOINT SOURCE: Arise mainly from specific categories of general land use. Sources could be run off and under drainage from agricultural land; seepage of land fill leachates etc. As in the case of coastal systems, point of access of pollution cannot be located and no person or corporate body can be proved to wittingly permit the pollution to occur.

IV. TYPES OF DIFFUSE POLLUTION

A. ACIDIFICATION OF WATERS

1. Sources: acid rain.
2. Control measures.
   (a) Judicious reduction of the emission of pollutants.
   (b) Adding a neutralizing alkali to acid-sensitive areas.
   (c) Effects of acidification

B. NITRATES IN WATERS

1. Maximum permissible limit for nitrates in water is 50 mg l-1. Implications are more serious in case of ground water than surface waters.
2. Control Measures

   Reduce intensity of agricultural activity which produces this heavy nitrogenous loading.

C. FROM POLLUTED LAND

1. Leachates from solid wastes and sludges
2. Spillages from a variety of sources including sewage.

D. ORGANIC POLLUTION

1. Sources: Originate from domestic sewage (raw/treated), urban

run off, industrial effluents and farm yard wastes, forming suitable substrates for micro organisms.

2. Effect of organic pollutants on water that receive them
3. Treatment: Sewage effluent is the greatest source of organic materials to Fresh waters. There are 4 stages in the treatment processes;

   (a) Preliminary treatment (b) Primary treatment

   (c) Secondary treatment (d) Tertiary treatment

E. EUTROPHICATION

1. Increase in the rate of income of nutrients especially/mostly of nitrogen & phosphorus.
2. Sources: (a) Discrete: specific sewage outfall.

   (b) Diffuse: Farmland area within a catchment
3. Control:

   (a) Elimination of phosphorus as an essential component of detergents (about 50% of the phosphorus could be removed)

   (b) Sewage treatment.

   (c) Altering land-use practices.

F. TOXIC POLLUTION

1. Metals (Heavy)
2. Organic compounds such as pesticides and their derivatives
3. Gases such as chlorine & ammonia
4. Anions such as cyanides, fluorides, sulphides etc.
5. Acids & alkalies

V. MONITORING STRATEGIES

A. OBJECTIVES OF MONITORING

1. Health concerns 2. Preventive measures
3. Punitive measures

B. TYPES OF MONITORING

1. Source monitoring 2. Water monitoring
3. Biota monitoring

VI. ABATEMENT OF POLLUTION

1. Categories

   (a) Wastewaters with high chemical quality

   (b) Contaminated run off from roofs and yards at industrial premises.

   (c) Clean cooling waters.
   (d) Grossly contaminated wastewaters and waste chemicals.

2. Treatment of waste waters: Sewage and industrial
3. (a) To maintain and improve the utility values of water resources.
   (b) To reduce health hazards to consumers of water.

If We Do Not Plant Knowledge When Young, It Will Give Us No Shade When We Are Old

4. GROUND WATER POLLUTION

I. INTRODUCTION

A. Definition: Subsurface water that occurs below the water table in soils and geologic formations that are fully saturated.

B. Hydrology

1. Water cycle: Ground water is an integral part of the hydrologic cycle because the global cycle accounts for the water movement between oceans, atmosphere, surface water & ground water. 2/3 of total precipitation is evaporated or transpired & 1/3 only is retained.
2. Aquifer: A ground water bearing formation, sufficiently permeable so as to transmit and yield water in usable quantities.
3. Types of Aquifers
   (a) Unconfined: absence of a semi/non-permeable surface above the water which restricts flow.
   (b) Confined: a water bearing formation between two confining layers of rock.
   (c) Perched: This is a temporary aquifer,when wateris collected on a flow restricting layer.This phenomena is known as Ponding'.
   (d) Leaky: These lose water due to downward vertical seepage through permeable/semi-permeable layer below.

II. GROUND WATER POLLUTION

A. Sources

1. Purposes
   (a) to discharge substances.
   (b) to store, treat & discharge substances
   (c) to retain substances during transmission or transport
   (d) discharging substances as consequences of other planned activities.
   (e) Naturally occurring sources.
2. Types of sources
   (a) Point sources: at specific points
   (b) Diffuse sources: over a large area

B. Types of pollutants

(a) Bacteria, viruses & other pathogens
(b) Non-metals (eg N, P, K)
(c) Metals (including heavy metals)

(d) Organics
(e) Pesticides & other agricultural run offs.
(f) Radionuclides

C. Transport & fate of Pollutants

This can be estimated by using the following methods:

(a) Leachate testing: Evaluating ground water potential
(b) Ground water tracers: Using specific tracers for specific pollutants
(c) Facilitated transport: Variation in speeds of pollutants under certain conditions

III. EFFECTS

A. On plants

1. Reduced growth
2. Poor productivity
3. Reduced resistance to diseases
4. Chlorosis
5. Necrosis

B. On Animals

1. Diseases due to pathogens
2. Diseases due to accumulation & concentration of some specific pollutants

C. Humans

1. Methaeomoglobinaemia: The 'blue baby' syndrome
2. Pathogenic diseases
3. Brain disease (Lead poisoning)
4. Long term effects of chronic heavy metal poisoning.

IV. MANAGEMENT

A. International aspects

1. U.S.A.-16 Federal statutes related to ground water quality anagement.
2. W.H.O. - The same rules pertaining to surface water apply here also

B. Control

1. At source
2. Interceptor systems
3. Surface water control
4. Impermeable barriers
5. Waste water treatment

C. Treatment

1. Physical treatment
2. In situ chemical treatment
3. In situ biological treatment
4. Surface technologies: Pumping water out & then treating it.

5. INDOOR POLLUTION

1. INTRODUCTION

Indoor air in buildings can be polluted with many types of materials and activities in the houses. For instance smoking inside the houses and furnishing materials used in rooms cause indoor pollution. Burning of wood for cooking exposes people especially children and women to indoor pollution. Pollutants produce headaches, coughing, sneezing, nausea burning eyes. Respiratory illnesses are cause of death.

2. HAZARDOUS HOUSEHOLD CHEMICALS

Corrosive drain openers, acidic products like toilet cleaners, house hold chemicals are toxic, e.g. Asbestos and lead

Asbestos: Asbestos is a component of floor and others.
Exposure to it results in asbestosis and lung cancer.

Lead: Sources of lead are water pipes and wall paints use cool water instead of hot H2O in which lead is dissolved.

3. HOUSE-HOLD HAZARDOUS WASTE

Some of the hazardous wastes are antifreeze, are sweet tasting and can poison animals and children.

4. HOW CAN EXPOSURE TO HAZARDOUS PRODUCTS BE REDUCED

Should read labels and directions. Handle them with care and minimize the use of hazardous substances, wear safety glasses.

(a) Toxic use reduction: Use should be minimized and use the alternative or not use them in closed rooms, use exhaust fan.

(b) Radon as a source of indoor air pollution:

Water from deep wells, municipal water are sources of radon. Radon emits radiation, when exposed results in damage to genetic material, DNA. and in long cancer.

(c) Reducing pollution from radon: It can be driven from house by a fan. It can be reduced by sealing the openings in basement floor.

5. COMBUSTION PRODUCTS AS INDOOR POLLUTANTS

Cigarette smoking is a major sources of combustion products.

Carbon monoxide and nitrogen oxides produced from kerosine heater and gas stoves. Smoking causes lung cancer and respiratory diseases. Stoves causes dizziness. Emissions of pollutants from the combustion sources depends on (i) types of fuel and (ii) combustion conditions.

6. VOLATILE ORGANIC COMPOUNDS AS A SOURCE OF INDOOR POLLUTION:

Paints, varnishes, turpentine, nail polish, hairspray are sources of Volatile compounds. chronic effects possible when products used without ventilation. Formaldehyde is a common chemical. It irritates eyes, nose, throat, Headache drowsiness are seen.

Air microbes as indoor pollutants uncontrolled sources of moisture generates microorganisms. Modern appliances provide standing water. evaporative coolers, self defrosting refrigerators and flush toilets have potential for contamination.

7. CONTROL MEASURES

(a) Maintenance of low relative humidity

(b) Elimination of dampness or standing water.

8. BIOLOGICAL POLLUTANTS

Includes biological matter other than microbes. Pollen, dust, faeces, dirty carpets are the sources, cause respiratory diseases like asthma, allergic reactions etc.

9. AIR POLLUTION DUE TO PERFUMES, LIQUORS, WINES, ROTTEN SMELLS

10. SOLUTIONS FOR INDOOR POLLUTION

(a) Houses and work places have to be ventilated to out side air for reducing pollution.

(b) source control

(c) use alternatives

(d) Don't smoke.

(e) Stoves and fire places are properly ventilated.

(f) Reduce Pesticide use.

6. NOISE POLLUTION

I. INTRODUCTION

Progress in man meant predominance of industrialization, technology & transport leading to urbanization & mercantilism. All of these caused pollution and threatened - the ecological security of man.

A. **PARADOX OF PROGRESS:** They still continue to do so

B. **BYEPRODUCTS OF POLLUTION:** Environmental pollution is classified into - Land Atmospheric, Water and Noise

C. **NOISE SYNDROME:** Source & causes of noise pollution are

1. Increasing population
2. Poverty
3. Illiteracy
4. Customs & religious fanaticism
5. Lack of civilities
6. Lack of policing

D. Institute of Road Education has statistics indicating the increase of noise in Indian cities. Delhi is the noisiest followed by Calcutta, Bombay & Madras.

E. Noise pollution needs to be controlled by the community's norms and legal action.

II. THEORITICAL CONSIDERATIONS

A. **HISTORY**

1. First hearing risk from forging & fashioning implements & weapons during bronze age.
2. Second risk from gun-powder in the 14th century.

B. **ETYMOLOGY:** Origin of the word noise

Latin - nansea, French – noyse, Greek - navisa.

C. **DEFINITIONS:** Noise is an "Unpleasant sound" Noise pollution is environmental noise of sufficient loudness to be annoying or physically harmful.

III. PRACTICAL ASPECTS

A. **SOURCES:** Broadly the sources are

1. Industrial - machinary, motor vehicles, explosives, satellites, telecommunications etc.
2. Non-industrial- loud speakers, radios, public gatherings.

B. **CLASSIFICATION**

1. The quality of noise in DB are
   (a) Soft range 40-60 DB
   (b) Risk range 60-100 DB
   (c) Danger range 1000 DB.

2. Based on the duration of exposure
   - (a) Occupational (b) Seasonal (c) Diurnal
   - (d) Discontinuous (e) Choice

C. EFFECTS

1. Hearing
   - (a) Temporary hearing loss
   - (b) Prolonged loss of hearing
   - (c) Permanent loss of hearing
   - (d) Irreversible acoustic trauma
   - (e) Acoustic accidents
   - (f) Ototic blast.
2. Other systems
   - (a) Psychological imbalances
   - (b) Vascular problems
   - (c) Improper digestion & ulcers
   - (d) Embryological disturbances
   - (e) Pediatric syndromes

D. CONTROLS

1. Self control 2. Social control
3. Legal control: Hearing disability on the WISCONSIN scale is an internationally accepted compensatable loss hence

IV. LEGAL CONSIDERATIONS

A. CONSTITUTIONAL PROVISIONS

1. General pollution :acts 39 (c), 47, 48 (A) and 51 (9)
2. There is a noticeable lack of proper perspective on the subject of noise.

B. LAW OF TORTS: Considers two kinds of nuisance

1. Public
2. Private - unlawful interference of a man's use of his property, health, comfort or convenience.
3. However to actually obtain relief it is cumbersome & interpretations differ.

C. CRIMINAL LAWS: Individual law suits.

1. Chapter XIV of Indian Penal Code sections 268, 270, 278, 279, 287, 288.

D. MOTOR VEHICLE ACTS 1988

1. Under sections 110 & 111 the central & state govts. are empowered to make specific provisions in controlling noise.

2. Sections 53, 56, 184 & the motor vehicle rules for reducing noise 119, 120, 121.

E. LABOUR LAWS: Section II of the Factories Act 1948 provide relief from nuisance - though nothing very serious or anything related to noise.

F. ENVIRONMENTAL PROTECTION ACT

1. Only act dealing with noise pollution as well in accordance with section 6 (2)
2. It however doesn't define noise, its effects, measurements or remedies.

V. OTHERS

1. Need for specific legislation
2. Suggestions for the act.
   (a) Quantification
   (b) Types of noise
   (c) Restrictions
   (d) Silent zones
   (e) Surprise checks.
   (f) Discourage audio at religious gatherings
   (g) Noise during elections
   (h) Stringent rules for public Undertakings too.
   (i) Location of airports
   (j) Scientific aspect to legislation. Medical knowledge essential.
   (k) Voluntary / N.G.O. support & participation.
   (l) Offences must be checked
   (m) Mobile patrols & courts must be introduced

7. SOLID-WASTES

1. Pollution is defined as an indescribable change in the Physical, Chemical or Biological characteristics of our air, land and water that may or will harmfully affect human life or that of other desirable species and mans activities. Solid Waste, one such pollutant is any unwanted or discarded material from residential, community, industrial, mining and agricultural societies that cause environmental problems.
2. Hence increasing population and fast industrialisation has lead to an increase in production of solid wastes, which is pronounced in developed countries.
3. In India Calcutta, Bombay, Delhi, Madras Bangalore and Hyderabad, Ahmedabad Produce the maximum amount of solid wastes.
4. The solid wastes should be treated so that they may not become seats of pollution. Before the disposal the collecting and transportation should be done carefully and equally. The wastes should be disposed using suitable methods which includes composting, (sanitary) and fills, incineration and pyrolysis and Recyling and reuse.
5. Composting is usually done for organic substances. The process involves the decomposition of organic matter present in the refuse by micro-organisms, primarily bacteria and fungi.
6. The wastes are (dumped) buried by consigning them with earth (every day). This method is called "Sanitary land fill". Here the complex organic wastes are slowly degraded or decomposed by the soil microorganisms. Hence the selected site should be well above the ground water table to avoid pollution by leachates.
7. Incineration is a process of controlled combination of the waste, so as to connect them into some residue and gaseous products. Very hygienic but expensive. Another thermal process is pyrolycis.
8. Recycling is a method by which the waste materials are converted into resources by recovery of usable products both material and energy. Papers, plastics, metals etc can be exampled.

   Recycling saves a lot of energy, the pollution is reduced, ground water contamination is reduced.
9. In strict sense, there is no waste, as the waste of one industry can well be the raw material for the other. So integrated industrial planning and system approach have to be adopted for recycling 'waste'. Recycling has immense hence fit to the community. It avoids pollution and at the same time provides resources and raw material for development.

8. SEWAGE POLLUTION

1. INTRODUCTION

The race among various countries to develop has resulted in unlimited exploitation of natural resources. This has resulted in disruption of ecological balance and also release of many man-made pollutants. These wastes have transformed natural water bodies into sewage depots destroying those eco-systems.

2. SEWAGE POLLUTION

The domestic wastes like human excreta, paper, cloth, soap, detergents etc. when dumped into water bodies, destroy selfpurifying ability and have also caused outbreak of various diseases. Mixing of sewage with water have made it unfit for drinking and domestic purposes.

3. SEWAGE CHARACTERISTICS:

Sewage quality is defined in terms of suspended solids, BOD and Ammonia. A second definition has been given according to its sources.

(a) Physical characteristics: Fresh sewage has a slightly soapy or oily odours, cloudy, and contain recognisable solids, of considerable size. Stale sewage smells of hydrogen sulphide and is dark grey in colour.

(b) Chemical characteristics: The sewage consists of inorganic contents which increase subsequently and organic contents in the disposed wastes.

(c) Microbiology of sewage: Microorganisms like bacteria, protozoans, worms and fungi are present in sewage water.

4. COMPOSITION OF SEWAGE

Sewage is 99.9% water and 0.1% of solids out of which about 2/3rd are organic compounds like proteins, urea, carbohydrates, fats-soap, cooking oil and greases. The inorganic components include chloride, metallic salts and road grit.

5. EFFECTS OF SEWAGE POLLUTION

(a) Health effects: Micro organisms present in sewage water spread diseases like Typhoid, dysentry, tuberculosis, gastroenteritis, cholera, diarrhoea, respiratory illness, paralysis, heart diseases, meningitis etc. when they contaminate the ground water.

(b) Effects on fresh water Ecosystems: Cultural eutrofication by human & animal wastes that have caused eutrophication and algal blooms in lakes; the addition of sewage leads to depletion of oxygen levels, which are reflected in terms of BOD of water. The 3 stages of BOD fluctuations are also described.

(c) **Effects on Marine Ecosystems:** Due to high level of dilution, the effects on marine ecosystems is considerably less except for the closure of beaches in some places due to sludge deposition.

6. MONITORING

(a) **Direct methods:** By assessing the amount of dissolved oxygen, suspended Solids, hardness and chemical oxygen demand.

(b) **Biological indices:** BOD indicates the extent of sewage pollution as proportional to organic load in the system. MPN (maximum probable number) of total coliform, faecal coliform, faecal streptococci and E. coli; others shehas chironomus, Tubifex, Dytiscus, Diatoms etc, occur in sewage polluted waters

7. SEWAGE TREATMENT:

(a) Preliminary treatment is to remove large debris by passing sewage along constant velocity channels or through grit chamber.

(b) Primary treatment where the suspended solids load is reduced up to 50% in large sedimentation tanks.

(c) Secondary treatment where the organic compounds are subjected to biologically mediated oxidation and decomposition in trickle filters, oxidation ponds or by the activated sludge process.

(d) Tertiary treatment or 'polishing' of effluents includes the chemical precipitation of specific substances, prolonged secondary treatment, stabilisation ponds, artificial wetlands and fluidized bed filter systems.

8. SLUDGE DISPOSAL

Sludge after digestion is reduced in volume by 2/3 rd and is used as land fill, dumped in sea, incinerated or used as manure.

9. REMOVAL OF PATHOGENS

Length of retention time during treatment, chemical composition of wastes and their state of degradation, antagonistic forces in the biological flora, PH and operational temperature govern the reduction of pathogen in sewage treatment process.

10. SEWAGE FOR AGRICULTURE

Certain species of fish like carps and Tilapia grow extremely well in sewage fertilized ponds. To achieve the microbial standard of effluents quoted by WHO, the sewage should be treated in an anaerobic and a facultative pond prior to discharge into fishpond (as fertilizer).

11. CONCLUSION

The world not being ideal, the sewage has to undergo secondary treatment to break up into sludge and water. But, the constituents of sewage are changing and increasing with time and the present treatment processes grow more and more incompetent. The only solution to all pollution problems vests in change of peoples attitudes and not by improving technology.

What ever is good to know is difficult to learn

9. POLLUTION BY PESTICIDES

I. INTRODUCTION

A. Definition: Any material useful for mitigation, control or elimination of plants or animals detrimental to human health or economy

Pesticides may be classified as insecticides, herbicides, rodenticides, molluscides, acaricides and nematocides.

(a) Definition of pesticide

(c) Usage of pesticides in general

(b) Classification

(d) Toxicity of pesticides and awareness

B. History

1. First ever reported chemical - 'arsenical paris green' against colorado potato beetle.
2. Other indications from classical greek literature etc.
3. Discovery of potential of Bordeaux mixture
4. 1945 - carbamates in Britain, switzerland.
5. Organochlorines
6. 1950-1960 - second generation insecticides.
   Organophosphates. Pyrethroids etc.
7. 1955: First appearance of Herbicides.

C. Role of pesticides in agriculture

1. Growing population demanded increase in food production
2. Cultivation of High yielding varieties
3. Mechanisation - which demanded crops varieties of similar life span so single variety cultivation in vast stretches
4. High input agriculture
5. Cultivating same crop round the year
6. These lead to pest outbreaks.

D. Production and Consumption

1. The growth of pesticide market between 1945 - 1975.
   1945 - 0.13 m Tonnes
   1955 - 0.44 m Tonnes
   1965 - 1 m Tonnes
2. Financial terms market has grown from $ 900 m (in 1960) to $ 7560 ml (1978).
   (a) British market - 1976 $ 238
   1986 $ 1539.

(b) USA. is responsible for 1/3rd of the total pesticide production in world.

(c) Indian consumption. 395 gm/hectare (1985 data) in India
1800 gm/hectare USA.
2000 gm/hectare Europe.
10.000 gm/hectare Japan.

II. POLLUTION DUE TO PESTICIDES

1. Philosophy of Better living through Chemistry and pesticides
2. Case of over use of pesticides or pesticide accidents eg. Pesticide spill in Rhine river, etc.
3. every year 40000 to 2 million pesticides Poisoning occur in world (stated of the the world 1988)
4. 10,000 to 40,000 of such exposures causes death.
5. case of D.D.T. and B.H.C. - banned in Europe and U.S. But exported to third world.
6. DDT in milk of mothers - all 75 samples were positive in Punjab. Estimated through mother's milk, daily intake of babies are 21 times the allowed level.
7. Nicaraguan mothers breast milk contain 45 times greater DDT content than the permitted level.
8. 'Circle of poison' due to trade and consumption.
9. A recent estimation tells us that chances of cancer has increased to 5,800 cancer/1 million people, While the permitted one is just 1 person / 1 million.
10. Drinking water contamination. eg. Atrazine - A herbicide - An Identified potential carcinogen found at levels 3 times the maximum permited levels in east England.
11. Ground water U.S. 50 pesticides are Identified
12. Biomagnification and food chain
13. Human society and Natural communities.
14. Occupational exposure etc.

III. EFFECTS

A. SOIL: Pesticides are toxic and therefore assumed that they will change or alter fundamental soil processes such as

1. Organic matter decomposition
2. Nitrogen transformation,
3. Sulphur transformation,
4. Phosphate availabilities,

5. Trace element availability and
6. Soil enzyme activity, which influence soil fertility and productivity.

B. WATER: The factors which influence the presistence of pesticides in water are solubility, bottom mud, organic matter, temperature and pH.

C. AIR: The pollution of the atmosphere can be either by volatilization of chemicals where filling, loading, mixing and spraying operations are done or through drift and wind erosion of soil particles laden with absorbed residences.

D. BIOTIC SYSTEMS: Pesticides disturb the equilibium existing between insect pests and their parasites or predators. Perhaps 90% of all the animals live as predators and feed on living matter; only a few live as true saprophytes. These predator and prey populations generally evolve a balanced supply & demand economy.

E. Classification of pesticides :

1. Mode of action
   - (a) Repellents and anti-feedants
   - (b) Fumigants
   - (c) Stomach poisons
   - (d) Ephemeral contact poisons
   - (e) Residual poisons
   - (f) Systemic poisons
2. Target organisms
   - (a) Insects: Insecticides
   - (b) Nematodes: Nematicides
   - (c) Molluscs: Molluscicides
   - (d) Mites: Acaricides
   - (e) Microbes: Bactericides
   - (f) Rodents: Rodenticides
   - (g) Fungus: Fungicides
   - (h) Herbs (weed): Herbicides
3. Chemistry

IV. TOXICOLOGY OF PESTICIDE ACTION

A. General toxicology

1. Exposure phase
   - (a) Factors
     - Dose (concentration)
     - Duration of exposure
     - Route of exposure
     - Nature of chemical

(b) Routes of exposure
- dermal
- gastro intestinal
- respiratory system.

2. Toxico kinetic phase. (pharmaco kinetic)
   (a) Absorption
   - Active transport
   - Passive transport

   (b) Distribution
   - Hydrophilic
   - liophilic

   (c) Metabolism
   - Biotransformation
   - Detoxification - Degradation
   - conjugation - Toxification

   (d) Detoxification reactions
   - Hydrolysis
   - Oxidative degradation
   - Reduction.

   (e) Excretion versus Retention
   - Biological half life.
   - Routes of Excretion - skin, Lungs, gastro-intestinal and kidneys

3. Toxico dynamic phase.
   (a) Inactivation of enzymes.
   (b) Interference with certain types of proteins.
   (c) Interference with small molecule synthesis.
   (d) Interference with oxygen transport
   (e) Interference with hemoglobin synthesis.
   (f) Interference with immune mechanism.

4. Dose response relationships

B. ECOTOXICOLOGY OF VARIOUS PESTICIDE GROUPS

1. Organophosphorous insecticides.
   (a) A brief account
   (b) Adverse effects
   (c) Acute effects - symptoms
   (d) Chromic effects - symptoms

(e) Environmental effects - mechanisms.

(f) Avifaunal - Teratogenic effects.
- Carcinogenic
- behavioral changes in gulls, decreased
- nest attending early migration, second nesting
- Local or global extinction of populations.

2. Carbamate insecticides:
   (a) Clinical toxicology
   (b) Sublethal dosages in human - symptoms.
   (c) Environmental
       - Behavioral changes in birds
       - Teratogenicity in Rabbits and Monkeys.
3. Organochlorine insecticides:
   (a) Persistant nature
   (b) Biomagnification - Ecotoxicology.
   (c) Ratio of concentration in a native organism to the concentration in its surroundings is known as biomagnification factor
   (d) Lipid solubility - food chain effects case study of fish eating birds
   (e) Trophic level I sea weeds - 0.001 ppm of Dieldrin
   (f) Trophic level II Animals - 0.027 pp m of dieldrin
   (g) Trophic level III Herrings - 0.057 ppm
   (h) Fish eating Bird - 0.5 ppm.
   (i) Dangers of food chain reaching to man -
4. Natural and synthetic Pyrethroids:
   (a) Physical & chemical properties
   (b) Chronic and Acute exposures
   (c) Lack of study in the field.

V. FATE OF PESTICIDES IN THE ENVIRONMENT

Further more, the persistance of pesticides in the environment is dependent upon many factors such as the nature of the pesticides, temperature, light, humidity, air movement, activity of micro-organisms and factors which influence the break-down and dispersion of these chemicals etc.

Three major problems are dealt with

(a) Resistance developed by certain pests.

(b) Persistance of certain pesticides causing environmental damage

(c) Harm to non-target organisms, flora and fauna.

To avoid these problems, degradable pesticides should be used.

VI. RESIDUE

A. INTERNATIONAL STANDARDS: The FAO/WHO "codex alimentarius" commission has established to protect the health of consumers and to ensure gain practices in the food trade and to fix maximum limits for pesticide residue.

B. INVERTIBRATES: Many invertebrates such as crustaceans, molluscs and fish collected from the river Jamuna in Delhi showed high residues of DDT varying from 0.06 to 7.57 ppb.

C. RESIDUES IN FOODS OF ANIMAL ORIGIN

1. Meat and Eggs
2. Milk and Milk products :

D. RESIDUES IN FOODS OF PLANT ORIGIN

1. Vegetables
2. Cereals and pulses
3. Spices
4. Oil seeds and oils.

E. RESIDUES IN HUMAN TISSUES AND SECTIONS

1. Adipose tissue.
2. Blood.
3. Breast Milk.

VII. HEALTH HAZARDS OF PESTICIDE RESIDUES

Since our food articles contain excessive amount of DDT and BHC,it is not surprising that Indian Population has unusally high amounts of these insecticides in the body. Other source such as air, water and direct contact with cantaminated surfaces may also contribute of some extent to DDT or BHC. burden in human body.

VIII. PROTECTION OF ENVIRONMENT

As a consequence of the environmental hazards associated with the use of pesticides most advanced countries of the world like the USA, Germany, Japan, Canada, etc. have enacted laws enforcing the safe use of pesticides.

IX. POISONINGS FROM PESTICIDES

1. As mentioned previously, toxicity or poisoning is a relative term and depends mainly on the chemistry of the compound.
2. Class I A - Extremely hazardous.
   Class I B - Highly hazardous.
   Class II - Moderately hazardous.
   Class IV - Slightly hazardous.
   Class V - Without any hazard.

3. Human poisonings
4. Mass poisonings in India

X. SAFE USE OF PESTICIDES

1. International efforts for controlling pesticides (mis) use
   (a) 1962: Codex Alimentarius commission. 120 member nations.
   (b) 1968: Codex committee on pesticide residues (CCPR)
   (c) Agrements on Internationally acceptable minimum limits of pesticide residues
      1. CMRLS - Corlex Maximum Residue Limits.
      2. ADI - Acceptable Daily Intakes
      3. CCPK Proposed on MRLs.
   (d) 1978 (FAO/WHO 1978)
      1. 2000 Residue food combinations have been proposed.
      2. 'Guide lines' - for good management for pesticides.

XI. ECOLOGICAL ALTERNATIVES OF PESTICIDES

1. Role of diversity in Agroecosystem stability: Monoculture, Mono-strain/var culture and pest outbreak etc.
2. Alternatives for broadly toxic pesticides
   (a) Biological options.
      1. Classical biological controls deliberate introduction and establishment of natural enemies.
      2. Augmentative release of Natural enemies. release of enemies after rearing artificially. i.e. periodic release of large number of natural enemies.
      3. Cover crops and living mulches.
      4. Genetic improvement of natural enemies.
      5. Microbial agents - as parasites including, Bacteria, fungi, virus, protozoa and nematodes.
      6. Host plant resistance - plant breeding
      7. Management of natural enemies of pests. By changing crop patterns so that efficiency of natural enemies increase.
      8. Autocidal controls: Tactics for causing the pest to reduce its own population. eg. by releasing more reproductively defective males
   (b) Cultural options
      1. Classical crop rotation: Deliberate planting of specific crop sequences to make the year to year survival of soil dwelling pests difficult or impossible.

2. Physical control: Physical barriers like Solarisation, Artificial mulches, row covers and sticky barriers.
3. Sanitation: Any practice that removes over wintering refugea or alternative refugea where pest can survive when the crop is not in the field.
4. Irrigation management.
5. Pruning and canopy management to reduce the habitability of crops to pests.
6. Strategic choices of soils, location of the filed, time of planting etc.
7. Regulatory management practice: Practice that must be instituted area wise in order to be effective eg. Mandatory Host free peside etc.

(c) Chemical options:

1. Synthetic organic pesticides.
2. Oil soaps and other fatty acids.
3. Botanical insecticides
4. Semio chemicals, including allomones, kairomones and pheromones.
5. Pesticide application technology
6. Treatment threshholds.

(d) Related education economic and policy increase.

1. Education about pest management.
2. Economic comparisons.
3. Policy issues.

XII. Pesticides and Soil Fauna

1. Pesticide used to control particular pest like namatode, fungus, insect, mite or ultimately gets into the soil and affect non target fauna.
2. Degradation of pesticides in soil
3. Pesticide persistence and residue in soil
4. Effects

(a) Soil microflora (b) Nematodes

(c) Earth worms (d) Snails and slugs

(e) Soil Arthropods

DEGRADABLE PESTICIDES

(a) Study on pesticides very recent in India
(b) Types of degradation in different soil types
(c) Toxicity of phorate on target and non-target organisms.
(d) Chemical degradation
(e) Soil factors controlling degradation.
  - soil pH, surface acidity, cation saturation.
(f) Study on effect of pesticide on plants.
(g) Microbial decomposition of pesticide.

Degradation by microbes

(a) Metabolic processes in micro-organisms
(b) Reactions with pesticides in soil to form metabolic products
(c) List of bacteria degrading pesticides.
(d) List of fungi
(e) List of pesticides which are commonly degradable
(f) Polymerisation of compounds.

Natural organic insecticides

(a) Important sources of insecticides -plant materials
(b) Types of insecticides- contact, dust, spray
(c) Effects of a few important insecticides.
(d) List of insecticides used as degradable pesticides.

Microbial Metabolism

(a) Bio chemical degradation by soil organisms.
(b) Matabolism of DDT
(c) Degradation of organophosphates, organic fungicides.

Integrated Pest Management

(a) Definition and purpose
(b) Integration of chemical, biological & cultural methods.
(c) Pest and pesticide management.
(d) Basic criteria of IPM.

Conclusion

(a) Contamination of environment and effects -cancer, Mutations,
(b) Degradation possible to a large extent.
(c) Awareness and scientific research in this field

10. THERMAL POLLUTION

1. **Introduction**

   Thermal pollution is the effect of heat generated by Industries in the environment.

2. **Second law of Thermodynamics**

   It says that any process using heat & convert it to mechanical energy, it cannot utilize fully, resulting in considerable loss of heat.

   (a) Seam electric plant works under this law with 80% efficiency.

   (b) Heat produced by fuel combustion: This is the fact, but the efficiency matters here.

   (c) Expansion principle: If any expansion is done adiabaticaly, it is with an atmospheric medium.

   (d) Spent steam: This step gives how heat is lost.

   (e) Average efficiency of steam electric plant: At present (1980-90) the efficiency is ca 34.00% where heat lost is (ca 90%).

3. **Sources of Thermal Pollution**

   (a) Nuclear power plant: Heat energy is generated with controlled nuclear fission reaction.

   (b) Power Industry: Its contribution to thermal pollution is 2/3 of it. (Both Nuclear 2 S.E.P).

   (c) Cooling Towers: They are the current media through which heat is liberated to the atmosphere.

4. **Effects of Thermal Pollution on Biota**

   (a) Health risks to Humans: To a greater extent the effect on Human beings is indirect.

   (b) Air saturation value: Any rise in temperature in water decreases its air-saturation value.

   (c) Effects on Flora: Rise in temperature will modify all existing biological activities of floral community.

   (d) Effect on Fauna: Here there are more possiblities for causing death of animals exposed.

   (e) Planktons: These primary producers in the trophic level of aquatic food chain are inhibited in their activity thereby collapsing the food chain.

   (f) Oxygen content: Alteration of temperature results indirect effect on oxygen content & reduces its value.

(g) Physiology: It deals with functional aspects. Any rise in temperature which alter the functions & resulting in abnormality of living organism & also death.

(h) Ecological balance: There is no detrimental effect on balance (ecological). But extreme conditions (760 c) will be adverse.

5. Thermal pollution over Urban Systems

We scan the effects of Thermal Pollution over urban areas where industries are high. Major effects are Climate change and, Health hazards.

6. Possible longrange impacts of Thermal Pollution

(a) Micro-study of Long range Impact: It is a case study on effects on climates in 20th & 21st centuries. This is the on basis three scenarios and results are estimated. years accounted are 1st Scenario - 1975, Second - 2050 - Third - 2100

7. Management of Thermal Pollution

Problems of thermal pollution can be alleviated by using artificial cooling lakes, ponds, improving the efficiencies of the power industries etc. some of major abatement technologies are:

(a) Cooling ponds: Water is let to cool before leaving into main stream.

(b) Developed Power Industries: Heat loss can be reduced by increasing efficiency of the power industries.

(c) Heating buildings: This is best in winter where the institution has its own power plant, can use the heat lost for heating the buildings.

(d) Deicing water ways: This is helpful in Northern climates to extend navigation. Both these may affect natural ecosystem in long-run.

(e) Desalination: Helpful in freshening sea water and even brackish waters.

(f) Aquaculture: From production point of view some warm condition is required which can be met with heat loss from industries.

11. RADIATION POLLUTION

I. RADIATIONS

A. Definition

1. Natural - earth
2. Manmade - Nuclear power
3. Deliberate - diagnostic
4. Accidental - Exposure at work.

B. Types

1. Electromagnetic - UV rays, X rays, Gamma rays
2. Particulate - Electrons, Protons - a-particles, Neutrons, & Mesons.

C. Response of cells: Oxygen higher - damage higher

Germ cells more susceptible

1. Hierarchial status
2. Age
3. DNA
4. LET

II. RADIOACTIVITY AND NUCLEAR REACTIONS

A. Concepts

1. Atomic Number - Number of protons
2. Mass number - Number of protons + Number of neutrons.
3. Alpha emitters
4. Beta emitters
5. Gamma emitters
6. Radioactive decay
7. Half life

B. Nuclear fission

$^{235}_{92}U + n - {}^{135}_{57}Te + {}^{97}_{40}Zr + 4n$

III. DOSE RATE, DOSE DISTRIBUTION

A. Definitions of Red, Gray & Sievert

B. Methods of Measurement

1. Thermoluminiscence - using Li crystals
2. Photographic emulsions - Ag halide
3. Scintillation detectors
4. Glass & Plastic
5. Semiconductors
6. Ferrous sulphate
7. Calorimetry.

Dose rate - Rate at which radiation dose is given

C. Distribution of Dose in Biological Material.

1. Relative Biological Effectiveness (RBE)
2. Linear Energy Transfer (LET).

IV. SOURCES

1. Uranium
2. Radium 226
3. Phosphate fertilizer
4. Gypsum & Ca silicate slag
5. Coal
6. Induced Radionuclides
7. Cosmic level dose
8. Mineral springs
9. Monazite sands.
10. Radioluminescent paints
11. Thorium

V. BIOLOGICAL EFFECTS OF RADIATION

A. Cellular Effects
   1. Stage of Cell cycle.
   2. Repair - Sublethal Damage (SLD)
   3. Potentially Lethal Damage (PLD)

B. Tissue Level
   1. Effects - growth retardation, Prenatal / perinatal death congenital malformations, CNS damage
   2. Dose - 36 y.

C. Genetic
   1. (a) One hit
      (b) two hit: Chromosome effect
   2. Gene mutations
      (a) Dominant - Anomalies of nerves, skin, cartilage, haemophilia, muscular dystrophy etc.
      (b) Recessive - Phenylketonuria, cystic fibrosis, albinism, deafness.
      (c) Sex Linked - Down's syndrome, Kleinfelter (XXY), Turner (XO), Spina bifida
      (d) Milltifactoral - Diabetes, Mental Retardation.
   3. Radiation and cancer.

VI. LATE EFFECTS OF RADIATION

Life shortening.

VII. MODIFYING EFFECTS

Chemical - Sensitisers (02), Protective (Cysteine)

Biological - Age, Proliferative state, repair mechanisms.

VIII. RADIOACTIVE WASTE MANAGEMENT

A. Low level wastes

1. Uranium mill tailings

2. Generated in cleanings of Uranium, Thorium, Radium plants
3. Disposed by shallow land burial.
   (a) Shallow coastal waters.
   (b) Compaction.

B. High Level wastes

1. Defense wastes - concrete steel drums below ground level
2. Transuranic - shallow burial
   - Retrieval storage for transfer to permanent repository.
3. Civilian High level wastes - commercial Reactors.

C. Gaseous, Highly soluble long-lived Nuclides.

1. Tritium - Half life 12.3 years. Reacts with Zirconium and becomes Zr H2.
2. Krypton 85 - Half life 10.7 years.

IX. NUCLEAR EXPLOSION AND FALLOUT

A. Short term Effects.

B. World wide Effects.

C. Behaviour of Individual Radionuclides

1. Sr - 90 - > 1.0 - hazardous dose
2. Cs - 137 - half life 28 yrs.
3. C - 14 - 5730 years - transmutations
4. Plutonium 239/238

X. NUCLEAR ACCIDENTS

A. March 1 1954 - Thermonuclear Detonation - Bikini atoll.

B. October 1957 - Windscale Reactor 1 UKAEE England.

C. November 1959 - Oakridge

D. January 1961 - Army stationary, low power

E. March 28 1979. Three Mile Island

F. April 26 1986: CHERONOBYL

1. Description - 4 X 1000 MWe unit.
2. Accident - Switching off of safety procedure. etc.
3. Damage - 31 Deaths due to Burns
4. 30 km radius -8 radiation 1000 mr/he I-131-25- 250 rads.
5. Russia - 14 Mci

   8 dose of 0.74 rem that yr. 2.5 rem - 50 yr dose.
6. W. Europe - 130 - 2 m rem.

XI. SAFETY STANDARDS

1. ICRP: Recommended 5 rem for workers, as the limit
2. UK - 0.5 rem (public)
3. USA - 0.25 rem (Public)

XII. NUCLEAR WEAPONS AND NON PROLIFERATION TREATIES

A. USA USSR

B. NPT - 1968

C. In 1989 - 138 signatories NPT and Other treaties

SUMMARY

1. Historically, radioactivity and x - rays were widely used in medicinal fields.
2. There are two types of Radiations - Ionizing and non - ionizing radiations.
3. The term radioactivity includes both naturally occurring radiations and man made radiations.
4. Naturally occurring radiations may be electro magnetic or particulate.
5. The sources of radioactive pollution may be varied like Natural, Environmental and Anthropogenic.
6. Radiations have pronounced effect on molecules and cells. The effects can be of three types - Immediate Delayed and Genetic.
7. Preventive measures for pollution and the methods of waste disposal.

11. MARINE POLLUTION

I. INTRODUCTION

A. **MARINE RESOURCES:** A brief overview of the resourcefulness of the sea and its complexity and diversity of life forms.

B. **FOCUSSING PERSPECTIVES:** Focussing the varied perspectives of naturalists, environmentalists, conservationists and economists and the potential of the marine environment as they perceive it.

C. **EXPLOITATION OF MARINE RESOURCES:** A review of major landmarks in marine use and exploitation in recent historical times.

II. ORIGIN OF WASTE WATER

The pathways that lead to marine pollution - rivers and coastal outflows; atmospheric transports; direct and indirect inputs from ships, oil rigs and off-shore structures. Their relative contributions to local and diffused pollution.

III. TYPES OF POLLUTANTS

A systematic discussion of the various categories of pollutants, their sources, impact on biota and local habitats and the stages and processes involved.

A. **OXYGEN DEMANDING WASTES:** Sewage, food processing plants, pulp and paper mills, tanning operations and other organic waste producing activities.

B. **SYNTHETIC ORGANIC COMPOUNDS:** Pesticides, synthetic organic chemicals, detergents and the non-biodegradable effluents of major industries.

C. **PLANT NUTRIENTS:** Nitrogen and Phosphorus compounds entering water in large quantities because of large scale fertilizer use, by products of sewage treatment and processing of biological materials like textiles and food.

D. **INORGANIC CHEMICALS AND MINERALS:** Includes inorganic salts, mineral acids, finely divided metals and metal compounds.

E. **SEDIMENTS:** Soil, sand and mineral particles washed into the aquatic environment by storms & floods. This category also includes particulate matter carried in by rain.

F. **RADIOACTIVE SUBSTANCES:** Disposal of radioactive wastes, bio-accumulation and related concepts.

G. **THERMAL DISCHARGES:** Effects of heat on local biota around sources of water used as coolants in power plants.

H. **OIL:** Industrial effluents, oil refineries, spills and wastes.

IV. **EFFECTS ON BIOTA:** Effects of the above mentioned pollutants on specific taxa.

A. AUTOTROPHIC ORGANISMS:

1. Phytoplankton
2. Marine micro-algae
3. Higher Plants

B. HETEROTROPHIC ORGANISMS:

1. Zooplankton
2. Bivalves
3. Crustaceans
4. Fish

The importance of the above mentioned taxa as indicators of pollution and their role in bio-accumulation is significant

V. WATER POLLUTION LAWS AND STANDARDS

Acts, laws and legislative organisations equipped with handling, curbing, controlling, preventing or managing marine pollution. Policies and decisions regarding pollution at National and Global levels.

VI. TREATMENT OF WASTE WATERS

A. **BASIC PROCESSES OF WATER TREATMENT:** Physical, chemical and biological processes; Primary, secondary tertiary and advanced water treatment methods.

B. **DISPOSAL VERSUS REUSE:** Effectiveness of recycling waste material to combat disposal problems.

C. **USING ALTERNATIVE MATERIALS:** The success of substituting toxic compounds used in manufacture of essentials and its drawbacks.

D. **OCEAN DISPOSAL VERSUS LAND DISPOSAL:** Comparative study of ocean and land dumping of wastes.

VII. RESEARCH NEEDS

Sampling and analysis of marine pollution methods and technologies available.

VIII. CASE STUDIES

A. **MINAMATA:** Industrial metal contamination in waters coastal (Japan) - a very brief report of impacts.

B. **SAN FRANCISCO BAY (USA):** Effects of coastal outflow on local marine environment.

C. **RICHARDS BAY (SOUTH AFRICA):** Possible impacts of a proposed industrial unit along the coast.

12. INTRODUCTION TO TOXICOLOGY

Toxicants are substances that are unwanted in the environment, causing damage to the living beings wholly or partly. These are otherwise named " pollutants". These are devided in 3 types

1. Based on the System affected [Soil, Air etc.]
2. Nature of pollution [Physical, Chemical, Radiation, etc]
3. Nature of Particles [Gas, liquid, Solid]

The study of toxicants is known as toxicology. It is divided into 3 divisions namely

Systemic Toxicology	*Genetic Toxicology*	*Ecological Toxicology*
	Clinical toxicology	Inductive logic
	Environmental Toxicology (Non clinical)	Deductive logic

Toxicology of the environment is known as environmental toxicology. Toxic substances may move from one to another ecosystem, or one to another organism - Ecotoxicology. They may affect the Genetic System - Genotoxicology.

Somatic cells	99% of Cancers
Reproductive cells	leads to hereditary diseases

They also affect different systems and organs of the organism - Systemic Toxicology. In the case of drugs, we find they are sometimes toxic to the same system meant for therapy or other systems [side effects] - Clinical Toxicology where one knos the toxicants. On the other hand the effects only are known and the causes are to be deduced from many inferences.

I. BASIC TENETS

A. History

1. Toxinology, Toxicology and determinism
   - Antiquity, medieval times, current times, Poisons, Empirical Science of medicine

B. Causes

1. Biological
   - Pollen, microbes, insects, worms, others
2. Chemical
   - drugs, pesticides, naturals, food additives, dyes etc
   - Industrials - raw materials, intermediates Byeproducts, endproducts and wastes

3. Physical
   - Radiations - alpha, beta, gamma & ultraviolet

C. Chemical world

1. 4.5 million chemicals
2. No toxicity data for most
3. Most information comes from drugs (Medicine) and pesticides (agriculture)
4. Most Produced Chemicals
   Sulphuric acid, Nitric acid, Ammonia chlorine, benzene, phosphoric acid

D. Exposures

1. Usage, occupation, consumption
2. Ecology and Accidents
3. Chronic and acute
4. Dosages and concentrations
5. Lethal, sub lethal, LD 50, LC 50

E. Symptomatology

1. Immediate and warning signals
2. Gradual, lagphase, chemical properties, latency, cell biology
3. Late, but sudden or gradual

F. Consequences

1. Long term or short term
2. Reversible or Irreversible
3. Tolerance, threshold and resistance
4. Intensity of effects
5. Target Vs non-target effects (origins of ecotoxicology)

G. Responses

1. Plants 2. Animals 3. microbes 4. Humans

H. Ecogenetics

1. Variations in responses among the individuals of a population.

I. Role of Metabolism

1. Entry routes - nasal, dermal and oral
2. Removal of toxic effects
   (a) excreation, (b) barriers of entry,
   (c) inactivation, (d) activation,
   (e) replacement of affected tissues
3. Enzyme actions in mouth, stomach, liver, etc

J. Monitoring

1. Indicator systems - mocrobes to Primates in vivo, in vitro, in situ & ex situ.
2. Human epidemiology.

II. THE TAXONOMY

A. CONVENTIONAL VS MODERN TOXICOLOGY

From Poisons to Ill health to Continuous health

From Occasional and rare to constant companionship with toxins.

B. GENERAL TOXICOLOGY

Agents known and effects monitorable

1. Animal Responses
   - (a) Dermal toxicity
   - (b) Occular toxicity
   - (c) Nephrotoxicity
   - (d) Hepatotoxicity
   - (e) Neurotoxicity
   - (f) Pulmonary toxicity
   - (g) Immunotoxicity
   - (h) Genetic toxicity
2. Plant Responses
   - (a) Photosynthesis
   - (b) Productivity
   - (c) Development and renascence
   - (d) Pathogenesis

C. ENVIRONMENTAL TOXICITY

Agents unknown and effects monitorable

1. Biological, chemiccal and physical
2. Seasonality, periodicity & role of climate
3. Ambient levels, occupational levels and mixtures
4. Origins and progress of 'diseases' - etiology and epidemiology

D. ECOTOXICOLOGY

Agents "unknown and effects not "monitorable"

1. Terrestrial: Plants, animals and microbes
2. Aquatic: Animals, plants and microbes
3. Avain: Connecting link with land, water and air conditions
4. Chemical Dynamics
   - (a) Tolerance and resitance
   - (b) Biotransformation and Bioaccummulation
   - (c) Magnification through food chain
5. General Effects
   - (a) Selection pressure
   - (b) Adaptability
   - (c) Reproductive fitness
   - (d) Population structure

(e) Breeding systems (f) Behaviour
(g) Disappearance of population (h) Chain effects

E. GENOTOXICOLOGY

Agents are both known and unknown. Effects are equally unmonitorable and predictable.

1. 5 million chemicals, radiations, different dosages and exposures
2. Affect multiplying systems in development and reproduction - DNA, Chromosomes, Segregational systems
3. Effects: slow, Irreversible, No warning signals, latent
4. Consequences
   (a) Teratogenesis b. Carcinogenesis c. Heretable diseases
5. International efforts to monitor and control ICPEMC, IPCS
6. Monitoring the cellular and genetic endpoints in any biological system/but not the ultimate effect ?

The great aim of education is not knowledge, but action

13. GENERAL, GENO - AND ECOTOXICOLOGY

I. FIELD MONITORING

A. Introduction

1. Real world situation
2. Total effects at individual, population & higher levels
3. Approach utilitarian or empirical
4. Applications of baseline knowledge from Laboratory experiments

B. Human systems

1. Epidemiology: Associating the likely causes with the perceived effect

   (a) Social surveys (b) Medical surveys (c) Case histories

C. Animal systems and Plant systems

1. Denizen approach in situ
2. Sentinel approach in situ
3. Habitat testing in situ and in vitro
4. Concentrator approach in situ and in vitro
5. Use of microbes

D. Examples - Animals

1. Crustaceans
2. Polychaetes
3. Insects: Orthopterans
4. Moluscans: Mussels
5. Amphibians
6. Fishes
7. Mammals
8. Aves
9. Mammals: Rodents, Squirrels

E. Others

1. Any endpoint of any system affected by any causes
2. Management of the problem
3. Pinpointing cause very difficult

II. LABORATORY MONITORING

A. Introduction

1. Determinism, in the Cause-Effect relationship
2. Variations in the determinism and difficulties in evaluations.
3. Regulatory Practices in the Human Health Protection
4. Approach Mechanistic

B. General Toxicology

1. Basic criteria
   - (a) Fast results
   - (b) Comparability to human systems
   - (c) Amenability for allviation testing
   - (d) Maintainability in captivity (i.e. Animal House, Aquaria, Lycimeters, etc.)
   - (e) Baseline information on the test system
2. Examples
   - (a) in vivo Systems: Mice, rats, hamsters, Rabbits, Pigs, Dogs, Monkeys, chicken, Pigeons
   - (b) in vitro Systems: Mammalian and Human cell lines
3. Qualitative and Quantative Characteristics
4. Endpoints - End responses or Endprocesses or both (process/mechanism ignored) (end response ignored)

C. Genetic Toxicology

1. Basic criteria
   - (a) Marker facility
   - (b) Short life cycle
   - (c) Uniqueness of representing some genetic phenomenon
   - (d) Baseline information on the organism or the cell lines
2. Examples:
   - (a) Microbes: Escherichia, Salmonella, Bacillus, Saccharomyces, Neurospora, Aspergillus, etc.
   - (b) Insects: Drosophila, Bombax
   - (c) Mammals: Mus, Rattus
   - (d) Plants: Allium, Vicia, Hordeum, Tradescantia
   - (e) in vitro systems: Mammalian and human cell lines
3. Qualitative and Quantative
4. Endpoints - Final response and Final process monitoring

D. Ecotoxicology

1. Approaches
   - (a) Organismic effects
   - (b) Periodically transfers organisms to laboratory
   - (c) Simulation of Ecosystems
   - (d) Enormous variables - Controlled conditions very difficult

2. Examples
    (a) Agroecosystems: simulalted models
    (b) Lycimeter approach with plants
    (c) Aquaria tests with fishes etc.

What sculpture is to a block of marble, education is to the soul

14. TOXICITY TO THE ORGANS

Liver, Kidney and Skin

I. LIVER

A. Introduction

1. Natural Susceptibility of liver to damage
   (a) Xenobiotics entering the body through the gastrointestinal tract are transported to liver by the hepatic portal vein
   (b) Xenobiotics produce a variety of metabolites which can induce lesions.
2. Some chemicals directly or after activation are toxic to liver.

B. Types of injury

1. Fatty Liver: Triglycerides accumulate abnormally
2. Necrosis: Cell death, cell membrane rupture, edema
3. Cholesterosis: Suppression of the bile flow, accumulation of bile salts, e.g., Jaundice
4. Cirrhosis: Collagen formation
5. Hepatitis: Inflammation of the whole liver

C. Mechanisms

1. Alteration of Cell membranes
2. Depletion of metabolites, e.g., Cofactors
3. Inhibition of enzymes
4. Bioactivation of chemicals from innocuous to reactive nature

D. Toxicants

1. Carbon Tetrachloride is activated to highly active free radical by Cytochrome P450-dependent mono oxygenase system.
2. Bromobenzene produces centrilobular hepatic necrosis through the formation of reactive epoxides.
3. Over dose of acetaminophen causes acute centrilobular hepatic necrosis.

II. KIDNEY

A. Introduction

1. Being excretory it has ability to concentrate chemicals - therefore very sensitive.
2. Renal blood flow is the most important factor in this sensitivity.
3. Bioactivation of chemicals increases toxicity Glutathione levels in the tissue has an important role.

B. Toxicants

1. Metals: Heavy metals are generally nephrotoxic
   (a) Cadmimum: long half life(20-30 years)- bio accumulate to toxic levels. Excreted as metallothione complex
   (b) Lead: Taken up by proximal tubule cells damage mitochondria by inhibiting their functions.
   (c) Mercury: Binds to the -SH groups of the membrane enzymes in the proximal tubule cells and inhibits Sodium reabsorption.
2. Antibiotics
   (a) Aminoglycosides nephrotoxic- Streptomycin, Neomycin and gentamycin - Gentamycin accumulates in the lysosomes of the proximal tubule. When threshold is reached, lysosome ruptures releasing hydrolytic enzymes which cause cell necrosis.
   (b) Polymycins are surface active, bind to phospholipids and may disintegrate the membrane.
3. Metabolites: Acetaminophen, Bromobenzene etc. are activated in the Kidney by the Cytochrome P-450 monooxygenase system to produce free radicals.

III. SKIN

A. Introduction

1. Skin consists of epidermis, dermis and an intervening basement membrane.
2. Epidermis consists of melanocytes and is a protective layer.
   Dermis has collagen and elastin.
3. Others are: hair follicles, sweat glands, sebaceous glands, small blood vessels and neural elements.

B. Effects

1. Irritation: Initial skin irritation at the site of action – soaps, detergents
2. Phototoxicity and Photoallergy: Both are light induced.
   Photoallergy involves immune reactions (e.g. Fentichlor, multifungin, Chloropropamide. Phototoxicity more common (e.g., coaltar, pyridine, sulfonamides)
3. Contact: Urticaria
   (a) Non-immunologic mechanism: the local urticaria appears quickly induced by the histamine, bradykinin, etc.

(b) Immunologic mechanism: local urticaria as well as generalised urticaria appear involving anaphylartoid reactions.

(c) Uncertain mechanisms: Ammonium persulphate an active ingredient of hair bleach causes erythema, urticaria and shock.

4. Cutaneous cancer: Soots, Coaltar, Creosite oils cause skin cancers in animals and humans

5. Epidermal adnexa

   (a) Antimitotic agents used in cancer chemotherapy affect a phase of hair growth resulting in hair loss.

   (b) Antimitotic agents and CNS depressants cause necrosis of sweat gland which secrete lipids (hormone dependent)

   (c) Chlorinated hydrocarbons cause various skin lesions.

The education of a man is never completed until he dies

15. NEUROTOXICITY

I. INTRODUCTION

1. Neurotoxicology: Detection, occurrence, properties, effects and regulation of toxic substances. Acute - effect observed after brief exposure.
2. Behavioural toxicology: Effects of toxicants on human and animal behaviour.
   (a) Periperal and Central Nervous system (PNS & CNS)
   (b) Other organ systems like endocrine glands.
3. Behaviour represents nervous system output or functioning of CNS. Therefore tests for behavioural changes are used to monitor damage to NS.
4. History: Prior to World War II only anti CHE agents (Physostigmine) was known -nerve gases (Sarin) - less toxic OPs (Malathion) for pest control - DFP (Di isopropyl fluro phosphate.
5. Nervous system shielded by protective mechanism - blood brain and blood nerve barriers.
6. Susceptibility
   (a) Metabolic rate
   (b) Little capacity for anaerobic metabolism
   (c) Longer length of axon - greater susceptibility
   (d) Due to electrical excitability integrity of cell membrane easily lost.

II. STRUCTURE OF NERVOUS SYSTEM

1. CNS: Brain, Spinal cord
2. PNS: Cranial & spinal nerves (SNS, PSNS)
3. CNS: Glia -
   (a) Astrocytes - Support BBB
   (b) Oligodendroglia - myelin sheath - electrical insulation
   (c) Microglia - macropages
4. PNS: Schwann cells -Myelin sheath
5. NT (neuro transmitters) - Acetylcholine, norepinephine
6. BBB: Protect from certain NT
   (a) Impermeable to substances of molecular weight 40,000
   (b) Lipid soluble only permeable
   (c) Absent where hormones act as chemoreceptors
   (d) Stops many NT- Diptheria, tetanus, staphylococcus, Hgcl2, etc.

7. BNB
   (a) Peripheral nerves
   (b) Interlace endoneurium with peri- and epineurium
   (c) Not as effective as BBB

III. MECHANISM

```
                 A            C            E
Receptors ——>Central ——>Effector ——>Behaviour
                 B Nervous      D organs
                   System
```

A: input cables (Afferent neurons)

C: output cables (Efferent neurons)

B & D: chemical messengers (hormones)

E: motor system

IV. TOXICANTS

1. Chemicals disrupt neural input/output relationships directly or indirectly through other organs
2. Types of Toxicants
   (a) Choline esterase inhibitors: nerve gases, insecticides
   (b) Overstimulation of cholinergic system: OPs
   (c) Blockade of cholinoreceptors: Tubo courarine (chondrodendron)
   (d) Non release of Acetyl choline: Botulins (Clostridium)
   (e) Blockade of Na channels in axon: Tetrodotoxin (Puffer fish)
   (f) Increasing permeability of resting membranes to Na : Batrachotoxin (Phyllobates) S. American frog

V. TYPES OF DAMAGE

1. Neuronopathy: glucose and O 2 impeded
   (a) Barbiturates: induce anoxia in brain
   (b) CO: induces selerosis of white matter
   (c) Cyanide, azide: inhibit cytochrome oxidase - cytotoxic anoxia
   (d) Methyl Hg: penetrates BBB (lipophitic) and affect ribosomes
   (e) Doxorubicin: breakdown of helical DNA
2. Axonopathy: damage the axon (cell) during its formation
   (a) Proximal: neurofilament transport impaired - accumulates in proximal axons- swelling and demyelination.
   (b) Distal: neurofilament proliferation- poly neuropahty – swelling (Impairment of glycolytic enzymes)

3. Blockade of Impulse conduction
    (a) Na pump blocked - action potential of membrane blocked (Tetrodotoxin, saxitoxin of Gonyaulox)
4. Blockade of Synaptic transmission
    (a) Blocks release of ACh from motor nerve ending muscles impaired - Paralysis (Botulin the most potent biological toxin)
    (b) Tetanoplasmin (Tetanus), CS2, DDT, Dieldrin, Born hydrides
5. Myelinopathy
    (a) Injury to oligodendrocytes and Schwann cells
        1. Ca transport in Schwann cells (Pb)
        2. Chelation (Cuprizone)
        3. Myelin sheath disrupted (triparanol)
        4. Myelin/myelinating cells affected (Diphtheria, Ethedium Bromide)
    (b) Affects myelin sheath
        1. Disruption of membrane structure: isoniazid, Pb
        2. Inhibition of Carbonic anhydrase
        3. Inhibition of oxidative phosphorylation enzymes
        4. Chelation of metals
6. Extracellular edema
    (a) Pb & Hg damage endothelial cells
    (b) As: edema, haemorrage in brain
7. Cellular edema
    (a) axon affected: CN, CO
    (b) nerve endings affected: Quabin methyl sulfoxine

VI. TESTS

1. Behavioural test: detection by observation
2. Neuropathological methods: at medulla and tibial nerves - and myelinopathy can be detected.
1. Biochemical tests - B - glucoronidase, B- galactosidase ChE inhibition

VII. CONCLUSIONS

1. Dangerous - immediacy
2. Neurotoxicity is most complex

16. RESPIRATORY TOXICITY

I. INTRODUCTION

1. Inhalation of airborne gases, vapours, liquid droplets, solid particulates affect the respiratory tract.
2. Respiratory Tract
   (a) Nasopharynx: Removes large particles, adds moisture, moderates temperature
   (b) Tracheal and Bronchial tract: airway to the alveoli, lined with epithelium and covered by a thin layer of mucus.
   (c) Pulmonary Acim: Sites where oxygen and Carbon dioxide are exchanged between blood and air.
3. Alveoli in the respiratory tract consists of
   (a) Cell type I: thin cytoplasm and large surface area.
   (b) Cell type II: Cuboidal, maturing into the above type
   (c) Endothelial cells
   (d) Macropages
   (e) Fibroblasts
4. Respiratory system regulates blood concentration of
   (a) Angiotensin b. Biogenic amines c. Prostaglandins

II. TOXIC EFFECTS

1. Systemic effects: toxic gases can be absorbed by the alveoli through simple diffusion
2. Effects on Lungs
   (a) Local irritation: Ammonia and chlorine cause bronchial contraction and edema
   (b) Cellular damage and edema
      1. NO2 and Ozone causes peroxidation of membrane - permeability increases - edema results
      2. Xylene and perchloroethylene spread throughout the body - Form reactive metabolites - covalent binding with macromolecules
   (c) Necrosis of clara cells - located where alveolar ducts branch from bronchioles. e.g. Ipomeanol- produced by Fusarium solani
   (d) Fibrosis and Emphysema: Quartz, Asbestos, coal dust, talc, Al carbides rupture lysosomal membrane of macropages releasing the silica, repeatedly

- Cigarette smoke, Al, Cd, O3, Nx induce emphysema.

(e) Allergy response: Spores, bacteria, cotton dust may lead to chronic bronchitis and fibrosis.

(f) Lung Cancer : Carcinogens in cigarette smoke, As, Cr, Ni, etc. cause cancer.

III. UPPER RESPIRATORY TRACT

NiO2, Asbestos, Cr, Toluene cause hyperemia, squamous or cell metaplasia, hyperplasia, ulceration and carcinoma in the nasal passages

IV. EFFECTS FOLLOWING OTHER ROUTES OF EXPOSURE

1. Ingested paraquat causes lung damage
2. Bleomycin, Bisulfan, Cycloheximide, Mitomycin induce pulmonary fibrosis
3. Methotrexate and streptomycin cause pulmonary eosinophilia
4. Phenyl butazone and Oxyphenyl butazone cause pulmonary edema.

V. TEST PROCEDURES

1. in vivo animal models subjected to inhalation of toxicants suspended in the air.
2. in vitro culture of isolated cells exposed to various toxicants - effects monitored.

Pulmonary diseases from Toxicants

S. No	*Toxicant*	*Disease*	*Site*	*Acute Effect*	*Chronic Effect*
1.	Aluminium	Aluminosis airways	upper shortness Alveolar interstitium	cough, fibrosis of breath	Interstitial
2.	Ammonia		upper airways	Irritation of upper & lower tract	Edema and Chronic bronchitis
3.	Arsenic		upper airways	Bronchitis	lung cancer Bronchitis laryngitis
4.	Asbestos	Asbestosis chyma	Paren-	fibrosis	Pulmonary Plural Calcification lung cancer
5.	Chlorine		upper airways	Cough Broncho pneumonia	
6.	Cotton dust	Byssinosis	upper airways wheezing	Tightness in chest	Chronic bronchitis

(Contd...)

7.	Ozone		Bronchi and Alveoli	Pulmonary edema	Emphysema
8.	Silica	Silicosis	Lung paren-chyma lymp nodes		Pulmonary fibrosis
9.	Toluene		upper airways	Acute Bronchitis	Edema
10.	Xylene		lower airways	Pulmonary edema	

Education's purpose is to replace an empty mind with an open one

17. REPRODUCTIVE & DEVELOPMENTAL TOXICITY

A. DEFINITION

1. Gross structural or anatomical defects by agents acting during organogenesis.
2. Developmental Toxicity due to exposure to chemicals prior to conception or during development. Offspring abnormal
3. Reproductive Toxicity: emphasis on parental generation, i.e., prematuring period
4. Teratology: abnormal fetal development

B. DEVELOPMENTAL HAZARDS

1. Incidence of reproductive failure and developmental defects: very large
2. Failure of human conceptions: 50%
3. Newborns with malformations: 3%
4. Reduced birth weight: 7.5%
5. Defects of unknown origin: 65-70%
6. Experience of infertility or spontaneous abortions = 50 - 60%
7. Causes: varied
8. Etiology: unknown
9. Genetic factors: 25%
   Environmental factors: 10%

C. CAUSATIVE FORCES

1. Chemicals evaluated for safety: very few
2. Exposure of humans high: environmental agents
3. Genetic and nutritional factors
4. Infectious agents

D. TYPES OF MANIFESTATIONS

1. Infertility
2. Spontaneous abortion
3. Premature births
4. Low birth weight
8. in utero or neonatal deaths
5. Infant mortality
6. Congenital physical defect
7. Mental retardation
9. Developmental stage, agent, dose, duration determines manifestation

E. IDENTIFYING HAZARDS

1. in vivo mammalian assays
   (a) First pathway
   (b) Background/control data

(c) Stage specificity (d) Dose-response relationship
(e) Materno-embryonic transfer (f) Identification of toxic agents
(g) Mechanisms (h) Extrapolation to humans

2. in vitro experiments
   (a) Initial screening (b) Elucidation of mechanisms
3. Human Surveys
   (a) Case reports (b) Epidemiological studies

F. RISK ASSESSMENT PROCESS

1. Hazard identification

   Qualitative evaluation of all human and animal data, experimental studies, analysis of molecular structure
2. Exposure assessment

   Populations exposed, their size and composition, types, magnitude, frequencies and durations of exposure.
3. Dose response assessment relationship between dose and effect
4. Risk characterisation

   Measure of risk for toxicity based on the above.

G. HUMAN SURVEYS

1. Final proof of safety or risk
2. Reference information for evaluation of in vitro and in vivo screening methods
3. Risk indicators

   thalidomide - teratology
   anaesthetics - abortions
   DES - teen-age cancers, aggressiveness
   Hydrocarbons (parents) - Child cancers
4. Methods
   (a) Follow up or cohort study (b) Case reference study
5. Spontaneous abortions
   (a) 20 - 40%
   (b) Related to the last menstrual period
   (c) Rates more in exposed women
6. Susceptible population
   (a) Workers with sterilizing agents antineoplastic agents
   (b) Pharmaceutical, Plastics, chemicals, rubber industries
   (c) Smelting and Soldering

7. Leading cause of child mortality in North - leukaemias, brain tumours, Neuroblastomas - low birth weights

H. CONCLUSION

1. Limitations of epidemiological studies cause - effect relationship
2. Systematic surveillance programmes - prenatal exposures and outcomes

One good school master is worth thousand priests

18. ECOTOXICOLOGY - TERRESTRIAL SYSTEMS

I. INTRODUCTION

1. Chemicalisation of habitats
2. Calsification: pesticides, drugs, etc.
3. Classification: Air, soil, food, water, etc.
4. Toxicity: Plants, animals, humans, Microbes.
    1. Pollutants in air and soil
    2. Seasonal, periodical variations in occurrence and concentration
    3. Food chains cause complications
    4. Culture of animals in waste waters for various purposes

II. AIR POLLUTION

A. HISTORY

1. With the use of fire, coal - heat and cooling
2. Domestic and industrial combustions
3. Automobiles and fossil fuels
4. Many calamities - Smog in London and Los Angels

B. TYPES

1. Unpolluted air

   Hypothetical - of natural point sources (Volcanoes, forest fires) and anthropogenic agents were absent.
2. Gaseous pollutants
    (a) Gases at normal temperature and pressure
    (b) Vapours of liquids and solids
3. Particulates
    (a) Fine solids or liquid droplets suspended in air
    (b) Dust, fumes, mist, smoke, aerosols.

C. SOURCES

1. Natural

   a. Volcano eruption b. Forest fires c. Dust storms d. Respiration
2. Anthropogenic
    (a) Mobile sources: Transport - automobiles - burning of fossil fuels - oxides of carbon and Nitrogen, Lead, Hydrocarbons.
    (b) Stationary sources: Industrial combustion, domestic activities, fly ash, sulfur, carbon, oxides of carbon and sulfur and others related to manufacturing processes.

D. HUMAN HEALTH EFFECTS

1. Irritation of respiratory tract. Children and the aged more sensitive due to insufficient development in the former and poor functioning in the latter. People with cardiovascular diseases such as asthma, emphysema and heart disease are also susceptible.
2. Sx: irritation of mucous membranes and bronchial constriction
3. Nx: pulmonary irritants
4. Lead: Impairment of nervous systems, mental retardation and blindness

E. ENVIRONMENTAL EFFECTS

1. Plants (crops, forests and vegetation)
   - (a) Bleaching, necrosis, colour changes.
   - (b) Alterations in growth and reproduction
     1. Growth and biomass
     2. Water relations between soil and plant
     3. Pathogenesis of various kinds
     4. Variations in the phenotype
2. Animals (including Domestic)
   - (a) Carcinomas in the external and internal organs
   - (b) Toxicity to various symptoms of the organism
   - (c) Variations in the phenotype - developmental polymorphism
   - (d) Behaviour - motility, reflexes to stimuli
   - (e) Rhythmic activity with extraneous
     1. Chronic exposure - Symptoms as in man.
     2. Cattle, sheep, Swine: Fluorides in water cause bone lesions, mottled and soft teeth.
3. Material and Structures
   - (a) Building materials soiled and blackened
   - (b) Acids in air damage marble.
   - (c) Ozone cracks rubber materials
   - (d) Sulphur oxides crack and tear paper and leather.
4. Atmosphere
   - (a) Atmospheric haze by suspended particles
   - (b) Reduced visibility by suspended particles

5. Acidic Deposition
   (a) Fishes in lakes affected
   (b) Release toxic metals (e.g. Alluminium)
   (c) Reduced tree growth, foliage burning
   (d) More effects where no buffering, by soil or humans is available
   (e) Neutralised by dissolving materials in the soil such as Al, Ca, Mg, Na, and K which are leached into surface waters.

III. SOIL POLLUTION

A. INTRODUCTION

1. Ultimate sink for anthropogenic materials
2. Basis for productivity
3. Host for the stationary land water filtered

B. SOURCES

1. Industrial: organic and inorganic wastes – byeproducts neither disposed nor conserved properly.
2. Agricultural: Pesticides, Fertilizers
3. Urban life: Pesticides, detergents, metals
4. Enter food chain from soil and water

C. POLLUTANTS

1. Metals: Industrial effluents- irrigation for plants- to man and animals by consumption
2. Pesticides: organochlorines poisonous due to persistance - biomagnification organophosphates more poisonous but short-lived.
3. Inorganics: Nitrates and Phosphates from fertilizers
4. Others
   (a) Increases periodically
   (b) Phenols, cyanides, solvents, dioxins, PCBs, PAHs, etc.

D. GENETIC CONSEQUENCES

1. Phenotypic variations in the population - genetic polymorphism
2. Transmissibility of changes to the subsequent
3. Generations

E. ECOLOGICAL CONSEQUENCES

1. Selection pressure on various stages of development
2. Reproductive fitness of the individuals and populations
3. Population structure

4. Behavioural patterns among themselves and towards others
5. Disappearance of populations due to selection

F. AGROECOSYSTEMS

1. Susceptibility of crops to pestilence
2. Resistance of pests and fungi to pesticides
3. Food chain passage of chemicals until man
4. Soil fertility losses
5. Productivity of the crop

The Only Real Education Comes From What Goes Counter To You

19. ECOTOXOCOLOGY: AQUATIC SYSTEMS

I. INTRODUCTION

1. Qualitative and quantitative effects of chemicals on aquatic organisms.
2. Transport, distribution, reactions and fate of chemicals.
3. Impacts of physical, chemical and biological factors.
1. Food chains
2. Dissolving, suspending and sedimenting substance
3. Variations in concentrations and dilutions dispersion
4. Rhythmic activity of animals
5. Salinity, hardness and nutrient status of the medium

II. ENVIRONMENT

1. Freshwater, marine, stationary, running.
2. Biotic and Abiotic components.
3. Concentration, duration of pollutant inputs.
4. Location specificity essential for establishing cause effect relations.

III. TOXICITY

1. Entry from sources direct or indirect.
2. Effects: lethal, structural or functional.
3. Concentration - Response relationships, Thresholds.

IV. CONCENTRATION FACTORS

1. Concentration, reaction and fate of chemicals controlled by properties of chemicals and ecosystems.
   (a) Physical and chemical properties of chemicals and their concentrations.
   (b) Physical, chemical and biological properties of ecosystem.
2. Biotransformation, Bioaccummulation and Bioavailability, Biomagnification.
3. Persistence depend on its half life.
4. Movement of chemical, reactions and products.

V. TOXICITY FACTORS

1. Exposure - route, duration, frequency of exposure and concentration.
2. (a) Acuteness - Single or multiple dosage in short periods - effects immediate or delayed.

   (b) Chronic - low dose, continuous or periodic - effects immediate or delayed.
   (c) Subchronic - intermediate in duration.
3. Frequency and thresholds.
4. Organism - sensitivity, accessibility, metabolic rates, diet, age, genetic,.
5. External environment
6. Physical and chemical properties, impurities
7. Structure - activity relationships.
8. Selective and Nonselective toxicity - targets presence, biodiversity

VI. EFFECTS

A. General
   1. Acute chronic/Subchronic
   2. Lethal/Sublethal
      Physiology, behaviour, histology, biochemistry, genetics.
   3. Immediate/delayed.
   4. Reversible/Irreversible
   5. Local/Systemic
   6. Sequential/Simultaneous
   7. Toxicological interactions - Synergism and Antagonism

B. Animal Responses
   1. Mobility and territoriality
   2. Sensitivity to light and temperature
   3. Behavioural patterns
   4. Carcinomas in the phenotype
   5. Annelids, polychaetes, Crustaceans, Molluscans, Echinoderms, Fishes, Amphibians and others

C. Plant Responses
   1. Growth and biomass
   2. Seed production and Reproductibility
   3. Lower plants, a few angiosperms

D. Genetic Consequences
   1. Knowledge in the formative stage
   2. Polymorphism and speciation, possible

E. Ecological Consequences
   1. Selection pressures
   2. Migrations

3. Population structure
4. Depletion of population
5. Interactions within the communities

F. Consequences to Society
1. Effects on food supplies
2. Trade imbalances
3. Competition among technologies for catching fish
4. Uncertain causal relationships lead to social strife
5. Conflicts among local people
6. Illegalities and violence
7. Transboundary issues

VII. CONCENTRATION - RESPONSE RELATIONSHIPS

1. Similar to dose - response relationships
2. Relationship may be graded with increasing concentration
3. Minimum effective dose - threshold
   Maximum tolerable dose - curves
4. Similar for species of similar age and health
5. Extrapolatable to others on weight basis

VIII. TOXICITY TESTING

1. Concentration and duration of exposure to produce the criterion effect
2. Identification of toxic chemicals
3. Controls - negative (untreated and solvent)
   - positive (references agent)
4. Exposure systems
   (a) Static test - still water exposure
   (b) Recirculation test - control water only circulated
   (c) Renewal test - Both renewed periodically - but static
   (d) Flow through test - Solutions flow through in and out of test chambers
5. Acute Toxicity Tests - time dependent mortality, immobility, growth cessation
6. Chronic toxicity tests - sublethal concentrations, long - term covering partial or complete life cycle.
   (a) Daphnia magna - water flea
   (b) Pimephales promelas - Fat head minnow

7. Early life stage test
8. Bioconcentration test
9. Sublethal tests - Behaviour and physiology
10. NOEC - No - Observed Effect Concentration
    LOEC - Lowest Observed Effect Concentration

The Result Of The Educative Process Is Capacity For Further Education

20. OCCUPATIONAL HEALTH

I. SOCIETAL CONCERN

1. Introduction

The objective of occupational health is the prevention of health impairment that may result from exposure to chemicals at workplace which may differ from person to person and place to place.

2. History

The need for health and safety in the workplace for employers and employees have been recognised since long when Hippocratus described toxic properties of lead. Greek historian 'Strebo' described the air in mines. Ramazzini published a book on occupational medicine.

3. Need for occupational health and safety

With the break of industrial revolution, many new industries have come up with untrained and unskilled workers. As they work for long hours they suffer from many health problems without any proper medical facilities. So compensation laws were finally passed.

4. Legislations

(a) Occupational health and safety act of 1970: this act guaranteed a safe and healthy workplace and granted employees the rights to be notified by the employers when they were exposed to harmful physical agents. Also fines for violation.

(b) Department of occupational safety and health administration They were charged with
- setting standards for safety in the workplace.
- enforce regulations.
- allow workers to register complaints and call for inspection

5. Occupational Health team consists of

(a) Occupational health nurse who is responsible for the care of illness and injuries occurring at workplace.

(b) Occupational physician performs pre -employment physicals on prospective employees.

(c) Industrial hygienist assess and control environmental hazards and toxic substances.

(d) Safety Engineer is concerned not only with the prevention of accidents but also with hazard control system based on environmental and human factor analysis.

(e) Industrial health educator has many responsibilities like educate the workers, counsel the workers, conduct epidemiologic studies, survey etc.

6. Routes of Exposure

Three major routes of exposure or entry of chemicals are contact, inhalation and ingestion.

7. Permissible levels of exposure can be expressed by

(a) Threshold limit value which is again sub-divided into

- Threshold limit value - Time weighted average
- Threshold limit value - Short term exposure limit
- Threshold limit value ceiling

(b) Biological limit Values

8. Occupational diseases may be due to

(a) Biological hazards: Main agents which may produce infection

(b) Occupational conditions

1. Overt - Hg, Pb
2. Subtle = others, delayed in nature
3. loss of hearing: noise
4. fibrosis of lungs: dust
5. Cancer
6. Shorter life span
7. Other Diseases

(c) Epidemiological data: distribution and determinants of disease frequencies in populations (associations not cause & effect)

1. Pneumocomosis : Coal workers
2. Bagassosis : dust of S. cane
3. byssinosis : dust cotton
4. Silicosis : dust Silica
5. Asbestosis : dust Asbestos
6. Scrotal cancer : English Chimmey Sweepers = 1870 s
7. Skin Cancer : Chromium workers = 1900 s
8. Other cancer : AS, VC, Radiation = Recent

(d) Dimension of the problem :

1. 1971 onwards NIOSH (USA) - 23,000: toxic substances
2. EMICNL 12,000: known toxicity
3. 7000 new chemicals / week being introduced

II. OCCUPATIONAL HEALTH HAZARDS

1. Chemicals and dust in combination with noise, heat, stress - physical & biological
2. Routes of entry
   (a) Ingestion: Oral, workers eating or smoking. For all consumer products this is essential.
   (b) Skin Absorption: more insidious & hazardous (Not seen).
   (c) Inhalation: nasal more general hazard no visible contact. Air currents imp.
3. Disease
   (a) acute or chronic
   (b) long latency period is more dangerous
   (c) Asbestosis: U.S.A.
   (d) 400,000 out of 1,000,000 will ultimately die due to cancer.
4. Occupational cancer.

Disease	*Contributing agents Occupational*	*Non-Occupational*
Heart	Many chemicals	Age & Heredity (A & H)
	Solvents	Sex (S)
	Irritants (Pulmonary)	Smoking (Sm)
	Tem(p)	Obesity (O)
		Drugs (D)
Deafness	Noise	A & H
	Nasopharyngeal	D
	Irritants	Wax
		Infection (I)
Arthritis	Dampness, cold	A & H
	Improper posture,	O
	listing	I
Pulmonary	Dusts	A & H
Diseases	gases	S, Sm
	humidity	Air pollution
	Improper O2 supply	I,
		Allergy

III. ENVIRONMENTAL EXPOSURES AND DISEASE

1. In USA

		1900	Now
(a) Heart disease	(4th)		
(b) Cancer	(8th)		1st
			2nd

   (c) It is estimated that 25% of population will ultimately develop a form of cancer.

2. Excess health risk in industrialised area
   - (a) life style : consumption tobacco etc.
   - (b) Occupation : working with pollutants
   - (c) environment : air and water pollution
   - (d) Unidentified and
   - (e) combinations
3. 60-90% of all cancers may be related to the environmental factors.

IV. INDUSTRIAL TOXICANTS

1. 'Silent killers': toxic substances everywhere
2. Minamata disaster: Fishing port of S. Japan 192 died Fertilizer manufacturer Water Bay Fish – Fisher folk Mercury
3. Kepone Factory & James River (Virginia): Kepone (thousands of pounds) Poisoning of workers in the Factory.
4. Hazards:
   - (a) Latent periods before a disease or suffering appears or seeks medical attention.
   - (b) Coupling by Temperature or Humidity
   - (c) Complexity due to cumulative effect of several agents. e.g. 40 years after the etiological agent exposure.
5. What is a Toxicant ? (NIOSH)

Potential to induce	tumors	age, sex
	transmissible change	
	Physical defects	exposure
	death via eye, mouth,	
	skin, breathing	any dose
	irritation	any duration
	behaviour alterations	
	mental un-alertness	
	ageing	

6. Many workers in different occupations subjected to the same pollutants e.g. Arsenic, Beryllium, Asbestos, Silica, CO

V. CATEGORISATION OF INDUSTRIAL POLLUTANTS

1. Allergins: Antigens that induce allergic symptoms :
   - (a) Pollen, animal hair, fungi, plant hairs, nasal and sinus disease
     1. dermatitis 2. Bronchial asthma
     3. pulmonary irritants - SOx , NOx, O3, Cl, NH3

(b) house dust, barn dust, coal dust, cotton dust

(c) Plastic industry: Isocyanates high amounts in air & when bust release toxic gases.

2. Fibrogens: Fibrosis is caused

(a) tissue scarring in lung tissue

(b) Rock quarry, amine, sand blasting, metal grinding, iron dust, cobalt (heart & hygiene) cotton dust.

3. Granulo(ma)gens: Sarcoidosis in lungs, multiple build up of cells as nodules

(a) Berrylium (Bicycles)

(b) Zirconium (nuclear reactors)

4. Fererogens: fatigue, headache, chills, coughing, dryness Metal fumes: Mn, Zn.

5. Asphyxiating agents :

(a) prevents hemoglobin from carrying O2 CO

(b) Paralyses brain & limits respiration. H2 S

6. Systemics: disrupt the total system

(a) Pb USA lead content in gasoline reduced to 0.5 gms/Gallon 1979

(b) Hg,Cd

(c) Fluorides - excepting NaF prevents dental decay

(d) Se, Va (Vanadium)

B, Ti (Titanium)

P, Te (Tellurium)

(e) Vc (Vinyl chloride) plastics (angio sarcoms of the liver) not only the worker but also people around the factories.

7. Radioactive agents: Cancer, genetic defects

8. Oil

(a) Petroleum hydrocarbons affect marine organisms in the aquatic environment.

(b) 1-100 ppm lethal

Plantation	wetlands	fish
Estuaries	birds	

(c) Skin irritation - human factors

(d) Fire hazards - Handling of oil

1. Torrey canyon tanker 1968 grounds of Santa Barbara
2. Alaskan pipeline explosion – 1977

VI. NOISE

A. Unwanted sound

1. Pollution temporary/permanent hearing impairment
2. USA 26% production workers 90 decibel starter

   59% production workers 85 decibel starter

   50 - normal conversation

   60 - laud conversation

   70 - Telephone conversation

   80 - annoying

   75-80 db: loud Rock Music
3. Sonic boom Supersonic air craft cone-shaped shock wave ground charge in air pressure exceeded 2 lbs/sq fort
4. Industry: textile, lumber, wood, food, building, etc.
5. disturbs sleep, retarded learning verbal/nonverbal, stress, blood pressure, heartbeat, endocrine secretions,
6. Ear protectors, ear plugs, ear muffs

VII. PESTICIDES

1. In spite of environmentalists and government, farmers use more pesticides, without which crop yields would be 15% less and some fruits and vegetables impossible to be produced.
2. Widespread contamination by the 32,000 pesticide products - 400 base chemicals
3. Aldrin/dieldrin, DDT, Endrin & Toxaphane - highly toxic to fish, animals and humans.
4. Muscle weakness, exhaustion, asthma, gastroenteritis, brain haemorrhage
5. Bioaccummulation: Toxaphane

F. Residues in food-stuffs

6. Mercury based ones are banned as seed treatments and paint constituent (mildew)
7. Secondary poisoning, PCBs in fish and mother's milk
8. Immunological defense system may also be affected.

VIII. WASTES: SEWAGE, LAND POLLUTION

1. Dumping into landfills or oceans or large bodies of water- Outcry.
2. City Dumps where the drainage reaches creeks and rivers pollution is so much that livestock, fishing etc. out of bounds.
3. Wastes are a menace to health - act slowly over a time

(a) nervous system, cancer, birth defects

(b) many persist due to non-degradability

4. In USA

(a) 10 million tons of hazardous wastes/year (non-radioactive)

(b) 5-10% annual increase

(c) 90% liquid form - metals, salts, acids, bases, organics, heavy metals, flammables and explosives

(d) Synthetic organic wastes: halogenated organic pesticides, pesticide containers, plasticizers, solvents

(e) Hospitals-pathological materials, drugs, bandages, organ-Remains

(f) Biological warfare materials

(g) Dumping, Burying, ocean submersion, burning: Public health Better procedures: Recycling by extraction of useful metalslandfills cut off from the ground water ;

(h) Municipal sewer systems: 50,000 industrial plants discharge

1. Treatment of waste water difficult\

2. Some hazardous pollutants may enter drinking water.

(i) Most of the solid wastes are convertible to energy.

(j) Sewage sludge - fertilizer and land conditioning

K. Sewage Agriculture in France 1893 onwards. But there are some dangerous chemicals - e.g. Heavy metals.

21. COMMUNITY HEALTH

1. INTRODUCTION

According to who exports community health refers to the health status of the members of the community, to the problems affecting their health, and to the totality of health can provided for the community, community health emphasis on community diagnosis and treatment.

2. HEALTH CARE AND HEALTH SERVICE

Health care includes traditional public health services, medical, nursing and dental services, provided to the individuals or communities, to promote, maintain, thonitor and restore health

The term health services refers ot the permanet country wide system of established instituation (hospital, health centre, health laboratories, research institutes), the objective of which is to cope up with various health needs and demands of the population.

3. STUDY OF COMMUNITY

The guidelines for studying a community systematically are as follows

(a) Physical characteristic of the area

(b) Demographic characteristics

(c) Environmental survey.

(d) Socio-economic Services.

(e) Health problems

(f) Health Knowledge

(g) community organization

(h) Channels of communication

(i) Community resources j. leader ship.

4. HEALTH CARE REVOLUTION

The Principles that has be recognized by all government in the provision of health care are as follows:

(a) Health care should be relevant - i-e- it should be based on the health needs and demands of the people.

(b) It should be adequate.

(c) It should be accessible

(d) should be based on social equity.

(e) Should be effective

(f) should be efficient.

(g) Should be based on community participative

5. PRIMARY HEALTH CARE

Primary health care is the essential health care given to individuals and acceptable to them, through their full participation and at a cost that the community and country can afford.

6. ELEMENTS OF PRIMARY HEALTH CARE ARE AS FOLLOWS

(a) Education of the people about the prevailing health problems and methods of preventing and controlling them.

(b) Promotion of food supply and proper nutrition.

(c) Adequate supply of safe water and basic sanitation

(d) Immunization against major infections diseases.

(e) Prevention and control of locally endemic diseases.

(f) Appropriate treatment of common diseases and injuries.

(g) Provision of essential drugs.

7. PRINCIPLE OF PRIMARY HEALTH CARE

According to who expert committee then are give principles for primary health care. they are as follows:

(a) Equitable distribution.

(b) Community involvement.

(c) Appropriate technology.

(d) focus on prevention .

(e) Multi Sectural approach.

8. ROLE OF NURSES IN PRIMARY HEALTH CARE

(a) Accessing the health status of the community and individuals

(b) Mobilising the community involvement

(c) Providing integrated health care including the treatment of emergencies and making references.

(d) Training and supervising health workers.

(e) collaborating with other development Sectors.

(f) Monitoring progress in primary health care.

9. HEALTH EFFECTS OF AIR POLLUTION

Effects include both immediate and delayed. Immediate effect include acute bronchitis. Chronic bronchitis and long cancer is the delayed effect of air pollution.

10. EFFECTS OF NOISE POLLUTION

(a) Deafness, Which may become Permanent if the noise exposure is too high.

(b) Interference with speech. (c) Inability to concentrate.

(d) Accidents in industries. (e) Physiological changes in the body.

(f) Loss of speech and disturbance to sleep.

11. THE HEALTH HAZARDS OF IMPROPER EXCRETA DISPOSAL

(a) Soil Pollution (b) Water Pollution

(c) Contamination of foods. (d) Fly breeding.

The disease associated with improper extracts disposal are: typhoid and paratyphoid fever, diarrhea, and dysentery, intestinal worm such as round worm and hook worm, cholera, polio, viral hepatitis etc.

12. FAMILY PLANNING SERVICES

(a) Treatment of sterility. (b) Marriage counseling and guidance.

(c) Sex education. (d) nutrition and home economics.

13. HEALTH EDUCATION

Health education has been described as cement that binds together the bricks of the health programma. The WHO formulated the aims of health education as follows:

(a) Health is valued as an asset in the community.

(b) To equip the people with skills knowledge and attitude to enable them to solve their health problems by their own actions and efforts.

(c) To promote the development and proper use of health services

22. MANAGEMENT STRATEGIES

I. INTRODUCTION

A. Roots of Environmental Degradation

1. Depletion of existing resources
2. Pollution air, waters, soil, noise
3. Increasing poverty, population
4. Changing attitude to natural environment

B. Need for Management strategies

1. Why ? Common problems, widespread effects to and for 'magic' plan globally, act regionally.
2. Several approaches to issues from micro-conservation of resources; increasing biodiversity; people's welfare etc.

II. GLOBAL AWARENESS AND SUSTAINABLE DEVELOPMENT

1. 1800s: Nature conservation in the colonies and Britain
2. 1900s: ecology in planning (UNESCO in '46 & IUCN in'56 etc)
3. Rise of environmentalism in second half of 1900s with 'Spaceship Earth' (Boulding). Club of Rome (Peccei) etc.
4. Important Milestones are world conservation strategy of (WCS) 1980, Bruntland Report 1987.

III. GOVERNMENT, ENVIRONMENT AND POLICY MAKING

1. Causes for continued degradation - no market for sustainability, open access to resources; no evaluation of resources etc.
2. Forging sound development policies
   (a) people - oriented in targets
   (b) trade policy liberalisation (GATT)
   (c) Economic incentives to even technology
   (d) Polluter pays policy
3. Some problems in implementing the above
   (a) Political economy - political and public lobbying mostly in dramatic areas, not necessarily most important
   (b) Lack of knowledge and awareness amongst public and information sustained to few.
   (c) Public attitudes and involvement - including snobbery of officials, mental blocks, need for more effort and money and hence no inputs.

IV. GLOBAL LEVEL POLICY MAKING

A. World Bank's Approach.

1. promote most effective use of sources by influencing developing nations & Assessment of projects supported
2. Track record
   (a) Takes into account economic and not ecological costs.
   (b) assessment of environment and conservation planning for post-project phase only
   (c) Stalls gross functioning as in Narmada Valley Project.

B. UNEP approach

1. act as catalyst and think tanks
2. conscience of UN agencies.
3. Funds from 'environmental fund' to which contributions are voluntary.
4. Effectiveness to far poor even on others UN agencies.
5. Achievements: Regional seas programme 1974.
6. GEMS 1975.
7. UN conference on Desertification 1977.
8. Commissioned IUCN in 1977 to formulate 'world conservation strategy'.

V. MANAGEMENT IN INDIA

A. Government policies.

1. Constitutional provisions
   (a) articles 48A and 51A am 'duty' of citizens to protect environment.
   (b) no emphasis on planning or legal protection
2. Five year plans
   (a) Only from 6th plan any mention of water, forest, Biosphere reserve etc.
   (b) 7th plan had National conservation strategy - research encouraged, information systems established.
   (c) 8th plan - stress on protection, monitoring and restoration of degraded ecosystems.
3. Environmental Laws.
4. Institutional Framework.
   (a) DOEF (Jan. 1985)
       - survey of flora, fauna, - research, - restoration

(b) Central pollution control Board (1974).
- Control & check pollution
- legal authority to penalise.

(c) Other institutions - wildlife institutions of India, Indian Institutions of Technology etc. Mainly to provide 'Science & technology' knowledge to 'Managers'.

B. Perspective in India.

1. Stabilisation of population growth
2. Integrated land use and water management
3. Conservation of biological diversity
4. Sustainable energy resource utilisation
5. Pollution control
6. Improvement of human habitats
7. Vague, only on paper, no infrastructure, need to back up.

Education is the transmission of civilization

23. BIOMONITORING OF POLLUTION

I. INTRODUCTION

A. BASICS

1. The biosphere & its constituents.
2. Natural feed back system and natural time scale over which effects of disturbances are dissipated.
3. Artificial feed back system, viz. monitoring of changes in the environment, using biological indicators.

B. DEFINITIONS

1. Monitoring 2. Biological monitoring 3. Biological indicators

C. OBJECTIVES OF BIOLOGICAL MONITORING

1. Recommendations of the International Union of Biological Sciences (IUBS), 1982:
   (a) Encouragement of scientific and national bodies to develop methods.
   (b) Interdisciplinary & international cooperation in standardising methods.
   (c) Encouragement of exchange of research results amongst the labs of the world.
   (d) Conferences on indicators at cellular, individual and population and ecosystem level.
2. Monitoring is undertaken for the following reasons:
   (a) Basic for management of biological resources for sustainable development.
   (b) Conservation of ecosystems and populations.
   (c) Knowledge of dynamics of ecosystem.
   (d) Insert pests of agriculture and forestry can studied for means of control.
3. Classification of questions regarding data collection:
   (a) Who undertakes or supports programme ?
   (b) Aims and objectives ?
   (c) What methods are being used ? Are they the most appropriate ones ?
   (d) What is the time scale for monitoring ?
   (e) Choice of variables and processes to be studied - do they fulfill the objectives of the programme ?

4. Health surveillance
   (a) Evaluation of health status.
   (b) Identification of individuals undergoing adverse health effects
   (c) Environmental Monitoring programmes for creating awareness .
   (d) Aim of the programme is to develop methods to indicate impacts on human health, its related to environmental factors end.
   (e) Conventional pollutant monitoring as a biological dose measures.
   (f) The development of methods of determining biological dose
   (g) Application of the methods in biological monitoring and used as indicators of biological effects.
   (h) Environmental health monitoring should be focused on indicators of reversible effects.

II. BIOLOGICAL INDICATORS

1. Community changes (change in species composition of the biotic community) can be used to monitor current status of the environment.
2. Predictive statements based on previously documented community changes.
3. Biological material and indicator species used for monitoring range from cells, tissues and organs to whole oroganisms (to the plants and animals).

III. PLANTS AS INDICATORS

1. (a) Presence or absence as indicator of environmental conditions
   (b) Community indicators such as characteristic flora of certain soils and water availability.
   (c) Specific plant taxa used as indicators. Lichens, Mosses, fungi, Higher vascular plants advantages and disadvantages.
      1. Use of species combination as indicators
      2. Structure & life form as indication.

IV. MONITORING POLLUTION

In two ways, through effects on individuals or through effects on the ecosystem.

A. EFFECT ON INDIVIDUALS

1. Biological Monitoring of Exposure To Chemicals

   Definition of permissible levels of exposure.

   Regular assessment of health risk associated with exposure limits.

   (a) AMBIENT MONITORING

   - Measurement of external expourse to chemical ie, through concentration in air, food, water etc.
   - Presence of health hazard estimated by reference to environmental exposure limits eg. threshold limit value and tissue - weighted average.

   (b) BIOLOGICAL MONITORING

   - The quantitative risk evaluation of carcinogens involves estimating a Virtually Safe Dose (V.S.D.)
   - Use of animal dose - response data.

B. EFFECTS ON ECOSYSTEMS

1. REASONS FOR LONG-TERM STUDIES

   (a) Basic ecological knowledge for understanding processes of many ecosystems.

   (b) Baseline for management.

   (c) Understanding synergistic and commulative effects of man-made perturbations.

   (d) Early detection of potentially harmful effects

2. LEVELS OF BIOLOGICAL ORGANIZATION

   Most monitoring studies concentrate on species level - single species may be unreliable predictors of response at higher level of organisation.

3. LOCALITIES FOR ECOSYSTEM MONITORING

   (a) Localities for long term monitoring should be severs - perturbations should be minimized.

   (b) Impacts of present should be important in the monitoring programme.

   (c) National Science Foundation reports (NSF, 1977, 1978) give guidelines for choosing sites with the following characteristics:

   - Where productive & useful short term research has already been carried out.

- Representative of major ecosystems and populations.
- chemical variables can be monitored.

C. TYPES OF INDICATORS OF POLLUTION

1. Sentinels: Organisms introduced into the environment as early warning systems.
2. Detectors: Species occuring naturally in the area, showing a measurable response to change.
3. Exploiters: abundance due to lack of competition from eliminated species.
4. Accummulators: organisms taking up chemicals in measurable quantities.
5. Bioassay organisms: organisms used as lab reagents to :
   - detect presence and / or
   - concentration of pollutants,
   - rank pollutants in order of toxicity
6. Limitations
   (a) Sensitive species gets eliminated if any stage of environmental conditions become adverse helps us monitoring the adverse environmental conditions.
   (b) Living organisms used to monitor different pollutants.
   (c) requires new & upcoming techniques of biomonitoring to prevent further degradation of the environment.

V. ETHICAL ASPECTS

1. Defining essential and non-essential research so as to limit the use of vivisection (animal-testing) only to essential research.
2. Impossible to put an end to production of harmful chemicals and radiations. It is possible to control their escape into the environment where they can interact with living human systems.
3. Monitoring procedures involving humans must be without health risks and should be done only with informed consent.

VI. INDICATORS

Assessment of environmental hazards on air, soil and aqueous environments, using biological methods. The various reasons of using Bio-indication. The various levels & integration of life forms used as biological Indicators.

1. **Introduction: It contains the following aspects.**
   (a) Concept of sustainability
   (b) Role of science-importance of biomonitoring in risk hazards indices (RHI)

(c) Requirements for a biomonitor - General, Biomarkers, social and regulatory Considerations.

LIMITATIONS

The use of organisms as indicators is restricted by limitations arising form the four following main laws :

1. The law of Bass Becking - Beyerinck
2. The law of the physiological & ecological amplitude.
3. The law of relative site constancy
4. The complex characters of factors (environmental)

2. Bioindicators of global environmental change

(a) Importance of plants and animals as indicators

(b) Insects as a indicator

(c) Physiological markers as indicator.

(d) Types of Bioindicators

1. True indicators 2. Scales of Indicator species 3. Accumulators

3. In situ Biological monitoring of pollutions.

(a) concentration of pollution and its effects on species at a specific sive exhibits differences in physiology and morphology.

(b) Relative ship between concentration of a melal in all organism and the abiotic sample.

(c) Dangers of not conducting insite biomonitoring.

(d) Marine approaches to onsite biomonitoring of pollution.

4. Community effects.

(a) Changes in the abendance of speaces due to contamination.

(b) Response shower in an comunity due to effects of pollution.

(c) Biological effect of pollution

(d) Pollutants affecting flore and fource the terrestrial ecosystems.

(e) Asessing the degree of pollution in freshwater ecosystems with respect of biotic , approach and by river invertabrate predictains and classification.

(f) Effects of pollutants on marine organisms

5. Bio accumulation of pollutants.

(a) Measuring pollutant levels in organisms

(b) Pollutants are assessed by the length of time spent feeding as the contaminated give in a niglatory species.

(c) Laboratory analysis for the contamination of plants in terestrial ecosystems.

(d) Earth worms are found to be one of the most important groups of monitor pollution.

(e) Difficulties in the assessment of pollution in fresh water ecosystems.

(f) The difficulty of analysing many pollutants in the marine ecosystems.

6. Effects of pollutants on organisms.

(a) Different pollutants affecting organisms are different parameters.

(b) Effects of pollutant on organisms of terrestrial ecosystems

(c) Effects of pollutants on organisms of fresh water ecosystems

(d) Effects of pollutants on organisms of marine ecosystems

7. Genetically bused resistance to pollution.

(a) plants possess genetically bused resistance to pollutants

(b) Invertabrates that are genetically resistance to pollutants

(c) 5 R's in insiter biomonitoring organisms.

8. Biomonitors of microbial contaminations of the enviroment:

(a) Micro organisms that can be used to indicute whether pathogens are present or hot.

(b) Sources of microbial contaminations

(c) Consepts of air indicater organism

(d) Industriral Indicaters as biomonitors of microobial contamination like total fecal coliforms, fecal stoeptococci, thererobic bacteria.

(e) New indicators like bacteriophages as a bioindicator

9. Biomonitoring of Aquatic systems.

(a) Pollution monitoning in aquatic enviroument

(b) There groups of indicator organisms that are fitted into aquatic systems

(c) Biomanicers in aquatic monitoring.

10. Biomonitoning of Terrestrial systems.

(a) PAHS as pollutants present in the soil

(b) Biomonitoring of PAHS and its effects

(c) Use of bio indicators for monitoring the pollutant effects

11. Bio Indicators of Air pollution

(a) Air pollution in relation of vegetative and its effects.

(b) Monitoring of air pollution.

(c) Monitoring of biological effects of pollutants of air by plants

(d) Non-plant bioindicators used as bio indicators of air pollution.

(e) Specification & examples of the usage of higher plants as indicators.

TABLE 1. Animals in Toxicity Testing: Aquatic Invertebrates

S.N(o)	*Scientific name*	*Common name*	*Taxonomy*	*Tested for*
A. Fresh water				
1.	Physa integra	Snails	Mollusca	Acute toxicity
2.	Chironomus	Midges	Arthropoda Diptera	Egg viability
3.	Daphnia magna D. pulex D. pulicaria	Daphnids	Arthropoda Crustacea Brachiopoda	Acute and toxicity
4.	Gammanis lacustris G. faxiatus G. pseudoli-mnaeus	Amphipods	Arthropoda Crustacea Malacostroca	Chronic effects of detergents
B.Marine				
1.	Cranostrea Virginica C. gigas	Oyster Bivalvia	Mollusca	Acute toxicity
2.	Acartia tonsa A. clausi	Copepods	Arthropoda Crustacea Copepoda	Acute toxicity (heavy metals)
3.	Penaeus setiferus P. duorarum P. azteuis	Shrimp	Arthropoda Crustacea Decapoda	Acute toxicity
4.	Palaemonetes pugio P. vulgaris	Grass shrimp	Arthropoda Crustacea Decapoda	Dodecyl sulfate bioassay
5.	Homanus americanus	American lobster	Arthropoda Decapoda	Toxicity of copper
6.	Uca s(p)	Fiddler crab	Arthropoda Crustacea	Acute toxicity testing
7.	Capitalla capitata	Poly-chastes	Annelida Polycheata	Acute toxicity (Heavy metals on laboratory populations)
C. Estuarine				
1.	Mysidopsis bahia	Mysid shrimp	Arthropoda Crustacea Decapoda	Pollutant toxicity to life cycle
2.	Asellus	Isopod meridianus	Arthropoda Crustacea Malacostrace	Tollerance to copper and lead

TABLE 2. Animals In Toxicity Testing: Terrestrial Invertebrates

S.N(o)	*Scientific name*	*Common name*	*Taxonomy*	*Tested for*
1.	Leptinotarse decenlineata	Colarodo potato beetle	Arthropoda Insecta Coleopteta	Toxicity of Pesticides
2.	Culex pipens	Mosquito	Arthropoda Insecta Diptera	Effect of DOT on malaria
3.	Anopheles s(p)	Mosquito	Arthropoda Insecta Diptera	Effect of DOT on malaria
4.	Drosophila melanogaster	Fruitfly	Arthropoda Insecta Diptera	All toxicities

TABLE 3. Animals in Toxicity Testing: Aquatic Lower Plants

S.N(o)	*Scientific name*	*Common name*	*Taxonomy*	*Tested for*
A. Fresh water				
1.	Selenastrum	Green algae	Chlorophyta	Acute toxicity
2.	Anabaena	Blue green algae	Cyanophyta	Acute toxicity
3.	Navicula	Brown algae	Chrysophyta	Acute toxicity
B. Marine				
1.	Chlorella s(p)	Green algae	Chlorophyta	Acute toxicity
2.	Isochrysis galbana	Brown algae	Chrysophyta	Acute toxicity
3.	Porphyridium cruentum	Rhodophyta	Rhodopyta	Acute toxicity

TABLE 4. Animals in Toxicity Testing: Aquatic Vertebrates

S.N(o)	*Scientific name*	*Common name*	*Taxonomy*	*Tested for*
A. Fresh water				
1.	Lepomis macrochirus	Bluegill	Pisces	Partial chronic tests
2.	Pimephales promelas	Fat head minnow	Pisces	Reaction to reference toxicants
3.	Salmo gairdneri	Rainbow trout	Pisces	Acute toxicity
4.	Salvelinus fontinalis	Brook trout	Pisces Osteichthyes	Partial chronic tests
B. Marine				
1.	Cyprindon veriegatus	Sheeps head minnow	Pisces	Life cycle toxicity
2.	Fundulus heteroclitus	Mummichog	Pisces	Teratogenesis
3.	Fundulus setiferus	Longnose Killifish	Pisces	Acute toxicity
4.	Menidia mennidia s(p)	Sivler side	Pisces	Toxicity of cadmium
5.	Channa punctatus	Midges	Pisces	General toxicity
6.	Tilapia mossambica		Pisces	General toxicity
C. Amphibian				
1.	Rana tigrina	Common frog	Amphibia	Nephro toxicity
2.	Xenopus	Common laevis	Amphibia frog	tertogenicity

TABLE 5. Animals in Toxicity Testing: Terrestrial Vertebrates

S.N(o)	*Scientific name*	*Common name*	*Tested for*
A. Aves			
1.	Gallus domesticus	Domestic fowl	Terratogenicity and neurotoxicity of pesticides
2.	Columba livia	Common pigeon	neurotoxicity of pesticides
3.	Anas platyrhyncha	Pekin duck	Spongy generation of white matter by some toxicants
B. Mammals			
1.	Oryctolagus uchiculus	Rabbit	Placental transport Teratogenicity Dermal cancer Lung toxicity
2.	Mus musculus	Mouse	Nephrotoxicity Respi- toxicity Infertilityy Teratogenicity Placental transport Neurotoxicity
3.	Rattus norvegieus	Laboratory rat	Nephrotoxicity Infertility Carcinogenesis Teratogenesis
4.	Mesocricetus auratus	Syrian hamster	Respiratory toxicity
5.	Meriones unguiculatus	Mongolian Gerbil	Behavioural toxicity
6.	Cavia porcellus	Guinea pig	All toxicities
7.	Canis familiasis	Dogs	Baldder tumors Pesticide neuro toxicity
8.	Folix catus	Domestic cat	Organomercurial toxicity
9.	Sus scrofa	Pig	Skin penetration studies
10.	Copra hircus	Goat	Organophosphate toxicity
11.	Bos terurers	Cattle	Reproductive toxicity
12.	Macaca mulatta	Rhesus Monkey	Neurotoxicity Drug effects

24. LAWS FOR POLLUTION CONTROL

I. ENVIRONMENTAL LAW: GLOBAL SCENARIO

1. Growth of awareness of environmental degradation & need for a proper Environmental policy & Management.
2. 1972 Stockholm conference: 'Magna carta' of our environment laid firm foundation for Environmental policies
3. Various other conferences eg. UNCED etc. contributed to growth of an Environmental policy.

II. THE INDIAN SCENARIO

1. Degradation of environment due to a huge population.
2. Growing problem of pollution of air, water, soil etc.
3. Need for a workable LEGO-ADMINISTRATIVE MACHINERY
4. Environmental policies started as early as Kautilya's times

III. ENVIRONMENTAL LAWS

A. DEFINITION: Legislation aimed at protection of the environment

B. SCOPE: These laws aim at specifying the role.

1. Regulation of pollutants, wastes etc.
2. Punitive action
3. Creating an authority to protect environment

C. FUNCTIONS

1. PRIMARY LAWS: Concerned with citizens & corporate bodies
2. SECONDARY LAWS: Concerned with Govt. Depts. & NGO s
3. TERTIARY LAWS: Concerned with activities of the state

D. CLASSIFICATION

Protective		*Planning*	
Humans	*Non-Humans*	*production*	*Distribution*
1. Water	1. Wild life	1. Land Utilization	1. Land ceiling
2. Air	2. Marine life	2. Irrigation	2. Town planning
3. Noise	3. Flora	3. Industry	3. Slums
4. Nuclear Radiation		4. Mining	4. Housing
		5. Grazing	5. Parks
5. Toxic subsystems		6. Estuaries et(c)	6. Sanctuaries etc.

IV. HISTORY OF ENVIRONMENTAL LAW IN INDIA

A. PRE - INDEPENDENCE TIMES

1. Strategy of 'policing the society'
2. no genuine interest in welfare of Indian environment, primary interest was exploitation
3. Some important laws passed by British are the criminal producers code, Factory Acts, nuisance Acts, Municipal Acts, Format Acts etc.

B. INDEPENDENT INDIA

1. 1947 - 1970s: Lackadaisical attitude to environment no concrete framework of policy
2. some important laws passed them were Factories Act (1948), Calcutta Municipal Act(1951), Insecticide Act 1968) etc.

C. TRANSITION TO A NEW AGE

1. Good leadership of Nehru, Mrs. Gandhi etc.
2. Influence of stockholm conference

D. 1970 S - 1990 S: AVALANCHE OF LEGAL ACTIVITY

1. 1972 - National Committee on Environmental Planning Formed.
2. 1980 - Tiwari committee Report.
3. 1980 - Dept. of Environmental set up. Likewise there was a growth of Environmental law - WATER ACT (1972),
   AIR ACT (1981), ENVIRONMENT ACT (1986),etc.

E. 1990 S: NEW 'BASE OF LIFE' TO LAW DUE TO RIO SUMMIT

F. INDIAN CONSTITUTION & ENVIRONMENTAL LAW

1. Constitution has guidelines for a sound Environmental policy
2. Eg. Articles 47, 51, 42, 43, 48, 49, etc.

V. EVOLUTION OF ENVIRONMENTAL LAW IN INDIA

A. TIWARI COMMISSION: (1980)

1. Inspected lego-administrative aspects of environmental issues
2. Headed by Tiwari
3. Attributed three uses to bad conditions, large population & degraded natural resources
4. Recommended that there be
   (a) Biosphere Reserves, Forests
   (b) Protection of endangered species

(c) better land use
(d) control of Toxic substances & Noise
(e) Dept of Environment.

5. Criticized the existing legal framework as being outdated, inconsistent, in adequate etc.

B. ENVIRONMENT PROTECTION ACT: (1986)

1. It dealt with all the aspects of each type of pollution
2. Standards for pollutants
3. Responsibility of each part (industry, govt. etc.)
4. Punishment for each environmental offence
5. Moreover there are many lacunae.
6. Does not include noise, radiation etc.
7. Implementation lough
8. Easy for offenders to escape due to loopholes

C. PROTECTIVE LAWS: The Indian Pinal Code forbids

1. Spreading of infectious agents
2. Fouling water
3. Public nuisance
4. Mischief
5. Making atmosphere conducive to health

D. AIR POLLUTION: SPECIAL

1. Motor Vehicle Act 1939
2. Air Act 1981
3. Environment Act 1986

E. WATER POLLUTION

1. Water Act 1974
2. Water Amendment Act 1978
3. Water cess Act 1977
4. Environment Act 1986
5. Important laws dealing with Marine pollution
   (a) Indian Port Act 1908
   (b) Merchant shipping Act 1958
   (c) Indian Dock Labourers Act 1934

F. LAND/SOIL POLLUTION

1. Factories Act 1948
2. Mines & Mineral Act 1957
3. Water Act 1974

4. Air Act 1981
5. Insecticide Act 1968
6. Industrial Act 1951
7. Environment Act 1986

G. **NOISE POLLUTION:**

1. no central law except that Articles 47, 48, 51, 39 indirectly deal with it
2. some states of Rajasthan, M.P., Bihar etc. have laws.
3. Lacuna in law dealing with Noise Pollution

H. **RADIATION POLLUTION**

1. Atomic Energy Act 1972
2. no other law dealing with Radiation Pollution

I. **PROTECTION OF WILD LIFE:**

1. Several Forests Acts & Wild Life protection act (1972)

VI. PARTICIPANTS IN ENVIRONMENTAL LEGISLATION

A. **CENTRAL & STATE GOVERNMENTS**

1. duty of each level of Govt. specified in all the Acts especially EPA.
2. some state Govt. make special laws if Noise - Rajasthan, Bihar etc.
3. The power to make laws depends on whose function the area comes in ie in Lest I (Union list), List II (state List) or List III (concurrent List)

B. **ROLE OF NG0s & VOLUNTARY AGENCIES**

1. Sierra club, Friends of the Earth, Green peace
2. India - Narmada Bachao Andolan (NBA) etc. "Watchdogs" of Govt. which breaks its own laws.

C. **ROLE OF JUDICIAL SYSTEM**

1. Courts responsibility most important
2. Eg. of RATLAM municipal case

VII. EVALUATION OF ENVIRONMENTAL LAW

Impotent- Punishment rare- litigation tough- corruption high- apathy high- laws vague, imprecise and inadequate

VIII. MAKING LAWS MORE EFFECTIVE

1. Better framed laws- direct, precise & extensive(fill lacunae)
2. Provide personnel to implement laws
3. make courts more accessible to people.

4. Benefits (income tax) to pollution control activity
5. Enhance environmental awareness
6. More public participation
7. Rise of aggressive environmental activism & charge in political attitudes to environment.

IX. ENVIRONMENTAL LAWS

1. 1887 - Wild birds and animal Protection Act
2. 1927 - Indian Forest Act
3. 1952 - Indian Board for wild life established
4. 1961 - World Wild Life Fund instituted
5. 1972 - Conservation and International Trade on Endangered Species International law on trade
6. 1977 - Wild life conservation Act
8. 1982 - Forest conservation Act
9. 1988 - Forest Amendment Act

> *Try not to become a man of success, but a man of value*

25. MONITORING BY INSTRUMENTATION

I. MONITORING

A. MEASUREMENT OF PARTICLES

The title Instrument techniques involves the measurement of particles (particulate pollutants) present in the atmosphere. There are different types of techniques involved in the measurement of the particles varying in different sizes. The various methods are as follows.

1. High Voltage sampler: A known volume of air is sucked by a high speed blower thro a fire filter paper. Such filter paper is kept in hot air at 105 c for about 30 minutes. It is cooled and weight. The sampling is done for 24 hours. The filter paper after sampling is removed gently and transferred carefully to the laboratory. Final weight is taken after drying at 105 C for half an hour.
2. Tape sampler: This type of samplers reduce the sampling time, ot as 10 minutes per sample. The particulates are caught on a paper tape, which is automatically reeled through the instrument, and farm a black dot.
3. Cascade impactor: There are used to collect samples and not for air quality monitaring. A cascade impactor is used for this purpose, which consists of four tubes, each with a prozeressively smaller opening, thus forcing highes and highes velocities.

B. MEASUREMENT OF GASES

Gas can be collected from atmosphere either by adsorption or absarption. Adsarption is a surface phenomenon and activated carbon is usually the adsarbent. The activated carbon is coated with a chemical which either collects the gas for future elutionor undergoes a chemical and colour change. Thus providing a direct estimate of the gas concentration.

1. Gas Bubbler collector: The equipment used is ofter called a bubbler since the gases are bubbled thro the callecting liquid, Some gases can be collected by dissolving them in the liquid and then analysing the liquid by chemical means.
2. Photometric device: The gas to be evaluated is mixed with reagents and then automatically and continuously passed through a measurement section which usually is a photometric device.

C. TREATMENT DEVICES

The selection of the carrect treatment devices requires the matching of the characteristics of the pollutants and the features of the control devices.

1. Cyclone separatars: This class of separatars is the most common of a general group of separatars that are classified as centrifugal or inertial separatars. It depends on the contrifugal force instead of gravity to separate particles from the gas stream.
2. Fabric filters: They used the principle of filtration. The fabric filters are made in the farm of tubular bag or cloth envelops and are suitable for a dust loading of the order of 19/m2. They are capable of removing dust particles as small as 0.5 u also.
3. Electrastatic precipitatar: These are particulate collection devices that utilise electrical energy directly to arrist in the removal of the particulate matter. There are successfully used to remove fine dusts from all kinds of waste gares with very high efficiency.
4. Wet scrubbers: This is universal in that confunction as either or both particulate and gas control devices. There particulate control devices utilize a liquid to assist in the removal of particulaters from the carrier gas stream. In there devices water is the mostly used scrubbing liquid. In there wet collectors, the particulates are agglomerated with water and then separated into cleaned gas and contaminated liquid streams. Important scrubbers are, (i) Spray scrubber or towers, (ii) Venturi scrubbers, (iii) aplone scrubber & (iv) packed scrubber.

D. MEASUREMENT OF COLOR

The variation of the color of a system with charge in concentration of some component forms the basis of colorimetric analysis. colorimeter deals with the determinations of the Con. Of a substance by measurement of the relative absorption of light to a known con. of the substance to use colorimetric method quantitatively.

1. Photoelectric colorimeter: It contains a light source, a color filter element. A monochromatic light obtained from the color filter is directed thro a cell containing sample. The light after passing through the sample strikes the photoelectric cell which measures the absorbance. Photoelectric colorimeter

requires a separate color filter for each determination and range of application is limited.

2. Spectrophotometer: In spectrophotometer either a glass prison or a diffraction grafting are used top produce monochromatic light. The basic instrumentation is same for both spectrophotometer and photometric colorimeter except for the manner in which monochromatic light is produced.

E. ATOMIC ABSORPTION SPECTROPHOTOMETRY (AAS)

This method is useful in measuring trace quantities of most elements in water. It is very sensitive and the elements present as low as ' ppm may be determined. The main advantage of AAs is that the determination can be carried out in presence of other elements and separation of test elements from other elements is not necessary.

F. FLAME PHOTOMETRY

It is also called as flame emission spectroscopy. This technique is mostly used for the analysis of sodium and potassium especially in fluids and tissues.

G. GAS CHROMOTOGRAPHY

It is based on the differential adsorption of different constituents. It is based on the differential adsorption of different constituents in a mixture on various adsorbents. In this technique there are two phares. The different constituents in the mixture are separated on the basis of a difference in their rates of migration throw a stationary phare when carried by moving phase.

H. OTHERS

1. Measurement of flouride: There are two colorimeter methods and one electrode method using fluoride ion selective electrode for the measurement of fluoride ion con. Among the colourimetric methods 'spadus' methods tolerates many interferences and reasonably accurate.

   Spadns method: In this method acid zirconyl spadns reagent in used. This reagent is prepared by mixing zirconyl chloride, Hcl, and spadns solution. Fluoride ion changes the color of zir concium spadns complex, and other color change is proportional to the fluoride ion concentration. This method tolerates many interferences and determines fluoride in the range from 0.00 to 1.40 mg/l. The reaction occurs immediately and so no waiting time is required.

2. Thermistor: The temperature of pond water is measured by an instrument called thermistor, based on the principles of

thermocouples. The glan globule of thermistor is lowered at different depths in water with the heep of an electric cord. The needle of the potentiometer outside the water gives the temperature valveson The scale that can be directly read out.

3. PH meter: PH expresses the hydrogen ion activity. PH is determined by electrometric method which involves the measurement of the electromotive force of a cell comprising an indicator electrode sensitive to hydrogen ion and a regerence electrode. The instrument wed is called pH meter knowledge of pH is necessary in the application of chlorine and in the selection of coagulants for water purification.

II. INSTRUMENTATION

A. INTRODUCTION TO QUALITY MONITORING

Performance of chemical, physical and biological measurements in an environmental system (natural or man made) so as to make a realistic assessment of probable behaviour of natural and pollutant species.

B. AIR QUALITY MONITORING-PURPOSES

Detecting concentration of varied types of pollutants and abatement techniques for controlling them

1. **Air Pollution Control Equipments**
   (a) Settling chambers: Gravity settling of particulate matter is the basic principle of its working.
   (b) Inertial separators: Using the greater inertia of the disperiod to effect the particulate gas separation.

   Inertial separators types a. Battle type b. Lowra type c. Dirst trap.

   (c) Cyclone collectors: Centrifugal force is used to precipitate the particulate matter. Types - Involute and tangential inlet collectors.
   (d) Filters: Types are fabric or clother filters (use vertical bags for separation of particulate matter), Reverse jet filter (high velocity reverse flow of air to precipitate pollutant particulatles Envelope type fabric filter (cloth envelop supported on a wire screen frame is used)
   (e) Electrostatic precipitations: (Esps's) - Electrical charging of particulates and subsequent removal on the low potential electrode.

(f) Scrubbers or wet collectors: Work on one or combination of more than one of the mechanism, like Impingement, Interception, Diffusion, condensation. Types - spray towers, ventur, scrubbers, cyclone scrubbers, packed scrubbers and mechanical scrubbers.

2. Air pollution estimating equipments

(a) High volume samplers: Works on the principle of Stoke's law. Air containing particulate matter when subjected to suction fork turns atleast 90 before passing through a horizontal filter.

(b) Beta gauge Dust monitor: Collection of dust on a glass filter paper roll and estimating the concentration using beta rays.

(c) Sampling train: Gaseous pollutants concentration is estimated using impinger, trap, manometer, flow meter, value and function pump arrangement.

(d) Cr Fluorescence SO2 Analysis: The fluorescence property of SO2 upon exposure to UV radiation is used for estimation of concentration.

(e) Chemiluminescence NOx analysis: Uses chemiluminescence producted by the reaction between NOx, and O3 for detection of NOx levels.

(f) Co Analysis: Determination of co concentration using Iodine pentoxide or Indicator tybe method or gas chromatographio method.

C. PURPOSE FOR WATER QUALITY MONITROING

Need to identify, estimate and control the concentration of various pollutants.

1. Water quality control equipments

(a) Waste water treatment plant operation: Treatment depends upon the standards of purity and quality of raw water to be obtained. Various steps - Sedimentation, Aeration, Coagulation, Flocculation, Settling, Filtration, Chlorination.

2. Water quality estimation instruments

(a) pH meter: Used to measure hydrogenion concentration of water to classify it as acidic or alkaline.

(b) Conductivity meter: To measure the conductivity of a solution.

(c) Total solids(TS): Measure of the amount of all kinds of solids in water.

(d) Total suspended solids (TSS): To find out the suspended impurities present in water.

(e) Secthi disc: To find out light penetration.

(f) Jacksons -Turbidometer To find out the turbidity of water bodies.

(g) BOD and DO: To find out the Biochemical Oxygen Demand and Dissolved Oxygen.

(h) Spectrophotometer: Works on Beer and Lambert's law which states that when monochromatic light passes through a transparent medium the rate of decrease of intensity, with the thickness of the medium is proportional to the intensity of light. Used to determine minute concentration of minerals or chemicals in water bodies.

(i) Flame photometer: Used for estimating Na, K, Ca and Li.

(j) Atomic absorption spectrophotometer: Vapourisation of water contain pollutants of metals and subsequent emission of radiation by the metal, thus estimation of concentration of metal.

(k) Infra-red spectrophotometer: Infrared spectrun (wave length) of metallic pollutant in water.

(l) Von Dorn water sampler: Works on the principle of opening and closing of the sampler at desired depths to collect water samples at depths of water body.

(m) Simple laboratory made water sampler: Simpler version of Von Dorn water sampler.

D. SOIL MONITROING PURPOSES

1. Infra red spectrophotometer: Refer water pollution.
2. Atomic absorption spectrophotometer: Refer water pollution.
3. Plasma emission spectrophotometer: Refer water pollution instrumentation.
4. Flame photometry: Refer water pollution instrumentation.
5. Eckman dredge: Consists of two hinged lid with a fixed sectional area to sample soil.

E. INSTRUMENTS USED IN PLANT AND ANIMAL STUDIES

1. Flame photometer.
2. Spectrophotometer.
3. Atomic absorption Sepctrophotometer.
4. Infra red spectrophotometer.

Nine - tenths of education is encouragement

26. REMOTE SENSING

A. INTRODUCTION

Remote sensing is the science and art of obtaining information about an object, area or phenomenan through the analysis of data acquired by a device that is not in contract with the object, area or phenomenon under

B. REMOTE SENSING TECHNIQUE

Remote sensing on one of the latest techniques, having wide range of applications in resources industry, mapping and analysis. In the present study, this technique has been used for preparation of thematic maps and analysis of various omit resources to a certain the problems of omit degradation.

C. AN IDEAL REMOTE SENSING SYSTEM

Having introduced some logic concepts, are now have the elements necessary to conceptualize and ideal remote sensing system.

1. Uniform energy source
2. A mountaineering atmosphere
3. Energy interactions at the earth surface
4. A super sensor
5. A real line data handling system
6. Multiple data users.

D. CHARACTERISTCS OF REAL REMOTE SENSING SYSTEMS

Let us consider some of the basis short comings common to all real remote sensing system in order to better understand there general operation and ability.

1. The energy sources
2. The atmosphere
3. The energy interaction at the earths surface
4. The sensor
5. The data handing systems
6. The multiple data users

E. REMOTE SENSING DATA

1. Arial photograph
2. Satellite Images
   (a) Land sat Images

(b) Spot Images
(c) Indian remote sensing satellite (IRS-1A and IRS-1B)

F. Remote Sensing Data Interpretaion

1. Photo - Interpretation technique
2. Visual interpretation techniques
3. Digital analysis techniques

G. Remote Sensing Application

1. Environmental studies
2. Forest resources survey and mapping
3. Wild life habitat analysis
4. Land use land occur analysis
5. Agriculture and crop studies
6. Waste land mapping
7. Soil survey and mapping
8. Geological and geomorphological surveys and mapping
9. Land from analysis
10. Urban surveys and mapping and
11. Marine resources.

8

Environmental Mutagenesis

1. INTRODUCTION
2. HISTORY
3. CELL STRUCTURE AND FUNCTION
4. AGENTS IN THE ENVIRONMENT
5. PESTICIDES
6. CONSUMER CHEMICALS
7. AIR AND WATER POLLUTION
8. RADIATIONS
9. ROUTES OF EXPOSURE
10. SOCIAL CONSEQUENCES
11. CARCINOGENESIS
12. HERETABLE DISEASES
13. MONITORING AND ASSAY SYSTEMS
14. CELLULAR IMPACTS
15. CELLULAR INDICATIORS
16. ECOLOGICAL CONSEQUENCES
17. TEST SYSTEMS
18. MODULATORS OF THE EFFECTS
19. PERSPECTIVES
20. INDIAN SITUATION

Syllabus

A. THEORY

1. Introduction to Genetics: Mitosis, Meiosis, Chromosomes & Genes
2. Introduction to Toxicology: Organs, Systems and Genetic Material
3. Chemicals and radiations in human environment
4. Exposure due to accidents, usage, consumption, occupation & ecology
5. Genetic effects from chemicals and radiations
6. Clastogenecity, Aneugenecity and Mutagenecity
7. Promutagenesis, Comutagenesis and Supermutagenesis
8. Carcinogenesis, teratogenesis and heritable diseases
9. Human genetic syndromes
10. Modulations
10. Monitoring Principles
11. Laboratory and Field Assay systems: microbial, plant, insect, mammalian, human etc
12. In situ mutagenesis and Current Trends
13. Regulation: Legal, Social, Scientific, Education

References

1. Berg K(ed) 1979. Genetic damage in man caused by environmental agents. Academic press.
2. Brusick, D. 1980. Principles of Genetic Toxicology. Plenum
3. Crow, JF. 1983. Indentifying and Estimating the genetic impact of Chemical Mutagens. National Academy of Sciences, U.S.A.
4. de Serres, F.J and Hollaender, A. 1970-980. (eds). Chemical Mutagens. Vol. 1-14 + Plenum Press.
5. Kilbey, B.J. et al (ed) 1984. Handbook of Mutagenicity test procedures. Elsevier Sci. Publ.
6. Mendelsohn, M.L and Albertini, R.J. (eds) 1990. Mutation and the Environment (vols 1-5), Wiley-Liss.
7. Moutschen, J 1985. Introduction to Genetic Toxicology, Wiley
8. Sharma, C.B.S.R., et al 1984. Envrionmental Genetic Toxicology in India. A Survey. Environmental Mutagen Society of India. B.A.R.C., Bombay, India.

1. INTRODUCTION

A. DEFINITION

Chemicals and radiations in the environment enter organisations including man, directly or indirectly. They often affect the genetic material of the recepient systems altering their characteristics. Such alterations pose long term risks to human health, among others, without any forewarning. Therefore these agents - Genotoxins or Mutagens - carry an hitherto unprecedented hazard to human welfare.

1. Quantum of receipt
   (a) lethal, sublethal, acute, subacute, chronic
   (b) LD 50, Does response, Thresholds.
2. Change in the work objectives
   (a) Produce mutations for they may be useful in agriculture — hoping for positives
   (b) Screen for mutations for they may be harmful for man— hoping for negatives

B. TOXICOLOGY OF MODERN LIFE: HUMAN ACTIVITIES

1. Technology

(a) Industry : The cause
(b) Labour force : The effected
(c) Products : agents (?)
(d) Pollutants : air agents, Water,Soil

2. Human Settlements

(a) Hygiene : Disease: Drugs
(b) Life style : Dyes, cosmetics
(c) Consumption : Foods, food products, air, water, Naturals, contaminants of pesticidal origin

3. Ecosystems

(a) Agroecosystem : agriculture, aquaculture
(b) In situ situations
(c) example: USA
   1. 50,000 waste dumps 25 tons annually
   2. 14,000 of these turn dangerous doing the next 10-15 years
   3. Superfung to manage dumps

4. Bribing attempts on Sierra Leone (successful)
5. Toxic dump (1974-52) at Niagara falls

(d) Example: INDIA

1. 17 dumping cities,
2. 4,000 factories
3. 50% of foods contaminated; % above limits
4. Water is much contaminated and passes through food chain
5. Air is equally contaminated

C. CHEMICALS IN OUR LIFE

1. Some basic information
   - (a) about 4-5 millions, mostly during the last 40 years (i.e 10000/month) 10,000 added annually (1977)
   - (b) about 50 -70,000 in active use: for 80% no toxicity data
   - (c) less than screened, hardly 1% of these are mutagens
   - (d) carcinogens, 90% of which are mutagens (about 500 - 1000)
   - (e) most serious chemicals: 1000.
2. Routes of exposure - usage and consumption
3. Important chemicals of hazard potential thalidomide, Hycanthone,Cyclamates, furfury Furamide, Nitropyrenes, Chlossform, formadehyde, alcohol chloramphericol, ethycene glycol.
4. Strees indices of these chemicals vary pesticides maximum
5. Ist order risk in the west, Vth order risk in India
6. 204 chemicals in the air by 67 large companies in US
7. US production: 1940 - 2 Bkg
   1950 - 11 Bkg
   1979 - 114 Bkg
8. Actual number tested so far: 3,500 - gentoxicity
9. Actual number tested so far: 1,500 - tumrogenicity
10. Rs.55-60,000 crores to run tests on animals in Denmark

D. BASIC HAZARDS AND THEIR CHARACTERISTICS

1. Characteristics of toxicity - Old and New.

Conventional Toxicity	*New Toxicity* *Pestilence stealeth in darkness*
(a) Initiation is sooner Vertical transmission Horizontal Transmission	(a) Initiation taken long time through reproduction (the efi through food chain (the agent)
(b) Neither horrizontal nor vertical in transmission	(b) Often vertical
(c) Sources and impact of dosage, identity of toxins are known	(c) Often unknown, Arose due to chemcalisation of environment, food chain, consumerism, etc.
(d) Cause and effect relationship well established	(d) Cause of effect relationship difficult
(e) Responses vary - lethal, acute, subacute, sublethal and Threshold	(e) The effects are often chronic, independent of these
(f) Recoverable, cure usual	(f) No recovery, cure impossible. Irreversible Beginning of the end.
(g) Reflexes function as	(g) No warning signal alarm signals
(h) No latency period	(h) Time lag between exposure and effect (3-7 years)
(i) Non-genetic, population at risk will not multiply	(i) Genetic. Affected population at risk may multiply with each generation
(j) Inhalation, Dermal,Neuro Reproductive toxicities	(j) Carcinogenesis, Teratogenesis and hereditary diseases
(k) Temporary burden occupational, familial, social	(k) Lasting Social burden

2. Genetic Material is effected

Genotoxicity, causing Cancers birth defects and heretable diseases, sterility, senility, cataract, mental illnesses etc.

(a) Mutagenesis

1. 4,000 genetic abnormalities
2. Some naturally exist but detrimental only in homozygous state

(b) Teratogenesis

1. 2-5% of all births defective
2. Mental illness about 1%

(c) Carcinogenesis

1. 40-55% raise between 1960-80 in 28 developed countries (males)
2. By 2000 A.D. expected to be an epedimic in the developing world too
3. 20-40% of all future cancer deaths due to 6 compounds - asbestos As, Cr, Ni, Benzene, Petroleum factories
4. 35% causation from diet chemicalisation (Amer. Cancer Society)
5. About 500 are suspected to be carcinogens out of all scres (i.e. about 1-10%)
6. Less than 10% Cancer deaths only are due to commercial and industrial chemicals.
7. Diesel exhaust carcinogenic - in Japan

E. TRANSDISCIPLINARY NATURE

1. Cylology : many endpoints are cellular
2. Genetics : many effects are heretable
3. Medicine : many diseases currently treated are actually genetic or chemical toxic symptoms and not biotic
4. Biochemistry : many modulators are biochemical in nature; e.g. enzymes
5. Molecular Biology : many sites of action are actually DNA regions many essay systems resulted from molecular biology research
6. Ecology : many agents are ambient, in mixtures pass through food chain
7. Sociology : Ultimately all effects lead to a social burden; stress group identification.

F. DETRIMENT INDEX

The concept of detriment index was developed by an Indian born Dutch scientist Sankaranarayanan and a Hungarian Scientist Czizel based on the Hungarian Health Statistics, probably the best maintained in the world. According to this concept every genotoxic effect restricts the normal life of the victim by bestowing its characteristic effects. To this extent the individual suffers a detriment,i.e.loss of work, productivity, self improvement and ability to contribute to common development.

The detriment is expressed in three ways. 1.Years of lost life [LL]. 2. Potentially impaired life [PIL] and 3.Actually impaired life [AIL].These indicators are derived from the frequencies of 26 common multifactorial diseases [6500/100,000].These diseases are classified as very severe, moderately severe and less severe. With the aid of some complicated statistical and clinical analysis it was estimated that these diseases caused about 2700 years of LL, 96,000 years of PIL and 5800 years of AIL per 100,000 individuals of Hungarians. The multifactorial diseases seem to cause greater detriment than the mendelian ones.

Formal education will make you a living; self education will make you a fortune

2. HISTORY

A. ORIGINS: 1925-45

1. Occupational cancer of the scrotum due to root - Pott 1775
2. Discovery of mutagenesis through radiations
   (a) Muller: X-rays in Drosophila (b) Stadler: X-rays in M
3. Discovery of cell transformation in bacteria
   (a) Griffiths (1928) - Pneumococcus - Smooth = Rough / capsulated
4. Discovery of Cell Transduction
   (a) Hershey & Chase (1952) - E. Coli Bacteriophage T2

B. PERIOD OF INNOCENCE: 1945-65:

1. Discovery of chemical mutagenesis -
   (a) Robson & Auerbach
   (b) Oehlkers
   (c) Rappaport
      1. mustard gas acted like x-rays
      2. Nitrous acid mutagenic in Aspergillus
      3. Allyl isothiocyanate, uzethane & formaldehyde also are mutagenic
2. Major advances in molecular biology
   (a) Avery et al : DNA is the genetic material
   (b) Watson & Crick : DNA structure elucidated
   (c) Kornberg : Bio synthesis of DNA achieved
   (d) Ochoa : Bio synthesis of RNA achieved
3. Environmental sources of mutagenic agents
   (a) Chemical warfare
      1. Experiments during Second World War
      2. Vietnam
      3. Iran, Iraq
   (b) Atomic explosions
      1. After math of Hiroshima and Nagasaki
      2. Fall out from Nuclear tests at Bikini
      3. Chernobyl
   (c) Crow's committee
      (i) International Committee for protection against Radiation (ICPR) established

4. Pediatric survey for birth defects
   (a) UK (b) British Columbia
5. Many cancer drugs are mutagens
   (a) Many carcinogens are also mutagens

C. ADVENT OF SUSPICION 1965-70: Evidence Accumulation

1. Pesticides, Foods, Drugs
2. Pest resistance due to mutagenic pesticides
   (a) nitrosamines : linked to Cancer, UK
   (b) cyclamates : cancer in USA, banned
   (c) Thalidomide : birth defects in Europe
   (d) Pest resistance : all over world
3. Pesticides through food chain
   (a) Nitrosamines linked for Cancer
   (b) Pesticide residues get food bio-magnified
4. Naturals through food chain
   (a) Cycasin : activated
   (b) Aflatoxins : UK, USA and Thailand
5. Pediatric survey for genetic diseases in British Columbia and United Kingdom
6. Specific Episodes
   (a) Radiations from Nuclear Reactor : 3-mile island, USA
   (b) Radiations from Nuclear Reactor : Hokkaido island
   (c) Radiations from (fail out) Explosions : Bikini island
   (d) Radiations from a fire accident in the reactor. Several countries are affected : Chernobyl
   (e) Betel Quid habit : Oral Cancer in India
   (f) Habits: brew of Tea in West Indies : Qesophagal cancer
   (g) Aflatoxins from peanuts meal originating in Brazil : (i) Turkey and Fowl mortality in UK
   (ii) Fish hatcherie in USA, 1960
   (h) Aflatoxins from peanuts : Liver Cancer in Thailand

(i) Oesophageal cancer in a country in UK : Nitrosoamines
(j) Furfuryl fuarmide : Stomach cancer in Japan
(k) Cyclamates banned : Stomach cancers reduced
(l) Herbicides 3,4,5-T,2,4-D : Vietnam war
(m) Mercury from effluents Fish-Man : Minamata disease-Japan
(n) Wastes : Love Canal, USA

7. Soil (Plewa, Orton) Air (Schairer, Ichikawa, Fishbein) Sewage (Bond) Effluents (Klekowski): Mutagenic
8. Mutations relationship with hereditary diseases, Cancer and birth defects strongly suspected.

D. AGE OF UNDERSTANDING (1970-): Realisation of the hazard

1. ICEMs (1967 - 73, 77, 81, 85 & 89) Environmental Mutagen Society
2. ICPEMC: International Committee for Protection against Environmental Mutagens and Carcinogens
3. UN recognition - through WHO, ILO, IARC
4. Journals & Publications - initiated

E. MILESTONES: Important developments

1927 - Discovery of physical mutagenesis by Muller

1945 - Discovery of chemical mutagenesis by Auerbach

Replication, transcription, translation, regulation processes elucidated.

Antineoplastic drugs and mutagenecity inter-relationships suspected

1956 - Internatiomal Commission for protection against Radiation (ICPR)

1968 - Crow's article - Chemical risk to future generations

1970 - Gopal - Iyengar - Vegetation as a detector

1972 - Sparrow - Accidental gaseous mutagen at ORNL

1973 - Environmental Mutagen Information Centre (EMIC) established Activation of chemicals to mutagens

1975 - Ames test - mutation & Cancer concordance 80-90%, Sugimura - Matsushima circles

1973 - Sister chromatid Exchange test developed by Perry

1975 - Committee, 17 under Drake reviewed Mutagenic hazards

1977 - International Conference on Environmental Mutagens (ICMR).

1979 - International Commission for protection against Environmental Mutagens and carcinogens organised (ICPEMC)

1980 - Genetoprogramme initiated by the E.P.A of USA

1980 - National Toxicology programme initiated in USA

1980 - International Registry of potentially Toxic Chemicals (IRPTC)

1981 - ICEM International Conference on Envirnmental Mutagens (ICEM)

1983 - International Programme for Chemical Safety (IPCS)

1983 - Automation (flow cytometry introduced into Mutation Research

1983 - National Academy of Sciences (USA) reviewed the state of the art regarding environmental Mutagens (ICEM)

F. BREAK THROUGHS: Major Achievements

1. Consequences of genotoxicity - teratogenecity, carcinogenicity and heretable diseases - thoroughly established
2. Standardization of various test systems
3. Detoxification of mutagens is a possibility
4. Plant activation of pesticides suspected by plewa
5. Activation of non mutagens to mutagens via liver (Promutagens).
6. Synergism of certain chemicals to cause mutations (Comutagenesis)
7. Antimutagenesis of plant pigments, vitamins and placental factors
8. Supermutagenesis of hycanthone
9. Discovery of Nitropyrenes, nitrosamines as the most dreaded genotoxins
10. Banning of several chemicals - Cyclamates, Thalidamide, AF-2

G. INTERNATIONAL SCENE

1. Historical

(a) Edinburg : Institute of Animal genetics

(b) Moscow : Institute of Genetics

2. Pioneers

(a) Oak Ridge National Laboratory? USA

(b) Brookhaven National Laboratory, USA

(c) National Institute of Genetics
(d) University of Leiden, Holland

3. **Leaders:** Institutions
   (a) National Institutions of Environmental Health Sciences, USA
   (b) University of Leiden,Holland e. Bhabha Atomic Research Centre, India
   (c) National Institute of Occupational Safety and Health, USA
   (d) National Institute of Toxicology, USA
4. **Leaders:** Individual
   (a) Auerbach (b) Hollaender
   (c) Sobels (d) Deserres
   (e) Ames (f) Huberman
   (g) Loprieno (h) Evans
5. **Leaders:** Systems
   (a) Microbes : Kada (b) Yeast : Zimmermann
   (c) Drosophila : Sobels (d) Fish : Kligerman
   (f) Birds : Bloom (g) Humans : Obe, Evans
   (h) Plants : Grant
6. **Periodicals**
   (a) Environmental mutagenesis (presently Env. & Mol. mutagenesis)
   (b) Mutagenesis, Teratogenesis and Carcinogenesis
   (c) Newsletter of EMS USA
   (d) Newsletter of EMSI
   (e) Newsletter of EMIC
   (f) Newsletter of Mutagenesis
   (g) Mutation research

H. INDIAN SCENE

1. **Historical**
   (a) Mehra: Plant system b. Gopal Iyengar: in situ monitoring
2. **Pioneers**
   (a) Kalyani University (b) Calcutta University
   (c) Cancer Research Institute
   (d) Bhabha Atomic Research Centre
3. **Leaders:** Institutions
   (a) Osmania University (b) Calcutta University
   (c) Cancer Research Institute

   (d) Bhabha Atomic Research Centre
   (e) Industrial Toxicology Research Centre

4. **Leaders:** Individuals
   (a) Kesavan - New Delhi b. Vaidya - Poona c. Kaul - Jammu
5. **Thrust areas:** Agents
   (a) Radiations b. Pesticides c. Drugs
6. **Thrust areas -** Systems
   (a) Plants b. In vivo mammals
7. **Contributions**
   (a) EMSI (1947)
   (b) Annual Conference
   (c) News letters
   (d) Workshops
   (e) Symposia

A little knowledge that acts is worth infinitely more than much knowledge that is idle.

3. CELL STRUCTURE AND FUNCTION

A. GENERAL FRAME WORK:

1. Chief differences between plant & animal cells & unicellular organisms.
   (a) Cell wall, Centrosomes, pigments
   (b) Extra cellular architecture of unicellular organisms.
2. Various organelles of a 'typical' cell
   (a) Boundaries: Cell wall and plasmalemma
   (b) Cytoplasmic organelles & ground plasm: Ground plasm, Endoplasmic reticulum, ribosomes, dictyosomes, Lysosomes, mitochondria, plastids, vacuoles, Centrosomes.

B. BOUNDARY SYSTEMS

1. Cell wall:
   (a) Chemical composition: Cellulose, Pectin, Lignin etc.
   (b) Fibrillar organization,
   (c) Middle lamella and development of walls.
   (d) Nature of walls in different organisms
   (e) Permeability & mechanical strength.
2. Plasmalemma:
   (a) Lipoproteinous,
   (b) Semipermeability
   (c) Membrane lability for protrusions & invaginations.

C. CYTOPLASMIC STRUCTURES

1. Ground plasm:
   (a) Nature:homogeneous plasma;
   (b) Ectoplasm & endoplasm;
   (c) cytonemata;
   (d) Gelation & solution:
   (e) Theories of organization: Emulsion, Fibrillar, Granular & alveolar theories.
   (f) Function.
2. Endoplasmic reticulum:
   (a) Discovery: Palade & Porter (1954)
   (b) Occurrence: In most cells except in prokaryotes
   (c) Nomenclature

(d) Structure:
1. Tubular or Vesicular
2. Cisternae, Lumen, hyaloplasm;
3. Smooth or rough.

(e) Ultrastructure:
1. Interlacing hollow system;
2. Number & location vary;
3. Lumen & enchylema;
4. Accessory nuclei.

(f) Function:
1. Intracellular transport;
2. Protein & carbohydrate synthesis
3. Mitochondrial function during anaerobiosis

(g) Origin:
1. de noveo:
2. Invagination of plasmalemma:
3. From nuclear envelope.

3. Ribosomes
   (a) Terminology: Microsomes, ribosomes, polysomes.
   (b) Ribosomes:
      1. Discovery: Palade (1953)
      2. Synonyms: Ergastoplasm, Nissl bodies (nerve cells)
      3. Occurrence: Association with E.R., in all active cells.
      4. Properties & function:Basophily,Ribonucleoprotein, protein synthesis.
4. Lysosomes:
   (a) Discovery; de Duve (1950-57)
   (b) Occurrence: Kidney and spleen
   (c) Structure: Membrane bound, granular
   (d) Function: Lysia of foreign bodies and lysis of decrepit cells of an organism (tail of tadpole)
   (e) Comparison with phagosome
5. Golgi complex or dictyosomes:
   (a) Discovery: Golgi 1898; Lipochondria (Baker 1957), Dictyosomes (Heslop-Harrison 1965)
   (b) Structure :
      1. Smooth canalicular ystems with double membrane
      2. Vesicles with inflated extensions
   (c) Constitution:
      1. Fluidy interior 2. Phospholipids & Phosphatases.

(d) Occurrence:

1. Mostly in animals, less in plants
2. Polar, scattered, circumnuclear
3. Small, Large, reticulate

(e) Origin:

1. From nuclear envelope 2. Special differentiation of ER.

(f) Function:

1. Water balance, Secretary
2. Synthesis of mucilage, Hemicellulose
3. Cell wall matrix and phragmoplast (Heslop-Harrison 1965)

6. Centrosomes:
   (a) Occurrence: Animals, sperm cells of ferns & gymnosperms; in plants: Only as a diffuse polar body.
   (b) Structure: 2 Centrioles surrounded by 9 peripheral triplets.
   (c) Function: Spindle formation during cell division.
7. Microtubules
   (a) Characteristics: Ectoplasmic, closer to centrioles or scattered microfilaments, (Bajer & Mole-Bajer 1967).
   (b) Function: Skeletal, Contractile, chromosomal movement in dividing cells.
8. Vacuoles
   1. Plant cells have large central sap vacuoles
   2. Animal cells, Pinosomes, phagosomes, contractile vacuoles.
   3. Membrane bound.
9. Mitochondria
   (a) Occurrence:
      1. Universal, granular or rod-shaped
      2. Aggregations in characteristic manner in muscle, nerve and secretory cells.
      3. More active in dividing cells.
      4. Stained by Janus green B.
   (b) Chemistry: Protein (65-70%), Lipid (25-30%), DNA (0.5%) etc.
   (c) Structure: 1. Typical double membrance;
      2. Tubular or cylindrical
      3. Cristae

(d) Function: 1. Power house of the cell (Siekevitz 1957)
2. Energy supply to the cites of synthesis.

(e) Origin: 1. From mocrobodies:
2. From membrane system:
3. Transformation of symbiont into organelle.

(f) General information:
1. Division during cell division
2. Traces of DNA of a primitive nature
3. Symbiotic theory.

10. Plastids
   (a) Types: Leucoplasts, chloroplasts, Chromoplasts
   (b) Chloroplasts: 1. Shapes, number, size 2. Protein (56%) & Lipids (32%), chlorophyll (8%) & traces of DNA of a primitive type 3. Behaviour in hypotonic & hypertonic solutions 4. Disappearance in darkness 5. Structure: Lamellar, grana, stroma, quantasomes 6. Origin from amoeboid proplastids 7. relationship with motochondria 8. Transformation of a symbiont into organelle.

D. NUCLEAR ORGANELLES: Nucleus: nucleolus, chromosomes and nuclear membrane.

1. Nucleus:
   (a) Introduction: Discovery (Brown), Fundamental unit of life, prochromosomal and metachromosomal systems, eukaryotic, protokaryotic & dinokaryotic organisation, classification.
   (b) Morphology: Nucleocytoplasmic ratios, number, position & size variations, tazonomic value, nuclear uniformity, chromocenters, karyomeres.
   (c) Structure: nuclear membrane, nucleolus, chromosomes.
      1. Nuclear membrane: Elastic, 2-layered, lipoproteinous, continuous with E.R., significance.
      2. Nucleolus: Busch, Sirlin
         (a) Introduction: discovery,nonmembranous, movements, variablity occurrence, nucleolonema & pars amorpha.
         (b) Chemistry: RNA, RN protein turnover, relationship with cytoplasmic RNA.
         (c) Function: role in spindle organization, protein synthesis, Matrix, nucleolonema & ontomutation

(d) Formation: prenucleolar bodies & their assembly, Nucleolar organising chromosome.

3. Chromosomes

(a) Introduction: discovery, definition, role.

(b) Morpholoty: number, size variations, shapes & other characteristics, taxonomic importance of numbers, polidy levels & their significance.

(c) Karyotype: Chromosome complements, symmetrical & asymmetrical karyotypes.

(d) Structure: Brachea, Primary & secondary Construction

1. Primary construction: centromere, kinetochore, localised of diffused, or dicentric or polycentric, position characteristic, autonomous, structure: micell, spherule or granule theory, function: responsible for the diagnostic shapes of chromosomes & anaphase movements, chemistry.
2. Secondary construction: Olisthrzone, nucleolar or satellited, tertiary intercalary, heterochromatin, spiralisation.
3. Satellites: terminal or inter calary, micromacro and linear.
4. Telomeres: extremities of brachea, heterochromatic, affinity towards nuclear membrane.
5. Brachea: Matrix, chromation-eu-and heterochro-matin. Chromonemata-major and minor coils, coiled coil hetero-, homobrachial, heterochromatin & eu chromatin heterogeniety in banding and replication patpterns heteropyknosis, Nucleic acids & protein & their distribution, types of heterochromatin & their function, comings, Casperson, Lima-de-Faria, White.
6. Strandedness of chromosomes: 2,4, strands, multistranded, steffensen's model. Fibrils and their sizes. Ris, Mazia, Kaufmann.
7. Chromosome models: arrangement of chemicals in the chromosme (a. protein backbone hypothesis (b. Protein-bridge hypothesis (c. Super coil (d. rope (e. differential coiling hypothesis. Taylor, Steffensen, Dupraw.
8. Gene structure and chemical nature of chromosomes: Gene-DNA, RNA, Nucleoprotein, chromomere, interchromomere.

(e) Types of chromosomes:

1. autosomes
2. Sex 2- chromosomes
3. B-chromosomes
4. polytene
5. Lampbrush
6. Coccid-type chromosomes.

(a) Autosomes: brachea, primary & secondary constructions, satellites, telomeres.

(b) Sex chrosomes: Sex / Chromatin, X,Y,Z, etc; Mittwoch

(c) B-chromosomes:supernumarary or accessory, Maize Rye, Sorghum etc., acro-or metacentric; mitotically stable or unstable; origin; significance; Ostergren's parasitic theory' phenotypic effects: Muntzing, Hones, Ostergren, White.

(d) Polytene chromosomes: Discovery by Balbiani, occur in the salivary glands of Dipteran larvae; Drosophila: 6 strands of fused chromosomes; chromocenter; polyteny: painter, white & Gall; bands interbands, waists, doublets, capsules, puffs,-Beerman's work. Polytene chromosomes in plants.

(e) Lampbrush chromosomes: Diplotene chromosomes of oocytes in sharks, amphibians, reptiles and birds. Structure: Chromomeres, loops, their spinning out as functioning of the genes, dynamics of loop behaviour and heterozygosity, wooly nature, chemistry of the loop, chromomere and interchromomeric axis.

Analogy between lampbrush and polytene chromosomes and the role of polyteny and loops.

(f) Coccid-type: Luzula purpurea, Homoptera etc. Centromeric activity diffuse. Brown, Battaglia.

E. MITOSIS

1. Introduction: Nuclear division with equitable chromosomal distribution.
2. Discovery: Flemming, strassburger, Hertwig.
3. Mitotic rate, time and length of mitosis during which organisms frow depend upon adult size.
4. Mitotic components - chromatic and achromatic, mitotic stages.
5. Intranuclear mitosis in Barbulanympha mitotic durations in different organisms.
6. Cell division cycle: G1 S G2 M and C phase, and their relative durations in different systems — interphase— hydration—visibility and optical properties: Howard and Pete, Taylor, Kimber.
7. Characteristics of G1, S, G2, M and C phases.

F. PROPHASE:

1. Nucleus spherical, increases in turgidity, refractive index, surface tension and cytoplasmic pH.
2. Progressive dehydration and coiling increase chromosomal visibility.
3. Minimal chromosomal separation and relational and relic coils.
4. Nucleoli and nuclear membrane disappear.
5. Telomeric points of contact with nuclear membrane
6. Chromosome condensation and centrifugal movement.

G. PROMETAPHASE AND SPINDLENORGANIZATION:

1. Spindle organization from polar caps or centrosome
2. Types of spindle: pointed, truncated or flared out at the pole, unipolar multipolar, — continuous, chromosomal and interzonal fibres—Direct and indirect mitosis (Schrader 1953).
3. Nature of spindle, isolation of spindle (Mazia & Dan 1954)
4. Microtubules - cytoplasmic, centromeric and chromosomal microtubules. (Bajer and Mole - Bajer 1969).

H. METAPHASE:

1. Chromosome movements consist of Congression, Orientation and Distribution.
2. Diplochromosomes - paranemic or plectonemic - centromere division.
3. Chromosomal distribution - hollow spindle.

I. ANAPHASE:

1. Chromatid separation and their further movement towards poles - factors affecting movement - laggards and forwards - theories of chromosome movement.
2. Movement of chromosomes synchronous
3. Haplo chromosomes.

J. TELOPHASE:

1. Chromosomes decondense, converge, relic coils
2. Reverse of prophase, prenucleolar bodies, nucleolar organization.
3. DNA content half of prophase nuclei

K. CYTOKINESIS:

1. No cytokinesis in coenocytic algae
2. Can occur without karyokinesis - sea urchin

3. Plants cell plate formation - dictyosomes - phragmoplast- future middle lamella.
4. Animals: Furrowing by astral cleavage, or disjunctive.

L. SIGNIFICANCE:

1. Constancy of species maintained, transmission of same genetic material.
2. Linear heredity established
3. Failure of cytokinesis, breakage, unequal segregation of daughter chromosomes, if perpetuated, lead to diversity within species.

M. AMITOSIS: TAPETAL DIVISIONS

N. ENDOMITOSIS

Endoduplication, ploidy and DNA, endoprophase, and metaphase etc. differentialed tissues.

Deviations from normal behaviour:

1. Acceleration, depression, induction and inhibition of mitosis.
2. G1, S, G2 - initiated effects and their appearance in Mitosis = chromosomal and microtubular - spindle and cytokinesis.
3. Consequences of deviations.

O. MEIOSIS

1. Discovery by Hertwig, strassburger, Von Beneden, Weismann.
2. Meiosis is coexistant with functional bisexuality - an antithesis of fertilization.
3. Modification of two mitotic divisions where chromosomes divide only once.
4. Separation of homologous chromosomes of maternal and paternal origin.
5. Types: initial, intermediary or terminal
6. Stages: Prophase (leptotene, zygotene, amphitene, pachytene, diplotene dictyotene, diakinesis — prometaphase — metaphase— anaphase—telophase— cytokinesis, Riley, Bennett, Stern, Hotta.

Leptotene : Nuclei larger, DNA replication, beaded appearance, attraction between chromosome ends.

Zygotene: Mating thread stage, synapsis—proterminal, procentric, intermediate-between homologues.

Amphitene: Synezesis of synapsed chromosomes

Pachytene : long stage, nucleolus prominent, bivalents, 4- stranded chromosome contraction, crossing over of segments.

Diplotene : Wooly appearance, condensation, chiasmata— variability, beginning of terminalization, lampbrush chromosomes.

Dictyotene: Unusual, in mosses, sudden elongation (Dill)

Diakinesis: Maximum condensation and terminalization

Nature of chiasmata: Crossing over, chiasmata, chiasmata frequency, terminalization quotient, breakage - union, precocity, synaptinemal complex, equational - reductional nature, 3 - strand and 4 - strand doubles, chiasma interferrence; Moses, Moens, Darlington.

Prometaphase: dyad, bivalent, centromeres lying face to face, origin of spindle material, microtubules.

Metaphase I: dyads move to different poles, no centromere division maximum chromosome condensation, chiasmata completely terminalize-position of interchiasmatal loops.

Anaphase I: diplochromosomes, genetically reduced (where no crossing over took place) and genetically equational (crossing over took place). segregation of homelogues of paternal and maternal origin. May directly enter prophase - II or Metaphase II.

Telophase I: relaxation of chromosome coiling, regrouping of chromosomes. No synthesis of nucleolus. May directly enter prohpase II.

Cytokinesis I: phragmoplast formation, furrowing etc.

Successive type

Prophase II |
Metaphase II |
Anaphase II |—— as in mitosis
Telophase II |
Cytokinesis II |

End products of meoisis: eggs, spores, sperms, haploid organisms.

Cell cycle: Several days in Barley, wheat, G1, S, G2 phase S-phase in one of the early prophases, synthesis at the time of crossingover, importance of bud size, meiotic stages and biochemical phase correlations.

Genetic significance:

1. Logical necessity as an opposite of fertilization, in transmission of parental charactors.
2. Source of variability: segregational and recombinant.
3. Crossing over percentages and linkage groups

4. Study of homology between segments
5. Differential distribution of genes in the 1st. and 2nd. divisions: Equational as well as reductional.
6. Modification of 2 mitoses: (a) instead of 2 heplochromosomes of 2 homologues, diplochromosome of 1 only goes to pole (b) segments of these diplochromosomes partially changed and (c) contromere did not divide.
7. A force in evolution through variability | — slow and gradual-conservative |

P. CELLULAR DYNAMICS OF SOURCE, APPEARANCE AND CONSEQUENCES OF GENOTOXIC EFFECTS OF ENVIRONMENTAL CHEMICALS

Location of effect	*Appearance of phases*				*Consequence*
	p	*m*	*a*	*t*	
1. G1, S	Asynchrony *				Inhibition, Acceleration Retardation, Lesions
2. G2					MT dysfunction, Subchromatid exchanges
3. Sphase: Lesions					
a. Non rapair-deletion	Mn	K	fragment	Mn	Altered
b. Non restitutive repair-					
1. Invertion	-	-	bridge	bridge	linkage
2. Translocation	-	K	bridge	bridge	
3. Duplication	-	K	-	-	groups
4. Microtubule function					
a. Partial dysfunction	-	K NC, ND	Lagging forwards	Mn	2n-2 and Mn 2n-1
b. Centromere dysfunction	Non dis-junction				2n+1 2n+2
5. Cytokinesis	2p	2m	2a	4n	Aneugenesis(?)

Homologues Diplochromosomes linkage groups altered affect the daughter cells and gametes from deletions, additions and position effects.

K = Karytotype, NC = noncongression, ND = Nondisjunction,
Mn = Micronucleus. *Synchrony may be lost fully or partially.

4. AGENTS IN THE ENVIRONMENT

A. RADIATIONS

1. Medical, ecological, accidental exposure
2. UV rays naturally increase in some habitats South Africa Queensland
3. X-rays - medical doses - frequent exposure
4. Y-rays - nuclear leaks and accidents
5. Low ionized radiations - Natural - monozite - India

B. COSMETICS

1. Natural - Turmeric, Henna
2. Hairdyes - 2 Nitro-p-phenylenediamine(ZNOPD)-major component
3. Skin tanners
4. Amines in dyes and other aids
5. Heavy metals in some creams

C. DYES

1. Drugs, Cosmetics, foods
2. Acridines
3. Amines
4. Metanil Yellow

D. PESTICIDES

1. Agricultural residues
2. Dichlorvos
3. Triazines
4. Dioxins
5. PCBs - Sterility (100 million sperms/ml-60-20)

E. HABITS

1. Chewing Tobacco, areca nut
2. Alcoholism
3. Smoking: 1300 tons of Benzopyrenes in USA/Year

F. DRUGS

1. Overdosing, longer use side effects
2. Quinacrine (Atabrino) antimaterial
3. Isoniazid – antitubercular

4. Thalidomide - tranquilizer
5. Chllamphenicol – antibiotic
6. Hycanthon - Schistosomiasis
7. Psoralences - Skin diseases
8. Methyl pyrilene
9. Sedatives
10. Librium, Antabuse release nitrosamines

G. INDUSTRIES

1. Vinyl chloride – Polymers
2. Formaldehyde - Solvent
3. Iris
4. Dioxins - Pesticide
5. Benzo(a)pyrene - energy
6. heavy metals - electroplating
7. Styrene - Polymers
8. Pyrenes - Reprographics

H. NATURAL

1. Foods, Drugs, habits
2. Saffrole
3. Cycasin
4. Quercetin
5. Kaemferol
6. Psoralene
7. Alkaloids, flavanoids and other Natural Products. too

I. FOODS: 3000 agents approved for use of food addition, processing generatives, Metabolic modifiers.

1. Dyes
   (a) Metanil Yellow b. Amaranth - banned in Russia & West Germany
2. Beverages
   (a) Coffeine - no placental barrier, one of the most dangerous compound
   (b) nitrosamines in (Whisky, Beer-liquors)
   (c) native brews in West Indies
3. Sweetners
   (a) Sodium Cyclamate - Cyclo hexylamine
   (b) Saccharin - advantage for diabetics outweighed, No banning.
4. Naturals
   (a) Alakaloids, Flavonoids in edible plants
5. Preparation
   (a) Smoked fish, boiled steak
   (b) Pyrolytic products
   (c) Special methods in some areas of China - 100 fold Cancers

6. Preservative
   (a) NaNo2 - nitrosamines in the stomach. But inhibits sporegrowth of Clostridium, i.e. anti botulism.
7. Toxins
   (a) Due to Aflatoxins 100000 turkeys and fowl died in UK in 1960 following consumption of Peanut meal from Brazil
   (b) Fish hacheries in U.S.A.
   (c) Liver Cancer in Thailand.
8. Others
   (a) Beet & Carrot juice b. Chlorinated water c. Monosodium glutarate

J. ENERGY

Low temperature and less oxygen consumption more mutagens are produced.

1. First discovery in 1972 at ORNL in USA - Thermal Station emission caused mutations in Tradescantia
2. Pioneering work - ORNL in USA - Production, Conversion, use of energy
3. Sources Atomic, Oil, Thermal, Synfuel, Coal, Wood, Biogas
4. Wastes from any sources, mostly nitropyrenes domestic air of various cooking energy sources
   - Crude synfuel - Neutral fraction of synfuel
5. Assayed until 1984: Chemicals
   - 16 Nitro Piperidines
   - 10 fractions of Gasifier Condensates
   - Coolant & other wastes
   - Emitters in plants
   - Trimethyl phosphate added to gasoline to control surface ignition and spark plug fouling
6. Monozite industries at Always
7. 9 Nuclear Centres in India

K. POLLUTION

1. Ambient air
   (a) Differs from place to place and depends upon wind velocity and direction
   (b) absorbed by skin or inhaled c. Particulates, spores, dust

(d) Gases: C ,N ,S halogenated hydrocabons pyrenes, polycyclic aromatic hydrocarbons (PAHs)

(e) Radiations especially near nuclear reactor

2. Occupational air

   (a) Open air worksites - open mines roadlaying

   (b) Kitchens of homes and restaurants - fuel emissions Nitropyrenes, S, N , HC - Volatiles from the surfaces of food stuffs.

   (c) Inside factories - depends upon the nature of the work - Pesticides, gases, heavy metals, Pyrenes, hydrocarbons, dust

   (d) All surrounding areas near the factors

3. Water

   (a) Surface flowing water, stagnant or stored water

   (b) Agricultural channels and streams — Pesticides

   (c) Treated drinking water — chlorinated compounds

   (d) Underground water - wells and bore wells - at different depths & sites — quality variations

   (e) Treated water of effluents and sewage for reuse — complex mixtures

   (f) Water near factories, industries, mining sites, waste dumps — pollutants.

4. Soil

   (a) Wastelands and arable lands

   (b) Intensively cultivated lands - pesticides

   (c) Lands near factories, landfills, waste dumps

   (Niagara falls' dump (1947-52) at Love Canal

   (d) Lands irrigated by waste waters - pollutants

L. FACTORS

1. In situ Vs experimental
2. Ambient Vs actual
3. Synergism Vs antagonism
4. Detoxification Vs activation
5. Residues Vs excretion

5. PESTICIDES

A. INTRODUCTION

1. LDCs - Organochlorines - 50% waterbodies
   Carcinogenic Treatment more caroinogens
2. DBCP - Dibromochloropropane - banned in USA (1977) but appeared in Waters of
   Sterility: Occup - Exp. of California in 1981
   Cancers: Mammals ground water
3. Global projection of 100% more food by 2000 A.D. i.e. pesticide use also by 100%
4. Pesticide use will double by 2000 A.D.: India, Mexico & Argentina Excessive Annual increase of 9% in the third world.
5. Loss of protein from fish lossess in running waters irrigation channels, stremas, rivers, rice paddies, ponds of irrigated water in Asia, Africa and Latin America.
6. Shocks and surprises possible.
7. Indian 80,000 tons per 06/80,000,000 hectares 1982 -83 i.e. 1 ton per 06/1000 hectares.
8. Reference: Global 2000 Report.
   (a) Carcinogenic pesticides
   (b) Teratogenic pesticides
   (c) Mutagenic pesticides - Potential (microbes)
   (d) Mutagenic pesticides - Actual (mammals_
   (e) Banned pesticides
   (f) Episodes connected by pesticides – Seveso, Bhopal, Handigodu Cochin, Iraq
   (g) - Residues, - Impurities, - Degraded products
   (h) Genetic diseases in man
   (i) Genetic effects on other organisms - Pest Resistance
   (j) Genotoxicology
   (k) Agroecosystem instability
   (l) Pesticides & man & environment
   (m) Genetic ability to resist: many genes controlled
      1. intensive monoculture 2. multicropping

B. HISTORY

1. American use

(a) 12 times more than 30 years ago But crop losses before harvest doubled

(b) Lone canal incident surfaced 20 yrs after the dumping Therefore pesticide caused instability

(c) 1p1/ animal sp. disappearing everyday what then would be the rate of microbes

- disappearing or - new strain origin

2. India: Production & Use

(a) Pesticide units - largest produces in Afro-Asia next to Japan

25 = active ingredients

50 = formulations

350 = Small scale units - conventional formulations

(b) Use / Ha

1. gms 100-300-400- India: enormos poller., unscientific use/ silent process

   1500/1200 - USa *

   10000/1500 - Japan * INSPITE OF SCIENTIFIC USAGE

   2000 - Europe *

   1968 1974 55 districts

   India 400 mg 340 gm/Ha 5000 gmg/ga guntur, Ap

(c) Capacity 80,000 tons - about 30,000 tons for agriculture

(d) 325 pesticides listed in 1975 insecticide act

- All listed by WHO as toxics included

- 125 registered with central insecticide board for production

(e) New introductions in India

1. Decin - pyrethroid - French help 2. Isoprotouron - Herbicide

(f) Pests

1. Minor pests - karnal bunt - major - wheat
2. Yellow/burn rust - Punjab - epidemic - HYVsg wheat
3. Brown plant hopper (Victor also) - Kerala- Rice
4. Bust. Blight
5. Gallmidges
6. Tungro virus

Rice - either newpest strains or crops lost resistance genes

(g) Coasts higher due to airlift

Therefore

(i) blackmarketing (ii) downgrading from 50% downwards

(h) Adulteration: dimecron, furadon, Rogor, Tribunol, Dosanex, Tolkan

1. Al. phosphide against rats in India
2. EDB malthion storing proposes

3. India: Episodes

(a) Pesticide accidents

1958.	Kerala	Ethyl parathion	100	wheat
		rolisol	casualities	
1977.	UP	BHC	250	wheat
	(Lakhimpur - kheri)		Casualities	
	Sitapur - Hardn			
1977	Karnataka Handigodu	OC & Op	babies	crabs
			- young & old	fish

Dwarfs genetics environment insult on vulnerable people.

Resistance

1. 364 pests resistant to 9 major pesticides - UNEP 1979 Ann. Rep
   (a) 15 sp. of anopheles to DDT
   (b) 35 sp. of anopheles to dieldrin some to malathion also: Gujarat
   (c) MIC - honey bees
2. Resistance to pesticides from 1911 accelerated greatly from 1947
3. FAO panel experts on resistance
   1965 - first - 182 Res. Strains Cotton & rice: most aff.
   1968 - 2 - 228 Res. Strains geographical
   1977 - 3 - 364 Res. Strains arthropods
4. 223 agr. pests - Res. to 9 major groups of pesticides
5. Mosquitos and other arthropods (WHO)
   1968 - 102 15 sp. Mos - DDT - 1969
   1976 - 121 37 sp. Dieldrin - 1969
   43 " - 1976
   24 sp - DDT - 1976
6. Culex 19 – 41 between 1968 - 1975
7. Anopheles - Several cases of multiple resistance
8. Herbicides - 50% of all pesticides applied 1979

9. plant pathogens 1965-70 - negligible; 1978 -79- 35 sp. (concurrent with systemic fungicides)
10. Rodents 75p (R. norregi , R. rattus) resistant
11. Tribolium (flour beetle) multiple & cross resistance

C. AGROECOSYSTEM INSTABILITY

1. Introduction

(a) Genotoxicity and human health - teratogenicity, carcinogenecity, mutagenicity

(b) Genotoxicology and agroecosystem realities

2. Information and Inferences

(a) Indirect evidences- industrialization of agriculture in USA & in India

(b) Direct evidences

1. Mutations in rhizobia: Dube
2. Mutations in cyanophycae: Singh
3. changes in the behaviour of pollinators: Grant
4. Cotton leafworm resistance to insecticides in Egypt Hollaende & Flet
5. weeds developed resistance: Pinthes
6. Aberrant weeds recognised: Tomkins
7. spontaneous variations in plant populations in and around crop levels: Sharma, Grant
8. Experimental work in sorghum, Barley,Maize:Liang, Plewa, Singgh, Sharma
9. Experimental work in vegetables: Boyd, Stolz

(c) Circumstantial evidences

1. Mutant resistance: CSE
2. Mutant mosquitoes: CSE
3. Gypsy moth mutation in the wing colour: Ehalich
4. Strains of bugs changed from 182-364; CSE
5. Human genetic abnormalities in pesticide workers: Sasa, Park

(d) Consequences

1. Resistance to pesticides
2. Reduction of soil fertility
3. Breeding system may be modified
4. Crop perceptiblity to newer pests

5. Habit and habitat alteration of useful organisms
6. Biological balances may be upset
7. Others, yet unvisualised

3. Modulators

Acceleration and / or retardation of the original effect of pesticides depend on various factors, esecially the pesticide characteristics.

(a) direct action	:	captan, OPs: Wild, staule
(b) normal reactions	:	oxidation, reduction: Fishbein
(c) active groups	:	epoxides, phosphates halides, amines, diazos
(d) metabolites	:	diflubenzuron, fenaminosulf: Senferes, Sharma Ethylene dibromide Karenth, Scot
(e) impurities	:	CCL, DMN, EDB, Pa Dioxins
(f) interactions	:	I + H + F ——— ? Seiler Nitrosoamines
(g) plant activation	:	herbicides: Plewa
(h) detoxifications		
(i) residues	:	Biomagnifications
(j) adulteration	:	? (ink)
(k) adjuents	:	?

4. Special situations

(a) Storage practices

(b) Sewage agriculture

(c) Aquaculture

(d) Fertilisers and pesticides

1. Imbalances: hypothesis revisited
2. Humanhealth: Unsuspected hazards
3. Perceptions: Proper perspective

6. CONSUMER CHEMICALS

INTRODUCTION

The International Agency for Research on Cancer (IARC) situated at Lyon in France which is the relevent arm of the World Health Organization is steadily occupied in examining substances suspected of evoking cancer in human beings. So far they have examined 585 substances and of these only 147 presented evidence that they might cause cancer in man. They include naturally occurring substances in food, plants, chemicals, work environment, Bacteria and virus.

I. DRUGS

A. CLASSIFICATION: based on their utility (treatment)

B. DESCRIPTION OF THE FOLLOWING CLASSES OF DRUGS - PRODUCTION, CONSUMPTION & HEALTH EFFECTS

1. Acridines : Proflamine, Acriflamine. Acridine orange, 5-amino acridine and Acridine mustard.
2. Antibiotics : Mitomycin -C, Streptonigrin, Streptozotocin, Patulin, Phleomycin, Azaserine, daunomycin
3. Others : Ethidium bromide, 8-Quinolinol, Dithranol, Miracil- D, Steroid diamines, Nitrofurazone, LSD, Caffeine and 8- ethoxy caffeine.

Teratogenicity and carcinogenecity of various drugs

II. DYES

A. CLASSIFICATION: Based on mode of application, structure, etc.

B. DETAILED STUDY OF THE FOLLOWING AZO DYES REGARDING THEIR PRODUCTION, CONSUMPTION, TERATOGENECITY AND MUTAGENECITY.

Azobenzene, P-amino azobenzene, O-amino azotoluene Para-dimethyl amino azobenzene, Chrysoidine, Sudan-II Penceau MX, Trypan blue, Amaranth

C. COLOURS: indigoids and Triphenyl methane dyes in creams, shampoos, polishes, eyebrow pencils

III. COSMETICS

A. CLASSIFICATION BASED ON USAGE

B. DESCRIPTION OF THE FOLLOWING WIDELY USED COSMETIC CHEMICALS CONCERNING THEIR PRODUCTION, CONSUMPTION AND GENOTOXICITY

Styrene oxide, 1,3-propane sultone, Formaldebyde, Toluene Benzoyl peroxide, Trichloroethylene, Pthalic acid esters Fluorocarbons, Haloethers, Hydroquinone, Acetamide, Chloroform, Anthroquinone, acetamide, p-dimethylamino azobenzene.

IV. FOODS & FOOD ADDITIVES

Mutagens are so widespread in nature that even the food we eat has a great deal of them in it. Thus the different kinds of foods, feed and food additives may cause genotoxicity.

Classification based on origins: Natural / Man-Made

A. NATURAL MUTAGENS

1. Animal origin

   Foods having nitrites induce the stomach to produce dimethyl nitrosamine (Carcinogenic). Thus the mutagen is produced by the animal.

2. Microbial origin

   Products of fungi (mycotoxins) mostly food contaminants, growing on stored foods like grains, peanuts etc, or fermenting food stuffs eg. miso (fermented soyabean paste eaten by Japanese). Main mutagens are Aflatoxins from Aspergillus flavus. Most dangerous of these is Aflatoxin- B which is a confirmed hepato carcinogen. It alkylates causing DNA cross links etc.

3. Plant origin

   (a) Pyrrolizidine alkaloids eg. Monocrotaline, senecionine, lasicarpine & heliotrine etc. are mutagenic and need activation by the mixed function oxidases.

   (b) Cycasin - methylazoxymethanol B-D-glucoside from cycads activation into ultimate carcinogen by intestinal microflora. Consumed by some people.

   (c) Bracken toxin: Bracken fern (Pteridium agrilinum) eaten in Japan. carcinogenic in rats mutagenic in Drosophila etc.

   (d) Flavonoids: in green parts of commonly consumed plants. eg. Quercetin, Kaempferol, morin, fesetin, rutin etc.

   (e) Other Compounds: Allylisothiocyanate, Anthroquinone, xanthones Naphthaquinone, coumarins, cryptopleurine, Furanocoumarine, safrole Sesquiterpenes,

B. ARTIFICIAL MUTAGENS

1. Protein pyrolysis products: Pyrolysis of protein food (amino acids) produce potent promutagens (Trp-p-1 & Trp-p-2) and two comutagens (Harman & Norharman).eg. Tryptophan, Glutamic acid, lysine etc. These mutagens are thus seen in charred meat, smoke condensate, cigarette tar & natural foods. The mutagens & comutagens are activated by the mixed function oxidase and cause point mutations in DNA.
2. Lipid hydroperoxides: formed by autooxidation of unsaturated lipids leading to free radical formation causing damage to DNA structure. eg. 7,8 - dithydroxy - 9,10 epoxy -7,8,9,10. tetrahydrobenzopyrene
3. Lipid oxidation products: Malonaldehyde or intermediates in malonaldehyde formation by oxidation of lipids. Others like epoxides are also greatly mutagenic. High fat diet & high epoxide levels proved to be causes of a few cancers.
4. Carbohydrate products: from Maillard browning reaction of amino acids with carbohydrates seen in channel food like bread, biscuts etc. The aldose & ketose groups get rearranged into Amadori compound which on nitrosation gives N-nitroso compounds which are genotoxic. Caramalized sugar has thus great mutagenicity potential.
5. Cooked foods: Boiling, grilling & frying of food caused mutagen formation in them. Smoked meat has benzopyrene. Longer cooking time increases mutagenicity. Metallic cooking surfaces cause greater genotoxicity than ceramic
6. Processed food: Heating, freezing & irradiation cause the formation of mutagens in food. Finally their curing causes the retention of the mutagens in the food itself. Irradiated food contain traces of radioactivity which can cause genotoxicity.
7. Beverages: tea - Quercetin & kaempferol mutagenic. Coffee - caffeine mutagenic. Alcohol -Acetylene carcinogenic. tannin - cocarcinogenic with acetylene.
8. Food additives
   (a) Antioxidants - butylated hydroxyamisole
   (b) Sequestrants - EDTA - Chromosomal aberrations
   (c) Colouring agents - flavonoids - Quercetin, morin, kaempferol etc. Tannins - cocarcinogenic. Quinones - Anthra & naphtha, Xanthones , Safrole, carcinogenic.
   Synthetic colours - coal tar derivatives.

(d) Flavones
(e) Curing agents: Sodium nitrite - Promutagen
(f) Flavour improvers: Chlorine, benzoylperoxide,
(g) Sweetners: Saccharin, cyclamate - carcinogens.
(h) Preservatives: epoxides - ethylene oxide, Dielthylpyro-carbonate, ethylcarbomate (carcinogens), tetracyclins teratogenic

V. NATURAL COMPOUNDS

A. NITRATE ACCUMULATING PLANTS: Spinach, beets, cabbage, carrot, celery, lettuce and raddish, Mithanenogalobinaemia.

B. TOXIC PROTEINS: Soyabean and Kidney bean, Haemagglutinin (glycoproteins)

C. TOXIC AMINOACIDS: Lathyrus sativus, lathyrogen

D. CYANOGENETIC GLYCOSIDES IN PLANT PRODUCTS: Almonds, apricots, peeaches, plums and cherries, Amygdalin.

E. SULPHUR CONTAMING TOXICANTS: Cabbage, Cauliflower, Mustrad and Allylisothio cyanate.

F. NARCOTICS
   1. Coccaine: Erythroxylon coca
   2. Cannabis, Marijuana, Hashish

G. MUSHROOMS: Amanita contains Muscarine, Bufotemin, psilocin and psilocylin.

H. MITOMYCIN -C: Natural origin, Teratogenic and carcinogenic.

I. DAUNOMYCIN, DOXARUBICIN AND DAUNORUBICIN: Anthracyline antibiotics,

J. MYCOTOXINS: citrinin, ochrotoxin Rubrotoxin,

K. VINBLASTINE AND VINCRISTINE: Vinca sp.

VI. INDUSTRIALS

Mustard gas	: Mutagen,CBW
Benzene	: Leukemia, Malignant lymphoma
Benzidine	: Bladder tumors.
Naphthyl amine	: Blood cancer, Bladder tumor
Acetaldehyde	: Oral carcinoma in human,
Butylated hydroxyamide	: papillomas,
Vinyl chloride	: Liver samer, lung, brain

VII. HABITS: alcohol, smoking, chewing betel quid etc.

VIII. SPICES: nutmeg, cloves, turmeric, ginger, chillies, safrole

IX. MUTAGENS IN CONSUMABLES AND EATABLES

A. BOILING, GRILLING AND FRYING OF FOODS,

B. BARBECUED BEEF, GRILLED STEAK, SMOKED FISH & HAM HAVE PAHS. BROWN CRUST OF FRESHLY BAKED BREAD HAS PREMELANOIDIN.

C. CRUST OF CHARCOAL BOILED BEEF STEAK HAS BP.

D. AZOQUINOLENES IN POTATOES, CAKES, BISCUITS, BREAD, ETC

Learn from yesterday, live for today, hope for tomorrow

7. AIR AND WATER POLLUTION

I. INTRODUCTION

Pollution is an undesirable change in the physical, chemical or biological characteristics of our air, land and water resulting from the activity of man and which significantly interferes with the well being of man and causes widespread damage to the ecosystem. Toxicology is the study of the nature and mechanism of toxic effects of substances on living organisms and other biological systems.

II. CLASSIFICATION OF POLLUTION

Air, soil and water

III. AIR POLLUTION

A. SOURCES OF AIR POLLUTION

1. Natural: (a) Volcanoes (b) Accidental (c) Oceanic spray (d) Pollen
2. Man made: (a) Industrial (b) Utility source (c) Personal

B. OCCUPATIONAL HAZARDS & ACCIDENTS

1. Bhopal gas tragedy
2. Chernobyl Nuclear mishap
3. Heavy metal toxicity

C. POLLUTANTS IN AMBIENT AIR

1. Coal fly-ash from coal-fired power plant, home-heating and coke production is a source of ambient pollution of air

   EFFECTS: Mutagenic activity seen in microbial assays.
2. Natural fly ash (Volcanic), commercial and home oil-fired heating units, spark ignition gasoline combustion engines are also sources.

   EFFECTS: Mutagenicity & transformation were demonstrated for solvents extracts in vitro using target cells.

IV. WATER POLLUTION

A. SOURCES OF WATER POLLUTION

1. Sewage pollution
2. Industrial pollution

   (a) Pesticide (b) Oil (c) Heavy metals (d) other Chemicals
3. Thermal pollution
4. Radioactive & Nuclear wastes

B. OCCUPATIONAL HAZARDS

C. POLLUTION IN THE AMBIENT WATER BODIES

V. GENOTOXIC EFFECTS

Differences in toxic effects are seen from one species to another, due to differences in individuals.

A. SPECIES AND STRAINS

B. SEX, HORMONAL STATUS AND PREGNANCY

C. AGE & NUTRITIONAL STATUS

D. ENVRIONMENTAL FACTORS

E. CHEMICAL INTERACTION

1. Additive
2. Synergistic
3. Potentiation
4. Chemical antagonism
5. Functional antagonism
6. Competitive antagonism
7. Non-competitive antagonism

VI. GENETIC EFFECTS OF AIR POLLUTION

A. ON PLANTS

B. ON ANIMALS

1. Aflatoxins,
2. Trimethyl phosphate
3. Mustard gas
4. Aziridine
5. Formaldehyde
6. Acrolein

C. ON MAN

1. Epichlorohydrin
2. Benzidine
3. Vinyl chloride
4. Quinoline
5. Chloroprene
6. Sulphur dioxide
7. Nitrosamines

VII. GENETIC EFFECTS DUE TO WATER POLLUTION

A. ON PLANTS

1. Cadmium chloride
2. Mercuric chloride
3. Mercuric oxide

B. ON ANIMALS

1. Radioactive pollutants
2. 2,4 - Diaminotoluene
3. Quinoline
4. 1,4 - Dioxane

C. ON MAN

1. Methyl hydrazine and derivatives
2. 3,3 - Dichlorobenzidine (DCB)
3. N - Nitrosopiperidine

VIII. IN SITU MUTAGENESIS

1. Definition: Mutagenesis among organisms living in their own habitats due to stress.
2. Organisms likely to be affected: Plants, animals, microbes and humans.
3. Types of changes occurring: Clastogenesis, Aneugenesis & mutagenesis
4. Types of changes monitorable: all except mutagenesis
5. Causes: ambient pollution
6. Consequences: Additive to variations occurring through normal channels of segregation and recombination of linkage groups.
7. Significance
   (a) Epidemological warnings genotoxic air and water to human populations
   (b) Concentration of habitat genotoxins
   (c) Acceleration of evolutionary processes
8. Monitoring strategies
   (a) Denizen approach: all organisms
   (b) Sentinel approach: mostly plants
   (c) Habitat sampling: all , mostly microbes
   (d) Auto -,& Allocoupling assays: All concentrators and microbes with Bioconcentrators

8. RADIATIONS

I. SOURCES OF RADIATION

A. NATURAL SOURCES

B. ARTIFICIAL SOURCES

C. MISCELLANEOUS SOURCES.

II. CLASSIFICATION

A. IONIZING RADIATION: RADIATIONS CONTAINING SHORTER WAVE LENGTH & HIGHER ENERGY THAN WAVE LENGTH.

Eg. x-rays, r-rays, cosmic rays.

B. NON-INOIZING RADIATION: ELECTROMAGNETIC RADIATIONS

Eg. Visible light, U.r-rays, Infra-red rays.

* Natural * Man Made * Deliberate * Accidental

C. NON-PARTICULATE

Electro magnetic radiation X rays UV rays

D. PARTICULATE

1. Protons
2. Newtrons
3. Mesons
4. Electrons
5. Radioactive isotopes

E. ELECTROMAGNETIC RADIATION

- Scattering
- Absorption
- Recoll & Nuclear Interactions

F. PHYSIOCHEMICAL & BIOLOGICAL CHANGES RESULTING FROM RADIATION.

G. LOW LEVEL AND BACKGROUND RADIATION

III. PROPERTIES

A. RADIOACTIVITY AND NUCLEAR REACTIONS

B. PHYSICAL CHANGES AFTER ABSORPTION OF IONISING RADIATION

Absorption of Alpha, Beta Neutrons, Photons, Xr ays, alpha rays

C. CHEMICAL CHANGES

D. BIOLOGICAL CHANGES

IV. DOSE, DOSE RATE, DISTRIBUTION

V. RADIATION PROTECTION STANDARDS

A. MAXIMUM PERMISSIBLE DOSE

B. HOW PROTECTION LIMITS ARE ESTABLISHED

C. STANDARDS – GRAPHS

VI. RADIOACTIVE POLLUTION

A. FOOD CHAIN

(a) Soil (b) Foliar Deposition (c) Metabolic Pathway

B. AQUATIC SYSTEMS

(a) Oceans (b) Rivers, Estuaries, coastal H2O

VII. NATURAL RADIOACTIVITY

A. PHOSPHATE FERTILIZERS

B. BUILDING MATERIALS

C. FOSSIL FUELS

D. COSMIC RAYS

E. EXTRAMATERIAL

F. MINERAL SPRINGS G. MONAZITE SANDS

VIII. OTHER SOURCES OF EXPOSURES

A. RADIUM

B. RADIOLUMINISCENT PAINTS

C. URANIUM

D. RADIONUCLIDES

IX. BIOLOGICAL EFFECTS

A. CELLULAR LEVEL & SUBCELLULAR LEVEL

B. TISSUE LEVEL

C. EFFECT ON SKIN

(a) Melanocytes melanin (b) Radiation Burns

(c) Langerhans

D. Radiation & Cancer

(a) Dose response curves (b) Human Data

(c) Radiation Biology (d) Radiotherapy

E. Genetic Effects

(a) Teratogenesis (b) Carcinogenesis (c) Heritable diseases

X. EFFECTS ON ECOSYSTEMS & EVOLUTION

XI. INTERACTION WITH CHEMICALS

A. OZONE DEPLETION

B. GREENHOUSE EFFECT & GLOBAL WARMING

C. VISIBLE LIGHT & PSORALENE

XII. LATE EFFECTS OF RADIATION

XIII. RADIOACTIVE WASTE MANAGEMENT

A. HIGH LEVEL

B. LOW LEVEL

C. GASEOUS HIGHLY SOLUBLE LONG LIVED RADIONUCLIDES

XIV. NUCLEAR EXPLOSIONS & FALLOUT

A. NUCLEAR FALL OUT

B. NUCLEAR ENERGY

C. SHORT TERM EFFECTS

(a) Physical Problems (b) Recovery

D. WORLD WIDE EFFECTS

(a) Radioactive Debris

(b) Behaviour of Individual Radionuclides

XVI. ACCIDENTS

A. HISTORY (TMI)

B. TMI -2

1. The Accident 2. Causes & Effect 3. Extent of damage

C. CHERNOBYL

D. NUCLEAR WEAPONS

1. The treaties 2. Star wars 3. Accidents

E. MARINE POLLUTION

XVII. NUCLEAR WEAPONS & THE NON-PROLIFERATION TREATIES

- WORLD STATISTICS ON WEAPONS CROW: The Above relation at Hiroshima & Nagasaki

XVII. THE FUTURE

A. SAFETY RECORD

B. RISKS - ACTUAL & PERCEIVED

9. ROUTES OF EXPOSURE

A. ACCIDENTAL

1. Oil tanker explosion
2. Nuclear reactor leakage
3. Chemicals, radiations and wastes

B. CONSUMPTION

1. Foods, additives, toxins, adulterants
2. Pyrolytic products, drugs, naturals
3. Metals, beverages, sauces, foodchain (Nv)
4. Non-vegetarian, pickles, mycotoxins

C. ECOLOGICAL

1. Atomic power stations, other energy sources
2. Food chain magnifications of toxins, pesticides
3. Air-worksites, ambient air
4. Water - Ground and surface water, treated water
5. Wastes - waste dumps, sewage, hospital refuses
6. Homestead

D. OCCUPATIONAL

1. Chemicals in each industry
2. Energy source chemicals 3. Worksite air
4. Homestead atmosphere - kitchen, etc.
5. Paints, varnishes, detergents

E. USAGE

1. Perfumes, dyes, cosmetics
2. Whiteners, fire retardants
3. Others at home and work place
4. Pesticides

10. SOCIAL CONSEQUENCES: DETRIMENTS, TERATOGENESIS

I. DETRIMENTS

A. INTRODUCTION

1. Personal, familial and social burdens increase as a result of genotoxicity load in the human populations. Burden will be in the form of Carcinogenicity, Teratagenicity- birth defects and heritable diseases.
2. In western countries, it is a 1st order risk. In developing countries it is of 5th order.
3. 25% of all deaths are expected to be due to Cancer in the next 10-20 years.
4. Mutation load increased from 2.5 to 7.5 during the last 20 years.
5. Concept of Detriment index is developed in Holland and Hungary.

B. DETRIMENT INDEX

The concept of detriment index was developed by an Indian born Dutch scientist Sankaranarayanan and a Hungarian Scientist Czizel based on the Hungarian Health Statistics, probably the best maintained in the world. According to this concept every genotoxic effect restricts the normal life of the victim by bestowing its characteristic effects. To this extent the individual suffers a detriment,i.e.loss of work, productivity, self improvement and ability to contribute to common development.

The detriment is expressed in three ways. 1. Years of lost life [LL]. 2. Potentially impaired life [PIL] and 3. Actually impaired life [AIL]. These indicators are derived from the frequencies of 26 common multifactorial diseases [6500 / 100,000]. These diseases are classified as very severe, moderately severe and less severe. With the aid of some complicated statistical and clinical analysis it was estimated that these diseases caused about 2700 years of LL, 96,000 years of PIL and 5800 years of AIL per 100,000 individuals of Hungarians. The multifactorial diseases seem to cause greater detriment than the mendelian ones.

II. TERATOGENESIS

The most susceptible stage is embryogenesis or morphogenesis. Entry routes of Chemicals and various barriers that they must encounter to reach target cell. Innumerable Drugs and other Compounds are being administered to pregnant women most of which could be genotoxic [smoking,alcoholism etc].

Children borne with congenital birth defects may impose/constitute a heavy familial burden and even entail heavy social costs.

1. Abnormalities recognised at birth or shortly after
2. These can be slight or serious or lethal
3. About 3% of all live births have some defect in the western countries
4. Mutagenesis due to
   (a) Viruses - German measles (b) Radiations - X rays
   (c) Chemicals - Thalidomide, Hycanthone, Pesticides
5. Genotoxic accidents - Seveso, Bhopal, Love Canal, 3-Mile Island, Chernobyl
6. Examples
   (a) Azaserine - deformed limbs, Syndactyly in rat
   (b) Nitrogen mustard - Hypotrophy, Brachynetia in chick
   (c) Cyclophosphamide - Hypognathina, Hypotrophy, Cleft Palate in rabbit
   (d) Chlorambicil - Syndactyly, reduction in the number of ribs in rat
   (e) Actinomycin D - Exencephaly, Spina bifida, Cleft palate in rat
   (f) Thalidomide - Limb deformities in man

III. SUSCEPTIBLE STAGES

A. INCIDENCES OF ANOMALIES: Anomaly refers to any form of gross anatomic, histopathologic or molecular changes. Statistics of anomalles reported world over. 5% of all births in the U.S have birth defects.

B. FETUS: Status of fetus during early embryogenesis. Routes of chemical entry. Labour-delivery and prelabour delivery stages. Responses of the mother and placenta to Teratogens. Effects of Drug administeation during and before Pregnancy.

C. PERINATAL IMMUNOTOXICOLOGY: Sensitivity of the immune system to toxic insult.

D. CENTRAL NERVOUS SYSTEMS VULNERABILITY: Effect of alcoholism, Phenytoin drug etc. on the central nervous system and brain.

E. PLACENTA: Significance of placenta as a site of injury, susceptibility, natural barriers. Types of placenta; protective functions of placenta.

F. PREIMPLANTATION EMBRYO: A critical stage of development susceptible to external injury.

External interference cause malformations and deformation of organs.

IV. MECHANISMS

A. CELL PROLIFORATION: Effect of methyl mercury and other compounds on the process of cell proliferation.

B. CELL LOCATION: Involves the movement of cells to specific alloted locations. Effect of compounds on this movement.

C. CELL LOSS: Necrosis and its role in shaping and formation of organs. Abnormal production of Necrosis by cytotoxic agents.

D. CELL SIZE: Teratogenic alterations due to alternation of cell size. Hypertrophy and Hypotrophy.

E. CELL DIFFERENTATION: An important stage of development. Neoplasia, adenocarcinomas etc. use of diethyl stilbesterol and abortions. Various maternal malformations and effects.

F. TISSUE INTERACTION: Effect of mutagens on tissue interaction and morphogenesis.

G. POST IMPLANTATION EMBRYO: Called the period of organogenesis.

V. AGENTS AND EFFECTS

A. RADIATION: Susceptibility of the latter stages of embryo to radiations and effects. Permanent and temporary deformations, doses of radiation.

Effect of radiation on organogenesis.

B. MERCURY: Occurrance of the metal and its effects. Methyl Mercury; threshold units.

C. LEAD: Reported deformations caused by lead. Occurrance and mechanism of action.

D. THALLIUM: Thallotoxicosis, occurance, susceptible stages, effects.

E. CADMIUM: Target organs, mechanism, occurrance, effects.

F. DRUGS: Use of drugs, administration, effect on mother and embryo.

VI. REVIEW OF SELECTED INCIDENCES

A. THALIDOMIDE

B. ALCOHOL

C. PESTICIDES

D. TOXICITY OF ANTINEOPLASTIC DRUGS

VII. EXPERIMENTAL MODELS

A. *IN VIRO*

B. *IN VITRO*

Education consist mainly of what we have unlearned

11. CARCINOGENESIS

I. INTRODUCTION

Carcinogenesis is the process by which a tumour or a cancer is induced.Uncontrolled proliferation of cells form malignant neoplasm leading to a cancer or tumour. Agents causing cancer are called Carcinogens.Carcinogens cause mutations and structural variations in the genetic material as seen in the chromosomes of cancer cells,like deletions, rings, translocations, inversions

Uncontrolled prolieration of differentiated tissues lead to Cancers. Most cancers are frightening to the carrier and socially a costly burden.

25% of all deaths in the West, 9% of which are environmental especially through food chain

1. Stages of Carcinogenesis
   (a) Initiation: Production of an irreversible cellular change
      - Necessary for Cancer development, but not enough.
      - Reversible (Metastasis-7)
      - Initiation act in low doses.
   (b) Promotion: Tumour is caused in a tissue where initiation has occured already.
      - Irreversible
      - Promoters act in high doses.
      - Co-carcinogen is often refered to as promoter
2. Mechanisms
   (a) Genetic: here table changes in DNA, Chromosome and / or gene
      - direct modification of DNA - mutagenesis
      - deletion, repetetion, translocation of DNA segments or whole groups - turbagenesis and clastogenesis
   (b) Epigenetic: non genetic changes
      - Cause permanent changes in the transcription of DNA
      - Virus genomes, oncogenes
      - Preferential proliferation of existing proneoplastic cells

II. CLASSIFICATION OF CARCINOGENS

Physical,Chemical& Biological agents	DNA reacting carcinogens
Epigenetic carcinogens	Unclassified

A. PHYSICAL AGENTS

1. Ionizing radiations

   Y and X-rays cause breaks in DNA - causing cancers like leukemias.

   Sources: X-ray machines, radiotherapy, uranium mining, Radioactive thorium from Monazite in Kerala, atomic fallout of Hiroshima, Bombing etc.

2. Non-ionizing radiation

   UV induces skin cancer. Heat causes breakage of DNA.

B. CHEMICAL AGENTS

Directly genotoxic or enzymatically activated.Many are electrophiles. They are of following types.

1. Alkylating agents

   Introduce an alkyl group into DNA & may cross link DNA. Cycasin, pyrrolizidine alkaloids, Dialkylnitrosamines, carbon tetrachloride, nitrogen and uracil mustard, ethylene imine, halogenated hydrocarbons like chloroform, DDT, etc. ethylene oxide, Aflatoxins, mitomycin-C, nitroso compounds like MNNG, streptozotocin, etc.

2. Aromatic amines & amides

   These are activated by the N-hydroxylation reaction into carcinogens. eg. esters of N-hydroxy-2-Acetyl aminofluorene, N-benzoyloxy-N-methyl-4-amino azobenzene, acridine orange

3. Nitroso compounds

   Compounds which get converted into carcinogenic hydroxylamines eg. 4-nitroquinoline-1-oxide to 4-hydroxyaminoquinoline-1-oxide

4. N- Hydroxypurines, 3-hydroxyxanthine & guanine 3-N-oxide yield potent electrophiles upon esterification.

5. Polycyclic aromatic hydrocarbons.

   Their derivatives bind covalently to DNA after metabolic activation by formation of attacking groups like epoxides and radicals. Phenanthrene, benz (a) anthracene, dibenz(a,h)-anthracene, 7-hydroxymethyl-12-methyl benz (a)- anthracene.

6. Hydrazine

   Causes development of leukemias, Sarcomas, lung adenomas etc. in mice after metabolic activation.

7. Metals

   Iron - containing compounds, salts of cobalt, lead, calcium chromate, Beryllium, Cadmium, Nickel are carcinogenic.

8. Atmospheric mutagens
   (a) Polynuclear aromatic hydrocarbons like benzo (&) pyyreme
   (b) Benzene - (marrow cancer)
   (c) Olefins - automobile exhausts: get converted to hydroperoxides, peroxides, epoxides, etc.
   (d) Ozone - (adinomas, squamous, metaplasia)
   (e) Asbestos - Carcinomas of respiratory tract.
   (f) Halogenated hydrocarbons:Vinyl chloride, Ccl4, chloroform, DDT.
   (g) Chloroprene(rubber industry): Skin & lung cancer in factory workers
   (h) Bromoalkanes: ethylene dibromide, 1,2,-dibromide-3-chloropropane (DBCP).
9. Pesticides

   DDT, ethylene oxide, thio-TEPA
10. Food & food additive carcinogens

    Lipid oxidation products like malonaldelyde, &-epoxides. (breast & prostate cancers). Cholesterol may help in inducing skin cancer. Maillard browning reaction products-

    Amadori compounds get nitrosated in stomach to N-nitroso compounds. Alcohol causes production of carcinogenic acethyldelyde, other cigarette smike, betel quid, aflatoxins, cycasin, bracken toxins, safrole, sodium nitrite, butylated hydroxy anisole, tannins, limonene, sacharin and cyclamate, epoxides diethyl pyrocarbonate.

C. BIOLOGICAL AGENTS

There are viruses which cause malignant neoplasms-sarcomas, carcinomas & leukemias etc. in different animals. The viruses are capable of inducing cancerous growth known as oncogenic viruses. They are of two types,

1. RNA, 2. DNA

1. RNA viruses - cause changes by synthesising DNA in cytoplasm, then integrating it into host chromosome which induces malignancy. Leukosis viruses like lymphomatosis viruses, myeloblastosis viruses, erythroblastosis virus & Rous virus and murine leukosis virus like Leukemia virus, sarcoma virus & Bittner's virus.

2. DNA viruses - The identity of the virus is lost in this kind, in the cell due to integration with host genome. These are of 4 types Papova, adeno-Herpes and Pox viruses
   (a) Papova viruses - eg. papilloma virus, polyoma virus & simian virus 40 - (SV-40)
   (b) Adeno viruses - eg. Human types, simian, cattle and avian types.
   (c) Herpes viruses - Luckes carcinoma virus, lymphoma virus
   (d) Pox virus - Fibroma-myxoma virus. yaba virus & Molluscum contagiosum virus.
3. Examples
   (a) Occupational Substances
       - Soot, tar, pitch, oil
       - Asbestos, vinyl chloride
       - PCB, Benzidine, 2 Naphthylamine Skin, lung, bladder cancers 4-amino bi phenyl
   (b) Drugs
       - Analgesics
       - Diethylsibesterol   Bladder cancer
       - Chlornaphazine
   (c) Foods
       - Butylated hydroxyamisole: Gastric cancers in Chile, Ireland,
       - Nitrates: Japan
   (d) Natural Containtant
       - Aflatoxin   Liver cancer in Britain and Thailand
   (e) Natural
       - Azoglucoside (Cycads)   Liver cancer in Guam
   (f) Habits
       - Tobacco chewing   Oral cancer in Asia
       - Smoking   Lung, Bladder Pancreas all over world

III. GENETIC MECHANISMS

1. Individual cells have genes which are similar to cancer causing sequences in viruses and are called Oncogenes, which when mutated induce neoplasm formations. Thus an environmental insult to cell by radiation, virus or chemicals can cause translocations or monosomy etc. giving it selective advantage & it multiplies.
2. Most carcinogens need activation metabolically to become ultimate carcinogens (electrophile) which attack nucleophilic groups like DNA. Thus an initiation step & a 'promotion' step are observed in carcinogenesis.
3. p53 - oncogene, which controls full proliferation, when mutated, promotes the cell proliferation and cause nearly 50% of human cancers.

IV. ANTICARCINOGENS

1. Indoles (in cruciferous vegetables like cabbage etc). lactones (eg. coumarine). Vitamins A. E. C. riboflavin etc. Antioxidants like Vitamin E (Tocoferol).
2. New Anticarcinogen - Lipo polysaccharide from bacteria infected wheat by Japanese Scientists.

12. HERETABLE DISEASES

1. Genetic disease express at different times during the life history
2. The disease load compounds with each generation. Mild effects coverting large population will have greater public health impact than severe or fatal ones.
3. The severe ones may be eliminated within a short time.
4. Sterility, senility, Cataract, Skeletal deformities, enzyme deficiencies
5. About 4000 genic syndromes have been recorded with different frequencies. e.g. Xeroderma Pigmentosum, phenyl ketonuria Sickle cell anemia
6. Duchenne's nucular dystrophy: most common(?) hereditary disease - 5 - 100,000, i.e. 0.005%
7. Thalidomide dister: 6,000 deformed children
8. 2.5% children genetically aberrent: congenital Anomalies
9. Hugarian statities 60% genetic disease
10. Detriment index more in the genetic diseases than in cancer
11. Bhopal 100 women gave deformed children 1400?
12. Phatassaemia: most common 9en diseases(?)
13. Cystic fibrosis: 1 in 5,000 in Europe, in 30,40,000 children. Out of 23 million borne in on year, 13m die within to year.

I. CHROMOSOMAL

A. AUTOSOMAL

1. Numerical: Euploidy and Aneuploidy - Monosomy,Trisomy
   (a) Turner's syndrome (b) Klinefelter's syndrome
   (c) Down's syndrome (d) Patau's syndrome
   (e) Edward's syndrome
2. Structural
   (a) Cri-du-chat syndrome (b) Philadelphia
   (c) Chromosome 3 - duplication-deletion syndrome.

B. SEX LINKED HERITABLE DISEASES

1. XY linked heritable diseases
   (a) Haemophilia (b) Colour blindness
2. Y-linked heritable diseases - a. Hypertrichosis
3. X-linked Heritable diseases
   (a) Baldness (b) Duchenne Muscular dystropy

(c) Hunter's syndrome
(d) Lesh-Nyhan syndrome
(e) Optic atropy

Discription, Frequency & effects of the above mentioned examples

II. GENIC

A. CHROMOSOMAL

1. Sex-chromosomal: Sex linked, Sex influenced and Sex limited.
2. Autosomal: Numerical and Structural

B. GENIC INHERITANCE

1. Monogenic: dominant or recessive
2. Digenic inheritance
3. Polygenic inheritance.

III. MONOGENIC AND DIGENIC INHERITANCE

A. AUTOSOMAL DOMINANT INHERITANCE

1. Neurofibromatosis
2. Huntington's chorea
3. Hepatic porphyria
4. Achondroplasia
5. Retinoblastoma
6. Chondrodystrophy
7. Cruozou's cranofacial dysostosis

The above disorders are studied with respect to their characteristics, frequency, health effects and medical treatment.

B. AUTOSOMAL RECESSIVE INHERITANCE

1. Sickle-cell anemia
2. Phenylketonuria
3. Galactosaemia
4. Diabetes mellitus
5. Xeroderma pigmentosum
6. Albinism
7. Fanconi's syndrome

The above disorders have been studied with refernece to its characteristies, frequency, health effects and medical treatment.

IV. POLYGENIC INHERITANCE: Refers to inheritance which is controlled by several genes. Examples

1. Cleft lip and palate
2. Some heart diseases
3. Schizophrenia
4. Pyloric stenosis
5. urinary tract malformations
6. Club foot
7. Aneucephaly/meningmyelocele
8. Hypertension.

The above disorders have been studied with refernece to their characteristics, frequency, health effects & medical treatment.

1. Gates 1927		Waltzing mouses (genetic methods) Chromosome aberration (nondis-function)
2. Painter 1927		Cytological analysis of the above
3. Tijo & Levan 1956		2n = 46
4. Ford & Hamerton 1986		2n = 46 confirmation
5. Lejeune et al 1959		Chromosome aberration. Correlea-ted to Humandiease Monglolism T21.
6. Jacobs et al 1959		Chromosome aberration. Correlated to Humandiease Mongloslism T21
7. Jacobs & strong 1959		Kleinfelter
8. Ford et al 1959		Turner
9. (a) T-21	:	1 - 700
(b) T-D group	:	1 - 10,000
(c) T-E group	:	1 - 4,000
(d) T-X	:	1 - 10,000 funds
(e) Turner	:	1 - 5,000 funds
(f) Kleinfelter	:	1 in 400 males
(g) Double X	:	i in 250 males
10. 25% of all miscarriages are due to chromosome errors (Carr 1963).		
11. Incidence of chromosome aberrations in abortuses 50 times > than at birth.		

1,136,971 syndromes out of 202 million .48% in1969.

Heller, J.H. 1969. Human chromosome abnormalities as related to physical and mental dysfunction. J. Hered. 60: 239-248.

Mertens, TR. Human Genetics, John Wiley

V. MENDELIAN GENETICS IN MAN

System	*Dominant*	*Recessive*
A. SKIN		
	(a) Piebald akin (Spotted with white)	(a) Self colour.
	(b) Pigmwnted skin.	(b) Albin.
	(c) Scaly skin (Peal of Ichthosis)	(c) Normal.
	(d) Tcickened skin (in parts come out, palms and soles, tylosio)	(d) Normal
B. HAIR		
	(a) Piebald.	(a) Self colour
	(b) White forelock	(b) Self colour
	(c) Dark hai(r)	(c) Light hair
	(d) Non-red (black)	(d) Red hair
	(e) Curlly hair	(e) Straight.

(*Contd...*)

(f) Wooly hair.	(f) Non-woolly.
(g) Abundant body hair.	(g) Little body hair
(h) Early baldness.	(h) Normal.
C. TEETH	
(a) Absent teeth.	(a) Normal
(b) Defective Dentin.	(b) Normal
D. EARS	
(a) Free ear lobe(s)	(a) Adherent ear lobes.
E. EYES	
(a) Brow(n)	(a) Blue or grey.
(b) Pigmented Iris.	(b) Albino
(c) Drooping eyelids.	(c) Normal
(d) Normal	(d) Myopia (near)
(e) Hyperopia (far)	(e) Normal
(f) Cataract (opaque lens)	(f) Normal
F. SKELETON	
(a) Dwarsism.	(a) Normal
(b) Polydactyly (extradigits)	(b) Normal
(c) Brachydactyly (short digits)	(c) Normal.
G. MUSCLES	
(a) Harelip	(a) Normal
(b) Rupture susceptibility to (5 times more in men)	(b) Normal
(c) aberrabt long palmar muscle.	(c) Normal
H. CIRCULATORY SYSTEM	
(a) Nose bleed.	(a) Normal
(b) Hemorrhoids.	(b) Normal
(c) Normal.	(c) Allergy.
I. RESPIRATORY SYSTEM	
(a) Resistance to Tuberculosis.	(a) Susceptibility.
J. EXCRETORY SYSTEM	
(a) Polystic kidney. (cavities within nephritis)	(a) Normal.
K. ENDOCRINE SYSTEM	
(a) Diabetes insipidus. (Excessive urination sugar)	(a) Normal
(b) Normal.	(b) D. Mellitus (sugar absence)

(*Contd...*)

L. DIGESTIVE SYSTEM

(a) Normal. | (a) Pylonic phenosis.
1. Stomach lower and contracted.
2. Normal food exct.
3. Vomiting caused.
4. Infant death.

(b) Ulcers. (excessive Hcl) | (b) Normal.

M. REPRODUCTIVE SYSTEM

(a) Hypospadias. | (b) Normal

Urethral opening of penis is undersurface than at the exo fit; due to failure of groove.
(as children regarded as os)
Female intersexuality.
Pseudohermaphroditism.
Met. rate more in 10 till 16 (in o +, stored as fat)
3% till 10 and 12% till 16.

N. TUMOURS

(a) Breast cancer.
(b) Nerve cancer (spine symathetic nervous system etc.)
(c) Prostate cancer.
(d) Cancer of digestive tract.
(e) Cancer of eye (dom)

O. NERVOUS SYSTEM

(a) Normal | (a) Deafness

(b) Otosclerosis. | (b) Normal
at 40 or so deafness.

(c) Normal. | (c) Schizophrenia.

eccentricity

hebephrenia — Unexplained laughter, hallucinations, autoversion

Cateronia — loss of desire to talk, assumption of fixed postures.

Paranoia — delusions of persecution.

VI. HUMAN GENETIC SYNDROMES

S.No.	*Disease*	*Symptoms*	*Detection*	*Prequency*
A.	**CHROMOSOMAL**			
1.	Cri-du-chat	Abnormal physical mental retordation not lethal,continous crying in young children like cat	Deletion of chromosome 5 (shortarm) translocation of chr 5	
2.	Buckling effect	-	Part of chromo-some missing	
3.	Philadelphia	Chronic granulocytic leukemia of a	Lack of long arm single chromo-some fragment No.22	
4.	Bloom			
B.	**GENOMIC**			
1.	Trisomic			
(a)	Down's Syndrome (Mongolism)	Short broad hands short stature, mental retardation broad head.	47 chromosome, 2 breakes in 14 & 21	1/700
(b)	Edwards	Malformed ears, small mouth & nose, shoe shappd kedney die 6th month	47, 18th chromosome	1/4000-1/18000-
(c)	Patau's	mental deficiency deafness, clefts lip	47,13th chromosome	1/5000
(d)	Trible-x	Frequent mental re-tardation,limited infertility,irregular combination of sex chromosome	XXX - 47 chromosome	1/500
(e)	Cleft-lip	Cleft-lip	D-group of chromosome XYD	
(f)	Klinefelter's	Deficiency of male harmone level, small testicles & high pitched voice,feminine voice easily death.	47- XXY	
(g)	Bloom's	Diated blood vessel, abnormal facial tratil stunted growth	Frequent chromosomal breakage	
2.	Monosomic			
(h)	Turner's	Failure of secondary sex charactetrs, short staure shield chest	45,XO (x is missing)	

C. GENIC

1.	Comptodactyly	Stiff-little finger penetranee of gene	incomplete
2.	Vender brachy (Blue sclerotics)	Thin bluish outer wall of the eye	incomplete penetrance of dominent gene
3.	Minor brachy dactyly	Second finger is very short	
4.	Epiloia	Abnormal growth of skin, heart	sublethal gene
5.	Colour blindness	Prolonopes - lack of real prgment deuto-topes- lack of green pigtment tritanopes lack of blue pigment	Abnormal x-linked
6.	Cystic fibrosis	Abnormal secretions of lungs, pancrease intertines, liver	heterozygotes
7.	Laurence -moon Biedl	Mental depciening, obesity, extrafinger in toes, subnormal development of geneital organs.	Expression of single primary genic activity.
8.	Sickle cell anemia	Decreased preasure of 02 in blood, Hameloysis Jaudic(e)	Abnormal hemoglobin gene 465
9.	Retinoblas-toma	Tumour of the retina	Abnormal dominent allele
10.	Ataxia	Normal surival of cells	Intermediate cells excise of DNA bases.
11.	Fanconi's anemia	cells highly sus-ceptiple of living increased chromatid breakage	Normal SCE frequency
12.	Xeroderma pigmentosum	Lack of dark pigments pigments in haris skin	gene become strongly freckled

D. BIOCHEMICAL SYNDROMES

1.	Alkaptonuria	darkening of urine qrthritis	Homogenetisic acid oxidase
2.	Fhenylketo-nuria	mental retardation excretion of phenyl alanine.	Phenylalanine hydroxylase

(Contd...)

3.	Tay-sachs	mental & motor retardation death by 2-4 years.	B-D-N- acetyl hexosaminidase
4.	calactosemia	Errors in carbolydrate metabrorism transferase	calactose -1 phosphate uri 1
5.	Glcycogen storage disease type 1 or vongierikes disease	Low blood sugarcone accumulate high glyogen in liver & kidny death	Glycose -6-phosophatase
6.	Glyopen - storage disease type II or pompes disease	Abnormal lysosomes	-1, 4- glycosidase
7.	Cytinuria	Excrete large amount of qrginine, ornithine tysiver, damage to kidney	Homogeygons for abnormal gene.
8.	Aminoacidnia	Excrete large quanity of aminoacids	Homoygous abnormal gene donot absorb cystine, arginine, lysine.
9.	Hypogammaglobu linemia	- Inability to produce globulin, unable to produce antibodies	
10.	Hemophilia	Patient void of 10 quarts of urine daily	deficiency of pitutary hormone
11.	Brown teeth (or) (Lesh-nylan)	Neurological disborder, inactive metabolism	Absence of anzyme hypoxanthire ger-amine-phosphoric-bosyl transferase (HEPRT)
12.	Cystic fibrosis	exerction of highly viscous mucas exocrive gland deficiencies	Beta glucosidase
13.	Albinism	lack of malaniye pigment.	Absence of tyrosinase
14.	Thelessemia	Hb disease, not easily	Homozygons recessive clot lethal
15.	Achoncho-plastic	suppressed growth deficiency of pitang hormone	dominant in heter ozygous form
16.	Darry's	loss of hand movements loss of speech, late blindness narrow	vaniated lumphsytes from cells in bone

13. MONITORING AND ASSAY SYSTEMS

1. EPIDEMIOLOGICALASSAY

(a) To explore if a genetic based disease is associated with any select group in the society

(b) Deduce the causes or identify agents inducing the genetic effects

(c) Survey of Medical records, Peripheral leucocyte for culturing for testing

2. EXCRETION ASSAYS

(a) To know whether or not mutagens or present in the urine and fecal matter

(b) Identify he likely mutagens or promutagens consumed by the subject through food and/or water

(c) Microbial Tests of urine and fecal matter

3. METABOLIC TRANSFORMATION ASSAYS

(a) To know whether any tissue activates or inactivates agents

(b) Correlate tissues activating some nonmutagens and inactivating some mutagens

(c) Ames assays with different tissue homogenates

4. PROPENSITY ASSAYS

(a) To evaluate the susceptibility/resistance of Select groups of subjects to genotoxic influences

(b) Discover the Select groups resistant or prone to common genotoxins. The groups may suffer from specific diseases such as diabetes, xeroderma pigmentosum,Psoriasis have specific habits such as smoking, alcoholism, chewing occupy specific environment depending upon their occupation

(c) *in vitro* assays for SCE, MN, and Biochemical endpoints

5. TARGET TISSUE ASSAYS

(a) To evaluate the vulnerability of the relevant tissue receiving an agent Determine if Lung or Liver or Stomach and Intestine susceptible for air pollutants, drugs and food respectively

(c) in vitro Cultures of the relevant tissues for SCE, Mn and other endpoints; Ames Assay with the homogenates of these tissues

6. IN SITU ASSAYS

(a) Know whether ecological situations - ambient and occupational air, water and soil carry genotoxins

(b) Discover habitats of genotoxic potential such as specific industries with occupational ambient polluted air, water resources and soil with chemical pollution

(c) - Assay of native flora and fauna
- Maintaining specific plant monitors
- Screening human peripheral leucocytes

7. LETHALITY ASSAYS

(a) To know if the agents are severely genotoxic, for the survivors may pose enormous long term burden.

(b) Whether genetic lethality is expected, the agent should be evaluated for low dose chronic effects(Subchronic).

(c) Dominant or Recessive, autosomal or sex-linked lethality in Drosophila and Rodents.

14. CELLULAR IMPACTS

I. CLASTOGENISIS

A. CLASTOGENISIS: Chromosomal Structural Variations due to breakage of chromosome or chromatid leading to an alteration in the chromosome integrity

B. GENETIC CONSEQUENCES

Alteration of the linkage group(s) of the cell - deletion, inversion, translocation, duplication.

C. MECHANISM

1. Breakage of the chromosomes at G1 stage, of chromatid at S and subcromatid at G2 stages of cell cycle. Mostly during S pbgase when DNA synthesis takes place and therefore susceptible for lesion.
2. Due to repair processes, inversion, translocation or duplication may occur depending upon the number of chromosomes involved in breakage and their relative proximity to each other.

D. CELLULAR INDICATORS

1. Gaps in the chromosome continuation
2. Sister chromatid Exchanges
3. Fragments at met a& anaphases
4. Exchanges at metaphase
5. Heteromorphic/diplochromosomes at metaphase
6. Bridges at anaphase
7. Micronuclei at telophase

E. Phenotypic Consequences: Some syndromes

1. Bloom 2. Cri-du-chat 3. Philadelphia 4. Buckling

F. Causative agents: Some examples

1. Actinomycin D 2. Mitomycin 3. Isoniazids 4. Benomyl

II. ANEUGENESIS

A. CHROMOSOMAL NUMERICAL VARIATIONS

B. DEFINITION: Turbulence in the dividing cells leading to abnormal chormosome numbers in the resulting cells

C. MECHANISM

1. Dysruption of spindle mechanism and/or centromere function
   - Nondisjunction of the diplochromosomes during anaphase
   - Lagging or precocious movement of haplochromosomes during anaphase

2. Dysfnction of cytokinesis - Nonfunction of phragmoplast

D. CELLULAR INDICATORS

1. Binucleation 2. Tetrapoidy 3. Aneuploidy
4. non-disjunction 5. laggards 6. forwards
7. Micronuclei 8. diplochromosmes 9. non congression
10. Desynapsis

E. PHENOTYPIC CONSEQUENCES - SYNDROMES IN MAN

1. Down (21) 2. Kleinefelter (x)
3. Turner (x) 4. Patau (+13)
5. Edward

F. CAUSATIVE AGENTS ACTING ON

1. Spindle: - Colchicine - Thurengiensin - Vinblastine
2. Cytokinesis: Caffeine - Aminopyrene - Thuringiensin - Fensulfothion

III. MUTAGENESIS

A. DEFINITION

Alteration of the gene as a whole or in pary by causing lesions in the functional DNA and/or in its activity .

B. CLASSIFICATION

The mutation may occur

1. in Somatic or Germinal tissues of the higher organisms
2. spontaneously or induced artificially
3. leading to micro or macro-changes

C. MECHANISM

1. Transition: Pu —Pu/Py — Py
2. Transmission: Pur — Py/Py — Pu
3. Substitution: Purine or Pyrimidine substituted
4. Lesion: Parts of DNA removed
5. Misrepair: lused DNA segment are not repaired properly

D. CHARACTERISTICS

1. Randomness of occurrence, i.e. unpredicbility
2. Recessiveness: muntant is always dominated by its original allele
3. Reversibility: mutations are unstable and revert to normalcy
4. Repeated Occurrence: Same locus often tend to undergo mutation

E. PHENOTYPIC CHANGES

1. Lethality
2. Organs change - petaloidy in cotton, Homeostatic changes
3. Morphological characteristics
4. nutritional requirements
5. Resistance
6. enzymatic activity

F. CAUSATIVE AGENTS

1. Experimental agents : EMS, EI, NgA, HA
2. Industrial agents : formaldehyde
3. Consumptive agents : cyclamates, hycanthone, AF 2
4. Pollutants : Benzopyrene, styrene Oxide

The important thing is not to stop questioning

15. CELLULAR INDICATIORS

A. ANEUGENESIS

Genomic endpoints suggest the vagrancy of chromosomes which lead to an altered chromosome number in the resultant cells. The can be monitored during mitoais and meiosis.

1. Lagging 2. Precocity 3. Noncongression
4. Nondisjunction 5. Centric fusion 6. Micronuclic
7. Binucleation 8. Arrested metaphases

Microtubule binding of the agent is suggestive of the above endpoints

B. CLASTOGENESIS

Endopoints at chromosomal level suggest lesion in the chromosomes which lead to an altered chromosome structure in the resultant cells. These can be monitored during mitosis and meiosis.

1. Gaps 2. Fragments 3. Bridges
4. Micronuclei 5. Deletions 6. Exchanges
7. SCES 8. Centric fission

Unscheduled DNA synthesis is suggestive of the above endpoints

C. MUTAGENESIS

Changes in the DNA are indicated by altered characters. These can be monitored during the life history of the organism.

1. The characters may be
   a. Lethality
      - dominant - recessive
   b. Specific markers
      - morphological - biochemical - nutritive
2. The direction of inheritance may be
   (a) Forward b. Backward
3. The control of characters may be
   (a) Monogenic (b) Digenic (c) Polygenic
   (d) Pleiotropic (e) multiple allelic

D. OTHER PHENOMENA

1. Mutations in the cytoplasmic DNA 2. Mitotic crossing over

E. INDICATORS

1. Aneugenesis: Higher plants, Animals, Tissue culture
2. Clastogenesis: Higher plants, Animals, Tissue culture
   (a) Allium, Vicia (b) Orthopterans

   (c) Amphibians, Fishes, Rodents
   (d) Culture of Rodent and human tissues

3. Mutagenesis: Higher Plants, Animals, Tissue Culture, Microbes
   (a) E. coli, S. typhimurium, B. subtilis
   (b) A. nidulans -
   (c) Tradescantia, Maize, Barly, Glycine
   (d) Rodents
   (e) Culture of Rodent and human tissues

College Is Like A Fountain Of Knowledge – And Students Are There To Drink

16. ECOLOGICAL CONSEQUENCES

I. AGRO - ECOSYSTEMS

A. INTRODUCTION

1. Pesticides are designed to be toxic in order to ensure public health and to protect the agricultural outputs.
2. Genetic injuries in human from mutagenecity, clastogenicity lead to teratogenecity, heritable diseases, still births, abortions, sterility, mental retardation besides cancer
3. Pesticides: About 400 basic pesticidal chemicals are in use all over the world constituting a few thousand formulations as a conservative reckoning. Other estimations range between 800-1500 basic chemicals and 100,000 formulations. It is also estimated that about 20 billion tons of them are used annually around in USA alone which is the most premier consumer in the world. In India, about 80 pesticidal chemicals are in use.

B. DYNAMICS

1. All the pesticides that are sprayed did not reach the target. Where did the rest go. They did not disappear but was subjected to dissipative forces including bulk movement as spray drift, volatilization from surfaces, adsorption into soil and dissolution in water. The initial reactions after spraying of pesticides are nonbiological and are followed by similar bio-chemical metabolism in plants, microorganisms and animals.
2. Routes of absorption.
   (a) Gastro intestinal absorption
   (b) Pulmonary absorption
   (c) Dermal absorption
3. Bio-chemical alteration of chemicals by living organisms.
   (a) Phase I Reactions include,
      1. Oxidation 2. Reduction 3. Dehalogenation
      4. Hydrolysis
   (b) Phase II reactions include,
      1. Gluconide conjugation
      2. Sulphate conjugation
      3. Amino acid conjugation
      4. Glutathione conjugation

5. Methylation
6. Acetylation.

C. GENOTOXICITY

1. Almost every pesticide is a potential mutagen or carcinogen. This is estimated through various biassays in bacteria Salmonella typhimurium or Escherichia coli and mitotic recombination and unscheduled DNA repair synthesis in human fibro blasts. Pesticides like Nitrofen, Ethylene Dibromide, Chloropurin, Methyl bromide etc. are proved to be mutagenic. The electorphilic reactivity has emerged as an important chemical characteristic common to many mutagens including those with functional groups such as epoxide, hydroxylamine, phosphate, sulphate, halide and diazo.
2. Some Genotoxic electrophilic groups :

Group	Electrophilic	Example
O		
El-C = C	Cl - C - C	Vinyl chloride
ArNO2	ArN - OH	4 - Nitrophenyl
R1 - oco NHR	CoN - OH	Ethyl carbamate
Ro3 Po	oPo - R	Trimethyl phosphate
CO - NH	CO - N - OH	Carbaryl
SPo - R	OPO - R	Parathion
R - Cl	X - R	Nitrogen Mustard

3. Resistance of Pesticides
   (a) Pathogenic fungi, nematodes and arthropods became resistant from many synthetic pesticides. Consequently becoming increasingly difficult to control
   (b) Resistance may be defined as the added ability to withstand an insecticide acquired by breeding of those individuals which survive exposures to that particular chemical.
   (c) Hundreds of species of insects have developed resistance against Pestiecides. Resistance in expressed in relative degrees such as 'folds'.
   (d) Mechanism of Resistance development
      1. Genetic considerations: Pesticides are not mutagenic agents, therefore the changes that occur in a population when exposed to insecticides must be due to mutation occuring for the reasons other than insecticide-exposure.

         The mutation in a population is probably due to the spread of genetic character present in a small part of the original population. eg. To housefly the resistance to DDT is ude to a recessive gene called Kdr.

2. Physiological considerations:
   - Conversion of insecticides to non-toxic metabolites
   - Excretion of toxicant
   - Dietary factors
   - Storage of toxicant
4. Host Susceptibility

   Crop plants may develop vulnerability to the pathogens to which they are usually resistant
5. Crop Yields and Purity

   Agronomic characters, including yield may be reduced if important genes mutated e.g. Triazines in Sorghum
6. Soil Fertility

   Soil fertility reduction may be due to mutations in the nitrogen fixing bacteria and blue green algae of the soil.
7. Breeding System

   It may be affected if the organs or behaviour of biota involved in the system are altered e.g. 5B System in Wheat
8. Food Chain Enigmas

   Organisms all along the food chain may carry the mutagenic substances from the ecosystem. e.g. Biomagnification of PCBs

II. VECTORS & PARASITES

A. INTRODUCTION

Vectors developing resistance to pesticides and parasites to drugs has been widely reported. Are these due to the mutagenicity of these chemicals? Basic understanding of these organisms is necessary

B. COMMUNICABLE DISEASES

1. Airborne communicable disease
2. Water-borne communicable disease

   (a) Viral (b) Bacterial (c) Protozoan

   (d) Helminthic (e) Leptospiral

C. PARASITES

1. Microparasites

   (a) directly transmitted microparasites

   (b) Vector transmitted microparasites

2. Macroparasites
   (a) directly transported macroparasites
   (b) Indirectly transported macroparasites
3. Ecology of Parasites
4. Parasites and diseases
5. Host -Parasite relationships
6. Control of Parasites
7. Effects due to Control: Genetic and Ecological

D. VECTORS
1. Taxonomy, Biology and Ecology of Vectors
2. Control of Vectors
3. Effects due to Control: Genetic and Ecological

> *Teachers open the door but you must enter by yourself*

17. TEST SYSTEMS

A.

1. **Plants**
   (a) Crepis, Hordeum, Vicia, Allium, Pisum
   (b) Tradescatia
   - Staminal hair colour mutation
   - Micronucleic in the tetrads
   (c) Maize
   - Revertances in pollen nature
   (d) Glycine
   - Somatic crossing over in the leaf
   (e) Arabidopsis
   - Seed nature in the pods
   - Biochemical markers of mutation
   (f) Hordeum
   - Turbagenic, clastogenic endpoints in the meristems and meiocytes
   - Mutations of monogenic and polygenic control
   (g) Osmunda
   - Chromosomal and mutational effects in the prothalli
2. **Microbes**
   (a) Bacteria
   -E.Coli, B. Subtilis, S. typhimurium
   Resistance/Susceptibility to drugs
   monogenic inheritance of nutritionla requirements,
   Resistance/Susceptibility to drugs
   - revertance to normaly
   (b) Yeast
   - Sacharomyces, Schizosaccharomyces
   - Monogenic inheritance of nutritional requir ements,
   - Somatic crossing over
   (c) Fungi
   - Aspergillus nidulans, Neurospore Crassa
   - Nutritional requirements, Resistance/Sucseptibility to drugs
   - revertance to normalcy

3. Insects

(a) Orthopterans

- Meiotic chromosome assay for turbagenicity and clastogencity

(b) Bombyx

- Ooyte colour mutation

(c) Drosophila

- Sex linked characters
- Eye colour
- Sex linked lethality
- Bivalves, Annelids(mytilus sps) (Polychacte worms)

4. Amphibians

(a) Rana, Bufo

- SCE, MN, aberrations during mitosis

5. Pisces

(a) Umbra limi

- SCE in the gills and other dividing tissues

(b) Snakes

- Banded krait
- changes in banding patterns - Dermal exposure mutation

6. Mammals

(a) In vivo systems of Rat, Mice, Hamster

- SCE & MN in the bonemarrow
- Cell division in the bonemarrow and spermatocytes
- Sperm abnormality
- Skeletal abnormality
- Dominant lethals

(b) In vitro systems of leucocytes, primary hepatocytes fibroblasts and ovarian Tissues of Rat, Mice Hamster, Muntjac, Monkey and Humans

- SCE, MN, aberrations during mitosis
- unscheduled DNA synthsis
- transformation from normally to malignancy
- Biochemical markers such as nutritional requirements, resistance/to drugs and enzymes activity

7. **Humans- *in situ***
    - Pollutant air ambiently or occupationally (accidentally)
    - Consumption of specific foods, drugs and water preferentially
    - Peripheral leucocyte cultures of humans under stress
    - Unscheduled DNA synthesis
    - SCE, MN, aberrations during mitosis

B. TEST SYSTEMS

1. **Plants**

    (a) Crepis, Hordeum, Vicia, Allium, Pisum

    (b) Tradescantia
    - Staminal hair colour mutation
    - Micronuclei in the tetrads

    (c) Maize
    - Revertances in pollen nature

    (d) Glycine
    - Somatic crossing over in the leaf

    (e) Arabidopsis
    - Seed nature in the pods
    - Biochemical markers of mutation

    (f) Hordeum
    - Aneugenic, clastogenic endpoints in the meristems and meiocytes

    (g) Osmunda
    - Chromosomal and mutation effects in the prothalli

2. **Microbes**

    (a) Bacteria
    - E.Coli, B. Subtilis, S. Typhimurium
    - Monogenic inheritance of nutritional requirements, Resistance/Susceptibility to drugs
    - revertance to normalcy

    (b) Yeast
    - Saccharomyces, Schizosaccharomyces
    - Monogenic inheritance of nutritional requirements,
    - Somatic crossing over, Gene conversion

    (c) Fungi
    - Aspergillus nidulans, Neurospora Crassa

- Nutritional requirements, Resistance / Susceptibility to drugs
- revertance to normalcy

3. **Invertebrates**
   (a) Orthopterans
   - Meiotic chromosome assay for aneugenicity and Clastogenicity

   (b) Bombyx
   - Oocyte colour mutation

   (c) Drosophila
   - Sex linked characters
   - Eye colour
   - Sex linked lethality

   (d) Annelids: Polychaete worms

   (e) Bivalves etc (Mytilus)
4. **Amphibians:** Rana, Bufo- SCE, MN, aberrations during mitosis
5. **Pisces:** Umbra limi- SCE in the gills and other dividing tissues
6. **Reptiles:** Branded krait: banding pattern, dermal mutation
7. **Mammals**
   (a) In vivo systems of Rat, Mice, Hamster
   - SCE & MN in the bonemarrow
   - Cell division in the bonmarrow and spermatocytes
   - Sperm abnormality
   - Cataract
   - Specific loci
   - Skeletal abnormality
   - Dominant lethals

   (b) in vitro systems of leucocytes, primary hepatocytes fibroblasts and ovarian Tissues of Rat, Mice, Hamster, Muntjac, Monkey and Humans
   - SCE, MN, aberration during mitosis
   - unscheduled DNA synthsis
   - transformation from normalcy to malignancy
   - Biochemical markers such as nutritional requirements, resistance to drugs and enzyme activity
8. **Humans**
   (a) in situ and in vitro
   - Pollutant air ambiently, occupationally or accidentally

- Consumption of specific foods, drugs and water preferentially
- Peripheral leucocyte cultures of humans under stress
- Unscheduled DNA synthesis
- SCE, MN aberrations during mitosis

18. MODULATORS OF THE EFFECTS

A. PHYSICAL

1. Temperature 2. Light 3. PH

B. CHEMICAL

1. Activation, i.e Promutagenesis
2. Detoxification, i.e Antimutagenesis
3. Antagonism, i.e Antimutagenesis, Desmutagenesis
4. Synergisim, i.e Comutagenesis

C. CELLULAR

1. Differential target sensitivity i.e. Supermutagenesis,

D. NEGATIVE

1. Deposition - PVC, asbestos
2. Accumulation - Pesticides crossing thresholds
3. Comutagenesis (Synergism) - Harman & Norharman
4. Interactions - an enigma
5. Latency - detection is escaped
6. Effective low doses -
7. Ageing -
8. Activation -

E. POSITIVE

1. Desmutagens - Incapaciation of mutagens
2. Antimutagenesis - Prevention of activation of promutagens
3. Detoxification - Liver metabolism
4. Inactivation - Stomach, mouth enzymes
5. Excretion - Kidney, Intestinal activities.
   - Chlorophyl & fibre have a role
6. Barriers - Placenta, Testes
7. Cytotoxicity - an alarming signal
8. Male - Randomness in activity due to prodigaltiy of production of gametes
9. Female - monthly rejection
   - abortions of defective embryos

F. EXAMPLES OF MECHANISMS

1. Pseudomutagenesis
   (a) high toxicity and low mutagenicity, if at all. e.g Pesticides
2. Promutagenesis
   (a) Converted to mutagens - Dimethyl benzathracene, Pheanthrene Phenonobarbitol, Dimethyl nitrosamine Diphenylnitrosamine
3. Supermutagenesis
   (a) Low toxicity and high mutagencity - Hycanthone, EMS, EI, NaAc
4. Interactive Mutagenesis
   (a) Synergistic or antagonistic to mutagenicity, i.e. initiate or destroy decrease or increase
   (b) Initiate
      - Singly nonmuagenic. Together mutagenic
      - Comutagenesis of Harman and nonharman
   (c) Decrease
      - Clastogenesis in the food
      - antioxidants Vitamin C & E decreased stomach Cancers in by 30% - 60%
   (d) Increase
      - Cyclamates, Phenobarbitol, Saccharin
   (e) Destroy
      - Antimutagens
      - Desmutagens
      - Retinoids, Vitamins B,C, Enzymes, Carotene, Biometals
      - Human plancenta

G. ROLE OF PLANTS

1. Residues
   (a) Pesticides in Plants
2. Concentration
   (a) Mushroom, Vegetables, Crops
   (b) Eichhronia
3. Activation
   (a) Flavonoids of many plants
   (b) Herbicides modified by Maize

4. Antimutagens
   (a) Biometals
   (b) Pigments
5. Desmutagens
   (a) Antagonists

H. ANTIMUTAGENESIS

1. Definition: reduction or prevention of genotoxic effocts
2. Examples: SH - compounds some, vitamins, some aninoacid refinods, natural compounds. L- cystein, VitA, Riboflavin, L. Glutamic acid.
3. Toxins where activities were shaffled Trenimon, bisulfan, BP, X-rays, 8-oxy guinoline sulphite, 7, 12- dimethyl bwnz (a) antherozone (DMBA), 4-dimethyl amino azobenzene naphthalyl DC - sutamic acid.
4. Advantage: Prophylactic measure. Dietary supplement of these protective agents asbestos, pesticides, alkylatruip agent etc.
5. Mechamisms
   (a) Direct reaction between antimutagen and mutagens
   (b) Action on drug metabolism activity - decrease or inhibition
   (c) Competction for binding sites by the activity
   (d) Stimulation of repair synthesis.

19. PERSPECTIVES

A. REGULATION

1. Testing for end points in various systems
2. Assessment of effects in various systems
3. Risks involved to humans
   (a) Occupation exposure b. Epidemiology c. Gene pool
4. Benefits from the Chemical Vs risk
5. Decisions
   (a) Ignore
      - harmless
   (b) Alternate processes
      - New Sweetners
   (c) Protect
      - Pyrenes
   (d) Warn
      - Habits - Tobacco
      - Alcohol - Areca nut
   (e) Tolerate
      - Saccharin, necessary for diabetics
      - Sodium nitrite, release nitrosamines but prevents botulism
   (f) Ban
      - Cyclamates
      - Furfuryl furamide

B. CURRENT TRENDS OF RESEARCH

1. Exposures
   (a) Complex mixtures, low does, chronic exposure
   (b) Minimum effective dose, thresholds
2. Systems
   (a) Tier system approach to screening specific agents
   (b) Battery system
3. In situ Assays to identify hazardous habitats
4. Modulating process, to enhance, to multiply, to reduce the potential effects.
5. Tissue specificity in cellular modulations
6. Enzymatic effects on chemicals and bio-activation

7. Stress indices of chemicals
    (a) to identify the risk groups
8. Detriment indices.

C. OTHERS

1. Many spontaneous mutations may be due to environmental sources
2. Chronic, interactive & low doses of chemicals
    (a) Worst culprit
    (b) Un-monitarable until damage is done
3. Daily intake of chemicals should be minimised

Learning Is Not Child's Play; We Cannot Learn Without Pain

20. INDIAN SITUATION

A. BIRTH DEFECTS

1. High in South India due to consanguiny 60 - 25,000, i.e 0.25% defective prof in metabolism
2. - 2.02% genetic defects I K Verma AIIMS
   - 1 in 30 second
   - 0.86 per million births
   - 1 million out of 1000 million = 0.1%

     Ten years 10 x 11 / 2 = 5.5

     Therefore 2000 AD = 2.02 + 5.5 = 7.52

     Global 0.5 — 10.5
3. Mentally ill in India = 1%

B. CANCERS

1. National cancer eradication programme

   1.5m = now (1987)

   0.5m = Every year
2. Fish cancer - 100% cods - Industrial pollution

C. CHEMICALS IN INDIA

1. Factories : 8826(1986)
2. Drugs : 40,000 formulations
3. Dyes : 73

   Per capita consumption = USA = 10.8

   UK = 7.7

   India = 0.22
4. Pesticides

   > 150

   55 only = of 500 distructs

   Guntur = 50, 000gm / hectare

   BHC - HCCH = 50%

8. Alcohol — Aldehyde

D. INDUSTRIES / OCCUPATIONAL

1. Indian Rare Earths Ltd, Kerala: Cancers reported among workers
2. National Fuel Complex, Hyderabad. Radiation burns at waste dump sites

3. Tarapur - higher natural radioactivity
4. Coimbatore
   (a) Polynosic fibre factory using Formaldehyde closed for an year during 1982
   (b) 60 groups of industries use formaldehyde
   (c) 0.2 million workers exposed by working in industries where formaldehyde is used
   (d) Formaldehyde - autoexhaust - cigarettes
5. Reprographies - arenes, pyrenes - mutagenic tricholorethylene
6. Bhopal: 100 women gave birth to deformed children ?

E. AGRICULTURE

1. Grape fields near Hyderabad - abortions and syndrome
   1-50: major commonly
   1-100: unifactional
   1-200: chr. abnormality
2. Pesticides - 70% of all tonnage on Indian farms, banned in the West
   - Jaggery, Rice parboiling, stored grains

F. WASTES

- Waste dumps in 17 major cities

G. HABITS

1. Betel guid - oral cancer
2. Pan masala - Highest sales and oral cancer in Kanpur
3. Indian diet - Childern as promoters, Turmeric, pepper, cinnamon = Antimutagenic

H. FOODS AND CONSUMABLES

1. 3000 food additives
2. Pine apple flavour = 17 compounds
3. 30% food adulterated
4. Processed food Industry Rs.15000 (1980) Cr.— 20,000 (1990)

I. ENERGY

1. Dungcake, wood - pyrene - 20 packs of cigarettes

J. ECOLOGY

1. Pesticides through food chain
2. Pyrenes in the ambient air
3. Pollutants in water
4. Chlorinated compounds in treated water

> *Education is a progressive discovery of our own ignorance*

9

Environmental Philosophies, Politics and Activism

1. CONCEPTUAL FRAMEWORK
2. SCIENCE OF ECOLOGY
3. ECOSPASMS: PROBLEMS OF CONCERN
4. ANCIENT ECOLOGICAL WISDOM
5. PHILOSOPHICAL CONSIDERATIONS
6. RELIGIOUS VIEWS ON NATURE AND HUMANKIND
7. BIOSPHERE PHILOSOPHIES AND PHILOSOPHERS
8. KALKI IN THE CONTINENT OF CIRCE
9. HISTORICAL IMPLICATIONS
10. LEGISLATIVE AND LEGAL ASPECTS
11. ECONOMIC ASPECTS
12. ECOLOGICAL LIMITS TO GROWTH
13. SOCIOLOGICAL CONSIDERATIONS
14. HUMAN SOCIETIES IN INDIA
15. SCIENTIFIC WORLDVIEW TO ECOLOGICAL WORLD VIEW
16. POLITICAL POLICIES AND MECHANISMS
17. POLITICAL PREREQUISITES FOR AN ECOLOGICAL AGE
18. SCIENCE, TECHNOLOGY AND AGRICULTURE
19. INTERNATIONAL RELATIONS
20. NEOIMPERIALISM: ECOLOGICAL AND ENVIRONMENTAL
21. ALTRUISTIC ACTIVITIES FOR CONSERVING EARTH

SYLLABUS

1. Philosophical Considerations
2. Religions on ecology and environment
3. Religious worldview vs.Scientific worldview vs.Ecological world view
4. Historical Implications: Past, Present and Futures
5. Economic Aspects: W T O Regimes
6. Sociological Considerations: Divisions and Conflict
7. Levers of Society: Consumerism and Poverty,
   Trade And Tourism
   Poor nations, Poor people, Women and Children
8. Legislative and Legal Aspects
9. Political Policies and Mechanisms
10. Green philosophies and People's movements
11. Science, Technology and Agriculture
12. International Relations
13. Neoimperialism: Ecological and Environmental
14. International Efforts

References

1. Barney, GO(ed) 1982. The Global 2000 Report to the president. Penguin Books, Hammonds worth, U.K
2. Brown LR 1974. The Global Politics of Resource Scarcity.
   Overseas Development Council, Washington DC.
3. Caldwell, LK 1990. Between two Worlds: Science, the Environmental Movement and Policy choice, Cambridge University Press, Cambridge.
4. Capra F and Spretnak C 1984.Green Politics,Dutton,New York.
5. Gorz A 1980.Ecology as Politics. South End Press, Boston.
6. Huntington, E. 1945 Mainsprings of Civilisation, wiley.
7. Stretton, H. 1976. Capitalism, Socialism and the Environment, Cambridge University Press.
8. Ward, B and Dubois, R. 1972. Only one Earth: The Care and Maintenance of a small planet. W.W. Norton, New York.
9. Westing, AF [ed]1986. Global Resources and International Conflict:Environmental Factors in Strategic Policy and Action. Oxford University Press, Oxford and New York.

1. ENVIRONMENTAL POLITICS: Conceptual Framework

A. THEORETICAL CONSIDERATIONS

Environment, Ecology, Natural Resources

1. Anthropogenic View vs. Evolutionary view
2. Realistic vs. Idealistic approaches
3. Environment: Hydro + Geo + Bio + Atmos + strato Spheres, i.e. Natural Resources + Ecology
4. Ecology: Interactions, Interdependences Inter relationships in time and space —> Ecosystem

Basic Tenets

1. Providential Ecology - NR as Man's Political Reality
2. Political Reality - Societies need organisation
3. NGO's: failure of political Parties and mechanisms
4. Ecocentric/Anthropocentric/Management for welfare
5. Political Mechanism: Aristotalian Definition

   People — Representatives — Leadership

   Voters — Assembly/Parliament — Ministry

   Political Views 2 Parties

   Advisors Executives

   Specialist Representative

6. EXCEPTIONS: Forms of Leaderships

   Types of representation Types of Advisors

7. NON-GOVERMENTAL AGENCIES OF CHANGE AND PROTEST

   Political activity of change - taken over

   Failure of Parties Failure of Governance

B. PRACTICAL EXPERIENCES

1. Greens of Germany - 5% Minimum - Then and Now
2. Green agenda in Political Parties vs Green Parties

   USA: India, 1:300 in NR use per Head

3. Indonesian Smog - Timber - Japan - Europe
4. India: Drain Theory of Naoroji

   Kaveri

   Narmada

   Chittagong and Jharkand

C. POLITICAL PARTIES

D. ACTIVITIES OF POLITICAL PARTIES

1. Campaign promises of development – false
2. Plans for ecological security - Do they have
3. LPG gradually destroys - imminent.

   All parties are for these; how do they plan to face them

D. IMPACTS OF ELECTIONS

1. Paper
2. Deforestation
3. Petrol consumption
4. Air Pollution with emissions
5. Noise pollution
6. Less work - Least work
7. Human ecological balances i.e. destruction of environmen(t)
8. Promises of developments once again,

E. INCOMPETENCE VS VOLUNTARISM

Good and Bad over a score of Practical Experiences

1. Greens of Germany - 5% Minimum - Then and Now
2. Greens' agenda in European Parties vs Greens' Party in USA: 1:300 NR use: India
3. Indonesian Smog - Timber - Japan - Europe
4. India: Drain Theory of Noiroji, Kaveri, Narmada, Chittagong and Jharkand
5. 1947 Episode of 10-16 millions Human Ecology
6. Timber politics and Recent Haze from Indonesia
7. South American Rain Forests - Hamburgers
8. Nepal - India - Bangladesh
9. Cauvery and Narmada
10. Rheine - Maine - Danube
11. Germany - Club of Rome(NGO) - Greens - Manifest stealing by others - greens are back.
12. India: Drain theory of Naoroji
13. Atomic Energy ———— Political Decision on Science, Education Technology, Social needs

    Environmental Adversity
14. Club of Rome – Intentions

F. PARADOXES OF NGOS

1. Dubious / Benami ones: Electioneering
2. Genuine ones - silent or neutral or platitudinous
3. Genuine ones - campaign against destruction of environment

G. ENVIRONMENTALISM, ECOISM AND ECOLOGISMS

1. Environmentalism: Wealth of Resources
2. Ecoism: Wealth of interrelationships
3. Anti Negativism = Prevention of negative Actions
4. Protectionism = Positive Approach of conservation & Resource renewal
5. Ecologisms: Basic tenets, Underlying principles of ecology, Adages

H. ECOLOGICAL LIMITS TO CONSUMERISTIC GROWTH

1. Open Ended Growth Impossible living on a LImited sphere, Growth has to be limited.
2. Club of Rome Inferences
   (a) Populations, Resource Depletions, Pollution, Energy Crunch, Hygiene & Sanitation
   (b) Industrialists, Economists, Social scientists, etc.
   (c) Politics, Economics, Technology,
3. Ecospasms
   (a) Ecological crises and Social crises
   (b) Pollution of air, water & soil, Soil erosion, floods & Deforestation, ozone depletion, green house effect and acid rain, occupational health, Biodiversity, Resource depletion, etc.
   (c) Human migrations, subhuman habitats, health & education illfare, Children & women injustice.

I. ORIENT/OCCIDENT/OLD WORLD/NEW WORLD/WEST/ EAST NORTH & SOUTH

J. PAGANISM TO RELIGIONS TO SCIENCE TO WHAT NEXT

Passage of civilizations: Ecological world View

K. 1. Forward into Past Knowledge 2. Deductive or Inductive logic
3. Unified goal human Welfare 4. Approaches diverse
5. Past and future. 6. Thought + word + Action
7. Information - Knowledge – Wisdom

L. ARRAY OF WISDOMS

1. Ancient Societies, Ancient literatures, Religious wisdoms, Aryan, Dravidian, Greek, Roman, Egyptian, Palestine, Jain, Babylonian, Hindu, Buddhist, Christian, Muslim outlooks and legacies
2. Natural Resource Conflicts - among people, societies and Polities. Colonialism & Neocolonialism. Global Scenarios
3. Heritages, literatures, philosophies, Prophecies -Optimism, Pessimism, Fatalism, Existentialism, Realism
4. Action in the last two decades - Realities on the ground - Hopes and Despair. The philosophic bases of actions and actions leading to the unfolding of motives and designs.
5. Lessons from philosophies, history and Current events
6. Environmentalism in India.

Interrelationships

UNITED NATIONS ENVIRONMENT PORGRAMME
ENVIOREMENT PROTECTION AGENCY U.S.A., EUROPE
INSTITUES OF TECHONLOGIES-ORGINS
COUNTRIES OF TERCHONOLOGYS' ORGINS/ TRANSFERS
NATIONAL INSITUTE OF TECHNOLOGY
SIMILAR INDUSRTIES IN INDIA
CENTRAL POLLUTION BOARDS
SCIENTIFIC JOURNALS

Consequences

of ecological disvalues and
academic crimes

ACADEMIC CRIMES (Increase)
HUMAN RESOURCE (Decrease)
ENVIRONMENTAL QUALITY (Decline)
ECOLOGICAL BALANCES (Destroy)
SOCIO-ECONOMIC CRIMES (Increase)

Divisions, Violence, Political Decisions

HUMAN ECOLOGY (Degeneration)
PESTILENCE & MISERIES (Acceleration)
ECOLOGY OF HABITATS (Destruction)
HATRED AND VIOLENCE (Stabilize)

2. SCIENCE OF ECOLOGY

A. INTRODUCTION

(1) What is Science?

(a) Counting Elephant's teeth: Directness

(b) Emperor's New cloths: Innocence.

2. What are the problems to which Scientific method in Applied?

(a) Depletion of Resources : why (excessive use)

(b) Degradation of Ecosystems, habitats & Inberitence : why (Exploitation beyond repair capacity)

(c) Imbalances among living and non-living constituents : why interacting subjects varnish or deplete)

3. Depletion heads to degradation and both to imbalance, because all constituents are interconnected therefore interdependent.

B. IMBALANCES

(1) Children's Story : The un-dried Fish and the Ant Hill Negative effect of a small error

2. Tale from Mahabharata : Drop of honey and hunter are leader further in the chain

3. Biology plus History : Spinster and the naval might positive effect of a small deed

C. INVISIBLE ROOTS OF THE VISIBLE: ECOLOGICAL WEBS.

1. Brazilian crop fields and poultry price in England

2. American Hamburgers and deforestation

D. CAUSE HERE AND EFFECT THERE: ECOLOGY AT PLAY

1. Acid rain : Canada and Scandinavia and Baltics

2. Oil Pollution : Tanker Break in North Atlantic - Fish death in the Columbian Pacific !

E. YOU CAUSE THE GROWTH, YOU LOOSE THE SUBSISTENCE

1. Uncle Ton's Cabin : ecology wronged - you have no coal, for you loose the job in the colliery The production is excessive.

2. Triple Troubles in Rural ecosystems you migrate from village, As you last the land to the lender, of cant line the despite more population

F. CULPRIT AS WELL AS VICTIM UNDER BOOMERANG:

1. Green house effect : North responsible, North South both get global warning
2. Ozone Depletion : North responsible, the whole planet suffer froth ray impacts

G. COMMUNITY JUSTICE: Every one gives what it can and Takes what it need all lead to free life of choice cant to monkey.

Man needs nature, nature does not need man !

H. MOTHER EARTH CONCEPT: Prithvi suktam, Bhoomata, Bhoodevi

1. Seven Ages of woman and seven stages of work
2. Man becoming woman, therefore becomes divide
3. Seven ages of man and seven ages of a tree.
4. The Tree, The land, The woman, The Mother If angry, beyond endurance Calamities befall.

I. CONCLUSIONS

1. Justice 2. Righteousness 3. Humanism feminism)
4. Spirituality

3. ECOSPASMS: PROBLEMS OF CONCERN

A. INTRODUCTION

Our life today

B. ECOLOGICAL BALANCE

1. Undried fish and the Anthill
2. Honey and the hunter
3. Spinsters and the Navy
4. Brazilian Groundnut and British Poultry

C. BALANCES TO BACKLASHES

D. ECOLOGY AND ENVIRONMENT

E. GATHERING STORMS: A CHECKLIST

1. Depletion of ozone layer
   Causes, responsibility, effects, solutions
2. Greenhouse Effect
   Causes, responsibility, effects, Solutions
3. Mutations in the Biosphere
   Genetic diseases, Cancer in humans; Chemicals, and radiation exposure.
4. Germplasm depletion
   Microbial, Plants and Animals as resources
   Biological death becoming genetic death leading to Ecological demises.
5. Acid Precipitation
   Acidic rain, oxides of C, N&S. affection wildlife forestry, Water resource.
6. Drinking water crises
   Enormous water resources, Rivers, rainfall, Ier grow water Many places water availability, polluted water ground water depletion, Water transportation
7. Soil erosion degradation of agricultural soil, deforestation, wind and water erosion.
8. Chemicalisation of habitats
   Pollution of air, water, soil and consumables, Pesticides heavy metals Radiations, health effects
9. Insanitation and diseases,
   Communicable diseases, epidemics, compounded by pollution by increasing pathogen and vector populations.

10. Human populations explosion, migration, gender injustice, child labour, poverty, birth and death rates.
11. Degradation of habitats new chemicals and radiations in balanced excessive resource exploration, chains and herbs snap, prodigality, Carrying capacity, buffering ability, density if reduces leading to ecological death.

    Forest, Aquatic systems, semiarid tropics, mountain systems and even human settlements.
12. Sea water intrusion

    Excessive ground water extraction near coast lines, Dependability for potable water increases
13. Episodic spasms

    Droughts of varying durations, floods of varying intensity in r* parts. Accidents of Chernobyl pollution of air and water - oil tanker explosions, gas leakages - sources, ecological connections, stability and food chain ranbicalsis.

F. CAUSATIVE FACTORS

1. Development

   use of natural Resources, Science, Technology, economic and political process for better housing, clothing, food, transport, education and heath produce by bye products which can cause a chain of reactions depletion forth, degradation later or vice versa all other.
2. Consumerism

   Hedonistic psyche leads to pleasurable usages and consumptions determining the direction of development processes. Purchasing ability creates a demand for their upplies of pleasure and luxury - obviously to a few. Resource fall monopolised by a few - the rest get pollutions after, and not getting products of development

G. SOLUTIONS

1. Limiting development to Resource availability their Life span, renewability / cyclability and congueres
2. Controlling consumerism by controlling the demands from purchasing ability by reducing this ability to buy and by controlling the supplies - political economy.
3. Control consumer numbers
4. Instead - there are efforts to raise new sources
5. Psyche: Man a part of environment and not its master.

H. HOPES

1. Efforts of governments - mostly half - hearted
2. Efforts of inter governmental agencies of the U N O
3. Voluntary activities of state, intellectuals, Journalists, and organisations awareness Campaigns to practical action.

I. DESPAIRS

1. Nimbyism, Nimylhism and Nodmytism
2. Searches for new resources and were efficient technologies for maintaining the ethos of consumerism
3. Non Reduction of consumption by rich countries and by rich sections of poor countries.

J. CONCLUSION

1. Evolutionary Endowment: Resources for use by Humankind.

   Diverse Ecology is the check against loss of resource Future totally assumed.
2. Ecology, checks in the forms of chain, links, webs are broken. The balanced resourcefulness

   (balances among resources) is therefore enlarge
3. In stead of repairing, "managing somehow" is resorted.

   This Will not lost long
4. Human kind is destined to bc conflict ridden and violent prone

4. ANCIENT ECOLOGICAL WISDOM

A. INTRODUCTION

1. Ancient historical inferences: archaeology literatures
2. Ancient Conservation strategies
   - (a) Before Christ
   - (b) Until Islam
   - (c) Islam and Industrial revolution
   - (d) Industrial Revolution and Colonialism
   - (e) Colonialism and political freedom
   - (f) Neocolonialism and decline of freedom

B. HISTORICAL / CULTURAL EVOLUTION

1. Continuous Civilizations
   - (a) Indian (b) Chinese

   2. Discontinuous Civilizations
   - (a) Mesapatopian (b) Egyptian
   - (c) Roman (d) Greek
3. Extinct
   - (a) Aztec (b) Inca (c) Maya
4. Ecological Factors
5. Human Factors

C. EVOLUTIONARY / ECOLOGICAL

1. Conservative Strategy: Revolution with environment
2. Biological and social evolution
3. Anthropological Remains
   - (a) Asia (b) Africa
   - (c) North America (d) South America
   - (e) Europe

D. TOOLS OF STUDY

1. Archaeology 2. Art history 3. Literatures
   - (a) Pali, Prakrit and Sanskrit
   - (b) Hebrew, Greek, Latin
   - (c) Arabic, Persian (d) Tamil
   - (e) Others (f) Later day Discoveries

E. INFERENCES

1. Natural Resources utilized within limits of Renewal and Tolerance, i.e. sustainable limits
2. Human fecundity: Civilizations on habitats where carrying capacity was inherent
3. Consumption without Ecological Imbalances.

F. LEADERSHIPS OF KNOWLEDGE SYSTEMS

1. Asceticism: Simple living and high thinking
2. Service: Others first, self later
3. Ethics (Morality & norms): Common justice

G. SANATANA DHARMA OF INDIA

1. Mother earth concept - Prithvi Suktam
2. Ecological harmony
3. Roots of Feminism

H. BUDDHISM & JAINISM

1. Ecological Equity, Reverence for life,
2. Ahimsa Concept, gratitude to nature - Ashoka

I. CHRISTIANITY: PROVIDENTIAL ECOLOGY

J. OTHER RELIGIONS: IMPORTANCE TO NATURE

K. CONCLUSIONS

1. Past wisdom as warnings on future
2. Religion as a means of environmental action
3. Religiosity is essential for environmental recovery

5. PHILOSOPHICAL CONSIDERATIONS

A. DEFINITIONS

1. Environment: Sum total of biota and materials around mankind - Resources, Ecology, Habitats, Subsistence Systems
2. Politics: Maintaining Public affairs such that people tend to live as a community.

B. PREHISTORIC THOUGHTS

1. Hunter - Gatherer - Agriculture
2. Primitive Societies Barter

C. RELIGIONS AND ENVIRONMENT

1. Buddhism and Jainism : austerity
2. Christianity : Lone and charity
3. Islam : Commitment
4. Hinduism : Ethics - inevitability of destruction
5. Providential ecology

D. MEDIEVAL TIMES - NATURAL RESOURCES - BARTERS

Trade Routes - Conquests - Maritime history

E. BACONIAN PRINCIPLES - AGE OF SCIENCE - DARWINISM

1. Industrial revolution - ownerships
2. International politics - Colonialism
3. Social Darwinism

F. GROWTH OF WARS, WARS FOR GROWTH AND LIMITS TO GROWTH

1. World War 1, 2, 3, 4, 5
2. 3 Worlds turning into 6

G. DOOMISTS, BOOMISTS AND EXISTENTIALISTS

1. Hardin, Paddock
2. Simon, Kahn
3. Boulding, Ward
4. Steady States
5. Space Ships, Life boats, Sinky Arks, Gaia, Green Philosophies, Eco-theocracy

H. MARX AND GANDHI

1. Ownership of resources
2. Depletion of resources
3. Degradation of environment
4. Sources appropriation as Equity
5. Trusteeship and Non violence

Tell me and I'll forget; show me and I may remember; involve me and I'll understand.

6. RELIGIOUS VIEWS ON NATURE AND HUMANKIND

A. INTRODUCTION

1. What is religion : A just way of life
2. Why was religion : Preservation ofToday, Fear of tomorrow
3. Origins of Religion : Ageless Hinduism, India & Palestine
4. Routes of March : Philosophy, literature, theology, Centre of power -Gods and Goddesses, prophets and followers, mutatios.

B. EMPIRICAL BASES

1. Domestication of human male and female - cohabitation
2. Domestication of plants and agriculture, concept of Bhoomata
3. Domestication of animals and concept of Gomata
4. Ecosystems : Chains, webs, cycles, energy flows, heredity variation, utilities and assets, liabiities and hazards, disasters - all mysteries
5. Ignorance of Forces : Creation of God, subsidiary Gods, goddesses. Fear, hope, respect, desire, worship, conservation, exploit.
6. Origin of Right livelihood concept, righteousness, pilgrim's progress, commonalty of all religions.

C. PROVIDENTIAL ECOLOGY

1. Providence created all biota on the planet.
   Providence established interrelationships
   Man is one among the above
2. Nature should not be disturbed but used with reverence, ancient Indian thought
3. Man alone was endowed with intelligence leading him to use the environmental resources for his growth and welfare: Christianity

D. CONSEQUENCES OF MISUSE

1. Boomerang in the form of ecospasms that will ruin Kalki concept of Hinduism - the only religion that predicted demise of mankind due to greed and vain glory.
2. All elements needed - all worshipful - multitheism - plurality - idolatry to continue.

7. BIOSPHERE PHILOSOPHIES AND PHILOSOPHERS

A. PROPHECIES BASED ON EXPERIENCES DATA AND KNOWLEDGE.

B. HOLISTIC VIEWS

1. Boomist Outlooks
   (a) Gaia hypothesis: Earth's infinite capacity to recover, Concept of Prithvi as Mother and Goddess in Hindu view of life, precedes.: Lovelock and Margulis
   (b) Resourceful Earth: Resourcefulness of earth is everlasting if science and technology are intelligently used: Kahn & Simon
2. Doomist Outlooks
   (a) Life Boat Ethics (Sinking boat)

   By the Ecological principle of exclusion, there will not be enough place on earth for all people. If all enter the boat, it sinks, therefore the life boat will accommodate only some.: Hardin,

   (b) Sinking Ark

   This is same as life boat ethics of Hardin but for terminology. This however supposes that the world is already a Noah's Ark. Even this may sink if selection of survivors is not made This concept of selecting a few to survive a deluge has first appeared in the Hindu thought, several Centuries or a few millinia before the biblical allusion.: Myers,

   (c) Triage Philosophy

   The global strong has to make a choice of rescuing some among the weaker societies. They would like to help out those who can positively respond. Those who cannot and those who do not need may be left out. Nearly half of the world had to be left by this reckoning.: Paddock

   (d) Kalki Concept

   Hindu wisdom predicted the doom of human society as a suicidal consequence to human greed and divorse from virtue.
3. Existentialistic Views
   (a) Spaceship Earth - Common future

   The planet is a spaceship. Any problem anywhere in it will burst the whole. Global cooperation is an imperative.

   : Ward, Boulding, Stevenson

1. **Free Market Growth**

   Market forces will determine wealths and poverties.

2. **Protectionist development**

   Rich nations shall endeavour to help out the weaker nations by reducing their own luxuries and help the others subsist.

   This approach is more relevent to individual countries as a natural policy

   : Keynes, Brown, Eckholm, Brandt

(b) Ecosystems Approach - Multiple futures - Common endeavour

1. Ecological Development

   Each country should develop based on or limited by its own resources - their renewability and carrying capacity. Reduction of luxuries, moderate outlook regarding standards of life, enrichment of common properties, simplicity in life and protection of life supporting systems.

   : Marx, Gandhi, Goldsmith, Greens and most NGOs

C. SECTORIAL CONSIDERATION

1. Population Bomb: Ehrlich
   - (a) Excessive populations increase consumers of finite sources
   - (b) Question of gerontocratic society
   - (c) Over populations, child labour, women inequality, illiteracy, social fears, are due to absence of growth.
2. Technology is the culprit: Commoner
   - (a) Products of technology used up for consumption. Byeproducts pollute people. Common resources depleted for the few. Many do not get the products. People thus are divided.
   - (b) Monopoly of technology divides nations
   - (c) Science and technology are a natural corollary of human cultural evolution. Their evils can be mitigated only by ethics and humanism.
3. Disarmament essential: Brandt
   - (a) Most resources, including human intelligence, go to make weapons. Weaponry consumes half of world's quantified inputs. A mere waste. Psyche of fear, unnatural competition, power greed are promoted.
4. Feminism (Greer, Kelly, Greens)
   - (a) If earth is treated as Mother, as per heritage and culture, the question of gender emerges

(b) Female has been a worker without wages yet with virtues par excellence

(c) The dominion over female is akin to the dominion over nature, mother earth, which has brought us to near ruin

(d) It is imperative to shake off earth from shackles of man and superman. In effect the human female must be liberated from man's tentacles of selfishness.

(e) But the female has to liberate herself from the psyche of subordination to man and assess the terms of equity, equality and identities vis-a-vis man. For this the female must understand the origins, roots and routes of male dominion over herself.

5. Others

   (a) Pollution of air, water and soil

   (b) Chemicalisation

   (c) Radiations

   (d) Politics of dominion

The aim of education is the knowledge not of fact, but of value.

8. EMERGING KALKI IN THE CONTINENT OF CIRCE

I. INTRODUCTION

1. Word common, Understanding uncommon
2. The Paradox of existence, the Dickensonian times
3. Sense of the passing time, yesterday, today, tomorrow and the day tomorrow

II. HISTORICAL ROOTS

A. **Ancient Times**

   1. Origin of life and Man: The Genetics and Evolution spread of the Nomad.
   2. Man's dependence on Nature: The environment civilisation strikes a balance.
   3. Growth of Populations,Creation: The culture of Religion and God, Empirical Science.

B. **Medieval Times**

   1. Trade routes and maritime powers old world and new world.
   2. Colonialism and open veins.

      North America, South America, Africa, Asia
   3. Science and Technology for resource exploitation
   4. Economics and Politics, Religion and Science in pursuit of Resources.

C. **Modern Times**

   1. World War I
      (a) Genesis of the conflict
      (b) Origin of the Second World theme
   2. World War II
      (a) Genesis of the conflict
      (b) Victors and Vanquished at the same end
      (c) Origin of the Life boat Ethic
         1. Comradery of the Adversaries
         2. Struggles for Political Freedom
         3. First,Second and Third Worlds
         4. The crevices in the Third World

3. World War III
   (a) The Definition: Former Colonisers vs Dominions
   (b) The First, Second and Third Worlds
      1. The First World 2. The Second World
      3. The Third World 4. The seeds of the Fourth World
   (c) Regional wars
   (d) Environmental ethic
      1. Club of Rome
      2. Limits of growth
      3. Environmental concerns - The ongoing 4th world war

D. Current Times - World War IV self regulation

1. G7 - G77, North vs South

III. CURRENT TIMES AND FUTURE TRENDS (1972-92) & 1992-

A. Resource projections of world's resources by 2000 AD

B. Social and Political Scenario

1. Perestroika and glasnost in USSR
   (a) The Question and the answer
   (b) The North-South Divide;
   (c) The beleagured South & the Looming Violence
2. The Exclusion Principle in an unipolar world
   (a) The choices for the North - Exclusion from the Ark
   The Philosophy of Triage in action
   South America Africa Asia - South Asia - India
   (b) Dominion over the world - The New Global commons - Consumerism and Ethics - The New paradigm

IV. PHILOSOPHIES OF THE EARTH

A. Life Boat Ethics B. Spaceship Earth
C. Gaia D. Existentialism - Steady State
E. Earth is Bountiful F. Providential Ecology
G. Marxism H. Gandhism

V. LABOURS OF SISYPHUS?

A. Light A Candle

1. Early prophets to Club of Rome
2. Dubois 3. Enrich 4. Commoner
5. Hardin 6. Boulding 7. Brown & Eckholm

B. They only Serve

1. Friends of the Earth
2. World Watch
3. Earth Scan
4. Green Peace
5. SAM
6. Greens
7. CSE
8. W.W.F
9. Blue Print for Survival

C. United We Stand

1. UNEP
2. U.N. Organisations

VI. THE INDIAN SCENE: ALL THE WORLD IS HERE

A. Realities on the Ground

1. Resources and compulsions
2. Social and Political Scenarios
3. The New Policy of 1991-92.

B. Retrieval in Sight?

1. Imperatives of the New Policy
2. A CIS on the Subcontinent?

VII. ETHOS AND ETHIC OF HINDUISM FABRIC

A. Ancient wisdoms: Sanskrit & Tamil

B. Tribals and Bishnois

C. Sacred groves and God's Lands

D. The Rigours of Hinduism to delay the inevitable?
Man's psyche will ultimately ruin nature & self
(Levi Strauss: Earth will end, as it began, without man)

E. The Philosophy of Kalki - A warning or a Conclusion

9. HISTORICAL IMPLICATIONS

A. WHAT IS HISTORY

1. Wars, Conquests, dates
2. Times, peoples, quality of lifestyles
3. Effects of conquests and subjugations
4. Effects of lifestyles on resources
5. Today's worlds 1,2,3,4, or 5!

B. SOURCES OF HISTORICAL INFORMATION

1. Archeology
2. Prehistoric literature: Sanskrit, Tamil, Greek, Latin, Hebrew
3. Literature until the advent of Scientific age
4. Archives of colonial powers
5. Literature in various fields from 17th century

C. INTRODUCTION

1. Origin of human settlements, growth of civilisations
2. Trade - Science and Technology - Struggles and Co-Operation.
3. Wars - Campaigns - Quest for Resources.
4. Maritime history - Science and technology - exploitation - Colonisations - violence.

D. MECHANISMS OF APPROPRIATION

1. Military strength - Fanaticism of faiths. Urges of trading for "Pleasures" of life - Industrial Revolution - Science and Technology.
2. Shifting precious metals - Buy goods at no / low prices - sell at high prices - non-sharing of science and technology - fulfill European desires in the colonies - generate European needs in colonies.
3. Competition among the exploiters for quality of life - i.e. owning up. Foreign resources.
4. Sharing the spoils among some competitors.
5. North America : Natives at low level of evolution, but conscious of self preservation - Exterminated.
6. South America : Natives at lower level of social organisation - Habitats inaccessible - coastal tribes exterminated.

7. Africa : Natives at the lowest level of social organisation - Enslaved for labour.
8. Asia : Natives at a high level of evolution and organisation - Traded, divided and tricked into submission.
9. Australia et(c) : Vacant lands - vast spaces, penal colonies. Natives killed.
10. Competitions among European countries lead to local, regional and extra regional conflicts with or without armies.

E. FIRST WORLD WAR/ GLOBAL WAR I

1. Causes and characteristics: Colonialists vs colonialists
2. Results or Consequences: Seeds for next war
3. Peace efforts and treaties: Sharing Spoils and crumb to the vanquished
4. Emergence of the 2nd World

OTHERS

1. Competition among European countries for colonial resources.
3. Colonies were slightly involved
4. S & T accelerated.
6. Origin of freedom movements in the colonies
7. Africa: borders altered.
8. Arctic treaty doling privileges on the defeated powers.
9. Geographically regional, ecologically global.

F. SECOND WORLD WAR / GLOBAL WAR II

1. Characteristics and causes: Colonialists vs Colonialists
2. Results and Consequences: Seeds for next war - Economic
3. Peace efforts and treaties
4. Emergence of the 3rd World

OTHERS

1. Repetition of the first world war with minor changes
2. War between two colonialist coalitions.
3. Colonies were actively involved.
4. S & T greatly accelerated.
5. Origin of the nuclear power
6. Origin of the third world
7. Acceleration of Freedom movements for Independence.

8. Origin of East - West Cold War, Alliances, Pacts.
9. Neocolonialism: Excessive development of Europe unjust exploitation of the colonies.

G. PREGLOBAL WARS

1. Non colonial 2. Colonial

H. THIRD WORLD WAR: (1950-70AS) / WORLD WAR III

1. 1945-1970: Marshall Plan
2. Neocolonialism: Colonialists vs Former colonies
3. Cold war

OTHERS

1. Developed first world dominate the entire third world economically and politically through science, technology, trade and political mechanisms.
2. Marshall plan for Europe.
3. Development of the third world on colonial models.
4. First world assisted through selective science, technology trades, aid - exploitative and self interests.
5. Interventions by the second world
6. Civil Wars, regional & Local wars as markets for military industrial complexes to siphon out capital wealth.
7. Pollution of the entire global resources, depletions, crunches, over population and ill health.
8. Imbalance between countries and within countries. Irrevocability of the bad impacts even on the exploiter.

I. FOURTH WORLD WAR (1972-92)/ WAR IV

1. 1970-1990
2. Global commons: War against self for self preservation
3. World War III objectives continued

OTHERS

1. War against self indulgence everywhere for corrective steps lest all may end up vanquished - Boomerangs. War between past and present and future generations.
2. Conservative / reformative / co-operative strategies.
3. Poor nations, poor people, resource depletion, poverty raise, population raise, pollution, ecosystem degradation, trade imbalances, payment imbalances (dept), netgrowth decline, inferior

science and technology. Falling values and failing economics, insecurities, escapism, bleak futures, conflicts and violence.

4. Concern for future, altruism in thought word action.
5. Intellectuals - Clubs of Rome - Global Models - Governmental actions - Intergovernmental actions - voluntary activities - North and South Dialogues and cooperations.
6. UNCHE - UNEP - UNCHE - UNCED
   (72) (76) (82) (92)
7. Third world war activities continued covertly / overtly while lip service only was lent for altruistic objectives both in North as well as South countries.

J. INFERENCES

1. Exploiters also cannot escape environmental backlashes.
2. Development models cannot be borrowed or implanted. They must depend on local conditions and history of society and ecosystems.
3. There cannot be an open ended growth as envisaged by capitalism and communism.
4. Politics cannot be left or right but front conscious of the problems in the front.
5. Values cannot be neutral but righteous. Means are as important as ends. Agro-eco systems determine futures to much greater extents
6. Realistic solutions appear to be the idealistic ones.

K. CONSEQUENCES

1. Second world broke into several Third world countries.
2. First world reformed itself into G7 and others.
3. Third world became 3 groups - Nova Rich-G15 and others. (ASEAN) 3 worlds - 5 to 6 worlds
4. G18 are the countries where the entire national product is inadequate to pay debts' annual interest. (7th world)
5. Fifth world war is initiated.
6. Intensive environmentalism, altruism, pluralistic thoughts, words and actions.
7. Crisis psyche, violence - values and Decadence in North and South countries - massive divisions into Ethnic groups

L. FIFTH WORLD WAR (1992-) / WORLD WAR V

1. 1990
2. Principle of Triage in a Unipolar World
3. Triage in each country: the local North and Souths
4. Extensive violence in most world
5. Presentation affluence in selected pockets

OTHERS

1. Cold wars become hot ecological wars.
2. North and South each country, selective social Darwinism
3. Global north and South become 7 worlds.
4. Philosophy of triage in operation. Between coalitions, countries and within each.
5. Social violence adds of ecological disquiet - Ecospasms
6. Options:
   (a) Ecospasms: Kalki
   (b) Social Revolution: Gandhi
   (c) Economic Revolution beyond smith and Marx: Keynes plus Buddha / Christ.
   (d) ecological marxism: Guevera
   (e) fundamentalism
   (f) existentialism, Hardinism and triage
7. Nimby-ism, Nimylt-ism, Nodmyt – ism

M. WHAT AWAITS THE III WORLD

1. IV World: Tottering economics, stabilise gradually
2. V World: Debt Traps and grand slide
3. VI World: Ecopasms-Economic disasters and Ecological disasters
4. Internal North and South

N. WELFARE STATE OR ILLFARE STATE COMMON SENSE 2

1. Mill, Smith, Marx, Keynes and Tom Paine
2. Ecological Common sense: Unadulterated ethics

M. ENVIRONMENTAL HISTORY

1. Archeology, Paleo-ethno-ecology
2. Ethno-ecology
3. Historical records, Archives
4. Natural History
5. Yesterday and Today influence Tomorrow - Regeneration of Ecology

10. LEGISLATIVE AND LEGAL ASPECTS

A. HISTORICAL ROOTS

1. Mauryan times
2. Other periods in India
3. Other periods in the world

B. ORIGIN OF THE MODERN LAW MAKING

1. The colonial Rules
2. Marxist laws
3. European efforts
4. American efforts

C. ENVIRONMENTAL PROTECTION AGENCY

1. USA as a model

D. NATURE OF THE ENVIRONMENTAL LAWS

1. Land and Soil
2. Water - Rivers - Resources and systems
3. Water - Sea - Resources and systems
4. Atmosphere: Warming, Ozone
5. Habitat Systems: Urban, rural systems, Housing Policy
6. Subsistence Systems: Agriculture, Aquaculture, Animal husbandry
7. Pollutions: Air, water, soil, noise
8. Health: occupational vectors
9. Forests - Major and minor products, Global sinks
10. Toxic Substances
11. Endangered Animals and Plants
12. Trade Practices

E. ROLE OF UN ORGANISATIONS IN LAW AND LEGISLATION,

1. Guidelines, examples, Conventions: honest brokery or Midwifery

F. ROLE OF PEOPLE'S MOVEMENTS IN LEGISLATION OF LAWS

1. NGOs as articulators

G. GEOGRAPHICAL SCOPE: INTERNATIONAL LAWS

H. NATIONAL LAWS

1. EPA as a model
2. Local wisdom - Traditional

I. LOCAL LAWS

Implementation at grass root level

J. CONCLUSION - THE FUTURE

1. Crime - law - Implementation - Rights of Victims
2. Trans-boundary issues

K. POLLUTION CONTROL IN INDIA

A. ENVIRONMENTAL LAW: THE WORLD SCENARIO

1. Growth of awareness of environmental degradation & need for a proper Environmental policy & Management.
2. 1972 Stockholm conference: 'Magna carta' of our environment laid firm foundation for Environmental policies
3. Various other conferences eg. UNCED etc. contributed to growth of an Environmental policy.

B. THE INDIAN SCENARIO

1. Degradation of environment due to exploitation by a huge population.
2. Growing problem of pollution of air, water, soil etc.
3. Need for a workable LEGO-ADMINISTRATIVE MACHINERY to safeguard the environment.

C. ENVIRONMENTAL LAWS

1. DEFINITION: Legislation aimed at protection of the environment.
2. SCOPE: These laws aim at specifying the role.
   (a) Regulation of pollutants, wastes etc.
   (b) Punitive action
   (c) Creating an authority to protect environment.
3. CLASSIFICATION

Protective		*Planning*	
Humans	*Non-Humans*	*Production*	*Distribution*
(a) water (b) Air (c) Noise (d) Nuclear Radiation (e) Toxic subsystems	(a) Wild life (b) Marine life (c) Flora	(a) Land Utilization (b) Irrigation (c) Industry (d) Mining (e) Grazing (f) Estuaries et(c)	(a) Land ceiling (b) Town planning (c) Slums (d) Housing (e) Parks (f) Sanctuaries etc.

D. FUNCTION OF ENVIRONMENTAL LAW

1. PRIMARY LAWS: Concerned with citizens & corporate bodies

2. SECONDARY LAWS: Concerned with Govt. Depts. & NGOs
3. TERTIARY LAWS: Concerned with activities of the state

E. HISTORY OF ENVIRONMENTAL LAW IN INDIA

1. PRE-INDEPENDENCE TIMES:
   (a) Strategy of 'policing the society'
   (b) no gemune interest in welfare of Indian environment, primary interest was exploitation
   (c) Some important laws passed by British are the criminal producers code, Factory Acts, nuisance Acts, Municipal Acts, Format Acts ect.
2. INDEPENDENT INDIA
   (a) 1947 - 1970 s: Lackadaisical attitude to environment no concrete framework of policy
   (b) some important laws passed them were Factories Act (1948), Calcutta Municipal Act (1951), Insecticide Act (1968) etc.
3. TRANSITION TO A NEW AGE:
   (a) Good leadership of Nehru, Mrs. Gandhi etc.
   (b) Influence of stockholm conference
4. 1970 s - 1990 s: Aravalche of legal activity :-
   (a) 1972 - National Committee on Environmental Planning Formed.
   (b) 1980 - Tiwari committee Report.
   (c) 1980 - Dept. of Environmental set up. Likewise there was a growth of Environmental law - WATER ACT (1972), AIR ACT (1981), ENVIRONMENT ACT (1986),etc.
5. 1990 s: New 'base of life' to law due to Rio summit
6. INDIAN CONSTITUTION & ENVIRONMENTAL LAW
   (a) Constitution has guideliness for a sound Environmental policy
   (b) Eg. Articles 47, 51, 42, 43, 48, 49, etc.

F. EVOLUTION OF ENVIRONMENTAL LAW IN INDIA

1. TIWARI COMMISSION 1980)
   (a) Inspected lego-administrature aspects of environmental issues
   (b) Headed by Shri N.D. Tiwari

(c) Attributed uses to bad bring conditions, large population & degraded natural resources
(d) Recommended that there be
   1. Biosphere Reserves, Forests
   2. Protection of endangered species
   3. better land use
   4. control of Toxic substances & Noise
   5. Dept of Environment.
(e) Criticized the existing legal framework as being outdated, inconsistent, in adequate etc.

2. ENVIRONMENT PROTECTION ACT :(1986)
   (a) It dealt with all the aspects of each type of pollution
   (b) Standards for pollutants
   (c) Responsibility of each part (industry, govt. etc.)
   (d) Punishment for each environmental offence
   (e) Moreover there are many lacunae.
   (f) does not include noise, radiation etc.
   (g) implementation tough
   (h) easy for offenders to escape due to loopholes
3. PROTECTIVE LAWS: The Indian Pinal Code . forbids
   (a) Spreading of infectious agents
   (b) Fouling water
   (c) Public nuisance
   (d) Mischief
   (e) Making atmosphere conducive to health
4. AIR POLLUTION: SPECIAL
   (a) Motor Vehicle Act 1939 b. Air Act 1981 c. Environment Act 1986
5. WATER POLLUTION
   (a) Water Act 1974
   (b) Water Amendment Act 1978
   (c) Water cess Act 1977
   (d) Environment Act 1986
   (e) Important laws dealing with Marine pollution are :
      1. Indian Port Act 1908
      2. Merchant shipping Act 1958
      3. Indian Dock Labourers Act 1934

6. LAND/SOIL POLLUTION:
   - (a) Factories Act 1948
   - (b) Mines & Mineral Act 1957
   - (c) Water Act,1974
   - (d) Air Act ,1981
   - (e) Insecticide Act 1968
   - (f) Industrial Act 1951
   - (g) Environment Act 1986
7. NOISE POLLUTION:
   - (a) no central law except that Articles 47, 48, 51, 39 indirectly deal with it
   - (b) some states of Rajasthan, M.P., Bihar etc. have laws.
   - (c) Lacuna in law dealing with Noise Pollution
8. RADIATION POLLUTION
   - (a) Atomic Energy Act 1972
   - (b) no other law dealing with Radiation Pollution
9. PROTECTION OF WILD LIFE:
   - (a) Several Forests Acts & Wild Life protection act (1972)

G. ROLE OF PARTICIPANTS IN ENVIRONMENTAL LEGISLATION

1. CENTRAL & STATE GOVERNMENTS
   - (a) Duty of each level of Govt. specified in all the Acts especially EPA.
   - (b) some state Govt. make special laws if Noise - Rajasthan, Bihar etc.
   - (c) The power to make laws depends on whose function the area comes in ie in Lest I (Union list), List II (state List) or List III (concurrent List)
2. ROLE OF NG0s & VOLUNTARY AGENCIES
   - (a) Sierra club, Friends of the Earth, Green peace
   - (b) India - Narmada Bachao Andolan (NBA) etc. "Watchdogs" of Govt. which breaks its own laws.
3. ROLE OF JUDICIAL SYSTEM
   - (a) Courts responsibility most important
   - (b) Eg. of RATLAM municipal case

H. EVALUATION OF ENVIRONMENTAL LAW :

Impotent- Punishment rare- litigation tough- corruption high- apathy high- laws vague, imprecise and inadequate

I. MAKING LAWS MORE EFFECTIVE ......

1. Better framed laws- more direct, precise& extensive (fill lacunae)

2. Provide personnel to implement laws
3. make courts more accessible to people.
4. Benefits (income tax) to pollution control activity.
5. Entrance environmental awareness.

J. FUTURE

1. Greater awareness
2. More public participation
3. Rise of aggressive environmental activism & charge in political attitudes to environment.

Tell me and I'll forget; show me and I may remember; involve me and I'll understand.

11. ECONOMIC ASPECTS

A. INTRODUCTION

Relations between resources & goods - Smith vs Marx vs Keynes: Outlooks

1. All relations are economic. All inter-relationships are ecological Humanistic - Welfare. Inhumanistic - Illfare
2. The above was borne when Marx wanted to dedicate Das Capital to Darwin. The conception took 120 + years to be borne and 20 years more to be realised in India. Are we progressing? At least with current currents in knowledge system? So rich, so sick, so poor, so lone, so disturbed and Yet!
3. Chief of Baltimore on Rainbow warriors. It is the Economists who make these warriors. The relation came from 1970s. Club of Rome & Limits to growth. Noble prize in Economics
4. Hard Facts, Rigourous analysis, No pet theories, Realities on ground-Global 2000, The Models.
5. Economics and Ecology are too close and interactive- Economy in nature: Ecology - Ecology of mankind with resources; Autarkism - Ecosystem; Human Ecology -Transaction costs; Wastes and surplus values. S&T efficiency leads to Value of source and increase output.
6. Atavism -Ontogeny repeats phylogeny. Development reminds history.
7. Limits to growth warnings: The Five cardinal principles of future. Some growth is better than NO growth. But no growth is better than bad growth. Limitations

   No growth > Poverty
   Good growth > Complacence, consumption
   Bad growth > Inequalities, violence

8. Ecosystems and Human Societies. New Economics-Econo-mysticism-Mythos-Entropy in life-Ecospasms
9. Gaia- Optimistic note on the retrieval from entropy.

B. ECOLOGY AND ECOSYSTEMS: Evolutionary Endowments, about 40 Balanced inter-relationships

1. forests
2. deserts
3. grass lands
7. marine systems
8. coastlines
9. islands

4. savannahs
5. wetlands
6. inland waters
10. agriculture
11. aquaculture
12. silviculture

C. RESOURCES IN THE ECOSYSTEMS: Constituents of Ecology

1. water
2. fauna
3. land and soil
4. minerals
5. flora
6. air
7. energy
8. human

   1. Values and costs
   2. Non-renewable resources
   3. Renewable resources
   4. Reproductivity Span - Biology and ecology

D. ENVIRONMENT: Developed Ecology

sequels and consequences.
feedbacks and backlashes

   1. Depletions
   2. Population
   3. Pollutions
   4. Energy
   5. Hygeine

      (a) Exploitation of Natural Resources
      (b) Development of human expertise
      (c) Role of Science
      (d) Role of Technology
      (e) Role of Man power
      (f) Role of Institutions

E. MECHANISMS

1. Goods, Markets, Transports - internal and external movements
2. Purchasing process - Barters - Exchanges
3. Demands - Needs - Supplies - Purchasing power

F. DOMINANCE OF MARKET PLACE ON

1. sales: Purchasing power
2. production, demands specific items
3. Institutions, priorities alter towards consumer tastes
4. Science and Technology, Change towards consumer tastes
5. On Resources, deplete or replenished or owned up

G. TRADE PRACTICES

1. Exports and Imports
2. GATT and the vaginas
3. Natural Resources - the Silent acquiser
4. Endangered Species - step towards extinction
5. G7 going G8 - Global ownership
6. G77 - Numbers increased , impact lessoning
7. G15 - better among the worse
8. COMECON - defunct but may rise again
9. ECC - The Global Arbiter
10. ASEAN - Regional success
11. SAARC - Still borne child
12. IATP - Mexico - USA - Canada, biggest trade zone

H. BYEPRODUCTS

1. Nature of bye products: Pollutants
2. Value and costs - New technology to avoid toxicity

I. POLICIES

1. Development pressure on efficiency
2. Demands dominate needs, the needy cannot demand
3. Groups and classes in society determine policies
   (a) Political Economy - Economic Policies are linked with Political ideologies, policies, forces and mechanisms
   (b) Environmental Economy - Resources depletion and degradation from pollution is dealt with.
   (c) Ecological Economy - Autarkism, life style is determined by the Resources

J. TERMINOLOGY

Accounting, Valuing, Costing, Pricing, C-B-Ratios, Private - Public - Commons, Input-Output, Transaction, Transportation Costs, Intrinsic - Market - Exchange values

K. A CHECK LIST

1. Labour -Skilled-Unskilled-Women-Children -Artisans-Heritage
2. Wetlands
3. Excreta
4. Bovine & Other milk animals
5. Plant Waste
6. Organic Farming
7. Veg/Non vegetarian Food
8. Biomass/Biogas
9. Biodiversity

10. Crops -old & new - germplasm
11. Tiger /Elephant/Crocodile
12. Minor Forest Products
13. Major Forest Products
14. Wild life Products
15. Seeds /Fertilizers Pesticides/ Water
16. Sources >Scourge Scavenging animals and Humans
    Water[irrigation] > Flood
    Heat [aeration] > Drought
17. Tanks vs Borewells.
18. S & T and Economics - Human Ecology as Economics

    > S & T

    Prices <

    > Resources

L. INDIAN ECONOMICS

1. Loosing sight of responsibilities and duties and rights to accept challanges and avail opportunities thrown by history. Those who ignore history will be condemned to repeat its mistakes.
2. Rush for degrees, papers, extra incomes, Upman-ships and using each others have made people myopic.
3. The value of the mind's eye
    Two eyes > One eyed > Poor Vision
    Squint eyed > Blind > Pretensions?
4. Sukhmoy, Dasgupta, Amartya Sen, Bhagawati, Dandekar, CSE, MIDS, People who brought great name to Indian Intellectual tradition and courage of making sorties into uncharted seas.
5. Kanchan Chopra, Anant, Gautam Sethi, Narinder Singh, Parikh, Nadkarni Agricultural economists.
6. India - Modelling of COR efforts [Even a Latin American Model LAM exists] Global 2000 Economy & Resources.
7. Economics of Dishonesty = Ecology vs Economy vs Honesty

M. IMPERATIVES

1. Mastering data– Global 2000
2. Projections of future
3. Health -disease-death
4. Detriment
5. Byeproducts - wastes
6. Recycling
7. MEF and ICSSR

N. TIME SCALES

- Short term economic benefits often leads to longer term eco system degradation. Benefits prove illusory.
- Political initiatives and economic factors in determining
- resource uses tend to be useful only in short run.
- the politician who does not produce observable results and the economist who forecasts demand, supply and prices too far ahead looks foolish when time arrives.
- Resource economics stresses immediate, short term use and de-emphasizes long term, less quantifiable social needs.
- Ecologists are concerned with the long term effects of factors that may show little evidence of operating at all in the short run.

No free lunch; Everything is connected to every thing else; Ecosystems Give what they can and Take what they need; From every one according to his abilities and to every one according to his needs is Marxist Utopia.

The aim of education is the knowledge not of fact, but of value.

12. ECOLOGICAL LIMITS TO CONSUMERISTIC GROWTH

A. GUIDING PRINCIPLES IN EXPLOITING THE BIOSPHERE FOR DEVELOPMENT

1. Carrying capacity: Since resources are limited population cannot grow beyond the size established by the resource limit. Malthusian logic.
2. Stability and Diversity: More genetic diversity, more ecological stability. Agriculture: Reduction of crop losses due to modernisation may never materialise. "Ecological Nightmare".
3. Ecological Buffering: Biological matter buffers air and the geologic surface. If this matter is not in sufficient quantity, carrying capacity will be reduced Warmer climates.

   All the above may be site specific

B. CLUB OF ROME (CR)

June 1970, Volkswagen Foundation, Peccei, King, Pestel

C. MODELS PREDICTING BACKLASHES & ADVOCATING A RE-PATTERN OF GROWTH.

1. World I Model: (Worldwide)
   (a) Forrester: Population, Capital, Resources, Pollution, Food.
   (b) Forrester and Pestel: World Dynamics 1971
2. World II model: (worldwide)
   (a) Meadows et al (MIT): Limits to Growth (1972)
   (b) Meadows & Meadows (MIT): Dynamics of Growth in a Finite World (1974)
3. World Integrated Model (WIM)
   (a) Mesarovic - Pestel (1974): Mankind at the Turning Point (Hanover) (Cleveland)
   (b) Interactions - Many aspects
   (c) Global Cooperation to avoid Catastrophies,
   Division & Conflict, hatred & violence imminent
4. Model of Integrated Relations in Agriculture (MOIRA)
   (a) Bruckmann (ed): "MOIRA: Food and Agriculture Model" (1975)
   (b) Linnemann, (Amsterdam): Model of Integrated Relations in Agriculture

5. Latin American World Model
   (a) Herrera et al (Rio de Janeiro) 1976
   (b) Catastrophe or New Society
   (c) Socio-Political power
       Exploitation & Destructive Values in Society
   (d) Poor peoples & Poor Nations (PPPN) vs. Rich Peoples & Rich Nation (RPRN)
6. UN World Model
   (a) W1, W2, W3, & WIM are frightening and unpalatable to the poor nations
   (b) Strategies to improve PPPN through economy
   (c) Leontief (Brandeis U. & Harvard U.) 1973
   (d) Carter, Petri, Stern: Physical limitation to Economic growth
7. Improvement of World Economy
   (a) Growth rates of Agriculture in High Income regions: 200%
   (b) Growth rates required in the low Income regions 500% - Latin America & Asia 4-5000 - Africa & China
   (c) 9 Critical geologic sources by 2000 AD

Copper(Cu)	Iron(Fe)
Nickel(Ni)	Manganese(Mn)
Lead(Pb)	Zinc(Zn)

   70% remain in 2000 AD. Most critical by 2020 AD
8. Government Global Model (1982): Resource depletion and Effects

D. RESOURCES DEPLETION & EFFECTS BY 2000AD

1.	Population	: 6.5 billion (2000AD). More effects on L.D.C.s 10 billion (2030)
2.	Arable land	: Increase by 4%
3.	Food	: Increased Yields, only source
4.	Higher yields	: Fertilizer, pesticides, power for irrigation, fuel for machinery: Energy?
5.	Energy from food	: 25% increase only possible, Bleak prospects. Needs 25% more than supplies
6.	Fossil energy	: Coal, gas, oil, oil-shale, tar-sands, Uranium - finite - economic disparities among countries - environmental impacts everywhere

7. Non-fossil Minerals : 1/4 of the DC absorbs 3/4 of the total resources of the world
8. Water :
   - more severe in many regions
   - 50% world already needs 100% increase
   - deforestation is the major culprit
9. Forests :
   - Timber sources decline by 50% - 20 million hectares/year - disappear annually.
   - Most losses: Africa, Asia, South America 40% will totally go
10. Agricultural Soils :
    - deterioration serious
    - erosion, organic matter, salinisation,
    - water logging, alkalisation
    - desert-like conditions.
11. Air :
    - Carbon-di-oxide increase
    - Ozone depletion
    - Acid rain
12. 9 Critical geologic Sources : Cu, Ni, Mn, Coal, Petroleum, Natural Gas
    Pb & Zn may be used up by 2000 A.D.
    70% only remain in 2000 A.D.
    Most Critical by 2020 A.D.
13. Wastes :
    - Radioactive
    - Non-Radioactive
14. Extinction of : 20% of existing tropical forests irretrievably germplasm lost
15. Future of the world economy
    (a) Growth rate of agriculture now less than 200% in the high income countries
    (b) Requirements in the low income regions
        1. 500% - Latin America
        2. 4-500% - Africa, China, Asia
        3. 950% - Middle East

13. SOCIOLOGICAL CONSIDERATIONS

A. INTRODUCTION

1. Ecological communities and diversity
   Biogeography and evolution
2. Human communities and diversity
   Anthropology, civilizations

B. EVOLUTIONARY ASPECTS

1. Races and Migrations
2. Ancient societies
3. Major civilizations and Environment
4. Native people in the North and South

C. CULTURAL ASPECTS

1. Religions and Environment: Nurture of Nature, Reverence
2. Colonialism and Environment: Resources meant for the strongest
3. Imperialism and Environment: Ownership through law
4. Science and Environment: Understanding intricacies of Nature, balancing and harmony
5. Social life and Environment: Today's Society, very complex

D. MODERN SOCIETY

1. Rural Ecosystems : Basics of Subsistence
2. Urban Systems : Parasites
3. Women : Marginalised by Nature, evolution and society
4. Poverty : Bad Environment produces poverty which further destroys Nature
5. Children : Sacrificed goats of ecological degradation

E. EDUCATION

1. Conventional: Ethics mentioned
2. Non-conventional: Success oriented, value neutrally

F. SCIENCE AND TECHNOLOGY

1. Ecology of Science and Technology Individuals work to countries policies: Class outlook or Hedonism
2. Development: Science and Technology indispensable

G. CONCLUSIONS

Environmental agenda in Social Reformers - Women's rights, Ethics for social equity

14. HUMAN SOCIETY IN INDIA

I. INTRODUCTION

- First regular census in India - 1881
- Census 1981: India's population 685,184,692
- India accounts for 2.4% of total world area and accuntants for about 15% of the worlds population
- India

II. STATISTICS

1.	Population in millions	1960	1990	2025
		442.3	853.4	1,445.6
2.	Average annuval	1965-70	1975-80	1985-90
	Population charge(%)	2.28	2.08	2.08
3.	Average annuval increment	1965-70	1975-80	1985-90
	to the population (thousands)	11,951	13,631	16,838
4.	Average annuval growth	1960-70	1970-80	1980-90
	of labour force (%)	1.5	1.7	2.0
	- World Resources	1990-91.		

The large population along with problems of distribution and allocational of services and resources has resulted in a divessity of problems.

III. POPULATION CONTROL NEACTH AND SANITATION

1. Family planning
2. Medical education
3. Communication programes
4. Health ceatres
5. Sanitation
6. Other welfare programmes.

IV. SCIENCE AND TECHNOLOGY

1. Third longest pool of scientific man power in the world.
2. Brain drain.
3. Training institutes
4. Laboratories and research centres.

V. CULTURES AND LINGUISTICS

1. Dravidian aryan culture.
2. Influences of various other culture through invasiens
3. Evolution of and amalgam of culture
4. Coexistence and meeting place of tradition modernity
5. Import of electronic and print media films etc

VI. MINORITIES

- Concept of minorities debatable
- Language, religion, population criteria
- Tribal population - Emerging majorities
- Revivalism of Hinduism - Reservation policies
- Linguistics recognitions - Benefits and concessions

Some of the situation manifested by the above are

1. Sikhs in Punjab
2. Shiv sena-Maharashtra
3. Kannada chatrinaligans - Karanataka
4. Secessionists' movements - NE states

VIII. URBAN GROWTH

1. Concentration of population in urban areas
2. Pressure in urban infrastructure and services increasing in slum areas
3. Of the 3,119 towns and cities only 8 have sewage disporsel and treatment facilities. 209 have partial facilities.
4. Cities major centre for resource degradation

IX. AGRICULTURE

1. Green revolution in 1960s
2. Increase in food production from 50 million tons in 1950 to over 150 million tons in 1980
3. Land reforms, agricultural subsidies, grants and loans.
4. Impact of soil erosion, pollution and deforestation
5. Impact of urban migration
6. Problems of distribution

X. ECONOMICS AND LABOUR

1. Growth of industrial labour force slow
2. Source of labour affected by
   (a) Size of population and its composition
   (b) Immigration
   (c) Emigration
3. Unemployment and under employment
4. Women and child labour
5. Overlap between poverty and unemployment
6. Parameters of economy
   (a) Investment state (Increase shows more capital for development)

(b) Capital output ratio (decrease shows inefficiency)

7. Policies concerning small scale and village industries.

XI. INDIAN EMIGRANTS IN NORTH AMERICA

1. Citizens of Canada
2. Americans
3. First generation parents
4. Second generation children born and brought up in urban North America
   (a) Number of South Asian Imigrants on the increase
   (b) Changing income and status
   (c) Family concerns
   (d) Approaches in dealing with children
      1. The fight response
      2. Authoritarian control response
      3. No control response

XII. FORESTS AND PEOPLE

1. Perceptions of forest crisis amd resource scarcity lead to normative government statements of policy and the imposition of cumulative layers of formal control.
2. Policy mechanisms are too complex and incoherent to function well.
3. Sectoralism and Polarisation of views increase with the uncertainity and complexity of forest issues.
4. Pro-timber emphasis concentrated wealth.
5. Gulf in communications and perceptions between local forest and national policy makers.
6. Informal policy.
7. Policies from outside the forest sector have more influence than forest sector policy.

15. SCIENTIFIC WORLDVIEW TO ECOLOGICAL WORLD VIEW

A. INTRODUCTION

1. No world View: Living as a part of nature
2. Religious World View: God, Creation, Ethics and Codes of living and interactions, providential ecology.
3. Scientific World View: Determinism, Cause and effect, logic and reason, Materials in a flux progress irreversible

B. CONSEQUENCES OF RELIGIOUS WORLD VIEW

1. Great thoughts, Treaties, Civilisations and cultures.
2. Division of the world into religious groups
3. Sub grouping of religions on ethnic or geographic bases
4. Wars for the spread of the gospels
5. Philosophies, Literatures, Unity of all religions
6. A tool in the armoury of Imperialists

C. CONSEQUENCES OF SCIENTIFIC WORLD VIEW

1. Great deeds, and civilizations
2. Quality of life improved systematically
3. World becomes small, knowledge and awareness growing
4. World on the brink, Nations in peril many times
5. Collapse was imminent, but for the recent detantes
6. World divided into very Rich, Rich, Poor, very Poor etc.
7. Planet itself in danger of sustainable disaster

D. ECOLOGICAL WORLD VIEW

1. Sequel to the bad effects of science as practiced by its masters
   (a) Wastage of resources for armaments and excessive consumerism
   (b) Appropriation of resources by some societies
   (c) Balancing forces in most societies destroyed
   (d) Even the profited societies unable to escape the bad effects of the above
2. An alternative for Union and Synthesis in place of religion and science - incorporating their vitality, good features - No particular authorship but a dozen forerunners can be identified
3. Ecological wisdom exists as Ethno-ecology as a part of all religions and as an end product of science itself.

4. Exclusiveness of religions and science replaced by communionism and interdependence.
5. The thesis: The Biosphere, ecosystems, communities, populations and therefore individuals of plants, animals and humans need the planet, Humans need all others and all others do not need humans! Therefore humans shall maintain all others, enriched through interactions. For this all human societies have to empower themselves first though interactions and coactions. This is possible with a need based thinking replacing a greed- based one - a voluntary effort for equity with empathy and renouncing the suicidal baggage excessive comforts, consumerism and security.
    1. Pre-Stockholm - Stockholm - Nairobi - Rio de Janeiro - what next warning signals sent everywhere
    2. Green Philosophies - Variants in Ecological world views, Greens. Eco-theology, Spaceship Concepts, Ecological Marxism
    3. Now or never for many peoples

A liberal mind is a mind that is able to imagine anything

16. POLITICAL POLICIES AND MECHANISMS

A. INTRODUCTION

1. What is Politics: Helping People live as a Community
2. Change through Policies: Legislative mechanisms
3. Mechanism of change: Beurocracy

B. THE POLITY

1. People, Country, Geography, Voters, Constituencies
2. Representative Bodies
   - local - Regional - National
3. Institutions
   1. Executive: Policy makers and changes are initiated
   2. Judiciary: Sentinels of equity and law
   3. Legislature: Law makers
   4. Beurocracy: Implementation

C. THE CHANGE IN SOCEITY

1. Legislature, Executive, Beurocracy and Judiciary - Policy making, Execution and surveillance
2. Local bodies - People and Governments implementation of policies

D. LEGISLATIVES AND ENVIRONMENTAL LAW

1. Regional Assemblies 2. National Parliaments

E. PRESSURE GROUPS, LOBBIES, SECTIONAL INTERESTS

1. Farm lobbies
2. Labour Union
3. Capitalists
4. Elite Groups
5. Artisans
6. Special groups

F. PEOPLE'S MOVEMENTS

1. Chipko and Appiko
2. Greens in Europe
3. Green peace
4. Other NGO's

G. CONCLUSION

Necessity of Reform in the Political processes and the Manpower

17. POLITICAL & SOCIAL IMPERATIVES FOR AN ECOLOGICAL AGE

A. INTRODUCTION

1. Agents of change - Government, Bureaucracy, Parties, women, Intellectuals
2. Political Paarties and doctrines
3. Voluntary social Action: Altruism

B. NEGATIVE PREREQUISITES

1. Vacuum of inaction by the responsible
2. Bankruptcy in doctrinaire politics, Historical compromises, reconciliations, volte faces impossible
3. Unrealistic practical politics
4. Social unrest, chaos and violence: No direction
5. Apathetic Middle classes
6. Violation of Human Rights
7. Unaccontability and free for all

C. POSITIVE PREREQUISITES

1. Messiah: psyches of hope and action
2. Voluntary action groups: Small hopes
3. Grass roots mutineers: Revolt possible
4. Neutral Military: oppression by force ruled out
5. Expanding/Expansive Economy: Development possible
6. Natural Resources a plenty: Commons, interference-less
7. Absence of Transboundary diversions: External
8. Cultural and literary heritage: Uphold the great bygones
9. Enlightened Religious systems: Ethics alive.

D. ANTAGONISIMS TO ECOLOGICAL AGE

1. Consumeristic middle class: Make hay when sun shines
2. Psyches of fear, and / or unrealistic hope: superstitions
3. Growth of crime and Mafias for success: Lawlessness
4. Absence of Intellectual leadership: Escapism
5. Absence of patriotism and National identity: Multination / ethnic states
6. Absence of social consciousness in women: The historical under dogs

7. Narcicism, Hedonism, Absence of Altruism: The Expanse Corrupt
8. Nimbyism: Insensitivity and Unaccountability

E. CONCLUSION

1. Different Scenarios in the world: all the above exist several futures or the several worlds
2. Justice with classes vs Dictatorship of the proletariat
3. The Choices: Ecological Euthanasia or Ecological Murder

F. INTERVENTION BY SOCIAL FORCES

1. Altruism, radical humanism – social actions
2. Assertion of rights: Civil rights movements
3. Revolts against injustice – Million mutinees

G. SOCIAL FORCES

1. Women in homesteads, workspace, cumulative effects
2. Workers in various sectors
3. Peasants and agricultural coolies
4. Intellectuals

H. MECHANISM OF SOCIAL CHANGE

1. Altruism and Service:" Intellectual Reformists Co-operatives, Educators and Teachers
2. Assertions and Service: NGO's, People's Movements, women, workers, peasants, Unionism
3. Revolts and Sacrifice: Pickers, strikes, Disobedience, Civil and Uncivil, Armed rebellions, Extremism and its toll.

18. SCIENCE, TECHNOLOGY AND AGRICULTURE

A. INTRODUCTION

1. Science and Environment
2. Technology and Environment
3. Agriculture and Environment
4. The Politics: Good and bad actions towards the needy recipients

B. SCIENCE, ENVIRONMENT AND POLITICS

1. Information on Resource quality, Monitoring, Biotechnology
2. Training on techniques of sensing, quantification
3. Collaboration on all fronts - Exchange programmes,
   Visitor-ships, scholar-ships, interactions
   First vs Second World's attitudes
4. The reality of recipient not catching up in self reliance Patriotism receding

C. TECHNOLOGY, ENVIRONMENT AND POLITICS

1. Information - long gaps
2. Training - Selective
3. Collaboration - outdated
4. Realities:
   (a) Recipients No self reliance
   (b) Donor's self interest in our back datedness
   (c) Institutes of Technologies in India: Manpower
   (d) Industries: Manpower
   (e) Private and Public Institutions
   (f) Patents: Buying and Royalties
   (g) Competitions and Betrayals

D. AGRICULTURE, ENVIRONMENT AND POLITICS

1. Information: Latest varieties, pesticides, Biotechnology
2. Training: Biotechnology, Pesticides, Degradation, Residues
3. Collaborations: Rothamstead to IBM's Biotechnology
4. Realities
   (a) Germplasm capture
   (b) Pesticide Dumping
   (c) Expertise nil to negligible

E. THE FUTURE OR FUTURES

National Organizations, International agencies, Scientific societies, NGO's Ethoses and Ethics, Classes and interests

F. EXAMPLES

1. European Science and Colonial Science
2. Science and Technology from 2nd World to 3rd World
3. Aswan Dam
4. Siberian Pipeline
5. Nuclear Physics
6. Biotechnology
7. Rocketry
8. Bhilai and other Steel plants
9. Defence Industry and Military
10. Disarmament - Science, Technology and Environment
11. IRRI, Cymmyt, etc.
12. Eco-agriculture
13. Appropriate Technology
14. Blacket, Haldane, Borlaug
15. Rosenberg, Fuchs, Khan
16. Empirical Sciences and Technologies
17. Medicinal Plants

GREEN REVOLUTION

A. INTRODUCTION

1. The importance of agriculture in the Indian Economy
   - (a) Share of national income
   - (b) Role in employment
   - (c) Links with other section
2. The agriculture development strategy
   - (a) History
   - (b) Particulars - Salient features of the approach
     1. Methods to increase land yeild.
     2. Use of modern inputs
   - (c) Self sufficiency in food grain production
     1. Increase of avilability per capita
     2. Increase in production
     3. Decrease in imports.

B. THE POLITICAL ASPECTS OF THE GREEN REVOLUTION

1. History

   The two strategies

   1. K.M Munshi

      -Detail of approach

      -Methodology bottom up approach

   2. C Subramaniyam

      -details of approach

      -Methedology - Centralized, top to bottom

2. Why the Green Revolution

   (a) Role of aid agencies and the U.S

      1. World bank
      2. US Aid
      3. US government.

   (b) Role of multinational Foundations

      1. Ford foundation
      2. Rockefeller foundation

   (c) Other vested interests

      1. National else
      2. MNCs producing fertilizers and pesticides

   (d) Thc rolc of fatc

      1. The 1966 drought
      2. Failed crops
      3. Dependance on US for food

   (e) The role of the intelligentia

      1. IARI and its directions (History)

         - A.B. Joshi - MS Swaminathan

      2. America returned agricultural scientists
      3. The initial Economic Costs

         (a) Devaluation of the Rupee to obtain WB Credit

         (b) Conditions and terms for foreign investment

         (c) Import liberalization

         (d) Elemination of domestic control

      4. The socio - political costs

         (a) The landless, marginal & small peasants

         (b) Capitalist nature of the GR.

1. Highly centralized
2. Concentration of political power

(c) Forced dependence on the west

(d) Highly capital intensive nature

C. THE ECOLOGICAL DESTRUCTIONS

1. Artificial ecosystem approach

   Result requirement of huge inputs

   1. Fertilizers (2) Irrigation
   3. Pesticides (4) Exotic seeds
   5. Machinery

2. Nature studies back

   (a) Land degradation via salinity

   (b) Depletion of nutrients

   (c) Depletion of ground water tables

   (d) Over-exploitation of marginal lands

D. IMPERATIVES FOR THE AGRO ECOLOGISTS AND POLITICIANS

1. Urgency for land reforms.

   (a) Effect of equity due to skewed land holding

   (b) The examples W. Bengal and Kerala

2. Political Prerequisites

   (a) The necessity of a new political order

3. The challenge for agro-ecologists

   (a) Regenerating depleted and degraded soils

   (b) Reducing expensive inputs

   (c) Maintaining an sustained productivity

4. Now or never

   (a) The threat of the vicious cycle of

   1. Increasing population is bad
   2. Increased degradation of land by expansion of GR

   (b) The rays of hope

   1. The awakening of the intelligentia
   2. Increased research in

      (a) Agro ecosystems (b) Alternative agriculture

   (c) The issue attracting the attention of

   1. Policy makers 2. Journalists.

19. INTERNATIONAL RELATIONS

A. INTRODUCTION

1. Political Boundaries: The African Absurdities
2. Ecological Boundaries: Riverine
3. Geographical Boundaries: Seas, Mountains
4. Multinational Countries: USSR, India
5. Multi-state Nationalities: Slav countries
6. Scattered Nationalities: Palestines, Kurds

B. INTERNATIONAL RELATIONS

1. Historical & cultural: The Roots, Europe, Asia
2. Stability vs Flux: Central Eurasia, Africa

C. INTERNATIONAL CONFLICTS

1. Oil exploration, pricing: OPEC vs others
2. Forestry products - Trading and Piracy: Japan & ASEAN
3. Land claims: Border disputes
4. Water - Rivers across countries: Many
5. Seas - fishing: Many
6. Migration, Refugees, Famine, genocides
   Divisions, conflicts, violence, wars

D. INTERNATIONAL CO-OPERATIONS

1. Regional Treaties and conventions
2. Regional Understandings, groups, activities
3. Concept of Global commons: Role of Powers
4. International co-operations
   (a) Wars and treaties
   (b) League of nations
   (c) United Nations and its organs
   (d) Conventions on Global commons
   (e) Rights to life and development imperatives for the North towards South
   (f) Charities vs global duties International activity outside UN - GATT, WB, IMF, ADB

E. BIPOLARITY TO TRIPOLARITY TO UNIPOLARITY

1. Impacts on conflicts and co-operations
2. Hedonism and Triage

F. TRADE AND TECHNOLOGY VS RESOURCES RIGHTS, DUTIES

1. The Growth of Ecological Fascism
2. Pre Marxian scenario by the turn of Century - History repeats itself 1900 to 2000 A.D.

G. EXAMPLES

1. Cuban Sugarcane
2. Ghanian Cocoa
3. Brazillian forests
4. Zairean copper
5. Water stoppage by Turkey
6. Water pollution by Germany
7. Air Pollution by USA, Europe Technology, Science
8. Vietnam War
9. PL480
10. Mineral Technology
11. Indian Cow - Islamic Meat!
12. Politics of Climate
13. Espionage
14. Crop failure in USSR
15. Oil resources in USA
16. Metal Stocking in USA
17. Oil Technology – Trans Siberian Pipeline
18. Consequences of Detante, Employment,
19. Japan's Ecofascism
20. Antarctic, Seabed, Outer space
21. Rhine -Maine -Danube
22. North Sea oil
23. Protectorates: Papua, Namibia

LEAGUE OF NATIONS

1. Formed after the I World War
2. Could not prevent the II World War
3. Body to maintain Status Quo
4. US refused to join
5. Failure due to disinclination to utilise the organisation as an instrument of peace

6. Expelled the U.S.S.R. in 1939 from its membership after the Soviet Union's attack on Finland

UNITED NATIONS

1. Came into existence on 24th October 1945
2. Organisation of the UN
   (a) General Assembly
   (b) Secretariat
   (c) Security Council
   (d) Trusteeship Council
   (e) Economic and Social Council
   (f) International court of Justice
3. Head quarters
   (a) First Avenue
   (b) UN Plaza
   (c) New York City
   (d) N.Y. 10017
   (e) USA
4. New members in UN
   (a) Nauru
   (b) Tonga

   Total Membership – 188

UNEP - UNITED NATIONS ENVIRONMENTAL PROGRAMME

1. Established in1972
2. Active in wide variety of programme to protect the environment
3. Recent major achievement of UNEP was sponsorship of the 1992 earth summit
4. Their initiatives
   (a) Afforestation Programmes
   (b) Protection of seas
   (c) Coasts from degradation

GATT NEGOTIATIONS: "THE ELEVENTH HOUR"

European leaders practice brinkamanship in Brussels. A GATT agreement will be come Wednesday evening at 11:59 and a half - Britain's Chancellor of the exchequer Kenneth Clarke said Korean Lawn makers cut their hair to protest opening up rice markets to imports.

IMF - INTERNATIONAL MONETARY FUND

1. Established on 27 December 1945
2. Independent International Organisation

ILO - INTERNATIONAL LABOUR ORGAN ISATION

1. Established in 1919
2. Autonomous part of the League of Nations
3. Inter governmental Agency

ASEAN - THE ASSOCIATION OF SOUTH EAST ASIAN NATIONS

1. Regional Organisations formed by the Governements of
   (a) Indonesia (b) Malaysia (c) Philippines (d) Singapore (e) Thailand
2. AIMS:
   To accelerate economic progress and maintain the economic stability of South East Asia
3. HEAD QUARTERS:
   (a) Jakarta in Indonesia

WTO - WORLD TRADE ORGANISATIONS

1. Permanent International trade body
2. Replaced GATT - General Agreement on Tariff's and Trade

CITES-CONVENTION INTERNATIONAL TRADE IN ENDANGERED SPECIES

1. 1989 - Elephants added to CITES list - Meeting in the Geneva
2. Ivory exports and imports banned

20. NEOIMPERIALISM: ECOLOGICAL AND ENVIRONMENTAL

A. INTRODUCTION

1. Appropriation of resources created unbridgeable hiatuses among nations and within peoples of some nations.
2. First, Second, and Third worlds became Fourth, Fifth and Sixth worlds - one planet and many worlds. Highest developed seven to highly developed dozen to moderately developed score to a lowly developed scores to the lowest developed score (i.e. -developing) to the degrading dozen = 175 countries.
3. Sections within each countries: Women, children, poor, native people and the artisans.

B. POOR NATIONS

1. Historical degradation - Bangladesh, Ethiopia, Sudan, Laos, etc.
2. Condemned by Ecology - Chad, C A R, Somalia, Ethiopia
3. War Torn economics - Cambodia, Laos
4. Bad Internal Policies - Nigeria, Mexico, Uganda, Malawi, Nepal
5. Bad External Policies - Burma
6. Disadvantageous geography - Mangolia, Bhutan, Mauritania, Sahel
7. Ecospasms

C. POOR PEOPLE

1. Owners of the commons which get privatised. Do not have purchasing power. Loose the ability to demand the supply of needs. Purchasing power is lost due to commons at zero costing become goods of higher value and costs. How to give them purchasing power? To how many?
2. The poor from rich nations, the poor are better off than those from poorer nations due to state's wealth getting to them as doles for unemployment which works as an incentive for private enterprise - some purchasing power is given.
3. Rich nations: Population controlled by self realisation. Richness due to history, Patriotism, Science, Technology, Trade and unity among similar nations. Low population reduces sharers.
4. Poor nations: Histroical reasons, Low patriotism, Absence of unity within the country and among similar countries, Science and Technology not advanced. Low literacy. High populations.

5. Poor nations: Poor people worst hit, degrees of poverty varies Poverty line: Euphemism when earning ability does not provide purchasing ability to sustain for a day with basic needs of food, shelter and clothing. Sometimes earning ability is absent. Sometimes opportunity to earn is absent.
6. Bottom rung occupied by starring people, Ethiopia, Somalia, Sahel
7. Shelter: Slums, pavements, etc. - Afro, Asian, South America
8. Cloths: Half naked or in tatters – Afro-Asia, South America
9. Lower rung go much lower, environmental bye products of Development -land and water degradation pollution, insanitation, etc., affects these most.

D. WOMEN

1. Among poor people worst hit are women. While suffering all that from poverty in addition, these sections, suffer more work, less wages, gender descrimination at work as well as home.
2. Illiteracy more. Physically weaker. Therefore suffer brutal domination.
3. Being at homesteads more often and longer, they are butts of stagnant insanitation and environmental degradation. Depending upon their history, the types of suffering, hardships and exploitation varies - bringing water and firewood from miles away, kitchen air to child rearing.
4. Women among the rich in poor nations also carry the social burdens of unused literacy, male domination at home and/or workplace. Affluence with historical legacies of subjugation.
5. Women among rich nations, despite economic and social emancipation, yet carry in their stride the gender descrimination - Perhaps unavoidable due to inheritant lower level of physical strength Pregnancy and child care - the inevitable minimum.
6. Uterus has made all the difference: The 9th month Disease and life long weakened status.
7. Feminism, Movements for emancipation/Liberation

E. CHILDREN

1. Poor Children in rich nations: Neglect at the formative - otherwise best resources available for growth.
2. Poor children in poor nations: Maximum neglect. Child labour - household to Industrial workers. Little or no education - Delinqencies and crimes. Breadwinners for families.

3. Rich children in poor nations: Personifications of selfishness
4. Schools - Nonexistant - or Dropsout - Economic necessity of erning to purchase subsistences!
5. Diseases and Mortality high. Subhuman living conditions. Slums and Sun Roofs.
6. Female of the poor child: Worst. Even parents condemn them to work and earn. Education is denied even by the parents - Tradition, Economic Necessity, wrong perceptions of the future. Female infanticide.
7. Despite science and better living standards inhumanism.

F. NATIVE PEOPLES

1. Tribals of Rich nations mostly exterminated. Survivors limited to settlements. Not in the mainstream USA, Australia, Canada, New Zealand.
2. Tribals of other countries vary in cultural status - Nagas of India to Sentenalese of Andamans, Papuans, etc.
3. Nature's protectors and dependents Forests, Mountains - subsists on nature's resources. Low or no literacy. Languages not developed - culture various from the mainstreams.
4. Lands taken away, forests owned up. Sometimes displaced by irrigation projects.
5. Empirical knowledge on Nature's resources - Ethnoscience - Partly exploited and confirmed by modern Science.
6. Deprivation of sources and comforts of Nature - Consequences various.

G. TRADITIONAL ARTESANS

1. All over the ancient civilizations and countries exist in numerous numbers - Native Crafts.
2. Industrialisation erased native crafts. Non traditionals gradually entered replacing the age old professionals.
3. Migrations to urban areas for want of work at rural systems underselling, underemployment and employments in unskilled works.
4. Same story everywhere in the world - The concept of Gram swarajya - Village Self Reliance/Rule to obviate this.
5. Some artesanal crafts irreplaceable. So are some replacements. While traditional crafts are small scale, nature dependent the replacements are large scale and degrading environmentally and economically.

H. CONCLUSION

Basic reason is ownership of commons, Economic marginalisation of some sections while wealth grows through development. grows. Degradation of resource follows development and results in further degradation of these sections. Triple Trouble.

The original idea of a university was all about freeing the human mind

21. ALTRUISTIC ACTIVITIES FOR PRESERVING EARTH (NGOS)

A. INTRODUCTION

1. Degradation of the environment, i.e. Natural Resources and Ecology(depletion and imbalances).
2. Governmental inadequacies - Escapism - Vested interests - Incompetence necessitate private activity - which cannot be done without a philosophy.
3. Political forces: Adding to the "goods", oblivious of "bads": irony of the electoral forces
4. Ideology: Philosophical bases of action - For Right or Wrong, Exploitation or retrieval - Thoughts - word - Action Continuum. Ethics, Equity, Empathy - Humanism.
5. Helping to hope is a Responsibility. Reaction to helplessness, Failures, Irresponsibility, Oppression. etc.
6. Prevention of Violence from people whose subsistence is threatened
7. Global, Regional and local Variations.

B. TAXONOMY OF ALTRUISM

1. Voluntary organizations: own fund, own activity
2. Public Trusts: Own funds (activities) Aid others
3. Autonomous Bodies: National or international
4. Non governmental organisations:
   (a) Government Dependent
   (b) Government supported
   (c) Trust Dependent / supported
5. Scale: Small or big
6. Scope: Regional National, International.
7. Activity Profile: Educational, Social or Political

C. MOTIVE FORCES

1. Humanism: Social consciousness, Reaction to injustice
2. Spirituality, Religious motives
3. Self propelsion - Social and political upward mobility
4. Objectives: Resistance of negative actions / Promotion of positive actions

D. SENSITIVITY TO PROBLEMS

1. A check list
   (a) Slavery of the illiterate, women, children and other Adults

   (b) Depletions of natural resources
   (c) Pollution and ill-health
   (d) Unsustainable development
   (e) Unjust Policies and /or Implementation
2. Objective Clarity
   (a) Subsistences from minimum standards.
   (b) Recipients of goods and bads of development.
   (c) Bells must toll: For whom? Judgement required
   (d) Light at tunnel's end: For whom?

E. KNOWLEDGE BASE

1. Information - Knowledge - Wisdom relationship
2. Back ground knowledge on the following necessary
   (a) History: Social, political & ecological
   (b) Political forces and actions
   (c) political economy
   (d) Ecological Principles
   (e) Science and Technology Policies & Practices
   (f) Human subsistence systems
   (g) Human Consumptions, usage & Trade practices
   (h) Education and Journalism

F. EXAMPLES OF CONCERTED ACTIVITY

1. Global examples.
   (a) Club of Rome : Pioneer, forecasting, Alert the world
   (b) World Wide Fund : Wild life conservation
   (c) Friends of the Earth : Campaigns, Crusades
   (d) World watch Institute : Data, Alerts, Forecasts, Journalism
   (e) World Resource Institute : Resource monitoring, Alerts
   (f) Green Peace : Crusaders
   (g) APPEN : Asiatic problems, FOE model
   (h) Greens : Pioneers, Crusaders, Political Forces, Feminism
   (i) UNEP : Policies, coordination.
2. Indian examples
   (a) Centre for Science & Environment : Pioneer, Journalism, Policy

(b) Development Alternatives : Field works, Planners

(c) Center for Environment & Education: : Education, Awareness Campaigns

(d) Kerala Sastra Sahitya Parishad : Awareness Campaigns, Crusaders

(e) MSS Foundation : Scholastic pursuits, Field works

G. CHOICES IN INDIA

1. Gandhi, Kumarappa, Mukherjee (RK), Jaiprakash, Vinoba
2. Marx, MN Roy, Mao, - Food for work Policies
3. Spiritual / Religion - Hindu, Jain, Buddhist ways of living with nature; Christian Activism, Arabindo etc.
4. Heritage and Nationalism - Vedic heritage, sanskrit literature, Cultural renaissance
5. Free Market Environmentalism

H. INDIAN PANORAMA OF ACTIVITIES

1. Specific Attention
   - (a) Bishnoi tradition
   - (b) Chipko Movement against tree felling
   - (c) Chotanagapur Resistance to fuel trees
   - (d) Women's uprising in A.P against Arrack
   - (e) Tehri Dam construction
   - (f) Narmada Oustees' rehabilitation
   - (g) Silent Valley conservation
2. General Attention
   - (a) Tree Planting
   - (b) Trekking for ecosystem knowledge
   - (c) Wildlife watching
   - (d) Clean up of nuisances
   - (e) Pollution Petitions, litigations
   - (f) Education / Awareness Campaigns
3. Antagonism
   - (a) Deforestation
   - (b) Pollution
   - (c) Soil erosion
   - (d) Wastes

4. Advocacy / Defence
   (a) Conservation of wetlands, Forests, organic farming, and germplasm, Indigenous systems, water, soil
   (b) Recycling of wants
   (c) Restorations of degraded habitats
   (d) literacy, education, Awareness

I. VOLUNTARY ORGANISATIONS

1. What are NGO's - Non Governmental Organisations.
2. No clear stratagic development.
   - The varius VOs do not co-ordinate their activities with one another or with the governmental agencies, WB or IMF.
3. VO's self -assessment
   - Symposium on "Development Alternatives" The challange for NGO's, held in London in March 1987.
   - Meeting in June 1989, in Manila, led to the Manila Declaration
4. Three types of third - party organisations
   - Government, business, voluntary.

     (threat power, economic power, integrative power, resp. to obtain resources.
5. Peoples Organisations (PO's)
   - They have a liberty to integrate use of cheap, economic and integrative power
   - Need for PO's (Line no 35,Pg No.101)
6. Public service contractors(PSCs)

   Driven more by market considerations than values.
7. GONGO (Governmental Non governmental Organisations)
   - Created by governments to channel funds from major international assistance agencies.
8. Individual as a volunteer.
9. Individual or - community citizen

   National citizen, Global citizen

J. FROM RELIEF TO PEOPLES MOVEMENT

- NGO's moving towards an attack on fundamental causes, from being an assistance agency.
- Generation one, generation two, generation three, fourth generation.

1. Generation one the NGO provides immediate relief characterized an humanitarian assistance. eg. In 1947, Settlers who were victims

of wars with Indian, in North America, were sent food by the Irish Protestants.

2. Generation two. The NGO's concentrate on developing the capacities of the people through self-reliant local action.
3. Generation three. The NGO's try to obtain changes in some policies and institutions at the local, national and International level.

   eg. In India, Samakhya and Multi-coops Associations carried out an extensive state and national campaign using courts, media, lobbying, public demonstrations to force Andhra Pradesh government to restore free elections to co-operatives
4. Social movements and global changes.

   Towards people - entered development on global scale.
5. To kill a Movement.

   The VO becomes bureacratized due to large amounts of financing of funds

   Some of the Non Governmental Orgnisations are:-

Name	*Objective*
(a) Arthik Samata Mandal	Socio-economic equality
(b) Van Vasi Seva Kendra	Socio-economic development of hill people.
(c) Sarvodaya Kendra Pindval	Welfare of tribals.
(d) State Social Work & Research Centre	Socio - natural economic development.
(e) Centre for Human Development & social change	Rural developmental programme.

K. PRESCRIPTIONS

Background as foundations; History of exploitation of natural resources; Ecospasms: Origins, progression and consequences; Activities of other Altruist activities.

1. IDEOLOGY

1. Selection of the agenda for action
2. Social and political objectives
3. Service on the ground
4. Education, journalism and populism
5. Niche selection: Area of operations

2. CHARACTERISTICS OF THE SELECTED NICHE:

1. History: Political, Social, Economic
2. Ecosystems: status, productivity
3. Resource: s-w-a-m-p-e-a soil-water-animals-Minerals-plantsenergy- air
4. Folklore and Traditions: Religion, Legends, Myths, Arts
5. Human Resources:
   (a) Individuals: Artists, Doctors, Writers, Intellectuals
   (b) Authorities, Beaurocracy
   (c) People's representatives
   (d) Educational Institutions
   (e) Hospitals.
6. Industries: Raw materials, Products, Byeproducts, Pollution
7. Agriculture: Productivity, Diversity
8. Problems: Any problem or all of them

3. ACTIVITY PROFILES:

1. Educational: Formal
2. General Awareness: Popular Campaigns
3. Field Studies: Wildlife, Ecosystems, tourism, Linkages
4. Social Service: Waste clean up, hygiene, restoration
5. Lobbying for right policies. Authorities and Representatives
6. Legal actions on wrong policies or activities
7. Agitational approaches
8. Political actions and Mechanisms

4. AGENDA FOR ACTION:

1. Tourism impacts
2. Developmental activities and sequels
3. Resource depletion. SWAMPEA
4. Human settlements
5. Work places: Women, Children
6. Pollution: Ill health
7. Systems degradation
8. Restoration of habitats

5. SELECTION OF THE AGENDA:

1. Ideology: Education / awareness build up necessary
2. Urgent and topical: Immediate action
3. Varied Popularity but topical: Articulation

6. METHODS OF ACTION:

1. Advertisements: Stickers, Pamphlets, Posters, Slides.
2. Aesthetic appeals: Theatre, Music Cinema
3. Educational methods: Films, Exhibitions, Meetings, Library,
4. Agitational techniques: Petitions, legal actions, processions, Protests, (fasts, pickets, strikes)
5. Political Processes: Lobbying, pressure groups, electioneering

7. ORGANISATIONAL ASPECTS

1. Infrastructure
   - (a) Office with furniture and secretarial equipments
   - (b) Staff committed to the objectives and incidental salaries
   - (c) Library and exchange activity
2. Financial:
   - (a) Donations as seed grants
   - (b) Grants-in-aid for specific projects
   - (c) Membership fees
   - (d) Tourism fees
   - (e) Other Earnings
   - (f) Accounts and Audits
3. Personnel:
   - (a) Leadership and associates
   - (b) Resourcefulness
   - (c) Simplicity - Accessibility, Unselfishness
   - (d) Ehichs, Equity and Empathy

8. CONCLUSIONS

Beware of Tourism - Beware of economic boons

1. Ethos of the Family Norm: Good To-day, Better Tomorrow
2. Service to the other children of the earth
3. Ultimate ideology: Vande Mataram.
4. Voluntary: How long? How far? Need for Private Enterprise in Altruism
5. Altruists Private Ltd!
6. Association of NG Dos - Bargaining Power, Lobbying Power, Influencing Power, Protecting power - vis-a-vis the objectives.
7. Political Activities or Ecolising the political parties
   - (a) Successes as agents of change, political forces as lobbyists, as educational activists etc. - prefixing with green & Eco

- Ecodevelopment, Ecospasm, Ecowar, Ecoespionage, Ecofascism, Ecologisms, Ecoisms, Green watch, Green trade, Green technology etc. Environment - friendly.

(b) World's progression: Triage, Ecospasms, Kalki in action

(c) Alternatives

(1) National Socialisms: Fascism

(2) Religiosity & Traditionalism

(3) Revolutions: Gandhi & Guevera

(4) Humanism

(d) Knowledge of Current events and histories of all Crises of intensive environmentalism.

(e) From club outlook, profession or hobby to Radical humanism.

Scientists dream about doing great things. Engineers do them

10

Applied Ecology

1. PRINCIPLES AND CONCEPTS

APPROACHES

2. BIOLOGICAL BASES
3. SOLVING OF PROBLEMS
4. LESSONS FROM EPISODES/ EVENTS
5. CLUES FROM LITERATURE
6. CLUES FROM MEDIA

CULTURES

7. ECOLOGICAL VALUES OF PLANTS
8. CULTURES AS APPLIED ECOLOGY
9. MONOCULTURES / POLYCULTURES
10. AGRICULTURE
11. AQUACULTURE
12. TREE CULTURES

MONITORING

13. BIOMONITORING OF POLLUTION

RESTORATION

15. SOIL: NUTRIENTS, WASTELANDS
16. ECOLOGY IN PRACIICE AT AUROVILLE

Syllabus

1. Applications of plan and animal ecologies: Agriculture, Animal Husbandry, vermiculture, Sericulture, Apiculture and other mono cultures. Companion and alternate cultures. Shifting agriculture.
2. Restoration of Soil Quality through remedial Practices - Biological chemical and Physical - Role of Mycorrhiza, bacteria, algae and organic manures.
3. Water quality recovery through ecological methods involving biota and cycling - aquaculturing recovery of Thames, Rhine and Danube as Examples. Ganga Action Plan
4. Social Forestry, Silviculture, Afforestation, Soil Binding - Usage of Plants appropriate to habitats, niches, problems and Environment
5. Biotechnology, Genetic Engineering, Gene Ecology and Ecological Genetics: Interrelations. Role of Genecology and Ecogenetics in the use of genetically modified crops.
6. Sustainable Development and Ecological Development Developmental Models based on local Ecosystems, Cultures and Selection Pressures.
7. Biological and Ecological warfare. Portents from Human Genome Projects and animal ecology researches carried out by Defense Departments
8. Aves as Monitors, Vectors, Predators of Agriculture, Pest Carriers and Nutrient suppliers.

References

1. Butterworth, F.M, Linda, B.C & Judith, G.R.1995. Biomonitors: Biomarkers of Environmental Change
2. Cairns, J: Recovery of Damaged Ecosystems, Virginia University Press.
3. Horn B.J. 1994. Ecological Approach to Pest Management, Elsevier
4. Mitchell & Jorgensen, S [ed] Ecological Engineering: Introduction to Ecotechnology, Wiley
5. Normon, M.J.T. pearson, C.J,searle, P.G.E; the ecology of tropical food crops (1984); cambridge university press
6. Saylor, G.S, Sansverio, J & Davis, K. L. 1997. Biotechnology in the Sustainable Environment
7. Widdowson, R.W. 1987. Towards Holistic Agriculture. Pergamon Press

1. PRINCIPLES AND CONCEPTS

A. INTRODUCTION

Applications of human relevance are based on the governing principles of the Planet Earth covering the Geological Cycles, Chemical Cycles and Biological Cycles i.e., Atmosphere, Chemosphere, Geosphere, Lithosphere, Hydrosphere and Biosphere.

The above pertain to Latitude, Altitude, Soil, Climate and Habitat on the non-biological side and Life Cycles, Reproductive Cycles, Successional Cycles and Food Chains on the biological side.

B. WHAT IS ECOLOGY

Balanced coexistence : Inter relationships, Inter connections, Interactions, Interdependences

1. Levels of Ecology : Planetary, Geographical, Ecosystems, Communities, Populations, Individual
2. Approach 1: Principles and Applications
3. Approach 2: Problems on Ground - What needs to be done
4. Approach 3: Ecological Thinking / Wisdoms

C. WHY APPLIED ECOLOGY ?

1. Productivity in Ecosystems - both Natural and Managed - is an endpoint, a Product, an ecological output. It is tangible and therefore vital for human existence. This happens by a careful balancing of all natural components and forces.
2. Conversion of Nature, Development, affects these balances and thus affect productivity negatively. These ecological disturbances therefore need ecological solutions, Restorations
3. Other Developments / Contingencies also needed Inputs from ecological knowledge systems
4. Backgrounds and skills needed to apply ecology for human welfare

D. PARTICIPATORY, INTERACTIVE AND INTEGRATIVE

What are the values of Ecosystems. How are they overexploited. How systems are degraded. How are they restored to normalcy. What are the Ecological Principles.

A. WATER RELATIONS : Marine & Non-Marine, Moving and Stationary Water Bodies, Biology and Ecology

Aquacultures - All Possible Types

Restorations - All types of degraded water bodies

B. SOIL RELATIONS : Quality, Landscape and use, Biology Erosions, Amendments & Remediations

C. PLANT ECOLOGY : Individuals, Populations, Communities Agriculture - Companion & Alternate, Soil - Crops - weeds - litter - pests - irrigation
Reforestation, Afforestation, Social Forestry, Silviculture, Soil Binders

Budgets: Water, Nutrient, Energy - Light and Temperature
Physiognomy: Habit, Density, Frequency
Phenology: Seed to seed in time and space
Interactions :

Plant/plant : habitat - weeds, Competition
Plant/Animal : Reproduction - Pollination, Dispersal
Plant/soil : Nutrition - Nitrogen fixation, aeration by worms
Plant/water : Drought, Salinity, nutrient uptake, evaporation & transpiration

D. ANIMAL ECOLOGY : Individuals, Populations, Communities Domestication, Animal Husbandry, Predators, Monitors, Vectors, Parasites, Nutrient Contributors, Bio-energy, Fish & Bird Models

E. CYCLES

1. Life Cycles : Vegetative and Reproductive; Ephemeral, Annual, Biennial and Perennial
2. Vegetative Cycles : Once, Twice, Repeated, week [s] or months
3. Reproductive Cycles : Once, Twice, Repeated, week [s] or months Pollination Strategy and Seed Output
Dispersal, Banking, Dormancy, Viability
4. Succesional Cycles : Seasonalities

F. INTERACTIONS WITHIN AND BETWEEN HABITATS & BIOTA

Pest Control, Vermiculture, Sericulture, Apiculture, Pollination and Seed Dispersal

G. FOOD CHAINS / WEBS: Efficiency, Water relations, Habits - herb, shrub, climber, tree, nutrition, Gaseous / chemical exchange

H. ILLFARE APPLICATIONS: Biological and Ecological warfares, Researches of Defense Departments

I. WELFARE APPLICATIONS: Biotechnology, Genetic Engineering, G M Crops, Gene-ecology, Ecological Genetics

J. CASE STUDIES : Problems and Solutions

Many intractable Cases were solved by ecological knowledge

K. EVENTS OF HISTORICAL VALUE: Fables, Parables, Episodes & Events can now be explained from ecological standpoints

A university is what a college becomes when the faculty loses interest in students

2. APPROACH-1: BIOLOGICAL BASES

A. PLANT ECOLOGY

1. Root Ecology
   - (a) Sprinkler Irrigation
   - (b) Drip irrigation
   - (c) Underground Barricades against erosion
   - (d) soil binding on the surface and sub-surface
2. Autecology
   - (a) Companion Cropping
   - (b) Weed management,
   - (c) Nutrient Cycling and Rotation [alternate] Cropping
   - (d) Nutrient Physiology & Productivity Interactions
3. Production Ecology & Nutrient Physiology
   - (a) Monocultures: Leaves, Stems -overground, Stems - underground, Flowers, Fruits-Unripe, Fruits-Ripe, Seeds,
4. Others
   1. Agriculture
   2. Horticulture & Gardens
   3. Silviculture
   4. Green belts
   5. Wind breaks
   6. Soil erosion
   7. Draining bogs [water logging]
   8. Social forestry, Agroforestry
   9. Forest protection, working plan 10. Seed technology
   11. Hybridisation & Extinctions: Habitat Loss / Over Exploitation
   12. Restoration Ecology
   13. Biofertilizers
   14. Plant Introductions: applied Phytogeography
   15. Cactus & Euphorbia Monocultures in California
   16. Dry land Agriculture [Israel],
5. Keywords: Gardens, wind, erosion, soil, bogs, forestry, agroforestry, social forestry, energy plantations, plantations, wood, seed banks, weeds, wood, hybrids

B. ANIMAL ECOLOGY

GENERAL

1. Husbandry of cattle, rabbits, laboratory animals

2. Zoos, Captive breeding, Game farming
3. Snakes, Frogs - Cultures and maintenance
4. Insect Biology - Many Applications
5. Behavioral Ecology in Neurosciences and Training of Animals
6. Impact of exotic species on Ecosystem
7. Milk, Meat & Energy: Goat, Buffaloe, Cow, Pig, Poultry, Horse, Mule, Camel, new foods
8. In situ and Ex situ Conservation, Gene bank
9. Effect of Exotic competitions on native fauna
10. Theory of national park design
11. Ecotourism

Key Words: zoos, pets, reptiles, insects, fish, birds, guano, bees, lac, vectors, parasites, hybrids

ORNITHOLOGY

1. Poultry, Ostrich - etc. rearing and Farming
2. Bird pets
3. Guano
4. Biological Warfare

Key Words: guano, migration, game birds, cage birds, trade

DOMESTICATED ANIMALS

1. Domesticated animals - dogs, cats, birds, etc.

C. AQUATIC ECOLOGY

1. Pisciculture
2. Mariculture
3. Algal cultures
4. Aquarium
5. Capture Fisheries
6. Culture of Molluscans, Crustaceans, etc.

Key Words: crabs, prawns, lobsters. oysters, spirulina, artemia

D. PEDOLOGY

1. Temperature
2. Porosity
3. Nutrients
4. Biota
5. Erosion
6. Desertification
7. Conservation
8. Soil formation
9. Soil Pollution
10. Reclamation of Alkaline Soil

E. MICROBIOL ECOLOGY

1. Antarctica - cold resistant
2. Heat resistance
3. Microorganisms - pesticides
4. Bioremediation

F. PLANT & ANIMAL INTERACTIONS

GENERAL

1. Biological Controls of Pests based on Predator-prey relationships;
2. Vector Parasite Management;
3. Wood-termite relationship in Plant Protoplast Fusions;
4. Frugivorous habit helped increase Tree Populations in Madagaskar;
5. Sericulture: Mulberry and Silk worm - Animal product
6. Apiculture: Bee and the Flower interaction - plant product
7. Lac-Culture
   (a) Sericulture (b) Apiculture (c) Lac culture
   (d) Biopesticides (e) Predator -prey relationships
   (f) Vermiculture, Organic farming

VECTORS AND PARASITES MANAGEMENT

1. Communicable disease: social and preventive medicine
2. Vector management practices

G. PLANT-ANIMAL-SOIL-WATER

1. Agriculture - crop, weed, pest, pathogen, IPM, Land Use
2. Integrated farming - birds, cattle
3. Forest Management
4. Water Management

H. ILLFARE ACTIVITIES

1. Drawing others Waters / liquid minerals from underground
2. Germ warfare
3. Carriers, Delivery Systems
4. Pest and Pathogen, Pesticide and pollutant warfare

I. CONSERVATION, RECLAMATION, RESTORATION

1. Waste lands, salt marshes, Mangroves, saline lands, Degraded lands, polluted lakes, tanks, rivers
2. Reforestation
3. Rare Species Conservation, Distribution

K. WASTES' Utilisations / Conversions and Disposals

1. Liquid waste-water, solid waste - sludge
2. Identification of Waste Potentials - organic / Chemical

L. BIOTECHNOLOGY

1. Genetic engineering for Ecology, Genes as resources
2. Water Economy, Salinity resistance, Adventitious Rooting
3. Genetic engineering for Productivity, exchange of Germplasm
4. Homoclimes, Gene-ecology
5. Cloning
6. Plastics degrading Microbes - Exploration or Engineering

M. ENGINEERING

1. Civil - Check Dams, Ground Water, Rain water Harvesting
2. Chemical Processes, Treatment of Pollutants from Industry
3. Treatment and application of sewage and sludge

N. OTHERS

1. Local People - Local Resources - Sustainability
2. Tradition, Culture and Civilisation
3. Geopolitics: Homoclimes, Conflicts, Co-operations
4. Ecofeminism
5. Ecotourism, Sustainable Development, Insular areas.
6. Urban ecology, Exploitation of Community Knowledge, Ethnobotany
7. Fire

"concern for MAN and his fate must always form the chief interest of all technical endeavours in order that the creation of our minds shall be a blessing and not a curse".

Einstein

Good teaching is one-fourth preparation and three-fourths theater

3. APPROACH-2: PROBLEMS AND SOLUTIONS

1. Thames River Clearance
2. Ganga Action Plan
3. Population Raising Projects: Tiger, Crocodile etc
4. USAR land Restoration
5. Mining Soil Restoration
6. North Sea Salmon and Rhine Pollution
7. Integrated Pest Management
8. Sewage Reuse
9. MSW Recycling
10. Restoration of Ecosystems - Auroville
11. Remediation of Soils
12. Air Pollution Abatement
13. Oil spill Clearance

Education is a better safeguard of liberty than a standing army

4. APPROACH-3: EPISODES/HISTORICAL EVENTS

1. **Spinsters made Britain Great**
   Plant-Animal Interactions —> Predator-Prey Relations —> Rural/urban —> Domestication —> Nutritive Value —>Physiology
2. **Pandavas were ignorant of their own surroundings**
   Krishna: Honey —> Ants —> Frogs —> Snake —> Eagle —> Hunter
3. **Brazilian Ground Nut increased the Prices of Turkey in Britain**
   Political Activity —> Social Survey —> Scientific Analysis —> Bioassays —> Fractionation —> Organic Chemistry —> Identification of New Compounds —> Genotoxicity Testing —> Smaller Mammals
4. **Cormonants of Chile saved Europe**
   Fish Eating Birds —> Guano on Andes —> Shipment to Britain —> European Soils obtain Phosphorus / Sulphur Amendments —> Britain captures the sea fish —> Processes locally and imports —> Birds loose food source and DIE —> Guano lost and birds too - Chile lost the resource
5. **Industrialised Agriculture blew Dakota Soil into Chicago**
   Extensive agriculture in Mid-plains —> top soil lost adhesion —> wind blew it off —> Fertility lost —> researches restored fertility after many years
6. **Ant Hill and the Undried Fish**
   Fish did not dry —> No Sunshine —> Haystack —> Cow did not Eat—>Not let Out —>Child Crying from Ant sting —> Anthill attacked
7. **Reaping the Harvest 4 decades after Sowing the Seed at Love canal**
   Niagara Water Falls —> Waste land —> Filling of Toxic Waste —> Decades later —> Housing Colony —> Diseases —> Traced to Ground Water —> Carcinogens from the Wastes
8. **Pakistan's Actions against India**
   (a) Ravi Water flow Direction altered —> Erosion on Indian side
   (b) Tunneling through soft soil and open into thick and long grass vegetation
   (c) Falcons used to carry cameras by feet and photograph Indian Installations
9. **Tashirojima island of North Japan**
   Silk industry affected – larvae eaten by mouse – cats introduced to eat the mice – cats need new food – beach fish and fish wastes became substitutes – 800 cats for 100 people

5. CLUES FROM SPCIALISED LITERATURES

A. PLANT ECOLOGY

1. Silviculture 2. Horticulture 3. Gardens
4. Green belts 5. Wind breaks 6. Soil erosion
7. Draining bogs 8. Social forestry

B. ANIMAL ECOLOGY

1. Husbandry of cattle, rabbits, laboratory animals
2. Zoos
3. Snakes, Frogs - Cultures and maintenance
4. Insect Biology - Many Applications
5. Behavioral Ecology in Neurosciences and Training of Animals

C. AQUATIC ECOLOGY

1. Pisciculture 2. Mariculture
3. Algal culture 4. Aquarium
5. Capture Fisheries 6. Culture of Molluscans, Crustaceans, etc.

D. PEDOLOGY

1. Erosion 2. Porosity 3. Nutrients 4. Biota

E. ORNITHOLOGY

1. Poultry, Ostrich - etc. rearing
2. Bird pets 3. Guano 4. Biological Warfare

F. PLANT AND ANIMAL INTERACTIONS

1. Sericulture 2. Apiculture 3. Lac culture
4. Biopesticides
5. Predator -prey relationships

G. PLANT-ANIMAL-SOIL-WATER

1. Agriculture - crop, weed, pest, pathogen
2. Integrated farming - birds, cattle
3. Forest Management

H. WARFARE AND ALLIED USES

1. Drawing others Waters / liquid minerals from underground
2. Germ warfare
3. Carriers, Delivery Systems
4. Pest and Pathogen, Pesticide and pollutant warfare

I. VECTORS AND PARASITES MANAGEMENT

1. Communicable disease: social and preventive medicine
2. Vector management practices

J. RECLAMATION

1. Waste lands, salt marshes, saline lands, Degraded lands, polluted lakes, tanks, rivers
2. Reforestation

K. WASTES' Utilisations / Conversions and Disposals

1. Liquid waste-water, solid waste - sludge

L. MICROBIOL ECOLOGY

1. Antarctica - cold resistant
2. Heat resistance
3. Microorganisms - pesticides

M. BIOTECHNOLOGY

1. Genetic engineering for Ecology
2. Water Economy, Salinity resistance, Adventitious Rooting
3. Genetic engineering for Productivity
4. Homoclimes
5. Gene-ecology

N. SCIENCE OF PETS

1. Domesticated animals - dogs, cats, birds, etc.

O. ENGINEERING

1. Civil, Chemical - Check Dams, Processes in Industry

P. OTHERS

Local people - local resources - sustainability tradition, culture and civilization geopolitics: homoclimes, hostilities and cooperation ecofeminisim

> "To every thing there is a
> season and a time to every purpose"

Ecclesiaster

6. LEADS FROM PRINT AND VISUAL MEDIA

A. RESOURCES

1. Soil & Land
2. Minerals
3. Plants
4. Animals
5. Humans
6. Water
7. Ecosystems
8. Energy -Nuclear
9. En-Phytomass –Petro-plants
10. En-Muscle - Animal, Human
11. En-Biogas
12. En-Coal
13. En-Hydro
14. En-Oil, Gas
15. En-Others: solar, wind, , geo

B. DEVELOPMENT - Cultures

1. Agriculture
2. Aquaculture
3. Food
4. Social Forestry
5. Gardening
6. Others

C. DEVELOPMENT - Projects

1. Irrigation
2. Energy
3. Industrial
4. Others

D. ENVIRONMENT - Scenarios

1. Biodiversity, Germplasm
2. Soil & Land
3. Chemicals, Pesticides
4. Consumerism & Adulteration
5. Radiations
6. Poll-air
7. Poll-water
8. Poll-soil
9. Acid rain
10. Green house
11. Ozone depletion
12. Climate changes
13. Health

E. ENVIRONMENT - Disasters

1. Drought/famine
2. Floods/Storms/Tides
3. Wars-CBW, Nuclear
4. Accidents
5. Degradations
6. Deforestation
7. Poaching

F. ENVIRONMENT - Social

1. Trade
2. Tourism
3. Rural
4. Urban
5. People

G. MANAGEMENT - Monitoring

1. Remote sensing
2. Indicators

H. MANAGEMENT - Action

1. Ecoagriculture
2. Conservation / protection: afforestation, Wild life
3. Reserves, Parks, Sanct.Gardens, Zoos
4. Reclamation/restoration
5. Sewage, Solid wastes
6. Civic Environmentalism

I. MANAGEMENT - Social

1. Education
2. NGO's, Activism, Movements
3. Parties, Govt. & law

J. SCIENCE

1. Biology
2. Medicine
3. Biotechnology
4. GenoToxicology

K. EDUCATION

1. Sci.& Tech.
2. Universities
3. Disvalues

L. INDIAN SOCIETY

1. History, Heritage,
2. Futures
3. Politics
4. Economics
5. Philosophy
6. Corruption

M. GLOBAL SOCIETY: Other Countries

7. ECOLOGICAL VALUES OF PLANTS

I. HIGHER PLANTS

A. INTRODUCTION

B. CLIMATE - VEGETATION RELATIONSHIP

C. ENVIRONMENTAL ROLES OF PLANTS

1. Physical Roles
   - (a) Maintaining vegetative cover
   - (b) Filtering dustfrom the air
   - (c) Reducing noise
   - (d) Cooling the air
   - (e) Pollution control
   - (f) Controlling wind erosion
   - (g) Wind breaks
2. Physiological Roles
   - (a) Watershed preservation
   - (b) Adding oxygen to the air
   - (c) Removing carbon dioxide from the air d. Nitrogen fixation
3. Intermediate Roles
   - (a) Organic mulches
   - (b) Wildlife support
   - (c) Food chain roles
   - (d) Nutrient cycling
   - (e) Pollination
4. Special Roles
   - (a) Grass lands
   - (b) Forest trees
   - (c) Mangroves

II. LOWER PLANTS

A. Classification

B. Ecological condition

C. Ecological uses of bryophytes

D. Seed beds

E. Erosion prevention

F. Sponges for acid rain

G. Treatment & waste water

H. Nitrogen fixing

I. Indicators of air pollution

J. Indicators of water pollution

III. PLANTS AND ANIMAL INTERACTIONS

A. Plant and animal intraction for human welfare

B. Plants benefit from animals

DISPERSAL

C. Pollen transport of cross pollination

D. Distribution of plants

HONEY

E. Nector of the plant

F. Apiculture - artificial making

PREDATOR–PREY

G. Predator - prey relationship

H. Prey distribution

I. Advantage of predator and prey relationship

BIOPESTICIDES

J. Biopesticides

K. Biopesticides of mosquito

L. Dragon fly numphs

M. Fishes like gambusia, minnows etc eat mosquito larvae.

N. Pest eating pests m. Advantages of biopesticides

COMMUNICABLE DISEASES

O. Plague

P. Malaria

Q. Gambia fever

R. Cholera

S. Parasites -amoebic dysentry

CONTROL OF VECTORS AND PARASITES

8. MONOCULTURES AND POLYCULTURES

I. CULTURE

A. INTRODUCTION
B. POLYCULTURE
C. MONOCULTURE
D. AGRICULTURE
E. HORTICULTURE
F. AQUACULTURE
G. SILVICULTURE
H. ARBORICULTURE

II. SERICULTURE

A. TYPE OF SILK
B. ORIGIN
C. SERICULTURE IN INDIA
D. RAW SILK PRODUCTION
E. STRATEGIES FOR SILK WORK BREEDING
1. Objectives for silk worm breeding
2. Development strategy for cocoon production technology
3. Strategy for raw silk and fabric production

F. ENVIRONMENTAL CONDITIONS
G. DEVELOPMENT PROBLEMS
1. Trends in world raw silk output
2. Global production of textile fibres
3. Raw silk production by variety
4. Mulberry silk production in india (MAJOR STATE)

III. TISSUE CULTURE

A. INTRODUCTION
B. TECHNIQUES
1. Micro propagation
2. Clonal propagation

C. APPLICATIONS
1. Plant pathology
2. Production of genetically variable plants
3. Viral eradication
4. Plant breeding, plant improvement
5. Production of useful bio-chemicals

D. PEST CONTROL IN MONOCULTURES
E. USE OF ORGANIC WASTES FOR FISH CULTURE
F. NEED TO VITALIZE INDIA'S CULTURE AND ENVIROMENT

"The greatest service that can be rendered to any country is to add a useful plant to it's culture"

Jefferson

9. AGRICULTURE AS APPLIED ECOLOGY

A. INTRODUCTION

1. The ecosystem concept
2. Agricultural ecology
3. Biochemistry of agro-ecosystem
4. The world food balance
5. Source of energy
6. Energy flow & biogeochemical cycles

B. ORIGIN OF AGRICULTURE

1. The chinese centre
2. The Indian centre
3. The central Asian centre
4. The near eastern centre
5. The Mediterranean centre
6. The Abyssinian centre
7. The middle American centre
8. The south American centre

C. HUMAN POPULATION & FOOD DEMAND

1. Cultivable Area
2. Classification Of Land
3. Types Of Soils

D. HUMAN FOOD PRODUCTION SYSTEMS

1. Agricultural Operations
2. Cropping Pattern
   (a) Inter- cropping. Companion cropping, alternate cropping
   (b) Organic farming
   (c) Integrated farming systems
   (d) Low external input sustainable agriculture (leisa)
   (e) Shifting cultivation
3. Cropping Pattern-2
   (a) Ley farming
   (b) Intensive cropping
   (c) Stubble retention
   (d) Traditional agriculture
   (e) Sustainable agriculture
4. Food crops:
   (a) Paddy
   (b) Herbs
   (c) Millets
   (d) Maize
   (e) Sugarcane
   (f) Pulses
   (g) Green
   (h) Fruits
   (i) Potatoes etc
5. Commercial crops:
   (a) Tea
   (b) Coffee
   (c) Rubber
   (d) Oil Seeds
   (e) Jute
   (f) Cotton
   (g) Tobacco
   (h) Cashew
   (i) Spices etc

6. Agricultural Implements
   (a) Traditional (b) Modern
7. Seeds, Manures and Fertilizers
8. Plant protection measures
   (a) Chemical (b) Mechanical (c) Physical (d) Cultural (e) Biological
9. Plantation of tree Belts Around Fields
   (a) Farm produce
      1. Farm Yard Manure 2. Urine
      3. Slurry 4. Compost
      5. Green Manuring
   (b) Non-Farm Produce
      1. Blood Meal 2. Bone Meal
      3. Guano 4. Hoof and Horn
10. Bio conversion of Agricultural Wastes

E. AGRICULTURAL LAND & FOOD PRODUCTION SUBSISTANCE AGRICULTURE

1. Soil, water & nutrients
2. The ecology of domestication
3. Pastoralism
4. Shifting cultivation
5. Permanent non-mechanised agricultural system
6. Chiampa cultivation in the valley of mexico
7. Desert run off agriculture

F. ECOLOGICAL FEATURES OF INTENSIVE CULTURE

1. Continuity 2. Adaptability
3. Ecosystem regulation & subsidization

G. THE DYNAMICS

1. Climate & agriculture
2. Impacts of irrigation & fertilizer
3. Soil & plant microbiology
4. Maintenance of the soil ecosystem
   (a) The nature of agricultural pest problems
   (b) Chemical pest control
   (c) Biological control of pest
5. Host Resistance & Integrated Pest Management

H. IMPACTS OF CULTIVATION AND GRAZING ON SOIL

1. Over grazing & desertification
2. Impacts of irrigation
3. Acid rains
4. Impacts of monoculture

I. FORESTRY: CLEAR CUTTING VS SELECTIVE CUTTING

1. Agroforestry
   - (a) Cropping (b) Lopping (c) Pruning
   - (d) Subsistence griforestry
   - (e) Commercial agroforestry
   - (f) Intermediate agroforestry
2. Social forestry
   - (a) Urban forestry
   - (d) Commercial form forestry
   - (b) Non-Commercial form forestry
   - (e) Community forestry
   - (c) Individual beneficiary oriented
   - (f) Community beneficiary oriented

J. OUTLOOK FOR INCREASING FOOD PRODUCTION

1. Available land
2. Water
3. Plant & animal breeding
4. Salt tolerant plants
5. Modifying old plants by new technologies
   - (a) Genetic vulnerability & germ plasm resources
   - (b) Breeding for improved performance

K. NEW SOURCES OF FOOD PRODUCTION

1. New Wild Plants To Agriculture / Plant Revival
2. Plants in enclosed environment outer space
3. Food from sea
4. Fish farming, aquaculture & mariculture
5. Eating lower on the food chain
6. Synthetic food

L. WHY AGRICULTURAL BELTS IN THE PAST HAVE FAILED?

M. WILL THE PRESENT ONES ALSO FAIL?

N. MAJOR SPROUTS & FALLS IN AGRICULTURE

O. THE GREEN REVOLUTION

The job of an educator is to teach students to see vitality in themselves

10. AQUACULTURE

A. DEFINITION

B. CLASSIFICATION OF AUQACULTURE

1. Fresh water
   - (a) Composite aquaculture
   - (b) Air breathing fish culture
   - (c) Integrated fish farming
   - (d) Larvivorous fish culture
   - (e) Ornamental fish culture
2. Brakish water

C. DIFFERENT FORMS OF AQUACULTURE

1. Fish culture in ponds
2. Using net pens, cage and enclosures
3. Vertical culture
4. Fish culture in irrigation canals and paddy fields

D. ECOLOGY OF A FISH POND

1. Water 2. Temperature 3. Turbidity 4. Light

E. MAINTENANCE OF AQUACULTURE

1. Breeding 2. Hatching 3. Feeding 4. Testing
5. Harvesting

F. CONSTRUCTION OF A FISH FARM

G. PRODUCTIVITY OF A FISH POND

H. FISH CULTURE IN BRACKISH WATER

1. Eel culture 2. Crab culture 3. Prawn culture

I. OTHERS

1. Mullets 2. Common carp 3. Indian carps
4. Labyrinths 5. Pikes and Perches
   - (a) Shrimp (b) Oyster (c) Mussels (d) Frog

J. PLANTS

1. Fresh water plants 2. Sea-weeds

K. BIOTECHNOLOGY APPROACH

1. Improved Diagnostic Reagents
2. Genetic Manipulations
   - (a) Chromosome Set Manipulation
   - (b) Gene Transfer

   (c) Selection of Gene for Transfer
   (d) Cryo-preservation Technology
3. Concerns raised by Biotechnology Approach
4. Social Issues in Aquaculture
   (a) Objectives
   (b) Aquaculture in India
   (c) Social Issues

L. INDUSTRY & NATIONAL BANKS IN AQUACULTURE DEVELOPMENT

Time is a great teacher, but unfortunately it kills all its pupils

11. TREE CULTURES

I. INTRODUCTION

A. **PERMACULTURE** B. **POMOCULTURE**

C. **FLORICULTURE** D. **OLERICULTURE**

E. **SERICULTURE** F. **MORICULTURE**

G. **AGROFORESTRY,** H. **SOCIAL FORESTRY,**

I. **ENERGY PLANTATIONS**

II. HIGH FOREST SYSTEMS

A. **HIGH FOREST SYSTEMS**

1. Clear Felling Sytem (a) Advantages (b) Disadvantages
2. Clear strip system
3. Alternative strip system 4. Uniform system
5. Group system 6. Shelter Strip System
7. Eberhands wedge system
   (a) Selection system
      1. Advantages 2. Disadvantage
   (b) Accessory systems

B. **COPPICE SYSTEM**

III. EVEN-AGED STANDS

IV. UNEVEN-AGED STANDS

A. **NATURAL FOREST OR PLANTATION**

B. **BENEFITS TO LOCAL PEOPLE**

C. **SILVICULTURAL SYSTEM IN PRACTICE**

D. **PLANTATIONS**

1. Silvicultural
2. Reasons for plantations
3. Development of plantation forestry
   1945 - 1965 :Three main trends influenced plantations.
   1966-present day.
4. Purpose of plantation
5. List of crops (plants) used in plantations and gardens

E. **THE CLEAR CUTTING SYSTEM**

1. Systems of concentrated regenerations
2. Seed -tree method

3. Agro-forestry
4. Agro-silvicultural system
5. The irregular shelter wood system:
   (a) The strip of group system
   (b) The uniform system
   (c) The group system
   (d) The shelter wood strip system
   (e) Wagner's blenders annschlay
   (f) Edwards wedge system
6. Allessory systems
   (a) Two -storied high forest system
   (b) High forest with vennus systems
   (c) Improvement fellings system

F. THE SELECTION SYSTEM

1. The uniform system
2. The group system
   (a) The selection system
   (b) The group selection systems
   (c) Coppice System

G. THE COPPICE SYSTEM

1. SILVO-PASTURAL SYSTEM
2. AGRO-SILCO PASTORAL SYSTEM
3. TAUNGYA
   (a) The simple coppice system
   (b) The shelter wood coppice system
   (c) Coppice with standards system
   (d) Selection coppice systems
   (e) Polluted system

H. FOREST GENETICS AND BREEDING

I. SELECTION OF GENETIC RESOURCES

J. ADVANCED GENERATION BREEDING

K. LARGE SCALE PRODUCTION OF VEGETTIVE PROPAGULES

1. Clone development approach
2. Tissue culture propagation
   Agrosilviculture - Silvipastoral - Agrosilvipastoral etc.

12. BIOMONITORING OF POLLUTION

Things are so strictly related, that according to the skill of the eye, from any one object the parts and properties of any other may be predicted Ralph Waldo Emerson (1803 - 1882).

I. INTRODUCTION

A. OBJECTIVES OF BIOLOGICAL MONITORING

B. EFFECTS ON ECOSYSTEMS

Reasons for long-term studies; Localities for ecosystem monitoring

1. Biological interactions with pollutants
   - (a) Bioaccumulation Magnification
   - (b) Measurement of tropical response against exposure levels / doses
   - (c) Advantage
2. Biotic indices
   - (a) Pollution factors and changes in trophical characteristics
   - (b) Direct measurement of biotic characteristics
   - (c) Farms of biotic indices classes of indices based on:
     1. Changes in function of an ecosystems
     2. In community structure if biota in an ecosystem
     3. Combinations of functional and community changes
3. Measures of the functions of the ecosystem:
   - (a) Changes in respiration photosynthetic ratio
   - (b) Changes in oxygen consumption
   - (c) Changes in concentration of 1. ADP 2. Lipids
   - (d) Changes in filtering rates
   - (e) Changes in Reproductive rates
   - (f) Changes in nutrient cycling rates
4. Measures of community Structure
   - (a) Identification, classification and quantification of biota
   - (b) Simple structural biotic index: the number of higher taxa, facilities, genera or species in an area.
   - (c) Sets of "Indicator species" different levels of pollution Limitations.
5. Indicator species
   - (a) why biological indication

     Types of bio indicators

Limitations to the use of bio indicators

Integrated use of plant, vegetation & land indication

(b) Ecological indicator species: Particular species which are selectively adapted to certain pollution conditions (either heavy or clean), (resistance) whose presence or absence is used to indicate pollution conditions.

(c) Chemical indicator species: Organisms that accumulate toxic substances present in trace amounts.

1. Indicators of Sewage Pollution
2. Indicators of Air Pollution
    (a) Epiphytic lichens
    (b) Higher Plants
    (c) Animals of indicators
        1. Health surveillance
3. Indicators of Climate
4. Agricultural Indicators
5. Indicators of potential productivity of Land pollution of surface water
6. Indicator of soil and other soil characteristic plant communities as indicators of ecological conditions
7. Indicators of Fire
8. Indicators of Petroleum
9. Indicators of adequate oxygen in water
10. Indicators of Overgrazing

6. Eco-toxicology of pollutants
    (a) Deoxygenating substances: EFFECTS OF REDUCED DISSOLVed oxygen and associated factors on communities and ecosystems.
    (b) Nutrient enrichment and entrospicaton: Ecosystem changes.
    (c) Pesticides
        1. Toxic effects on organisms
        2. Ecosystem response
        3. Overall ecosystem effects
    (d) Petroleum and related hydro carbons
        1. Uptake and metabolism by larger biota
        2. Biological and transfer and bio-magnification

3. Sub-lethal effects.
4. Ecosystem effects

(e) Metals and SALTS

1. Transport and transformations in biota.
2. Toxic effects on individuals
3. Ecological effects

(f) Atmospheric pollutants

(g) Thermal pollution

1. heated effluents
2. Discharges from dams and reservoirs

(h) Radio-nuclides

1. Physiological effects of radiation.
2. Effects on communities, populations and ecosytems

(i) Suspended solids and silt

1. Effects on individuals
2. Ecological effects

7. Conclusions

(a) Basic knowledge required for bio-monitoring exposure to chemicals

(b) Criteria for selecting the biological tests.

(c) Confounding factors in biological monitoring.

(d) Monitoring strategies and assessment.

(e) Analytical aspects

(f) Ethical aspects

POSSIBLE ANIMAL CANDIDATES

Ameca Splendours (fish),	Platichothys flesus
Ictalurus, mebulosus (Brown Bull Heab)	American oyster
Pomatoeeros triqueter	Winter founder
Asiatic clans Corbicula s(p)	Rainbow tank
Scorldculana plana - borrowing bivalve -	Pleuroelelus watl - newt
(Heavy metals)	Pangrellus Neauthes arnaceodenlata
Grassotera gigas - Pacific oyster	Ictalurus mebulosus
Grassotera Virginia American oyster	pet dogs
Macona Bralthica - clams - Ag 8 Cu Accum	Donax
Rangia Cunelata - Clams	Umbrapygmaea
Anadonta Cygnea (anatna) - fresh water	purpuratus
muscel	Pleurodeles watl
Unio Elegangotulus - Fresh water muscel	Ellipto Complanatus

(*Contd...*)

Homous americam - Lobsteres
Cancer Urroratus - Role crab
Lamp silis ventricosa-Pochet boole mussel 1
Heteropmenste fossilis (fish)
Littorina saseatilis - peinimble
shrump (accum)
Neries Vireus - Polychael
Hydra - Alteniata ? 146
Gnathonenims petrisi - electrifish
Peromysilus polionotus - old field mouse
Dalphina - Brocare
Bulinius - fresh water snail
(fresh water mud)
Poecilocerus pictus (grasshopper
Littorura littorea
Macoma balthica (class)
Lig techinus pictus
stizo sledion candense
Coturnix Japanica - Japanese quael
Notho branchino rachaivi
Caenor habdetes elgan(Mematode)
Venerupis japonica - Short necked clam
Hemigraspus nudus - shorecrabs
Palemonelas pugio (grass shrump)
Poccilia reliculata-guppy
Mya arenaria - softshell clam
Diplodon chilensis chilensis
Notobranchius achoivi (Fresh)
Sea urchin - Stronglyo controtus
Smeteria mollisuma
Zebra fish
Habrobracion
Golisa fasciatus
Nephthys incisa
Panagellus rediannus
Nolopterus nolopletus

Raccoons
Umbralim
Cluck embryos
Chironomus
Meno hystera
Micropertalama
Diplolaime bruciee
Mytilus edulis
Augulla, (EEP)
Mytulus gallo SCE
Drosophila
Nibea mit Sukuri (Goaler)
Oryzias lalopes (Medaka)
Rerrulus Marmoratus
Boleophalmus dussumieri
Rana catas beiana
Scarbeculari plana
Homarus amenanus lobster
Alburnus alburnus
Nitoera spempes
Atlanta Macteral eggs
Parophrys vetu lus
Grassostera gigas
Cancer magester
Sharks - accumulatoss
Ostrea edulis
Abra alba
Neries Vireus
Peromyscus Lencopus
Sigmedon lisjudus
Momedon monoceros
Para phrys vetulus
Mus musculus

13. BIOLOGICAL INDICATORS

I. INTRODUCTION: Why Biological Indication

A. BASICS

1. The various reasons of using Bioindication
2. The various levels & integration of life forms used as biological Indicators.

B. LIMITATIONS OF THE USE OF BIO-INDICATORS

The use of organisms as indicators is restricted by limitations arising form the four following main laws :

1. The law of Bass Becking - Beyerinck
2. The law of the physiological & ecological amplitude.
3. The law of relative site constancy
4. The complex characters of factors (environmental)
   (a) The biosphere & its constitutents.
   (b) Natural feed back system and natural time scale over which effects of disturbances are dissipated.
   (c) Artificial feed back system, viz. monitoring of changes in the environment, using biological indicators.

C. DEFINITIONS

1. Monitoring
2. Biological monitoring
3. Biological indicators

D. OBJECTIVES OF BIOLOGICAL MONITORING

1. Recommendations of the Inter. Uni. Biol. Sci.(IUBS), 1982
   (a) Encouragement of scientific and national bodies to develop methods.
   (b) Interdisciplinary & international cooperation in standardising methods.
   (c) Encouragement of exchange of research results amongst the labs of the world.
   (d) Conferences on indicators at cellular, individual and population and ecosystem level.
2. Monitoring is undertaken for the following resons:
   (a) Basic for management of biological resources for sustainable development.
   (b) Conservation of ecosystems and populations.

(c) Knowledge of dynamics of ecosystem.

(d) Insert pests of agriculture and forestry can studied for means of control.

3. Classification of questions regarding data collection:

   (a) Who undertakes or supports programme?

   (b) Aims and objectives?

   (c) What methods are being used? Are they the most appropriate ones?

   (d) What is the time scale for monitoring?

   (e) Choice of variables and processes to be studied - do they fulfill the objectives of the programme?

4. Health surveillance

   (a) Evaluation of health status.

   (b) Identification of individuals undergoing adverse health effects.

5. Types of Bioindicators

   (a) True indicators

   (b) Scales of Indicator species

   (c) Accumulators

6. Biological monitoring - various criteria to be met.

   (d) Integration of chemical monitoring & Biological monitoring.

II. BIOLOGICAL INDICATORS

A. Community changes -change in species composition of the community) can be used to monitor current status of the environment

B. Predictions based on previously documented community changes

C. Biological material and indicator species used for monitoring range from cells, tissues and organs to whole oroganisms of plants and animals

D. Various levels & integration of life forms used as biological Indicators. Intergration of chemical & Biological monitoring.

E. Limitations of the use of Bio-indicators: The use of organisms as indicators is restricted by the following

   1. The law of Bass Becking - Beyerinck

   2. The law of the physiological & ecological amplitude.

   3. The law of relative site constancy

   4. The complex characters of factors (environmental)

III. TYPES OF INDICATORS

1. Sentinels: Organisms introduced into the environment as early warning systems.
2. Detectors: Species occuring naturally in the area, showing a measurable response to change.
3. Exploiters: abundance due to lack of competition from eliminated species.
4. Accummulators: organisms taking up chemicals in measurable quantities.
5. Bioassay organisms: organisms used as lab reagents to :
   - detect presence and / or
   - concentration of pollutants,
   - rank pollutants in order of toxicity

IV. PLANTS AS INDICATORS

Lichens, Mosses, fungi, Higher plants; advantages & disadvantages

A. 1. Presence or absence as indicator of environmental conditions.
2. Community indicators such as characteristic flora of certain soils and water availability.
3. Specific plant taxa used as indicators. Lichens, Mosses, fungi, Higher vascular plants advantages and disadvantages.

B. INTEGREATED USE OF PLANT - VEGETATION & LAND INDICATION

1. Use of species combination as indicators
2. Structure & life form as indication.

C. PLANTS AS INDICATORS OF PROCESSES & USES

1. Indicators of Agriculture
2. Indicators of Salinity
3. Indicators & accumulators of gaseous air pollution
4. Community indicators such as characteristic flora of certain soils and water availability.

D. BIOINDICATORS AND CHEMICAL POLLUTION OF SURFACE WATERS

1. Use of Direct & indirect method of Indication.

E. BIOLOGICAL INDICATION OF AIR POLLUTION

1. Higher plants as Indicators & accumulators of gaseous air pollution
2. Specification & examples of the usage of higher plants as indicators.

F. **PLANTS AS INDICATORS OF ECOLOGICAL CONDITIONS**

1. Indicators of Agriculture
2. Indicators of Salinity

IV. MONITORING POLLUTION

In two ways, viz. through effects on individuals or through effects on the ecosystem.

A. EFFECT ON INDIVIDUALS

1. Biological monitoring of exposure to chemicals

   Definition of permissible levels of exposure.

   Regular assessment of health risk associated with exposure limits.

   (a) Ambient monitoring

   1. Measurement of external expourse to chemical ie, through concentration in air, food, water etc.
   2. Presence of health hazard estimated by reference to environmental exposure limits eg. threshold limit value and tissue - weighted average.

   (b) Biological Monitoring

   1. The quantitative risk evaluation of carcinogens involves estimating a Virtually Safe Dose (V.S.D.)
   2. Use of animal dose - response data.

V. EFFECTS ON ECOSYSTEMS

1. Reasons for long-term studies

   (a) Basic ecological knowledge for understanding processes of many ecosystems.

   (b) Baseline for management.

   (c) Understanding synergistic and commulative effects of man-made perturbations.

   (d) Early detection of potentially harmful effects.

2. Levels of biological organization

   Most monitoring studies concentrate on species level - single species may be unreliable predictors of response at higher level of organisation.

3. Localities for ecosystem monitoring

   (a) Localities for long term monitoring should be severs - perturbations should be minimized.

(b) Impacts of present should be important in the monitoring programme.

(c) National Science Foundation reports (NSF, 1977, 1978) give guidelines for choosing sites with the following characteristics:

1. Where productive & useful short term research has already been carried out.
2. Representative of major ecosystems and populations.
3. Chemical variables can be monitored.

VI. ANIMALS AS INDICATORS

1. Behaviour and physiology of animals as indicators of environmental change.
2. Disadvantages and biases.

VII. ETHICAL ASPECTS

1. Defining essential and non-essential research so as to limit the use of vivisection (animal-testing) only to essential research.
2. Impossible to put an end to production of harmful chemicals and radiations but possible to curb their escape into the environment and prevent interactions with human systems.
3. Monitoring procedures involving humans must be without health risks and should be done only with informed consent.

14. MONITORING SYSTEMS IN THE FIELD

A. INTRODUCTION

1. Real world situation
2. Total effects at individual, population & higher levels
3. Approach utiliterian or empirical
4. Applications of baseline knowledge from Laboratory experiments

B. HUMAN SYSTEMS

1. Epidermiology: Associating the likely causes with the perceived effect
    (a) Social surveys
    (b) Medical surveys
    (c) Case histories

C. ANIMAL SYSTEMS AND PLANT SYSTEMS

1. Derizen approach in situ
2. Sentinel approach in situ
3. Habitat testing in situ and in vitro
4. Concentrator approach in situ and in vitro
5. Use of microbes

D. EXAMPLES - ANIMALS

1. Crustaceans
2. Polychaetes
3. Insects: Orthopterans
4. Moluscans: Mussels
5. Amphibians:
6. Fishes:
7. Mammals:
8. Aves:
9. Mammals: Rodents, Squirrels

E. OTHERS

1. Any endpoint of any system affected by any causes
2. Management of the problem
3. Pinpointing cause very difficult

TABLE 1. Plants in Toxicity Testing: Aquatic Lower Plants

S. No.	*Scientific name*	*Common name*	*Taxonomy*	*Tested for*
A. FRESH WATER				
1.	Selenastrum	Green algae	Chlorophyta	Acute toxicity
2.	Anabaena	Blue green algae	Cyanophyta	Acute toxicity
3.	Navicula	Brown algae	Chrysophyta	Acute toxicity
B. MARINE				
1.	Chlorella	Green algae	Chlorophyta	Acute toxicity
2.	Isochrysis galbana	Brown algae	Chrysophyta	Acute toxicity
3.	Porphyridium cruentum	Red algae	Rhodopyta	Acute toxicity

TABLE 2. Aquatic Invertebrates in Toxicity Testing:

S.N(o)	*Scientific name*	*Common name*	*Taxonomy*	*Tested for*
A. FRESH WATER				
1.	Physa integra	Snails	Mollusca	Acute toxicity
2.	Chironomus	Midges	Arthropoda Diptera	Egg viability
3.	Daphnia magna D. pulex D. pulicaria	Daphnids	Arthropoda Crustacea Brachiopoda	Acute and toxicity
4.	Gammanis lacustris G. faxiatus G. pseudoli-mnaeus	Amphipods	Arthropoda Crustacea Malacostroca	Chronic effects of detergents
B. MARINE				
1.	Cranostrea Virginica C. gigas	Oyster Bivalvia	Mollusca	Acute toxicity
2.	Acartia tonsa A. clausi	Cope pods	Arthropoda Crustacea Copepoda	Acute toxicity (heavy metals)
3.	Penaeus setiferus P. duorarum P. azteuis	Shrimp	Arthropoda Crustacea Decapoda	Acute toxicity

(*Contd...*)

4. Palaemonetes pugio P. vulgaris	Grass shrimp	Arthropoda Crustacea Decapoda	Dodecyl sulfate bioassay
5. Homanus americanus	American lobster	Arthropoda Decapoda	Toxicity of copper
6. Uca s(p)	Fiddler crab	Arthropoda Crustacea	Acute toxicity testing
7. Capitalla capitata	Poly-chaetes	Annelida Polycheata	Acute toxicity (Heavy metals on laboratory populations)
C. ESTUARINE			
1. Mysidopsis bahia	Mysid shrimp	Arthropoda Crustacea Decapoda	Pollutant toxicity to life cycle
2. Asellus meridianus	Isopod	Arthropoda Crustacea Malacostrace	Tollerance to copper and lead

TABLE 3. AQUATIC VERTEBRATES IN TOXICITY TESTING:

S.N(o)	*Scientific name*	*Common name*	*Taxonomy*	*Tested for*
A. FRESH WATER				
1.	Lepomis macrochirus	Bluegill	Pisces	Partial chronic tests
2.	Pimephales promelas	Fat head minnow	Pisces	Reaction to reference toxicants
3.	Salmo gairdneri	Rainbow trout	Pisces	Acute toxicity
4.	Salvelinus fontinalis	Brook trout	Pisces Osteichthyes	Partial chronic tests
B. MARINE				
1.	Cyprindon veriegatus	Sheeps head minnow	Pisces	Life cycle toxicity
2.	Fundulus heteroclitus	Mummichog	Pisces	Teratogenesis
3.	Fundulus setiferus	Longnose Killifish	Pisces	Acute toxicity
4.	Menidia mennidia s(p)	Sivler side	Pisces	Toxicity of cadmium
5.	Channa punctatus	Midges	Pisces	General toxicity
6.	Tilapia mossambica		Pisces	General toxicity

(*Contd...*)

C. AMPHIBIAN				
1.	Rana tigrina	Common frog	Amphibia	Nephro toxicity
2.	Xenopus laevis	Common frog	Amphibia	tertogenicity

TABLE 4. TERRESTRIAL INVERTEBRATESIN TOXICITY TESTING

S.N(o) name	*Scientific name*	*Common*	*Taxonomy*	*Tested for*
1.	Leptinotarse decenlineata	Colarodo potato beetle	Arthropoda Insecta Coleopteta	Toxicity of Pesticides
2.	Culex pipens	Mosquito	Arthropoda Insecta Diptera	Effect of DOT on malaria
3.	Anopheles s(p)	Mosquito	Arthropoda Insecta Diptera	Effect of DOT on malaria
4.	Drosophila melanogaster	Fruit fly	Arthropoda Insecta Diptera	All toxicities

TABLE 5. TERRESTRIAL VERTEBRATES IN TOXICITY TESTING:

S.N(o)	*Scientific name*	*Common name*	*Tested for*
A. AVES			
1.	Gallus domesticus	Domestic fowl	Teratogenicity neurotoxicity
2.	Columba livia	Common pigeon	neurotoxicity
3.	Anas platyrhyncha	Pekin duck	Spongy generation of white matter
B. MAMMALS			
1.	Oryctolagus uchiculus	Rabbit	Placental transport Teratogenicity Dermal cancer Lung toxicity
2.	Mus musculus	Mouse	Nephrotoxicity Resp. toxicity Infertility Lung toxicity Teratogenicity Placental transport Neurotoxicity

3.	Rattus norvegieus	Laboratory rat	Nephrotoxicity Infertility Carcinogenesis Teratogenesis
4.	Mesocricetus auratus	Syrian hamster	Respiratory toxicity
5.	Meriones unguiculatus	Mongolian Gerbil	Behavioural toxicity
6.	Cavia porcellus	Guinea pig	All toxicities
7.	Canis familiasis	Dogs	Baldder tumors neuro toxicity
8.	Felix catus	Domestic cat	Organomercurial toxicity
9.	Sus scrofa	Pig	Skin penetration
10.	Copra hircus	Goat	Organophosphate toxicity
11.	Bos terurers	Cattle	Reproductive toxicity
12.	Macaca mulatta	Rhesus Monkey	Neurotoxicity Drug effects

15. SOIL: NUTRIENTS, WASTELANDS AND CONSERVATION

I. PLANT NUTRIENTS

A. INTRODUCTION TO PLANT NUTRIENTS

1. Macronutrients: carbon, hydrogen, oxygen; nitrogen, phosphorus, potassium, calcium, Magnesium, suphur.
2. Micronutrients: iron, manganese, copper, zinc, boron, molybdenum, chlorine.
3. Beneficial elements, include, cobalt, sodium and silicon, and nickle and vanadium in some cases.

B. FUNCTIONS OF NUTRIENT ELEMENTS IN PLANTS

C. MACRONUTRIENTS

1. Nitrogen
2. Phosphorus
3. Potassium
4. Calcium
5. Magnesium,
6. Sulphur

D. MICRONUTRIENTS

1. Iron
2. Manganese
3. Copper
4. Zinc
5. Boron
6. Molybdenum
7. Chlorine

E. BENEFICIAL ELEMENTS

1. Cobalt
2. Sodium
3. Silicon
   (a) Carbon dioxide availability
   (b) Light

F. BIOMASS: ROOT - SHOOT RATIO

G. PLANT TISSUE ANALTSIS OF MINERAL CONSTITUENTS

1. Total Ash content of plant tissue:
2. Wet oxidation of plant tissue:

H. METHODS OF ANALYSIS OF NUTRITIONAL ELEMETS

1. Phosphrus
2. Nitrogen
3. Potosium
4. Sulpher
5. Calcium
6. Magnesium
7. Iron
8. Managenese
9. Copper
10. Zinc
11. Boron
12. Molybdenum
13. Chlorine
14. Cobalt
15. Sodium
16. Silicon
17. Aluminium

II. FRAGILITY

A. INTRODUCTION

B. FORMATION OF SOIL

C. WEATHERING OF SOIL-FORMING ROCKS

1. Physcial weathering
2. Chemical weathering
3. Biological weathering

D. THE SOIL PROFILE

1. A generalized profile of soil
2. Classification of soil texture
3. Structure of soil
4. Soil colour
5. Properties of soil

E. PHYSICAL PROPERTIES

1. Soil Density
2. Porosity
3. Permeability of soil
4. Temperature
5. Water
6. Atmosphere

F. CHEMICAL PROPERTIES

1. Inorganic elements and compounds of soil
2. Organic matter of soil
3. Colloidal properties
4. Soil PH

G. PHYSICAL FACTORS

1. The restless Earth
2. The Soil Profile
3. Topography and Soil

4. Soils are changed by use
5. Seasonal changes in soil

H. ECONOMIC FACTORS

1. Soil depletion on sub-marginal farm land
2. Price Depression
3. Acidification chemical process that affects mineral soils

I. SOILS OF INDIA

J. COSTLY CONSERVATION

III. WASTELANDS

A. INTRODUCTION

1. Cultivated land affected by soil erosion
2. Water logged land
3. Saline and Alkaline lands
4. Degraded Forest
5. Sedimented land
6. Gullies and Ravines
7. Shifting cultivation
8. Wind eroded deserts
10. Barren and uncultivable land
11. Potentially arable land
12. Fallow land
13. Other types of waste land
    (a) Deep mines (b) Strip mines
    (c) Quarries (d) Industrial and domestic wastes
    (e) Natural wastelands

B. CONSEQUENCES OF DEPLETED LAND

1. Food resources 2. Fodder
3. Fire wood 4. Organic fertilizer
5. Medicinal plants 6. Timber
7. Water

IV. RESTORATION/ RECLAMATION

A. PRINCIPLES OF RECLAMATION

B. PHYSICAL PROBLEMS OF SOILS

C. CHEMICAL CHARACTERISTICS OF SOILS

1. Nitrogen 2. Phosphates 3. Toxicity

D. SPECIES INTERACTION AND ECOLOGICAL PROCESSES

E. DEFINITION AND CLASSIFICATION

F. RESTORATION AND MANAGEMENT

1. Natural man-made
   - (a) Restoration philosophies
   - (b) Nature conservation
   - (c) End uses of restored land
   - (d) Cost of land restoration
   - (e) Benefits of land restoration
   - (f) Planning

H. RESTORATION

1. Solutions
   - (a) Top soil conservation
     1. Sewage sludge
     3. Pulverised fuel ash
   - (b) Other materials
     2. Domestic sewage
     4. Chemical wastes
   - (c) Hydraulic seeding
   - (d) Direct improvement
   - (e) Grasses and legumes
   - (g) Trees and shrubs
2. Costs vs benefits
3. Reclamation potential
   - (a) Protective life support environment
   - (b) Waste assimilative environment
   - (c) Human - industrial environment
4. Conservation programs
5. Afforestation programs
6. Voluntary agencies in waste land development
7. Socio economic aspects
   - (a) Cost of land restoration
   - (b) Benefits of land restoration

16. ECOLOGICAL ACTIVITIES OF AUROVILLE

I. INTRODUCTION

II. ALTERNATIVE TECHNOLOGIES

A. Solar energy
B. Solar bowl
C. Biogas
D. Wind energy

III. BUILDING TECHNIQUES

A. Earth
B. Ferrocement

IV. WATER RESOURCES

A. Water management
B. Integrated watershed management
C. Water conservation research

V. WASTE WATER RECYCLING

VI. GREEN BELT & BIOREGION

A. Origins
B. Green belt and corridors
C. The aurobrindavan -hermitage area
D. Bioregional area

VII. AGRICULTURE

A. Farming operations
B. Service farming
C. Survey
D. Aurospirulina
E. Drip irrigation
F. Biological pest control
G. Annapurna - granary of auroville
H. Agriculture, man & ecology programme
I. Vermiculture using industrial waste

VIII. FORESTRY

IX. FISHERIES

X. VILLAGE ACTION AIMS AND OBJECTIVES

A. Aim
B. Objectives
C. Villages
D. Benefits to villagers
E. Village development
   1. Environment
   2. Health
   3. Economy
   4. Youth Clubs
   5. Education
   6. Environmental Education

XI. Development Of Auroville

A. Contributing human resources
B. Possibilities for students

Appendices

1. **VINTAGE TEXTS:** Essentials
2. **PROSPECTUS:** Hypocrisy
3. **SYLLABUS:** Common Good
4. **FACULTY:** Jekyll and Hyde
5. **EVALUATIONS:** Values Lurk

1. VINTAGE TEXTS IN ECOLOGY

Abelson, P.H. 1982. Energy and chemicals from trees.

Alexander,Maurice.1958.The place of aging in wildlife management. Amer.Sci.

Alexander, R.1967. Functional design in fishes. Hutchinson, London.

Alexander, R.M.1968. Animal mechanics, University of Washington Press, Seattle.

Allee, W.C., A.E. Emerson, O. Park, T. Park, and K.P. Schmidt. 1949. Principles of Animal Ecology. W.B. Saunders & Co.,

Allee, W.C. 1951. Cooperation among animals. Henry Schuman, New York.

Allee, W.C. and Karl P.Schmidt. 1951. Ecological animal geography. John Wily.

Allee,W.C.1931.Animal Aggregations.A Study in General Sociology. U.Chicago Press.

Allen, K.R.1980. Conservation and management of Whales. U. Washington Press,

Anderson, R.M. 1981. Population ecology of infectious disease agents. In: Theoretical Ecology: Principles and Applications, 2nd edn. Blackwell, Oxford.

Anderson, Edgar. 1948. Hybridization of the habitat. Evol. 2ool.

Andrewartha, H.G.and L.C. Birch.1954.The distribution and abundance of animals. U. Chicago Press,

Andrewartha, H.G.1961. Introduction to the study of animal population, U. Chicago Press.

Archley, W.R and D. Woodruff.1981.Evolution and speciation. Cambridge U. Press,

Ardrey, Robert. 1967. The territorial imperative, Atheneum, New York.

Arthur, W. 1987. The niche in competition and evolution. John Wiley

Askew, R.R. 1971. Parasitic insects. American Elsevier, New York.

Ashby, M. 1973. Introduction to Plant Ecology. Macmillan

Ashmole, N.P. 1971. Sea bird ecology and the marine environment. In:Avian Biology, Volume 1. D. S. Farner & J.R.King eds. Acadamic Press.

Atchley, W.R., and D. Woodruff, eds, Evolution and Speciation; Essays in Honor of M.J.D. White. Cambridge University Press, New York, 1981.

Baer, Jean G. 1951. Ecology of animal parasites. U. llinois Press, Urbana.

Bainbridge, P., Evans, G.C. and Rackham, O.(Eds). Light as an Ecological Factor. British Ecology Symposium no.6., Blackwells.Glasgo.

Baker, R.R. 1978. The Evolutionary Ecology of Animal Migration. Hodder & Stoughton, London.

Baker, R. R. 1982. Migration:Paths Through Time and Space. Hodder & Stoughton, London.

Barber, R.T. and F.P. Chavez. 1982. Biological consequences of El Nino.

Barbour, M.G., J.H. Burk,and W.D.Pitts.1980. Terrestrial plant Ecology. Benjamin / Cumming, Menlo Park, Calif.

Barbour,W.R.1956. South America. In S. Haden-Guest, A World Geography of Forest Resources. Ronald. New York.

Barclay, G.W. 1958. Techniques of Population Analysis, Wiley, New York.

Bartlett, M.S. 1960. Stochastic population models in Ecology and Epidemiology. Wiley, New York.

Barnes, R.S.K., 1984. Estuarine biology. 2nd ed. Edward Arnold, Londan.

Barnes, R.S.K., and R.N. Hughes. 1982. An introduction to marine ecology. Blackwell, Oxford.

Barnes,R.S.K. and K.H. Mann.1980. Fundamentals of aquatic ecosystems. Blackwell, Oxford.

Barrett, J.A. 1983. Plant-fungus symbioses. In: Coevolution. D.J. Fukuyama & M. Slatkin eds. Sinauer Associates. Sunderland, MA.

Bates, HenryWalter.1864.The naturalist on the river Amazons.John Murray, London.

Bates, Marston.1949. The Natural History of Mosquitoes. Macmillan, New York.

Bateson, W.1894. Materials for the study of variation. Macmillan Co. New York.

Bateson, P., ed.1983. Mate choice. Cambridge University Press, Cambridge.

Baver, L.D., W.H. Gardner, and W.R. Gardner. 1972. Soil physics. John Wiley

Bayly, I.A.E. and W.D.Williams.1973. Inland waters and their ecology. Longman,

Beattie,A.J.1985.The evolutionary ecologyof ant-plantmutualisms. CUP, Cambridge

Beard, J.S.1973. The physiognomic approach. In Ordination and classification of communities, ed. R.H.

Whittaker, Dr. W. Junk Publ. The Hague.

Beaufort, L.F. de 1951. Zoogeography of the land and inland waters. Sedgwick and Jackson, London.

Beagon, M.1979. Investigating Animal Abundance: Capture-Recapture for

Biologists. Edward Arnold. London.

Beagon, M. 1985. A general theory of life-history variation. In: Behavioural Ecology. R.M. Sibly & R.H. Smith eds. Blackwell. Oxford.

Beagon, M.& Mortimer, M.1986. Population Ecology: A Unified Study of Animals and Plants. Blackwell Scientific Publications. Oxford.

Bell, G. 1982. The masterpiece of nature: the evolution and genetics of sexuality. University of California Press, Los Angeles.

Belt. Thomas. 1873. The naturalist in Nicaragua. .M. Dent & Sons, London.

Belt, T. 1888. The naturalist in Nicaragua. Bumpus. London.

Berg, L.S. 1950. Natural regions of the U.S.S.R. Macmillan Co., New York.

Berryman, A.A. 1981. Populations Systems: A General Introduction. Plenum, New York.

Bertram, B.C.R. 1976. Kin selection in lions and in evolution. Pages 281-301. in P. Bateson and R. Hinds, eds. Growing points in ethology. Cambridge University Press, Cambridge.

Bertram, B.C.R. 1979. Serengeti predators and their special systems, 221-248 in A.R.E. Sinclair and M. Norton-Griffiths, eds. Serengeti: dynamics of an ecosystem. University of Chicago Press, Chicago.

Beverton, R.J.H., and S.J. Holt. 1957. On the Dynamics of Exploited Fish Populations. H.M. Stationery Office,London.

Billings, W.D. 1970. Plants and the Ecosystem, Wadsworth, Belmont.

Bligh,J,J.L.Cloudsley-Thompson and A. G. MacDonald, eds. 1976. Environmental physiology of animals.

Blower, J.G., L.M.Cook, and J.A. Bishop. 1981. Estimating the size of animal populations. Allen and unwin, London.

Bodenheimer, F.S. 1938 Problems of Animal Ecology, Oxford University Press.

Bogue, D.J. 1969. Principles of Demography. Wiley, New York.

Boughey, A.S. 1968. Ecology of populations. The Macmillan Co., New York.

Boughey, A.S. 1971. Man and the environment. Macmillan Co., New York.

Box, E.O. 1981. Macroclimate and Plant Forms: An Introduction to Predictive Modeling in Phytogeography. Jumk, The Hague.

Bradshaw,A.D. 1987. The reclamation of derelict land and the ecology of ecosystems. In: Restoration Ecology. W.R. Jordan III, M.E. Gilpin & J.D. Aber eds. Cambridge University Press.

Bradshaw, A.D. & Chadwick, M.J. 1980. The Restoration of Land Blackwell.

Bradshaw,A.D& McNeilly, T. 1981.Evolution and Pollution. Edward Arnold, London.

Braun-Blanquet, J. 1932. Plant sociology. McGraw-Hill, New York.

Braun,E.L.1950.Deciduousforests ofeastern North America, Blakiston Philadelphia.

Brewer, Richard.1960.A brief history of ecology. Part I pre-nineteenth century to 1919. Occ. Papers of the C.C. Adams Center Ecol. Stud., 1:1-18.

Brewer. R. 1988. Science of ecology.Saunders Co.Philadelphia, Pennsylvania, U.S.A.

Brock,T.D.1966.Principlesof Microbial Ecology.Prentice Hall,Englewood Cliffs, N.J.

Brockmann, H.J. 1984. The evolution of social behavior in insects. Pages 340-361 in J.R. Krebs and N.B. Davies, eds. Behavioral Ecology: an evolutionary approach. 2d. Sinauer, Sunderland, Mass.

Brody, S. 1945. Bioenergetics and Growth. Van Nostrand Reinhold, New York.

Brown, D. 1954. Methods of Surveying and Measuring Vegetation. Commonwealth Bureau of Pastures and Field Crops, Bull. 42. Hurley, England.

Brown, G.W., Jr. 1968. Desert biology. Academic Press, New York.

Brown, Harold W. and Minna E. Jewell.1926. Further studies on the fishes of an acid lake. Trans. America Micros. Soc. 45:20-34.

Brown, J.H. & Gibson, A.C. 1983. Biogeography. Mosby. St. Louis.

Brown, J. 1975 Geographical ecology of desert rodents. Pages 315-341 in M. Cody and J. Diamond, eds. Ecology and evolution of communities. Harvard University Press, Cambridge, Mass.

Brown, L.1981. Building a sustainable society. Norton, New York.

Brown, W.L., Jr. 1973. A comparison of the Hylean and Congo-West African rain forest ant faunas. Pages 160-185 in B.J. Meggers, E.S. Ayensu, and W.D.Duckworth, eds. Tropical forest ecosystems in Africa and South America: a comparative review. Smithsonian Institution Press, Washington, D.C.

Buffon, G.L.L., Compte De.1756. Natural History, General and particular (Trnasl. W. Creech, Edinburg, 17890).

Burdon, J.J. 1987. Diseases and Plant Population Biology. C U P Cambridge.

Burrows, F.M. 1986. The aerial motion of seeds, fruits, spores and pollen. In: Seed Dispersal. D.R. Murray ed. Acadamic Press. Sydney.

Buss, L.W. 1986. Competition and Community organization on hard surfaces in the sea. In: Community Ecology. J.Diamond & Y.J. Case eds. Harper & Row, New York.

Butzer, Karl W. 1971.Environment and archeology, an ecological approach to prehistory. Aldine-Atherton, Inc. Chicago.

Buxton, Patrick A. 1923. Animal life in deserts. Edward Arnold & Co., London.

Caborm, J.M.1957. Shelter Belts and Microclimates. Forestry Commission Bulletin 29. HMSO.

Cailliet,G.M, P.Y.Setzer and M.S.Love. 1971. Everyman's guide to ecological living. Macmillan & Co., NewYork.

Cain, S.A.1944. Foundations of Plant Geography. Harper & Row, New York.

Cain, S.A. and G.M. de Oliveria Castro 1959. Manual of vegetation analysis. Harper & Brothers, New York.

Calow, P. 1981. Resources utilization and reproduction. In: Physiological Ecology: An Evolutionary Approach to Resources Use. C.R. Townsend & P. Calow eds. Blackwell Scientific Publication. Oxford.

Calvin, M, and J.A. Bassham. 1962. The photosynthetic carbon compounds. Benjamin, New York.

Carlquist, S. 1965. Island Life. Natural History Press, New York.

Carlquist, S. 1974. Island Biology. Columbia University Press, New York.

Carson, Rachel. 1962. Silent spring. Houghton Miffin Co., Boston.

Carefoot, T. 1977. Pacific seashores. University of Washington Press Seattle.

Carpentr, J.R.1938. An Ecological Glossary. University Oklahoma Press. Norman.

Case,T.J. 1982.Coevolution in resource-limited competition communities. Theoritical Population Biology.

Caughley, G. 1976b. Plant-herbivore systems. In Theoritical Ecology, ed.R.M. May, Saunders, Philadelphia.

Caughley, G. 1977. Analysis of vertebrate Populations. Wiley, New York.

Caughley, G. & Lawton, J.H. 1981. Plant-herbivore systems. In: Theoritical Ecology: Principles and Applications. 2nd edn. R.M. May ed. Blackwell Scientific Publications. Oxford.

Chapman, Abel.1922. Savage sudan. Its wild tribes, big-game, and bird life. G.P. Putnam's Sons, New York.

Charlesworth, B. 1977. Populaltion genetics, demography, and the sex ratio. Pages 345-363 in Christianson and T.Fenchel, eds. Measuring selection in natural populations. Springer-Verlag, Berlin.

Charlesworth, B.1980. Evolution in age-structured populations, CUP, Cambridge.

Charnov, E.L.1982. The theory of sex allocation. Princeton U. Press, Princeton.

Chaturvedi, M.D. India. In S.Haden-Guest, A World Geography of Forest Resources. Ronald, New York.

Chesson, P.L. 1986. Environmental variation and the coexistence of species. In: Community Ecology. J. Diamond & T.J. Case eds. Harper & Row. New York.

Chipp, T.F. 1926. Aims and methods of study in tropicl countries with special reference to West Africa. In A.G. Tansley and T.F.Chipp. Aims and Methods in the Study of Vegetation, British Empire Veg. Comm, London.

Clapham, W.B. 1973. Natural Ecosystems. Collier-Macmillan, New York.

Clark, C.W. 1976. Mathematical bioeconomics. Wiley, New York.

Clark, C.W. 1976. Mathematical bioeconomics: The Optimal Managment of Renewable Resources. Wiley - Interscience, New York.

Clarke, George L. 1954. Elements of ecology. John Wiley & Sons, New York.

Clausen, J., D.D. Keck, and W.M. Hiesey. 1948. Experimental studies on the Nature of Species. III. Environmental Responses of Climatic Races of Achillea. Carnegie Inst. Publ. No, 581, Washington, D.C.

Clements, Frederic E. 1916. Plant succession. Carnegie Inst. Washington Publ.

Clements,F.E.1904. The Development and Structure of Vegetation. Woodruff-Collins. Lincoln.

Clements, F.E. 1905.Research Methods in Ecology. Woodruff- Collins. Lincoln.

Clements, Frederic E. and Victor E. Shelford 1939. BIo-ecology. John Wiley & sons, New York.

Cloudsley-Thompson, J.L.and M.J.Chadwick. 1964. Life in deserts. Foulis, London.

Cody, M. 1974. Competition and the structure of bird communities. Princeton University Press, New Jersey.

Cody, M.L. 1986. Structural niches in plant communities. Pages 381-405 in J. Diamond and T. Case, eds, Community Ecology, Harper and Row, New York.

Cohen,J.1966 A model of Simple Competition, Harvard University Press, Cambridge.

Cohen, J. 1978. Food webs and niche space. Princeton University Press, Princeton.

Colinvaux, P. 1973. Introduction to ecology. Wiley, New York.

Colinvaux, P. 1986. Ecology. John Wiley & Sons, New York

Colwell, R.K. & Winkler, D.W. 1984. A null model for null models in biogeography. In: Ecological Communities: Conceptual Issues and the Evidence. D.R. Strong, D. Simberloff, L.G. Abele& A.B. Thistle eds. Princeton University Press. Princeton, NJ.

Commoner, Barry. 1971. The Closing circle-nature, man and technology. Alfred A.Knopf, Inc., New York.

Connell, J.H.1974. Field experiments in marine ecology. R. Mariscal, ed, Experimental marine biology. Academic Press, New York.

Connell, J. H. 1975. Some mechanisms producing structure in natural communities: a model and evidence from field experiments. In: Ecology and Evolution of Communities. M.L. Cody & J.M. Diamond eds. Belknap, Cambridge, MA.

Connell, J.H.1979. Tropical rainforests and coral reefs as open non-equilibrium systems. In: Population Dynamics. R.M. Anderson, B.D. Turner & L.R. Taylor eds. Blackwell Scientific Publications. Oxford.

Connor, E.F and D. Simberloff. 1984. Neutral models of species' co-occurrence patterns. Princeton University Press, New Jersey.

Conway, G. 1981. Man versus pests. In: Theoretical Ecology. R.M. May, ed. Blackwell Scientific Publications, Oxford.

Conway, W.G. 1980. An overview of captive propagation. In: Conservation Biology: An Evolutionary-Ecological Perspective. M.E. Soule & B.A. Wilcox eds. Sinauer Associates, Sunderland, MA.

Coole, LaMont C. 1970. Playing Russian Roulette with Biogeochemical Cycles. The Environmental crisis ed. H.W. Helfrich, Yale University Press, New haven.

Cooley, R.A.1963. Politics and Conservation: The Decline of the Alaska Salmon. Harper & Row, New York.

Cooke, W.B. 1979. The Ecology of fungi. CRC Press, Boca Raton, Fla.

Coon, Carleton. 1962. The origin of races. A. Knopf, New York.

Costello, D.F. 1969. The prairie world. Crowell, New York.

Cooper, J.P. 1975. Photosynthesis and Productivity in Different Environments. Cambridge University Press. Cambridge.

Cormack, R.M., P.P. Ganapathi, and D.S. Robson. 1979. Sampling biological populations. International Coop. Publishing House, Fairland.

Cott, H.B. 1940. Adaptive coloration in animals. Methuen, London.

Cottam G, F.G. Goff and R.H.Whittaker. 1978. Wisconsin comparative ordination. In Ordination of Plant Communities (R.H. Whittaker, Ed.). W. Jumk, The Hague.

Coupland, R.T. 1979. Grassland Ecosystems of the World: Analysis of Grasslands and Their Uses. Cambridge University Press, Cambridge.

Coupland, R.T., R.Y. Zacharuk and E.A. Paul. 1969. Procedures for study of Grassland ecosystems. The ecosystem concept in Natural Resource Management ed. by Van Dyne, Academic Press New York.

Cox, C.B., Healey, I.N. & Moore, P.D. 1976. Biogeography. Blackwell,. Oxford.

Cox, G.W. 1985. Laboratory Manual of General Ecology. Brown, Dubuque, IA.

Crawely, M.J. 1983. Herbivory: The Dynamics of Animal- Plant Interactions. Blackwell. Oxford.

Crisp, D.J. 1975. Secondary productivity in the sea. In Productivity of World Ecosystems, National Academy of Sciencs, Washington,

Critchfield, H.J. 1966. General Climatology, Prentice-Hall

Crow, J. and M. Kimura 1970. An introduction to population genetics theory. Harper & Row, New York.

D'Ancona,Umberto. 1954. The struggle for existence. Biblio, Bioth. (Eng. Tran.)

Dajoz, R., 1977. Introduction to Ecology. Hodder and Stoughton.

Dansereau, Pierre. 1947. The distribution and structure of Brazilian forests.

Dansereau, P. 1957. Biogeography-an ecological perspective,Ronald Press, NewYork.

Darling, F. Fraser. 1937. A herd of red deer. Oxford University Press, London.

Darlington,P.J.1957.Zoogeography:Thegeographicaldistribution of animals. Wiley,

Darlington, P.J. 1965. Biogeography of the Southern End of the World. Harvard University Press, Cambridge, Mass.

Darwin, C. 1859. On the origin of species. John Murray, London.

Darwin, C. 1888. The Formation of Vegetable Mould through the Action of Worms. John Murray, London.

Daubenmire, R.F.1947.Plants and environment. John Wiley & Sons, Inc., New York.

Davies, N.B. 1978. Ecological questions about territorial behaviour. In: Behavioural Ecology: An Evolutionary Approach, J.R. Krebs & N.B. Davies eds. Blackwell Scientific Publications Oxford.

Dawkins, R., and J.R. Krebs. 1978. Animal signals: information or manipulation ? 292-309 in J.R. Krebs and N. B. Davies, eds, Behavioral Ecology. Blackwell,

Dawson, E. Yale 1966 Marine Botany: An Introduction. Holt, Rinehart and Winston.

Dawkins, R. 1976. The Selfish Gene. Oxford University Press, Oxford.

Dawkins, R. 1982. The Extended Phenotype. Oxford University Press, Oxford.

Day, P.R. 1965. Particle fractionation and particle -size analysis. American Society of Agronomy, Wisconsin.

Debach, P. 1964. Biological Control of Insect Pests and Weeds, Reinhold, New Haven.

Debach, P.1974. Biological control by natural enemies. Cambridge University Press,

Defant, Albert.1958. Ebb and flow; the tides of earth, air and water. University Michigan Press Ann Arbor.

Denno, R.F, and M.S. McClure. 1983. Variability: a key to understanding plant-herbivore interactions. in R.F. Denno and M.S. McClure, eds. Variable plants and herbivores in natural and managed systems. Academic Press, New York.

Detwyler, Thomas R. 1971. Man's impact on environment. McGraw-Hill, New York.

De Wit, C.T. 1960. On competition. Versl. Landbouwk. Onderzoek Wageningen,

De Wit, C.T.and J.Goudriaan.1978. Simulation of ecological processes. Wiley.

Dice, Lee R.1952. Natural communities. University Michigan Press, Ann Arbor:

Dirzo, R. 1984. Herbivory: a phytocentric overview. in R.Dirzo and J. Sarukhan, eds, perspectives on plant population Ecology. Sinauer, Sunderland, Mass.

Dixon, A.F.G. 1970. Quality and availability of food for a sycamore aphid population. In Animal Populations in relation to Their Food Supply, ed. A. Watson, Blackwell, Oxford, England.

Dobzhansky, Theodosius. 1951. Genetics and the origin of species. Columbia University Press, New York.

Douglass, A.E. 1928. Climatic cycles and tree growth. Carnegie Inst. Washington publ. 289.

Dodson, C.H. 1975. Coevolution of orchids and bees. in L.E. Gilbert and P.H. Raven,eds, Coevolution of animals and plants.University of Texas Press, Austin.

Doube, B.M. 1987. Spatial and temporal organization in communities associated with dung pads and carcasses. In: Organization of

Communities: Past and Present. J.H.R. Gee & P.S. Giller eds. Blackwell, Oxford.

Dunbar, Carl O. 1949. Historical geology. John Wiley & Sons, New York.

Dunbar, M.J. 1968. Ecological development in polar regions; a study in evolution. Prentice-Hall,

Dunson, W.A. 1975.The Biology of Sea Snakes. University Park Press, Baltimore,

Ebling, F.J. and Health, G.W. The Future of Man. Academic Press.

Edmunds, M. 1974. Defence in Animals:A Survey of Antipredator Defences. Longman.

Edney, E.B.1974. Desert arthropods. In Desert Biology. ed. G.W. Brown Jr, Academic Press, New York.

Edwards, R.Y. and C. David Fowle. 1955. The concept of carrying capacity. Trans. 20th N. Amer. Wildl. Conf.

Ehleringer, J, H.A. Mooney, R.W. Percy, and P.W. Rundel. 1989. Physiological plant ecology-field methods and instrumentation. Champan and Hall, London.

Ehrlich, P. Rand A.H.Ehrlich.1961.Howtoknowthe butterflies. Brown, Dubuque, Iowa.

Ehrlich, Paul R. and Anne H. Ehrlich. 1970. Population, resources, environment -issues in human ecology. W.H. Freeman and Co., San Francisco.

Ehrlich, P.R. and A.H. Ehrlich. 1981. Extinction: The causes and consequences of the disappearance of species. Random House, New York.

Ehrlich, P.R. A.H. Ehrlich, and J.P.Holdren, 1977. Ecoscience: population resources, environment. Freeman, San Francisco.

Ehrlich, P.R. R.W. Holm, and I.L. Brown, 1976. Biology and society. McGraw-Hill, New York.

Ehrlich, P.R., R.W. Holm and D.R. Parnell 1974. The process of evolution. McGraw-Hill, New York.

Ehrman, L. 1983. Endosymbioses. Pages 128-136 in D.J. Fukuyama and M. Slatkin, eds, Coevolution. Sinauer, Sunderland, Mass.

Eisenberg. J.F., 1981. The mammalian radiations: and analysis of trends in evolution, adaptation and behavior. University of Chicago Press, Chicago.

Eisenberg. J.F., 1970. Chemical defense against predation in arthropods. in E. Sondheimer and J.B. Simeone, eds.Chemical Ecology. Academic Press,

Ekman, S. 1953. Zoogeography of the sea. Sedgwick & Jackson, London.

Elliott, D.K., ed 1986. Dynamics of extinction. Wiley, New York.

Elton. C. 1927. Animal Ecology, Reprinted 1966 by Science Paperbacks, London.

Elton. C.S. 1966. Animal Ecology. Methuen.

Elton. C. 1942. Voles, Mice, and Lemmings, Oxford University Press, New York.

Elton. C. 1958. The Ecology of animals and plants, Reprinted 1966 by Science Paperbacks, London.

Elton. C.S. 1958. The Ecology of invasions by animals and plants, Methuen,

Elton. C. 1966. The Pattern of Animal Communities, Methuen Landscape, London.

Emlen, S.T., and S. Vehrencamp. 1983. Cooperative breeding strategies among birds. Pages 93-120 in A. Brush and G.A. Clark, Jr,eds. Perspectives in ornithology. Cambridge University Press, Cambridge.

Erdtman, G. 1943. An Introduction to Pollen Analysis. Chron. Botan, Waltham.

Etherington, J.R. 1975. Environmental and plant Ecology, Wiley, New York.

Eyre,S.R.1963.Vegetation and soils, a world picture. Aldine Publication Chicago.

Fao (Food and Agricultural Organization of the United Nations). 1972. Atlas of the Living Resources of the seas. Fao Department of Fisheries, Rome.

Feeny, P.P. 1976. Plant apparency and chemical defense. in J.M. Wallace and R.L. Mansell, eds. Biochemical interaction between plants and insects. Plenum,

Fenchel,T. 1987. Ecology-Potentials and Limitations. Ecology Institute, Germany.

Field, C. and H.A. Mooney. 1986. The photosynthesis-nitrogen relationship in wild plants. Pages 25-55 in P.J. Givinish, On the economy of plant form and function. Cambridge University Press, Cambridge.

Fisher, R. A. 1930. The genetical theory of natural selection, Clarendon, Oxford.

Fisher, J., and R.M. Lockley. 1954. Sea-birds. Collins, London.

Fitter, A. H & Hay,R.K.M.1987. Environmental Physiology of Plants. Academic Press,

Flattely, F.W. and C.L. Walton 1922. The biology of the sea-shore, Macmillan.

Flint, M.L., and R. Van Den Bosch.1981. A history of pest control. In Introduction to Integrated Pest Management, Plenum, New York.

Ford, E.B. 1931. Mendelism and Evolution. Methuen, London.

Ford, E.B. 1975. Ecological genetics. John Wiley & Sons, Inc.,New York.

Frankel, Gottfried S. and Donald L. Gunn 1940.The orientation of animals, Clarendon Press, Oxford.

Frankel, O.H. and M.E.Soule 1981. Conservation and Evolution. C U P,

French, N.R. 1979. Perspectives in Grassland Ecology. Springer-Verlag.

Frisch, K. von. 1950. Bees, their vision, chemical senses, and language. Cornell University Press Ithaca.

Frisch, K.von. 1967.The dance language and orientation of bees. Harvard U. Press.

Fry, C.H. 1977. The evolutionary significance of cooperative breeding in birds. in B. Stonehourse and C.M. Perrins, eds. Evolutionary Ecology. Macmillan,

Fukuyma, D.J. 1979. Evolutionary biology, Sinauer, Sunderland, Mass.

Fukuyma, D.J.& Slatkin,M. eds. 1983. Coevolution. Sinauer Associates, Sunderland,

Gates, D.M. 1962 Energy Exchange in the Biosphere, Harper and Row, New York.

Gates, D.M. 1975. Introduction: Biophysical ecology.D.M. Gates and R.B. Schmerl, eds. Perspectives of biophysical ecology. Springer-Verlag, New York.

Gauch, H.G.1982.Multivariate Analysis in Community Ecology.Cambridge U. Press,

Gause, G.F. 1934. The struggle for existence. Williams & Wilkins, Baltimore

Geist, V.1978. On weapons, combat, and ecology. An Aggression, Dominance,and IndividualSpacing, ed. L. Krames, P. Pliner, and T. Alloway, Plenum, New York.

Gibbons,J.H. 1980. Energy from Biological Processes. Office of Technology Assessment, Supt. Documents, U.S. Govt. Printing Office, Washington, D.C.

Gilbert, N.,A.P. Gutierrez, B.D.Frazer, and R.E.Jones.1976. Ecological Relationships. Freeman, San Francisco.

Gilbert, L.E. 1980. Food web organization and the conservation of neotropical diversity. Pages 11-33 in M.E. Soule and B.A. Wilcox, eds. Conservation biology, Sinauer, Sunderland, Mass.

Giller, P.S. 1984. Community Structure and the Niche. Chapman and Hall, London.

Gimingham, G.H.1976. An Introduction to Heathland Ecology. Oliver and Boyd.

Gleason, H.A.and A. Cronquist. 1964. The Natural Geography of Plants. Columbia University Press, New York.

Gleick, J. 1987. Chaos: Making a New Science. Viking, New York.

Goldsmith, F.B. and C.M. Harrison.1976. Description and analysis of vegetation. In methods in plant ecology, ed. S.B. Chapman, Blackwell, Oxford, England.

Good, R. 1964. The Geography of the Flowering plants, Longmans, London.

Gorman, M.L. 1979. Island Ecology. Chapman & Hall, London.

Goulding, M. 1980. The fishes and the forest: explorations in Amazonian natural history. University of California Press, Berkeley.

Graham, Samuel A. 1925. The felled tree trunk as an ecological unit.

Grace, J. 1983. Plant-Atmosphere Relationships. Chapman & Hall, London.

Gray, J.S. 1981. The Ecology of Marine Sediments: An Introduction to the Structure and Function of Benthic Communities, Cambride University Press, Cambridge.

Gray, A.J., M.J. Crawley, and P.J. Edwards,eds. 1987 Colonization, succession, and stability. Blackwell Scientific Publications, California.

Green, R. H.1979. Sampling Design and Statistical Methods for Environment Biologists. Wiley, New York.

Greig-Smith,P. 1983 Quantitative Plant Ecology, University of California Press,

Grodzinski, W. and A. Goreckl. 1967. Daily energy budgets of small rodents. In Secondary Productivity of Terrestrial Ecosyustems. Vol.1, ed. K. Petrusewicz, Polish Acad. Sci., Warsaw.

Grime, J.P. 1974. Plant Stragies and Vegitation Processes. Wiley, Chickester.

Gulland, J.A. 1962. The application of mathematical models to fish populations. In The Exploitation of Natural Animal Populations, ed. E.D. LeCren and M.W. Holdgate, Blackwell, Oxford,

Gulland, J.A. 1977. Fish Population Dynamics. Wiley, New York.

Gunn, D.L. and Stevens, J.G.R. 1977. Pesticides and Human Welfare. O.U.P.

Haden-Guest, S. 1956. World Geography of Forest Resources. Ronald, New York.

Hainsworth, F.R. 1981. Animal Physiology. Addison-Wesley, Reading, MA.

Hall, C.A.S. and J.W. Day, Jr. editors. 1977. Ecosystem modeling in theory and practice: An introduction with case histories. John Wiley & Sons, New York.

Hanson, Herbert C.1962. Dictionary of ecology.Philosophical Library Inc, NewYork.

Hardy, A.C. 1956. The open sea and the world of plankton. Collins, London.

Hardy, A., 1970. The Open Sea, Part II Fish and Fisheries, Collins New Nat.

Harley, J.L. 1971. Mycorrhizza. Oxford Biol Reader O.U.P. Ed. Heaad,J.J.

Harper, J. 1977. Population biology of plants. Academic press, New York.

Harper, J.L. 1960. The Biology of Weeds. British Ecology Symposium no.I. Blackwell.

Harper, J.L. 1981. The meaning of rarity. In: The Biological Aspects of Rare Plant Conservation. H. Synge ed. Wiley, Chichester.

Harper, J.L. 1982. After description. In: The Plant Community as a Working Mechanism. E.J. Newman ed. British Ecological Society Special Publications series, 1. Blackwell Scientific Publications. Oxford.

Harris, J. A. 1934. The Physico-chemical properties of plant saps in relation to phytogeography. University Minn. Press. Minneapolis.

Hartl, D.L. 1980. A primer of population genetics. Sinauer, Sunderland, Mass.

Hassell, M.P.1976. The Dynamics of Competition and Predation, Edward Arnold,

Hassell,M.P. & Anderson, R.M. 1989. Predator-prey and host-pathogen interactions. In: Ecological Concepts. J.M. Cherrett ed. Blackwell, Oxford.

Hastings, J.R.and R.M.Turner.1965. The Changing Mile. U. Arizona Press, Tucson.

Hartshorn, G.S. 1978. Tree falls and tropical forest dynamics. Pages 617-628 in P.B. Tomilinson and M.H. Zimmerman, eds. Tropical trees as living systems. Cambridge University Press, Cambridge.

Haurwitz, B. and J.M. Austin.1944. Climatology. McGraw-Hill. New York.

Haviland, Maud D.1926. Forest, steppe and tundra. Univ. Press, Cambridge.

Heape, Walter. 1931. Emigration, migration and nomadism. Heffer & Sons, Cambridge.

Henderson, L.J. 1913.The fitness of the environment, MacMillan, New York.

Hesse, Richard, W.C. Alle, and Karl P.Schmidt 1951. Ecologicalanimal geography, Wiley.

Hill, R.W. 1976. Comparative physiology of animals: and environmental approach. Harper & Row,

Holdgate, M.W. 1970. Antarctic ecology. Academic Press, New York.

Holdridge, L.R.1967.Life zone Ecology.Tropical Science center, SanJose, Costa Rica.

Holdren, J.P., G.Morris and I.Mintzer. 1980. Environmental aspects of energy sources. Ann. Rev. Energy 5.

Horn, D.J. 1988. Ecological Approach to Pest Management. Elsevier,

Horn, H.S. 1975b. Markovian properties of forest succession. in M.L. Cody and J.M. Diamond, eds. Ecology and evolution of communities, Harvard University Press, Cambridge, Mass.

Horn, H.S.1981.Succession,in TheoriticalEcology, ed. R.M.May,Blackwell, Oxford, Howard, H. Eliot, 1920. Territory in bird life, Dutton, New York.

Howe, H.F. & Westliey, L.C. 1986. Ecology of pollination and seed dispersal. In: Plant Ecology. M.J. Crawley ed. Blackwell Scientific Publications. Oxford.

Huffaker, C.B. and P.S. Messenger. 1964. The concept and significance of natural control. In Biological Control of Insect Pests and Weeds, ed. P. DeBach, Chapman & Hall, London.

Huntington, C.C. and Fred A. Carlson. 1934. The geographic basis of society. Prentice-Hall, Inc., New York.

Huntington, Ellsworth. 1924. Civilization and climate, Yale University Press,

Hutchinson, G.E. 1957. A treatise on limnology. I Geography, physics and chemistry. Wiley, New York.

Hutchinson, G.E. 1966. A treatise on limnology. Vol.2 Geography, physics and chemistry. Wiley, New York.

Hutchinson, G.E. 1967. A treatise on limnology. II. Introduction to lake biology and the limno-plankton. Wiley, New York.

Hutchinson, G.E.1975. A treatise on limnology. III. Limnological botany. Wiley,

Hutchinson, G.E.1978. An Introduction to Population Ecology.Yale University Press, New Haven, Conn.

Huxley, Julian.1943. Evolution, the modern synthesis, Harper & Bros., New York.

Hynes,J.S.H.B.N.1970.The Ecology of running waters. Liverpool University Press,

Ito, Y. 1980. Comparative Ecology. Cambridge University Press, Cambridge.

Ivens, J.D., and R.G. Barry. 1974. Arctic and alpine environments, Methuen,

Ives, J.D. 1974. Biological refugia and the nunatak hypothesis. In: Arctic and Alpine Environments. J.D. Ives & R.D. Berry eds. Methuen, London.

Jacks, G.V. 1959. Soil. Nelson.

Jennings, H.S.1906. Behavior of lower organisms. Colombia University Press, NewYork.

Janzen, D.H.1981.Evolutionary physiology of personal defence. In: Physiological Ecology: An Evolutionary Approach to Resource Use. (C. R. Townsend & P. Calow eds. Blackwell Scientific Publications, Oxford.

Jeffers, J.N.R. 1978. An introduction to systems analysis: With ecological applications. University Park Press, Maryland.

Jenny, H.1980. The soil resource: origin and behavior,Springer-Verlag, New York.

Jones, C.D. and R.J. Little, eds. 1983. Handbook of experimental pollination biology. Van Nostrand Reinhold, New York.

Johnson,C.G.1969. Migration and Dispersal of Insects by Flight.Methuen, London.

Jordan, W.R.III, Gilpin, M.E. & Aber, J.D.1987. Restoration Ecology. Cambridge University Press, Cambridge.

Karlin, S., and E. Nevo, eds. 1976. Population genetics and Ecology, Academic Press, New York.

Keast, A. 1970b. Food specialization and bioenergetic interrelations in the fish faunas of some small Ontario waterways, Pages 377-411 in J. Steele, eds. Marine food chains, Oliver and Boyd, Edinburgh.

Kershaw, K.A. 1973. Quantitive and Dynamic Plant Ecology. Elsevier, New York.

Kershaw, K.A. and J. H. Looney.1985.Quantitative and dynamic ecology. Edward Arnold.

Keith, L.B.1963.Wildlife'sten-year cycle.University of Wisconsin press, Madison.

Keyfitz, N., and W. Flieger. 1971. Population: facts and methods of demography. Freeman, San Francisco.

Kinne, Otto. 1970. Marine ecology. John Wiley & Sons Ltd., New York.

Kira,T.1975. Primary production of forests. In Photosynthesis and productivity in different environments, ed. J.P. Cooper, Cambridge University Press, Cambridge.

Kitazawa, Yozo. 1959. Bio-economic study of natural populations of animals

Klages, K.H.W. 1942. Ecological Crop Geography. Macmillan, New York.

Kleiber, M. 1961. The Fire of Life. Wiley, New York.

Klein, David R. 1970. Food selection by North American deer and their response to over utilization of preferred plant species. In Adam

Watson's, Animal populations in relation to their food resources. Blackwell.

Klopfer, P.H. 1969. Habitats and Territories, Basic Books, New York.

Kormondy, E.J. 1984. Concepts of ecology. Prentice-Hall, Englewood Cliffs,

Kozhow, M. 1963. Lake Baikal and its Life, Dr. W. Junk.

Kramer, P.J. 1983. Water relations of plants. Academic Press, New York.

Krebs, J.R., Stephens, D.W. & Sutherland, W.J. 1983. Perspectives in optimal foraging. In: Perspectives in Ornithology. G.A.Clark & A.H. Brush eds. Cambridge U. Press.

Kronick,D.A.1985. The Literature of the life sciences. ISI Press, Philadelphia,

Kubiena, W.L. 1953. The Soils of Europe, Madrid.

Kuchler, A.W. and I.S.Zonneveld. 1988. Vegetation mapping. Kluwer Academic Publishers, Hinham, Massachusetts, U.S.A.

Lack, D. 1947. Darwin's finches. Cambridge University Press, Cambridge.

Lack, D. 1954. The natural regulation of animal numbers, Oxford University Press,

Lack, D. 1966. Population studies of birds, Clarendon, Oxford University Press,

Lack, D. 1968. Ecological adaptations for breeding in birds, Methuen,

Lack,D. 1971. Ecological Isolation in Birds. Blackwell Scientific Publications,

Lack, D. 1976. Island Birds. Blackwell Scientific Publications, Oxford.

Ladd, Harry S.1959. Ecology, paleontology and stratigraphy. Sci. 129: 69-78.

Lagler,Karl F.1952. Freshwater fishery biology. Win. C. Brown Co.,Dubuque, Iowa.

Lappe, F. 1971. Diet for a Small Planet. Ballantine, New York.

Larcher,W.1975.Physiological plantEcology.M.A.Biederman-Thorson, Springer - Verlag.

Laws, R.M. 1984. Seals. In: Antarctic Ecology. Acadamic Press, London.

Leack, G.D.1976. Energy and Food Production. I.P.C. Science and Tech.

Lee, K.E. & Wood, T.G. 1971. Termites and Soils. Academic Press, London.

Legendre, L and P. Legendre. 1983. Numerical Ecology. Elsevier, New York.

Leigh, E. 1975. Population fluctuations and community structure. In: Unifying Concepts in Ecology. W.H. van Doben, R.H. Lowe-McConnell eds. Junk, The Hague.

Leopold, Aldo. 1936. Game Management, Charles Scribner, New York.

Leopold, A. Carl and Robert Ardrey 1972. Toxic substances in plants and the food habits of early man.

Lerner, I. Michael. 1954. Genetic homeostasis. Oliver and Boyd, London.

Lerner, I.M. 1958. The genetic basis of selection. Wiley, New York.

Levins, R. 1968. Evolution in changing environments. Some theoretical Explorations Princeton University Press, New Jersey.

Levinton, J.S. 1982. Marine Ecology. Prentice-Hall, Englewood Cliffs, N.J.

Li,Ching Chun. 1955. Population genetics, Chicago Univ. Press, Chicago.

Lieth, H. 1974. Phenology and Seasonality Modeling. Springer-Verlag, New York.

Lieth, H. and R.H. Whittaker, eds.1975. Primary production of the biosphere. Ecological studies, Vol. 14. Springer-Verlag, New York.

Likens, G.E. 1981. Some Perspectives of the Major Biogeochemical Cycles. Wiley,

Long, J.L. 1981. Introduced birds of the world. Universe, New York.

Lotka, A.J. 1925[1956]. Elements of physical biology. Dover, New York.

Lovelock, J.E. 1979. Gaia: a new look at life on Earth. Oxford University Press

Lowe-McConnell, R.H. 1977. Ecology of fishes in tropical waters, Edward Arnold,

Lundegardh, H.G. 1931. Environment and Plant Development. Edward Arnold. London.

Macan, T.T. and E. B. Worthington.1951. Life in lakes and rivers. Collins Co.,

Macan, T.T. 1974. Freshwater Ecology, Longmans, London.

MacArthur, R.H., and E.O.Wilson.1967. The theory of island biogeography. Princeton University Press, Princeton, N.J.

MacArthur, R.H. 1972. Geographical Ecology. Harper & Row,

MacFadyen, A. 1957. Animal ecology, aims and methods, Sir Isaac Pitman & Sons,

MacFadyen, A. 1962. Energy flow in ecosystems and its exploitation by Grazing, Grazing in TerrestrialandMarine environment, ed. D.J. Crisp, Blackwell, Oxford.

Magurran, A.E.1988. Ecological diversity and its measurement. Princeton University Press, New Jersey.

Malthus,T.R.1798.An Essay on the Principle of population.(Macmillan, New York.

Mani. M.S. 1968. Ecology and biogeography of high altitude insects, Ser. Ent. 4, Junk, The Hague.

Margalef, D.R. 1968. Perspectives in ecological theory. University of Chicago Press.

Mariscal, R.N. 1972. Behavior of symbiotic fishes and sea anemonesin H.E. Winns and B.L. Olla, eds. Behavior of marine animals Vol.2. Plenum, New York.

Marler, P.R. 1968. Visual systems. in T.A. Sebeck, eds. Animal communications. University of Indiana Press, Bloomington.

Marler, P.R., and P. Mundinger.1971. Vocal learning in birds, in H. Moltz. eds. The ontogeny of vertebrate behavior. Academic Press, New York.

May, R.M. 1973. Stability and complexity in model Ecosystems. Princeton niversity Press, Princeton, N.J.

May, R.M. 1975a. Patterns of species abundance and diversity, in M. Cody and J. Diamond.eds. Ecology and evolution of communities.Harvard University Press, Cambridge, Mass.

May, RM(ed0 1976. Theoretical Ecology: Principles and Application. Blackwell,

May, R.M. 1981. Models for two interacting populations. In: The Current Status and Future of Parasitology. K.S. Warren & E.F. Purcell eds. Josiah Macy, Jr., Foundation, New York.

Maynard Smith,J.1968. Mathematical ideas in Biology. Cambridge University Press.

Maynard Smith, J. 1978. The Evolution and the theory of games. Cambridge University Press, Cambridge.

Maynard Smith, J. 1972. On Evolution. Edinburgh University Press, Edinburgh.

Maynard Smith, J.1974. Models in Ecology. Cambridge University Press, Cambridge.

Maynard Smith, J. 1978. The Evolution of Sex. Cambridge University Press,

Mayr,Ernst. 1970. Population, species, and evolution. Harvard University Press,

McNaughton, S.J. and Wolf, L.L. 1973. General Ecology. Blackwell.

McGinnies, William G., Bram J. Goldman, and Patricia paylore 1968 Deserts of the world. University Arizona Press, Tucson.

McFarland, W.N., F.H. Pough, T.J. Cade. and J.B. Heiser. 1979. Vertebrate life. Macmillan, New York.

McKaye, K.R. 1981. Natural selection and the evolution of interspecific brood care in fishes. in R. Alexander and J. Tinkle, eds. Natural selection of social behavior. Chiron, New York.

McLean, R.C. and W.R.I. Cook. 1946. Practical Field Ecology. Allen & Unwin.

Merriam, C.H. 1898. Life Zones and Crop Zones. U.S. Dept. Agr. Div. Biol. Surv.

Mellanby, K. 1970. Pessticides and Pollution. Collins, New Nat.

Miller, Charles R. 1971. The Socio-economic roots of environmental pollution.

Miller, G.T.Jr. 1988. Environmental Science. Wadsworth, Belmont.

Monteith, J.N. 1973. Principles of environmental physics. American Elsevier,

Mooney, H.A., and M. Godron, eds.1983. Disturbance and ecosystems: components of response, Springer-Verlag, Berlin.

Moore, Hilary B.1958. Marine ecology. John Wiley & Sons, New York.

Moreau, R.E.1966. The bird faunas of Africa and its islands. Academic Press,

Moss, B.1980. Ecologyof Fresh Waters. Blackwell Scientific Publications, Oxford

Moss, B. 1989. Ecology of Fresh Waters: Man and Medium, Blackwell

Muller-Dombois,D. 1974. Aims and Methods of Vegetation Ecology. Wiley, New York

Munn, R.E. 1966. Descriptive micrometeorology. Academic Press, New York

Munn, R.E. 1970. Biometerological methods. Academic Press, New York.

Myers, W.L. and R.L. Shelton. 1980. Survey Methods for Ecosystem Management.Wiley.

Nobel,P.S.1983.Biophysical Plant Physiology and Ecology. Freeman, San Francisco.

Nouris, M.J.1987. SPSS Guide to data analysis. McGraw-Hill, New York.

Odum, H.T. 1983. Systems ecology: An introduction. John Wiley & Sons, New York.

Packham,J.R.&Harding, D.T.L.1982. Ecology of Woodland Processes. Edward Arnold,

Patil, G.P, E.P. Pielou and W.E.Waters. 1971. Statistical ecology. Vol.I, Spatial patterns and statistical distributions. Pennsylvania State University Press,

Pearl, R. 1928. The Rate of Living. Knopf, New York.

Peters, R.H.1983. The Ecological Implications of Body Size. Cambridge U. Press,

Philips, E.A. 1959. Methods of vegetation study. Henry Holt and Co., New York.

Pianka, E.R. 1983. Evolutionary Ecology, Harper & Row, New York.

Pianka, E.R.1986.Ecology and natural history of desert lizards. Princeton U.Press.

Pickett, S.T.A.& White, P.S.1985. The Ecology of Natural Disturbance as Patch Dynamics. Acadamic Press,

Pielou, E.C. 1975. Ecological Diversity. John Wiley & Sons, New York.

Pielou, E.C. 1977. Mathematical ecology. John Wiley & Sons, New York.

Pielou, E.C. 1979. Biogeography. Wiley, New York.

Pieloy, E.C. 1984. The Interepretation of Ecological Data. Wiley, New York

Pijl, L.vander 1969. Principles of Dispersal in Higher Plants. Springer-Verlag,

Pimm, S.L. 1982. Food Webs. Chapman & Hall, London.

Pitcher, T.J. & Hart, P.J.B. 1982. Fisheries Ecology. Croom Helm, London.

Platt, R.B. and J.F. Griffiths. 1964. Environmental measurement and interpretation Reinhold Publishing Corp., New York.

Poole, R.W. 1978. An Introduction to Quantitative Ecology. McGraw Hill, New York.

Prance, G.T. 1985. The Changing forests. In: Amazonia. G.T. Prance & T.E. Lovejoy ed. Pergamon Press, Oxford.

Price, P.W. 1980. Evolutionary Biology of Parasites. Princeton University Press,

Prosser, C.L. 1973. Comparative animal physiology. Vol.1.Environmental physiology. Saunders, Philadelphia.

Putman, R.J.1983. Carrion and Dung: The Decompsition of Animal Wastages. Edward Arnold, London.

Putwain, P.D. 1989. Resistance of plants to herbicides. In: Weed Control Handbook: Principles, Blackwell, Oxford.

Rabinowitz, D. 1981. Seven forms of rarity. In: The Biological aspects of rare plant conservation. H. Synge ed. Wiley, Chichester.

Ramade, F. Ecology of Natural Resources. Wiley, Chichester.

Ranwell, D.S. 1974. Ecology of Salt Marshes and Sand Dunes. Chapman & Hall, London.

Raymont, John E.G. 1963. Plankton and productivity in the oceans. Macmillan Co.,

Reichle, D.E, R.V. O'Neill and W.F. Harris. 1975. Principles of energy and material exchange in ecosystems. In Unifying concepts in Ecology, ed. W.H. Van Dobben and R.H. Lowe-McConnell. Dr.W. Junk Publ. The Hague.

Reiser, Oliver L.1937. Cosmecology: a theory of evolution.

Remmert, H.1980. Ecology: A textbook. Springer-Verlag, New York,

Rhoades, D.F, and R.G.Gates.1976. A general theory of plant antiherbivore chemistry. in J.W. Wallace and R.L. Mansell, eds. Biochemical interaction between plants and insects. Plenum,

Rhodda, Michael. 1967. Noise and society. Oliver and Boyd, Londan.

Rice, E.L. 1974. Allelopathy. Academic Press, New York.

Richards, P.W. 1952. The tropical rain forest. Cambridge University Press,

Richards, P.W. 1973. Africa, the "odd man out". in B.J. Meggers, J.E.S. Ayensu, and W.D. Duckworth, eds. Tropical forest ecosystems in Africa and South America: a comparative review. Smithsonian Institution Press, Washington.

Richards, B.N. 1974.Introduction to the Soil Ecosystem. Longman, Harlow.

Ricklefs, R.E. 1979. Ecology. Chiron Press, New York, U.S.A.

Ridley, H.N.1930.The dispersal of plants throughout the world. L.Reeve. Ashford, Kent, England.

Romans, R.C. ed. 1981. Vegetation maps for easter North America: 40,000 Years B.C. to the present. in Geobotany. II. Plenum, New York.

Rosenberg, N.J. 1974. Microclimate: The Biological environment. Wiley.

Rosenthal, G.A., and D.H. Janzen. 1979. Herbivores: Their Interaction with Secondary Plant Metabolites. Academic Press,

Rosswall, T.H. 1983.The major Biogeochemical Cycles and their Interactions, Wiley.

Roughgarden, J.1979[1987]. The theory of population genetics and evolutionary ecology: an introduction. MacMillan.

Roughgarden, J.,S. Gaines, and S. Pacala. 1987. Supply side ecology: the role of physical transport processes. In P. Giller and J. Gee, eds. Organization of communities: past and present. Blackwell.

Roughgarden, J. 1986. A comparison of food-limited and space-limited animal competition communities. In: Community Ecology. J. Diamond & T.J. Case eds. Harper & Row,

Runcorn, S.K. 1962. Continental drift. Academic press, New York.

Russell, E.W. 1950. Soil Conditions and Plant Growth, Longman,

Ruttner, F. 1963. Fundamentals of Limnology, translated by D.G.Frey and F.E.J.Fry, University of Toronto Press, Toronto.

Sale, P. 1978. Reef fishes and other vertebrates: a comparison of social structures in behavior: adaptations in the aquatic and terrestrial environments. Wiley,

Salisbury, E.J. 1942. The Reproductive Capacity of plants: Studies in Quantitative Biology. G. Bell, London.

Salisbury, E.J. 1961.Weeds and Aliens, Collins, London.

Salwasser, H. 1986. Conserving a regional spotted owl population. In: Ecological Knowledge and Environmental Problem-Solving. National Academy Press, Washington.

Sauer,C.O.1969. Agricultural Origins and Dispersals, M.I.T. Press, Cambridge.

Schimper, A.F.W.1903. Plant-Geography upon a physiological Basis, Clarendon Press

Schelderup-Ebbe,T. 1935. Social Behavior of Birds. A Handbook of Social psychology, ed. by Carl Murchison, Clark University Press, Worcester.

Schmidt-Nielsen, K.1964.Desert animals:physiological problemsof heat and water Clarendon, Oxford.

Schmidt-Nielsen, K. 1979. Animal Physiology: Adaptation and Environment. Cambridge University Press, London.

Schnieder, S.H and R.Londer,1984. The coevolution of climate and life. Sierra Club

Schultz, A.M. 1969. A study of an Ecosystem. The Arctic Tundra, The Ecosystem Concept in Natural Resource Managament, G. M. Van Dyne ed., Academic Press.

Schwarzbach, Martin.1963. Climates of the past. Van Nostrand Co. Ltd., New York.

Scott, J.A., N.R. French and J.W. Leetham. 1979. Patterns of consumption in grasslands. In Perspectives in Grassland Ecology, ed. N.R.French, Springer-Verlag.

Scriber, J.M. 1983. Evolution of feeding specialization, physiological efficiency and host races in selected Papilionide and Saturniidaein R.F. Denno and M.S. McClure, eds. Variable plants and herbivores in natural and managed systems, Academic Press, New York.

Seber,G.A.F.1982.The Estimation of Animal Abundance and Related parameters. Griffin.

Seton, Ernest Thompson 1909. Life histories of northern animals. Charles Scribner's Sons, New York.

Seton, Ernest Thompson 1912. The arctic prairies. Constable & Co., London.

Seton, Ernest Thompson 1925-28. Lives of game animals. Doubleday, Doran Co.

Shelford, V.E.1913.Animal communities in temperate America. University of Chicago Press, Chicago.

Shelford,V.E.1926. Naturalist's Guide to the Americas. Williams & Wilkins Co, Baltimore.

Shelford, V.E.1929. Laboratory and field ecology. Williams & Wilkins Co, Baltimore.

Shelford, V.E. 1963. The ecology of North America. Univ. Illinois Press, Urbana.

Sheppard, P.M. 1958. Natural selection and heredity. Hutchinson, London.

Shorrocks, B. ed.1984. Evolutionary ecology. Blackwell, Oxford.

Shorrocks, B.& Rosewell, J. 1987. Spatial patchiness and community structure: coexistence and guild size of Drosophila on ephemeral resources. In: Organization of Communities: Past and Present. J.H.R. Gee & P.S.Giller, eds. Blackwell, Oxford.

Shugart, H.H.1984. A theory of forest dynamics. Springer-Verlag, New York.

Shyrock, H.S, Siegel, J.S. & Stockwell, E.G. 1976. The Methods and Materials of Demography. Academic Press, New York.

Smith, J.M. 1974. Models in ecology. Cambridge University Press, Cambridge.

Sibly, R.M. & Calow, P.1985. An integrated approack to life-cycle and r/k theory. In: Behavourial Ecology. R.M. Sibly & R.H. Smith eds. Blackwell, Oxford.

Sibly, R.M.& Calow, P. 1986. Physiological Ecology of Animals. Blackwell

Silvertown, J.W. 1982. Introduction to Plant Population Ecology. Longman,

Simberloff, D. 1984. Properties of coexisting bird species in two archipelagoes. In: Ecological Communities: Conceptual Issues and the Evidence. D.R. Strong, D.Simberloff, L.G. Abele & A.B. THistle, eds. Princeton University Press,

Simberloff, D. 1986. Are we on the verge of a mass extinction in tropical rain forests ? in D.K. Elliot, ed. Dynamics of extinction. Wiley. New York.

Simpson, G. G. 1953. The major features of evolution. Columbia University Press, New York.

Simpson, G.G., A. Roe and R.E. Lewontin. 1960.Quantitative Zoology. Harcourt Brace Jovanovich, New York.

Sladen, B.K.and F.B. Bang 1969. Biology of populations. American Elsevier.

Slobodkin,LB.1961.Growth and regulation of animal populations. Holt,Rinehart and Winston, New York.

Smith VK (ed)1981. Ecology and Field Biology. Harper and Row. New York.

Smith, D.C., 1973. The Lichen Symbiosis and Symbiosis of Algae with invertebrates Oxford Biol Reader O.U.P. Ed. Head, J.J.

Sokal, R.R, and F.J. Rohlf. 1980. Biometry. W.H. Freeman Co., San Francisco.

Solbrig, O.T, and D. Solbrig. 1979. An Introduction to population biology and Evolution. Addison-Wesley, Reading, Mass.

Solbrig, O. ed.1980. Demography and evolution in plant populations. University of California Press, Berkeley.

Solomon, D. 1979. On a paradigm for mathematical modeling. In Contemporary Quantitative Ecology and Relational Ecometrics (G.P.Patil and M.L.Rosenzweig, Eds.) International Co-operative Publishing, Fairland, M.D.

Soule, M.E. 1986. Conservation Biology: The Science of Scarcity and Diversity. Sinauer Associates, Sunderland, MA.

Soule, M.E. 1987. Viable Populations for Conservation. Cambridge U. Press,

Soule, M.E. and B.A. Wilcox. eds. 1980. Conservation biology: an evolutionary-ecological perspective. Sinauer, Sunderland, Mass.

Southwood, T.R.E. 1966. Ecological methods. Methuen & Co. Ltd, London.

Southwood, T.R.E. 1977. The relevance of population dynamic theory to pest status. In Origins of Pest, Parasite, Disease and Weed Problems, ed. J.M. Cherrett and G.R. Sagar, Blackwell, London.

Southwood, T.R.E. 1966. Ecological methods: With Particular Reference to the Study of Insect Populations. Wiley, New York.

Sprent,J.I.1979. The Biology of Nitrogen Fixing Organisms. McGraw Hill, London.

Sprent, J.I.1987.The Ecology of the Nitrogen Cycle. Cambridge U.Press, Cambridge.

Stanley, S.M. 1975. A theory of evolution above the species level. Proc. Natl. Acad. Sci.

Stebbins, G.L.1950. Variation and evolution in plants, Columbia University Press,

Stebbins, G. L. 1966. Processes of Organic Evolution. Prentice-Hall

Stebbins, G.L. 1974. Flowering plants: evolution above the species level. Harvard University Press, Cambridge, Mass.

Stebbins, G.L.1982. Darwin to DNA: Molecules to Humanity. Freeman, San Francisco.

Steele, J.H. 1974. The structure of marine ecosystems. Harvard University Press,

Steele, F. and Bourne, A. 1976. The Man/Food Equation. Academic Press.

Stenseth, N.C. 1983. Causes and consequences of dispersal in small mammals. In: The Ecology of Animal Movement.I.R. Swingland, & P.J.Greenwood eds. O U P.

Stewart, Omer C. 1956. Fire as the first great force employed by man. In W. L. Thomas. Man's role in changing the face of the earth. U. Chicago. press, Chicago.

Stewart, W.D.P. 1967. Nitrogen-fixing plants.

Stott, P. 1981. Historical plant geography: an introduction. Allen and Unwin,

Stolp, H.1988. Microbial Ecology: Organisms, Habitats, Activities. Cambridge University Press, Cambridge.

Strong, D.R., D. Simberloff, L.G. Abele, and A.B.Thistle. 1984. Ecological communities: conceptual issues and the evidence. Princeton University Press, Princeton, N.J.

Strong, D.R.Jr. Lawton, J.H. & Southwood, T.R.E.1984. Insects on Plants: Community Patterns and Mechanisms. Blackwell Scientific Publications, Oxford.

Sullivan, W.1974. Continents in motion: the new Earth debate. McGraw-Hill.

Sukachev, V.and N. Dylis 1964. Fundamentals of forest biogeography. Oliver & Boyd,

Sutcliffe, J. 1977. Plants and Temperature, Edward Arnold, London.

Swan, Lawrence W. 1961. The ecology of the high Himalays. Sci. Amer. 205: 68-78.

Tansley, A.G.1946. Introduction to Plant Ecology. Allen & Unwin. London.

Tansley, A.G., and T.F. Chipp. 1926. Aims and Methods in the Study of Vegetation. British Empire Veg. Comm. London.

Tait, R.V. 1968. Elements of marine ecology. Plenum Press New York.

Tax, Sol.1960. Evolution after Darwin. Vol.1. The evolution of life. University Chicago Press.

Taylor, S.A. and G.L. Ashcroft. 1972. Physiological edaphology. W.H. Freeman Co.,

Taylor, Harden F. 1970. The optimum population for Britain. Academic Press,

Thayer, Gerald H. 1910. Concealing-coloration in the animal kingdom. Macmillan.

Thomas, William L.1956. Man's role in changing the face of the earth. University Chicago Press, Chicago.

Thompson, J.N. 1988. Evolutionary ecology of the relationship between ovipostion preference and performance of offspring in phytophagous insects. Entomologia experimential et applicata.

Tiger, Lionel and Robin Fox. 1971. The imperial animal. Holt, Rinehart and Winston, New York.

Tilman, D. 1982. Resource competition and community structure. Princeton University Press, Princeton, N.J.

Tilman, D. 1986. Evolution and differentiation in terrestrial plant communities: the importance of the soil resource: light gradientin J. Diamond and T. Case, eds. Community ecology. Harper & Row, New York.

Timofeeff-Ressovsky, N.W. 1940. Mutations and geographical variation. In Huxley's. The new systematics, Clarendon Press, Oxford.

Tinbergen, N. 1951. The study of instinct. Clarendon, London

Tinbergen, N. 1964. The evolution of signaling devices. in W. Etkin, eds. Social behavior and organization among vertebrates. U. Chicago Press, Chicago.

Topham, P.B.1977. Colonization, growth, succession and competition. M.R.D. Seaward, ed, Lichen ecology. Academic Press, London.

Townsend, C.R.1980.The Ecology of Streams and Rivers. Edward Arnold, London.

Townsend, C.R.& Calow, P. 1980. Physiological Ecology: An Evolutionary Approach to Resource Use.

Blackwell, Oxford.

Trewartha, G.T. 1954. An introduction to climate. McGraw-Hill, NewYork.

Trippensee, Reuben Edwin. 1948. Wildlife management. McGraw-Hill, NewYork

Tromp, S.W.1980.Biometerology. Heyden and Son, London.

Turk, Amos, J. Turk and J.T. Wittes.1972. Ecology, population, environment. W. B. Saunders Co., Philadelphia.

Udvardy,Miklos D.F.1969. Dynamic zoogeography. Van Nostrand Reinhold Co, New York.

Underwood, T. 1986. The analysis of competition by field experiments. In: Community Ecology: Pattern and Process. J.Kikkawa & D.J. Anderson eds. Blackwell.

Unwin, D.M.1980. Microclimate measurement for ecologists. Academic Press, NewYork.

U.S. Soil Conservation Service. 1938. Range Management Handbook. S.C.S. Region 9.

Uyeda, S.1978.The new view of the Earth: moving continents and moving oceans. Freeman, San Francisco.

Vandermeer, J. 1981. Elementary Mathematical Ecology. Wiley, New York.

Van Den Bosch, R. P.S. Messenger, and A.P. Gutierrez. 1982. An introduction to biological control. Plenum, New York.

Van Den Bosch, R.and P.S. Messenger. 1975. Biological Control. Intertext Books. Pesticides. ICI Education Publication.

Van Groenendael, J.M. 1985. DIfferences in life histories between two ecotypes of Plantago lanceolata. in J.White, ed. Studies on plant demography. Academic Press.

Vander Pijl, L. 1972. Principles of dispersal in higher Plants. Springer-Verlag.

Varley, George C.1970. The concept of energy flow applied to a woodland Community. In Adam Watson's,Animal population in relation to their food resources. Blackwell.

Varley, G.C, G.R. Gradwell and M.P. Hassell. 1973.Insect Population Ecology. Blackwell, Oxford, England.

Vavilov, N.I.1940. The new systematics of cultivated plants. In J.Huxley, The New Systematics. Clarendon Press, Oxford.

Vitousek, P.M. 1983. Mechanisms of ion leaching in natural and managed ecosystems. in H. A. Mooney and M. Godron, eds. Disturbance and ecosystems: components of response. Springer-Verlag, Berlin.

Vitousek, P.M, W.A. Reiners, J.M. Melilo, C.C. Grier and J.R.Gosz. 1981. Nitrogen cycling and loss following forest perturbation: the components of response. in G.W. Barrett and R. Rosenberg, eds. Stress effects on natural ecosystems. Wiley-Interscience, New York.

Vollenweider, R.A., ed. 1974. Primary production in aquatic environments. IBP Handbook No.23. Blackwell Scientific Publications, Oxford.

Wagner, Richard H.1970.Environment and man. W.W. Norton & Co., Inc., New York.

Wainwright, S.A, W.D. Biggs, J.D. Currey and J.M. Gosline. 1976. Mechanical design in Organisms, Wiley, New York.

Walford, Lionel A.1958. Living resources of the sea. Ronald Press Co. New York.

Wallace, A.R.1869. The Malay archipelago: the land of the orangutan and the bird of paradise. Harper & Row, New York.

Wallace, A.R.1876.The geographical distribution of animals. Vols I,II. Macmillan,

Wallace, A.R. 1878. Tropical Nature and Other essays, Macmillan, London.

Wallace, A.R.1880. Island life, or the phenomena and causes of insular floras and fauns. Macmillan, London.

Wallace, B. 1981. Basic population genetics. Columbia University Press, New York.

Wallwork, John A. 1970. Ecology of soil animals. McGraw-Hill, New York.

Waring, R.H. 1989. Ecosystems: fluxes of matter and energy. in: Ecological Concepts. J.M. Cherrett ed. Blackwell Scientific Publications, Oxford.

Waring, R.H.& Schlesinger, W.H. 1985. Forest Ecosystems: Concepts and Management. Academic Press, Orlando, FL.

Warming, E. 1895. Plantesamfund (Revised for English edition as Oecology of plants, 1909), Clarendon Press, Oxford.

Warming, E. 1909. Oecology of Plants. An Introduction to the study of plant communities, English Translation by P. Groom and I.B. Balfour, Oxford.

Warren, A. and Goldsmith, F.B. 1974. Conservation in Practice. Wiley.

Warner, R.R. 1978. Evolution of hermaphroditism and unisexuality in aquatic and terrestrial vertebrates. in E.S. Reese and F.J. Lighter, eds. Contrasts in behavior: adaptations in the aquatic and terrestrial environments. Wiley.

Watt, K.E.F. 1966. Systems analysis in ecology. Academic Press, New York.

Watt, K.E.F.1968. Ecology and resource management, McGraw-Hill, New York.

Weaver, J.E and Frederic E. Clements. 1938. Plant ecology. McGraw-Hill, New York.

Weaver, J.E. and F.W. Albertson. 1956. Grasslands of the Great Plains. Their nature and use. Johnsen Publ. Co., Lincoln,

Weaver, J.E.1968.Prairie plants and their environment.U.Nebraska Press, Lincoln

Weinberg, Alvin M. and R. Philp Hammond.1970.Limits to the use of energy.

Welch, Paul S.1952. Limnology. McGraw-Hill, New York.

Welty, J.C. 1979. The life of birds. Saunders, Philadelphia.

Went, F.W. 1970. Plants and the chemical environment, Chemical ecology ed. by E. Sondheimer and J.B. Simeone, Academic Press, New York.

Westlake, D.F. 1965. Some basic data for investigation of the productivity of aquatic macrophytes. In C.R. Goldman's, Primary productivity in aquatic environments, University California Press, Berkeley.

Whatley, J. W. & Whatley, F.R. 1980. Light and Plant Life. Edward Arnold, New York.

Wheeler, William Norton.1923. Social life among the insects. Harcourt, Brace & Co, New York.

White, M.J.D. 1978. Modes of speciation. Freeman, San Francisco.

Whitmore, T. C. 1982. On pattern and process in forests. In The Plant Community as a working mechanism, ed. E.I. Newman. Blackwell, Oxford.

Whittaker, R. H. 1962.The classification of natural communities.

Whittaker, R. H. 1970. The biochemical ecology of higher plants.Acadamic Press,

Whittaker, R.H. 1970. Communities and ecosystems. Macmillan Co., New York.

Whittaker, R.H.1975. Communities and ecosystems. Macmillan, New York.

Whittaker,R.H.(Ed.)1978. Ordination of Plant Communities.W.Junk,The Hague.

Whitton, B.A, ed. 1975. River ecology. Blackwell, Oxford.

Wickler, W. 1968. Mimicry in plants and animals. McGraw-Hill, New York.

Williams, C. B. 1964. Patterns in the balance of nature and related problems in quantitative Ecology. Academic Press, New York.

Williams,G.C.1966.Adaptation and Natural Selection. Princeton University Press,

Williams, G.C. 1975. Sex and evolution. Princeton University Press, Princeton,

Williamson, M.H.1972.The Analysis of Biological Populations. Edward Arnold,

Williamson, M.H.1981. Island Populations. Oxford University Press, Oxford.

Willis, J.C. 1922.Age and Area. University Press. Cambridge.

Wilson, E.O. 1975. Sociobiology: The new synthesis. Harvard University Press,

Wilson, E.O. and Bossett, W.H. 1971 A Primer of Population Biology. Sinauer.

Woodwell, G.M. 1980. Aquatic systems as part of the biosphere. In Fundamentals of Aquatic ecosystems, ed. R.K. Barnes, and K.H. Mann. Blackwell, Oxford.

Woodwell, G.M., R.H. Whittaker, W.A. Reiners, G.E. Likens, C.C. Delwiche and D.B. Botkin. 1978. The Biota and the world carbon budget.

Worthington, E.B.1975. Evolution of I.B.P. C U P, Cambridge.

Wrigley, G. 1982. Tropical agriculture: the development of production, Longman,

Wulff,E.V.1943.AnIntroductionto Historical Plant Geography. Chron.Bot. Walthan.

Wyatt, H.V. 1987. Information sources in the life sciences. Buttworth, London.

Wynne-Edwards,V.C.1962.Animaldispersionin relation to social behavior. Harrner.

Yonge, C.M.1949. The sea shore. (Reprinted 1963) Atheneum, New York.

Young, J.Z. 1971. An Introduction to the Study of Man. O.U.P.

Zaret, T.M. 1980. Predation and freshwater communities. Yale University Press, New Haven, Conn.

Zaret, T.M. and E.P. Smith. 1984. On measuring niches and not measuring them. In Evolutionary Ecology of Neotropical freshwater Fishes [T.M. Zaret,Ed.). W. unk, The Hague. 127-137.

Zelitch, I.1971. Photosynthesis, Photorespiration and plant productivity. Academic Press, New York.

Zenkevitch, L. 1963. Biology of the seas of the USSR.(Transl. from the Russian). Allen & Unwin, Ltd., London.

2. THE PROSPECTUS FOR M.S. IN ECOLOGY

The Pondicherry University

PONDICHERRY-605 001

The School of Ecology

Post-Graduate Programme-M.S.

1987—1989

PROSPECTUS

(APPLICATION FORM ENCLOSED)

* Spatially modified from the originals, which are in the Pondicherry University

T. N. Seshan, I.A.S.

सत्यमेव जयते

Ministry of Environment and Forests
Paryavaran Bhawan
C. G. O. Complex
Lodi Road
New Delhi-110 003

SECRETARY
Government of India

Dated : 22 . 3 . 1987

Message

The current pattern of man's efforts for development while producing economic gains, has wrought severe damage to natural eco-systems. As a consequence of disturbed habitats, diverse species of flora and fauna are becoming extinct from the face of the Earth. The natural resources of the earth-water, air, soil, plant and animal life-which are the basis of our very existence are getting degraded as a consequence of developmental activity not in harmony with the environment.

There is therefore urgent need to restore the ecological integrity to ecosystems; to develop and implement ecologically sound habitats; and to inculcate enduring attitudes and values of respect for the natural environment in all peoples.

As part of the broad response to this ecological crisis, there is a major need to mobilise educational forces and to help shape the knowledge, skills and values of future citizens. The 'School of Ecology' being started in the young University at Pondicherry, I am sure, will go a long way in producing ecologically educated citizens with basic knowledge of sound concepts so that they could learn to make environmentallywise decisions based on the detailed analysis of alternatives.

May the School grow from strength to strength.

T. N. SESHAN

PROSPECTUS

PONDICHERRY UNIVERSITY, SCHOOL OF ECOLOGY

1. UNIVERSITY

The Pondicherry University was established by the Parliament Act 53 of 1985 with effect from 16th October, 1985. This University is dedicated by our Prime Minister to strive to fulfill the scientific aspirations of the People" on the most innovative lines. The University is slated to be a Pioneer and Leader amongst institutions of higher learning and has al ready embarked upon the task of laying strong foundations required for National and International excellence.

The campus of the University is coming up in a sprawling 788 acres complex lapped by the Bay of Bengal on the scenic Pondicherry-Mahabalipuram Highway. The Campus development has been meticulously planned incorporating all the modern ideas for becoming a beehive of academic activity. The Building works are in progress with appropriate funding by the UGC. A building for the School of Ecology is being taken up. The building will incorporate most modern classrooms, well equipped audio visual facilities, extensive library and reading hall facilities together with modern retrieval systems.

2. SCHOOL OF ECOLOGY

Pondicherry University's innovative efforts are truly reflected in their new School of Ecology, lhe School of Ecology is the first of its kind in these parts to be devoted exclusively for the study of the world we live in so that we can preserve it as we have known it. In India, this is one of the few Schools with a specific theme and objective in this innovative branch of studies. The University of Pondicherry true to its commitment to the long term and larger interests of the nation has set up this School of Ecology to cater to the specific demand to preserve, protect and defend the basic resources upon which the people rely for their every existence.

3. GENESIS

It is common knowledge that humanity is tottering on the brink of a precipice. Under the guise of development, the resources have been abused to such an extent that the people may be snuffing out the very source of our existence. Lack of perception about the environment and the inter-dependence that is inherent in things natural is the root cause. Efforts have been made in India and abroad to attack these problems methodically. So far, the attempts made have been to bring. the basic sciences together in a loosely knit framework of Environmental sciences. But ours in Pondicherry is an effort at synthesising an integrative first step in the large context of environmental studies and is one of the first in India.

4. OBJECTIVES

Though there have been attempts to have viable programmes in Environmental Sciences in the recent past, these attempts, have not succeeded fully because of the loose organization of different disciplines such as Mathematics, Physics, Chemistry and Biology without any specific objective or thrust in a given direction. 'Ecology which links biological systems including man with the environment is a much more specific and directed approach and therefore should have formed the focal point for any School of Environmental Sciences. This has not, unfortunately, happened because of a definite lack of appreciation on our part so far about Ecology as a unifying concept in Environmental studies.

The definition of Ecology is to be understood in its broadest sense that includes plant and animal life and with MAN as the focal point for studies.

The University of Pondicherry has consciously taken a significant decision that is a radical departure from what has been attempted so far here and elsewhere.

With the Andaman & Nicobar Islands and Lakshadweep in our unit one of the main thrust areas will have to be centering around this island eco system which opportunity is not available for others.

A second thrust area will be centering around the urban ecosystem interactions in the main land with high population density in the rural belt added to the highly depleted natural resource base. The rural eco system meets urgent strategy for maintaining the balance. With a number of industries going up in urban centres, man's relationship with the environment here also is highly distorted. The result is pollution of the soil, water and air leading to universal destruction.

Rain forest eco system of Andaman & Nicobar Islands with reference to their eco physiology will be another thrust area, even in the rural urban eco system studies, the invasion of the casuarina and Bluegum culture and the impact of social forestry and agro forestry have to be studied in depth.

The above areas of study are only a few examples; the rest indicated elsewhere in the prospectus.

5. AREA

(i) Unmarred Pondicherry: Pondicherry is one of the few pockets on the Indian subcontinent that has managed to stay fairly well developed without scarring its face with developmental lesions. It still has within itself probably the last unpolluted wet land ecosystem-*Kaliveli Tank.* Again it is one of the few coastal areas where the sea-shore has not been converted into a garbage dump yet. However, efforts are being underway to rapidly industrialise and our School of Ecology will playa cardinal role in channelling this development into ecologically non-lethal variety.

(ii) Pristine Andamans: If there is any large area in this globe that has not yet suffered the ravages of development, it is these islands. They are pristinely pure yet. So, far, we have succeeded in preserving the natural balance. Now that the International situation is changing vis-a-vis Hong Kong and the face of Andaman and Nicobar may change as a result of NRl's coming over here it would be the privilege of the faculty of the School of Ecology to ensure that the face-lift does not leave scars but beautifies further this darling of the Bay of Bengal.

(iii) Unpolluted Lakshadweep: One more area of interests for the University will be the Lakshadweep Islands - the garland of the Arabian sea. Here again much work needs to be done' to keep up the ecological balance.

6. U. G. C.

The University approached the UGC for support of its efforts in starting the School of Ecology. The U. G. C. already approved the establishment of this school and this school had the privilege of being inaugurated by Prof. Yashpal, Chairman, U.G.C.

7. FACULTY

The School has in place expert faculty members like Prof. V. M. Meher Homji an Ecologist of International repute as Honorary Dean and Prof. Rauf Ali, formerly of the faculty of Mahidol University, Thailand and a noted IUCN expert as an adjunct Professor.

8. EXTENSION CAMPUS IN ANDAMAN AND NICOBAR ISLANDS AND COLLABORATION WITH FRENCH INSTITUTE

The University has plans for setting up an extension campus in Andaman and Nicobar Islands in an effort to set up a research station on the lines of the Smithsonian Tropical Research Institute in Panama.

The French Institute at Pondicherry under the leadership of Mr. Pierre Legris is collaborating with the Pondicherry University School of Ecology. The French Institute has done something significant already within the sphere.

9. M.S. IN ECOLOGY

This School offers a Master of Science (M.S) programme of two years' duration consisting of (a) Foundation Courses (b) Core Courses (c) Electives and (d) Research Projects.

(a) **Foundation Courses:** The Foundation Courses would be offered in the first semester depending on the background of each student as a special programme under the advice of a member of the faculty.

(b) **Core Courses:** The core courses are meant to give the students a basic grounding required of a good ecologist. These will be the following five:

* Environment Impact Assessment
* Biometry and Eco-system Modelling
* Population Ecology
* Geo-Sciences
* Eco Restoration and Resource Conservation

(c) **Elective Courses:** The student will be offered about 8 or 10 courses in the III Semester and they can choose any five. The initial choices could be from among.

* Socio Biology
* Marine Costal System
* Forest Ecology
* Wetland Ecology
* Biogeography
* Air and Water Pollution
* Vector Biology
* Biophysical Ecology
* Palynology
* Urban Ecology
* Eco Physiology
* Protected Ecosystem Planning
* Elective Project

(d) **Research Project:** The thrust of the programme is in the Research Project each student is required to take in the IV Semester. This project work will be intensively field study oriented and will attempt to tackle current problems faced in the Indian context.

10. BROAD AREAS FOR RESEARCH

The School's research efforts would be among the following areas.

Forest Ecology with special reference to Raw forest Eco System of Andamans

Wetland Ecology-Issues of Kaliveli Ecosystem

Human Settlement and their Impact

Industrial Pollution

Invasion of Casuarina and Bluegum. Culture in Rural Urban Eco System.

Water Resources Management and Hydrology

Ethology

Renewable Resources of Energy

Conservation of Resources

Eco-restoration

Ocean Ecology and Fisheries

Cauvery Ecosystem

Island Ecosystem

Systems Modelling

Marine Ecosystems

Palynology

Social and Agro Forestry

11. FACILITY

The School will have in place the best facilities for carrying out research like computers and other sophisticated scientific equipment. This University school would function in close collaboration with the two institutes of internationally renown-the Pondicherry Vector Control Research Centre (VCRC) and the French Institute Pondicherry as already stated.

12. ADMISSION AND ELIGIBILITY

Normally students with a high bachelors degree in any Science area may apply for th is unique programme. Exceptional candidates from other disciplines may also apply.

13. M. S. CORE COURSES CREDITS

Semester I: Bridge Courses of relevance to ecology.

Course	Credits
EC 301 Mathematics and Physics	3
EC 303 Statistics	2
EC 305 Computers	2

EC 307 Environmental Analysis	2
EC 309 Biology	3
EC 311 Ecology	4
Semester II: Core Courses	
EC 402 Biometry	3
EC 404 Population Ecology	3
EC 406 Aquatic and Wetland Ecology	3
EC 408 Natural Resources	3
EC 410 Pollution & Toxicology	4
Semester III: Core Courses	
EC 501 Biogeography and Forest Ecology	3
EC 503 Environmental Impact Assessment	2
EC 505 Ecosystem Management and Eco-development	4
EC 507 Evolutionary Ecology	3
EC 509 Technical Report Writing	2
EC 511 Systems Modelling	2

14. ELECTIVE COURSES

Anyone of these courses will be selected by each student in consultation with the Faculty

1. Marine Ecology
2. Tropical Forest Ecosystem
3. Limnology
4. Behavioural Ecology
5. Plant and Animal Interactions
6. Agro-ecosystems
7. Urban Ecology
8. Environmental mutagenesis
9. Environmental monitoring
10. Water treatment and Pollution control
11. Mathematical modelling
12. Ecological engineering

15. FACULTY

Prof V. M. Meher-Homji, Dean

Prof S. B. Chaphekar

Prof C. B. S. R. Sharma

Dr. Priya Davidar, Reader

Prof Rauf Ali, Guest Faculty

Prof S. A. Abbasi

Dr. A. K. Kumaraguru, Reader

Dr. K. V. Devi Prasad, Reader
Dr. N. Parthasarathy, Lecturer
Shri D. Ramamoorthy, Lecturer
Dr. G. Poyyamoli, Lecturer
Shri S. S. Sundaravel, Lecturer

16. FEES

The following fees are to be paid by the students per semester

		Rs.
(i)	Tuition fees	500
(ii)	Course materialsfees	300
(iii)	Special fees	100
(iv)	Library & Computer fees	100
		Rs. 1000
(v)	Matriculation. Registration recognition and magazine fees (one time payment)	Rs. 150

17. SELECTION

The application in the encased form should reach the Registrar, Pondicherry University on or before 1st June 1987. The students will be selected on the basis of an Entrance Examination in the form of an aptitude test. This test will be held at Pondicherry on June 21 1987. Selected short listed top ranking candidates will have an interview at Pondicherry on the 11th and 12th of July 1987 at their own cost. The first batch will consist of not more than 15 students.

3. COURSE STRUCTURE AND SYLLABUS*

M. S. COURSE, SALIM ALI SCHOOL OF ECOLOGY, PONDICHERRY UNIVERSITY

		Credits
Semester I: Bridge Courses		
EC 301	Mathematics and Physics	3
EC 303	Statistics	2
EC 305	Computers	2
EC 307	Environmental Analysis	2
EC 309	Biology	3
EC 311	Ecology	4
Semester II: Core Courses		
EC 402	Biometry	3
EC 404	Population Ecology	3
EC 406	Aquatic and Wetland Ecology	3
EC 408	Natural Resources	3
EC 410	Pollution & Toxicology	4
Semester III: Core Courses		
EC 501	Biogeography and Forest Ecology	3
EC 503	Impact Assessment	2
EC 505	Ecosystem Management and Eco-development	4
EC 507	Evolutionary ecology	3
EC 509	Technical Report Writing	2
EC 511	Systems Modeling	2
Semester IV: Electives and Research Project (5 credits)		
EC 602	A. Marine Ecology	
EC 602	B. Tropical Forest Ecosystems	
EC 602	C. Limnology	
EC 602	D. Behavioural Ecology	
EC 602	E. Plant and Animal Interactions	
EC 602	F. Agro-ecosystems	
EC 602	G. Urban Ecology	
EC 602	H. Environmental Mutagenesis	
EC 602	I. Environmental Monitoring	

* Spatially modified from the originals, which are in the Pondicherry University

EC 602 J. Water Treatment and Pollution control
EC 602 K. Mathematical Modeling
EC 602 L. Ecological Engineering
EC 604 Project Work (10 credits)

Dear colleagues,

Kindly give your suggestions, if any, to improve the enclosed material (on a separate sheet) preferably by Friday evening

(CBSR Sharma)

1. SBC - As per discussion with colleagues. 4.11
2. SAA -
3. PD - PD
4. KUD - I have no addition to suggest ... Nov 4, '87
5. AKK -
6. GP - ... - correction in my model (enclosed)
7. NP - ...
8. SS -
9. DR - ...
10. RA -
11. VMH -

My comments are attached (separate sheets). Minor changes are also indicated on page 3, 6, 10, 18, 19 & 10 of attached draft.
6.11.87
(Prof. S A Abbasi)

SYLLABUS

SEMESTER I

EC 301. MATHEMATICS AND PHYSICS (CREDITS: 2) (ALI, DEVI PRASAD)

Basis of calculus - functions of single variable, concept of limits, differential coefficients, differentiation of algebraic, trigonometric and exponential functions. Meaning of the derivative - maxima and minima, addition, multiplication. Linear algebra – matrices, inversion of matrices, Integration formulae of integration for algebraic, trigonometric and exponential functions. Integration by parts. Differential equations - solving equations of first and second order, examples from ecology.

Basic kinematics like motion of particle in one and two dimensions, projectile motion, kinetic and potential energy. The equivalence of heat and mechanical energy, the concepts of specific heats and heat capacities, the Laws of Thermodynamics and their special relevance to ecosystems. Basic electricity and magnetism: voltage, current and their relationships, electromagnetic radiation, EM radiation as energy input, ionising and non-ionising radiations. Concepts in nuclear physics - fission and fusion, radioactivity and radiation, biological effects of radiation.

References

1. Resnick, Halliday, 1977. Physics, Wiley & Sons, New York. 564 pp.
2. Sears et al, 1977. University Physics Addison Wesley.
3. Ayres Jr., 1972. Theory and Problems of Calculus, 2nd Ed. Shaum's Outline Series, McGraw-Hill Co., Singapore. 346 pp.

EC 303. Statistics (Credits: 2) (Ali, Sundarvel)

Set operations. Permutations and combinations. Sample spaces, events and partitions. Conditional probability and independence. Tree diagrams. Bayes Theorem. Random Variables in one and two dimensions. Frequency distributions. Mean, median, mode as measures of central tendency. Mean deviation, standard deviation, variance, covariance, Uniform, Normal and Poisson probability distributions. Simple hypothesis testing using non-parametric statistics.

References

1. Friend, 1987. Quantitative Methods, Longman Exam Guides.
2. Lipschutz, 1982. Theory and Problems of Statistics, Schaum's Outline Series, McGraw-Hill, Singapore. 153 pp.
3. Hamburg, 1985. Basic Statistics: A Modern Approach, Harcourt Jovanovich Publ., London.

EC 305. Computers (Credits: 2) (Devi Prasad, Sundarvel)

Computers - use of computers, operating system. Word processing and report preparing with computers. Data processing - higher languages, Data processing with Pascal. Features of Pascal - use of arrays, records and sets, repetitive loops, procedures and functions.

References

1. IBM PC Users guide and reference manual.
2. Gottfried, 1986. Theory and Problems of Programming with Pascal. Schaum's Outline Series, McGraw-Hill, Singapore. 407 pp.
3. Wirth, Jensen, 1986. Pascal Users Manual and Reports, Springer Verlag (Narosa Publishing, New Delhi). 266 pp.

EC 307. Environmental Analysis (Credits: 2)

(Abbasi, Kumaraguru, Parthasarathy, Ramamurthy)

pH, nutrients and their significance in ecological processes.

Basics of environmental analysis with special reference to potentiometry, volumetry, conductometry, spectrophotometry, atomic absorption and atomic emission spectroscopy etc.

References

1. APHA: Standard Methods for Analysis of Water and Waste water
2. Vogel's Quantitative Inorganic Analysis.

EC 309. Biology (Credits: 2) (Sharma, Poyyamoli, Parthasarathy)

Levels of biological organisation, plant and animal diversity. Morphology and systematic of major plant and animal groups. Principles of development, reproduction and inheritance, Mendelism, mitosis, meiosis, chromosomes, genes and DNA. Sources of genetic variation and fundamentals of evolution. Taxonomy, distribution and functions of microbes in the environment. Their significance in biodegradation, biochemical cycles, contamination and disease, Isolation and culture methods.

References

1. Buffaloe, 1964. Principles of Biology, Prentice Hall, India. 365 pp.
2. Hawkings,(ed) 1986.Encyclopedia of Indian Natural History, Oxford University Press, New Delhi,620p.
3. Parder, (ed) 1982. Synopsis and Classification of living organisms, McGraw-Hill, 2 Vols.

EC 311. ECOLOGY (Credits: 4)

(Chaphekar, Ali, Davidar, Kumaraguru, Poyyamoli, Ramamoorthy)

Ecology: definition, history and scope, atmosphere, lithosphere, hydrosphere and biosphere - their interactions and adaptations of organisms, environmental factors; autecology and synecology; ecological succession; biogeography; ecosystem concept, structure, diversity and functions, capture and transfer of energy in biosphere and ecosystems. Food chains, Ecological pyramids, Biogeochemical cycles, hydrological cycle and budgets, nutrient cycles and budgets; evolution of civilization and impact on ecological balances.

References

1. Deshmukh, 1986. Ecology and Tropical Biology. Blackwell Scientific Publications. 375 pp.
2. Odum, 1971. Fundamentals of Ecology, W.B. Saunders, Philadelphia, 574 pp.
3. Odum, 1983. Basic Ecology, W.B. Saunders, Philadelphia, 613 pp.

SEMESTER II

EC 402. Biometry (Credits: 3) (Ali, Sundarvel)

Correlation, Regression and Analysis of variance, discriminant analysis and Hotelings T for community classification and ordination. Modelling of community through multiple regression analysis, principal components analysis, factor analysis, cluster analysis, canonical correlation analysis and time series analysis. Measurements of species diversity. Field work, Exposure to computer based multivariate analysis.

References

1. Afifi, Clark, 1984. Computer-aided multivariate analysis, Lifetime Learning Publ., California.
2. Poole, 1974. An Introduction to Quantitative Ecology, McGraw-Hill Publ., London.
3. Sokal, Rohlf, 1969. Biometry, Freeman.

EC 404. Population Ecology (Credits: 3) (Ali, Davidar)

Genetics related to populations: fitness and selection; population processes. The concept of fitness; modelling of single-species population; intra-specific competition. Predation: optimal foraging theory, functional prey responses, co-evolution. Life history strategies, energy allocation, dispersal, reproduction, population regulation. Community structure: measurement of diversity and abundance, responses to disturbance, instability.

References

1. Begon, Mortimer, 1986. Population Ecology - A unified Study of Animals and Plants, Blackwell Publ.
2. Cody, Diamone, 1975. Ecology and Evolution of Communities, Harvard University Press, Cambridge, USA.

EC 406 Aquatic And Wetland Ecology (Credits: 3)

(Abbasi, Kumaraguru, Poyyamoli, Ramamoorthy)

Scope of studies, in aquatic and wetland ecology. Freshwater, estuarine and marine ecosystems. Physicochemical characteristics; freshwater, lakes, ponds and rivers. Brackish waters; estuaries; intertidal zone, sub-littoral zone and Oceans. Distribution and abundance of plants and animals, in relation to environmental factors, adaptations, productivity.

References

1. Dring, 1982. The Biology of Marine Plants, Edward Arnold, London, 199 pp.
2. Mellanby, 1986. Animal life in Fresh Water, Chapman and Hall, London.
3. Tonapi, 1980. Fresh Water Animals of India - An Ecological Approach, Oxford & IBH Publ., New Delhi, 341 pp.

EC 408 Natural Hesources (Credits: 3)

(Sharma, Poyyamoli, Parthasarathy)

Plants, animals, soils, water and minerals as resources. Different types of energy resources, Variation in resource quality, distribution and utilization. Human population growth and resource depletion; past, present and future scenarios. Natural resources of India. Principles governing the use of natural resources. The concept of renewability. Factors influencing the distribution and utilization of natural resources.

References

1. Ehrlich et al., 1977. Eco-science: Population, resources, environment, Freeman, San Francisco, 1051 pp.
2. Ranade, 1984. Ecology of Natural Resources, John Wiley & Sons, New York, 231p
3. World Resources Institute 1986. Basic Books Inc., New York, 353 pp.

EC 410 Pollution And Toxicology (Credits: 4)

Chaphekar, Sharma, Abbasi, Kumaraguru)

Pollution of land, air and water. Natural and man-made pollution. Nature of pollutants in air, water and soils. Their origin, distribution and effects on life and ecosystems. Deposition of solid wastes, leaching and contamination of water resources. Short term and long term effects at organismic, ecosystem and biospheric levels. Aerobiology and allergies - pollen calenders and forecasting of diseases. Noise pollution, Ecotoxicology and principles of toxicology; oral dermal, neuro, respiratory, reproductive toxicity of xenobiotics to human kind. Teratogenecity, Carcinogenicity and Mutagenecity.

References

1. Hodgson, Guthrie, 1980. Introduction to Biochemical Toxicology, Elsevier, New York.
2. Lu, 1985. Basic Toxicology, Hemisphere Publ., Washington, 276 pp.

SEMESTER III

Ec 501 Biogeoghaphy and Fohest Ecology (Credits: 3)

(Meher-Homji, Chaphekar, Parthasarathy, Ramamoorthy, French Institute)

History of vegetation. Principles of plant and animal distribution; vegetational types and floristic realms of the world. Vegetation mapping. Bioclimatology, bioclimatic classifications, macro-, meso-, microclimates. Bioclimatic variability, monsoon mechanism, vagaries of weather El Nino, concept of probable climate. Factors of climate - rainfall types, amount, distribution, seasons, temperature, dry period, xerothermic index, secondary factors. Forests and rainfall, Principles of Palynology and its role in phytogeography. Evolutionary convergence and divergence, age and area concept endemism; botanical provinces and vegetation and types of India. Soils - types, properties and distribution.

References

1. Cain 1976. Biogeography.
2. Good 1964. Principles of Phytogeography, Blackwell.
3. Simmons, 1979. Biogeography - Natural and Cultural, E. Arnold, 400 pp.

EC 503 Environmental Impact Assessment (Credits: 2)

(Abbasi, Sundarvel)

Micro, semi-micro and macro impacts of natural and human-induced activities on the environment: reversible/assimilative and irreversible impacts. Benefits and costs of developmental projects. Impact assessment methodology: frames of reference, identification of major vectors, impact quantification and trade-off analysis. Case studies: impact of major construction/industrial/mining/water resource and other developmental projects.

EC 505 Ecosystem Management And Ecodevelopment (Credits: 4)

(Chaphekar,Sharma, Davidar, Kumaraguru, Sundarvel)

Major natural and man-made ecosystems and responses to environmental stresses: freshwater, marine, estuarine, forest, grassland, desert, agricultural and urban ecosystems; prevention and management of ecological disasters. Concept of renewability and its relevance in resource management; restorative practices for reclamation and conservation of habitats and resources. Designing of green bolts. Land use planning, technological measures for pollution abatement. Peoples perceptions. Environmental education and legislation.

References

1. Centre for Science and Environment, 1985. The State of India's Environment.
2. Lohanil 1984.Environmental Quality Management, South Asian Publishers, NewDelhi.
3. O'Riordan, 1979. Progress in Resource Management and Environmental Planning, John Wiley.

EC 507 Evolutionary Ecology(Credits: 3)

(Ali, Davidar, Parthasarathy)

Intensive six week field based course on ecological principles and research methods. Topics covered: ecology, evolution and animal behaviour. Students will work in groups, pose hypotheses, design projects to test the hypotheses and present the results in a short seminar.

EC 509 Technical Report Writing (Credits: 2)

(Davidar, Devi Prasad)

Students will critically rend and discuss a scientific paper every week. The papers will be of uneven quality usually from one research area. Simultaneously the students will be given data or use data they have collected to individually write a technical report. These reports will be critically reviewed by the rest of the class and by the instructor.

EC 511 Systems Modelling (Credits: 2)

(Abbasi, Ali, Devi Prasad)

Why model? Models, their uses and limitations, complexity in ecosystems, nonlinearity, interaction, discontinuity models. Basics of modelling: defining the problem, identification of parameters, state variables, driving variables and output variables. Types of mathematical models, deterministic and stochastic models. Examples of dynamic and deterministic models: Lotka-Volterra models for interacting populations. Stochastic Models: examples; evaluation, verification and validation of models. Use of computers in modelling.

References

1. Halfon, 1979. Theoretical Systems Ecology, Academic Press.
2. Jeffers, 1979. Modelling, Chapman & Hall, London.
3. Smith, 1978. Models in Ecology, Cambridge University Press.

SEMESTER IV (EACH COURSE CARRIES 5 CREDITS)

ELECTIVES

EC 602 A Marine Ecology

(Chaphekar, Kumaraguru, Parthasarathy and French Institute)

Marine environment: Physico-chemical properties of sea water, zonation. Coastal environment: topography, water movement. Neritic province: plankton, adaptations, distribution, productivity. Life on rocky environment: life habits and adaptations, zonation, diversity and community organisation, productivity, Life in sediments: physical nature, protests, macrophytes, sea-grasses, macrofauna, meiofauna. Brackish water: types of estuaries, environmental features, biota, adaptations, productivity, food webs. Coral reefs: classification, morphology, zonation, nutrition and growth, species interactions, diversity and biogeography, productivity. Marshes and mangroves: salt marshes; zonation, flora and fauna, mangroves; distribution, zonation, fauna productivity.

References

1. Barnes 1984. Estuarine Biology, Edward Arnold, London 276 pp.
2. Kinne (ed) 1983. Marine Ecology. Vols I-V, Wiley.
3. Tait 1981. Elements in Marine Ecology. Butterworth's, London 376 pp.

EC 602B Thopical Fohest Ecosystems

(Chaphekar, Davidar, Parthasarathy and French Institute)

Forest types of India: physiognomy, structure and function, floristics, species diversity and plant demography; productivity and biomass; nutrient cycling; soil and vegetation systems; litter production; seasonality forest succession and regeneration. Deforestation and afforestation. Plantation forestry, social forestry, agro forestry. Conservation strategies, Sacred groves and biosphere reserves.

References

1. Agarwala 1985 Forests in Inqia. Oxford & IBH. New Delhi.

2. Holdridge et al 1971. Forests Life Zones in Tropical Environments. Pergamon Press.
3. Wenger 1984. Forestry Handbook. John Wiley, New York. 1335 pp.

EC 602 C Limnology

(Abbasi, Kumaraguru, Poyyamoli, Ramamoorthy)

Freshwater ecosystems: lentic and lotic habitats: energy flows, nutrients and limiting factors; hydrology, geomorphology, limnochemistry and limnobiology of lakes, rivers, ponds, springs, rock-pools, dug wells and reservoirs. Stresses in the limnic ecosystems; natural and induced succession; limnology vis a vis water resource

References

1. Welch 1952 Limnology. McGraw-Hill; NY. 538 pp.
2. Wetzal, 1975 Limnology. W.B. Saunders.

EC 602 D Behavioural Ecology (Ali, Davidar)

The concepts of reproductive success and fitness. Levels of selection. The advantages of group living. Group selection and kin selection. The theory of reciprocal altruism. Parental care and parent-off spring conflict, Game theory models and evolutionarily stable strategies. Strategies for dispersal and reproduction. Case studies from social insects, birds and mammals.

References

1. Clutton-Brock & Harvey. Readings in Socio biology.
2. Krebs & Paries Introduction to Behavioural Ecology. Oxford University Press.

EC 602 E Plant And Animal Interactions (Ali, Davidar)

Co-evolution of plants and animals: plant-pollinator, plant-frugivore and plant-herbivore interactions. Plant-pollinator relationships; flower function and pollinators; pollination syndromes; foraging behaviour; pollination success; out-crossing and inbreeding; seed set. Plant-frugivore relationships; fruit quality; dispersal agents and fruit preferences; seed dispersal; seed predation and seedling recruitment. Plantherbivore interactions: resource availability; plant defences; feeding specializations. Population biology of plant-animal relationships.

References

1. Futuyma & Slatkin (eds) 1983. Coevolution Sinauer Associates - Sunderland, MA.
2. Gilbert & Raven (eds) 1975.Coevolution of Plants and Animals. University of Texas Press, Austin.

EC 602 F Agroecosystems

(Chaphekar, Poyyamoli, Sundarvel, Ramamoorthy)

Monocultural practices and its attending problems. Population dynamics of pests on crop plants. Pests, Predators and principles of integrated pest management. Pesticides, fertilizers and soil ecology. Biomagnification of xenobiotics along food chains. Ecoagriculture - definition, concepts, components and methods in contrast with conventional agriculture, environmental and social impacts. Agricultural typology in India. Agro ecosystem of hills, deserts and coastal regions, drought prone and flood prone systems, jhum agriculture.

References

1. Dalton 1975. Study of Agricultural Systems. Applied Science Publishers Ltd. London. 441 pp.
2. Spedding 1975. The Biology of Agricultural Systems. Academic Press, London. 261 pp.

EC 602 G Urban Ecology (Chaphekar, Sundarvel)

Fundamentals of Urban Ecology. Settlements; heiarchy and order, entropy analysis, urban and rural - activities population and space. Towns, cities and metropolitan areas. Urbanization in India and its ecological implications. Slums, traffic, cogestion, solid and liquid wastes, air and noise pollution problems. Cities: distribution, structure, composition, land use and landscapes. Horizontal and vertical growth. Factorial ecology. Urban planning, conflict zones and land use plans. Preservation and conservation of natural and built-up environment. Development plants.

References

1. Collins 1984. Urban Ecology - 2 teacher's resource book Cambridge University Press.
2. Yadav 1987. Contemporary city ecology Concept. New Delhi.
3. Berry, Kasarda 1977. Contemporary Urban Ecology. Macmillan, London.
4. Hawley 1971. Urban Society; an ecological approach Ronald press, N.Y.

EC 602 H Environmental Mutagenesis

(Sharma, Kumaraguru)

Chemicals and radiations in human environment. Exposure of humans through accidents, usage, consumption, occupation and ecology. Genetic hazards from chemicals and radiations. Clastogenecity, turbagenecity and mutagenecity. Carcinogenesis, teratogenesis and inherited diseases. Human genetic syndromes. Assay systems; microbial, insect, mammalian, Piscean, human and plants; salient features; advantages and limitations of representative examples. Current trends in genotoxicology, promutagenesis, comutagenesis and supermutagenesis. Genetic hazards of human consumption practices.

References

1. Brusnick 1980. Principles of Genetic Toxicology, Plenum Press, New York. 279 pp.
2. Hollaender (ed) 1971-1987 Chemical Mutagens, vols. 1-10. Plenum, New York.
3. Sugimaria, Konda & Takena (eds) 1982. Environmental mutagens and Carcinogens. Tokyo University Press, 778 pp.

EC 602 I Environmental Monitoring (Chaphekar, Sundarvel)

Monitoring of stressed and unstressed environments. Environmental quality standards, choice of variables in a monitoring programme, monitoring networks. Advanced 8nvironmental analysis, high sensitivity and continuous monitoring. Chemical and physical methods: remote sensing, surveying of stress groups in society. Instrumentation, natural monitors, plant and animals in environmental monitoring.

References

1. Kopflu & Craun 1986. Environmental Epidemiology. Lewis Publishers, Inc. 284 pp.
2. Thomas 1974. Indicators of environmental quality Plenum Press, N.Y.

EC 602 J Water Treatment and Pollution Control

(Abbasi, Ramamoorthy)

Ecology and pollution control/waste water management; sources and characteristics of waste waters, quantification of waste water flows, treatment objectives, unit operations and unit processes, reactions, screening, sedimentation, filteration, coagulation, aerobic and anaerobic processes, disinfection, tertiary treatment.

References

1. Tchobanoqlaus Wastewater Engineering: Disposal and Reuse, McGraw-Hill, N.Y.
2. Sawyer, McCarthy 1978. Chemistry for Environmental Engineers, McGraw-Hill, N.Y.

EC 602 K Mathematical Modelling (Ali, Devi Prasad)

Models in ecology: approaches to models; problems, definition and objectives; choice of specific model. Deterministic and dynamic models; incorporating the relationships in terms of mathematical equations; identification of variables; methods of solutions; handling nonlinearity feedback. Matrix models; formulation of models in matrix notation; Eigen vectors and Eigen Values; Markov models. Stochastic models; identification of variables, use of variance analysis, regression analysis, identifying the need to use multivariate methods. Canonical correlation methods and other advanced techniques. Gama theory and catastrophe theory; their application.

References

1. Halfon 1979. Theoretical Systems Ecology. Academic Press.
2. Patten 1971. Systems Analysis and Simulation in Ecology. Academic Press.
3. Smith 1973. Models in Ecology. Cambridge University Press.

EC 602 L Ecological Engineering

(Abbasi, Ramamoorthy)

Ecological viability and effluent engineering systems – Water treatment with chironomids, daphnids, other invertebrates and teleosts – macrophytes and wetlands in the treatment and recycling of wastes – vermiculture – weed control through utilization systems – microcosms and waste management.

References

1. R. Dinges, Ecological Systems of water Pollution Control, 1979.
2. W.H. Smith and K.R. Reddy (eds) Wastewater Treatment for Pollution Control and Resource for Pollution Control and Resource Recovery, Magnolia pub., Florida, 1987.

4. FACULTY PROFILES

Meher-Homji, V.M.(b.1932), F.N.A., F.A.Sc., Honorary Dean. M.Sc Botany (Bombay), Ph.D (Bombay), D.Sc (Toulouse), Biogeography, Phytosociology. Teaching/Research Experience Plant Ecology, Phytosociology, Forest Ecology, Biogeography, Vegetation Cartography, Conservation, Environmental Education and Planning, Bioclimatology, Bibliography.

Ali, Rauf. (b.1954). Adjunct Professor B.Tech (BITS, Pilani), Ph.D. Behavioural Ecology (Bristol). Teaching/Research Experience Statistics, Basic Ecology, Animal Behaviour, Primate Ecology, Island Biogeography, Sampling Methods, design of Experiments.

Chaphekar S.B. (b.1935). Professor M.Sc Botany (Bombay), Ph.D Plant Ecology (Bombay). T02ching/Research Experience Plant Ecology, Phytogeography, Environmental Pollution and menitoring, Environmental Education.

Sharma C.B.S.R. (b.1942). Professor M.Sc. Botany (Rajasthan) Ph.D Plant Cytogenetics. (BITS, Pilani). Teaching/Research Experience: Autecology, cytogenetics, cell biology, economic botany, resource depletion, environmental quality, Environmental Impacts. Genotoxicity of sewage and pesticides; in situ genotoxicity assays in plants, animals and humans,

Abbasi S.A. (b.1950) Professor M.Sc Chemistry (Jabalpur), Ph.D. Freshwater Ecology/Water quality (III Bombay) D.Sc Environmental Engineering (Cochin) Teaching/Research Experience Limnology, Pollution Control and Waste Management, Bio-energy, Impact Assessment and Environmental Analysis.

Davidar, Priya (b.1952). Reader M.Sc Botany (Madras) S.M. Vector Biology, (Harvard) Ph.D. Zoology (Bombay). Teaching/Research Experience Evolutionary Biology, Pollination ecology, Host-Parasite Interactions immunological techniques.

Kumaraguru A.K. (b.1953). Reader M.Sc Marine Biology (Annamalai) Ph.D. Heavy Metal Pollution. (Annamalai), Ph.D Pollution and Bioenergetics (Guelph). Teaching/Research Experience Environmental Biology, Pollution and Toxicology. Aquaculture, Fish Energetics, Marine Biology/Ecology.

Devi Prasad K.V. (b.1957). Reader M.Sc Physics(IIT Madras) Ph.D. Theoretical Biophysics. (Purdue) Teaching/Research Experience Solid State Physics, Computational Physics, Biological Physics, Numerical Modelling.

Poyyamoli G (b.1953). Lecturer M.Sc Marine Biology (Annamalai) Ph.D Insect Ecology (Madurai) Teaching/Research Experience Marine Clostridia, Emergence pattern of Aquatic Insects, Energy Plantations, Sampling of Techniques, Survey Methods, Integrated Rural Energy Plans.

Parthasarathy N (b.1959). Lecturer M.Sc Botany (Madras) Teaching/ Research Experience Plant Embryology, Forest Ecology, Vascular Plant Taxonomy, Botany, Plant Ecology, Marine Ecology.

Sundarvel S (b.1956). Lecturer M.A. Social work. (Madurai) P.G. Diploma in urban and research planning (Ahmedabad) Teaching/Research Experience Planning for Agro development & Human Settlements, Urban and Regional Planning, Computers.

Ramamoorthy D (b.1959). Lecturer M.Sc, M.Phil Botany (Annamalai) Teaching/Research Experience Crop-Weed Competition, Agro-ecosystems.

5. EVALUATIONS: COURSES

ANONYMOUS

A. SUBJECTS / PAPERS: Do you Wish to

1. INTRODUCE Any NEW Subjects:
   (a) Wild Life
   (b) GIS & Rem. Sensing
   (c) Human Ecology
   (d) Envi. Chemistry
   (e) Animal Biodiversity & Forest Zoology
2. Upgrade some SOFT Papers to Hard Category:
   (a) Applied Ecology
   (b) Ornithology
   (c) Environmental Politics
3. REMOVE / SHIFT some HARD papers to Soft Category:
   (a) Global Change
   (b) Agri. & Environment
   (c) Epidemiology
   (d) Integr. Coastal Management
   (e) Environmental Monitoring

B. SYLLABI REVISIONS: Do you think that

4. Syllabi of some papers need to be INCREASED
   (a) Statistical Ecology
   (b) Applied Soil Ecology
   (c) Principles of Ecology
   (d) Environmental Pollution
   (e) Environmental Monitoring
5. Syllabi of some papers need to be REDUCED
   (a) Ecosystem Management
   (b) Integr. Coastal Zone Management
6. Some syllabi need to be reorganised by REMOVING OVERLAPS
   (a) Health & Environment (b) Forest Botany

C. WEIGHTAGE: Do you think that

7. CREDITS of some papers need to be REDUCED
   (a) Popul. Ecology (b) Ecosys. Management
   (c) Principles of Ecology

8. CREDITS of some papers need to be INCREASED
   - (a) Natural Resources
   - (b) Behavioural Ecology

D. PRACTICES [Lab & Field] and SKILLS

9. PRACTICALS should be INTRODUCED / INCREASED in MANY papers
   - (a) Environmental Monitoring
   - (b) Plant Biodiversity
   - (c) Environmental Pollution
   - (d) Health & Environment
   - (e) Soil Ecology
   - (f) Epidemiology
   - (g) Terrestrial Biomes

E. ANY QUERIES YOU WISH TO MAKE ?

Will there be any improvement at all in our Education?

F. ARE YOUR EXPECTATIONS FROM TEACHERS FULFILLED

Yes = 3, No = 8 Do not Know =12

G. WHAT ARE THE SUBJECTS TO BE INCLUDED IN YOUR COURSE

1. Fresh Water Ecology
2. Marine Ecology
3. GIS & Modeling
4. Wild Life Ecology
5. Geography
6. Microbiology
7. Soil
8. FIELD WORKS

H. WHAT ARE THE SUBJECTS TO BE EXCLUDED IN YOUR COURSE

1. Ecophysics [KVDP]
2. Statistical Ecology [AMS]
3. Agriculture & Environment [DR]

I. WHAT ARE THE SUBSTANDARD PAPERS NEEDING IMPROVEMENT

1. Principles of Ecology & Environment[DR]
2. Ecotourism [GP]
3. Statistical Ecology [AMS]
4. Agriculture & Environment [DR]
5. Ecophysics [KVDP]
6. Basic Ecology [DR]

J. WHAT ARE THE BACKGROUNDS YOU WISH TO KNOW

Our University, School Teachers and Subject

K. YOU DESIRE RESEARCH GUIDES FROM PU/SASEES OR OUTSTATION

Local = 12 Outstation = 21

locally who is your PREFERRED advisor / guide

Davidar = 7 Anisa Khan = 2 Parthasarathy = 3

Sharma = 6 Reddy = 3 Poyyamoli = 1

L. ARE YOU SATISFIED WITH THE PROGRAMME ADVISORY COMMITTEE

Yes = 4 No = 9 Do Not Know = Others

M. ARE YOU SATISFIED STUDYING HERE OR NOT

Yes = 2 Leave if Possible = 7 Not Sure = Others

5. EVALUATIONS: STUDENTS

1. They differ from paper to paper.
2. The instructor will select what is suitable for his / her paper from the following
   - (a) Library Assignments
   - (b) Latest Developments from Scientific Journals
   - (c) Current Concerns from Print Media
   - (d) Question Bank
   - (e) Data Sheets from all sources
     1. Practical Assignments [Practice Schooling]
     2. Laboratory Exercises
     3. Field Exercises
     4. Field Survey
     5. Social Survey Excursions
   - (f) Open Book Examination / Take-Home Exercises
   - (g) Comprehensive Test with all types of Questions
   - (h) Seminars

5. EVALUATIONS: FACULTY (QUALITATIVE)

ANONYMOUS (1987-1990)

Perception of Students on Teaching in the School – Dominant opinions

Item	Name of the Teacher							
	CBS	GP	NP	AKK	SAA	ABC	PD	SSS
1. Pace	Slow(50)	Fast(50)	OK(55)	OK(45)	OK(40)	Slow(50)	OK(60)	OK(50)
2. Clarity	Good(90)	Low(30)	Average(75)	Average(55)	Good(50)	Average (40)	Average (50)	Low(70)
3. Depth of knowledge	Very good(90)	Low(50)	Very good (50)	Fair(50)	Very good (40)	Good(50)	Fair(30)	Inadequate (70)
4. Breadth of knowledge	Very good (75)	Inadequate (60)	Good(50)	Fair(30)	Very good (30)	Good(40)	Good(60)	Inadequate (60)
5. Lucidity	Very much	Not(50)	OK(70)	OK(50)	OK(40)	OK(60)	OK(60)	Not(60)
6. Captivating Impact	Very much	Not(80)	So so(70)	So so(40)	Very much (50)	So so(50)	So so((50)	Not (70)
7. Concern towards students	OK(50)	OK(45)	OK(65)	OK(65)	OK(50)	OK(60)	OK(85)	OK(60)
8. Appeal of style	Very much (60)	Change desired(70)	Not bad (30)	Not bad(30)	Very much (40)	Not bad (40)	Not bad (50)	Change desired(70
9. Teaching quality	Enlightening (90)	Bookish(90)	Bookish (30)	Bookish(40)	Specific(50)	Specific (30)	Specific (50)	Bookish (85)
10. Communication gap	No(50)	Not much (40)	Not much (50)	Very much (35)	Very much (30)	Very much (50)	Very much (50)	Not much (50)
11. Work load taken	Verry good	Good	Good	Least	Good	Good	Good	Minimum
12. Treatment of the subject	Conventional & good(90)	Conventional & bad(80)	Conventional &good(60)	Conventional & average (50)	Conventional & good (40)	Conventional & (30)	Conventional & good(50)	Conventional & bad(60) & bad(60
13. Overall standard	Best(90)	Average(50)	Average(40)	Average(40)	Best(50)	Average(60)	Average(50)	Average(40

* First and Second Batch of students(28)
( )% of students withthe dominant opinion
Dr Meher-Homji hardly took any classes(lesser than Dr AKK&DR)
Dr Rauf Ali is considered among the best, overall
Dr KVDP & DR not evaluated in this exercise

Abbreviations: SBC-S.B.Chaphekar;CBS-C.B.S.R.Sharma SAA-S.A.Abbasi;PD-PRIYA DAVIDAR;AKK-A.K.KUMARAGURU; KVDP-K.V.DEVI PRASAD;NP-N.PARTHASARATHY;SSS-S.S. SUNDARVEL;GP-G.POYYAMOLI;DR-D.RAMAMOORTHY

5. EVALUATIONS: FACULTY (QUANTITATIVE)

A COMPARATIVE ASSESSMENT OF TEACHING AND TEACHERS BY M.Sc STUDENTS

Anonymous (2000-2004)

ASPECTS [MARKS]	TEACHERS									
	CB	PD	VR	AB	KV	GP	NP	DR	SS	AM
	Marks %									
A. PAPERS [240] CRITERIA 20	84	76	61	45	48	65	71	40	40	43
Syllabus Quality Background,Summary Study Material										
B. INSTRUCTION [400]	80	77	60	43	52	58	72	33	38	44
Coverage, Knowledge Concepts, Discussions Innovations										
C. TEACHER [560]	82	69	61	46	45	54	72	43	38	46
Knowledge, Ability Interest, Principles Evaluation Student Concerns Res. Guidance										
D. IMPACTS [240]	81	60	55	39	43	45	67	39	35	33
Boredom, Enjoyable Inspiration Skills										
E. Total [1440]	82	74	62	44	47	55	71	39	38	43
	A	B	C	-	-	D	B	-	-	-
Grade	-	-	-	F	F	-	-	F	F	F

[TOTAL=510; Average 51]

Marks:Excellent =A Good =B Above Average =C Average =D Below Average =E Poor =F

Student Sigantures

Confessions

Crossing the **SEVEN** ages of Shakespeare I enter the Terminal Roll.
On the banks of ***VAITARINI*** truth should be revealed to the
advantage of criminals and sinners to redeem themselves

A. UNIVERSITY AND THE FIRST VICE CHANCELLOR

1. A University at Pondicherry in the memory of Sri Aurabindo was promised by Indira Gandhi, but had to wait until Rajiv Gandhi. Even then, it could not be named after the sage, due to local protests.
2. Act and Statutes were drafted officially by Peri Sastry, the then Election Commissioner, but actually by K.Venkatasubramanian, the demoted Director of School Education, TN, tipped for the future VC post.
3. The search Committee has recommended KVS as the last preference. And he only was selected. So much for the honesty of the Committee, the Minister President Jail Singh, the Gnani and the backroom operations of Venkataraman, the Vice President.
4. KVS never studied in a University. His belated Doctoral thesis was Ghost-written. He was demoted by the government for indulging in moral turpitude. And with a bang he is back in power.
5. The local government offered him 3 sites to start a University – On Cuddalore Road, On Dindivanam Road, and in Lawspet. But he went for the 4th one on Markanam Road, as it is the farthest from town –safest for permissive conducts. What a great foresight!

B. SALIM ALI SCHOOL OF ECOLOGY

6. There was a growing concern about environment. And suddenly Salim Ali died, It was politically opportune to start a Salim Ali School of Ecology. Post haste, MHRD granted the School; sanctioned many posts and gave generous grants.
7. The ground work was prepared by two inexperienced men, but readily available locally – one from Auroville, Rauf Ali, and another from French Institute, Meher-Homji.

They prepared a compendium of Priority Areas, guidelines for Student Admission and Faculty Recruitment.

C. SELECTION COMMTTEE AND SELECTIONS

8. A Selection committee for the appointment of Faculty was formed – the foundation for future. The Committee consisted of [1] The Vice Chancellor [2] The Honorary Dean, Homji, who never taught and always avoided responsibilities [3] Rauf Ali, Lecturer – Reader level Free Lancer [4] The Registrar of Madras IIT and [5] an Assistant Professor teaching Under Graduate Courses. This is a wrong Committee with the last three not qualified.

9. Out of 500 applicants, 200 were called for interview for 3 Professors, 3 Readers and 4 Lecturers posts. Among the 10 selected are:

   [1] a Senior lecturer level Scientist devoid of Teaching and Research guiding experiences, was catapulted to the highest level due to the props from a Chief Minister and a Lady Judge who became a Governor later, despite his family's prominence in Intelligence Records.

   [2] A Research Fellow of a State U., was given a Reader post, due to proximity to VC, as a Nephew of his former colleague sharing moral turpitude charges.

   [3] An America- returned Doctorate irrelevant to Ecology was suddenly parachuted here from administration. Equally fast he was married off with a girl from a neighbouring department. From VC's initiative. Mysterious! He eventually became a never working scourge of the Department and University, an evil genius.

   [4-7] The 4 Lecturers, none qualified, came due to personal favoritism of Homji, Arabindo Ashramites, a Minister from Tamilnadu, and a local MLA, all super-selfish and burdens on the University, one facing absconding charges.

   Any VC with shady antecedents will recruit only depraved people. Soon they became autonomies and their indiscipline was shielded by the two honorary appointees. What else is the rationale for their appointment when there are 10 regular faculty? Department soon became scandalous. Foundations for crime and failure are laid. Dramas began to cover up their crimes. All wanted power, profit, pleasure and popularity without working. Soon this culture spread to many departments.

Venkataraman, KVS, Vayyapuri, Aranganayakam, Kandasamy, CLGupta, Farooq, Fatima Biwi, Meher-Homji, Gloria Land, Mahendra Pal, Kubera laterly have all poisoned Ecology, University and Society. All these are strengthened by the next VC Agnanam.

D. DANCE MACABRE BEGINS, WITHOUT EVEN A COMMA, SALIM ALI SCHOOL OF ECOLOGY DURING 1987 – 2004 AND BEYOND

These drain-pipe entries soon segregated into two groups, G-1 [Cassius +Shylock+ Moriarty, a Tri-hybrid Dracula] and G-2 [Hell emptied – Devils Dushtachatushtayam] Barring one lady the rest had no teaching experience or a holistic knowledge of Ecology. The leader of G-1 was a double Jumper with a shady past. The G-2 are all locals with rabid prejudices and jingoism. Both follow their own rules!

Both indulged in my character assassination due to a fear of discipline and exposure generated by their inferiority, entry routes and unfair desires. Fortunately for me, G-1, got exposed, due to an investigation by the then Chief Rector, the LG, General R.S.Dayal – I got vindicated. The G-2, being local caused greater damages. Both these gangs with a presiding VC accelerated their frauds, crimes, Dis, and Mis-informations. They had only two objectives – **self aggrandizement** and **stifling the righteous**. Their **Sins, Crimes, Social, Financial, Academic and Legal Offences covering Students, Research Scholars, University System, Funding agencies and Me**, never ended. They continue unexposed and profit endlessly. Only god may punish them–Mortals cannot. They must await retributions.

Kumaraswamy's Ghost and Semi- Ghosts of Pandian, Mahadevan, Venugopal, Chakravarty, Pathak, Bhat, Vishnupriya, Ganesh, Raghu, Shaji, Amruth, Babu, Anil, Jahnavi Pai, Rajasekar, Tiwari, Manimekalan, Sudhakar, Subba Rao, Satyanarayana, Sundaram, Belliappa, Srinivasan, Manali, Amerigo, etc, are hovering waiting to see a retribution visiting these criminals and their accomplices.

E. WHY TARGETTING ME

The "**Dossier of Falsehoods**" [DoF] maintaining since 3 decades and the **"False FIR on a Reverse Me-Too Case,"** used for 2 decades by the gangs to harm me as they please, are to be judged by their mothers, wives and children along with my "**Pension Obstructions**".These are in addition to "**Copying my works**" and at the same time **Spreading Disaffections** to any one suspected to be even talking to me. This alienating technique rendered me unbearably lonely, as if under solitary confinement for life.

These gangs pushed me into depression for long. They tortured me daily forenoon in my own room, for some months before retirement. They drove me to the verge of suicide. Generally inscrutable, they are intolerant of the traditional principles. Most faculty prostrated to these Cannibals and Necrophiles, when only asked to bend. I did not. And that made all the difference, because

I got my Qualifications, HONESTLY.
I got all my Jobs, HONESTLY.
I did my Teaching, HONESTLY.
I did my Research, HONESTLY.

This is the difference between me and all others in the department and most others in the University. The root of all my problems

They empower themselves using NERLICOFISM – NEpotism, REgionalism, LInguism, Communalism & Favoritism- ruining students and institutions without their knowledge. Needless to say the righteous become solitary Jokers. My colleagues and 2 VCs were wild rendering me helpless and later hopeless. Nehru lamented:

Animals kill other animals for food.
They also kill them for protection.
Man also kills animals.
But wilder is that man
Who kills the spirit of man in others?

Such a conversion of *Homo sapiens* to ***Homo cannibalis*** *has been predicted by Churchill 70+ years ago and feared by our founding fathers.* ***Churchill*** *prophesied in 1946:*

Power will go to the hands of
Rascals, rogues, freebooters
All Indian leaders will be of
Low caliber & men of straw

They will have sweet tongues and silly hearts
They will fight amongst themselves for power
India will be lost in political squabbles

IN EVERY WALK OF LIFE

F. WHAT I DID TO DISCOURAGE SINS

I talked to KVS to correct matters. He Listened; agreed; but too many limitations for a Brahmin! He brought his successor, AGnanam for protecting his interests. He is suave and scheming. He wanted to earn both profits and fame. And he made. He was acceptable due to his localism. I also argued with him on wrongs. He justified. I made 3 attempts to goad people into correct paths. They recoil:

1. The first one *"A Collapsing National University"* was given to the Chancellor personally, which ultimately resulted in a CBI case, from which he escaped with the help of the 2nd VC, which is a different story, [published in my book, SHARKS ON CAMPUS]]
2. Finding Gnanam to be mean, I published an article in Indian Express ***"Cradle is the Grave".*** Through Prabhu Chawla, Widely appreciated, I received about 40 congratulatory letters. But AGnanam and his devils wanted legal action on me [see the Public Domain].
3. Crimes accumulated under CBCS. The VC appointed a Committee to enquire under my chairmanship. We did our work and submitted. This 20p report contained details of functioning of this system at PU, until 2004. : ***"Committee Report on Choice Based Credit System at Pondicherry University"*** [Every Department was given a Copy]

   All were guilty. All profited and harmed me for being right, enjoying the credibility and trust of most. Students, University and Funding Agencies were all cheated. The unqualified, the incompetent, anti-work, but full of desires seek short cuts through crime. This is a psychic issue at a time of transitions. Unfortunately I was brought by destiny to cross their path! As Guru Nanak prescribed, such minority men should be sent away from the evil majority's midst!

   God sees everything, but waits, said Tolstoy. How long? .Meanwhile my academic output and utility were terribly strangulated by the 2 gangs, their friends and patrons. Who gives me my stolen Future?

G. ULTIMATE RESULT - LOW ACADEMIC OUTPUT IN RESEARCH

(a) Papers

1. <u>31</u> Research Papers in U.K, USA, Holland, Switzerland, Italy, Germany, Japan = **230p**
2. <u>51</u> Research Papers in India = **445p**

(b) Reviews: Chemicals, Pollutants and Mutagenesis =154p

1. 1971 – India – CSIR Journal =**17p**
2. 1987 – Malaysia – SAM-APPEN = **15p**
3. 1990 – U S A – CRC Critical Reviews =**34p**
4. 1990 – U K – Mutagenesis = **21p**
5. 1993 – On ***in situ*** Mutagenesis, UNPUBLISHED = **67p**

(c) Reports / Projects*

1. Monozite Belt Floristics -**UGC**
2. Maize Germplasm Collection for CYMMYT at Mexico - **CYMMYT**
3. **Phulbani**: Medicinal Plants used by Tribals - **UGC**
4. **Drugs with Heavy Metals:** Genetic Toxicity in Rodents - **ICMR**
5. **Fungicides**: Genetic Toxicity of Commonly used Fungicides -**CSIR**
6. ***In situ* mutagenicity; *VCs and Colleagues destroyed this mid stream* - DOEF**
7. **Small Water bodies:** Most successful and Appreciated Report- **UNDP**
8. **East Coast of Tamil Nadu:** Not compiled into a Formal Report: **INTACH, CAG, & PU**
9. **Vision 2020 Pondichery, GOP,**

*** Assisted by 12 Students, 8 obtaining Doctorates**

H. ULTIMATE RESULT- LOW OUTPUT IN BOOKS FOR PUBLIC

(a) Published

1. **Sharks on Campus:** Compilation of **41 Articles** on Higher Education; p371, **2015,** Notion
2. **Ecology, Environment and Politics**: Compilation of **38 lectures** in Ecology & Environment in 35 Institutions in India; p412, **2018,** Kalpaz
3. **Teaching Labours of Sisyphus**:Synopses of **190 Class Lectures** From 10 Branches of Environmental Sciences, p802, **2019,** Gyan

(b) Forthcoming

4. From Genetic Toxicology To Environmental Mutagenesis
5. Irrigation Tanks In The **Tamil Country**

6. Keeping The **Asphidistra** Alive
7. Ecography of Tamil Nadu Coast
8. Plants in Medicine, Energy, Crop Protection and Environmental Monitoring

---

I feel I am guilty of their crimes
because I was unable to influence or correct or stop them from their misdeeds but evoked jealousies, prejudices, fears and vengeances.
Their tortures made my life miserable, helpless,
hopeless and not worth living.
These 'Necrophiles' would lie even in a Dying Declaration